THE WILEY BICENTENNIAL–KNOWLEDGE FOR GENERATIONS

Each generation has its unique needs and aspirations. When Charles Wiley first opened his small printing shop in lower Manhattan in 1807, it was a generation of boundless potential searching for an identity. And we were there, helping to define a new American literary tradition. Over half a century later, in the midst of the Second Industrial Revolution, it was a generation focused on building the future. Once again, we were there, supplying the critical scientific, technical, and engineering knowledge that helped frame the world. Throughout the 20th Century, and into the new millennium, nations began to reach out beyond their own borders and a new international community was born. Wiley was there, expanding its operations around the world to enable a global exchange of ideas, opinions, and know-how.

For 200 years, Wiley has been an integral part of each generation's journey, enabling the flow of information and understanding necessary to meet their needs and fulfill their aspirations. Today, bold new technologies are changing the way we live and learn. Wiley will be there, providing you the must-have knowledge you need to imagine new worlds, new possibilities, and new opportunities.

Generations come and go, but you can always count on Wiley to provide you the knowledge you need, when and where you need it!

William J. Pesce
President and Chief Executive Officer

Peter Booth Wiley
Chairman of the Board

www.wiley.com/college/microsoft *or*
call the MOAC Toll-Free Number: 1+(888) 764-7001 (U.S. & Canada only)

www.wiley.com/college/microsoft *or*
call the MOAC Toll-Free Number: 1+(888) 764-7001 (U.S. & Canada only)

Microsoft® Official Academic Course

Windows Vista® Configuration Microsoft® Certified Technology Specialist Exam 70-620

Craig Zacker

Credits

EXECUTIVE EDITOR	John Kane
SENIOR EDITOR	Gary Schwartz
DIRECTOR OF MARKETING AND SALES	Mitchell Beaton
MICROSOFT STRATEGIC RELATIONSHIPS MANAGER	Merrick Van Dongen of Microsoft Learning
GLOBAL MOAC MANAGER	Laura McKenna
DEVELOPMENT AND PRODUCTION	Custom Editorial Productions, Inc
EDITORIAL ASSISTANT	Jennifer Lartz
PRODUCTION MANAGER	Micheline Frederick
CREATIVE DIRECTOR/COVER DESIGNER	Harry Nolan
TECHNOLOGY AND MEDIA	Lauren Sapira/Elena Santa Maria
COVER PHOTO	Corbis

Wiley 200th Anniversary logo designed by: Richard J. Pacifico

This book was set in Garamond by Aptara, Inc. and printed and bound by Bind Rite Graphics.
The covers were printed by Phoenix Color.

ISBN-13 978-0-470-11592-3

Printed in the United States of America

10 9 8 7 6 5 4 3 2

www.wiley.com/college/microsoft *or*
call the MOAC Toll-Free Number: 1+(888) 764-7001 (U.S. & Canada only)

Foreword from the Publisher

Wiley's publishing vision for the Microsoft Official Academic Course series is to provide students and instructors with the skills and knowledge they need to use Microsoft technology effectively in all aspects of their personal and professional lives. Quality instruction is required to help both educators and students get the most from Microsoft's software tools and to become more productive. Thus our mission is to make our instructional programs trusted educational companions for life.

To accomplish this mission, Wiley and Microsoft have partnered to develop the highest quality educational programs for Information Workers, IT Professionals, and Developers. Materials created by this partnership carry the brand name "Microsoft Official Academic Course," assuring instructors and students alike that the content of these textbooks is fully endorsed by Microsoft, and that they provide the highest quality information and instruction on Microsoft products. The Microsoft Official Academic Course textbooks are "Official" in still one more way—they are the officially sanctioned courseware for Microsoft IT Academy members.

The Microsoft Official Academic Course series focuses on *workforce development*. These programs are aimed at those students seeking to enter the workforce, change jobs, or embark on new careers as information workers, IT professionals, and developers. Microsoft Official Academic Course programs address their needs by emphasizing authentic workplace scenarios with an abundance of projects, exercises, cases, and assessments.

The Microsoft Official Academic Courses are mapped to Microsoft's extensive research and job-task analysis, the same research and analysis used to create the Microsoft Certified Technology Specialist (MCTS) exam. The textbooks focus on real skills for real jobs. As students work through the projects and exercises in the textbooks they enhance their level of knowledge and their ability to apply the latest Microsoft technology to everyday tasks. These students also gain resume-building credentials that can assist them in finding a job, keeping their current job, or in furthering their education.

The concept of life-long learning is today an utmost necessity. Job roles, and even whole job categories, are changing so quickly that none of us can stay competitive and productive without continuously updating our skills and capabilities. The Microsoft Official Academic Course offerings, and their focus on Microsoft certification exam preparation, provide a means for people to acquire and effectively update their skills and knowledge. Wiley supports students in this endeavor through the development and distribution of these courses as Microsoft's official academic publisher.

Today educational publishing requires attention to providing quality print and robust electronic content. By integrating Microsoft Official Academic Course products, Wiley*PLUS*, and Microsoft certifications, we are better able to deliver efficient learning solutions for students and teachers alike.

Bonnie Lieberman
General Manager and Senior Vice President

www.wiley.com/college/microsoft *or*
call the MOAC Toll-Free Number: 1+(888) 764-7001 (U.S. & Canada only)

Preface

Welcome to the Microsoft Official Academic Course (MOAC) program for Microsoft Windows Vista. MOAC represents the collaboration between Microsoft Learning and John Wiley & Sons, Inc. publishing company. Microsoft and Wiley teamed up to produce a series of textbooks that deliver compelling and innovative teaching solutions to instructors and superior learning experiences for students. Infused and informed by in-depth knowledge from the creators of Microsoft Office and Windows Vista™, and crafted by a publisher known worldwide for the pedagogical quality of its products, these textbooks maximize skills transfer in minimum time. With MOAC, students are hands on right away—there are no superfluous text passages to get in the way of learning and using the software. Students are challenged to reach their potential by using their new technical skills as highly productive members of the workforce.

Because this knowledgebase comes directly from Microsoft, architect of the Windows Vista operating system and creator of the Microsoft Certified Technology Specialist (MCTS) exams, (www.microsoft.com/learning/mcp/mcts/default.mspx), you are sure to receive the topical coverage that is most relevant to students' personal and professional success. Microsoft's direct participation not only assures you that MOAC textbook content is accurate and current; it also means that students will receive the best instruction possible to enable their success on certification exams and in the workplace.

The Microsoft Official Academic Course Program

The *Microsoft Official Academic Course* series is a complete program for instructors and institutions to prepare and deliver great courses on Microsoft software technologies. With MOAC, we recognize that, because of the rapid pace of change in the technology and curriculum developed by Microsoft, there is an ongoing set of needs beyond classroom instruction tools for an instructor to be ready to teach the course. The MOAC program endeavors to provide solutions for all these needs in a systematic manner in order to ensure a successful and rewarding course experience for both instructor and student—technical and curriculum training for instructor readiness with new software releases; the software itself for student use at home for building hands-on skills, assessment, and validation of skill development; and a great set of tools for delivering instruction in the classroom and lab. All are important to the smooth delivery of an interesting course on Microsoft software, and all are provided with the MOAC program. We think about the model below as a gauge for ensuring that we completely support you in your goal of teaching a great course. As you evaluate your instructional materials options, you may wish to use the model for comparison purposes with available products.

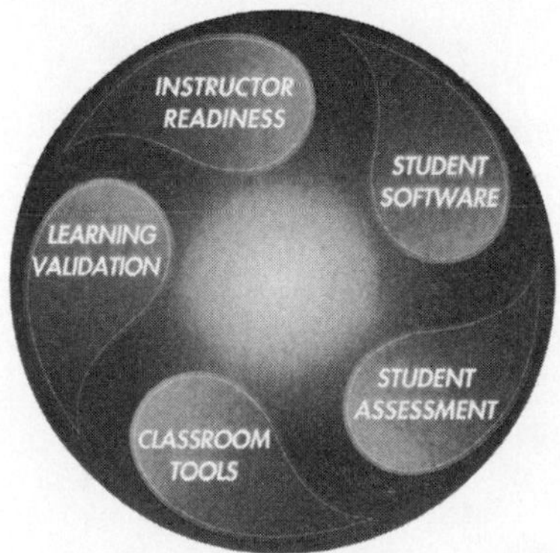

www.wiley.com/college/microsoft *or*
call the MOAC Toll-Free Number: 1+(888) 764-7001 (U.S. & Canada only)

Illustrated Book Tour

■ Pedagogical Features

The MOAC textbook for Windows Vista is designed to cover all the learning objectives for that MCTS exam, which is referred to as its "objective domain." The Microsoft Certified Technology Specialist (MCTS) exam objectives are highlighted throughout the textbook. Many pedagogical features have been developed specifically for *Microsoft Official Academic Course* programs.

Presenting the extensive procedural information and technical concepts woven throughout the textbook raises challenges for the student and instructor alike. The Illustrated Book Tour that follows provides a guide to the rich features contributing to *Microsoft Official Academic Course* program's pedagogical plan. Following is a list of key features in each lesson designed to prepare students for success on the certification exams and in the workplace:

- Each lesson begins with an **Objective Domain Matrix.** More than a standard list of learning objectives, the Domain Matrix correlates each software skill covered in the lesson to the specific MCTS "objective domain."
- Concise and frequent **Step-by-Step** instructions teach students new features and provide an opportunity for hands-on practice. Numbered steps give detailed, step-by-step instructions to help students learn software skills. The steps also show results and screen images to match what students should see on their computer screens.
- **Illustrations:** Screen images provide visual feedback as students work through the exercises. The images reinforce key concepts, provide visual clues about the steps, and allow students to check their progress.
- **Key Terms:** Important technical vocabulary is listed at the beginning of the lesson. When these terms are used later in the lesson, they appear in bold italic type and are defined. The Glossary contains all of the key terms and their definitions.
- Engaging point-of-use **Reader aids,** located throughout the lessons, tell students why this topic is relevant (*The Bottom Line*), provide students with helpful hints (*Take Note*), or show alternate ways to accomplish tasks (*Another Way*). Reader aids also provide additional relevant or background information that adds value to the lesson.
- **Certification Ready?** features throughout the text signal students where a specific certification objective is covered. They provide students with a chance to check their understanding of that particular MCTS objective and, if necessary, review the section of the lesson where it is covered. MOAC offers complete preparation for MCTS certification.
- **Knowledge Assessments** provide three progressively more challenging lesson-ending activities.
- **Student CD:** The companion CD contains the worksheets that accompany each lesson.

www.wiley.com/college/microsoft *or*
call the MOAC Toll-Free Number: 1+(888) 764-7001 (U.S. & Canada only)

Lesson Features

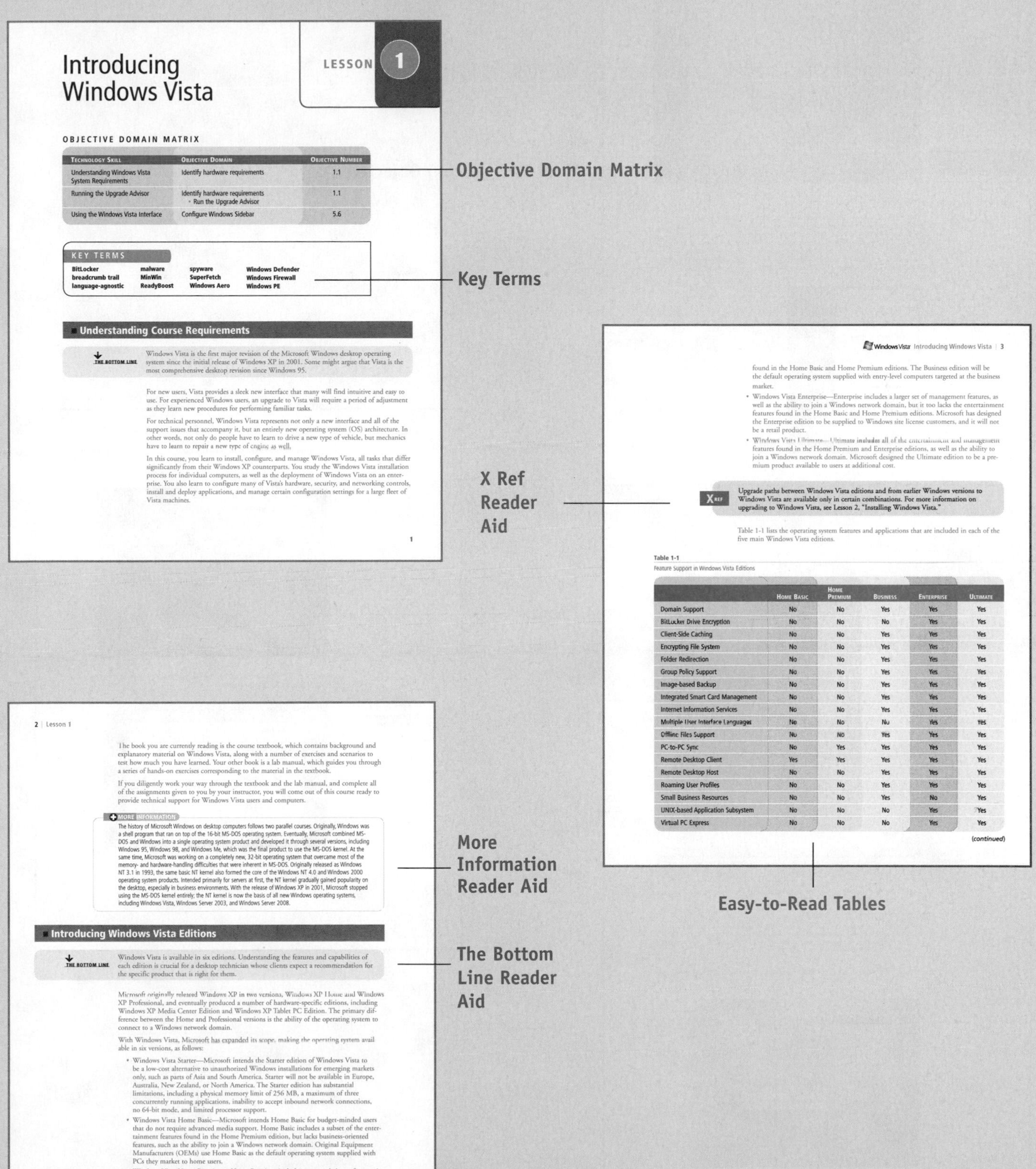

Introducing Windows Vista

LESSON 1

OBJECTIVE DOMAIN MATRIX

Technology Skill	Objective Domain	Objective Number
Understanding Windows Vista System Requirements	Identify hardware requirements	1.1
Running the Upgrade Advisor	Identify hardware requirements • Run the Upgrade Advisor	1.1
Using the Windows Vista Interface	Configure Windows Sidebar	5.6

KEY TERMS

BitLocker	**malware**	**spyware**	**Windows Defender**
breadcrumb trail	**MinWin**	**SuperFetch**	**Windows Firewall**
language-agnostic	**ReadyBoost**	**Windows Aero**	**Windows PE**

■ Understanding Course Requirements

THE BOTTOM LINE: Windows Vista is the first major revision of the Microsoft Windows desktop operating system since the initial release of Windows XP in 2001. Some might argue that Vista is the most comprehensive desktop revision since Windows 95.

For new users, Vista provides a sleek new interface that many will find intuitive and easy to use. For experienced Windows users, an upgrade to Vista will require a period of adjustment as they learn new procedures for performing familiar tasks.

For technical personnel, Windows Vista represents not only a new interface and all of the support issues that accompany it, but an entirely new operating system (OS) architecture. In other words, not only do people have to learn to drive a new type of vehicle, but mechanics have to learn to repair a new type of engine as well.

In this course, you learn to install, configure, and manage Windows Vista, all tasks that differ significantly from their Windows XP counterparts. You study the Windows Vista installation process for individual computers, as well as the deployment of Windows Vista on an enterprise. You also learn to configure many of Vista's hardware, security, and networking controls, install and deploy applications, and manage certain configuration settings for a large fleet of Vista machines.

1

2 | Lesson 1

The book you are currently reading is the course textbook, which contains background and explanatory material on Windows Vista, along with a number of exercises and scenarios to test how much you have learned. Your other book is a lab manual, which guides you through a series of hands-on exercises corresponding to the material in the textbook.

If you diligently work your way through the textbook and the lab manual, and complete all of the assignments given to you by your instructor, you will come out of this course ready to provide technical support for Windows Vista users and computers.

MORE INFORMATION: The history of Microsoft Windows on desktop computers follows two parallel courses. Originally, Windows was a shell program that ran on top of the 16-bit MS-DOS operating system. Eventually, Microsoft combined MS-DOS and Windows into a single operating system product and developed it through several versions, including Windows 95, Windows 98, and Windows Me, which was the final product to use the MS-DOS kernel. At the same time, Microsoft was working on a completely new, 32-bit operating system that overcame most of the memory- and hardware-handling difficulties that were inherent in MS-DOS. Originally released as Windows NT 3.1 in 1993, the same basic NT kernel also formed the core of the Windows NT 4.0 and Windows 2000 operating system products. Intended primarily for servers at first, the NT kernel gradually gained popularity on the desktop, especially in business environments. With the release of Windows XP in 2001, Microsoft stopped using the MS-DOS kernel entirely; the NT kernel is now the basis of all new Windows operating systems, including Windows Vista, Windows Server 2003, and Windows Server 2008.

■ Introducing Windows Vista Editions

THE BOTTOM LINE: Windows Vista is available in six editions. Understanding the features and capabilities of each edition is crucial for a desktop technician whose clients expect a recommendation for the specific product that is right for them.

Microsoft originally released Windows XP in two versions, Windows XP Home and Windows XP Professional, and eventually produced a number of hardware-specific editions, including Windows XP Media Center Edition and Windows XP Tablet PC Edition. The primary difference between the Home and Professional versions is the ability of the operating system to connect to a Windows network domain.

With Windows Vista, Microsoft has expanded its scope, making the operating system available in six versions, as follows:

- Windows Vista Starter—Microsoft intends the Starter edition of Windows Vista to be a low-cost alternative to unauthorized Windows installations for emerging markets only, such as parts of Asia and South America. Starter will not be available in Europe, Australia, New Zealand, or North America. The Starter edition has substantial limitations, including a physical memory limit of 256 MB, a maximum of three concurrently running applications, inability to accept inbound network connections, no 64-bit mode, and limited processor support.
- Windows Vista Home Basic—Microsoft intends Home Basic for budget-minded users that do not require advanced media support. Home Basic includes a subset of the entertainment features found in the Home Premium edition, but lacks business-oriented features, such as the ability to join a Windows network domain. Original Equipment Manufacturers (OEMs) use Home Basic as the default operating system supplied with PCs they market to home users.
- Windows Vista Home Premium—Home Premium includes an extended set of cosmetic and entertainment features, but lacks business features, such as the ability to join a Windows network domain. OEMs supply Home Premium as an upgrade on PCs they market to home users.
- Windows Vista Business—Business includes a basic array of management features, as well as the ability to join a Windows network domain, but it lacks the entertainment features

Windows Vista Introducing Windows Vista | 3

found in the Home Basic and Home Premium editions. The Business edition will be the default operating system supplied with entry-level computers targeted at the business market.

- Windows Vista Enterprise—Enterprise includes a larger set of management features, as well as the ability to join a Windows network domain, but it too lacks the entertainment features found in the Home Basic and Home Premium editions. Microsoft has designed the Enterprise edition to be supplied to Windows site license customers, and it will not be a retail product.
- Windows Vista Ultimate—Ultimate includes all of the entertainment and management features found in the Home Premium and Enterprise editions, as well as the ability to join a Windows network domain. Microsoft designed the Ultimate edition to be a premium product available to users at additional cost.

XREF: Upgrade paths between Windows Vista editions and from earlier Windows versions to Windows Vista are available only in certain combinations. For more information on upgrading to Windows Vista, see Lesson 2, "Installing Windows Vista."

Table 1-1 lists the operating system features and applications that are included in each of the five main Windows Vista editions.

Table 1-1
Feature Support in Windows Vista Editions

	Home Basic	Home Premium	Business	Enterprise	Ultimate
Domain Support	No	No	Yes	Yes	Yes
BitLocker Drive Encryption	No	No	No	Yes	Yes
Client-Side Caching	No	No	Yes	Yes	Yes
Encrypting File System	No	No	Yes	Yes	Yes
Folder Redirection	No	No	Yes	Yes	Yes
Group Policy Support	No	No	Yes	Yes	Yes
Image-based Backup	No	No	Yes	Yes	Yes
Integrated Smart Card Management	No	No	Yes	Yes	Yes
Internet Information Services	No	No	Yes	Yes	Yes
Multiple User Interface Languages	No	No	No	Yes	Yes
Offline Files Support	No	No	Yes	Yes	Yes
PC-to-PC Sync	No	Yes	Yes	Yes	Yes
Remote Desktop Client	Yes	Yes	Yes	Yes	Yes
Remote Desktop Host	No	No	Yes	Yes	Yes
Roaming User Profiles	No	No	Yes	Yes	Yes
Small Business Resources	No	No	Yes	No	Yes
UNIX-based Application Subsystem	No	No	No	Yes	Yes
Virtual PC Express	No	No	No	Yes	Yes

(continued)

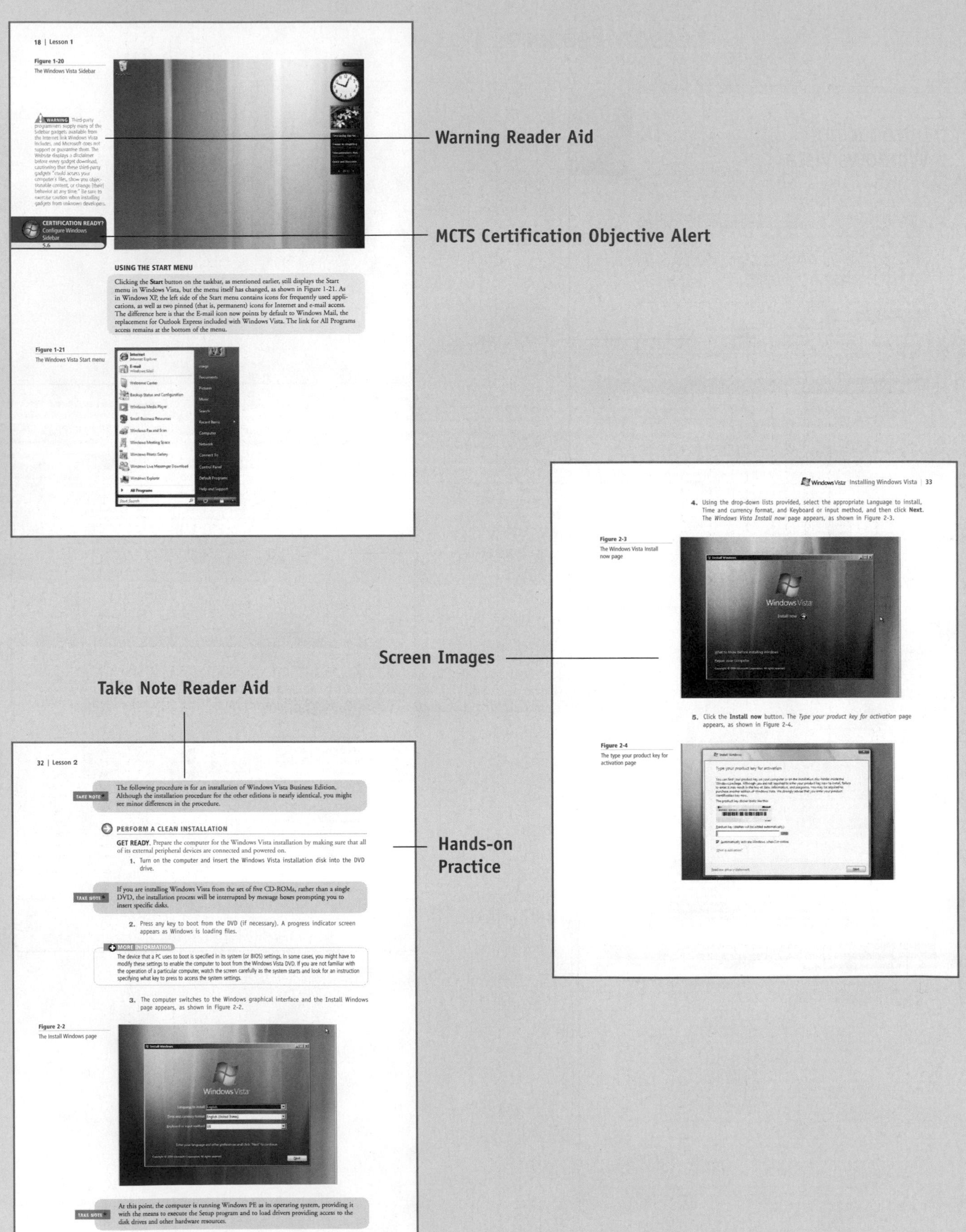

www.wiley.com/college/microsoft *or*
call the MOAC Toll-Free Number: 1+(888) 764-7001 (U.S. & Canada only)

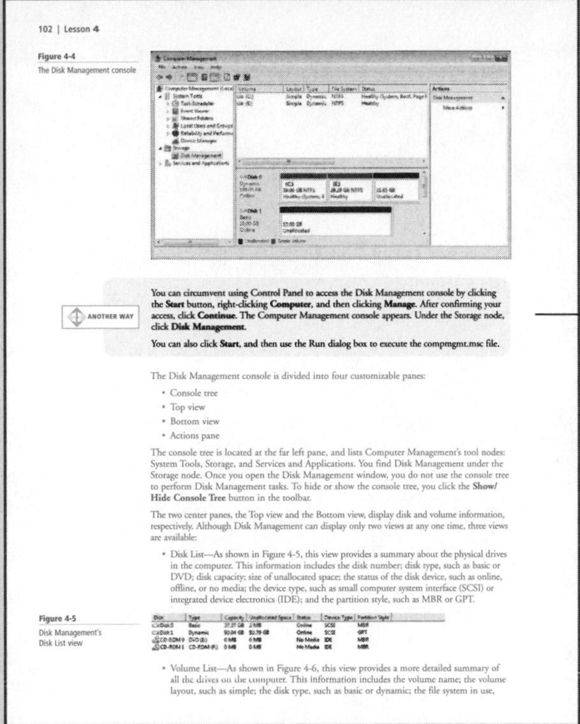

Figure 4-4
The Disk Management console

ANOTHER WAY

You can circumvent using Control Panel to access the Disk Management console by clicking the Start button, right-clicking Computer, and then clicking Manage. After confirming your access, click Continue. The Computer Management console appears. Under the Storage node, click Disk Management.

You can also click Start, and then use the Run dialog box to execute the compmgmt.msc file.

The Disk Management console is divided into four customizable panes:

- Console tree
- Top view
- Bottom view
- Actions pane

The console tree is located at the far left pane, and lists Computer Management's tool nodes: System Tools, Storage, and Services and Applications. You find Disk Management under the Storage node. Once you open the Disk Management window, you do not use the console tree to perform Disk Management tasks. To hide or show the console tree, you click the **Show/Hide Console Tree** button in the toolbar.

The two center panes, the Top view and the Bottom view, display disk and volume information, respectively. Although Disk Management can display only two views at any one time, three views are available:

- Disk List—As shown in Figure 4-5, this view provides a summary about the physical drives in the computer. This information includes the disk number; disk type, such as basic or DVD; disk capacity; size of unallocated space; the status of the disk device, such as online, offline, or no media; the device type, such as small computer system interface (SCSI) or integrated device electronics (IDE); and the partition style, such as MBR or GPT.

Figure 4-5
Disk Management's Disk List view

Disk	Type	Capacity	Unallocated Space	Status	Device Type	Partition Style
Disk 0	Basic	37.27 GB	2 MB	Online	SCSI	MBR
Disk 1	Dynamic	93.04 GB	52.79 GB	Online	SCSI	GPT
CD-ROM 0	DVD (E:)	0 MB	0 MB	No Media	IDE	MBR
CD-ROM 1	CD-ROM (F:)	0 MB	0 MB	No Media	IDE	MBR

- Volume List—As shown in Figure 4-6, this view provides a more detailed summary of all the drives on the computer. This information includes the volume name; the volume layout, such as simple; the disk type, such as basic or dynamic; the file system in use,

Another Way Reader Aid

Case Scenarios

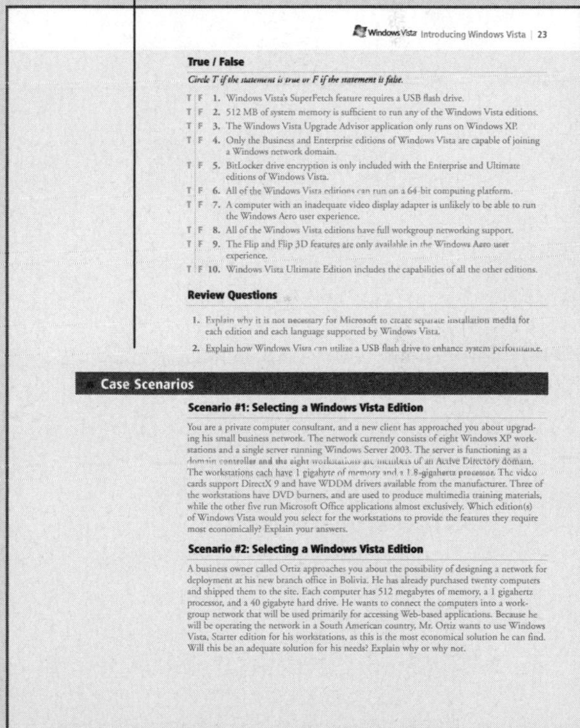

True / False

Circle T if the statement is true or F if the statement is false.

T F 1. Windows Vista's SuperFetch feature requires a USB flash drive.
T F 2. 512 MB of system memory is sufficient to run any of the Windows Vista editions.
T F 3. The Windows Vista Upgrade Advisor application only runs on Windows XP.
T F 4. Only the Business and Enterprise editions of Windows Vista are capable of joining a Windows network domain.
T F 5. BitLocker drive encryption is only included with the Enterprise and Ultimate editions of Windows Vista.
T F 6. All of the Windows Vista editions can run on a 64-bit computing platform.
T F 7. A computer with an inadequate video display adapter is unlikely to be able to run the Windows Aero user experience.
T F 8. All of the Windows Vista editions have full workgroup networking support.
T F 9. The Flip and Flip 3D features are only available in the Windows Aero user experience.
T F 10. Windows Vista Ultimate Edition includes the capabilities of all the other editions.

Review Questions

1. Explain why it is not necessary for Microsoft to create separate installation media for each edition and each language supported by Windows Vista.
2. Explain how Windows Vista can utilize a USB flash drive to enhance system performance.

Case Scenarios

Scenario #1: Selecting a Windows Vista Edition

You are a private computer consultant, and a new client has approached you about upgrading his small business network. The network currently consists of eight Windows XP workstations and a single server running Windows Server 2003. The server is functioning as a domain controller and the eight workstations are members of an Active Directory domain. The workstations each have 1 gigabyte of memory and a 1.8-gigahertz processor. The video cards support DirectX 9 and have WDDM drivers available from the manufacturer. Three of the workstations have DVD burners, and are used to produce multimedia training materials, while the other five run Microsoft Office applications almost exclusively. Which edition(s) of Windows Vista would you select for the workstations to provide the features they require most economically? Explain your answers.

Scenario #2: Selecting a Windows Vista Edition

A business owner called Ortiz approaches you about the possibility of designing a network for deployment at his new branch office in Bolivia. He has already purchased twenty computers and shipped them to the site. Each computer has 512 megabytes of memory, a 1 gigahertz processor, and a 40 gigabyte hard drive. He wants to connect the computers into a workgroup network that will be used primarily for accessing Web-based applications. Because he will be operating the network in a South American country, Mr. Ortiz wants to use Windows Vista, Starter edition for his workstations, as this is the most economical solution he can find. Will this be an adequate solution for his needs? Explain why or why not.

Sumnmary Skill Matrix

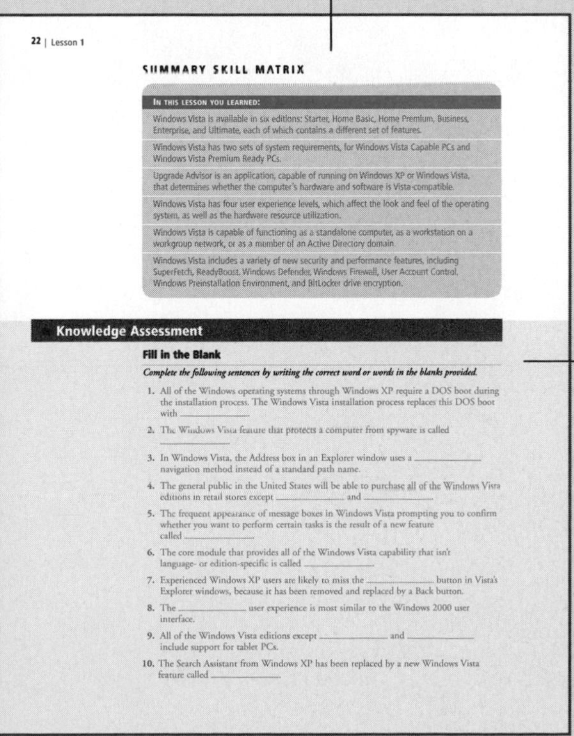

SUMMARY SKILL MATRIX

IN THIS LESSON YOU LEARNED:
Windows Vista is available in six editions: Starter, Home Basic, Home Premium, Business, Enterprise, and Ultimate, each of which contains a different set of features.
Windows Vista has two sets of system requirements, for Windows Vista Capable PCs and Windows Vista Premium Ready PCs.
Upgrade Advisor is an application, capable of running on Windows XP or Windows Vista, that determines whether the computer's hardware and software is Vista-compatible.
Windows Vista has four user experience levels, which affect the look and feel of the operating system, as well as the hardware resource utilization.
Windows Vista is capable of functioning as a standalone computer, as a workstation on a workgroup network, or as a member of an Active Directory domain.
Windows Vista includes a variety of new security and performance features, including SuperFetch, ReadyBoost, Windows Defender, Windows Firewall, User Account Control, Windows Preinstallation Environment, and BitLocker drive encryption.

Knowledge Assessment

Fill in the Blank

Complete the following sentences by writing the correct word or words in the blanks provided.

1. All of the Windows operating systems through Windows XP require a DOS boot during the installation process. The Windows Vista installation process replaces this DOS boot with ________.
2. The Windows Vista feature that protects a computer from spyware is called ________.
3. In Windows Vista, the Address box in an Explorer window uses a ________ navigation method instead of a standard path name.
4. The general public in the United States will be able to purchase all of the Windows Vista editions in retail stores except ________ and ________.
5. The frequent appearance of message boxes in Windows Vista prompting you to confirm whether you want to perform certain tasks is the result of a new feature called ________.
6. The core module that provides all of the Windows Vista capability that isn't language- or edition-specific is called ________.
7. Experienced Windows XP users are likely to miss the ________ button in Vista's Explorer windows, because it has been removed and replaced by a Back button.
8. The ________ user experience is most similar to the Windows 2000 user interface.
9. All of the Windows Vista editions except ________ and ________ include support for tablet PCs.
10. The Search Assistant from Windows XP has been replaced by a new Windows Vista feature called ________.

Knowledge Assessment Questions

www.wiley.com/college/microsoft *or*
call the MOAC Toll-Free Number: 1+(888) 764-7001 (U.S. & Canada only)

www.wiley.com/college/microsoft *or*
call the MOAC Toll-Free Number: 1+(888) 764-7001 (U.S. & Canada only)

Conventions and Features Used in This Book

This book uses particular fonts, symbols, and heading conventions to highlight important information or to call your attention to special steps. For more information about the features in each lesson, refer to the Illustrated Book Tour section.

CONVENTION	MEANING
NEW FEATURE	This icon indicates a new or greatly improved Windows feature in this version of the software.
THE BOTTOM LINE	This feature provides a brief summary of the material to be covered in the section that follows.
CLOSE	Words in all capital letters and in a different font color than the rest of the text indicate instructions for opening, saving, or closing files or programs. They also point out items you should check or actions you should take.
CERTIFICATION READY?	This feature signals the point in the text where a specific certification objective is covered. It provides you with a chance to check your understanding of that particular MCTS objective and, if necessary, review the section of the lesson where it is covered.
TAKE NOTE	Reader aids appear in shaded boxes found in your text. *Take Note* provides helpful hints related to particular tasks or topics.
ANOTHER WAY	*Another Way* provides an alternative procedure for accomplishing a particular task.
XREF	These notes provide pointers to information discussed elsewhere in the textbook or describe interesting features of Windows Vista that are not directly addressed in the current topic or exercise.
Alt+Tab	A plus sign (+) between two key names means that you must press both keys at the same time. Keys that you are instructed to press in an exercise will appear in the font shown here.
A ***shared printer*** can be used by many individuals on a network.	Key terms appear in bold italic.
Key My Name is.	Any text you are asked to key appears in color.
Click OK.	Any button on the screen you are supposed to click on or select will also appear in color.

www.wiley.com/college/microsoft *or*
call the MOAC Toll-Free Number: 1+(888) 764-7001 (U.S. & Canada only)

Instructor Support Program

The *Microsoft Official Academic Course* programs are accompanied by a rich array of resources that incorporate the extensive textbook visuals to form a pedagogically cohesive package. These resources provide all the materials instructors need to deploy and deliver their courses. Resources available online for download include:

- The **MSDN Academic Alliance** is designed to provide the easiest and most inexpensive developer tools, products, and technologies available to faculty and students in labs, classrooms, and on student PCs. A free 1-year membership is available to qualified MOAC adopters.

  Note: Microsoft Windows Vista Enterprise Edition can be downloaded from MSDNAA for use by students in this course
- **Windows Server 2003 Trial Software.** A 180-day trial version of the Windows Server 2003 software can be downloaded for use with this course from the Microsoft TechNet site (http://technet.microsoft.com/).
- The **Instructor's Guide** contains Solutions to all the textbook exercises and Syllabi for various term lengths. The Instructor's Guide also includes chapter summaries and lecture notes. The Instructor's Guide is available from the Book Companion site (http://www.wiley.com/college/microsoft) and from Wiley*PLUS*.
- The **Test Bank** contains hundreds of multiple-choice, true-false, and short answer questions and is available to download from the Instructor's Book Companion site (http://www.wiley.com/college/microsoft) and from Wiley*PLUS*. A complete answer key is provided. It is available as a computerized test bank and in Microsoft Word format. The easy-to-use test-generation program fully supports graphics, print tests, student answer sheets, and answer keys. The software's advanced features allow you to create an exam to meet your exact specifications. The computerized test bank provides:
  - Varied question types to test a variety of comprehension levels—multiple-choice, true-false, and short answer.
  - Allows instructors to edit, randomize, and create questions freely.
  - Allows instructors to create and print different versions of a quiz or exam.
- **PowerPoint Presentations and Images.** A complete set of PowerPoint presentations is available on the Instructor's Book Companion site (http://www.wiley.com/college/microsoft) and in Wiley*PLUS* to enhance classroom presentations. Approximately 50 PowerPoint slides are provided for each lesson. Tailored to the text's topical coverage and Skills Matrix, these presentations are designed to convey key Windows Vista concepts addressed in the text.

  All figures from the text are on the Instructor's Book Companion site (http://www.wiley.com/college/microsoft) and in Wiley*PLUS*. You can incorporate them into your PowerPoint presentations, or create your own overhead transparencies and handouts.

  By using these visuals in class discussions, you can help focus students' attention on key elements of Windows Vista and help them understand how to use it effectively in the workplace.

- **The Wiley Faculty Network** lets you tap into a large community of your peers effortlessly. Wiley Faculty Network mentors are faculty like you, from educational institutions around the country, who are passionate about enhancing instructional efficiency and effectiveness through best practices. Faculty Network activities include technology training and tutorials, virtual seminars, peer-to-peer exchanges of experience and ideas, personal consulting, and sharing of resources. To register for a seminar, go to www.wherefacultyconnect.com or phone 1-866-4FACULTY (U.S. and Canada only).

Wiley*PLUS*

Broad developments in education over the past decade have influenced the instructional approach taken in the Microsoft Official Academic Course programs. The way that students learn, especially about new technologies, has changed dramatically in the Internet era. Electronic learning materials and Internet-based instruction is now as much a part of classroom instruction as printed textbooks. Wiley*PLUS* provides the technology to create an environment where students reach their full potential and experience academic success that will last them a lifetime!

Wiley*PLUS* is a powerful and highly-integrated suite of teaching and learning resources designed to bridge the gap between what happens in the classroom and what happens at home and on the job. Wiley*PLUS* provides instructors with the resources to teach their students new technologies and guide them to reach their goals of getting ahead in the job market by having the skills to become certified and advance in the workforce. For students, Wiley*PLUS* provides the tools for study and practice that are available to them 24/7, wherever and whenever they want to study. Wiley*PLUS* includes a complete online version of the student textbook, PowerPoint presentations, homework and practice assignments and quizzes, image galleries, test bank questions, gradebook, and all the instructor resources in one easy-to-use website.

Organized around the everyday activities you and your students perform in the class, Wiley*PLUS* helps you:

- **Prepare & Present** outstanding class presentations using relevant PowerPoint slides and other Wiley*PLUS* materials—and you can easily upload and add your own.
- **Create Assignments** by choosing from questions organized by lesson, level of difficulty, and source—and add your own questions. Students' homework and quizzes are automatically graded, and the results are recorded in your gradebook.
- **Offer context-sensitive help to students, 24/7.** When you assign homework or quizzes, you decide if and when students get access to hints, solutions, or answers where appropriate—or they can be linked to relevant sections of their complete, online text for additional help whenever—and wherever they need it most.
- **Track Student Progress:** Analyze students' results and assess their level of understanding on an individual and class level using the Wiley*PLUS* gradebook, or export data to your own personal gradebook.
- **Administer Your Course:** Wiley*PLUS* can easily be integrated with another course management system, gradebook, or other resources you are using in your class, providing you with the flexibility to build your course, your way.
- **Seamlessly integrate all of the rich Wiley*PLUS* content and resources with WebCT and Blackboard**—with a single sign-on.

Please view our online demo at **www.wiley.com/college/wileyplus.** Here you will find additional information about the features and benefits of Wiley*PLUS*, how to request a "test drive" of Wiley*PLUS* for this title, and how to adopt it for class use.

MSDN ACADEMIC ALLIANCE—FREE 1-YEAR MEMBERSHIP **AVAILABLE TO QUALIFIED ADOPTERS!**

MSDN Academic Alliance (MSDN AA) is designed to provide the easiest and most inexpensive way for universities to make the latest Microsoft developer tools, products, and technologies available in labs, classrooms, and on student PCs. MSDN AA is an annual membership program for departments teaching Science, Technology, Engineering, and Mathematics (STEM) courses. The membership provides a complete solution to keep academic labs, faculty, and students on the leading edge of technology.

Software available in the MSDN AA program is provided at no charge to adopting departments through the Wiley and Microsoft publishing partnership.

As a bonus to this free offer, faculty will be introduced to Microsoft's Faculty Connection and Academic Resource Center. It takes time and preparation to keep students engaged while giving them a fundamental understanding of theory, and the Microsoft Faculty Connection is designed to help STEM professors with this preparation by providing articles, curriculum, and tools that professors can use to engage and inspire today's technology students.

* Contact your Wiley rep for details.

For more information about the MSDN Academic Alliance program, go to:

http://msdn.microsoft.com/academic/

Note: Microsoft Windows Vista Enterprise Edition can be downloaded from MSDNAA for use by students in this course.

Important Web Addresses and Phone Numbers

To locate the Wiley Higher Education Rep in your area, go to the following Web address and click on the "*Who's My Rep?*" link at the top of the page.

http://www.wiley.com/college

Or Call the MOAC Toll Free Number: 1 + (888) 764-7001 (U.S. & Canada only).

To learn more about becoming a Microsoft Certified Technology Specialist and exam availability, visit www.microsoft.com/learning/msbc.

www.wiley.com/college/microsoft *or*
call the MOAC Toll-Free Number: 1+(888) 764-7001 (U.S. & Canada only)

Student Support Program

Book Companion Website (www.wiley.com/college/microsoft)

The book companion site for the MOAC series includes the Instructor Resources, the student CD files, and Web links to important information for students and instructors.

Wiley*PLUS*

Wiley*PLUS* is a powerful and highly-integrated suite of teaching and learning resources designed to bridge the gap between what happens in the classroom and what happens at home and on the job. For students, Wiley*PLUS* provides the tools for study and practice that are available 24/7, wherever and whenever they want to study. Wiley*PLUS* includes a complete online version of the student textbook, PowerPoint presentations, homework and practice assignments and quizzes, image galleries, test bank questions, gradebook, and all the instructor resources in one easy-to-use website.

Wiley*PLUS* provides immediate feedback on student assignments and a wealth of support materials. This powerful study tool will help your students develop their conceptual understanding of the class material and increase their ability to answer questions.

- A **Study and Practice** area links directly to text content, allowing students to review the text while they study and answer. Access to Microsoft's Pre-Test, Learning Plan, and a code for taking the MCAS certification exam is available in Study and Practice. Additional Practice Questions tied to the MCAS certification that can be re-taken as many times as necessary, are also available.
- An **Assignment** area keeps all the work you want your students to complete in one location, making it easy for them to stay on task. Students have access to a variety of interactive self-assessment tools, as well as other resources for building their confidence and understanding. In addition, all of the assignments and quizzes contain a link to the relevant section of the multimedia book, providing students with context-sensitive help that allows them to conquer obstacles as they arise.
- A **Personal Gradebook** for each student allows students to view their results from past assignments at any time.

Please view our online demo at www.wiley.com/college/wileyplus. Here you will find additional information about the features and benefits of Wiley*PLUS*, how to request a "test drive" of Wiley*PLUS* for this title, and how to adopt it for class use.

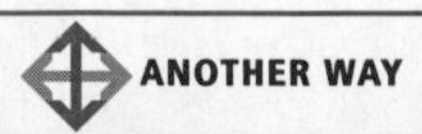

You can use the Search function in the Open dialog box to quickly find the specific file for which you are looking.

Wiley Desktop Editions

Wiley MOAC Desktop Editions are innovative, electronic versions of printed textbooks. Students buy the desktop version for 50% off the U.S. price of the printed text, and get the added value of permanence and portability. Wiley Desktop Editions provide students with numerous additional benefits that are not available with other e-text solutions.

Wiley Desktop Editions are NOT subscriptions; students download the Wiley Desktop Edition to their computer desktops. Students own the content they buy to keep for as long as they want. Once a Wiley Desktop Edition is downloaded to the computer desktop, students have instant access to all of the content without being online. Students can also print out the sections they prefer to read in hard copy. Students also have access to fully integrated resources within their Wiley Desktop Edition. From highlighting their e-text to taking and sharing notes, students can easily personalize their Wiley Desktop Edition as they are reading or following along in class.

Preparing to Take the Microsoft Certified Technology Specialist (MCTS) Exam

The Microsoft Certified Technology Specialist program is part of the new and enhanced Microsoft Business Certifications. It is easily attainable through a series of verifications that provide a simple and convenient framework for skills assessment and validation.

For organizations, the new certification program provides better skills verification tools that help with assessing not only in-demand skills on Windows Vista, but also the ability to quickly complete on-the-job tasks. Individuals will find it easier to identify and work towards the certification credential that meets their personal and professional goals.

To learn more about becoming a Microsoft Certified Technology Specialist and exam availability, visit www.microsoft.com/learning/mcp/mcts.

Microsoft Certified Technology Specialist (MCTS) Program

The Microsoft Certified Technology Specialist certifications enable professionals to target specific technologies and distinguish themselves by demonstrating in-depth knowledge and expertise in their specialized technologies.

A Microsoft Certified Technology Specialist in Windows Vista, Configuration possesses the knowledge and skills to configure Windows Vista for optimal performance on the desktop, including installing, managing, and configuring the new security, network, and application features in Windows Vista.

By becoming certified, you demonstrate to employers that you have achieved a predictable level of skill in the use of the Windows Vista operating system. Employers often require certification either as a condition of employment or as a condition of advancement within the company or other organization. The certification examinations are sponsored by Microsoft but administered through exam delivery partners like Thomson Prometric.

Preparing to Take an Exam

Unless you are a very experienced user, you will need to use a test preparation course to prepare to complete the test correctly and within the time allowed. The *Microsoft Official Academic Course* series is designed to prepare you with a strong knowledge of all exam topics, and with some additional review and practice on your own. You should feel confident in your ability to pass the appropriate exam.

After you decide which exam to take, review the list of objectives for the exam. You can easily identify tasks that are included in the objective list by locating the Objective Domain Matrix at the start of each lesson and the Certification Ready sidebars in the margin of the lessons in this book.

To take the MCTS test, visit *www.microsoft.com/learning/mcp/mcts* to locate your nearest testing center. Then call the testing center directly to schedule your test. The amount of advance notice you should provide will vary for different testing centers, and it typically depends on the number of computers available at the testing center, the number of other testers who have already been scheduled for the day on which you want to take the test, and the number of times per week that the testing center offers MCTS testing. In general, you should call to schedule your test at least two weeks prior to the date on which you want to take the test.

When you arrive at the testing center, you might be asked for proof of identity. A driver's license or passport is an acceptable form of identification. If you do not have either of these items of documentation, call your testing center and ask what alternative forms of identification will be accepted. If you are retaking a test, bring your MCTS identification number, which will have been given to you when you previously took the test. If you have not prepaid or if your organization has not already arranged to make payment for you, you will need to pay the test-taking fee when you arrive.

www.wiley.com/college/microsoft *or*
call the MOAC Toll-Free Number: 1+(888) 764-7001 (U.S. & Canada only)

Acknowledgments

MOAC Instructor Advisory Board

We would like thank to our Instructor Advisory Board, an elite group of educators who has assisted us every step of the way in building these products. Advisory Board members have acted as our sounding board on key pedagogical and design decisions leading to the development of these compelling and innovative textbooks for future Information Workers. Their dedication to technology education is truly appreciated.

Catherine Binder, Strayer University & Katharine Gibbs School–Philadelphia

Catherine currently works at both Katharine Gibbs School in Norristown, PA and Strayer University in King of Prussia, PA. Catherine has been at Katharine Gibbs School for 4 years. Catherine is currently the Department Chair/Lead instructor for PC Networking at Gibbs and the founder/advisor of the TEK Masters Society. Since joining Strayer University a year and a half ago she has risen in the ranks from adjunct to DIT/Assistant Campus Dean.

Catherine has brought her 10+ year's industry experience as Network Administrator, Network Supervisor, Professor, Bench Tech, Manager and CTO from such places as Foster Wheeler Corp, KidsPeace Inc., Victoria Vogue, TESST College, AMC Theatres, Blue Mountain Publishing and many more to her teaching venue.

Catherine began as an adjunct in the PC Networking department and quickly became a full-time instructor. At both schools she is in charge of scheduling, curricula and departmental duties. She happily advises about 80+ students and is committed to Gibbs/Strayer life, her students, and continuing technology education every day.

Penny Gudgeon, CDI College

Penny is the Program Manager for IT curriculum at Corinthian Colleges, Inc. Until January 2006, Penny was responsible for all Canadian programming and web curriculum for five years. During that time, Corinthian Colleges, Inc. acquired CDI College of Business and Technology in 2004. Before 2000 she spent four years as IT instructor at one of the campuses. Penny joined CDI College in 1997 after her working for 10 years first in programming and later in software productivity education. Penny previously has worked in the fields of advertising, sales, engineering technology and programming. When not working from her home office or indulging her passion for life long learning, and the possibilities of what might be, Penny likes to read mysteries, garden and relax at home in Hamilton, Ontario, with her Shih-Tzu, Gracie, and husband, Al.

Jana Hambruch, School District of Lee County

Ms. Hambruch currently serves as Director for the Information Technology Magnet Programs at The School District of Lee County in Ft Myers, Florida. She is responsible for the implementation and direction of three schools that fall under this grant program. This program has been recognized as one of the top 15 most innovative technology programs in the nation. She is also co-author of the grant proposal for the IT Magnet Grant prior to taking on the role of Director.

Ms. Hambruch has over ten years experience directing the technical certification training programs at many Colleges and Universities, including Barry University, the University of South Florida, Broward Community College, and at Florida Gulf Coast University, where she served as the Director for the Center for Technology Education. She excels at developing alternative training models that focus on the tie between the education provider and the community in which it serves.

Ms. Hambruch is a past board member and treasurer of the Human Resources Management Association of SW Florida, graduate of Leadership Lee County Class of 2002, Steering Committee Member for Leadership Lee County Class of 2004 and a former board member of the Career Coalition of Southwest Florida. She has frequently lectured for organizations such as Microsoft, American Society of Training and Development, Florida Gulf Coast University, Florida State University, University of Nevada at Las Vegas, University of Wisconsin at Milwaukee, Canada's McGill University, and Florida's State Workforce Summit.

Dee Hobson, Richland College

Dee Hobson is currently a faculty member of the Business Office Systems and Support Division at Richland College. Richland is one of seven colleges in the Dallas County Community College District and has the distinction of being the first community college to receive the Malcolm Baldrige National Quality Award in 2005. Richland also received the Texas Award for Performance Excellence in 2005.

The Business Office Systems and Support Division at Richland is also a Certiport Authorized Microsoft Office testing center. All students enrolling in one of Microsoft's application software courses (Word, Excel, PowerPoint, and Access) are required to take the respective Microsoft certification exam at the end of the semester.

Dee has taught computer and business courses in K-12 public schools and at a proprietary career college in Dallas. She has also been involved with several corporate training companies and with adult education programs in the Dallas area. She began her computer career as an employee of IBM Corporation in St. Louis, Missouri. During her ten-year IBM employment, she moved to Memphis, Tennessee, to accept a managerial position and to Dallas, Texas, to work in a national sales and marketing technical support center.

Keith Hoell, Katharine Gibbs School–New York

Keith has worked in both non-profit and proprietary education for over 10 years, initially at St. John's University in New York, and then as full-time faculty, Chairperson and currently Dean of Information Systems at the Katharine Gibbs School in New York City. He also worked for General Electric in the late 80's and early 90's as the Sysop of a popular bulletin board dedicated to ASCII-Art on GE's pioneering GEnie on-line service before the advent of the World Wide Web. He has taught courses and workshops dealing with many mainstream IT issues and varied technology, especially those related to computer hardware and operating system software, networking, software applications, IT project management and ethics, and relational database technology. An avid runner and a member of The New York Road Runners, he won the Footlocker Five Borough Challenge representing Queens at the 2005 ING New York City Marathon while competing against the 4 other borough reps. He currently resides in Queens, New York.

Michael Taylor, Seattle Central Community College

Michael worked in education and training for the last 20 years in both the public and private sector. He currently teaches and coordinates the applications support program at Seattle Central Community College and also administers the Microsoft IT Academy. His experience outside the educational world is in Travel and Tourism with wholesale tour operations and cruise lines.

Interests outside of work include greyhound rescue. (He adopted 3 x-racers who bring him great joy.) He also enjoys the arts and is fortunate to live in downtown Seattle where there is much to see and do.

MOAC Windows Vista Reviewers

We also thank the many reviewers who pored over the manuscript, providing invaluable feedback in the service of quality instructional materials.

Microsoft® Windows Vista™ Configuring Microsoft® Certified Technology Specialist Exam 70-620

Sue Bailey, Ouachita Technical College
David Courtaway, DeVry University—Pomona
Jason Eckert, TriOS College
Rob Hillard, National Park Community College
Katherine James, Seneca College
Steven Singer, Kapi'olani Community College
Steve Strom, Butler Community College
Joyce Thompson, Lehigh Carbon Community College
Dennis Yeadon, CDI College—Brampton

Microsoft® Supporting and Troubleshooting Applications on a Windows Vista™ Client for Enterprise Support Technicians

Microsoft® Certified Information Technology Professional Exam 70-622

Mohan Bala, CDI College—Toronto
Brian Bordelon, Lantec Computer Training Center
Wendy Corbin, Baker College
Nanci Ford, Fanshawe College
Vijay Navghare, CDI College—Scarborough
Richard Tamme, Elgin Community College
Sam Valcaniant, Chattanooga State Technical Community College

Focus Group and Survey Participants

Finally, we thank the hundreds of instructors who participated in our focus groups and surveys to ensure that the Microsoft Official Academic Courses best met the needs of our customers.

Jean Aguilar, Mt. Hood Community College
Konrad Akens, Zane State College
Michael Albers, University of Memphis
Diana Anderson, Big Sandy Community & Technical College
Phyllis Anderson, Delaware County Community College
Judith Andrews, Feather River College
Damon Antos, American River College
Bridget Archer, Oakton Community College
Linda Arnold, Harrisburg Area Community College–Lebanon Campus
Neha Arya, Fullerton College
Mohammad Bajwa, Katharine Gibbs School–New York
Virginia Baker, University of Alaska Fairbanks
Carla Bannick, Pima Community College
Rita Barkley, Northeast Alabama Community College
Elsa Barr, Central Community College–Hastings
Ronald W. Barry, Ventura County Community College District
Elizabeth Bastedo, Central Carolina Technical College
Karen Baston, Waubonsee Community College
Karen Bean, Blinn College
Scott Beckstrand, Community College of Southern Nevada
Paulette Bell, Santa Rosa Junior College

Liz Bennett, Southeast Technical Institute
Nancy Bermea, Olympic College
Lucy Betz, Milwaukee Area Technical College
Meral Binbasioglu, Hofstra University
Catherine Binder, Strayer University & Katharine Gibbs School–Philadelphia
Terrel Blair, El Centro College
Ruth Blalock, Alamance Community College
Beverly Bohner, Reading Area Community College
Henry Bojack, Farmingdale State University
Matthew Bowie, Luna Community College
Julie Boyles, Portland Community College
Karen Brandt, College of the Albemarle
Stephen Brown, College of San Mateo
Jared Bruckner, Southern Adventist University
Pam Brune, Chattanooga State Technical Community College
Sue Buchholz, Georgia Perimeter College
Roberta Buczyna, Edison College
Angela Butler, Mississippi Gulf Coast Community College
Rebecca Byrd, Augusta Technical College
Kristen Callahan, Mercer County Community College
Judy Cameron, Spokane Community College
Dianne Campbell, Athens Technical College
Gena Casas, Florida Community College at Jacksonville
Jesus Castrejon, Latin Technologies
Gail Chambers, Southwest Tennessee Community College
Jacques Chansavang, Indiana University–Purdue University Fort Wayne
Nancy Chapko, Milwaukee Area Technical College
Rebecca Chavez, Yavapai College
Sanjiv Chopra, Thomas Nelson Community College
Greg Clements, Midland Lutheran College
Dayna Coker, Southwestern Oklahoma State University–Sayre Campus
Tamra Collins, Otero Junior College
Janet Conrey, Gavilan Community College
Carol Cornforth, West Virginia Northern Community College
Gary Cotton, American River College
Edie Cox, Chattahoochee Technical College
Rollie Cox, Madison Area Technical College
David Crawford, Northwestern Michigan College
J.K. Crowley, Victor Valley College
Rosalyn Culver, Washtenaw Community College
Sharon Custer, Huntington University
Sandra Daniels, New River Community College
Anila Das, Cedar Valley College
Brad Davis, Santa Rosa Junior College
Susan Davis, Green River Community College
Mark Dawdy, Lincoln Land Community College
Jennifer Day, Sinclair Community College
Carol Deane, Eastern Idaho Technical College
Julie DeBuhr, Lewis-Clark State College
Janis DeHaven, Central Community College
Drew Dekreon, University of Alaska–Anchorage
Joy DePover, Central Lakes College
Salli DiBartolo, Brevard Community College
Melissa Diegnau, Riverland Community College
Al Dillard, Lansdale School of Business
Marjorie Duffy, Cosumnes River College
Sarah Dunn, Southwest Tennessee Community College
Shahla Durany, Tarrant County College–South Campus
Kay Durden, University of Tennessee at Martin
Dineen Ebert, St. Louis Community College–Meramec
Donna Ehrhart, State University of New York–Brockport
Larry Elias, Montgomery County Community College
Glenda Elser, New Mexico State University at Alamogordo
Angela Evangelinos, Monroe County Community College
Angie Evans, Ivy Tech Community College of Indiana
Linda Farrington, Indian Hills Community College
Dana Fladhammer, Phoenix College
Richard Flores, Citrus College
Connie Fox, Community and Technical College at Institute of Technology West Virginia University
Wanda Freeman, Okefenokee Technical College
Brenda Freeman, Augusta Technical College
Susan Fry, Boise State University
Roger Fulk, Wright State University–Lake Campus
Sue Furnas, Collin County Community College District
Sandy Gabel, Vernon College
Laura Galvan, Fayetteville Technical Community College
Candace Garrod, Red Rocks Community College
Sherrie Geitgey, Northwest State Community College
Chris Gerig, Chattahoochee Technical College
Barb Gillespie, Cuyamaca College
Jessica Gilmore, Highline Community College
Pamela Gilmore, Reedley College
Debbie Glinert, Queensborough Community College
Steven Goldman, Polk Community College
Bettie Goodman, C.S. Mott Community College
Mike Grabill, Katharine Gibbs School–Philadelphia
Francis Green, Penn State University
Walter Griffin, Blinn College
Fillmore Guinn, Odessa College
Helen Haasch, Milwaukee Area Technical College
John Habal, Ventura College
Joy Haerens, Chaffey College
Norman Hahn, Thomas Nelson Community College
Kathy Hall, Alamance Community College
Teri Harbacheck, Boise State University
Linda Harper, Richland Community College
Maureen Harper, Indian Hills Community College
Steve Harris, Katharine Gibbs School–New York
Robyn Hart, Fresno City College
Darien Hartman, Boise State University
Gina Hatcher, Tacoma Community College
Winona T. Hatcher, Aiken Technical College

BJ Hathaway, Northeast Wisconsin Tech College
Cynthia Hauki, West Hills College – Coalinga
Mary L. Haynes, Wayne County Community College
Marcie Hawkins, Zane State College
Steve Hebrock, Ohio State University Agricultural Technical Institute
Sue Heistand, Iowa Central Community College
Heith Hennel, Valencia Community College
Donna Hendricks, South Arkansas Community College
Judy Hendrix, Dyersburg State Community College
Gloria Hensel, Matanuska-Susitna College University of Alaska Anchorage
Gwendolyn Hester, Richland College
Tammarra Holmes, Laramie County Community College
Dee Hobson, Richland College
Keith Hoell, Katharine Gibbs School–New York
Pashia Hogan, Northeast State Technical Community College
Susan Hoggard, Tulsa Community College
Kathleen Holliman, Wallace Community College Selma
Chastity Honchul, Brown Mackie College/Wright State University
Christie Hovey, Lincoln Land Community College
Peggy Hughes, Allegany College of Maryland
Sandra Hume, Chippewa Valley Technical College
John Hutson, Aims Community College
Celia Ing, Sacramento City College
Joan Ivey, Lanier Technical College
Barbara Jaffari, College of the Redwoods
Penny Jakes, University of Montana College of Technology
Eduardo Jaramillo, Peninsula College
Barbara Jauken, Southeast Community College
Susan Jennings, Stephen F. Austin State University
Leslie Jernberg, Eastern Idaho Technical College
Linda Johns, Georgia Perimeter College
Brent Johnson, Okefenokee Technical College
Mary Johnson, Mt. San Antonio College
Shirley Johnson, Trinidad State Junior College–Valley Campus
Sandra M. Jolley, Tarrant County College
Teresa Jolly, South Georgia Technical College
Dr. Deborah Jones, South Georgia Technical College
Margie Jones, Central Virginia Community College
Randall Jones, Marshall Community and Technical College
Diane Karlsbraaten, Lake Region State College
Teresa Keller, Ivy Tech Community College of Indiana
Charles Kemnitz, Pennsylvania College of Technology
Sandra Kinghorn, Ventura College
Bill Klein, Katharine Gibbs School–Philadelphia
Bea Knaapen, Fresno City College
Kit Kofoed, Western Wyoming Community College
Maria Kolatis, County College of Morris
Barry Kolb, Ocean County College
Karen Kuralt, University of Arkansas at Little Rock
Belva-Carole Lamb, Rogue Community College
Betty Lambert, Des Moines Area Community College
Anita Lande, Cabrillo College
Junnae Landry, Pratt Community College
Karen Lankisch, UC Clermont
David Lanzilla, Central Florida Community College
Nora Laredo, Cerritos Community College
Jennifer Larrabee, Chippewa Valley Technical College
Debra Larson, Idaho State University
Barb Lave, Portland Community College
Audrey Lawrence, Tidewater Community College
Deborah Layton, Eastern Oklahoma State College
Larry LeBlanc, Owen Graduate School–Vanderbilt University
Philip Lee, Nashville State Community College
Michael Lehrfeld, Brevard Community College
Vasant Limaye, Southwest Collegiate Institute for the Deaf – Howard College
Anne C. Lewis, Edgecombe Community College
Stephen Linkin, Houston Community College
Peggy Linston, Athens Technical College
Hugh Lofton, Moultrie Technical College
Donna Lohn, Lakeland Community College
Jackie Lou, Lake Tahoe Community College
Donna Love, Gaston College
Curt Lynch, Ozarks Technical Community College
Sheilah Lynn, Florida Community College–Jacksonville
Pat R. Lyon, Tomball College
Bill Madden, Bergen Community College
Heather Madden, Delaware Technical & Community College
Donna Madsen, Kirkwood Community College
Jane Maringer-Cantu, Gavilan College
Suzanne Marks, Bellevue Community College
Carol Martin, Louisiana State University–Alexandria
Cheryl Martucci, Diablo Valley College
Roberta Marvel, Eastern Wyoming College
Tom Mason, Brookdale Community College
Mindy Mass, Santa Barbara City College
Dixie Massaro, Irvine Valley College
Rebekah May, Ashland Community & Technical College
Emma Mays-Reynolds, Dyersburg State Community College
Timothy Mayes, Metropolitan State College of Denver
Reggie McCarthy, Central Lakes College
Matt McCaskill, Brevard Community College
Kevin McFarlane, Front Range Community College
Donna McGill, Yuba Community College
Terri McKeever, Ozarks Technical Community College
Patricia McMahon, South Suburban College
Sally McMillin, Katharine Gibbs School–Philadelphia
Charles McNerney, Bergen Community College
Lisa Mears, Palm Beach Community College

Imran Mchmood, ITT Technical Institute–King of Prussia Campus
Virginia Melvin, Southwest Tennessee Community College
Jeanne Mercer, Texas State Technical College
Denise Merrell, Jefferson Community & Technical College
Catherine Merrikin, Pearl River Community College
Diane D. Mickey, Northern Virginia Community College
Darrelyn Miller, Grays Harbor College
Sue Mitchell, Calhoun Community College
Jacquie Moldenhauer, Front Range Community College
Linda Motonaga, Los Angeles City College
Sam Mryyan, Allen County Community College
Cindy Murphy, Southeastern Community College
Ryan Murphy, Sinclair Community College
Sharon E. Nastav, Johnson County Community College
Christine Naylor, Kent State University Ashtabula
Haji Nazarian, Seattle Central Community College
Nancy Noe, Linn-Benton Community College
Jennie Noriega, San Joaquin Delta College
Linda Nutter, Peninsula College
Thomas Omerza, Middle Bucks Institute of Technology
Edith Orozco, St. Philip's College
Dona Orr, Boise State University
Joanne Osgood, Chaffey College
Janice Owens, Kishwaukee College
Tatyana Pashnyak, Bainbridge College
John Partacz, College of DuPage
Tim Paul, Montana State University–Great Falls
Joseph Perez, South Texas College
Mike Peterson, Chemeketa Community College
Dr. Karen R. Petitto, West Virginia Wesleyan College
Terry Pierce, Onandaga Community College
Ashlee Pieris, Raritan Valley Community College
Jamie Pinchot, Thiel College
Michelle Poertner, Northwestern Michigan College
Betty Posta, University of Toledo
Deborah Powell, West Central Technical College
Mark Pranger, Rogers State University
Carolyn Rainey, Southeast Missouri State University
Linda Raskovich, Hibbing Community College
Leslie Ratliff, Griffin Technical College
Mar-Sue Ratzke, Rio Hondo Community College
Roxy Reissen, Southeastern Community College
Silvio Reyes, Technical Career Institutes
Patricia Rishavy, Anoka Technical College
Jean Robbins, Southeast Technical Institute
Carol Roberts, Eastern Maine Community College and University of Maine
Teresa Roberts, Wilson Technical Community College
Vicki Robertson, Southwest Tennessee Community College
Betty Rogge, Ohio State Agricultural Technical Institute
Lynne Rusley, Missouri Southern State University
Claude Russo, Brevard Community College
Ginger Sabine, Northwestern Technical College
Steven Sachs, Los Angeles Valley College
Joanne Salas, Olympic College
Lloyd Sandmann, Pima Community College–Desert Vista Campus
Beverly Santillo, Georgia Perimeter College
Theresa Savarese, San Diego City College
Sharolyn Sayers, Milwaukee Area Technical College
Judith Scheeren, Westmoreland County Community College
Adolph Scheiwe, Joliet Junior College
Marilyn Schmid, Asheville-Buncombe Technical Community College
Janet Sebesy, Cuyahoga Community College
Phyllis T. Shafer, Brookdale Community College
Ralph Shafer, Truckee Meadows Community College
Anne Marie Shanley, County College of Morris
Shelia Shelton, Surry Community College
Merilyn Shepherd, Danville Area Community College
Susan Sinele, Aims Community College
Beth Sindt, Hawkeye Community College
Andrew Smith, Marian College
Brenda Smith, Southwest Tennessee Community College
Lynne Smith, State University of New York–Delhi
Rob Smith, Katharine Gibbs School–Philadelphia
Tonya Smith, Arkansas State University–Mountain Home
Del Spencer – Trinity Valley Community College
Jeri Spinner, Idaho State University
Eric Stadnik, Santa Rosa Junior College
Karen Stanton, Los Medanos College
Meg Stoner, Santa Rosa Junior College
Beverly Stowers, Ivy Tech Community College of Indiana
Marcia Stranix, Yuba College
Kim Styles, Tri-County Technical College
Sylvia Summers, Tacoma Community College
Beverly Swann, Delaware Technical & Community College
Ann Taff, Tulsa Community College
Mike Theiss, University of Wisconsin–Marathon Campus
Romy Thiele, Cañada College
Sharron Thompson, Portland Community College
Ingrid Thompson-Sellers, Georgia Perimeter College
Barbara Tietsort, University of Cincinnati–Raymond Walters College
Janine Tiffany, Reading Area Community College
Denise Tillery, University of Nevada Las Vegas
Susan Trebelhorn, Normandale Community College
Noel Trout, Santiago Canyon College
Cheryl Turgeon, Asnuntuck Community College
Steve Turner, Ventura College
Sylvia Unwin, Bellevue Community College
Lilly Vigil, Colorado Mountain College
Sabrina Vincent, College of the Mainland
Mary Vitrano, Palm Beach Community College
Brad Vogt, Northeast Community College
Cozell Wagner, Southeastern Community College

Carolyn Walker, Tri-County Technical College
Sherry Walker, Tulsa Community College
Qi Wang, Tacoma Community College
Betty Wanielista, Valencia Community College
Marge Warber, Lanier Technical College–Forsyth Campus
Marjorie Webster, Bergen Community College
Linda Wenn, Central Community College
Mark Westlund, Olympic College
Carolyn Whited, Roane State Community College
Winona Whited, Richland College
Jerry Wilkerson, Scott Community College
Joel Willenbring, Fullerton College
Barbara Williams, WITC Superior
Charlotte Williams, Jones County Junior College
Bonnie Willy, Ivy Tech Community College of Indiana
Diane Wilson, J. Sargeant Reynolds Community College
James Wolfe, Metropolitan Community College
Marjory Wooten, Lanier Technical College
Mark Yanko, Hocking College
Alexis Yusov, Pace University
Naeem Zaman, San Joaquin Delta College
Kathleen Zimmerman, Des Moines Area Community College

We would also like to thank Lutz Ziob, Sanjay Advani, Jim DiIanni, Merrick Van Dongen, Jim LeValley, Bruce Curling, Joe Wilson, and Naman Kahn at Microsoft for their encouragement and support in making the Microsoft Official Academic Course programs the finest instructional materials for mastering the newest Microsoft technologies for both students and instructors.

www.wiley.com/college/microsoft *or*
call the MOAC Toll-Free Number: 1+(888) 764-7001 (U.S. & Canada only)

Brief Contents

www.wiley.com/college/microsoft ***or***
call the MOAC Toll-Free Number: 1+(888) 764-7001 (U.S. & Canada only)

Contents

Lesson 4: Working with Disks 94

Lesson 5: Working with Users and Groups 145

Lesson 6: Working with Drivers and Printers 182

FOR INSTRUCTORS

Wiley***PLUS*** is built around the activities you perform in your class each day. With Wiley***PLUS*** you can:

Prepare & Present

Create outstanding class presentations using a wealth of resources such as PowerPoint™ slides, image galleries, interactive simulations, and more. You can even add materials you have created yourself.

Create Assignments

Automate the assigning and grading of homework or quizzes by using the provided question banks, or by writing your own.

Track Student Progress

Keep track of your students' progress and analyze individual and overall class results.

Now Available with WebCT

"It has been a great help, and I believe it has helped me to achieve a better grade."

Michael Morris,
Columbia Basin College

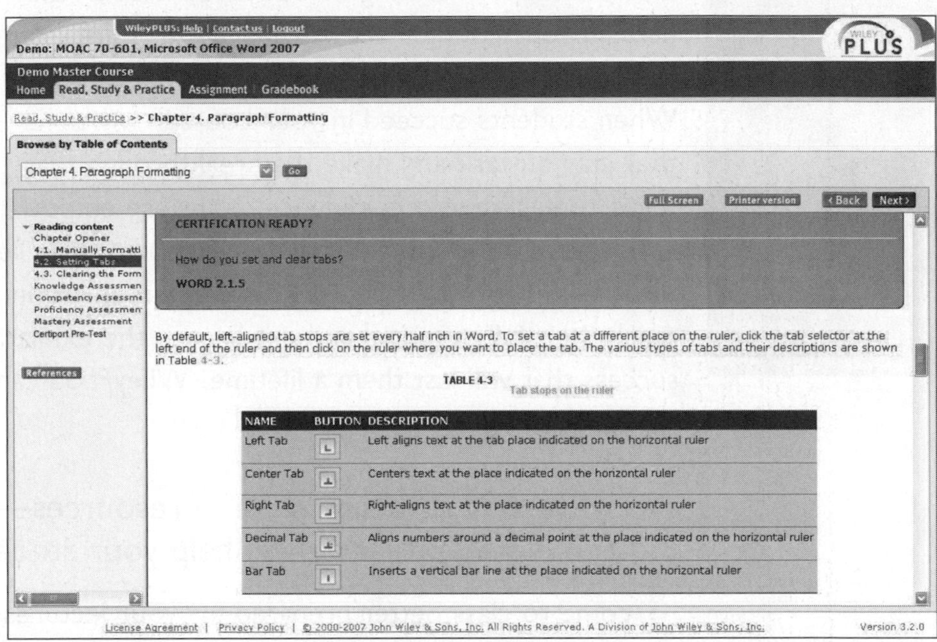

FOR STUDENTS

You have the potential to make a difference!

Wiley*PLUS* is a powerful online system packed with features to help you make the most of your potential and get the best grade you can!

With Wiley***PLUS*** you get:

A complete online version of your text and other study resources.

•

Problem-solving help, instant grading, and feedback on your homework and quizzes.

•

The ability to track your progress and grades throughout the term.

For more information on what Wiley*PLUS* can do to help you and your students reach their potential, please visit www.wiley.com/college/*wileyplus*.

76% of students surveyed said it made them better prepared for tests.*

*Based on a survey of 972 student users of Wiley*PLUS*

www.wiley.com/college/microsoft *or*
call the MOAC Toll-Free Number: 1+(888) 764-7001 (U.S. & Canada only)

Microsoft® Official Academic Course

Windows Vista® Configuration Microsoft® Certified Technology Specialist Exam 70-620

Craig Zacker

www.wiley.com/college/microsoft *or*
call the MOAC Toll-Free Number: 1+(888) 764-7001 (U.S. & Canada only)

Introducing Windows Vista

LESSON 1

OBJECTIVE DOMAIN MATRIX

Technology Skill	Objective Domain	Objective Number
Understanding Windows Vista System Requirements	Identify hardware requirements	1.1
Running the Upgrade Advisor	Identify hardware requirements • Run the Upgrade Advisor	1.1
Using the Windows Vista Interface	Configure Windows Sidebar	5.6

KEY TERMS

BitLocker
breadcrumb trail
language-agnostic
malware
MinWin
ReadyBoost
spyware
SuperFetch
Windows Aero
Windows Defender
Windows Firewall
Windows PE

Understanding Course Requirements

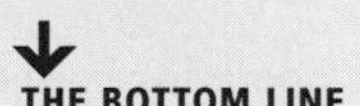

Windows Vista is the first major revision of the Microsoft Windows desktop operating system since the initial release of Windows XP in 2001. Some might argue that Vista is the most comprehensive desktop revision since Windows 95.

For new users, Vista provides a sleek new interface that many will find intuitive and easy to use. For experienced Windows users, an upgrade to Vista will require a period of adjustment as they learn new procedures for performing familiar tasks.

For technical personnel, Windows Vista represents not only a new interface and all of the support issues that accompany it, but an entirely new operating system (OS) architecture. In other words, not only do people have to learn to drive a new type of vehicle, but mechanics have to learn to repair a new type of engine as well.

In this course, you learn to install, configure, and manage Windows Vista, all tasks that differ significantly from their Windows XP counterparts. You study the Windows Vista installation process for individual computers, as well as the deployment of Windows Vista on an enterprise. You also learn to configure many of Vista's hardware, security, and networking controls, install and deploy applications, and manage certain configuration settings for a large fleet of Vista machines.

The book you are currently reading is the course textbook, which contains background and explanatory material on Windows Vista, along with a number of exercises and scenarios to test how much you have learned. Your other book is a lab manual, which guides you through a series of hands-on exercises corresponding to the material in the textbook.

If you diligently work your way through the textbook and the lab manual, and complete all of the assignments given to you by your instructor, you will come out of this course ready to provide technical support for Windows Vista users and computers.

The history of Microsoft Windows on desktop computers follows two parallel courses. Originally, Windows was a shell program that ran on top of the 16-bit MS-DOS operating system. Eventually, Microsoft combined MS-DOS and Windows into a single operating system product and developed it through several versions, including Windows 95, Windows 98, and Windows Me, which was the final product to use the MS-DOS kernel. At the same time, Microsoft was working on a completely new, 32-bit operating system that overcame most of the memory- and hardware-handling difficulties that were inherent in MS-DOS. Originally released as Windows NT 3.1 in 1993, the same basic NT kernel also formed the core of the Windows NT 4.0 and Windows 2000 operating system products. Intended primarily for servers at first, the NT kernel gradually gained popularity on the desktop, especially in business environments. With the release of Windows XP in 2001, Microsoft stopped using the MS-DOS kernel entirely; the NT kernel is now the basis of all new Windows operating systems, including Windows Vista, Windows Server 2003, and Windows Server 2008.

■ Introducing Windows Vista Editions

THE BOTTOM LINE Windows Vista is available in six editions. Understanding the features and capabilities of each edition is crucial for a desktop technician whose clients expect a recommendation for the specific product that is right for them.

Microsoft originally released Windows XP in two versions, Windows XP Home and Windows XP Professional, and eventually produced a number of hardware-specific editions, including Windows XP Media Center Edition and Windows XP Tablet PC Edition. The primary difference between the Home and Professional versions is the ability of the operating system to connect to a Windows network domain.

With Windows Vista, Microsoft has expanded its scope, making the operating system available in six versions, as follows:

- Windows Vista Starter—Microsoft intends the Starter edition of Windows Vista to be a low-cost alternative to unauthorized Windows installations for emerging markets only, such as parts of Asia and South America. Starter will not be available in Europe, Australia, New Zealand, or North America. The Starter edition has substantial limitations, including a physical memory limit of 256 MB, a maximum of three concurrently running applications, inability to accept inbound network connections, no 64-bit mode, and limited processor support.
- Windows Vista Home Basic—Microsoft intends Home Basic for budget-minded users that do not require advanced media support. Home Basic includes a subset of the entertainment features found in the Home Premium edition, but lacks business-oriented features, such as the ability to join a Windows network domain. Original Equipment Manufacturers (OEMs) use Home Basic as the default operating system supplied with PCs they market to home users.
- Windows Vista Home Premium—Home Premium includes an extended set of cosmetic and entertainment features, but lacks business features, such as the ability to join a Windows network domain. OEMs supply Home Premium as an upgrade on PCs they market to home users.
- Windows Vista Business—Business includes a basic array of management features, as well as the ability to join a Windows network domain, but it lacks the entertainment features

found in the Home Basic and Home Premium editions. The Business edition will be the default operating system supplied with entry-level computers targeted at the business market.

- Windows Vista Enterprise—Enterprise includes a larger set of management features, as well as the ability to join a Windows network domain, but it too lacks the entertainment features found in the Home Basic and Home Premium editions. Microsoft has designed the Enterprise edition to be supplied to Windows site license customers, and it will not be a retail product.
- Windows Vista Ultimate—Ultimate includes all of the entertainment and management features found in the Home Premium and Enterprise editions, as well as the ability to join a Windows network domain. Microsoft designed the Ultimate edition to be a premium product available to users at additional cost.

Upgrade paths between Windows Vista editions and from earlier Windows versions to Windows Vista are available only in certain combinations. For more information on upgrading to Windows Vista, see Lesson 2, "Installing Windows Vista."

Table 1-1 lists the operating system features and applications that are included in each of the five main Windows Vista editions.

Table 1-1

Feature Support in Windows Vista Editions

	Home Basic	Home Premium	Business	Enterprise	Ultimate
Domain Support	No	No	Yes	Yes	Yes
BitLocker Drive Encryption	No	No	No	Yes	Yes
Client-Side Caching	No	No	Yes	Yes	Yes
Encrypting File System	No	No	Yes	Yes	Yes
Folder Redirection	No	No	Yes	Yes	Yes
Group Policy Support	No	No	Yes	Yes	Yes
Image-based Backup	No	No	Yes	Yes	Yes
Integrated Smart Card Management	No	No	Yes	Yes	Yes
Internet Information Services	No	No	Yes	Yes	Yes
Multiple User Interface Languages	No	No	No	Yes	Yes
Offline Files Support	No	No	Yes	Yes	Yes
PC-to-PC Sync	No	Yes	Yes	Yes	Yes
Remote Desktop Client	Yes	Yes	Yes	Yes	Yes
Remote Desktop Host	No	No	Yes	Yes	Yes
Roaming User Profiles	No	No	Yes	Yes	Yes
Small Business Resources	No	No	Yes	No	Yes
UNIX-based Application Subsystem	No	No	No	Yes	Yes
Virtual PC Express	No	No	No	Yes	Yes

(continued)

Table 1-1 (*continued*)

	Home Basic	Home Premium	Business	Enterprise	Ultimate
Windows Aero	No	Yes	Yes	Yes	Yes
Windows DVD Maker	No	Yes	No	No	Yes
Windows Fax and Scan	No	No	Yes	Yes	Yes
Windows Media Center	No	Yes	No	No	Yes
Windows Movie Maker	Yes	Yes	No	No	Yes
Windows Shadow Copy	No	No	Yes	Yes	Yes
Windows Side Show	No	Yes	Yes	Yes	Yes

Understanding Windows Vista System Requirements

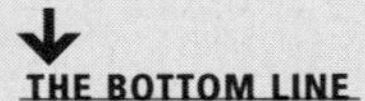

Many clients considering an upgrade to Windows Vista are likely to need hardware upgrades as well, and a thorough understanding of the Vista system requirements is essential for the desktop technician.

Because the various Vista editions differ primarily in the number and type of applications included with each product, the basic minimum system requirements are the same for all (except Starter) editions. Microsoft has created two designations for Vista system requirements, called Windows Vista Capable PC and Windows Vista Premium Ready PC. Table 1-2 shows the minimum hardware requirements for each of these designations.

Table 1-2

Minimum System Requirements for Windows Vista

Windows Vista Capable PC	Windows Vista Premium Ready PC
800 MHz 32-bit (x86) or 64-bit (x64) processor	1 GHz 32-bit (x86) or 64-bit (x64) processor
512 MB of system memory	1 GB of system memory
DirectX 9-capable graphics processor	DirectX 9- and WDDM-capable graphics processor, with Pixel Shader 2.0 and 32 bits per pixel
	128 MB or graphics memory
	40 GB of hard drive capacity with 15 GB free
	DVD-ROM drive
	Audio output capability
	Internet access capability

Microsoft permits PCs conforming to these specifications to display an official logo such as the one shown in Figure 1-1. However, the appearance of the logo on a new computer does not necessarily mean that a license for the Windows Vista operating system is included in the computer's price. You might still have to pay for the operating system separately.

Figure 1-1

The Windows Vista Capable PC logo

Apart from these minimum system requirements, there are also hardware limitations for each of the Windows Vista editions, as shown in Table 1-3.

Table 1-3

Hardware Limitations for Windows Vista Editions

	Starter	Home Basic	Home Premium	Business	Enterprise	Ultimate
32-bit or 64-bit Support	32-bit Only	Both	Both	Both	Both	Both
Max RAM (32-bit)	256 MB	4 GB	4 GB	4 GB	4 GB	4 GB
Max RAM (64-bit)	N/A	8 GB	16 GB	128 GB	128 GB	128 GB
Two-Processor Support	No	No	No	Yes	Yes	Yes
Windows Tablet PC Support	No	No	Yes	Yes	Yes	Yes
Peer Network Connections	0	5	10	10	10	10

While the official system requirements that Microsoft provides are a useful starting point, they do not provide the whole picture. Upgrading to Windows Vista is a subject that is sure to be on the minds of many Windows users, ranging from home users with a single computer to corporate executives responsible for thousands of workstations. For these users, simply falling within the system requirements is not enough. They want to be sure that Vista will be an improvement over their previous OS, and that requires them to consider the individual system components more carefully.

- Processor—Of the major computer components, the processor is likely to have the least effect on overall system performance. The 800 MHz and 1 GHz processors called for in the Vista system requirements are relatively outdated by today's standards. Most of the PCs in use today have processors much faster than 1 GHz, and even computers that are four or five years old will most likely meet the required speeds. The benefits derived from a faster processor depend largely on the applications the computer is running. Hardcore gamers are the users most intent on wringing every last GHz from their systems, but for general computer use, the requirements are not so heavy. For the purposes of upgrading to Windows Vista, it is probably not worthwhile to purchase a new computer just to get a faster processor.
- System memory—The memory requirements of the Windows operating systems have risen precipitously in recent years. The 512 MB minimum required for a Vista Capable PC is pushing the lower limit. You are likely to experience disappointing performance levels in Windows Vista with just 512 MB, and you certainly will not be able to multitask large applications. Memory is easy and inexpensive to upgrade, however; no other hardware upgrade will yield a more immediately detectable performance increase. The 1 GB of memory recommended for a Vista Premium Ready PC is sufficient for a general-purpose system, but memory-intensive applications such as video and image editing, as well as high-end games, could well benefit from more. Be sure to check your system documentation to determine what memory upgrades are possible for your computer.

- Hard disk space—Windows Vista requires much more hard disk space than earlier versions of Windows, but with the low prices and high capacities of today's hard disk drives, it is not difficult to meet or exceed the system requirements. For most users, the real disk space hog is not operating system files or even applications, but rather the collection of audio and video files that we all seem to accumulate. Another aspect to consider, however, is the performance level of the hard drive(s) in your computer. Older drives that spin at 5400 RPM can lead to palpably poorer performance than drives running at 7200 RPM or faster. In addition, if you plan to upgrade, you might consider using one of the newer Serial Advanced Technology Attachment (SATA) drives instead of the older Integrated Drive Electronics (IDE) models. If you do upgrade to SATA on an older computer, remember that you will probably have to purchase an SATA controller card as well as the drive itself.
- Video display adapter—The system component that is causing the most upgrade worries to potential Vista users is the video display adapter. Windows Vista is the first Windows operating system to require such specific graphics capabilities, compelling many users to take a crash course in video display adapter specifications as a result. The operating system feature that requires the capabilities stated in the Vista Premium Ready PC specification is ***Windows Aero,*** the interface element that gives the Vista desktop its glass-like, translucent look. On a Vista system running Windows Aero, the edges of all windows are translucent and contain a fuzzy image of the elements behind them. It is the process of rendering those fuzzy images while Aero is running that is so graphic intensive, and incidentally, consumes significant system resources as well. The result is impressive; an Aero desktop has a slick, modern appearance that enhances the Windows user experience. However, if your existing video adapter has been serving you well, you can certainly wait to upgrade it. The Aero features are mostly cosmetic, and your system is likely to perform better using the similar but less graphic-intensive Vista Basic interface instead.

For businesses running hundreds or thousands of workstations, the cost of these hardware upgrades can be enormous, so you should carefully consider the current state of your computers and what new hardware your organization will need to make a Windows Vista upgrade practical and productive.

Running the Upgrade Advisor

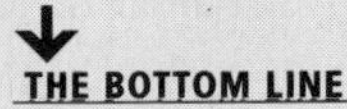

All desktop technicians should be familiar with the Upgrade Advisor application, as it is the surest way of determining whether a computer is capable of running Windows Vista.

CERTIFICATION READY?
Identify hardware requirements: Run the Upgrade Advisor
1.1

The easiest way to determine whether your Windows XP computer is capable of running Windows Vista is to use Microsoft's Upgrade Advisor application, which replaces the Hardware Compatibility List (HCL) associated with earlier Windows versions. Upgrade Advisor is a Windows XP and Windows Vista application that scans an individual computer's hardware and software to determine whether it is capable of running Windows Vista at peak efficiency.

RUN UPGRADE ADVISOR

GET READY. Before you run Upgrade Advisor, be sure to plug in and turn on any USB devices or other devices such as printers, external hard drives, or scanners that you regularly use with the PC you are evaluating.

1. Insert the Windows Vista installation disc in the drive. The Install Windows page appears, as shown in Figure 1-2.

Figure 1-2

The Install Windows page

2. Click the **Check compatibility online** arrow. The Windows Vista: Upgrade Advisor page appears, as shown in Figure 1-3.

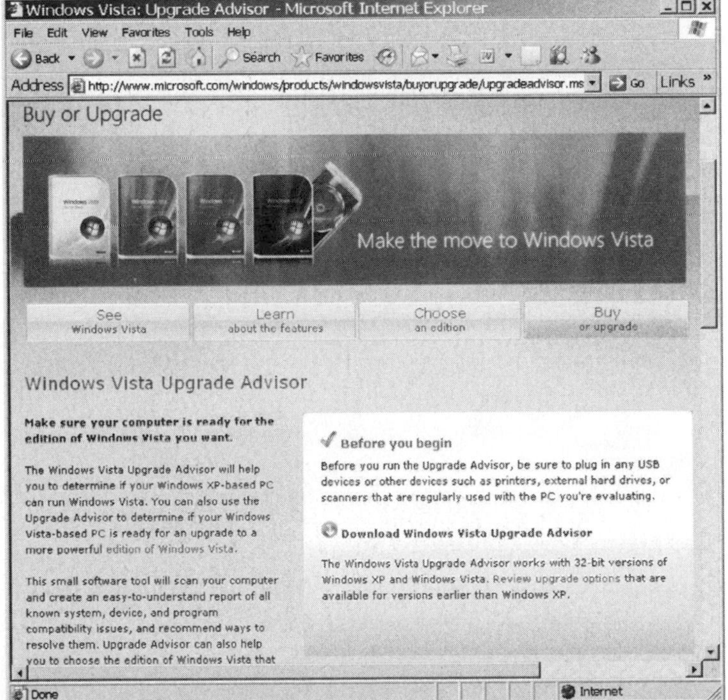

Figure 1-3

The Windows Vista: Upgrade Advisor page

TAKE NOTE*

If you do not have a Windows Vista installation disk, you can access the Windows Vista: Upgrade Advisor page directly by entering the following URL into your browser: *http://go.microsoft.com/fwlink/?linkid=60497.*

3. Click the **Download Windows Vista Upgrade Advisor** hyperlink. The Download Details: Windows Vista Upgrade Advisor page appears.
4. Click the **Download** button. A File Download–Security Warning message box appears.
5. Click the **Run** button. A progress indicator message box appears. Once the system has finished downloading the file, an Internet Explorer–Security Warning message box appears, asking if you want to run the software.

6. Click the **Run** button. The Welcome to the Windows Vista Upgrade Advisor Setup Wizard page appears, as shown in Figure 1-4.

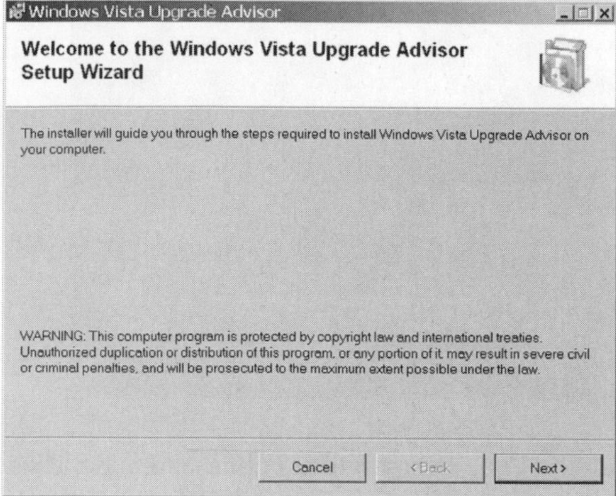

Figure 1-4

The Welcome to the Windows Vista Upgrade Advisor Setup Wizard page

7. Click **Next** to continue. The License Agreement page appears, as shown in Figure 1-5.

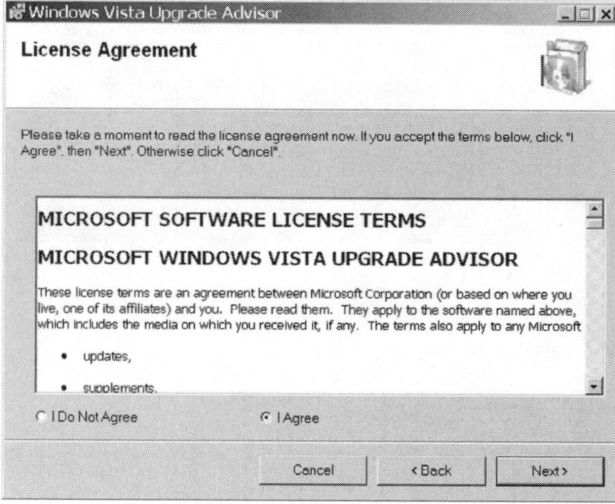

Figure 1-5

The License Agreement page of the Windows Vista Upgrade Advisor Setup Wizard

8. Select the **I Agree** radio button and then click **Next**. The Select Installation Folder appears, as shown in Figure 1-6.

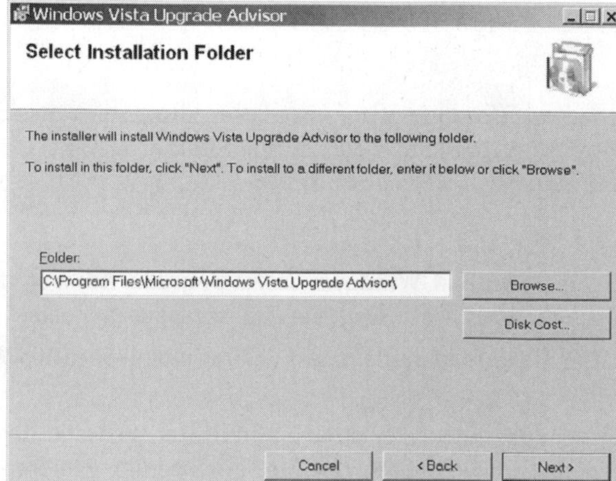

Figure 1-6

The Select Installation Folder page of the Windows Vista Upgrade Advisor Setup Wizard

9. Click **Next** to accept the default location. The Confirm Installation page appears, as shown in Figure 1-7.

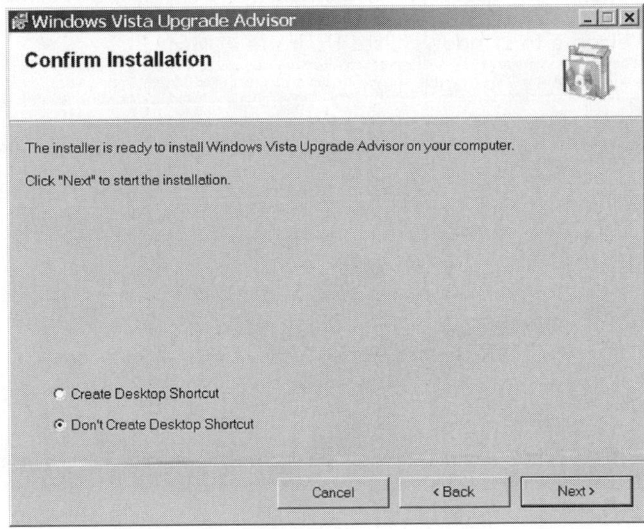

Figure 1-7

The Confirm Installation page of the Windows Vista Upgrade Advisor Setup Wizard

10. Select the **Create Desktop Shortcut** radio button, if desired, and then click **Next**. The Installing Windows Upgrade Advisor page appears, as the wizard installs the program.
11. The Installation Complete page appears, as shown in Figure 1-8. Leave the Launch Windows Vista Upgrade Advisor checkbox selected and then click **Close**.

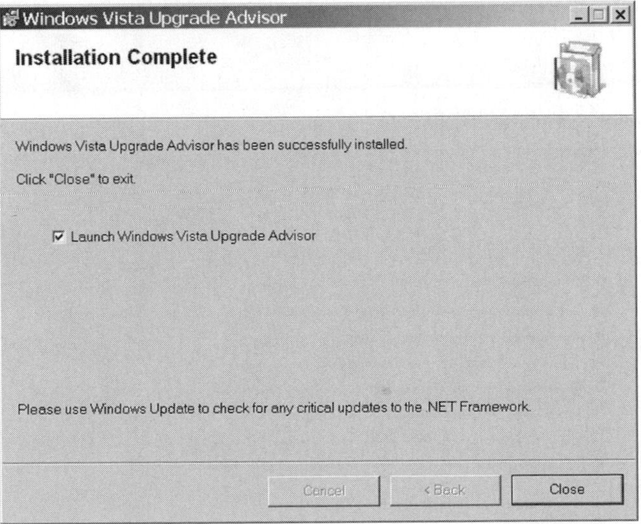

Figure 1-8

The Installation Complete page of the Windows Vista Upgrade Advisor Setup Wizard

12. The Upgrade Advisor program loads and then the Welcome to Windows Vista Upgrade Advisor page appears, as shown in Figure 1-9.

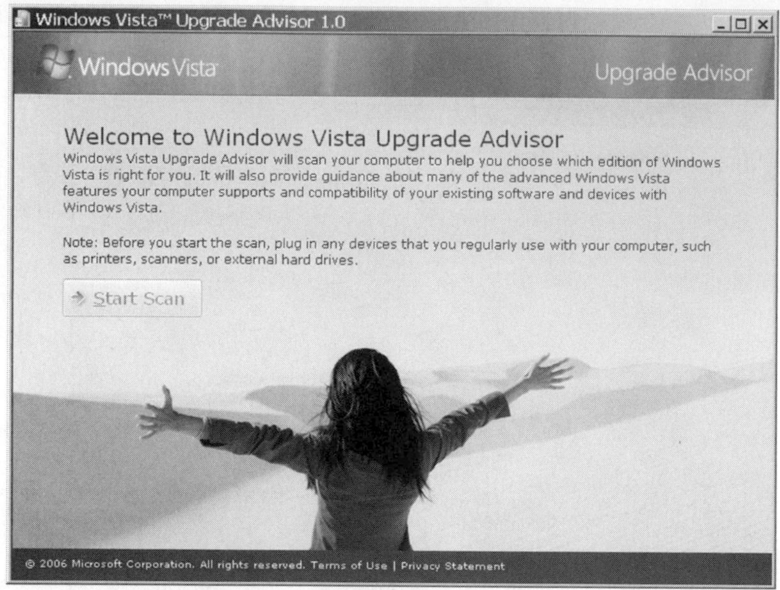

Figure 1-9

The Welcome to Windows Vista Upgrade Advisor page

13. Click the **Start Scan** button. As it scans the hardware and the software on your computer, Upgrade Advisor displays information about Windows Vista.
14. When the *Scan complete* page appears, as shown in Figure 1-10, click the **See Details** button. A screen appears, specifying whether your computer is capable of running Windows Vista and, if so, recommending a specific edition.

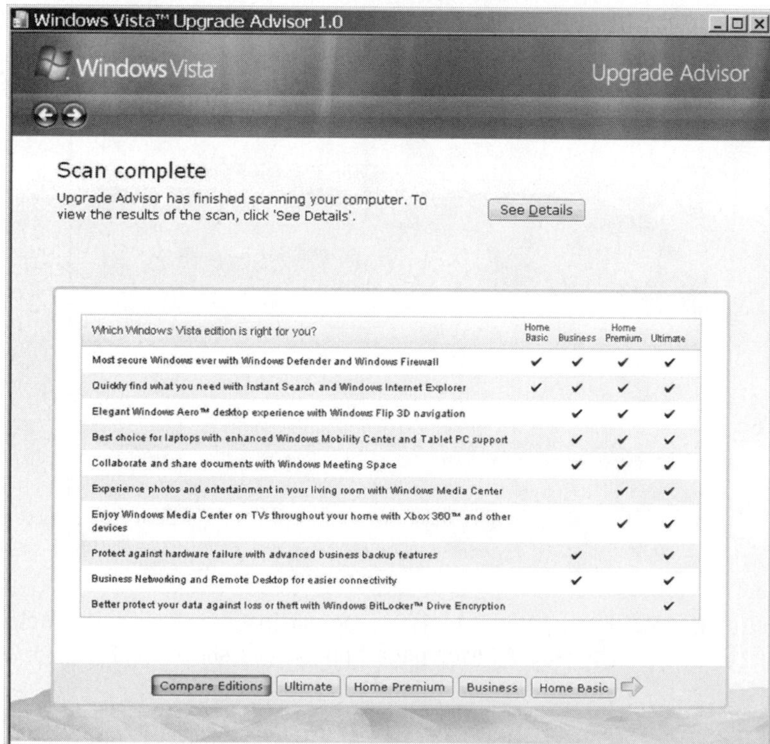

Figure 1-10

The Scan complete page

If your computer is not capable of running Windows Vista, Upgrade Advisor displays a list of the system requirements and/or devices that would prevent Vista from running. If your computer is capable of running Windows Vista, as shown in Figure 1-11, Upgrade Advisor might display system requirements and devices that you could improve, to provide better performance with Vista.

Figure 1-11

The Your computer can run Windows Vista page

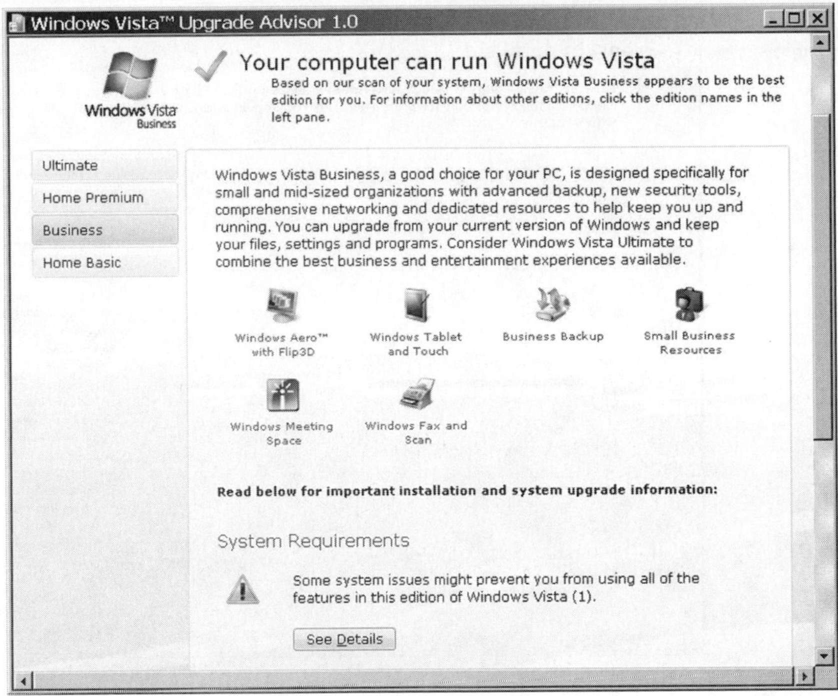

For example, if your computer has sufficient memory, hard disk space, and processor speed, Upgrade Advisor will indicate that an upgrade to Vista is possible, but if your video adapter is incapable of running the Windows Aero interface, the advisor will tell you so, as shown in Figure 1-12.

Figure 1-12

The Review these system issues for Windows Vista page

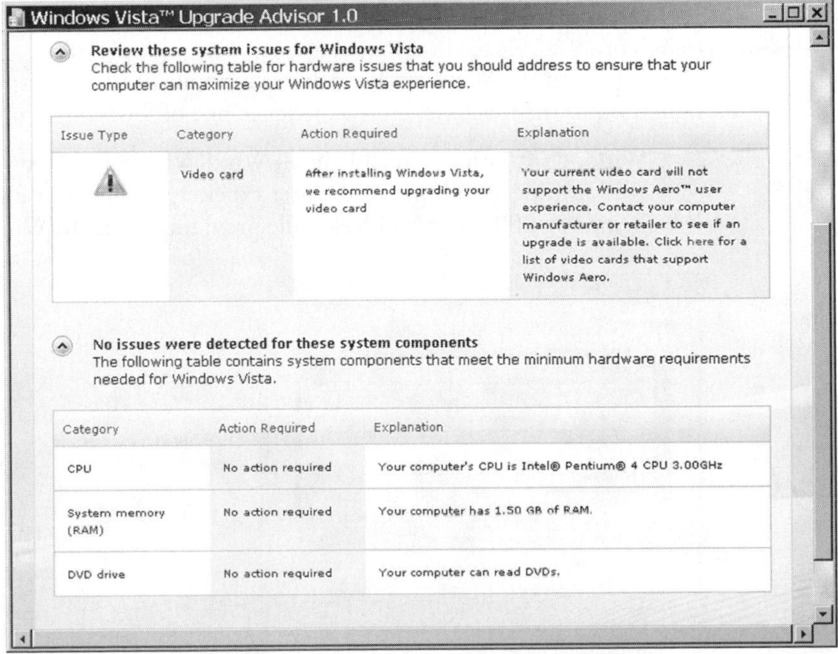

In addition to evaluating your hardware, Upgrade Advisor also scans the software on your computer and attempts to determine whether it will run with Windows Vista. As shown in Figure 1-13, the *Program details* page lists applications with both major and minor compatibility issues, and also lists the software products that have a Windows Vista logo, indicating that they have been tested with Windows Vista.

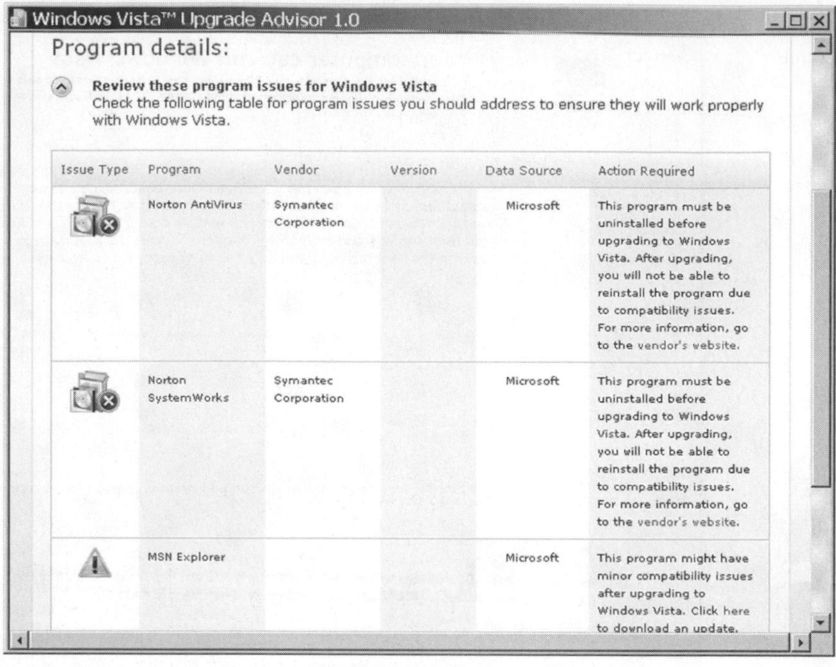

Figure 1-13

The Program details page

■ Introducing Windows Vista User Experience Levels

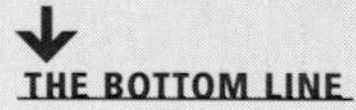

The Windows Vista user experience levels are liable to be a source of many technical support calls. Desktop technicians should be familiar with the levels, the hardware configurations that can alter them, and the controls used to configure them.

Depending on the Windows Vista edition installed on the computer and the hardware configuration of the machine, users experience one of four different interface levels, as follows:

- Windows Classic—Available in all Windows Vista editions (including the Starter edition), the Windows Classic user experience, shown in Figure 1-14, largely retains the Windows 2000 look and feel while providing access to Windows Vista features.

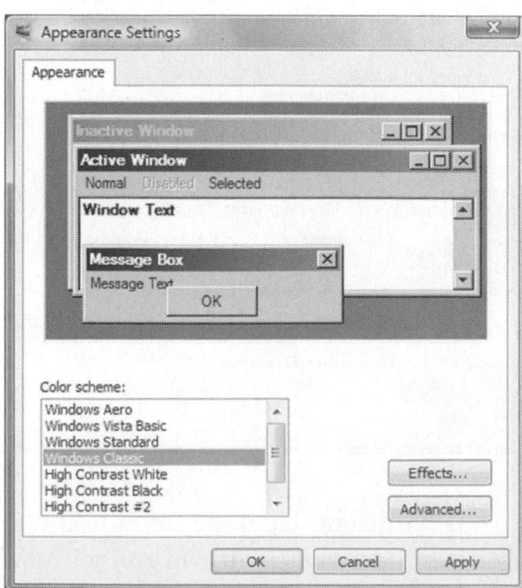

Figure 1-14

The Windows Classic user experience

- Windows Standard—Available in all Windows Vista editions except Starter, the Windows Standard interface, shown in Figure 1-15, retains the gray, square-cornered, two-dimensional look of the Windows Classic interface, but takes advantage of Windows Driver Display Model (WDDM) graphics hardware to provide smoother and faster window handling.

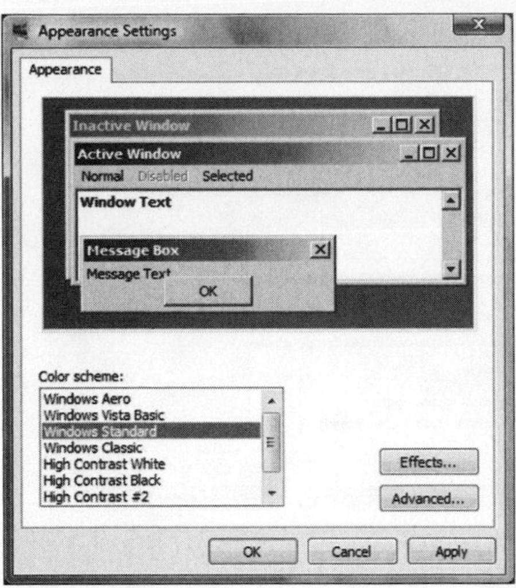

Figure 1-15

The Windows Standard user experience

- Windows Vista Basic—Available in all Windows Vista editions (including the Starter edition), the Windows Vista Basic user experience, shown in Figure 1-16, provides users with many of the new Vista interface features found in Windows Aero, but at a reduced detail level that has more modest hardware requirements. For example, Vista Basic windows have the same rounded edges as Windows Aero windows, but the edges are not transparent.

Figure 1-16

The Windows Vista Basic user experience

- Windows Aero—Available in all Windows Vista versions except Starter and Home Basic, Windows Aero is the most advanced user experience that Windows Vista can provide. Individual windows take on a translucent glass look around the edges, as shown in Figure 1-17, taskbars have live thumbnails, and the Windows Flip and Flip 3D views enable you to work with your windows in different ways. Windows Aero requires the most advanced hardware of any of the user experiences listed here, and consumes the most system resources.

Figure 1-17

The Windows Aero user experience

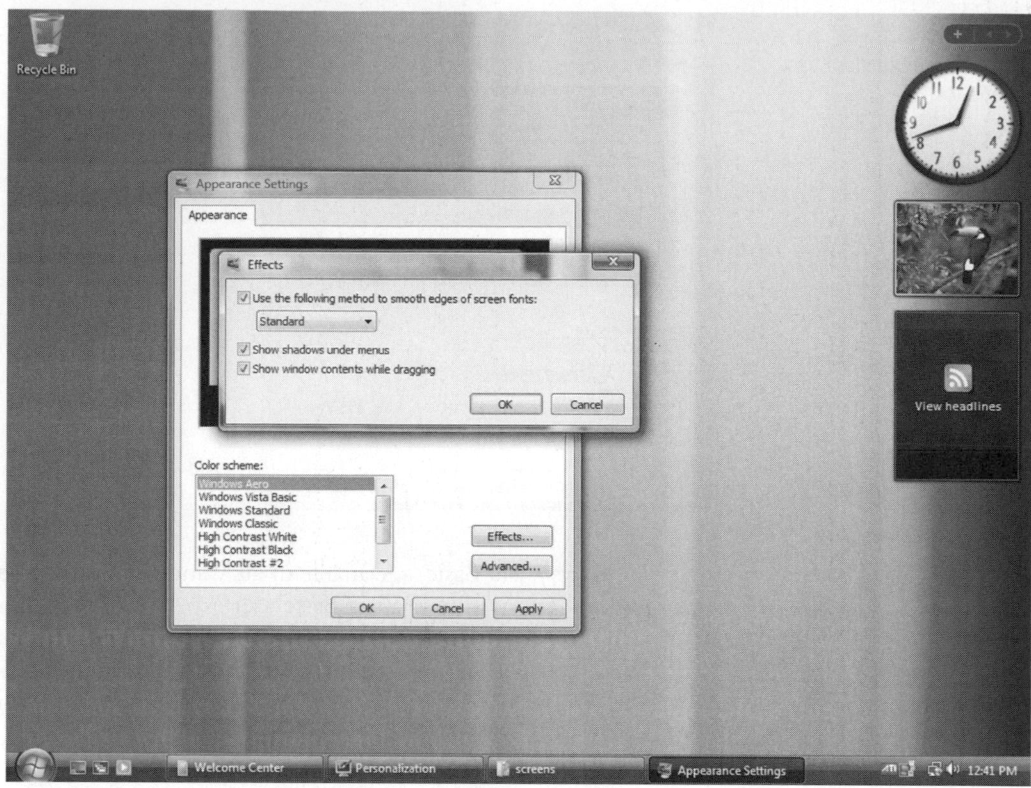

When you install Windows Vista, the Setup program configures the operating system to use the most advanced user experience level that your computer hardware can support by default. You can modify the default setting using the Personalization control panel.

For more information on customizing the look and feel of the Windows Vista user interface, see Lesson 3, "Configuring System Settings."

■ Understanding Windows Vista Organizational Roles

THE BOTTOM LINE

Windows Vista is capable of functioning as a standalone or network computer, and desktop technicians should be familiar with the peculiarities of both environments.

Based on the different types of applications and features they include, the various Windows Vista editions enable the operating system to function as a workstation in a number of organizational roles, as follows:

- Standalone—The Windows Vista Home Basic, Home Premium, and Ultimate editions are all suitable for running on a standalone workstation, such as that of a single home user connected only to the Internet. While many standalone users do run office productivity applications, such as word processors and spreadsheets, entertainment applications, such as media players, are more prevalent. That is why these three editions include more media-related applications, which are of greater importance to home users, and are more likely to be inappropriate for business users.
- Workgroup—All of the Windows Vista editions except Starter are capable of functioning as part of a workgroup network. A workgroup is a peer-to-peer network in which each computer can communicate with any other computer, without a central authentication or authorization facility. In most cases, workgroup networks enable users in homes and

small businesses to share resources, such as printers, backup devices, or Internet connections. In a workgroup, each computer is responsible for maintaining its user accounts and securing its own resources.

- Domain—The Windows Vista Business, Enterprise, and Ultimate editions are all capable of joining a Windows network domain. A Windows domain uses one or more Windows servers as domain controllers, that is, computers that authenticate the access credentials of domain users and authorize their access to domain resources. With this arrangement, network administrators can create and maintain a single, centrally located set of user accounts for the entire network. Windows Vista is not capable of functioning as a domain controller, but these three editions do include domain client capabilities. Because of the additional expense of running domain controllers and purchasing domain-capable editions of Windows, this organizational role is typically limited to medium and large businesses.

TAKE NOTE*

A Windows network domain is not necessarily the same as an Internet domain. A Windows domain consists solely of computers running Windows, each of which must be running client software that enables it to join and participate in the domain. An Internet domain can consist of computers running on any hardware platform and using any operating system. The primary function of an Internet domain is to assign friendly names to the computers and associate them with the IP addresses the computers use to communicate. For more information on domains and networking, see Lesson 7, "Configuring Network Connectivity."

■ What's New in Windows Vista?

Windows Vista includes a great many new features, some of which are hidden "under the hood" while others are immediately visible. Desktop technicians must familiarize themselves with these changes and try to anticipate how they will affect their duties.

As stated earlier, for technicians and users accustomed to Windows XP and/or Windows 2000, Windows Vista will require a period of acclimatization before you feel comfortable with all of the new features and procedures. However, in many cases, you will find that Microsoft has improved substantially on its earlier products in many ways.

Working with Windows Vista Distribution Media

You have seen already that Microsoft has increased the number of operating system editions available from two in Windows XP to six in Windows Vista. However, when you begin working with the installation media, you will soon notice that working with six versions of the operating system does not mean working with six different sets of installation disks.

Microsoft has chosen to release Windows Vista on DVD discs by default rather than on CDs as they did Windows XP (although a set of five CDs is available). The amount of code required to install Windows Vista is far too much to fit on one CD, so a single DVD was deemed preferable to a set of CDs. All new computers sold today come equipped with a DVD reader, and most users that already own computers have DVD support. For those that do not, aftermarket DVD-ROM drives are extremely inexpensive and easy to install.

TAKE NOTE*

All of the Windows Vista editions except Starter support both 32-bit (×86) and 64-bit (×64) processor platforms. Because the platforms utilize totally different sets of instructions, the 32-bit and 64-bit versions of the operating system are supplied on different discs.

For corporate customers with fleets of computers lacking DVD drives, it is possible to install Windows Vista over a network connection or by copying the installation files to a USB flash drive.

Understanding the Windows Vista Modular Architecture

You will notice that Microsoft is not distributing a different installation DVD for each Windows Vista edition. Technicians working with multiple editions will soon learn that all of the editions are included on a single disk. The operating system Setup program determines which edition to install from the product key you enter during the installation process.

These innovations in the Windows Vista distribution method are possible, and practical, because of the modular architecture that Microsoft has devised for the operating system. It has based all of the Windows Vista editions on a common core module that is sometimes called ***MinWin***. The MinWin module contains approximately 95 percent of the operating system functionality. All Windows Vista installations begin with the installation of the MinWin module; the additional installation of a secondary module containing the functionality of the product key designated edition follows.

The MinWin module, in addition to lacking all edition-specific code, also lacks all language-specific code. The module is therefore said to be ***language-agnostic***. For this reason, Microsoft does not have to produce multiple versions of Windows Vista for different languages. The installer selects the appropriate language during installation, which results in the application of a language module that supplies all of the text the operating system displays. Figure 1-18 illustrates the installation process and the application of the edition-specific and language-specific modules.

Figure 1-18

The Windows Vista modular installation process

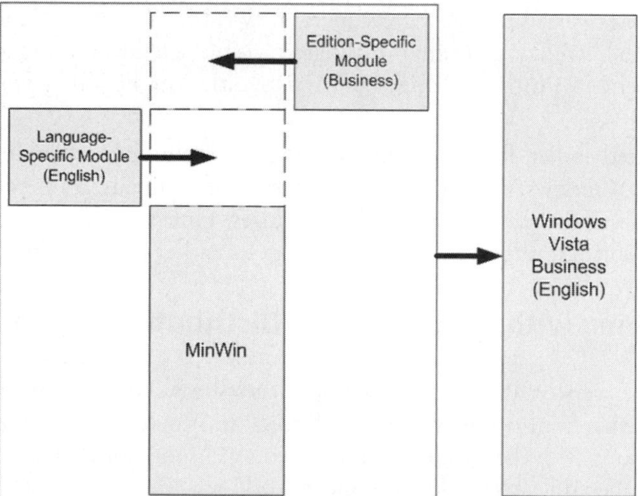

The single disc distribution medium also simplifies the process of upgrading Windows Vista to another edition or adding another language to the interface. The Windows Anytime Upgrade process consists of simply adding the appropriate edition or language module to the operating system from the same installation disc.

Using the Windows Vista Interface

When you look at a new installation of Windows Vista for the first time, you will notice that some of the familiar Windows screen elements have changed substantially in appearance.

USING THE TASKBAR

The taskbar remains the fundamental entry point for the Windows Vista interface, just as it was in Windows XP. The taskbar's Start button is now the Vista orb, as shown in Figure 1-19, in place of the familiar rectangular button present since the introduction of Windows 95. Clicking the orb displays the Start menu.

Figure 1-19

The Windows Vista taskbar

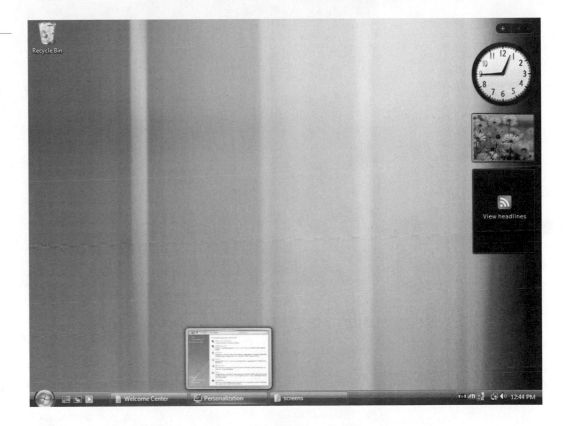

MORE INFORMATION

Windows Vista uses the same live thumbnail capability as the taskbar in the new Flip and Flip 3D features. When you press **ALT+Tab**, a task list appears, containing live thumbnails instead of just icons. Pressing the **Windows Logo+Tab** key combination arranges all of the currently open windows in a stack with a 3D appearance.

The taskbar also retains the familiar buttons representing all of the applications currently running on the computer. However, in Windows Vista, if the computer is running the Windows Aero user experience, mousing over a taskbar button displays a thumbnail of the application's current appearance. This thumbnail is "live," meaning that it contains a reduced version of the exact image you would see if you maximized the application. For example, if you mouse over a taskbar button representing a minimized media player, the thumbnail will contain the video currently playing, in full motion.

USING THE SIDEBAR

It seems that after finally eliminating all of the clutter from the Windows desktop, the developers at Microsoft could not resist creating a new way to load it up again. The Sidebar, shown in Figure 1-20, is a new desktop element that enables you to select small programs called gadgets that appear on the right side of your screen. By default, Vista places a selection of gadgets on the desktop, ranging from a clock to a headline news ticker to a slideshow of wallpaper images. You can easily add or remove gadgets at your discretion, choosing from the small selection installed with Vista or the ever-growing library of third-party gadgets accessible using the Internet link supplied in the gadget gallery window in Vista.

Figure 1-20

The Windows Vista Sidebar

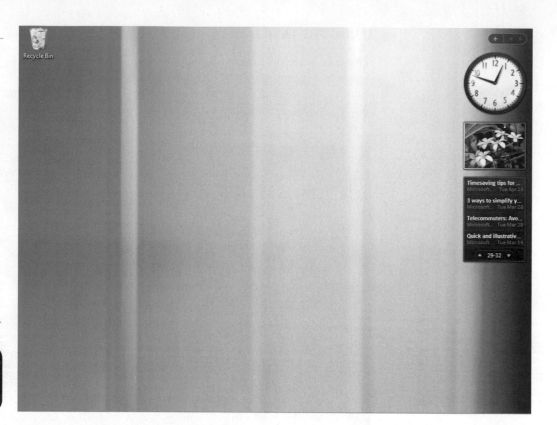

WARNING Third-party programmers supply many of the Sidebar gadgets available from the Internet link Windows Vista includes, and Microsoft does not support or guarantee them. The Website displays a disclaimer before every gadget download, cautioning that these third-party gadgets "could access your computer's files, show you objectionable content, or change [their] behavior at any time." Be sure to exercise caution when installing gadgets from unknown developers.

CERTIFICATION READY? Configure Windows Sidebar 5.6

USING THE START MENU

Clicking the **Start** button on the taskbar, as mentioned earlier, still displays the Start menu in Windows Vista, but the menu itself has changed, as shown in Figure 1-21. As in Windows XP, the left side of the Start menu contains icons for frequently used applications, as well as two pinned (that is, permanent) icons for Internet and e-mail access. The difference here is that the E-mail icon now points by default to Windows Mail, the replacement for Outlook Express included with Windows Vista. The link for All Programs access remains at the bottom of the menu.

Figure 1-21

The Windows Vista Start menu

On the right side of the Start menu, there are still links to various Windows features, but you will notice that Microsoft has changed the names of some familiar elements. For example, "My Computer" is now just "Computer" and "My Documents" is now just "Documents." These name changes are consistent throughout the Windows Vista interface.

USING EXPLORER WINDOWS

Microsoft has substantially redesigned the Windows Explorer application and the Explorer windows that appear when you access drives and folders in Windows Vista, as shown in Figure 1-22. These changes are likely to be among the first that technicians supporting Vista encounter.

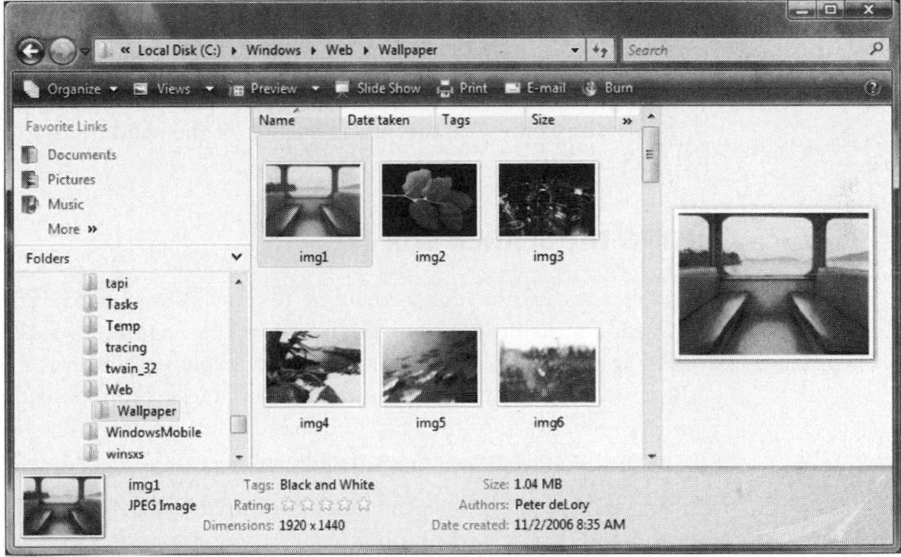

Figure 1-22
A Windows Vista Explorer window

When you open an Explorer window, the traditional Navigation pane appears on the left, beneath a new Favorite Links pane. By default, the Navigation pane displays the contents of the current user's user profile. You might have to scroll down to find the more familiar Computer and Network containers (remembering that the word "My" has been omitted).

At the top of the window, the Address box that used to specify the path name of the currently selected folder or file now contains a series of links to the selected folder or file's parent folders in the file system hierarchy. For example, the address of a selected folder in a Windows XP Explorer window might appear as C:\Program Files\Microsoft Office. In a Windows Vista Explorer window, the same folder appears as Computer > Local Disk (C:) > Program Files > Microsoft Office.

This is sometimes known as a *breadcrumb* navigation method, or a ***breadcrumb trail***, because the address is essentially a trail leading back to the source. Each of the breadcrumbs functions as a link directly back to a parent level in the file system. Because the breadcrumb mechanism provides complete access to any parent of the currently selected folder, Microsoft has removed the familiar Up button from the interface.

TAKE NOTE*

Users accustomed to clicking the **Up** button to move upwards through the file system are likely to be frustrated at first by its absence. However, the breadcrumb method actually provides more complete access to the file system, as well as a great deal of additional flexibility. In addition to clicking a breadcrumb, which can take you directly to any folder in the hierarchy, you can also click the arrows between the crumbs, which enable you to navigate downwards through the folders without leaving the Address box. For those inclined to resist change, the new Explorer window also has Forward and Back buttons to the left of the Address box, like those in a browser window. In many instances, the Back button provides the same function as the old **Up** button.

Directly beneath the Address box is the toolbar, which contains buttons (some with submenus) for the functions that users most often need when working with the currently selected item.

Another design change in the Vista Explorer window is the removal of the familiar menu bar containing the File, Edit, View, Tools, and Help menus. Fortunately, you can make the menu bar appear between the Address box and the toolbar at any time, simply by pressing the **Alt** key.

Beneath the toolbar are the panes that provide different views of the folder or file that you are currently exploring. In addition to the primary pane displaying the contents of the currently selected folder or container, you can choose to display any or all of the following:

- Navigation pane—Appears on the left side of the window and displays the computer's file system as an expandable tree of folders and containers.
- Preview pane—Appears on the right side of the window and displays an enlarged version of the selected file's contents in its native format.
- Details pane—Appears at the bottom of the window and displays metadata for the selected file or folder.

USING THE SEARCH BOX

Vista introduces a drastic overhaul in Window's search capabilities. Gone is the Search Assistant and its little cartoon characters, and in its place is a discreet little Search box, which you can find on the Start menu, on Explorer windows, in Windows Mail, in Windows Media Player, and in many other places throughout the operating system. This box is the interface to the new Windows Search Engine (WSE), which enables users to perform context-sensitive, metadata-based, as-you-key searches from almost anywhere.

Typing a character in the Search box causes the WSE to begin searching immediately for appropriate targets in the current context. For example, when you start a search from an Explorer window, WSE looks for files in the currently selected folder. Launching a search from the Start menu attempts to locate a program, document, or favorite starting with the specified letter. As you key additional letters in the Search box, the selection is winnowed down to only the targets matching the search string. WSE searches are also not limited to filenames. You can perform more complex searches based on file metadata using the Search pane, shown in Figure 1-23, which is also accessible from the Start menu, any Explorer window, and other places.

Figure 1-23

A Windows Vista Search window

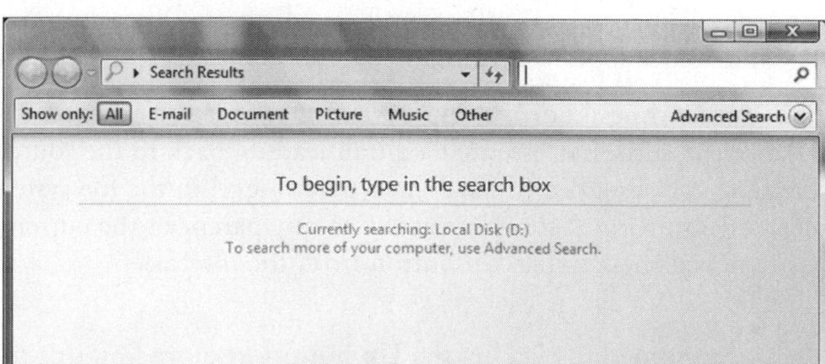

Introducing New Vista Features

In addition to its revamped architecture and modified interface, Windows Vista also includes a number of new and enhanced features and applications. Some of the most important performance and security features are as follows:

- SuperFetch—Windows XP first introduced the concept of *prefetching* to Windows, in which the operating system keeps track of the data that the system uses most frequently and stores in a special cache in system memory. ***SuperFetch*** is an enhanced method of prefetching in which the system maintains a more detailed profile of the computer's disk usage and can make far more educated guesses about what information to include in the cache. In combination with ReadyBoost, SuperFetch can provide a substantial enhancement to a Windows Vista system's performance.
- ReadyBoost—There is no condition that is more debilitating to a Windows computer than a shortage of memory. Earlier in this lesson, you learned how Vista can benefit from a memory upgrade, but even without a permanent upgrade it is still possible to give the system temporary access to extra memory using a new feature called ReadyBoost. ***ReadyBoost*** is a feature that enables Windows Vista to use the storage space on a USB flash drive as additional system memory. ReadyBoost uses a flash drive to store the SuperFetch cache, thereby freeing up the system memory where the cache would ordinarily be preloaded.
- Windows Defender—To prevent spyware from infiltrating your system and compromising your privacy, Windows Vista includes a new feature called Windows Defender. ***Spyware*** is a type of software that gathers information about computers and their users and sends it back to another system. ***Windows Defender*** blocks the installation of software that it suspects of being spyware and monitors the computer for signs of spyware activity.
- Windows Firewall—Introduced in Windows XP, ***Windows Firewall*** prevented unauthorized network traffic from entering the system. In Windows Vista, Windows Firewall is now bidirectional, meaning that it also prevents unauthorized traffic from leaving the system. Malicious individuals design many types of ***malware*** (malicious software) to install themselves on victims' computers and then send signals to a home computer on the Internet, enabling the malware's owner to take control of the victim's system. By blocking this outgoing traffic, Windows Firewall can prevent a computer from being co-opted by unauthorized parties.
- User Account Control—A new security feature that attempts to limit the damage that unauthorized programs and users can do to a system by limiting the capabilities of all the user accounts on that system.
- Windows PE—Starting with Windows NT, Microsoft was determined to create operating systems that did not run on top of the DOS kernel. However, even operating systems as late as Windows XP required a DOS boot at the beginning of the installation process, to copy the installation files to the computer's hard disk. Windows Vista finally eliminates DOS from the process completely by supplying its own preinstallation environment, called Windows PE 2.0. ***Windows PE*** is a subset of Windows Vista that provides basic access to the computer's network and disk drives, so that it is possible to perform an in-place or a network installation.
- BitLocker Drive Encryption—***BitLocker*** is a feature that Microsoft designed to address the problem of compromised data when a computer is lost or stolen. By encrypting the entire Windows volume, including swap and hibernation files, and performing an integrity check on the boot components, the data is protected, even if someone should attempt to access the drive using another operating system.

SUMMARY SKILL MATRIX

IN THIS LESSON YOU LEARNED:
Windows Vista is available in six editions: Starter, Home Basic, Home Premium, Business, Enterprise, and Ultimate, each of which contains a different set of features.
Windows Vista has two sets of system requirements, for Windows Vista Capable PCs and Windows Vista Premium Ready PCs.
Upgrade Advisor is an application, capable of running on Windows XP or Windows Vista, that determines whether the computer's hardware and software is Vista-compatible.
Windows Vista has four user experience levels, which affect the look and feel of the operating system, as well as the hardware resource utilization.
Windows Vista is capable of functioning as a standalone computer, as a workstation on a workgroup network, or as a member of an Active Directory domain.
Windows Vista includes a variety of new security and performance features, including SuperFetch, ReadyBoost, Windows Defender, Windows Firewall, User Account Control, Windows Preinstallation Environment, and BitLocker drive encryption.

■ Knowledge Assessment

Fill in the Blank

Complete the following sentences by writing the correct word or words in the blanks provided.

1. All of the Windows operating systems through Windows XP require a DOS boot during the installation process. The Windows Vista installation process replaces this DOS boot with ________________.
2. The Windows Vista feature that protects a computer from spyware is called ________________.
3. In Windows Vista, the Address box in an Explorer window uses a ________________ navigation method instead of a standard path name.
4. The general public in the United States will be able to purchase all of the Windows Vista editions in retail stores except ________________ and ________________.
5. The frequent appearance of message boxes in Windows Vista prompting you to confirm whether you want to perform certain tasks is the result of a new feature called ________________.
6. The core module that provides all of the Windows Vista capability that isn't language- or edition-specific is called ________________.
7. Experienced Windows XP users are likely to miss the ________________ button in Vista's Explorer windows, because it has been removed and replaced by a Back button.
8. The ________________ user experience is most similar to the Windows 2000 user interface.
9. All of the Windows Vista editions except ________________ and ________________ include support for tablet PCs.
10. The Search Assistant from Windows XP has been replaced by a new Windows Vista feature called ________________.

True / False

Circle T if the statement is true or F if the statement is false.

T | F 1. Windows Vista's SuperFetch feature requires a USB flash drive.

T | F 2. 512 MB of system memory is sufficient to run any of the Windows Vista editions.

T | F 3. The Windows Vista Upgrade Advisor application only runs on Windows XP.

T | F 4. Only the Business and Enterprise editions of Windows Vista are capable of joining a Windows network domain.

T | F 5. BitLocker drive encryption is only included with the Enterprise and Ultimate editions of Windows Vista.

T | F 6. All of the Windows Vista editions can run on a 64-bit computing platform.

T | F 7. A computer with an inadequate video display adapter is unlikely to be able to run the Windows Aero user experience.

T | F 8. All of the Windows Vista editions have full workgroup networking support.

T | F 9. The Flip and Flip 3D features are only available in the Windows Aero user experience.

T | F 10. Windows Vista Ultimate Edition includes the capabilities of all the other editions.

Review Questions

1. Explain why it is not necessary for Microsoft to create separate installation media for each edition and each language supported by Windows Vista.
2. Explain how Windows Vista can utilize a USB flash drive to enhance system performance.

■ Case Scenarios

Scenario #1: Selecting a Windows Vista Edition

You are a private computer consultant, and a new client has approached you about upgrading his small business network. The network currently consists of eight Windows XP workstations and a single server running Windows Server 2003. The server is functioning as a domain controller and the eight workstations are members of an Active Directory domain. The workstations each have 1 gigabyte of memory and a 1.8-gigahertz processor. The video cards support DirectX 9 and have WDDM drivers available from the manufacturer. Three of the workstations have DVD burners, and are used to produce multimedia training materials, while the other five run Microsoft Office applications almost exclusively. Which edition(s) of Windows Vista would you select for the workstations to provide the features they require most economically? Explain your answers.

Scenario #2: Selecting a Windows Vista Edition

A business owner called Ortiz approaches you about the possibility of designing a network for deployment at his new branch office in Bolivia. He has already purchased twenty computers and shipped them to the site. Each computer has 512 megabytes of memory, a 1 gigahertz processor, and a 40 gigabyte hard drive. He wants to connect the computers into a workgroup network that will be used primarily for accessing Web-based applications. Because he will be operating the network in a South American country, Mr. Ortiz wants to use Windows Vista, Starter edition for his workstations, as this is the most economical solution he can find. Will this be an adequate solution for his needs? Explain why or why not.

Lesson 2: Installing Windows Vista

OBJECTIVE DOMAIN MATRIX

Technology Skill	Objective Domain	Objective Number
Performing a Clean Installation	Perform a clean installation • Set up Windows Vista as the sole operating system.	1.2
Migrating to Windows Vista	Upgrade to Windows Vista from previous versions of Windows • Use Windows Easy Transfer to move files between machines.	1.3
Identifying Upgrade Paths	Upgrade to Windows Vista from previous versions of Windows • Identify valid upgrade paths.	1.3
Upgrading to Windows Vista	Upgrade to Windows Vista from previous versions of Windows.	1.3
Preparing to Upgrade	Upgrade to Windows Vista from previous versions of Windows • Identify application compatibility requirements.	1.3
Upgrading from Windows XP	Upgrade from one edition of Windows Vista to another edition • Perform an in-place upgrade.	1.4
Upgrading Vista Editions	Upgrade from one edition of Windows Vista to another edition.	1.4
Performing a Dual Boot Installation	Perform a clean installation • Set up Windows Vista to dual boot with Windows XP.	1.2

KEY TERMS

Clean installation
Dual boot
Multilingual user interface (MUI)
side-by-side migration
Windows RE
wipe-and-load migration

Selecting Installation Options

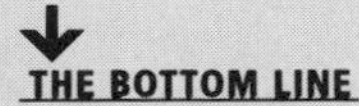

THE BOTTOM LINE

Before installing Windows Vista, or any operating system, whether on a single computer or a fleet of machines, you must first answer a number of questions to determine what type of installation to perform.

CERTIFICATION READY?
Installing and Upgrading Windows Vista
1

The planning phase before a Windows Vista installation varies depending on the complexity of the installation you are contemplating. For standalone home users, installing Windows Vista might mean thinking about what data to preserve, determining whether the hardware will work with the new operating system (OS), and finally purchasing the product itself. For corporate administrators responsible for hundreds or thousands of computers, an operating system upgrade represents a huge amount of testing and preparation, as well as a massive expense. However, the technicians supporting home users and corporate administrators ask themselves essentially the same questions, just on a different scale.

The following sections cover some of the most important questions.

Will the Hardware Support the New Operating System?

In Lesson 1, "Introducing Windows Vista," you learned about the various Windows Vista editions and their hardware requirements. The first question to ask yourself when a client is contemplating an operating system upgrade is whether the client's current hardware can run the new software effectively.

In many cases, this is not just a matter of whether the computer meets the software manufacturer's minimum hardware requirements. After all, the client wants the new operating system to run better than the old one, not worse. If the computer does not meet the Windows Vista Premium Ready PC hardware specifications, you should consider a hardware upgrade.

For the home user, a hardware upgrade might mean purchasing and installing a new memory module or two, or perhaps a video adapter. An experienced user might install the hardware him- or herself, while less savvy users might have you do it. Either way, the cost and time involved is relatively small.

However, to perform hardware upgrades like these, corporate administrators must multiply the cost and the installation time by hundreds or thousands of workstations, and factor in other elements such as lost productivity and overtime costs. Therefore, as with all aspects of a large-scale deployment, technicians in a corporate environment must plan and test carefully before even considering an upgrade to Windows Vista. For example, you might want to perform a series of test installations on differently configured computers to determine exactly what hardware upgrade provides the best performance at the lowest cost.

TAKE NOTE*

Some of Windows Vista's hardware demands are unusual when compared with previous Windows versions. The Windows Vista Premium Ready PC specifications for graphics capabilities are necessary only to run the Windows Aero user experience. Windows Aero is a major selling point for Windows Vista but it is essentially a cosmetic feature, and you should consider your client's needs carefully before recommending hardware upgrades. A home user is likely to want all of the "bells and whistles" that Windows can provide, and replacing a video adapter is typically a small enough price to pay for that experience. However, for a corporation considering an upgrade to Vista, the time and cost of replacing hundreds of video adapters is far more substantial, especially when the only result is the availability of a cosmetic feature that business users could easily do without.

Will the New Operating System Support the Existing Applications?

The second major consideration for a client contemplating a Windows Vista installation is whether the applications the client already owns will run on the new operating system. The last thing clients want to hear after the successful installation of a new operating system is that they need to purchase additional new software.

As with hardware upgrades, the prospect of upgrading or changing applications is far more daunting in the corporate environment than for the standalone user. Home users typically run commercial, off-the-shelf applications. The prices for upgrades supporting new operating systems typically fall soon after the release of the OS.

At the corporate level, however, you are more likely to find special-purpose or customized applications; these present greater difficulties. It might take time for developers to produce updates for special-purpose applications; for customized applications, it might be necessary to commission additional work from a programmer. Commercial applications can be extremely costly to upgrade, especially when you have to purchase hundreds or thousands of licenses.

In corporate environments, application testing is as important as hardware testing. Even if an updated version of an application is available, you must test it carefully with the new operating system to ensure that it functions properly. The alternative could be the failure of a mission-critical application across the entire enterprise, resulting in extended downtime and lost productivity.

Which Windows Vista Edition Should I Install?

You should select a Windows Vista edition based on several factors, including the tasks the client will be performing and, of course, the client's budget.

For home users, the choice between Home Basic and Home Premium is primarily economic. If a client wants to burn DVDs and spends a lot of time working with audio and video files, then Home Premium is generally worth the additional investment. Home Premium provides the Windows Aero user experience; Home Basic does not. Many new computers ship with Home Basic installed, so there is likely to be a large number of clients requesting upgrades to Home Premium.

TAKE NOTE *

The Windows Vista Starter edition is left out of consideration unless you have clients living outside of North America, Europe, or Australia and who are running rudimentary, low-end PCs.

Most corporate installations require their workstations to log on to a Windows network domain, which eliminates Home Basic and Home Premium as possible choices because they lack domain support. In most cases, the client's relationship with Microsoft determines the choice between Business and Enterprise. Windows Vista Business is a retail product, available in stores everywhere, while Enterprise is only available directly from Microsoft as part of a Windows Vista site license agreement.

Windows Vista Ultimate Edition is a premium product intended for users who require domain support and who want the features of the Home Premium edition. Home users for whom price is not a major concern are likely to opt for the Ultimate edition, but its adoption in the corporate world is likely to be limited to users requiring its multimedia capabilities.

Should I Perform an Upgrade or a Clean Installation?

The question of whether to install Windows Vista by performing an in-place upgrade or a clean installation depends on the amount and type of data stored on the computer, as well as the computer's current efficiency.

Obviously, new computers, or computers with new hard disk drives, require a ***clean installation***, in which you boot from the Windows Vista setup disk and create or select a blank partition where Vista will reside. If the computer is currently running Windows XP, you must consider whether it is preferable to wipe out the existing operating system and install Windows Vista from scratch or install Vista over the previous OS.

MORE INFORMATION

You can perform an in-place upgrade to Windows Vista only on computers running Windows XP or another edition of Windows Vista. It is not possible to upgrade to Windows Vista from Windows 2000, Windows Me, Windows 98, Windows 95, Windows NT, or Windows 3.1. For computers running these operating systems, you must perform a clean installation.

WARNING If you decide to perform a clean installation of Windows Vista on a home user's computer, be sure to question the user carefully about all possible data that might need to be backed up first. Many less experienced users are unaware, for example, that accessing their e-mail involves a server logon. Another technician might have set up the user name and password long ago, and all the user knows is to click the e-mail icon.

The primary advantage of performing a clean installation is that Windows Vista will achieve its best possible performance. Installing the operating system files on a blank disk means that they will be unfragmented, improving disk performance. A clean installation ensures that the user retains the maximum amount of disk space for applications and data. Of course, a clean installation also erases all existing data, so you must be careful to back up everything that the client wants to retain.

For home users, there is usually some data that the client wants to preserve, such as image or video files, or data files for specific applications. Fortunately, writable CDs and DVDs, USB flash drives, and external hard drives make it relatively easy to back up the client's essential data. What can be more problematic in a case like this is the loss of important configuration settings, such as user names, passwords, and customized application templates. Be sure to preserve this type of information before wiping out a partition to perform a clean installation.

Performing an in-place upgrade to Windows Vista means that whatever disk and registry clutter is present under the previous operating system will remain in place under Vista. Files might be extensively fragmented, even to the point of executing poorly, and outdated applications and data files could occupy significant amounts of disk space.

The advantage to performing an in-place upgrade is that all of the user's applications, data files, and configuration settings remain intact, but even this could be a problem. Upgrades can generate incompatibilities with drivers or applications that you must rectify before the computer can run properly.

In a corporate environment, it is more typical for users to store their data files on servers, as opposed to local drives. Also, a properly maintained corporate network should document all configuration settings and logon credentials. This minimizes the problem of potential data loss when you perform a clean installation.

Clean installations are generally preferable in the corporate world because they ensure that all of the computers are running an identical system configuration. This eliminates the technical support problems that occur when each computer is running a different configuration.

Should I Perform a Single or Dual Boot Installation?

One other solution to the problem of whether to perform an upgrade or a clean installation is to create a ***dual boot*** environment, in which you retain the old operating system installation on one disk partition and create a clean installation of Windows Vista on another.

Dual-booting enables a user to run either operating system at any time. The original operating system installation retains all of its existing applications and settings, but you must configure the new Windows Vista installation from scratch and install all of your applications.

The disadvantages to dual-booting include the following:

- You must have a separate disk partition available to install Windows Vista
- Two operating systems require twice as much disk space as one
- Switching from one operating system to another to perform a specific task takes too long

Dual-booting is not commonly found in corporate computing environments, but some home users employ it to test new operating systems or maintain configurations to support different applications.

Do I Have to Install Multiple Languages?

Before Windows Vista, each language required its own version of the operating system that had to be developed, maintained, and distributed separately. With Windows Vista, however, it is possible to install multiple language packs on a single computer so that individuals can work in multiple languages.

The main problems for multilingual users in the past has been the availability of the languages they need and the complex procedure for implementing multiple languages on a single computer. To use multiple languages on a Windows XP computer, you must begin with an installation of the English language Windows XP version. Then you install the ***multilingual user interface (MUI)*** pack and whatever additional language packs you need. Unfortunately, some of the language packs provide more complete support than others.

Windows Vista contains an entirely new MUI architecture that makes it easier to install multilingual support on a computer. In Windows Vista, the binary code that makes up the operating system is entirely language-neutral. During the Vista installation process, the Setup program installs the operating system and then applies a language pack containing the information needed to provide the localized user interface.

MORE INFORMATION

Because the Windows Vista binaries are language-neutral there is no need for language-specific service packs or other updates. Microsoft is therefore able to release each update in one generic version suitable for all Windows Vista computers around the world, regardless of the language they use.

Because the language packs for Windows Vista contain no binary code they are interchangeable. Therefore, it is no longer necessary for technicians to consider localization issues before installing the operating system. You can change a Windows Vista installation from one language to another at any time, or install multiple language packs that utilize the same binary code.

Understanding the Windows Vista Boot Environment

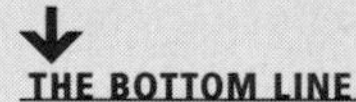

Windows Vista eliminates DOS from the installation process for the first time and provides a new boot environment: **Windows PE.**

Those who have performed clean installs of standalone Windows XP systems should recall that the very beginning of the process, immediately after the system boots from the installation CD-ROM, consists of several character-based (that is, non-graphical) screens, like that shown in Figure 2-1. On these screens, you opt to perform the installation, agree to the terms of the End User License Agreement (EULA), select the drive partition on which you want to install Windows XP, and then watch as the program copies the installation files from the CD-ROM to a temporary folder on the hard drive.

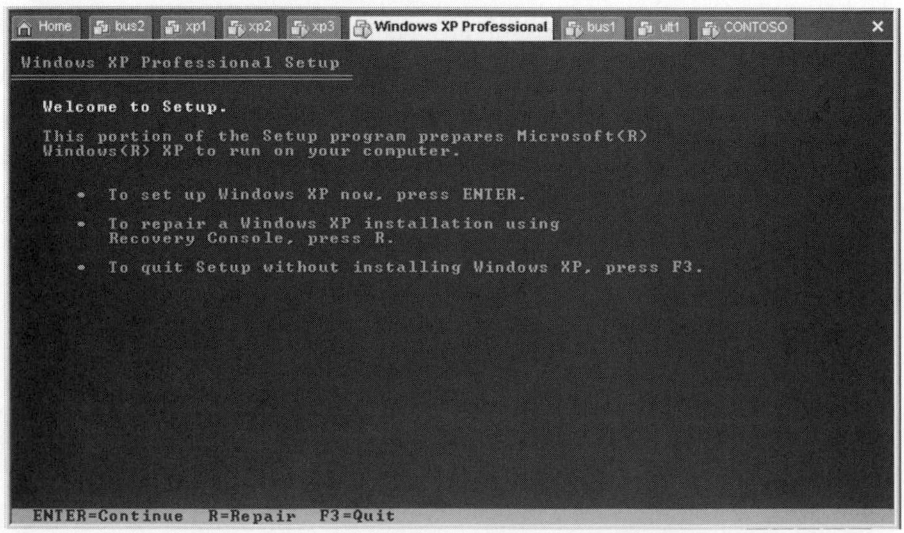

Figure 2-1

A character-based screen from the MS-DOS phase of a Windows XP installation

These screens are character-based because all of the Windows operating systems up to Windows XP required an MS-DOS boot at the beginning of the installation process. The MS-DOS boot was necessary because the computer required an operating system to run the installation program and to gain access to the disk drives.

For original equipment manufacturers (OEMs) and corporate customers, deploying Windows on a large number of computers typically required a boot from an MS-DOS system disk to provide access to the computer's drives and to provide access to a network share where the Windows installation files or a disk image was located.

This need for an MS-DOS boot has become increasingly problematic over the years for several reasons, including the following:

- Limited disk support—MS-DOS can provide access only to disk drives formatted using one of the File Allocation Table (FAT) formats. MS-DOS cannot provide access to the NTFS drives that most of today's Windows computers use.
- No internal networking support—MS-DOS has no internal networking support, and because it is a 16-bit operating system administrators must obtain and load 16-bit network adapter drivers (as compared to the 32-bit drivers that Windows uses), as well as a TCP/IP client, before they can access a share containing Windows installation files.
- Limited script support—MS-DOS has no internal support for any scripting languages except for rudimentary batch files.
- Boot device limitations—Many computers today, especially those in corporate environments, do not have floppy disk drives, and creating bootable MS-DOS CD-ROMs can be problematic.

Introducing Windows PE 2.0

Windows Vista might be the fourth major Windows release to eliminate the need for MS-DOS as an underlying operating system (after Windows NT, Windows 2000, and Windows XP), but it is the first to completely eliminate MS-DOS from the installation process. To replace MS-DOS in the installation process, Windows Vista includes the Windows Preinstallation Environment (Windows PE 2.0).

Windows PE 2.0 is a stripped-down operating system, based on the Windows Vista kernel, that enables system administrators to boot a computer that has no operating system installed and initiate the operating system setup process. When compared to MS-DOS, Windows PE has a number of distinct advantages, including the following:

- Native 32-bit or 64-bit support—Windows PE is a native 32-bit or 64-bit operating system (OS) that enables the computer to address memory just as the full Windows Vista operating system does. MS-DOS is a 16-bit OS and is relatively limited in its memory addressing capabilities.
- Native 32-bit or 64-bit driver support—Because Windows PE is a 32-bit or 64-bit OS, it can use the same drivers as a full Windows Vista installation. System administrators therefore do not have to search for antiquated 16-bit network drivers as they did with MS-DOS.
- Internal networking support—Windows PE includes its own internal TCP/IP networking stack and is capable of functioning as a Windows file sharing client. This means that after booting Windows PE, an administrator only has to supply a driver for the network adapter and the networking stack is complete.
- Internal NTFS support—Windows PE includes internal support for the NTFS 5.x file system used by Windows Vista, as well as the FAT file systems that MS-DOS supports. This means that when you boot a system using Windows PE, you can read from and write to

existing NTFS drives in the computer, as well as create and format new NTFS partitions. It is even possible to create and manage dynamic volumes using Windows PE.

- Scripting language support—Windows PE includes internal support for a subset of the Win32 application programming interface (API), meaning that it is possible to run some Windows programs in the preinstallation environment. Windows PE also includes optional support for Windows Management Instrumentation (WMI) and Windows Script Host, which makes it possible for administrators to execute virtually any Windows action using a script.
- Flexible boot options—Windows PE can boot from a variety of media, including CD-ROM, DVD-ROM, a USB floppy drive, or a Windows Deployment Services (DS) server. The computer can then run the Windows PE operating system from a variety of media, including the DVD, a temporary folder on a hard disk, a USB flash drive, a RAM disk, or a network share.

MORE INFORMATION

Windows PE 2.0 is available in both 32-bit and 64-bit versions. You must use the 32-bit version of Windows PE to install the 32-bit version of Windows Vista and the 64-bit version of Windows PE to install the 64-bit version of Windows Vista.

Understanding Windows PE 2.0 Limitations

Microsoft intends Windows PE to be a reduced subset of the Windows Vista operating system, only providing sufficient capability to perform certain installation, diagnostic, and recovery functions while running from a minimized hardware environment, such as a RAM drive.

Because there was never any intention for Windows PE to function as a full-time operating system, and to facilitate its rapid deployment and execution, there are certain inherent limitations in the product, such as the following:

- Windows PE does not support the entire collection of Win32 APIs as a full installation of Windows Vista does. Microsoft limits the APIs in Windows PE primarily to those providing disk and network input/output functions, as well as certain APIs that make it possible to run basic programs. Reducing the API support enables Windows PE to run in a smaller memory space than Windows Vista.

MORE INFORMATION

Because Windows PE requires a relatively small memory space, the entire operating system can run from a RAM disk. A RAM disk is a driver that allocates a section of active memory for use as a virtual disk drive, complete with drive letter. Because the RAM disk is based in memory it is much faster than a hard disk drive, but it is also volatile; all of its contents are lost when the computer restarts. Running the Windows Vista Setup program from a RAM disk enables all of the operating system file handles to remain open throughout the installation process. By contrast, running the Setup program directly from the DVD makes it impossible to remove the disk (to load third-party drivers, for example) without interrupting the installation procedure. In the same way, running the Setup program from a temporary folder on a hard disk interferes with partition creation and management functions that might be needed during the installation.

- Windows PE automatically stops and reboots after 72 hours of continuous operation. This deliberate limitation prevents individuals from using the product as a permanent operating environment.
- Windows PE networking support is limited to the TCP/IP and NetBIOS Over TCP/IP (NetBT) protocols. There is no support for IPX/SPX or any other network/transport layer protocols.
- While it is possible to modify the Windows PE registry when the operating system is running, all registry keys are reset to their default values each time the operating

system restarts. It is possible to make permanent changes to the registry, but to do so you must make the changes offline by manually editing the registry while Windows PE is not running.

- Windows PE does not have file server or Terminal Server capabilities, nor does it support the Microsoft .NET framework or the Windows on Windows 32 (WOW32), Windows on Windows 64 (WOW64), Virtual DOS Machine (VDM), OS/2, or POSIX subsystems.

Using Windows PE

In addition to functioning as a platform for individual installations of Windows Vista, Windows PE is useful for other scenarios that require a basic operating system with minimal resource usage.

Some of the other scenarios that can make use of Windows PE are as follows:

- Custom deployments—Windows Vista uses Windows PE during the default installation procedure, but it is possible for administrators to build their own unattended installation routines using Windows PE as a platform to run scripts and deploy customized disk images on fleets of workstations. You can even use Windows PE to deploy operating systems other than Windows Vista.
- System troubleshooting—If a Windows Vista computer fails to start, or if it crashes repeatedly, a technician can launch the Windows Recovery Environment (***Windows RE***), which is simply another name given to Windows PE on a computer with Vista already installed. In the Windows RE environment, the technician can use Vista's built-in troubleshooting utilities or run third-party or custom diagnostic tools.
- System recovery—Original equipment manufacturers (OEMs) who build their own computers typically supply their customers with a system recovery disk rather than a simple operating system installation disk. A system recovery disk contains image files that can restore the computer to its original state, just as it was after the operating system and applications were installed and configured. OEMs can use Windows PE to build recovery solutions that automate the process of setting up Windows Vista, installing specific drivers, installing applications, and configuring the entire system to create a standardized environment.

Performing a Clean Installation

A clean installation is the simplest way to deploy Windows Vista on a new computer or a computer with a partition that you are willing to reformat (losing all of the data on the partition in the process).

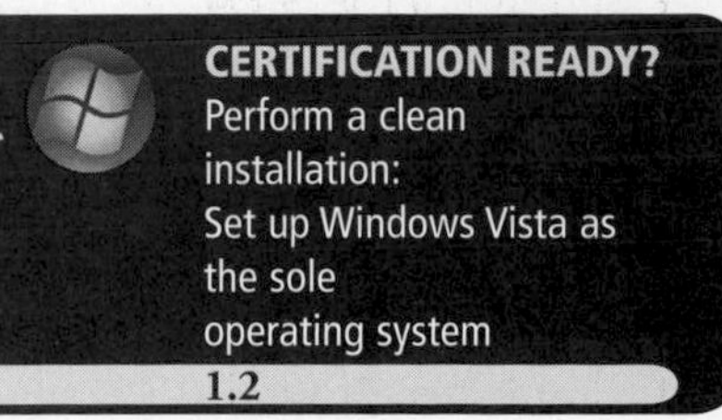

CERTIFICATION READY?
Perform a clean installation:
Set up Windows Vista as the sole operating system
1.2

If a computer is brand new and has no operating system installed on it, then it cannot start until you supply a boot disk, such as the Windows Vista installation disk. During the installation you will select the disk partition on which you want to install Vista, and the Setup program will copy the operating system files there.

If the computer has an operating system installed on it, and you have already backed up all of the data that the client wants to preserve, then you are ready to boot the computer from the Windows Vista installation disk. During the setup process you can erase a partition on the disk in preparation for installing Vista there.

TAKE NOTE* The following procedure is for an installation of Windows Vista Business Edition. Although the installation procedure for the other editions is nearly identical, you might see minor differences in the procedure.

PERFORM A CLEAN INSTALLATION

GET READY. Prepare the computer for the Windows Vista installation by making sure that all of its external peripheral devices are connected and powered on.

1. Turn on the computer and insert the Windows Vista installation disk into the DVD drive.

TAKE NOTE* If you are installing Windows Vista from the set of five CD-ROMs, rather than a single DVD, the installation process will be interrupted by message boxes prompting you to insert specific disks.

2. Press any key to boot from the DVD (if necessary). A progress indicator screen appears as Windows is loading files.

MORE INFORMATION

The device that a PC uses to boot is specified in its system (or BIOS) settings. In some cases, you might have to modify these settings to enable the computer to boot from the Windows Vista DVD. If you are not familiar with the operation of a particular computer, watch the screen carefully as the system starts and look for an instruction specifying what key to press to access the system settings.

3. The computer switches to the Windows graphical interface and the Install Windows page appears, as shown in Figure 2-2.

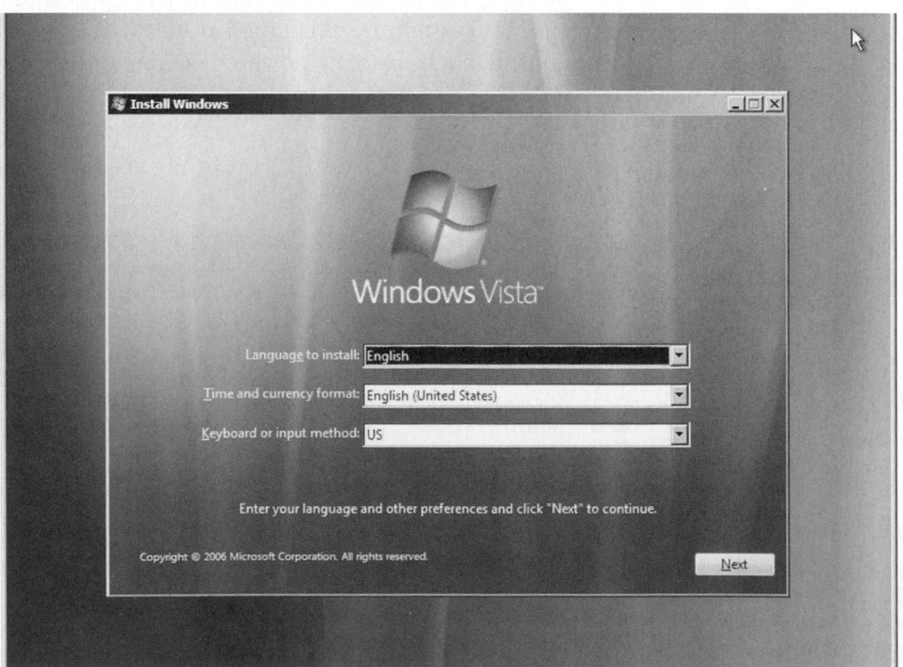

Figure 2-2
The Install Windows page

TAKE NOTE* At this point, the computer is running Windows PE as its operating system, providing it with the means to execute the Setup program and to load drivers providing access to the disk drives and other hardware resources.

4. Using the drop-down lists provided, select the appropriate Language to install, Time and currency format, and Keyboard or input method, and then click **Next**. The *Windows Vista Install now* page appears, as shown in Figure 2-3.

Figure 2-3

The Windows Vista Install now page

5. Click the **Install now** button. The *Type your product key for activation* page appears, as shown in Figure 2-4.

Figure 2-4

The type your product key for activation page

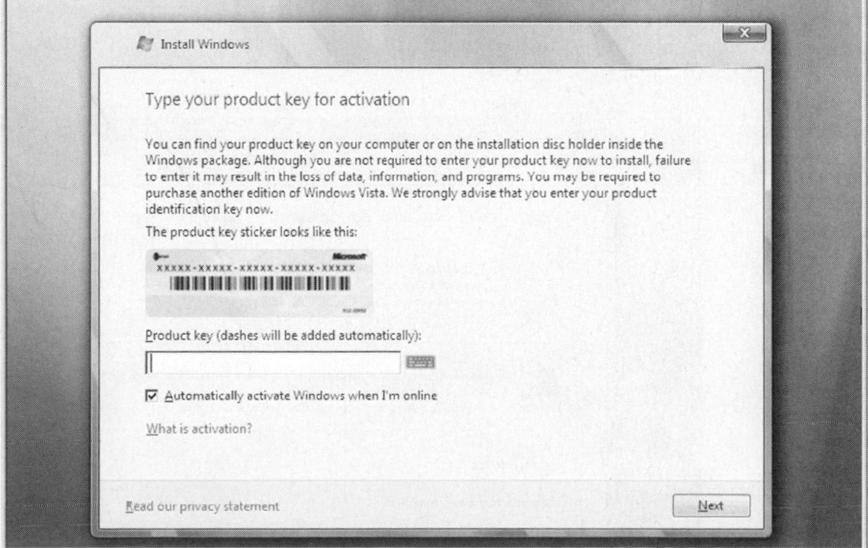

6. In the *Product key* text box, type the key code supplied with your copy of Windows Vista. Leave the *Automatically activate Windows when I'm online* checkbox selected, unless you know you will have to activate your computer by telephone or some other means. Click **Next** to continue. The *Please read the license terms* page appears, as shown in Figure 2-5.

Figure 2-5

The Please read the license terms page

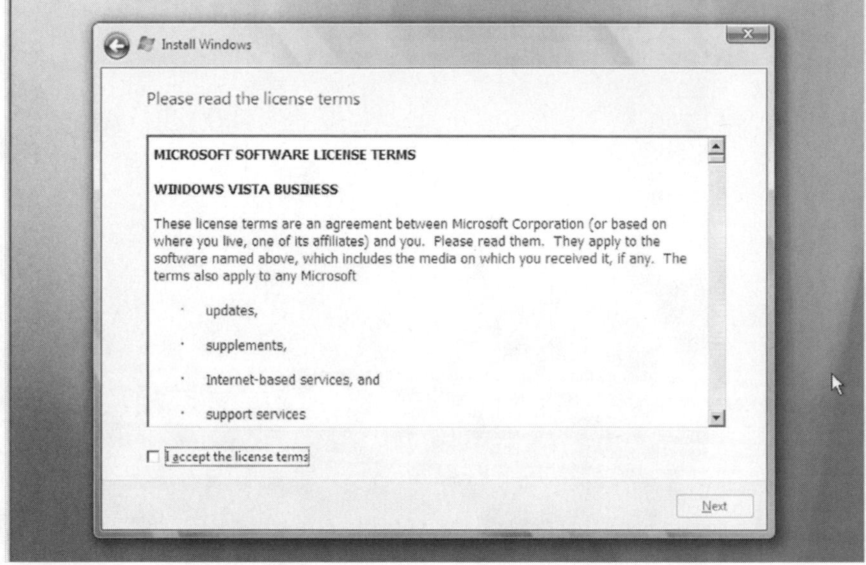

TAKE NOTE* The product key code you supply on this page determines which version of Windows Vista the Setup program will install on your computer.

7. Select the **I accept the license terms** checkbox and click **Next**. The *Which type of installation do you want?* page appears, as shown in Figure 2-6.

Figure 2-6

The Which type of installation do you want? page

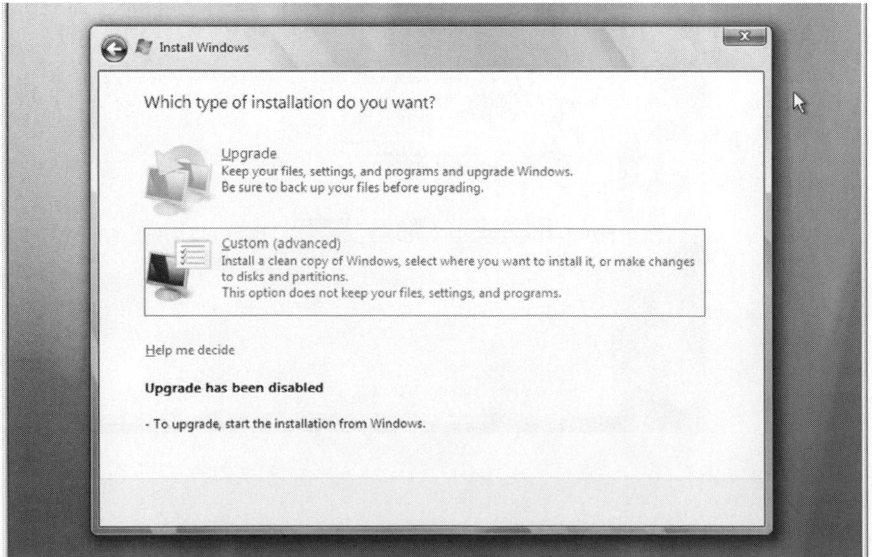

8. Click the **Custom (advanced)** option. The *Where do you want to install Windows?* page appears, as shown in Figure 2-7.

Figure 2-7

The Where do you want to install Windows? page

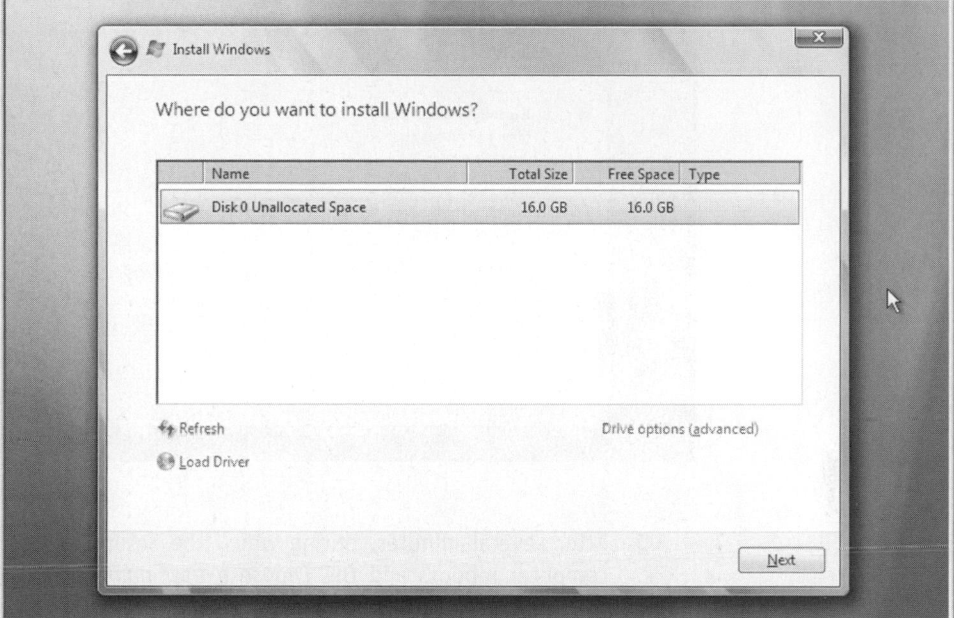

TAKE NOTE*

The Upgrade option is currently disabled because you booted the computer using the Windows Vista installation disk. For the Upgrade option to function, you must boot the existing Windows XP or Windows 2000 operating system and start the Windows Vista installation program from there. See "Upgrading to Windows Vista" later in this lesson for more information.

MORE INFORMATION

Unlike the wizards included in previous versions of Windows, which have Back and Next buttons at the bottom of nearly every page, Windows Vista wizards have only a Next button. However, note that you can still move backwards to the previous page of the wizard by clicking the left arrow button in the top left corner of the window, a convention adapted from Web browsers.

9. From the list provided, select the partition on which you want to install Windows Vista, or select an area of unallocated disk space where the Setup program can create a new partition. Then click **Next.** The Installing Windows page appears, as shown in Figure 2-8.

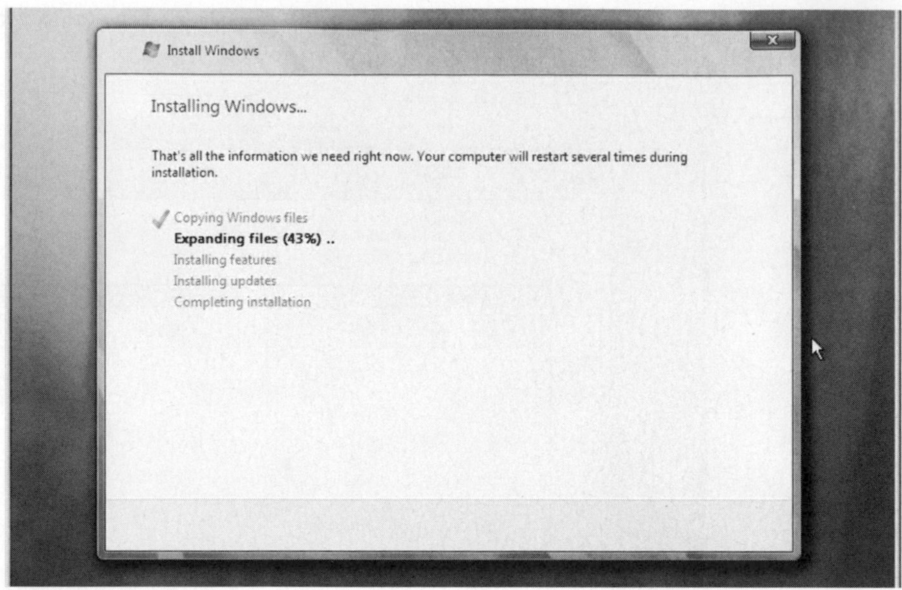

Figure 2-8

The Installing Windows page

10. After several minutes, during which the Setup program installs Windows Vista, the computer reboots and the *Choose a user name and picture* page appears, as shown in Figure 2-9.

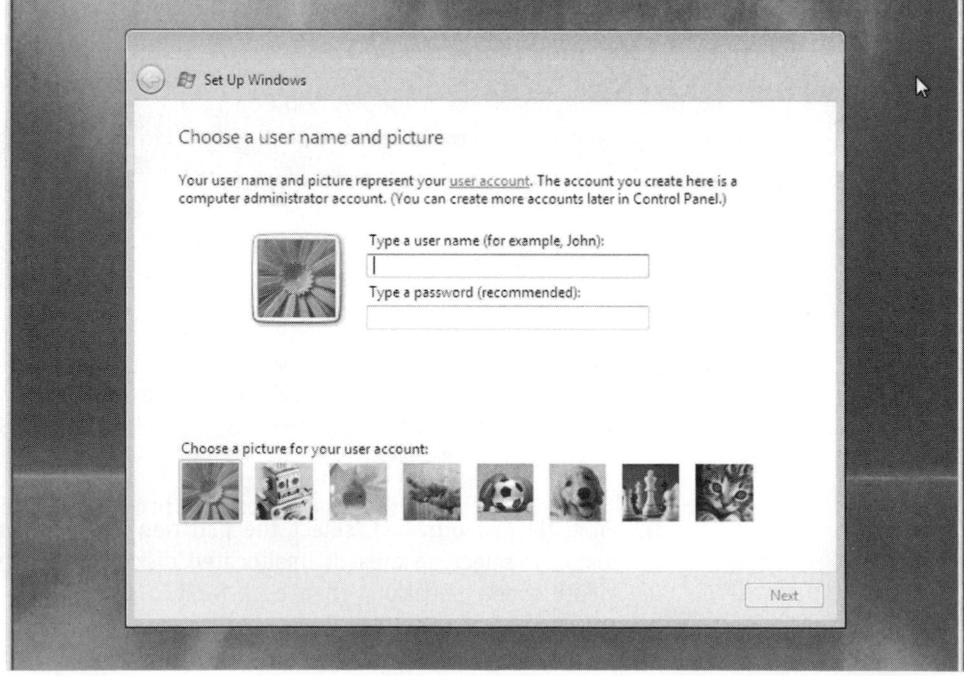

Figure 2-9

The Choose a user name and picture page

11. In the *Type a user name* text box, enter a name for the first user account on the system.
12. In the *Type a password* text box, enter the password to be associated with the user account. You can also click one of the thumbnails to select a picture that will be associated with the user account.
13. Click **Next** to continue. The *Type a computer name and choose a desktop background* page appears, as shown in Figure 2-10.

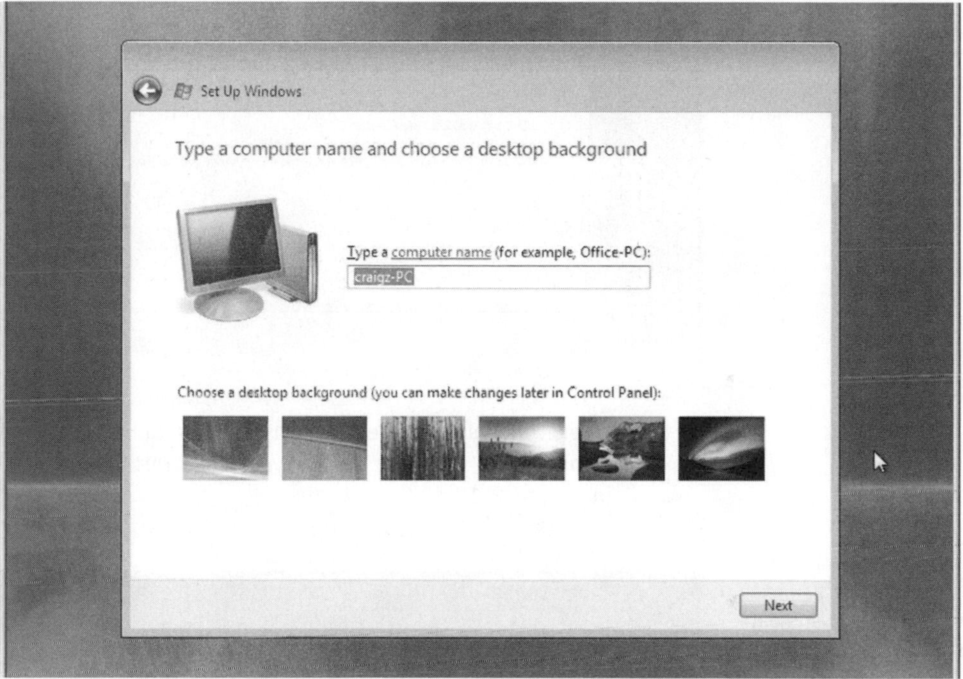

Figure 2-10

The Type a computer name and choose a desktop background page

14. In the *Type a computer name* checkbox, enter a name, no more than fifteen characters long, by which the computer will be known on the network.

TAKE NOTE* If the computer is connected to a Windows network, then the name you specify for the computer must be unique on that network.

15. Click one of the thumbnails to select a background image for your Windows desktop and click **Next** to continue. The *Help protect Windows automatically* page appears, as shown in Figure 2-11.

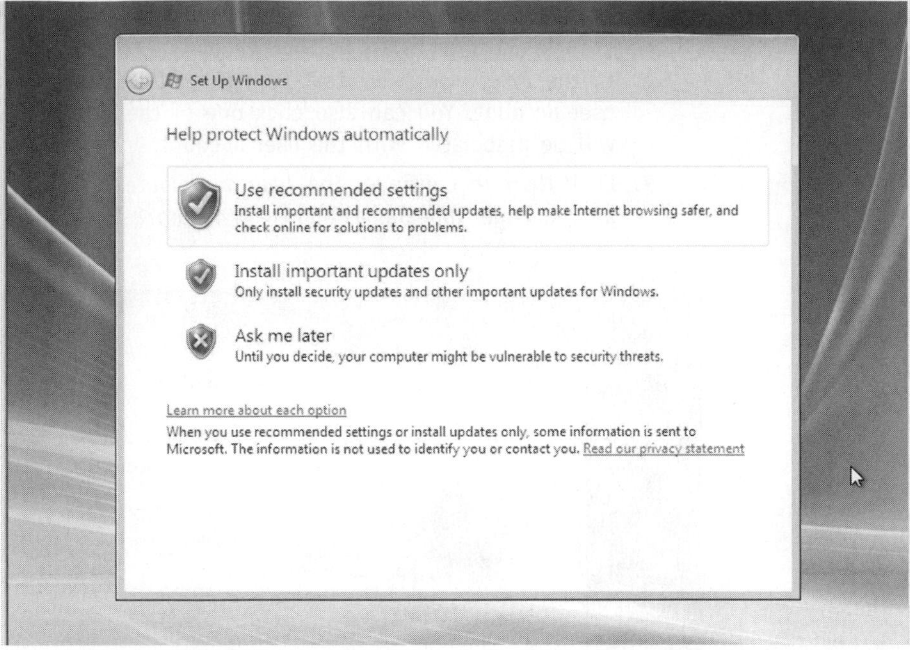

Figure 2-11

The Help protect windows automatically page

16. Select one of the three options specifying what security settings you want the computer to use. The *Review your time and date settings* page appears, as shown in Figure 2-12.

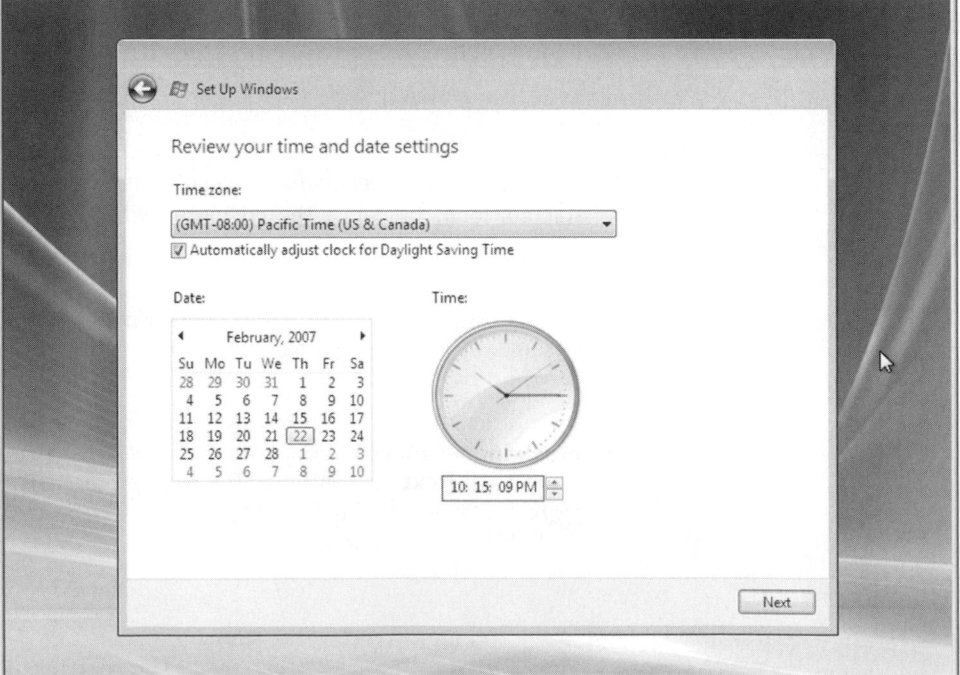

Figure 2-12

The Review your time and date settings page

TAKE NOTE*

As with most of the settings you configure during the Windows Vista installation, you can also select a different security option at a later time.

17. From the *Time zone* drop-down list, select the time zone in which the computer will be running. If the date and time specified in the calendar and clock are not accurate, or you want to prevent the computer from adjusting itself during Daylight Savings Time, correct the settings and click **Next.** The *Select your computer's current location* page appears, as shown in Figure 2-13.

Figure 2-13

The Select your computer's current location page

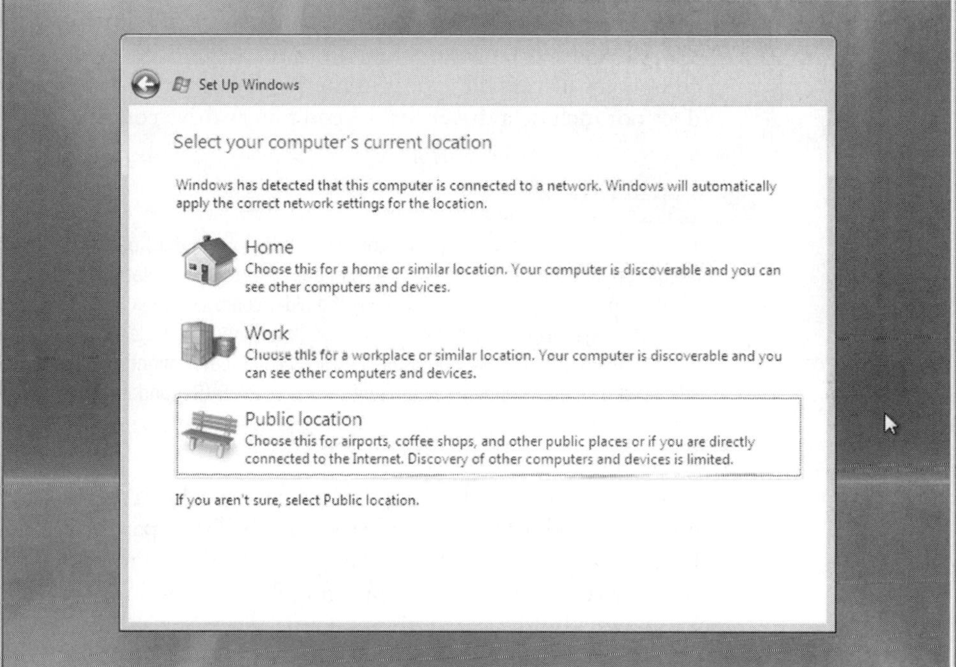

TAKE NOTE*

The *Select your computer's current location* page appears only when the Setup program successfully detects and configures a network connection. Otherwise, the Setup program omits it.

18. Click the appropriate option specifying the computer's normal location. A *Thank you* page appears.
19. Click **Start.** The computer runs through a series of optimization routines as it starts Windows Vista for the first time. A *Preparing your desktop* screen appears.
20. A few minutes later, the system completes its new startup routine and the Welcome Center window appears.

At this point, you can remove the installation disk from the drive. When the computer starts, it will load Windows Vista.

Installing Third-Party Drivers

During the Windows Vista installation procedure, the Setup program enables you to select the partition or area of unallocated disk space where you want to install the operating system.

The *Where do you want to install Windows?* page lists the partitions on all of the computer's disk drives that the Setup program can detect with its default drivers. In most cases, all of the computer's drives will appear in the list; if they do not, it is probably because Windows PE does not include a driver for the computer's drive controller.

MORE INFORMATION

There are several reasons why a computer might employ a third-party disk controller, rather than the one integrated into the motherboard. The computer might have a relatively old motherboard and more modern drives whose capabilities are not supported by the older controller. The computer might also be using SCSI (Small Computer Systems Interface) rather than IDE (Integrated Drive Electronics) hard drives, and a SCSI controller that is not supported by Windows PE. Finally, the computer might be using a specialized controller that provides advanced disk management technologies, such as RAID (Redundant Array of Independent Disks).

If the hard drives in the computer are connected to a third-party controller, rather than the one integrated into most motherboards, the list of partitions might appear empty, and you will have to supply a driver for the Setup program to see the drives. Check the controller manufacturer's Website for a driver supporting Windows Vista. If none is available, use the most recent Windows XP driver.

To install the driver, use the following procedure:

INSTALL A THIRD-PARTY DISK DRIVER

GET READY. If during a Windows Vista installation no disk partitions or unallocated space appear on the *Where do you want to install Windows?* page, you must install the appropriate driver for your disk controller using the following procedure before the installation can continue.

1. On the *Where do you want to install Windows?* page, click the **Load Driver** button. A Load Driver message box appears, as shown in Figure 2-14.

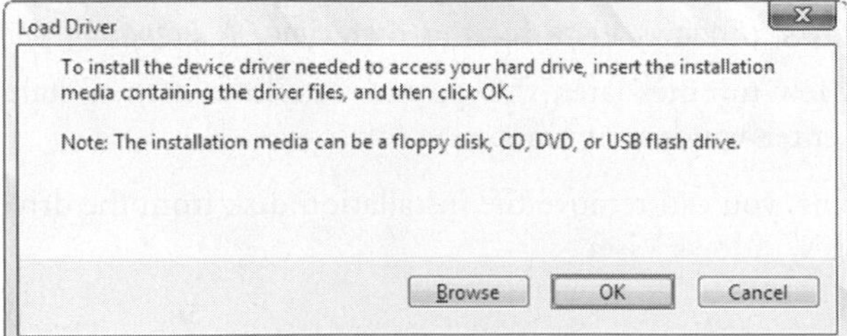

Load Driver
To install the device driver needed to access your hard drive, insert the installation media containing the driver files, and then click OK.
Note: The installation media can be a floppy disk, CD, DVD, or USB flash drive.
Browse
OK
Cancel

Figure 2-14

The Load Driver message box

2. Insert the storage medium containing the driver into the computer. You can supply drivers on a CD, DVD, floppy disk, or USB flash drive.

TAKE NOTE*

Because Windows PE is running on a RAM drive, it is possible to remove the Windows Vista installation disk from the DVD drive and insert another disk containing drivers. You will later have to re-insert the Windows Vista disk to complete the installation.

3. Click **OK** if the driver is in the root directory of the storage medium, or **Browse** if it is necessary to locate the driver in the directory structure of the disk. When the driver loads, the partitions and unallocated space on the associated disks appear in the list on the *Where do you want to install Windows?* page.
4. Select the partition or area of unallocated space where you want to install Windows Vista and then continue with the rest of the installation procedure, as covered earlier in this lesson.

Working with Installation Partitions

In addition to installing disk drivers, the *Where do you want to install Windows?* page enables you to create, manage, and delete the partitions on your disks.

Clicking the ***Drive options*** *(advanced)* button on the page causes four additional buttons to appear, as shown in Figure 2-15. These buttons have the following functions:

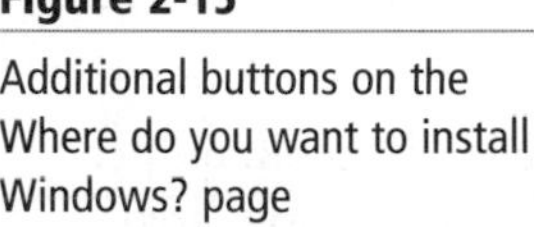

Figure 2-15

Additional buttons on the Where do you want to install Windows? page

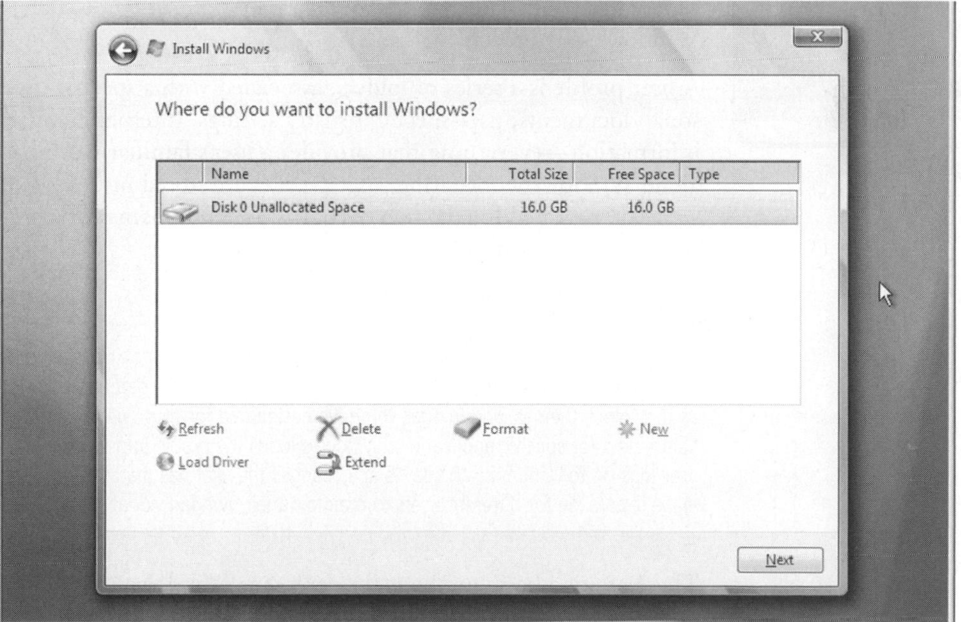

- Delete—Removes an existing partition from a disk, permanently erasing all of its data. You might want to delete partitions to consolidate unallocated disk space, enabling you to create a new, larger partition.
- Extend—Enables you to make an existing partition larger, as long as there is unallocated space available immediately following the selected partition on the disk.
- Format—Enables you to format an existing partition on a disk, thereby erasing all of its data. There is no need to format any new partitions you create for the install, but you might want to format an existing partition to eliminate unwanted files prior to installing Vista on it.
- New—Creates a new partition of a user-specified size in the selected area of unallocated space.

Migrating to Windows Vista

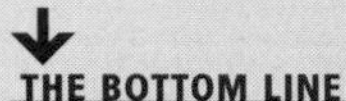

Just because you have performed a clean installation of Windows Vista on a client's computer does not necessarily mean that the user has to lose his or her files and folders, application settings, and Internet favorites. Using tools supplied with Windows Vista, you can migrate these system elements from one computer to another.

CERTIFICATION READY?
Upgrade to Windows Vista from previous versions of Windows: Use Windows Easy Transfer to move files between machines.
1.3

In some cases, supplying a client with a clean installation of Windows Vista is a perfectly adequate solution. The client might be using a computer for the first time, or might not have any important data to carry over from his or her previous workstation. However, most experienced computer users have data they want to retain, data that is typically stored in a Windows user profile.

A user profile is a series of folders, associated with a specific user account, that contain personal documents, user-specific registry settings, Internet favorites, and other personalized information—everything that provides a user's familiar working environment. On a standalone Windows workstation, user profiles are stored in the Documents and Settings folder, in subfolders named for the user accounts. On a domain workstation, the user profiles are also stored in a network server.

MORE INFORMATION

User profiles consist of files, such as a user's personal documents and Internet favorites, stored in appropriate profile folders, and settings stored in a registry file. The registry settings include basic display parameters, such as the colors, themes, and images you have designated for your Windows desktop, as well as configuration parameters for specific applications. Windows loads the profile information into memory each time that particular user logs on to Windows, and saves any changes the user has made to the profile when logging off. User profiles make it possible for different users to maintain their own individual settings on one Windows computer.

There are two basic methods for deploying Windows Vista to a client while retaining the user profile settings: upgrade and migration. In an upgrade, you install Windows Vista on the computer running an earlier operating system. Vista overwrites the old OS, but all of the user profiles already on the computer remain in place. In a migration, you copy the user profile information from the old operating system to some temporary medium and transfer it to a new computer on which you have performed a clean installation of Windows Vista.

Microsoft has created two different tools for migrating files and settings to new computers, which are as follows:

- Windows Easy Transfer—Designed for the migration of a single computer, Easy Transfer makes it possible to migrate user profile information for multiple users from one computer to another.

- User State Migration Tool 3.0—Designed for large-scale enterprise deployments, User State Migration Tool can migrate profile information for multiple users on multiple computers.

In the following sections, you learn the procedure for using Windows Easy Transfer to migrate user profile settings from an existing Windows XP workstation to a new Windows Vista workstation. You also learn some basic facts about using the User State Migration Tool.

X REF

For more detailed coverage of the User State Migration Tool, see Lesson 1 in *MOAC 70-622: Installing, Maintaining, Supporting, and Troubleshooting Applications on the Microsoft Windows Vista Client–Enterprise.*

Using Windows Easy Transfer

Windows Easy Transfer is a tool that migrates user profile information from an existing Windows computer to a new computer with a clean installation of Windows Vista.

The Windows Easy Transfer tool migrates user profile data from one computer to another in a variety of scenarios. As long as you are working with the user accounts from one single computer, Windows Easy Transfer can function in virtually any hardware configuration. Some of the options you can select are as follows:

- Number of computers—Windows Easy Transfer supports both side-by-side and wipe-and-load migrations. In a ***side-by-side migration***, you have two computers running simultaneously; one is the source computer containing the user profile information you want to transfer, and the other is the destination computer running Windows Vista to which you want to transfer the profile information. In a ***wipe-and-load migration***, you have only one computer, which initially contains the user profile settings you want to transfer. After saving the profile information to a removable storage medium, you perform a clean Windows Vista installation, wiping out all data on the drives, and then transfer the profile data from the removable medium back to the computer.
- Direct or indirect—When you are performing a side-by-side migration, you can use Windows Easy Transfer with the computers connected together directly, using a cable or a network, or connected indirectly, using a removable storage medium.
- Storage medium—Windows Easy Transfer can use virtually any storage medium to transfer profile data between computers, as long as it provides sufficient storage space and is accessible by both machines. You can use a writable CD or DVD, a USB flash drive, an external hard drive, or a network share. Floppy disks are not supported because they have insufficient capacity.

The procedure for migrating files consists of two basic elements: saving the user profile information on the existing computer and transferring the information to the new computer. Using the capabilities of Windows Easy Transfer, you should be able to satisfy the requirements of virtually any standalone user that wants to move to Windows Vista without performing an upgrade. The most common scenarios are likely to be the following:

- Scenario 1–A user purchases a new computer on which he wants to run Windows Vista, but he also wants to retain the files and settings from his existing Windows XP computer.
- Scenario 2–A user wants to install Windows Vista on her existing Windows XP computer and retain all of her files and settings, but she wants to avoid performing an upgrade to maximize her Vista performance.

The following sections describe the Windows Easy Transfer procedures for each of these scenarios.

Performing Migration Scenario 1

Ed is a longtime Windows XP user with a small network in his home. He has just purchased a new computer with Windows Vista preinstalled on it, and wants to migrate his files and settings from his XP computer to the Vista computer. The new computer came with recovery disks, but no Vista installation disk.

In this scenario, you perform a side-to-side migration with both computers connected to the user's home network. However, because you do not have access to a Windows Vista installation disk, you must add a third element to the procedure, in which you provide the XP computer with access to the Windows Easy Transfer program.

PERFORM MIGRATION SCENARIO 1

GET READY. Both computers must be powered on and connected to the home network. Create a network share on one of the two computers and make sure that both systems can access it.

1. On the Windows Vista computer, click **Start** > **All Programs** > **Accessories** > **System Tools** and then select **Windows Easy Transfer.** The Welcome to Windows Easy Transfer page appears, as shown in Figure 2-16.

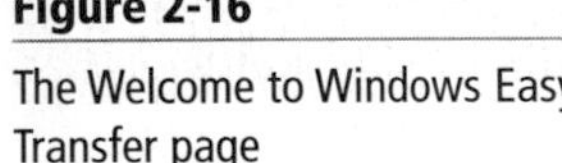

Figure 2-16

The Welcome to Windows Easy Transfer page

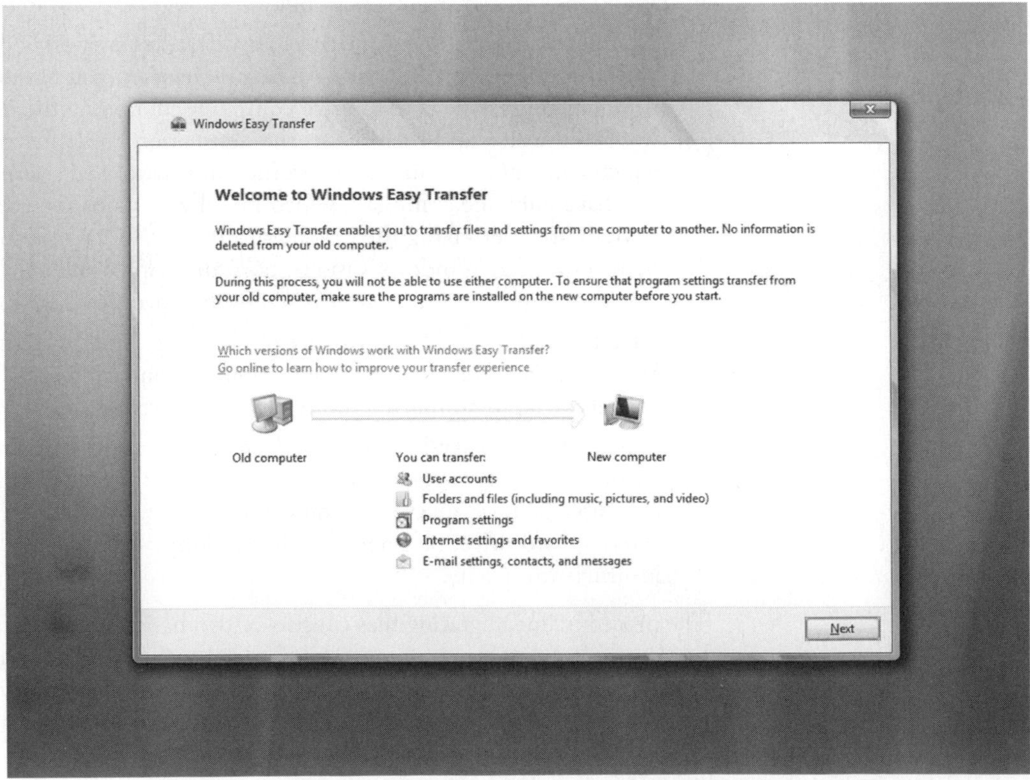

2. Click **Next.** The *Do you want to start a new transfer or continue one in progress?* page appears, as shown in Figure 2-17.

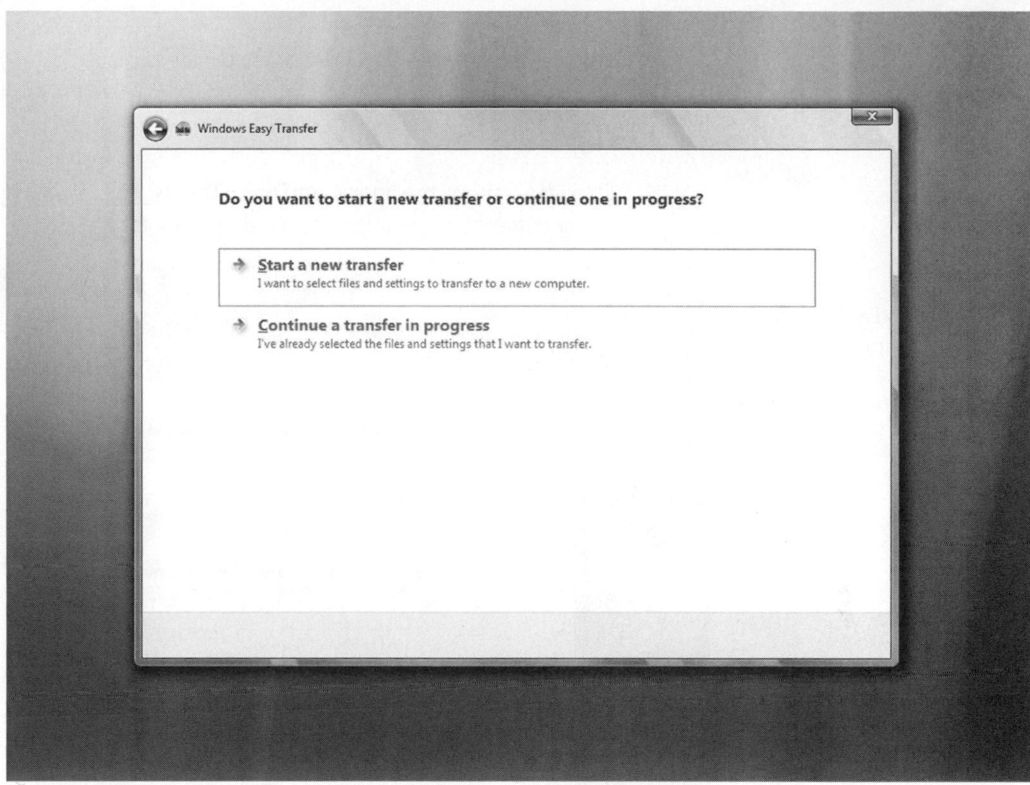

Figure 2-17

The Do you want to start a new transfer or continue one in progress? page

3. Click **Start a new transfer**. The *Which computer are you using now?* page appears, as shown in Figure 2-18.

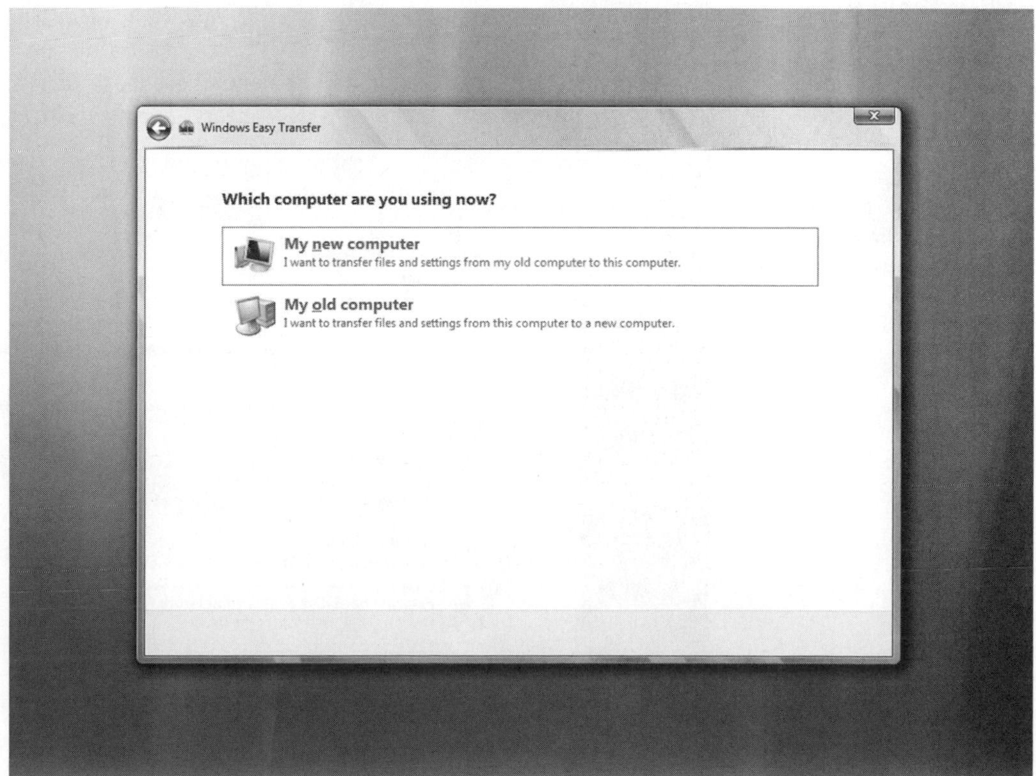

Figure 2-18

The Which computer are you using now? page

4. Click **My new computer**. The *Do you have an Easy Transfer cable?* page appears.

MORE INFORMATION

An Easy Transfer cable is a special USB cable that you can use to connect two Windows computers together solely for the purpose of using the Windows Easy Transfer utility. In this particular scenario, the user has a network available, which performs the same function.

5. Click **No, show me more options.** The *Is Windows Easy Transfer installed on your old computer?* page appears, as shown in Figure 2-19.

Figure 2-19

The Is Windows Easy Transfer installed on your old computer? page

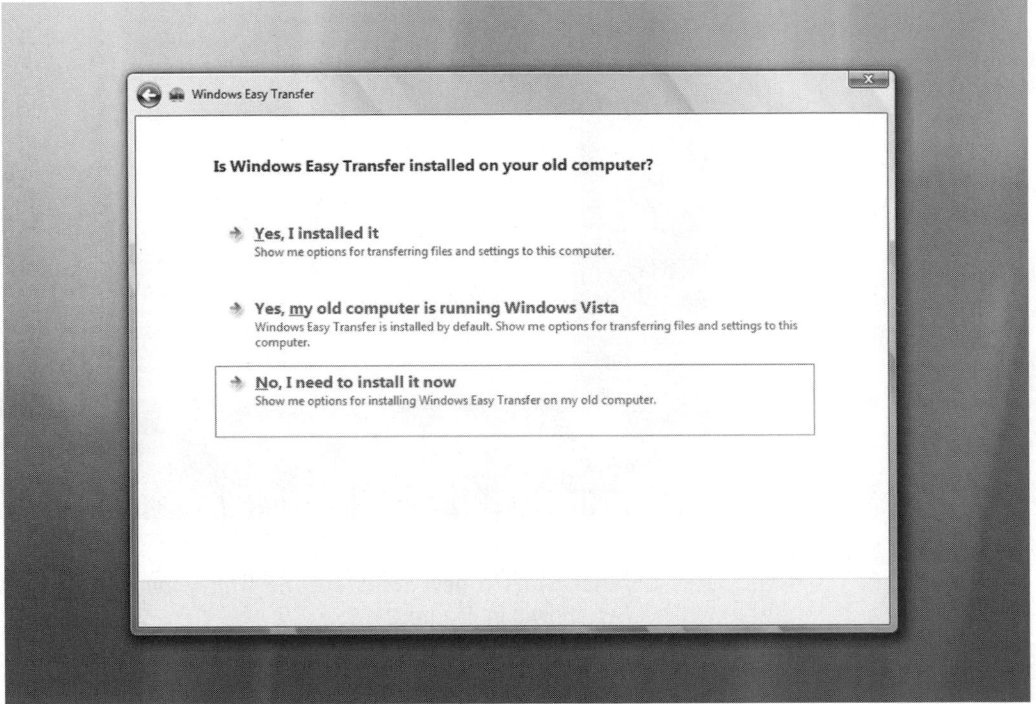

 **WARNING** To transfer user profile information to a Windows Vista computer, you must use the Windows Easy Transfer program supplied with Windows Vista. Windows XP has a Files and Settings Transfer Wizard that performs roughly the same functions, but this tool is not compatible with Windows Vista user profiles.

6. Click **No, I need to install it now.** The *Choose how to install Windows Easy Transfer on your old computer* page appears, as shown in Figure 2-20.

Figure 2-20

The Choose how to install Windows Easy Transfer on your old computer page

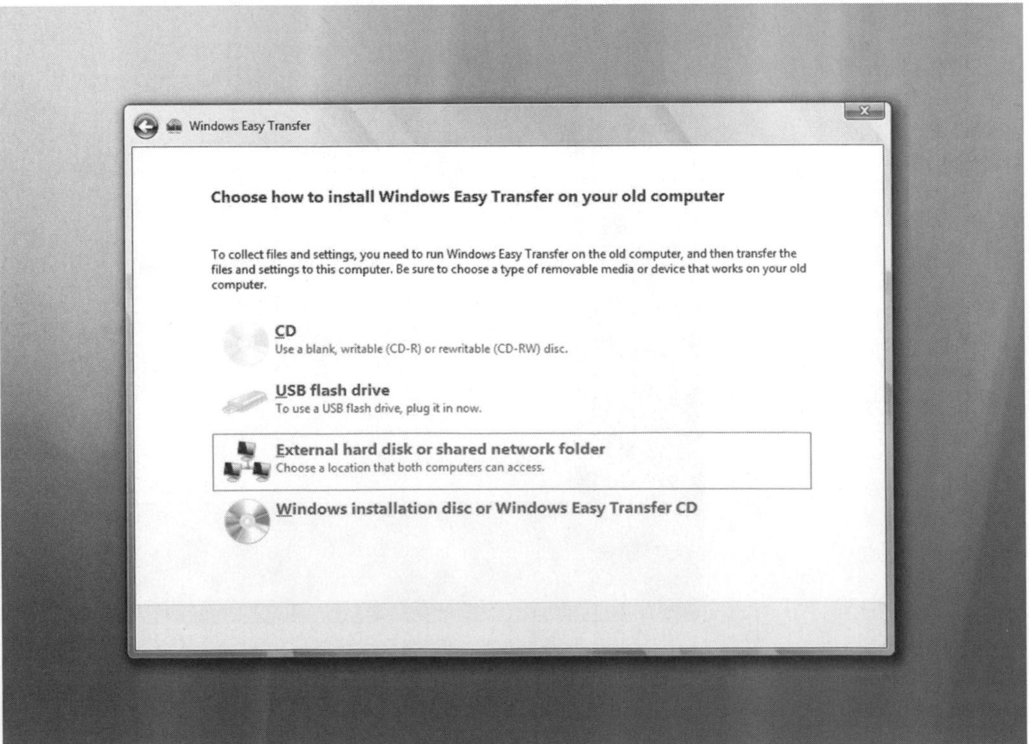

7. Click **External hard disk or shared network folder**. The *Choose an external hard disk or network folder* page appears, as shown in Figure 2-21.

Figure 2-21

The Choose an external hard disk or network folder page

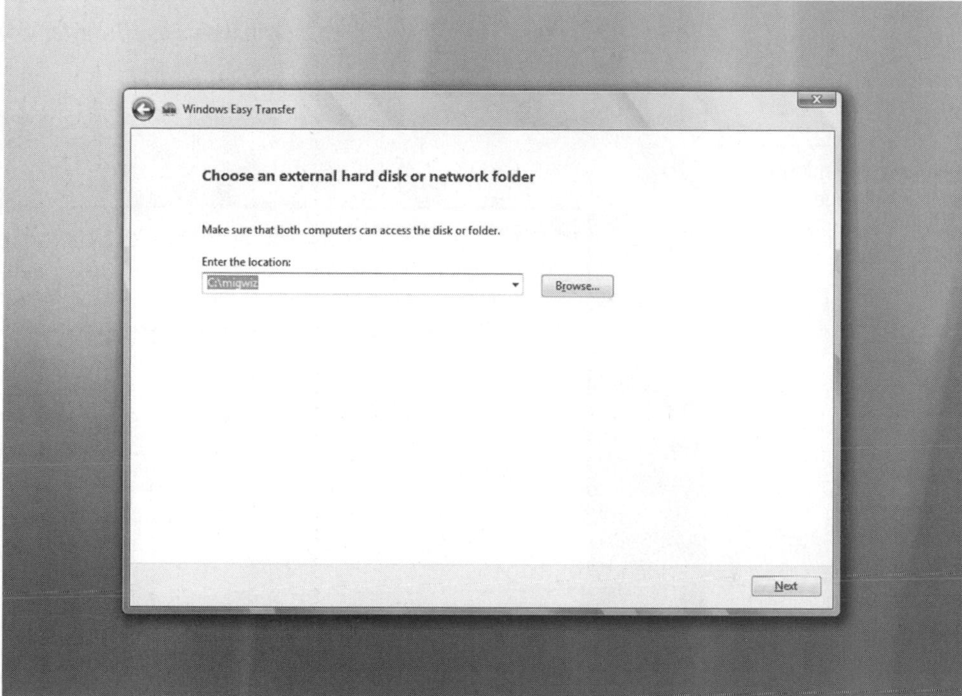

8. In the *Enter the location* text box, specify the location of the network share you created before beginning the procedure. Then click **Next**.

MORE INFORMATION

You can use any other storage medium to transfer the Windows Easy Transfer program to the Windows XP computer, such as a writable CD or DVD or a USB flash drive, as long as the XP computer is capable of reading it.

9. The *Copying the Windows Easy Transfer software* page appears as the wizard packages the software and copies it to the share. Then the *Are your computers connected to a network?* page appears, as shown in Figure 2-22.

Figure 2-22

The Are your computers connected to a network? page

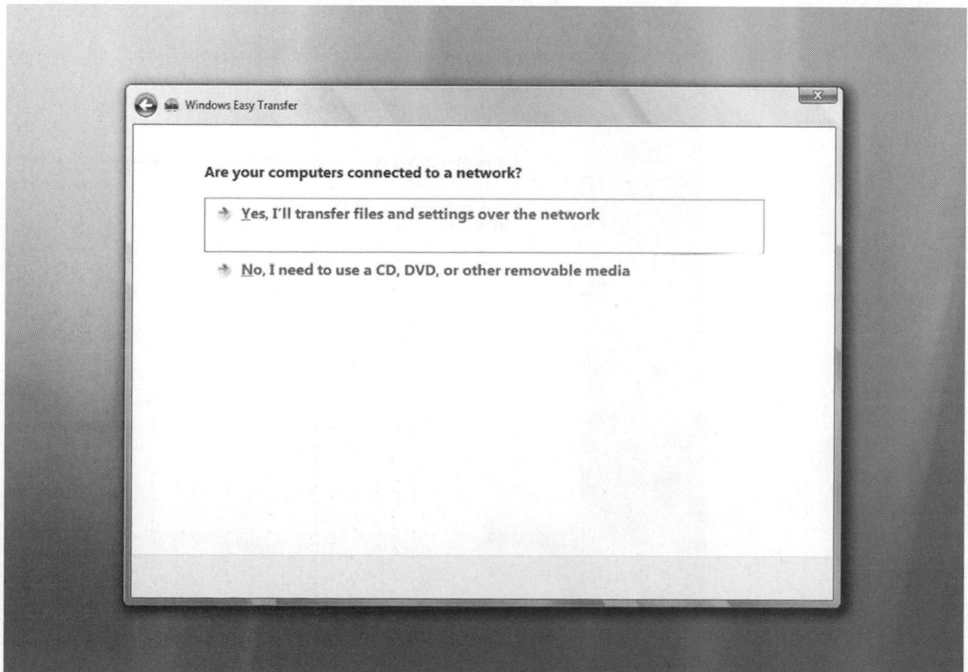

10. Click **Yes, I'll transfer files and settings over the network.** A Windows Easy Transfer message box appears, asking for permission to unblock the port needed for Windows Easy Transfer's network transmissions.
11. Click **Yes**. The *Do you have a Windows Easy Transfer key?* page appears, as shown in Figure 2-23.

Figure 2-23

The Do you have a Windows Easy Transfer key? page

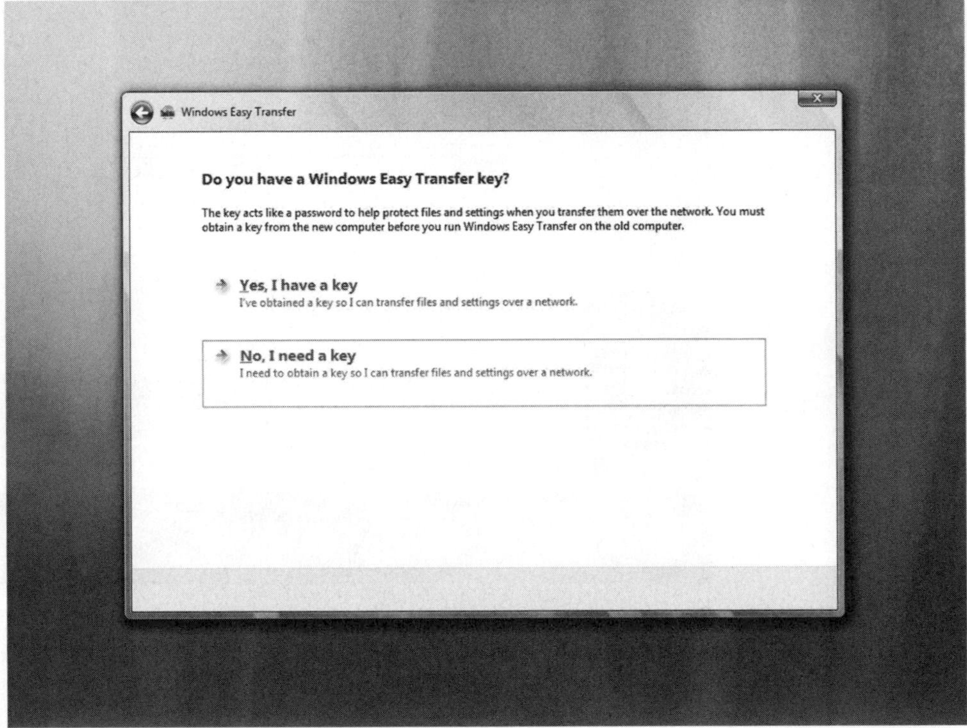

12. Click **No, I need a key.** The *Go to your old computer and start Windows Easy Transfer* page appears, containing the key, as shown in Figure 2-24.

Figure 2-24

The Go to your old computer and start Windows Easy Transfer page

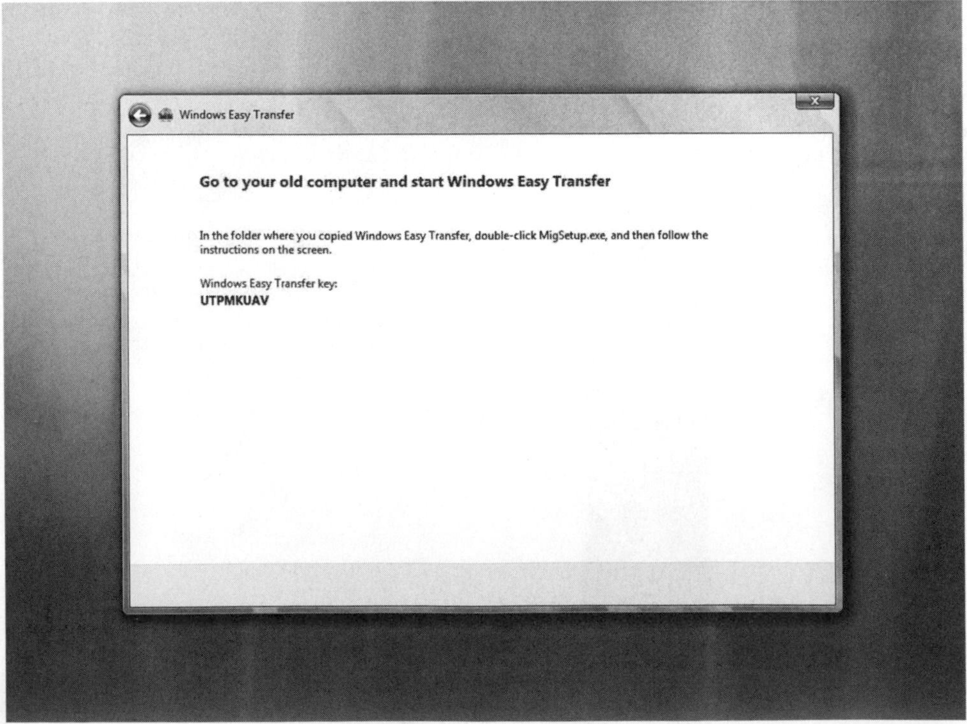

13. On the Windows XP computer, Click **Start > All Programs > Accessories** and then select **Windows Explorer**. A Windows Explorer window appears.
14. Browse to the network share you created before beginning the procedure and run the Migsetup.exe program that the wizard on the other computer created there. The *Close programs* page appears, instructing you to close any programs that are accessing user profile information.
15. Click **Close all**. The *Choose how to transfer files and settings to your new computer* page appears, as shown in Figure 2-25.

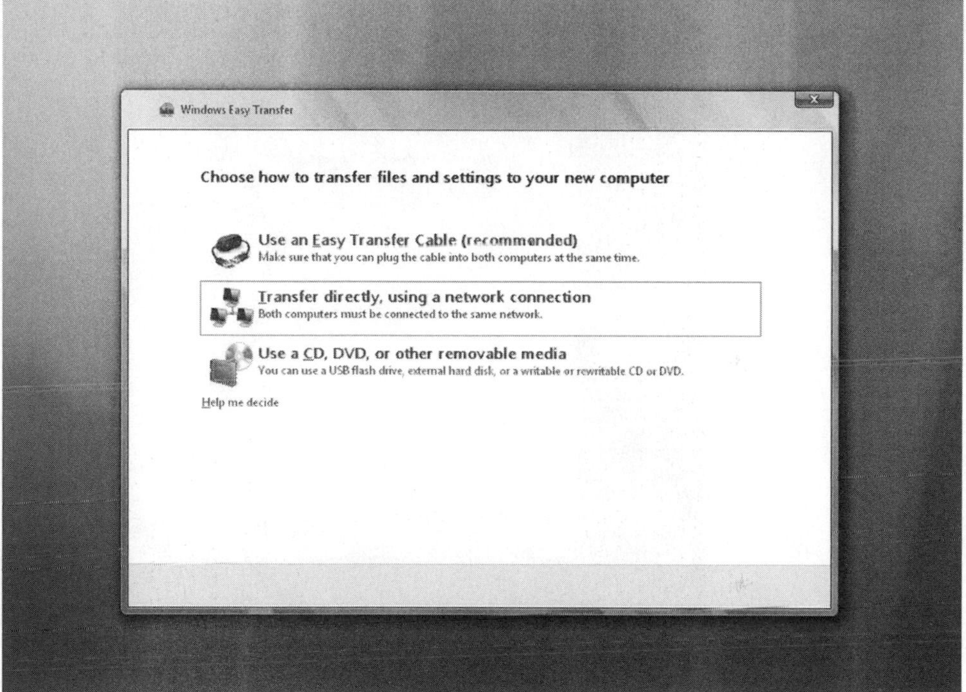

Figure 2-25

The Choose how to transfer files and settings to your new computer page

16. Click **Transfer directly, using a network connection.** The *Choose how to transfer files and settings over a network* page appears, as shown in Figure 2-26.

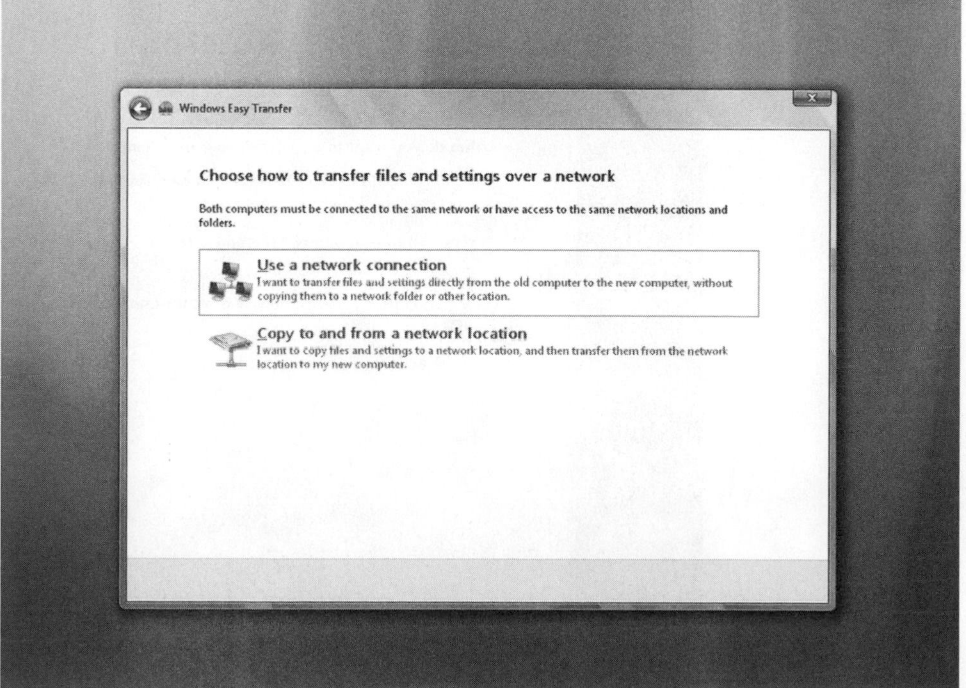

Figure 2-26

The Choose how to transfer files and settings over a network page

17. Click **Use a network connection.** The Windows Easy Transfer message box appears, prompting for permission to open the required firewall port.
18. Click **Yes.** The *Do you have a Windows Easy Transfer key?* page appears.
19. Click **Yes, I have a key.** The *Type your Windows Easy Transfer key* page appears, as shown in Figure 2-27.

Figure 2-27

The Type your Windows Easy Transfer key page

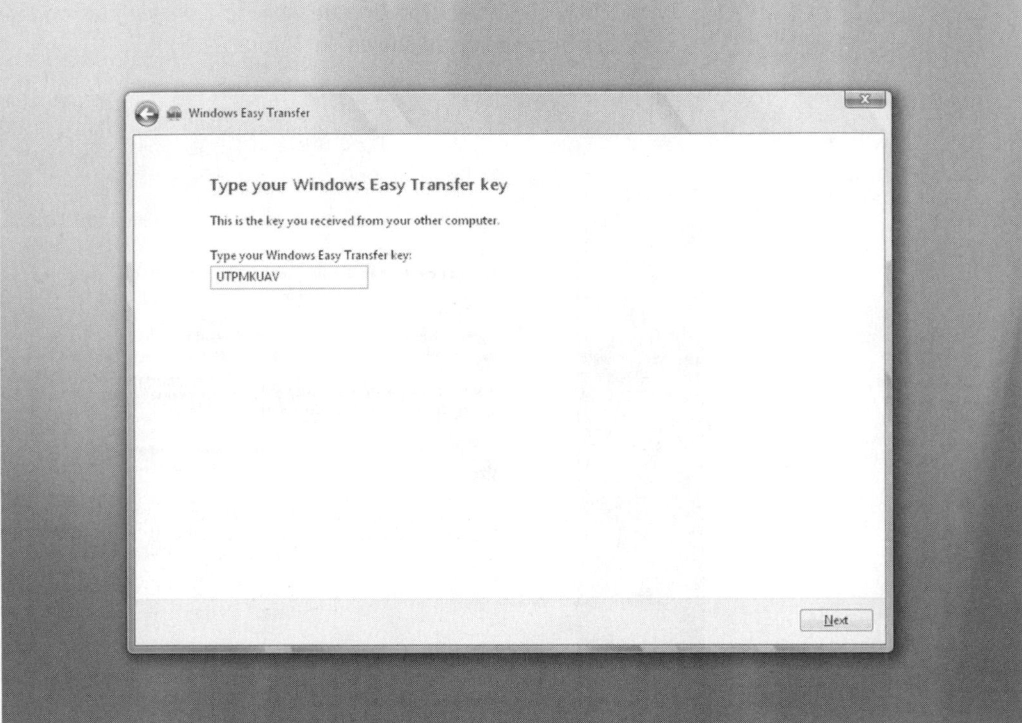

20. In the *Type your Windows Easy Transfer key* text box, enter the key the wizard provided on the other computer in Step 12, and click **Next.** The *What do you want to transfer to your new computer?* page appears, as shown in Figure 2-28.

Figure 2-28

The What do you want to transfer to your new computer? page

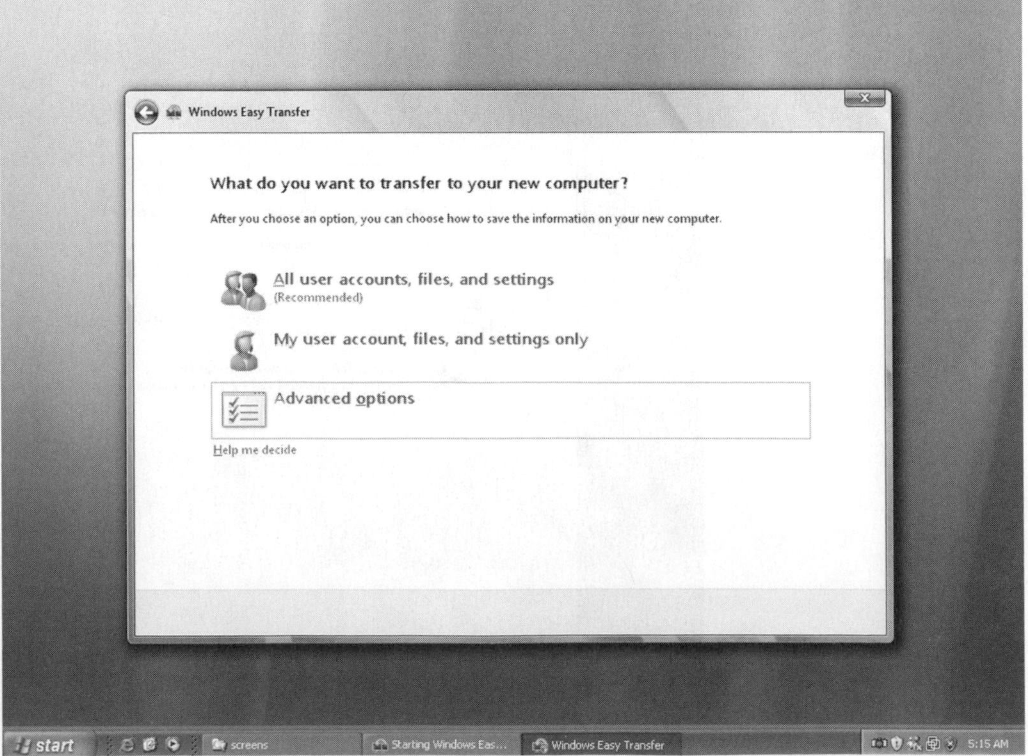

21. Click **All user accounts, files, and settings.** The *Review selected files and settings* page appears, as shown in Figure 2-29.

Figure 2-29

The Review selected files and settings page

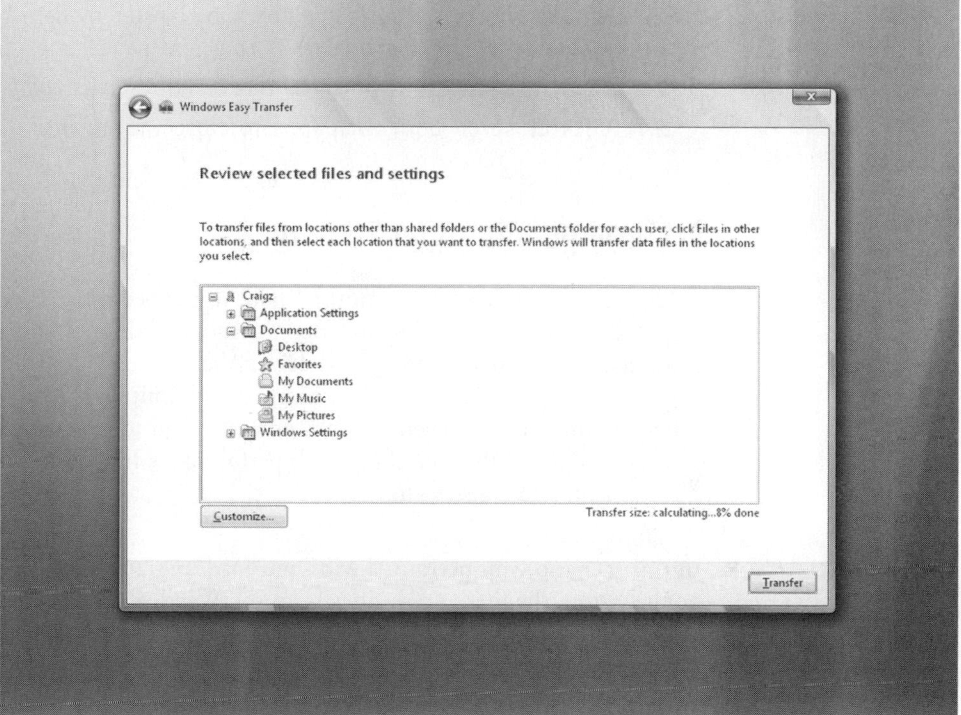

22. Click **Transfer.** The *Type a new user name or click a name in the list* page appears, as shown in Figure 2-30.

Figure 2-30

The Type a new user name or click a name in the list page appears

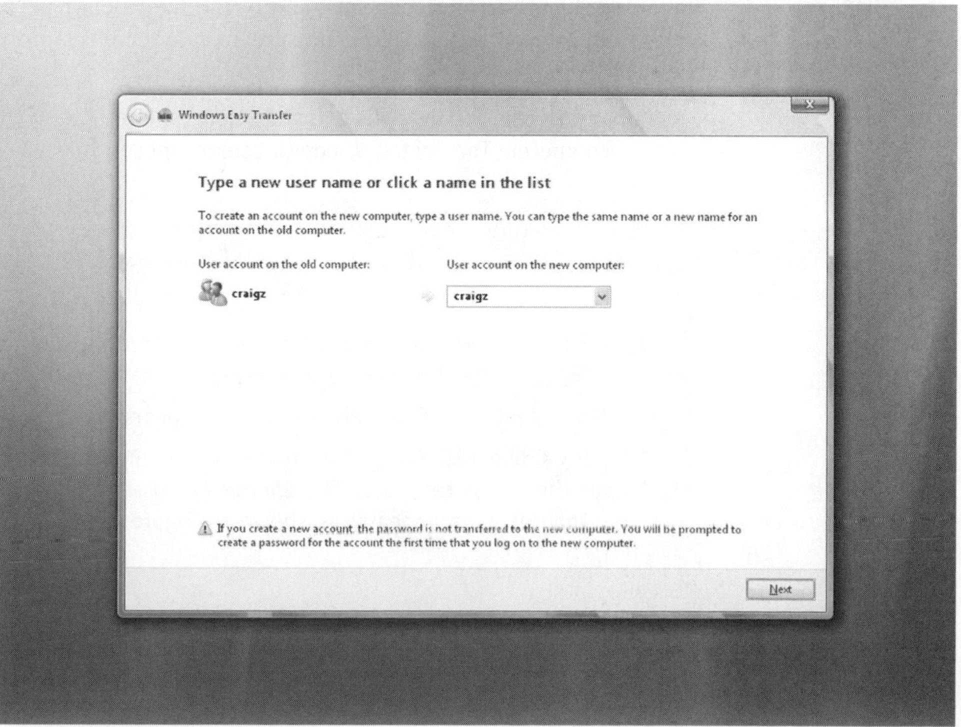

23. In the *User account on the new computer* dropdown list, select the user account to which you want to apply the files and settings found in the user profile specified under *User account on the old computer*. (You can also enter a name for a new user account instead.) Click **Next** to continue.

24. The *Please wait until the transfer is complete* page appears. When the process finishes, the *You're ready to transfer files and settings to your new computer* page appears.
25. On the Windows Vista computer, the transfer process begins automatically and the *Please wait until the transfer is complete* page appears.
26. When the process is finished, the *The transfer is complete* page appears.
27. Click **Close** on both computers to close the wizard.

Performing Migration Scenario 2

Alice has a Windows XP computer that she has been sharing with her roommates for several years. She recently purchased the retail version of Windows Vista, which came bundled with a free external hard drive. Alice wants you to install Vista, retaining the years of files and settings she has accrued and omitting the files and settings created by her roommates. However, she does not want you to perform an upgrade, because she has recently noticed that the computer's performance has degraded, possibly due to file fragmentation and registry clutter.

In this scenario, you perform a wipe-and-load migration using the external hard drive to temporarily store the files and settings from the Windows XP computer. Then, after performing a clean installation of Windows Vista, you transfer the files and settings from the external drive back to the computer. Because Alice has a Windows Vista installation disk, there is no need to transfer the Windows Easy Transfer program from a Windows Vista computer.

PERFORM MIGRATION SCENARIO 2

GET READY. Make sure that the Windows XP computer has Service Pack 2 installed and that the external hard drive is connected and operating. Then make a secondary backup of the client's important files as a safety measure, in case there is a problem with the migration procedure.

1. Insert the Windows Vista installation disk into the DVD drive of the Windows XP computer. The Install Windows screen appears.

Windows Easy Transfer can migrate user profile information only from computers running Windows 2000 SP4, Windows XP SP2, and Windows Vista.

2. Click **Transfer files and settings from another computer**. The Welcome to Windows Easy Transfer page appears.
3. Click **Next.** The Close Programs box appears.
4. Click **Close All**. All of the programs that are accessing the user profile information on the computer close. The *Choose how to transfer files and settings to your new computer* page appears, as shown in Figure 2-31.

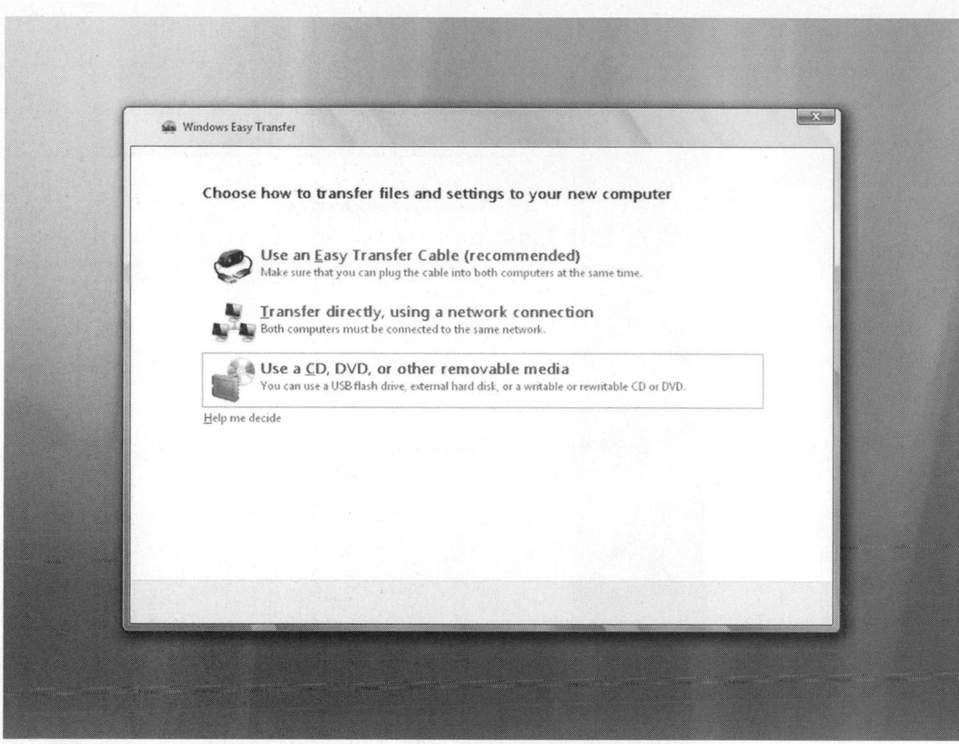

Figure 2-31

The Choose how to transfer files and settings to your new computer page

5. Click **Use a CD, DVD, or other removable media.** The *Choose how to transfer files and program settings* page appears, as shown in Figure 2-32.

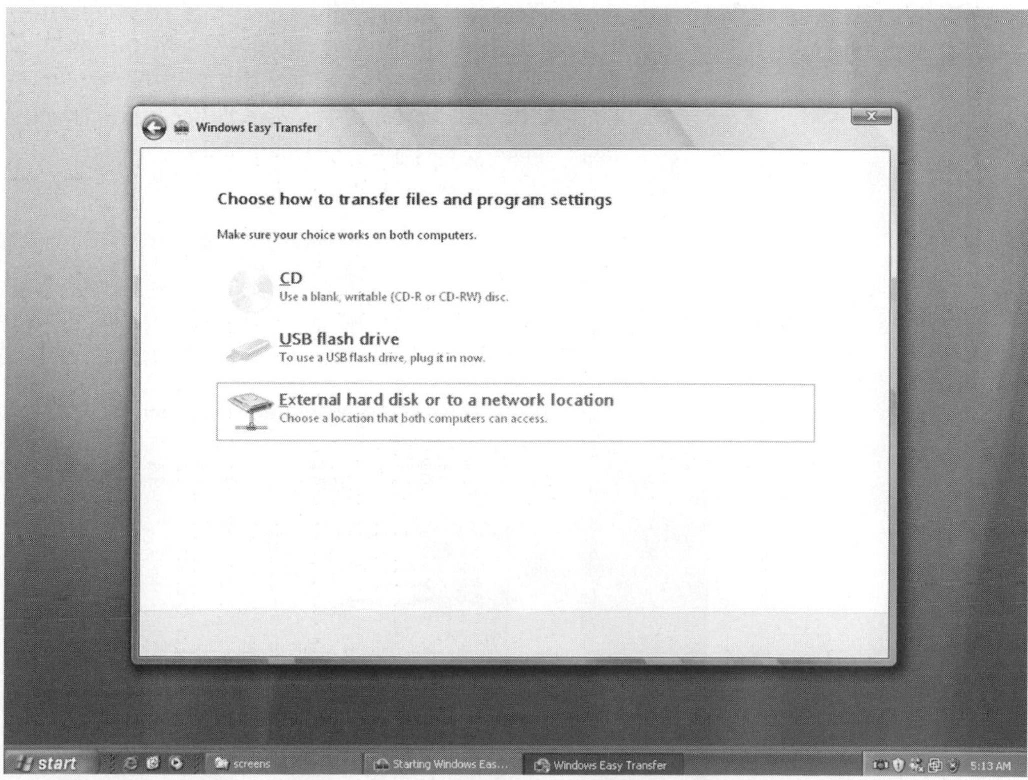

Figure 2-32

The Choose how to transfer files and program settings page

6. Click **External hard disk or to a network location.** The *Choose a network location* page appears, as shown in Figure 2-33.

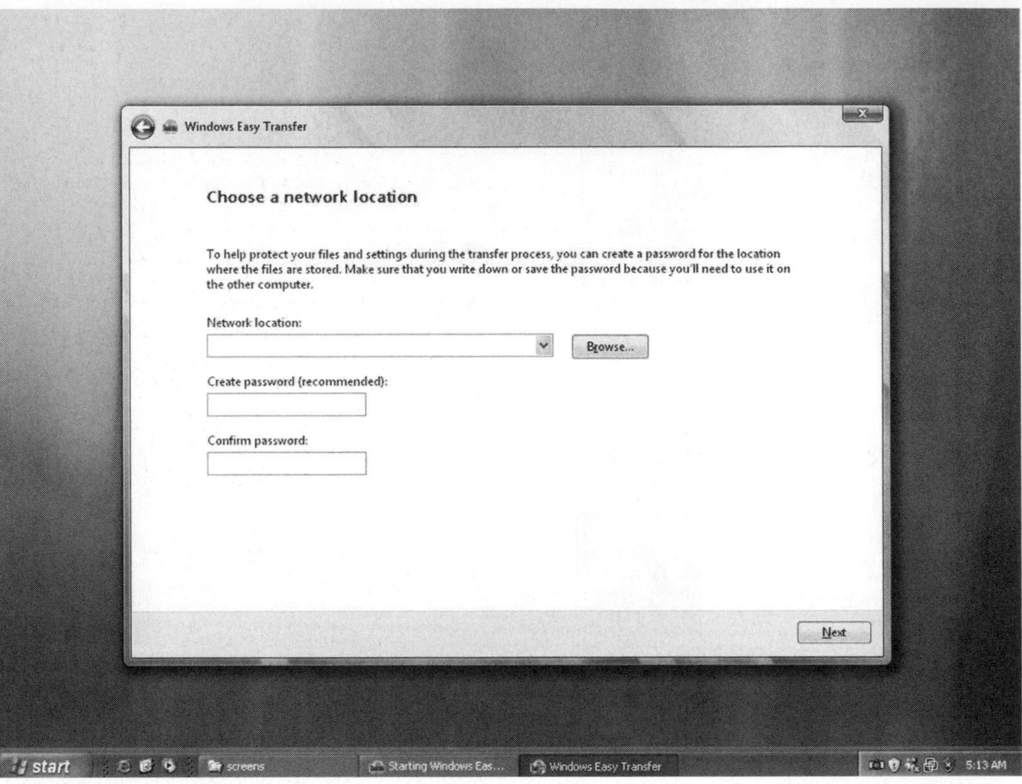

Figure 2-33

The Choose a network location page

7. In the *Network location* text box, enter (or browse to) a folder on the external hard drive. (You can also specify a password to protect the profile data, if desired.) Then click **Next** to continue. The *What do you want to transfer to your new computer* page appears.
8. Click **Advanced options**. The *Select user accounts, files, and settings to transfer* page appears, as shown in Figure 2-34.

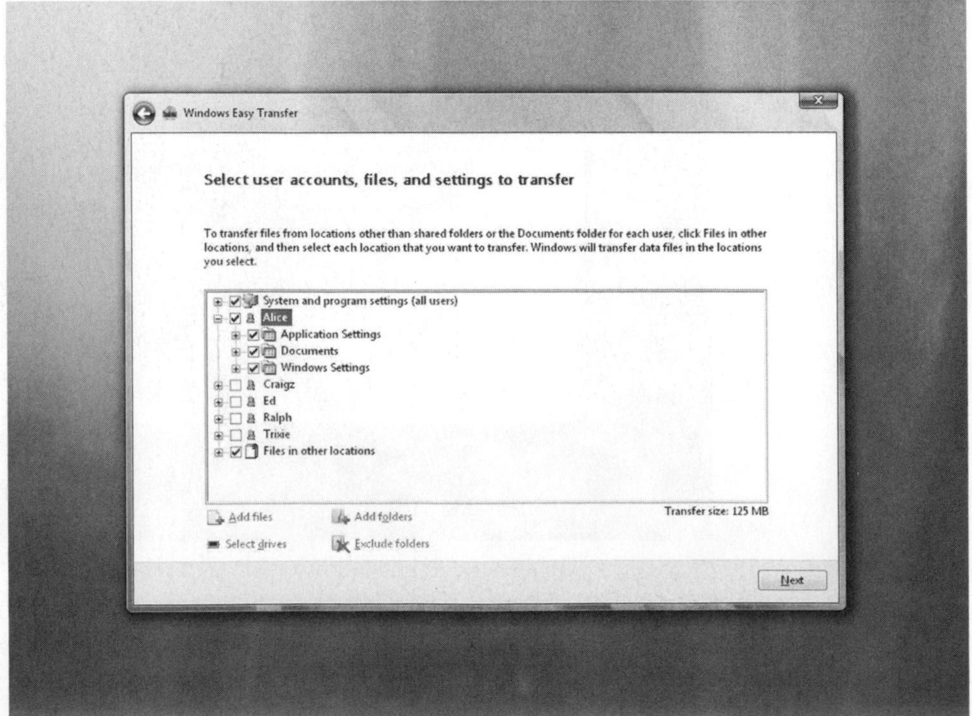

Figure 2-34

The Select user accounts, files, and settings to transfer page

9. Clear the checkboxes for all of the user accounts except Alice's, and then click **Next**. The *Please wait until the transfer is complete* page appears.
10. When the wizard finishes writing the profile data to the external hard drive, the *You're ready to transfer files and settings to your new computer* page appears.
11. Click **Close** to shut down the wizard.
12. Disconnect the external hard drive from the computer.
13. Perform a clean installation of Windows Vista on the computer, as detailed earlier in this lesson, erasing the partition on which Windows XP was installed.
14. Reconnect the external hard drive to the computer and make sure that it is functioning.
15. On the Windows Vista computer, click **Start > All Programs > Accessories > System Tools** and select **Windows Easy Transfer**. The *Welcome to Windows Easy Transfer* page appears.
16. Click **Next**. The *Do you want to start a new transfer or continue one in progress?* page appears.
17. Click **Continue a transfer in progress**. The *Are your computers connected to a network?* page appears, as shown in Figure 2-35.

Figure 2-35

The Are your computers connected to a Network? page

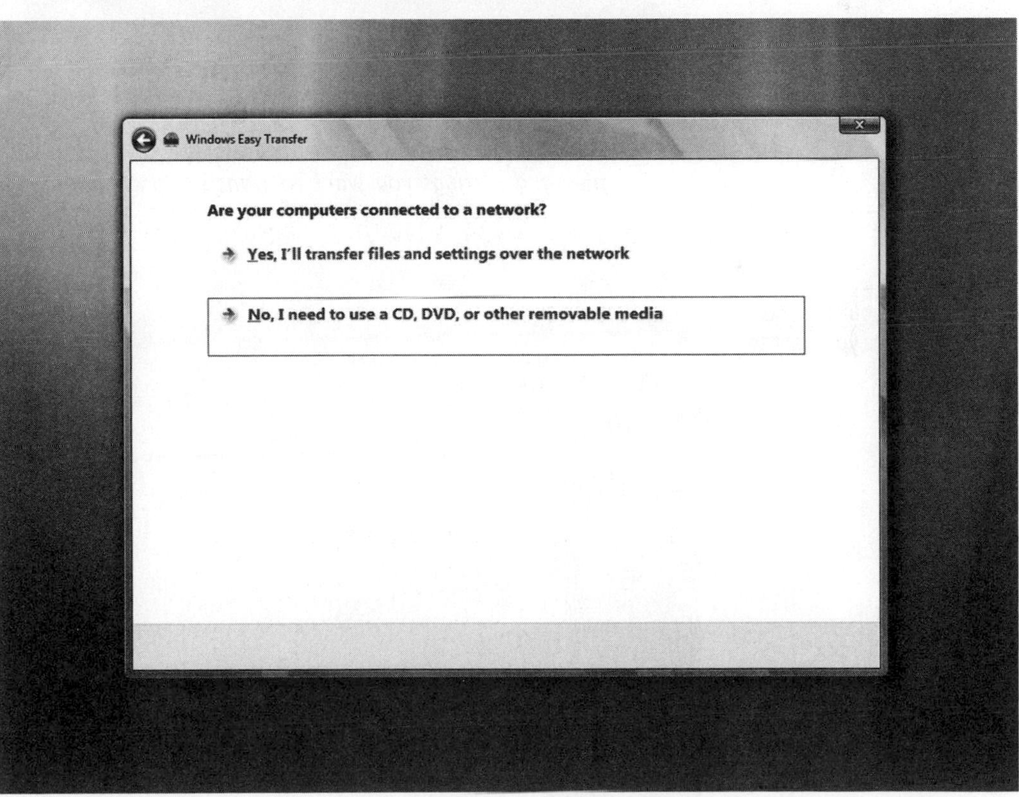

18. Click **No, I need to use a CD, DVD, or other removable media**. The *Where did you save the files and settings you want to transfer?* page appears, as shown in Figure 2-36.

Figure 2-36

The Where did you save the files and settings you want to transfer? page

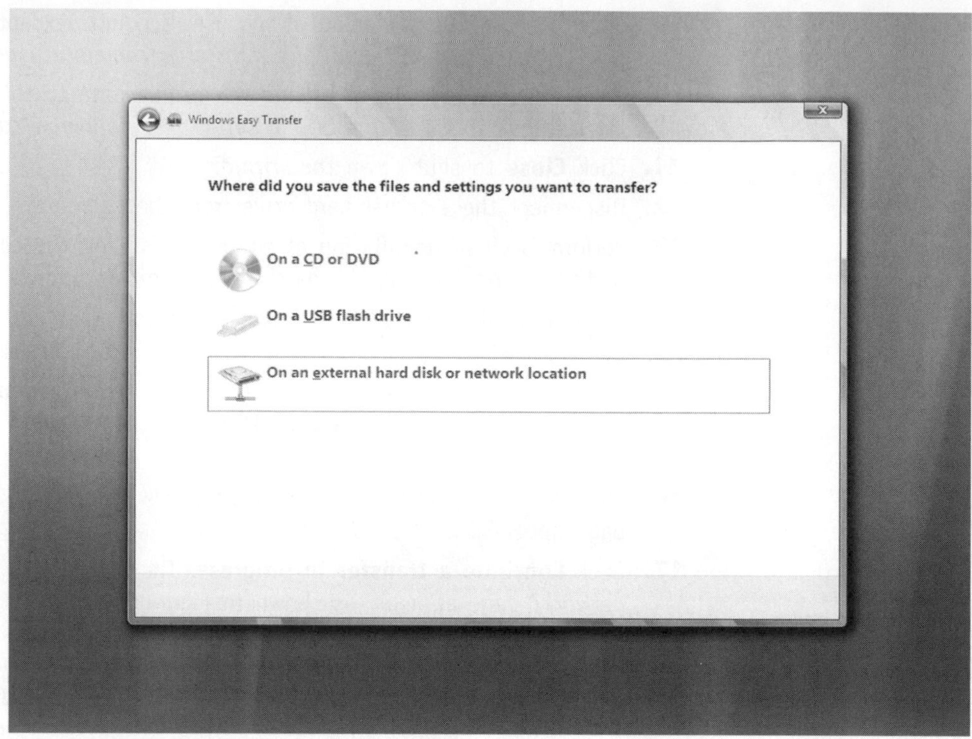

19. Click **On an external hard disk or network location.** The *Where did you copy the files and settings you want to transfer?* page appears, as shown in Figure 2-37.

Figure 2-37

The Where did you copy the files and settings you want to transfer? page

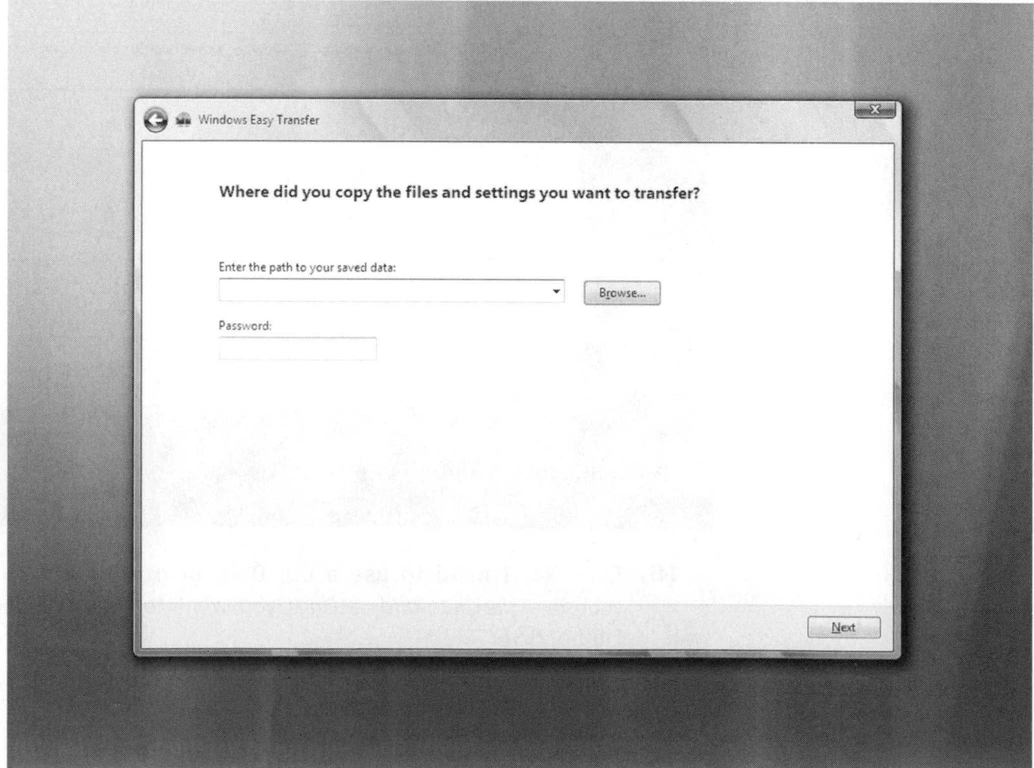

20. In the *Enter the path to your saved data* text box, enter the name of (or browse to) the folder on the external hard drive where you saved the Windows XP user profile information, specifying the password, if necessary. Then click **Next.** The *Type a new user name or click a name in the list* page appears.

21. In the *User account on the new computer* text box, enter **Alice** and click **Next**. The *Review selected files and settings* page appears.
22. Click **Transfer**. The *Please wait until the transfer is complete* page appears.
23. When the wizard is finished, the *The transfer is complete* page appears.
24. Click **Close**. A Windows Easy Transfer message box appears, stating that you must log off before the changes the wizard has made can take effect.
25. Click **Yes** to log off.

■ Identifying Upgrade Paths

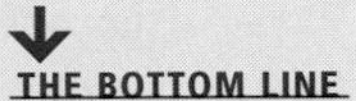
THE BOTTOM LINE

In many cases, the most convenient way to deploy Windows Vista on existing computers is to perform an upgrade from another operating system. However, there are a multitude of Windows versions, and not all of them support upgrades to Windows Vista.

CERTIFICATION READY?
Upgrade to Windows Vista from previous versions of Windows: Identify valid upgrade paths.
1.3

As noted earlier in this lesson, performing an in-place upgrade to Windows Vista is a quick and convenient way to provide clients with the new operating system without sacrificing the personal files and configuration settings that the users have built up over the years. When you perform an in-place upgrade, all of the files and settings on the computer remain intact, including installed applications. If you choose to install Vista to the partition that contains the old operating system, the Setup program renames the existing Windows folder to Windows.old, so that the old operating system is still recoverable.

IMPORTANT

When discussing operating system upgrades, it is important to distinguish between the purchase of an upgraded operating system license and the actual installation of the upgraded operating system. The term *in-place upgrade* refers to an installation of Windows Vista on an existing computer, retaining all applications, files, and settings. Some users, however, might be eligible for an upgrade to Vista, but can't perform an in-place upgrade. For example, Microsoft's Website indicates that licensed Windows 2000 users are eligible to purchase an upgrade version of Windows Vista at a reduced price, but this does not mean that they can install Vista with Windows 2000 in place. In fact, Windows 2000 systems require a clean installation to run Windows Vista.

Upgrading from Earlier Windows Versions

There are limits to the upgrade paths to Windows Vista from earlier Windows versions.

Only computers running the following operating systems are eligible for upgrades to Windows Vista:

- Windows 2000
- Windows XP
- Windows Vista (another edition)

These Windows versions are all eligible for purchase of a Windows Vista license at an upgrade price, but you can only perform an in-place upgrade on a computer running Windows XP. Windows XP has an architecture similar to that of Windows Vista, which makes it possible to convert its settings. However, the various editions of Windows XP are compatible only with certain editions of Windows Vista. Table 2-1 lists all of the operating systems that are eligible for upgrades to Windows Vista and indicates whether an in-place upgrade is possible for each path.

Table 2-1
Upgrade Paths to Windows Vista

	Home Basic	Home Premium	Business	Enterprise	Ultimate
Windows XP Home	In-place upgrade supported	In-place upgrade supported	In-place upgrade supported	In-place upgrade supported	In-place upgrade supported
Windows XP Professional	Clean installation required	Clean installation required	In-place upgrade supported	In-place upgrade supported	In-place upgrade supported
Windows XP Media Center	Clean installation required	In-place upgrade supported	Clean installation required	Clean installation required	In-place upgrade supported
Windows XP Tablet PC	Clean installation required	Clean installation required	In-place upgrade supported	In-place upgrade supported	In-place upgrade supported
Windows XP Professional x64	Clean installation required	Clean installation required	Clean installation required	Clean installation required	Clean installation required
Windows 2000 Professional	Clean installation required	Clean installation required	Clean installation required	Clean installation required	Clean installation required

TAKE NOTE* Windows Vista Enterprise is available only as part of a site license arrangement with Microsoft. It is not sold as a retail product, so upgrade packages are not available in stores.

If your clients' computers are running any of the following operating systems, they cannot upgrade to Windows Vista. They must purchase a full license and perform a clean installation.

- Windows 3.1
- Windows 95
- Windows 98
- Windows Me
- Windows NT 3.x or 4.0
- Windows 2000 Server
- Windows Server 2003

Upgrading from Other Windows Vista Editions

In some cases, Windows Vista enables you to upgrade to other editions of the operating system.

If Windows Vista is installed on your clients' computers, it is possible to upgrade to another Vista edition to take advantage of the additional features it provides. Because a Windows Vista installation disk includes the software for all editions, users only have to purchase the license for the upgraded version and obtain a product key. Microsoft refers to this as a Windows Anytime Upgrade. This feature is available in all Windows Vista installations.

There are limitations to the upgrades you can perform between Windows Vista editions, however. Table 2-2 lists the upgrade paths between Windows Vista editions and specifies which are eligible for Windows Anytime Upgrades.

Table 2-2
Windows Anytime Upgrade Paths

	To Home Basic	To Home Premium	To Business	To Enterprise	To Ultimate
From Home Basic	N/A	Yes	No	No	Yes
From Home Premium	No	N/A	No	No	Yes
From Business	No	No	N/A	Yes	Yes
From Enterprise	No	No	No	N/A	Yes
From Ultimate	No	No	No	No	N/A

TAKE NOTE*

The general rules of Windows Anytime Upgrade paths are as follows:

- You cannot "upgrade" to a lesser Vista edition (such as Home Premium to Home Basic), unless you perform a clean installation.
- The two home and the two business editions form separate upgrade paths. In other words, you cannot upgrade a home edition to a business edition or a business edition to a home edition.
- The Ultimate edition upgrade is available to all other editions.

For technicians supporting standalone systems, the Vista upgrade you are most likely to see is from Home Basic to Home Premium or Ultimate. Home Basic is the primary product for OEM computer manufacturers, and many home users are likely to want the additional cosmetic and multimedia features that an upgrade provides.

Upgrading to Windows Vista

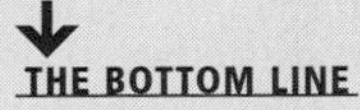

THE BOTTOM LINE

To the computer operator, performing an in-place upgrade to Windows Vista is a relatively simple procedure, but the procedure that the Setup program performs behind the scenes is highly complex.

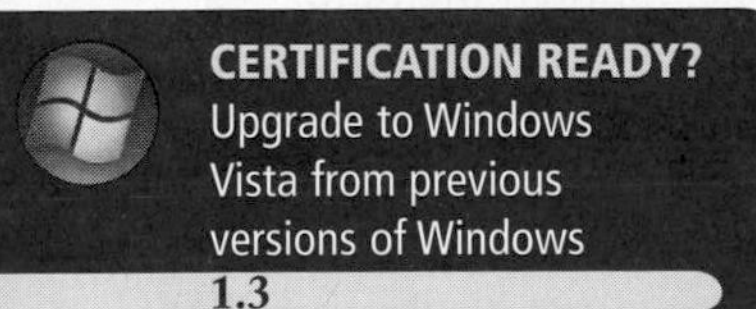

During the upgrade process, the Setup program creates a new Windows folder and installs the Windows Vista operating system files into it. This is only half of the process, however. The program must then migrate the applications, files, and settings from XP. This calls for a variety of procedures, such as importing the user profiles from the Documents and Settings folder, copying all pertinent settings from the XP registry to the new Vista registry, locating applications and data files, and updating XP device drivers with new versions.

While in-place upgrades usually proceed smoothly, the complexity of the upgrade process means that there are many things that can potentially go wrong. To minimize the risks involved, it is important for a technician to take the upgrade process seriously, prepare the system beforehand, and have the ability to troubleshoot any problems that might arise. The following sections discuss these subjects in greater depth.

TAKE NOTE*

An in-place upgrade from Windows XP to Windows Vista is much more complex than an upgrade from one Vista edition to another. All of the Vista editions use the same basic core files and architecture. Upgrades are primarily a matter of installing additional applications, which is not as invasive or dangerous.

CERTIFICATION READY?
Upgrade to Windows Vista from previous versions of Windows: Identify application compatibility requirements.
1.3

Preparing to Upgrade

Before you begin an in-place upgrade to Windows Vista, you should perform a number of preliminary procedures to ensure that the process goes smoothly and that the client's data is protected.

Consider the following before you perform any upgrade to Windows Vista:

- Run Upgrade Advisor—To be sure that the computer is capable of running the Windows Vista edition you plan on installing, run Upgrade Advisor and take note of its advisories regarding the computer's hardware and software. If it is necessary to perform hardware upgrades, do so before installing Windows Vista, making sure that the new hardware is operational before proceeding.

X REF For more information on running the Upgrade Advisor program and Windows Vista's hardware requirements, see Lesson 1, "Introducing Windows Vista."

- Check hardware compatibility—The Upgrade Advisor program can point out hardware inadequacies in the computer, especially in regard to the Windows Vista system requirements. If it is necessary to upgrade hardware, make certain that the products you purchase are certified for use with Windows Vista. The Upgrade Advisor program can also identify devices that might not function under Windows Vista. However, it is sometimes possible to make such devices run properly with a driver or firmware upgrade. It is a good idea to perform an inventory of the computer's primary components before you perform the upgrade, and consider the age and capabilities of each one. It is always best if you can warn a client of potential hardware incompatibilities before you perform the upgrade procedure.
- Search for updated drivers—As part of your hardware inventory, be sure to consider the age of the device drivers installed on the computer. Check hardware manufacturers' Websites for driver updates, especially those that are specifically intended to provide support for Windows Vista. In some cases it might be preferable to install the new drivers while XP is still running, but if the manufacturer provides separate XP and Vista drivers wait until Vista is installed. Even if no updates are available, it is a good idea to gather all of the drivers for the computer's hardware together and copy them to a removable storage medium, such as a writable CD or flash drive. This way, if the Setup program requires a driver during the upgrade process, you have it available.
- Print a Device Manager summary—The Windows XP Device Manager application provides a wealth of information about the hardware installed in the computer, including driver versions and system resource usage. It is a good idea to print out an *All Devices And System Summary* report before you begin the upgrade procedure. This way, if any hardware problems occur under Windows Vista, you have a record of a functional configuration for each device.
- Check application compatibility—Upgrade Advisor can point out possible application compatibility problems, but you can sometimes solve these problems by updating or upgrading the application. Create an inventory of the software products installed on the computer and check the manufacturers' Websites for updates, availability of upgrades, and announcements regarding support for Windows Vista. For example, if the computer is running Microsoft Office, use the Office Online Website to download the latest updates. Check the applications' system requirements as well. An application that has barely enough memory to run on Windows XP might not run at all on Vista, which has greater memory requirements for the operating system. Install any free updates that are available and notify the client of the possible need for paid upgrades. In a corporate environment, you should test all applications for Vista compatibility, no matter what the manufacturer says, before you perform any Vista upgrades. However, for standalone clients, testing usually isn't practical. The best you can do is to inform the client that

there might be problems with specific applications and warn them that there might be additional costs involved for new versions or different products.

- Check disk space—Make sure that there is at least 15 gigabytes of disk space free on the partition where Windows XP is installed. During the upgrade procedure, sufficient disk space is needed to hold both operating systems simultaneously. After the upgrade is complete, you can remove the old XP files, freeing up some additional space.
- Ensure computer functionality—Make sure that Windows XP is running properly on the computer before you begin the upgrade process. You must start an in-place upgrade from within Windows XP, so you cannot count on Vista to correct any problems that prevent the computer from starting or running the Setup program.
- Perform a full backup—Before you perform any upgrade procedure you should back up the entire system, or at the very least the client's essential files. You can use Windows Easy Transfer if no other tool is available. Removable hard drives make this a simple process, even if the client does not have a suitable backup device in the computer.
- Purchase Windows Vista—Be sure to purchase the appropriate Windows Vista edition for the upgrade, and have the installation disk and product key handy.

CERTIFICATION READY?
Upgrade from one edition of Windows Vista to another edition: Perform an in-place upgrade.
1.4

Upgrading from Windows XP

Once you complete the steps in the previous section, you are ready to perform an in-place upgrade from Windows XP to Windows Vista.

To upgrade a Windows XP computer to Windows Vista while preserving all files and settings, use the following procedure:

UPGRADE WINDOWS XP TO WINDOWS VISTA

GET READY. Turn on the computer running Windows XP and make sure you have the Windows Vista installation disk and product key ready.

1. Insert the Windows Vista installation disk into the DVD drive. The Install Windows screen appears.
2. Click **Install now**. The *Get important updates for installation* page appears.
3. Click **Do not get the latest updates for installation**. The *Type your product key for activation* page appears.

TAKE NOTE*

If the computer is connected to the Internet, you might want to click *Go online to get the latest updates for installation* to ensure that the computer's drivers and other software are up to date.

4. In the *Product key* text box, enter the product key supplied with your Windows Vista upgrade package. Then click **Next**. The *Please read the license terms* page appears.
5. Select the **I accept the license terms** checkbox and click **Next**. The *Which type of installation do you want?* page appears.
6. Click **Upgrade**. After a compatibility check, a *Compatibility repost* screen appears, listing any problems or potential problems with the computer's hardware or software configuration.
7. Click **Next**. The *Upgrading Windows* page appears.
8. After several minutes, during which the Setup program installs Windows Vista, the computer reboots and the *Help protect Windows automatically* page appears.
9. Select one of the three options specifying what security settings you want the computer to use. The *Review your time and date settings* page appears.

10. From the *Time zone* drop-down list, select the time zone in which the computer will be running and then click **Next**. The *Select your computer's current location* page appears.
11. Click the appropriate option specifying the computer's normal location. A *Thank you* page appears.
12. Click **Start**. The computer runs through a series of optimization routines as it starts Windows Vista for the first time. A *Preparing your desktop* screen appears.

A few minutes later, the system completes its new startup routine and the Welcome Center window appears.

CERTIFICATION READY?
Upgrade from one edition of Windows Vista to another edition
1.4

Upgrading Windows Vista Editions

One of the main advantages of the new architecture that Microsoft devised for Windows Vista is that it makes upgrades to other Vista editions incredibly simple.

There are two ways to upgrade a Windows Vista computer to another edition:

- Purchase an upgrade package from a retailer.
- Use the Windows Anytime Upgrade tool included with Vista.

To perform an in-place upgrade of Windows Vista, you must have an installation disk and a product key for the new edition. If you do not have an installation disk, which is possible if you purchased the computer with Windows Vista preinstalled, you must either order one from Microsoft (at minimal cost) or purchase a retail upgrade package, which contains the disk and a product key.

If you have an installation disk, you can use the Windows Upgrade Anytime tool to purchase the upgrade online and obtain a product key for the new edition.

UPGRADE THE VISTA EDITION

1. Click **Start** > **Control Panel**. The Control Panel window appears.
2. Click **System Maintenance** > **Windows Anytime Upgrade**. The *what do you want to do?* window appears, as shown in Figure 2-38.

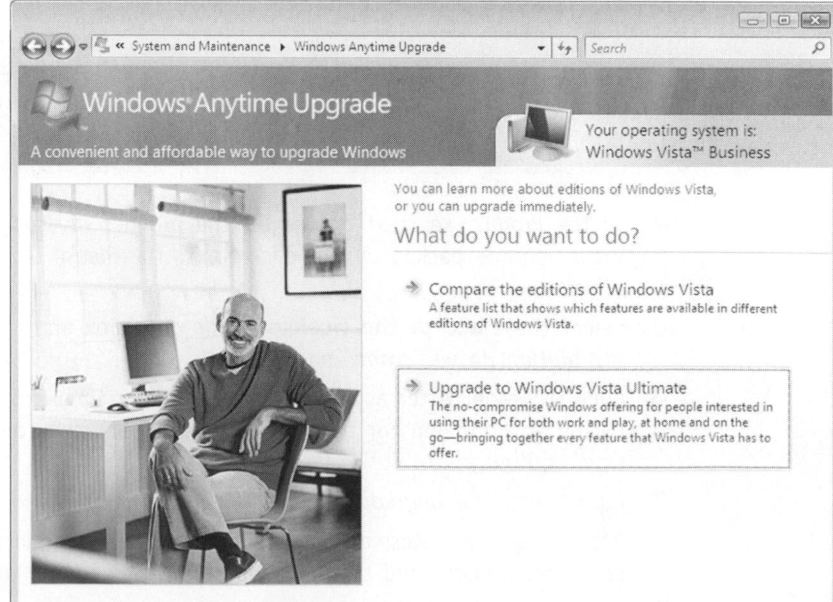

Figure 2-38

The What do you want to do? window

3. Click **Upgrade to Windows Vista Ultimate.** The *You've chosen to upgrade to Windows Vista Ultimate* page appears, as shown in Figure 2-39.

Figure 2-39

The You've chosen to upgrade to Windows Vista Ultimate page

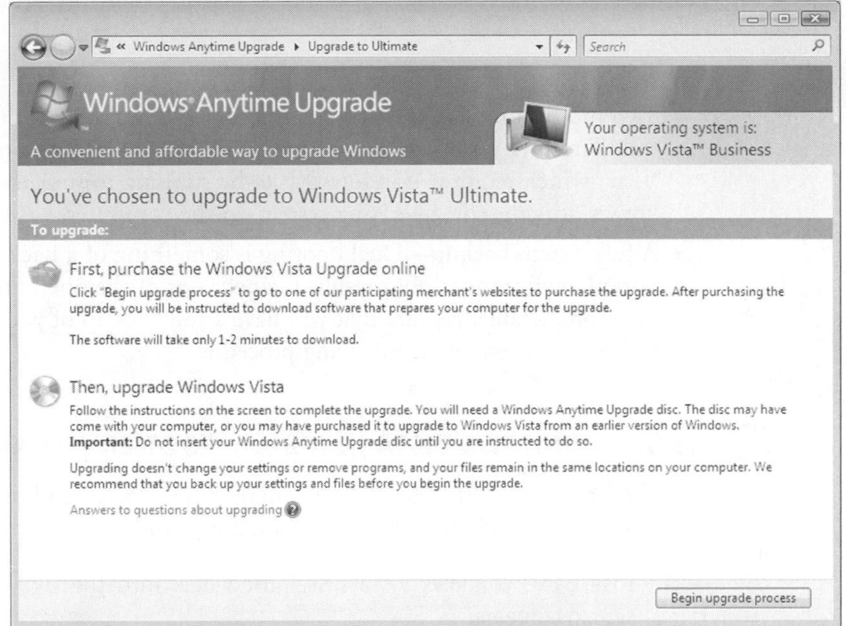

4. Click the **Begin upgrade process** button and then follow the instructions to purchase and install the upgrade.

■ Performing a Dual Boot Installation

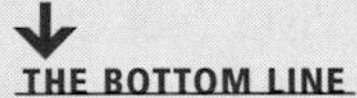

When a user wants to test Windows Vista without making a full commitment, or needs to maintain an older operating system for compatibility with specific applications, a dual boot environment can be ideal.

Although it has drawbacks, mainly in terms of disk space, many users rely on a dual boot environment to provide access to two independent operating system installations. In a dual boot environment, both operating systems are completely independent of each other, so restrictions regarding upgrade paths do not apply. You can dual boot any edition of Windows Vista with Windows XP.

To create a dual boot environment on a computer running Windows XP, you must have all of the following:

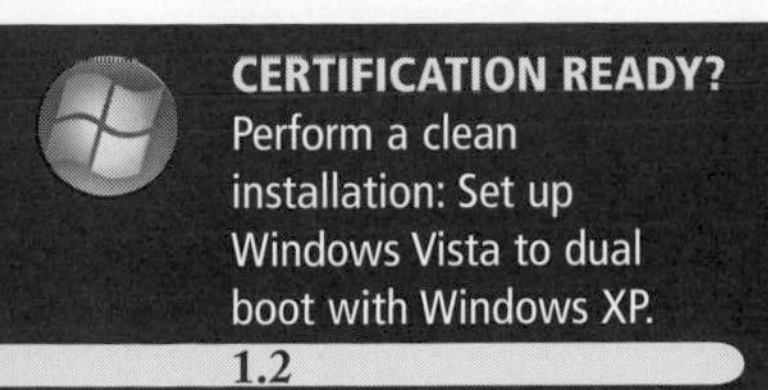

CERTIFICATION READY?
Perform a clean installation: Set up Windows Vista to dual boot with Windows XP.
1.2

- Two disk partitions—Windows does not support multiple operating systems on a single disk partition. Therefore, you must have two partitions to dual boot, one for the computer's original operating system and one for the Windows Vista installation. In addition, be aware that Windows Vista must be installed on a primary partition, not on a logical disk in an extended partition. Make sure that the partition where you intend to install Vista has sufficient disk space for a full installation.

TAKE NOTE*

If you have sufficient disk space for a Windows Vista installation on your computer's C: drive, but you have only one partition, there is no way to create a new primary partition out of that disk space using the tools in Windows XP without erasing the entire drive. You must use a third-party tool, such as Norton's PartitionMagic, to create the partition.

- Two full product licenses—From a licensing standpoint, a dual boot environment is a full Windows Vista installation, not an upgrade. Do not purchase an upgrade license for Vista, which requires Windows XP to be running to start the installation. As far as Vista knows, it is the sole operating system on the computer.
- A full system backup—Dual booting is something of a hack, and not an officially supported environment. As a result, the behavior of the operating systems can sometimes be unpredictable. Be sure that you have a full backup of your Windows XP installation before you attempt the following procedure.

INSTALL WINDOWS VISTA IN A DUAL BOOT ENVIRONMENT

GET READY. Turn on the computer running Windows XP and make sure you have the Windows Vista installation disk and product key ready.

1. Insert the Windows Vista installation disk into the DVD drive. The Install Windows screen appears.
2. Click **Install now**. The *Get important updates for installation* page appears.
3. Click **Do not get the latest updates for installation**. The *Type your product key for activation* page appears.
4. In the *Product key* text box, enter the product key supplied with your Windows Vista package. Then click **Next**. The *Please read the license terms* page appears.
5. Select the **I accept the license terms** checkbox and then click **Next**. The *Which type of installation do you want?* page appears.
6. Click **Custom (advanced)**. The *Where do you want to install Windows?* page appears.
7. Select the partition on which you want to install Windows Vista (not the partition where Windows XP is installed) and then click **Next**. The Installing Windows page appears. After several minutes, during which the Setup program installs Windows Vista, the computer reboots and the *Choose a user name and picture* page appears.

   Complete the installation process by following the "Perform a Clean Installation" procedure described earlier in this lesson, starting at Step 11.

WARNING If you select the partition on which Windows XP is installed, you will not get a dual boot environment. Instead, the Windows Vista Setup program will rename the Windows folder to Windows.old and create a new Windows folder for the Vista files. This is still a clean installation, however. The Setup program will not import the XP files and settings, and once the process is completed, you will no longer be able to boot to Windows XP.

Rebooting the system after completing the Windows Vista installation process causes the screen shown in Figure 2-40 to appear. From this menu, you select the operating system you want to start. "Microsoft Windows" refers to Windows Vista, and "Earlier Version of Windows" refers to Windows XP. To switch between operating systems, you have to completely shut down the one that is running, and then restart the computer.

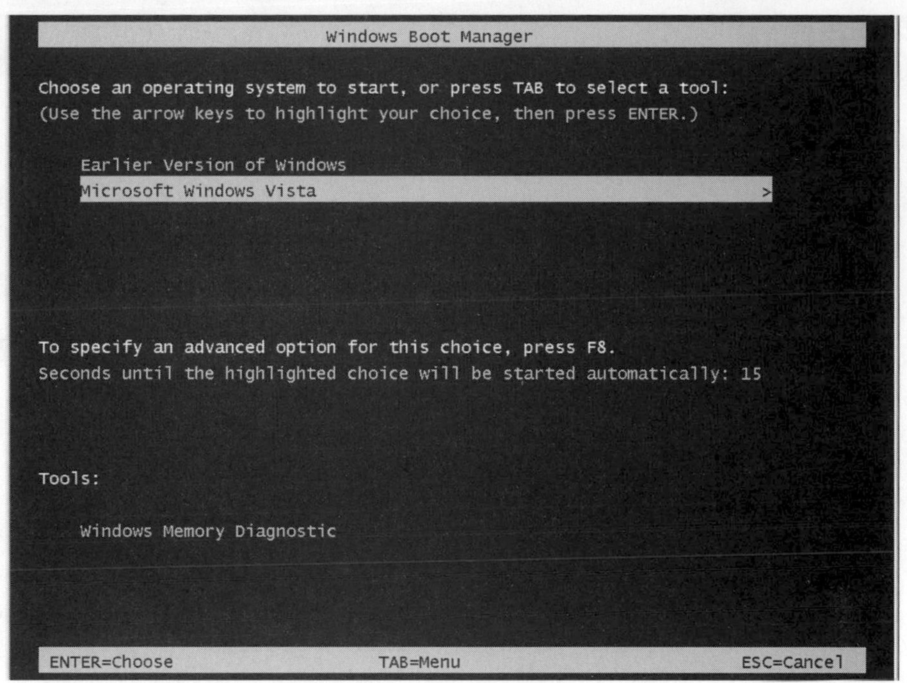
Windows Boot Manager
Choose an operating system to start, or press TAB to select a tool:
(Use the arrow keys to highlight your choice, then press ENTER.)
Earlier Version of Windows
Microsoft Windows Vista
To specify an advanced option for this choice, press F8.
Seconds until the highlighted choice will be started automatically: 15
Tools:
Windows Memory Diagnostic
ENTER=Choose
TAB=Menu
ESC=Cancel

Figure 2-40

The Windows Boot Manager page

SUMMARY SKILL MATRIX

IN THIS LESSON YOU LEARNED:
Windows Vista includes a new preinstallation environment called Windows PE.
In a clean installation, you boot from the Windows Vista Setup disk and create or select a blank partition where Vista will reside.
It is possible to migrate files and settings from an existing Windows installation to a newly installed Windows Vista installation using either Windows Easy Transfer or the User State Migration Tool.
Windows Vista supports in-place upgrades only from Windows XP or another Windows Vista edition.
To perform an in-place upgrade, you must launch the Windows Vista Setup program from within Windows XP.
To upgrade from one Windows Vista edition to another, you can use the Windows Anytime Upgrade tool found in the Windows Vista Control Panel.
A dual boot installation is one in which two operating systems are installed on separate disk partitions, providing access to both at boot time.

■ Knowledge Assessment

Fill in the Blank

Complete the following sentences by writing the correct word or words in the blanks provided.

1. Windows Easy Transfer supports two types of migrations, called ______________ and ______________.
2. When a serious problem occurs with Windows Vista, you might be able to repair it by starting the Windows PE operating system and running diagnostic tools. In this scenario, Windows PE is called by another name, which is ______________.
3. To migrate user profile information from one computer to another, you can use either ______________ or ______________.
4. A computer running Windows PE will automatically reboot after ______________.
5. Windows Easy Transfer supports migration using any removable storage medium common to the two computers except ______________.
6. The Windows Vista component that enables the computer to support more than one language is called the ______________.
7. The reason why it is possible to remove the Windows Vista installation disk to supply the Setup program with drivers is that Windows PE runs on a ______________.
8. To upgrade Windows 98 to Windows Vista, you must perform a ______________.
9. The files and settings that Windows Easy Transfer can migrate to a Windows Vista computer are primarily stored in ______________.
10. As a preinstallation environment, Windows PE is a vast improvement over DOS because it includes internal support for ______________ and ______________.

True / False

Circle T if the statement is true or F if the statement is false.

T | F 1. Windows PE is the latest version of the DOS operating system.

T | F 2. It is possible to perform an in-place upgrade of the 32-bit Windows Vista Ultimate Edition from any 32-bit version of Windows XP or Windows Vista.

T | F 3. To create a dual boot environment with Windows Vista, you must have two primary partitions on your computer.

T | F 4. Windows Vista Home Basic users can perform in-place upgrades to Windows Vista Business Edition without obtaining a new installation disk.

T | F 5. One way to perform an in-place upgrade is to boot from the Windows Vista installation disk, choose the Custom option, and then select the partition on which Windows XP is installed.

T | F 6. To create a Windows Vista workstation that supports multiple languages, you must begin by installing the English language version of Vista.

T | F 7. It is not possible to "upgrade" a computer running the Windows Vista Ultimate edition to the Enterprise edition without performing a clean installation.

T | F 8. Windows 2000 Professional users are eligible to purchase an upgrade version of Windows Vista, but they cannot perform an in-place upgrade.

T | F 9. To migrate the user profiles of multiple user accounts located on the same computer, you must use the User State Migration Tool.

T | F 10. Any program that can run on Windows Vista can run on Windows PE.

Review Questions

1. Give two detailed reasons why Windows PE 2.0 is a better installation environment for Windows Vista than MS-DOS.
2. Explain the difference between a side-by-side migration and a wipe-and-load migration, using Windows Easy Transfer.

Case Scenarios

Scenario #1: Upgrading Windows Vista Editions

You are working as a desktop support technician at a computer store, and a customer approaches you with a laptop computer he purchased six months ago. The computer came with Windows Vista Home Basic installed on it, and the customer now wants to use the computer to log on to the Windows domain at his office. He knows he cannot do this with Windows Vista Home Basic, and wants you to upgrade the computer to Windows Vista Business, without affecting his files and settings. Explain in detail the procedure you would have to use to fulfill the customer's request.

Scenario #2: Upgrading Windows Vista Editions

When you run Windows Upgrade Advisor on a client's computer, the report's only recommendation is that you upgrade the video display adapter after you upgrade the operating system to Windows Vista. What is likely to be the result immediately after you install Windows Vista on the computer and before you upgrade the video adapter?

Configuring System Settings

OBJECTIVE DOMAIN MATRIX

Technology Skill	Objective Domain	Objective Number
Configuring Windows Sidebar	Configure Windows Sidebar • Download and install Gadgets	5.6
Introducing Windows Aero	Configure and troubleshoot Windows Aero	2.2
Understanding Windows Aero Hardware Requirements	Configure and troubleshoot Windows Aero • Identify hardware requirements for Windows Aero	2.2
Troubleshooting Video Adapter Issues	Configure and troubleshoot Windows Aero • Troubleshoot graphics card issues • Identify WDDM drivers (using Win+Tab to check Aero is on)	2.2
Validating Windows	Configure and troubleshoot Windows Aero • Configure Windows Genuine Advantage	2.2
Running the System Performance Rating Tool	Configure and troubleshoot Windows Aero • Run the System Performance Rating tool	2.2
Updating Display Drivers	Configure and troubleshoot Windows Aero • Identify WDDM drivers (using Win+Tab to check Aero is on)	2.2
Enabling Aero Display Settings	Configure and troubleshoot Windows Aero • Change the desktop theme to Windows Aero	2.2

KEY TERMS

Desktop Window Manager (DWM)
DirectX
gadget
Graphic Device Interface (GDI)
graphics processing unit (GPU)
Windows Display Driver Model (WDDM)
Windows Genuine Advantage

Customizing the User Experience

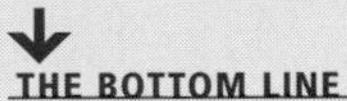

There are often additional tasks that desktop technicians must perform on a newly-installed Windows Vista computer.

As a technician installing Windows Vista, you are not necessarily finished when the Setup program closes. Depending on the needs of the client, you might need to perform a large number of configuration tasks before the job is done. For example, some clients might want you to configure Vista to use the more familiar interface from Windows XP or even Windows 2000. Others might want the computer to function in certain ways, but be unaware of which controls to use to implement those settings. Finally, you might be required to set up the computer to function in a business environment, in which the employer wants to impose certain restrictions on the computer users. It is up to you to gauge the needs and capabilities of your clients and provide them with an interface that is easy and convenient for them to use.

The following sections examine some of the most common configuration settings technicians have to adjust immediately after the Windows Vista installation process.

MORE INFORMATION

Computer technicians who are relatively new to servicing clients frequently have trouble distinguishing between their own preferences and the needs of their clients. As an experienced Windows user, you are probably accustomed to configuring a large number of controls in specific ways in order to customize an interface to your preferences. However, while these settings might be suitable for you, they could possibly make things more difficult for your clients. The changes you make to clients' computers should enhance their productivity without interfering with the normal operation of the Windows controls.

Customizing the Desktop

You can customize the Windows Vista desktop for productivity or cosmetic reasons.

There are two basic types of customizations that you are likely to perform on a new Windows workstation: those that enhance productivity and those that provide cosmetic alterations. This lesson concentrates mostly on the former. It is easy to spend hours playing with the colors, fonts, and images that make up the Windows interface, attempting to achieve the perfect look. However, your perfect look is not likely to be the same as that of your clients, so you are usually better off leaving them to explore the cosmetic settings themselves, rather than doing it for them. The most common exception to this rule, however, is the appearance of the desktop.

TAKE NOTE*

One might argue that Windows Vista takes a step backward by adding a new feature called Windows Sidebar to the desktop. For more discussion, see "Configuring Windows Sidebar" later in this lesson.

The desktop is the first thing a user sees after logging on, and it is probably going to be the source of the user's first reaction. Experienced users might marvel at what the computer can do, but for many beginners, if it's not pretty, they won't use it.

Early versions of Windows had all kinds of icons and controls on the desktop, and as the years passed, each ensuing version stripped some away. After all, the desktop is covered with windows most of the time, rendering those desktop icons inaccessible. In Windows Vista, only one icon remains: the Recycle Bin. Of course, everyone has their own preferences, and it is still possible to add icons to the desktop. Therefore, after a user logs on, the first thing he or she sees is the desktop background. Windows Vista includes a collection of desktop background images that is greatly improved over previous Windows versions. To change the desktop background, use the following procedure:

CHANGE THE DESKTOP BACKGROUND

GET READY. Turn on the computer and log on using one of the existing user accounts. Close any windows that appear on the desktop.

1. Right-click the desktop, and then from the context menu, select **Personalize.** The *Personalize appearance and sounds* page appears, as shown on Figure 3-1.

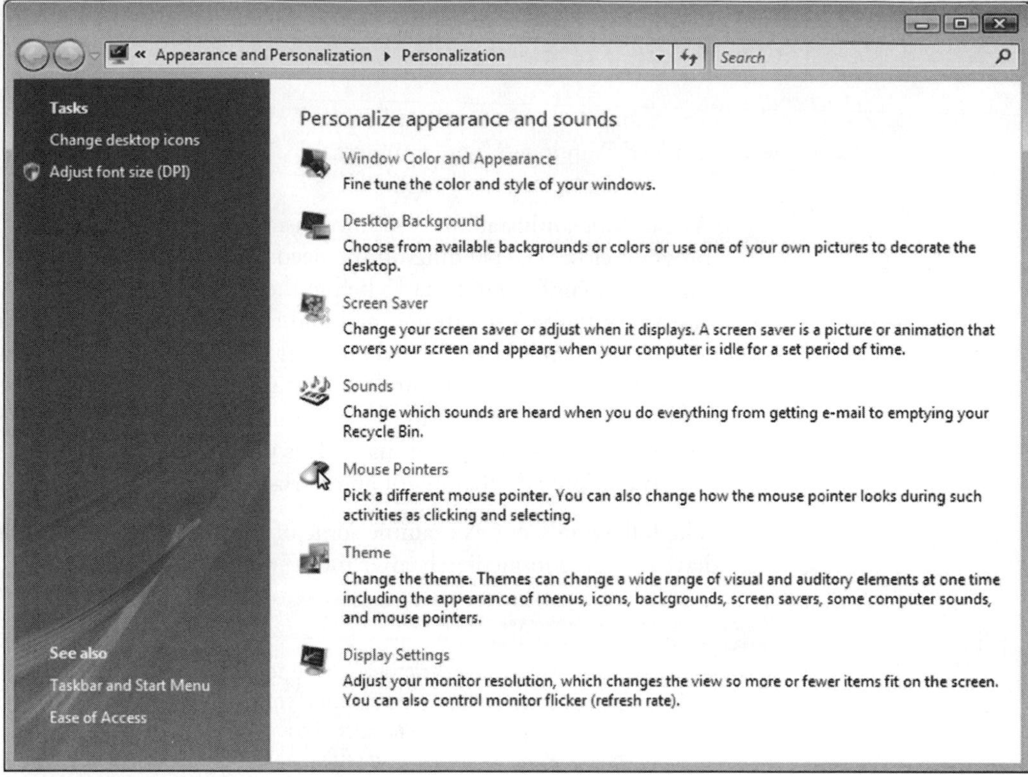

Figure 3-1

The Personalize appearance and sounds page

2. Click **Desktop Background**. The *Choose a desktop background* page appears, as shown in Figure 3-2.

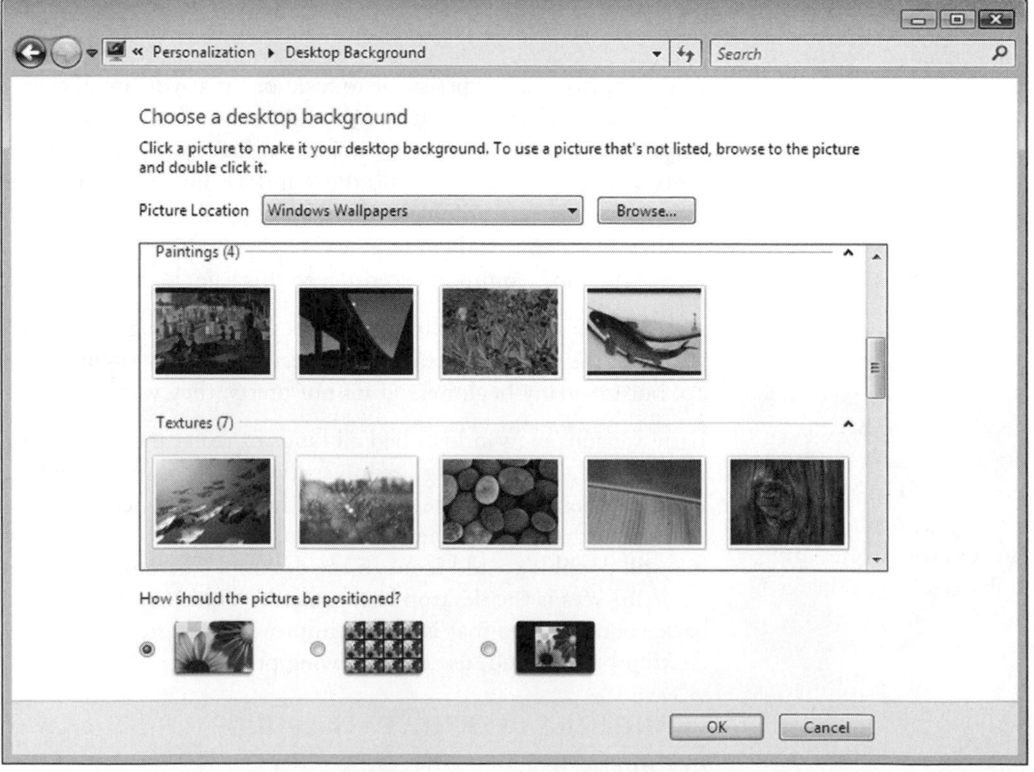

Figure 3-2

The Choose a desktop background page

3. Click one of the Windows Wallpaper thumbnail images that appears in the box to apply it to the desktop.
4. Click **OK** to close the window.

You can also click the **Browse** button to select an image of your own in any folder. If the image you choose is smaller than the desktop, you can select one of the three radio buttons at the bottom of the page to control how the image fills the screen. The options are as follows:

- Fit to screen—Windows stretches or compresses the image to fit the screen. If the image is too small or uses a different aspect ratio than your monitor, it might appear distorted.
- Tile—Windows repeats the image as many times as needed, both horizontally and vertically, to fill the screen. The smaller the image, the more tiles it will take.
- Center—Windows places a single instance of the image in the center of the screen. If the image is too large, it might be cropped.

Customizing the Start Menu

The Start menu is the primary mechanism for launching applications in Windows; you can make a number of modifications to increase its utility.

The Windows Start menu, shown in Figure 3-3, appears when you click the orb on the left side of the taskbar or click the **Ctrl+Esc** key combination.

Figure 3-3

The Windows Start menu

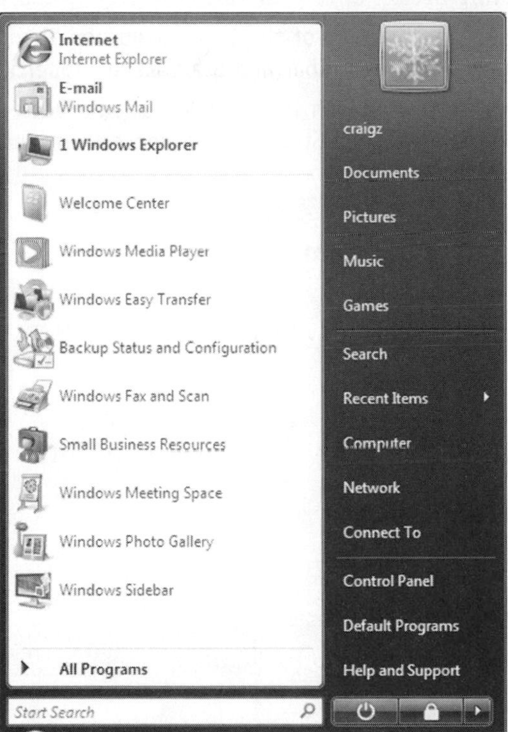

TAKE NOTE*

By default, Windows Vista configures the Internet and E-Mail shortcuts to open Internet Explorer and Windows Mail, respectively. However, you can associate different applications with these shortcuts using the Customize Start Menu dialog box, as discussed later in this lesson.

The Start menu consists of three sections:

- Right side—The right side of the Start menu contains links to commonly used Windows built-in features on a black background, including the current user's profile, the Control Panel, and the Search and Help engines.
- Upper left—The upper left side of the Start menu contains pinned icons on a white background, that is, icons that remain in place permanently. By default, Internet and E-Mail are the only pinned icons, but you can add others.
- Lower left—The lower left side of the Start menu contains the icons for the programs you access most frequently, on a white background.

At the bottom of the lower left section is an All Programs link that takes you to a series of cascading menus containing shortcuts to all of the applications installed on the computer.

There are a number of ways to customize the Start menu to increase its capabilities, as described in the following sections.

Adding Icons for Most Popular Programs

By default, the Start menu contains icons for the nine programs you run most often. If the computer user runs a lot of different applications, it is possible to increase this number to provide quick access to more programs.

To increase the number of icons displayed on the Start menu, use the following procedure:

ADD START MENU ICONS

GET READY. Turn on the computer and log on using one of the existing user accounts. Close any windows that appear on the desktop.

1. Click the **Start** button on the taskbar. The Start menu appears.
2. Right-click the background of the Start menu and then from the context menu select **Properties**. The Taskbar and Start Menu Properties dialog box appears.
3. On the Start Menu tab, with the Start Menu radio button selected, click the **Customize** button. The Customize Start Menu dialog box appears, as shown in Figure 3-4.

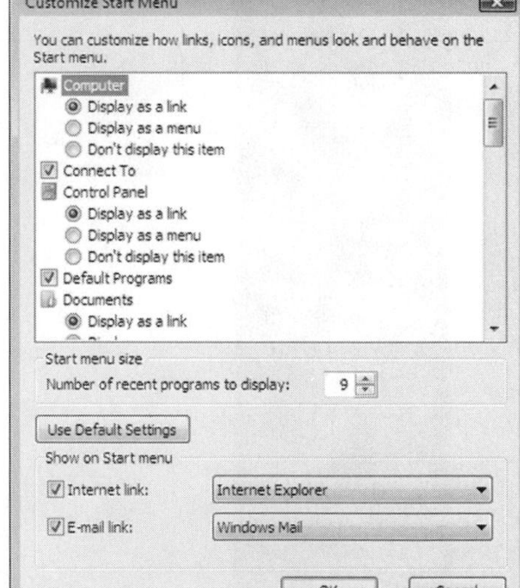

Figure 3-4

The Customize Start Menu dialog box

4. In the *Start menu size* box, adjust the *Number of recent programs to display* spin box to a number greater than nine.
5. To increase the number of icons that can fit in the Start menu, scroll down to the bottom of the list of settings and clear the Use Large Icons checkbox.
6. Click **OK** to close the Customize Start Menu dialog box.
7. Click **OK** to close the Taskbar and Start Menu Properties dialog box.
8. Click the **Start** button again. Notice that the icons in the Start menu are reduced in size and that there are more of them.

Adding Pinned Icons

Having the user's most popular programs appear on the Start menu is not a bad idea, but it can be troublesome. The icons appear in order of popularity, which means that the order is likely to change regularly. Some of the user's favorite programs might even drop off the Start menu entirely.

To create a Start menu with a list of programs that never changes, you can add shortcuts to the pinned icons section in the top left, using the following procedure:

ADD PINNED ICONS

GET READY. Turn on the computer and log on using one of the existing user accounts. Close any windows that appear on the desktop.

1. Click the **Start** button on the taskbar. The Start menu appears.
2. Right-click one of the shortcuts that appears in the lower left section of the Start menu, or click **All Programs** and then right-click one of the shortcuts found there.
3. From the context menu, select **Pin to Start Menu.**

The shortcut you selected now appears permanently in the top left section of the Start menu, as shown in Figure 3-5.

Figure 3-5

Additional pinned shortcut in the Start menu

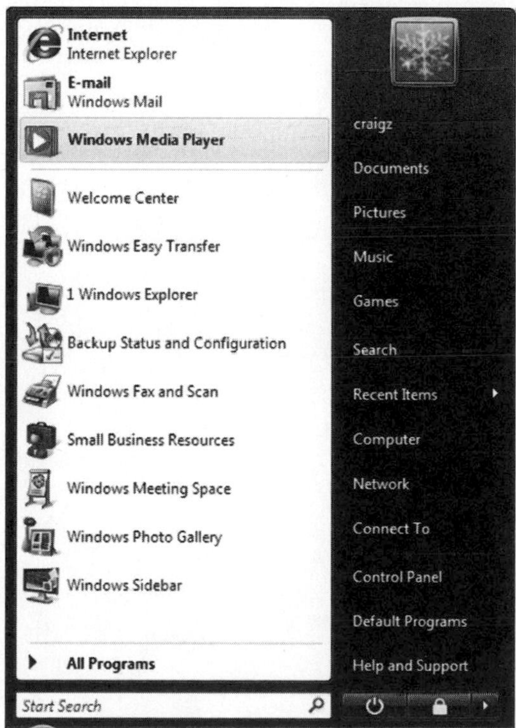

TAKE NOTE*

If your clients use a relatively small collection of applications, you might want to create a permanent Start menu configuration for them by reducing the number of shortcuts in the "most popular" section and adding all of their applications to the "pinned" section.

Converting Links to Menus

You can covert the Start menu links to menus, for ease of access to the elements they contain.

The right side of the Start menu contains links to common system elements, such as Documents, Computer, Network, and Control Panel. Placing links here is a convenient and accessible alternative to placing them on the desktop. Clicking one of these links opens the selected item in a new window.

One way to simplify the process of accessing some of these links is to convert them to menus, so that users can navigate down through submenus and select a specific item rather than open a new window. To convert links to menus, use the following procedure:

CONVERT LINKS TO MENUS

GET READY. Turn on the computer and log on using one of the existing user accounts. Close any windows that appear on the desktop.

1. Click the **Start** button on the taskbar. The Start menu appears.
2. Right-click the background of the Start menu and then, from the context menu, select **Properties**. The Taskbar and Start Menu Properties dialog box appears.
3. On the Start Menu tab, with the Start Menu radio button selected, click the **Customize** button. The Customize Start Menu dialog box appears.
4. Scroll through the list of settings and, for any or all of the following entries, select the Display as a menu radio button, as shown in Figure 3-6.

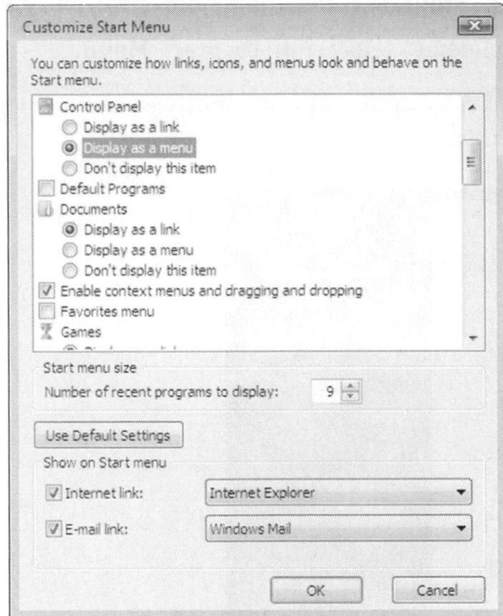

Figure 3-6

Converting links to menus in the Customize Start Menu dialog box

- Computer
- Control Panel
- Documents
- Games
- Music
- Personal Folder
- Pictures

5. Click **OK** to close the Customize Start Menu dialog box.
6. Click **OK** to close the Taskbar and Start Menu Properties dialog box.

The items you modified now appear as menus when you click them in the Start menu, as shown in Figure 3-7.

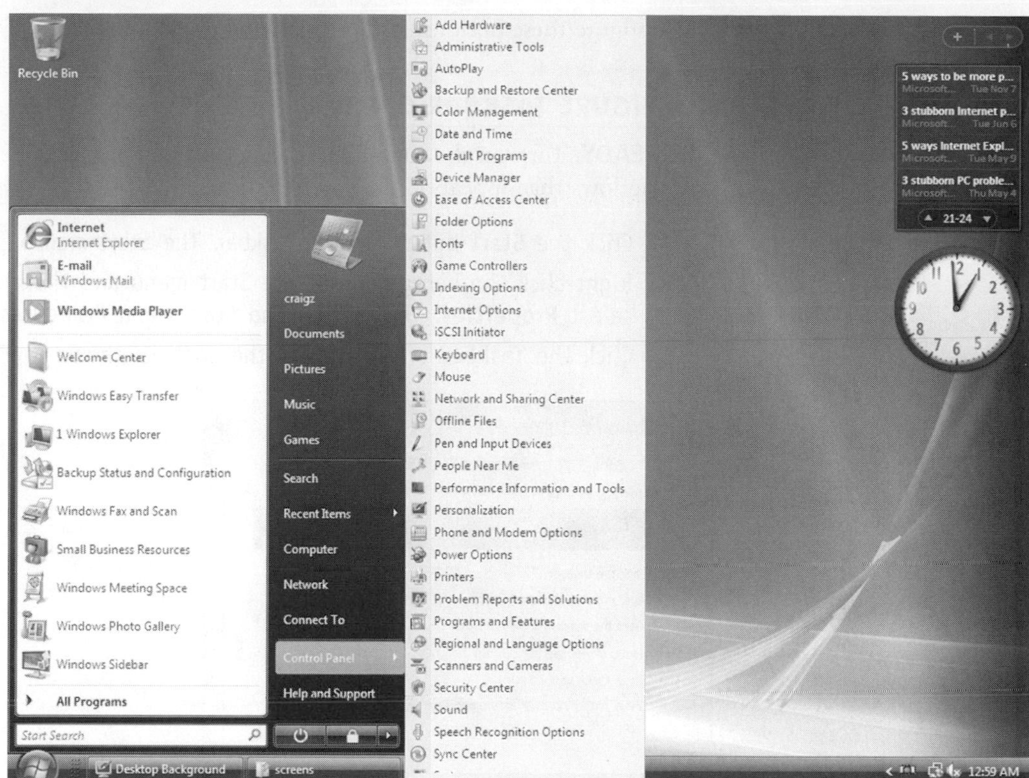

Figure 3-7

Submenus in the Start menu

MORE INFORMATION

In addition to the settings covered so far in this lesson, the Customize Start Menu dialog box contains a number of other controls that enable you to specify what features should appear on the Start menu, how they should appear, and how they should behave.

Configuring the Taskbar

The Windows taskbar contains a variety of elements that you can configure to your clients' specifications, only some of which are activated by default.

In its default configuration, the Windows taskbar contains the following elements, as shown in Figure 3-8.

Figure 3-8

The Windows taskbar in its default configuration

- Start button—An orb-shaped button that provides access to the Start menu
- Main taskbar area—The primary area of the taskbar, it contains a button for each program running on the computer
- Notification area—Once called the Tray, this area contains small icons that provide access to system tools and features. Developers can also design their applications to insert icons into the tray
- Quick Launch toolbar—A group of small shortcut icons that provide one-click access to applications and selected system functions

In the following sections, you learn how to configure the taskbar to provide users with improved access to system features.

Configuring Taskbar Options

The basic taskbar options control how and when the taskbar appears.

To configure these options, use the following procedure:

CONFIGURE TASKBAR OPTIONS

GET READY. Turn on the computer and log on using one of the existing user accounts. Close any windows that appear on the desktop.

1. Click the **Start** button on the taskbar. The Start menu appears.
2. Right-click the background of the Start menu and then, from the context menu, select **Properties**. The Taskbar and Start Menu Properties dialog box appears.
3. Click the **Taskbar** tab to display the controls shown in Figure 3-9.

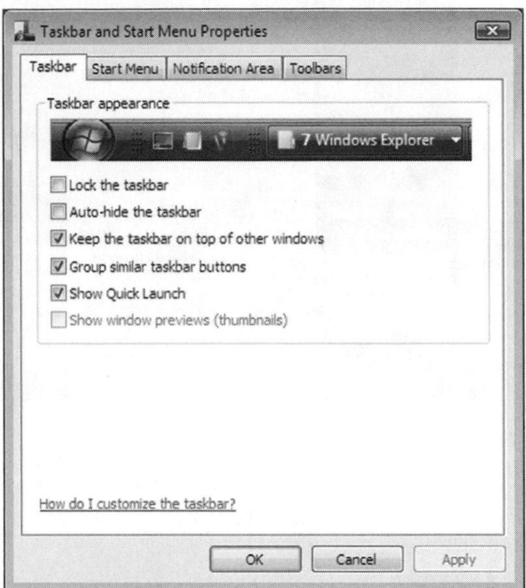

Figure 3-9

The Taskbar tab of the Taskbar and Start Menu Properties dialog box

4. Select or clear the checkboxes on the tab to control the options listed in Table 3-1.
5. Click **OK** to close the dialog box.

Table 3-1

The Taskbar Options and Their Default States

TASKBAR OPTION	DEFAULT STATE	FUNCTION
Lock the taskbar	Unselected	When selected, users cannot resize or move the taskbar or any of the taskbar toolbars.
Auto-hide the taskbar	Unselected	When selected, provides additional desktop real estate by causing the taskbar to disappear when the mouse cursor is not hovering over it. Moving the mouse cursor to the bottom of the screen causes the taskbar to re-appear.
Keep the taskbar on top of other windows	Selected	When selected, causes the taskbar to remain visible, even when you drag other windows over it.
Group similar taskbar buttons	Selected	When selected, causes multiple documents open in the same application to appear as a single taskbar button.
Show Quick Launch	Selected	When selected, causes the Quick Launch toolbar to appear.
Show windows previews (thumbnails)	Unselected	When selected, causes the taskbar to display a real-time thumbnail of a running application when you mouse over its taskbar button. This feature is only available on computers running the Windows Aero user environment.

Configuring Toolbars

The taskbar comes with six toolbars, one of which is the Quick Launch toolbar mentioned in the previous section.

Vertical lines separate each toolbar from the others; you can drag these lines to adjust the size of the toolbar. Although due to limited space it is unlikely that you will activate all six toolbars for a client, as shown in Figure 3-10, you can activate any combination, using the following procedure:

Figure 3-10

The Taskbar toolbars

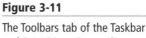

CONFIGURE TASKBAR TOOLBARS

GET READY. Turn on the computer and log on using one of the existing user accounts. Close any windows that appear on the desktop.

1. Click the **Start** button on the taskbar. The Start menu appears.
2. Right-click the background of the Start menu and then, from the context menu, select **Properties**. The Taskbar and Start Menu Properties dialog box appears.
3. Click the **Toolbars** tab to display the controls shown in Figure 3-11.

Figure 3-11

The Toolbars tab of the Taskbar and Start Menu Properties dialog box

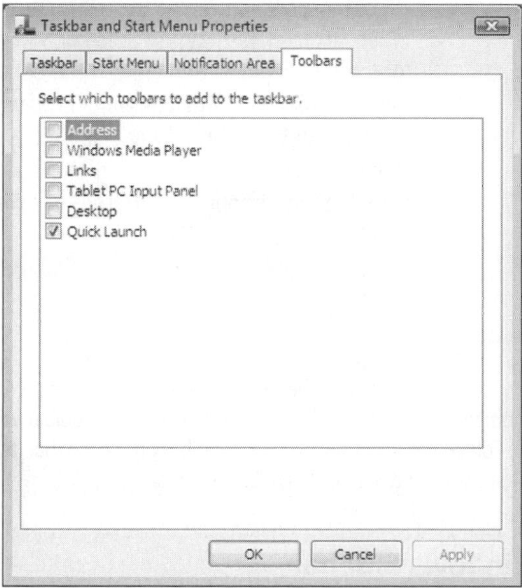

4. Select or clear the checkboxes on the tab to control the options listed in Table 3-2.
5. Click **OK** to close the dialog box.

Table 3-2

The Taskbar Toolbars and Their Default States

Taskbar Option	Default State	Function
Address	Unselected	When selected, adds a text box to the taskbar in which users can key a path name, URL (Uniform Resource Locator), or UNC (Universal Naming Convention) address. Clicking the arrow next to the text box opens the appropriate browser, application, or Explorer window and loads the address.
Windows Media Player	Unselected	When selected, minimizing a Windows Media Player window causes a Windows Media Player toolbar to appear on the taskbar.
Links	Unselected	When selected, adds a toolbar to the taskbar containing the standard set of links that appear in the Favorites menu. You can customize the Links toolbar by adding or deleting shortcuts to the Links folder under Favorites.
Tablet PC Input Panel	Unselected	When selected, adds a single button to the taskbar that displays the Tablet PC Input Panel.
Desktop	Unselected	When selected, adds a toolbar that contains an Internet Explorer shortcut, plus submenus for the personal, Public, Computer, Network, Control Panel, and Recycle Bin folders.
Quick Launch	Selected	When selected, displays an area containing single-click shortcut icons for Internet Explorer and Windows Media Player, plus two special icons that minimize all of the currently displayed windows and display the 3D Window Switcher (if Windows Aero is running) or the standard task switcher. You can add additional shortcuts to the toolbar by dragging and dropping them from the Start menu or an Explorer window.

MORE INFORMATION

You can also create new, custom toolbars on the taskbar by right-clicking an empty space on the taskbar, clicking the Toolbars submenu, and selecting New Toolbar. In the New Toolbar window that appears, select a folder and click Select Folder. The folder appears as a toolbar on the taskbar, and any files, documents, or shortcuts in the folder appear as buttons in the toolbar.

Configuring Windows Sidebar

Recent releases of Windows have gradually streamlined the desktop, removing all of the icons until finally only the Recycle Bin was left. However, Windows Vista adds a new feature to the desktop called the Windows Sidebar.

CERTIFICATION READY?
Configure Windows Sidebar: Download and install Gadgets
5.6

The Windows Sidebar is an area at the right side of the desktop, where you can place small applications called ***gadgets***. Gadgets are simple applications that display system information or function as push clients, continually receiving information from servers on the Internet and displaying it in a custom-designed interface.

By default, a Windows Vista installation places the following gadgets in the Windows Sidebar:

- Clock—A large analog clock that displays the current system time
- Slide Show—A small window that displays a cycling collection of images, to which you can add your own images
- Feed Headlines—A client application that receives news headlines from MSNBC

You can add Sidebar gadgets at will by using the following procedure:

ADD SIDEBAR GADGETS

GET READY. Turn on the computer and log on using one of the existing user accounts. Close any windows that appear on the desktop.

1. Click **Start**, and then click **Control Panel.** The Control Panel page appears.
2. Click **Appearance and Personalization.** The Appearance and Personalization page appears.
3. Under Windows Sidebar Properties, click the ***Add Gadgets To Sidebar*** link. The Gadget Gallery page shown in Figure 3-12 appears.

Figure 3-12

The Windows Sidebar gadgets provided with Windows Vista

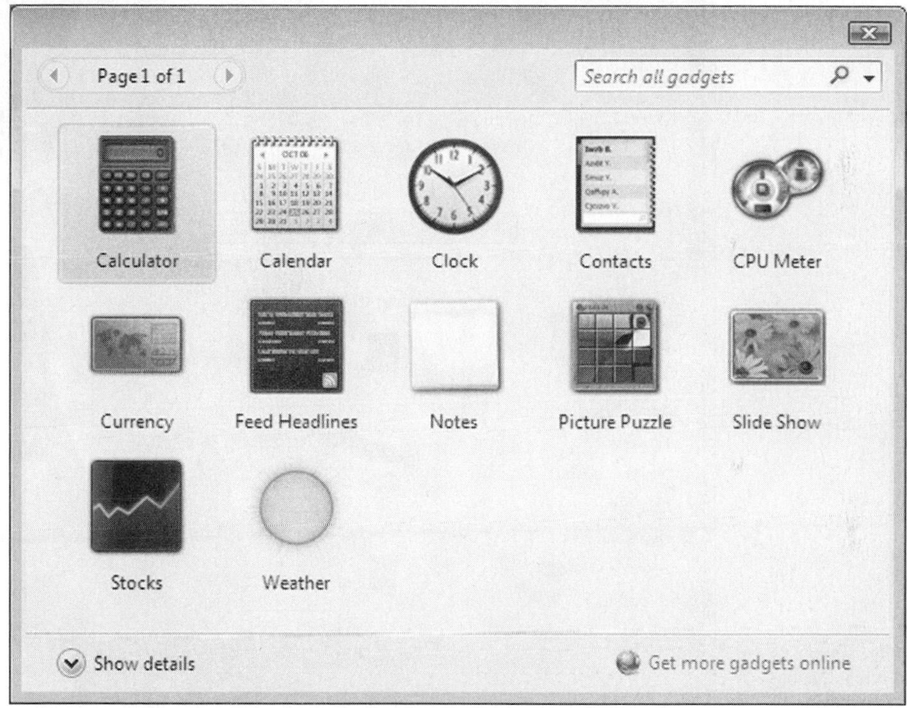

4. Select one of the gadgets shown on the page and then drag it to the Sidebar. The gadget is added to the Sidebar.

Once you have added gadgets to the Sidebar, you can manipulate them individually using the Options and Close buttons on each gadget, or by right-clicking a gadget and selecting commands from the context menu.

Windows Vista includes a small collection of simple gadgets, but Microsoft has established a Website where users and third-party developers can post gadgets of their own creation. To access this collection, use the following procedure:

DOWNLOAD SIDEBAR GADGETS

GET READY. Turn on the computer and log on using one of the existing user accounts. Close any windows that appear on the desktop.

1. Click **Start**, and then click **Control Panel.** The Control Panel page appears.
2. Click **Appearance and Personalization.** The Appearance and Personalization page appears.

3. Under Windows Sidebar Properties, click the ***Add Gadgets To Sidebar*** link. The Gadget Gallery page appears.
4. Click the ***Get more gadgets online*** link. An Internet Explorer window opens and connects to the Personalize Windows Vista Sidebar Web page (see Figure 3-13) at *http://vista.gallery.microsoft.com/vista/SideBar.aspx*.

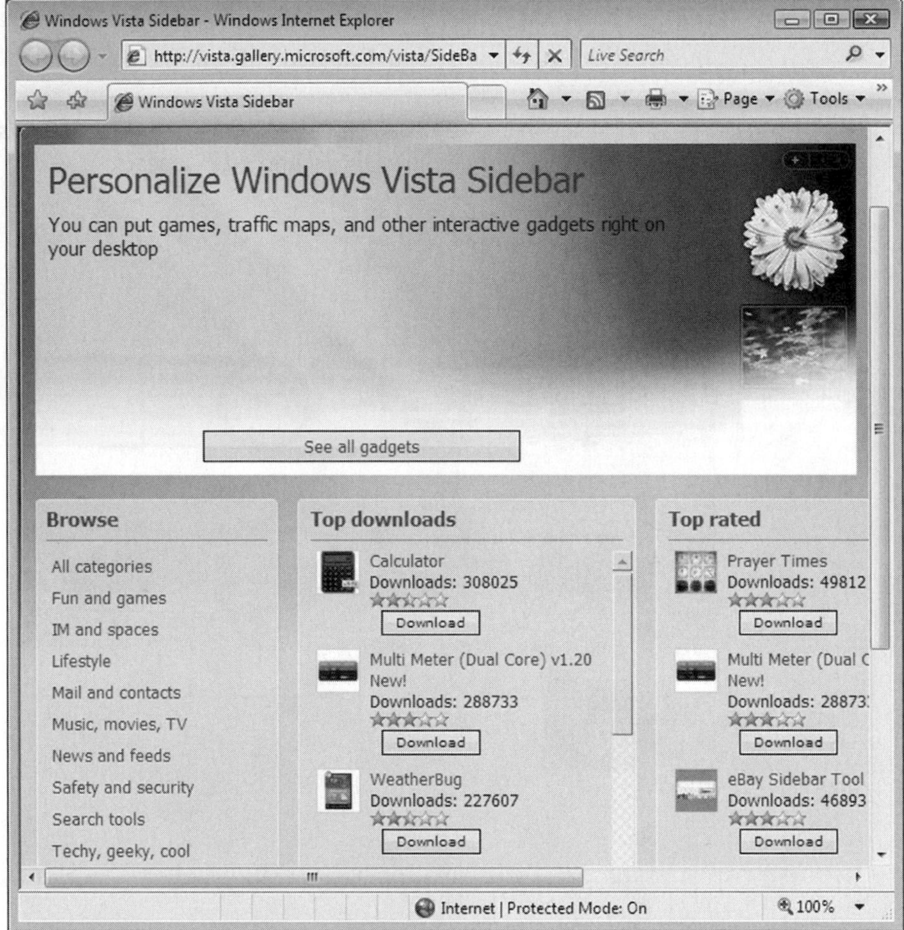

Figure 3-13

The Personalize Windows Vista Sidebar Web page

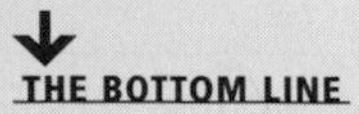
WARNING Keep in mind that, from a security standpoint, downloading and running applications created by unknown developers is a highly dangerous undertaking. The Windows Sidebar can be an open door into your computer that bypasses all of the Windows security measures. Only download and install gadgets created by developers you have reason to trust.

5. Choose one of the gadgets offered in the gallery and then click its **Download** button.
6. Click **OK**, **Open**, and then **Allow** to begin the download.
7. When the download is complete, click **Install** to add the gadget to the Sidebar. **CLOSE** the Internet Explorer window and the Gadget page.

Introducing Windows Aero

THE BOTTOM LINE Because the Windows Aero user experience level received a great deal of publicity during the Windows Vista rollout, a lot of users are interested in running this feature. However, because of its unusual hardware and licensing requirements, Aero fails to run on some new Windows Vista installations.

Technicians servicing standalone systems are likely to field a number of calls regarding newly installed Windows Vista computers that are failing to run Windows Aero. In fact, technicians might find the same problem occurring on computers they install themselves.

Understanding Windows Aero Hardware Requirements

Lesson 1 examined the two levels of system requirements that Microsoft has published for Windows Vista: those for a Windows Vista Capable PC and those for a Windows Vista Premium Ready PC. The primary difference between these two levels is the hardware required to support Windows Aero.

CERTIFICATION READY?
Configure and troubleshoot Windows Aero: Identify hardware requirements for Windows Aero
2.2

The additional system memory and main processor speed required for a Windows Vista Premium Ready PC help Windows Aero to run better, but they do not determine whether or not Aero can run at all. The requirements for the video display adapter, however, do determine whether the computer is capable of running Aero. To support Windows Aero, a video adapter must have two things: an adequate graphics processor and sufficient graphics memory.

The graphics processor must support the following:

- WDDM drivers
- DirectX 9
- Pixel Shader 2.0
- 32 bits per pixel

In addition, the adapter must have one of the following:

- 64 MB of graphics memory to support a single monitor at a resolution lower than 1,310,720 pixels (1280 x1024)
- 128 MB of graphics memory to support a single monitor at resolutions from 1,310,720 to 2,304,000 pixels
- 256 MB of graphics memory to support a single monitor at a resolution higher than 2,304,000 pixels

XREF
For more information on running Upgrade Advisor, see Lesson 1, "Introducing Windows Vista."

For most computer users, these requirements are meaningless. Microsoft's Upgrade Advisor application enables users to determine whether their existing computers have the hardware needed to run Windows Vista with Windows Aero. For desktop support technicians, there are likely to be a large number of clients with computers that do not have the graphic hardware needed to run Aero, and who want to upgrade to a video adapter that fulfills the stated requirements. How do you determine which of the many graphics cards on the market support Vista with Aero? First, you must understand what these requirements mean.

Understanding Graphics Hardware

Today's video display adapters are far more complex than those of just a few years ago.

Many video adapters are really self-contained computers, with their own processors and their own memory, all installed on an expansion card, as shown in Figure 3-14. Many of these cards even have their own fans to counteract the heat produced by the processor chip. The ***graphics processing unit (GPU)*** on a video adapter is not the same general-purpose type as the system processor on the computer's motherboard; it is a special-purpose processor designed to perform specific 3D graphic functions. The system processor could conceivably perform these functions, but the GPU can do them much faster. Offloading the graphics processing tasks to a separate chip removes a significant burden from the system processor, enabling it to concentrate on other tasks.

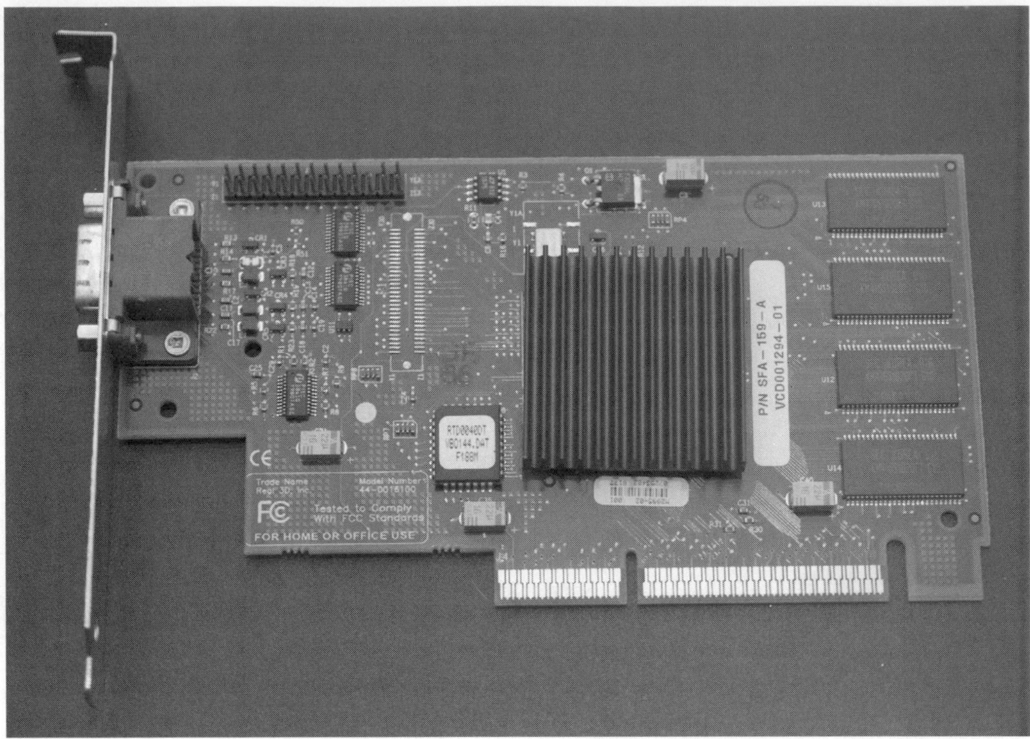

Figure 3-14

A typical video display adapter card

Just as with the computer's main components, a video adapter runs better if it has a faster, more capable GPU and more graphics memory. This is why Windows Vista requires a certain level of graphics processor and a certain amount of graphics memory to run Windows Aero.

Phasing Out GDI

In all of the Windows operating systems up to and including Windows XP, a subsystem called the ***Graphic Device Interface (GDI)*** handles the basic graphic tasks required by the operating system.

GDI is responsible for drawing the lines and curves, rendering the text fonts, and handling the color palettes used to produce the graphical windows that you see on the monitor. In Windows XP and Windows Server 2003, GDI is enhanced in a new version called GDI+, but like its predecessor, GDI+ is still a relatively limited 2D graphical environment. For example, the simple games included with Windows, such as Solitaire, can use GDI for their graphics functions. This is because these games do not require any complex animation or 3D rendering. Games and other applications that require the GPU can access it, but only one application at a time can do so.

MORE INFORMATION

One of the fundamental principles of the Windows operating systems is to isolate the computer hardware from the applications running on the system. For example, those who remember the days before Windows will recall that every DOS application required its own printer driver, whereas Windows has a single printer driver installed in the operating system, and all the applications use it. GDI functions in the same way, in that it isolates the applications from the graphics hardware. Application developers use specific calls to GDI or GDI+ classes, and the classes in turn make calls to the video display drivers.

GDI and GDI+ have limits because they use the main system processor and memory to perform their rendering tasks, sharing these resources with all of the other operating system and application functions running on the computer. GDI cannot utilize the dedicated GPU and memory found on even the most elaborate video adapters for desktop rendering. This is why Windows XP and earlier versions do not have specific graphics hardware requirements. A Windows computer does not use the rendering capabilities of the video adapter unless it is running an application that specifically calls for them, such as a 3D game or multimedia program.

Introducing WDDM

One of the big innovations in Windows Vista, and the reason why its developers are so excited, is that the operating system can now make use of the dedicated graphics hardware on the video adapter.

At some point, Microsoft's developers realized that, on many Windows computers, the high-powered graphics hardware that owners purchased at great expense is lying idle most of the time. Unless the user is running a 3D game or some other graphics-intensive application, GDI is responsible for the graphics appearing on the screen, and so are the main system processor and memory. If Microsoft could offload some of those everyday graphics-rendering tasks to the video adapter, the graphic capabilities of the operating system would improve and the reduced load on the main system processor would improve the overall performance of the computer.

Enter the ***Windows Display Driver Model (WDDM)***, a totally new display driver architecture developed by Microsoft and released for the first time in Windows Vista. WDDM provides the operating system itself, as well as the applications running on it, with access to the graphics hardware on the video display adapter. This is possible because WDDM enables various applications to share the GPU by scheduling access to processor resources. Windows Aero utilizes the GPU on a continual basis to render the desktop, but it is possible to run a 3D game or other graphical application at the same time.

MORE INFORMATION

WDDM is a completely new display driver design. In Windows XP, display drivers run in kernel mode, near to the core system code, and a driver problem can easily halt the entire computer. Microsoft has estimated that as many as 20 percent of the blue screen errors Windows XP users experience are attributable to display driver problems. In the WDDM model, display drivers consist of two parts: a small kernel mode driver and a user mode driver that does most of the work. Moving most of the code out of kernel mode protects the operating system. Display driver problems are more likely to occur in user mode, which can crash the application but not the operating system.

On a computer running the Windows Aero user experience, the ***Desktop Window Manager (DWM)*** application is responsible for drawing and updating the windows that appear on the desktop. DWM is essentially a Direct3D application that uses the graphics hardware on the video adapter to render each window in an offline buffer before sending it to the display. The resulting Windows Aero effect is an improvement over the other user experiences both in content and in quality. The greater capabilities of the GPU enable windows to have the glass-like transparency effect and the 3D window manipulation capabilities you see in Aero, and the offline buffering provides a smoother, cleaner desktop experience, without the window tearing and incorrect redrawing that can affect GDI renderings.

MORE INFORMATION

DirectX is a collection of application programming interfaces (APIs) that provide multimedia services to application developers. Direct3D is one of those APIs, used specifically for drawing 3D graphics like those used by Windows Aero.

WDDM 1.0, the version implemented in the initial release of Windows Vista, is designed to utilize GPUs that already exist on the market. These GPUs were not designed to multitask, so WDDM must use task scheduling as a workaround. Microsoft has recognized some shortcomings to this method and is currently working on WDDM 2.0, which will require true multitasking GPUs that are not yet available on the retail market.

Select a Video Display Adapter

For desktop support technicians, it can be difficult to determine whether the existing video adapter in a computer will support Windows Aero without using the Upgrade Advisor application. Although the WDDM driver standard is relatively new, the hardware capabilities defined in that standard are not. There are plenty of video adapters with compliant GPUs that were supplied with computers now several years old. In addition, there are a large number of video adapters on the market that are WDDM-compliant, but they do not say so on the package or in their specifications because they were marketed before the WDDM standard appeared. As long as the manufacturer has released a Windows Vista driver that complies with WDDM, the GPU should work with Aero.

The other GPU requirement for a Windows Vista Premium Ready PC is that it support the DirectX 9 standard with Pixel Shader 2.0. This is not a recent standard. DirectX 9.0, first released in December 2002, supports Pixel Shader 2.0, so there are plenty of adapters on the market with GPUs supporting this requirement. There have been several subsequent DirectX 9.0 releases since 2002, with 9.0c, supporting Pixel Shader 3.0, appearing in December 2004. In addition to these, Windows Vista also supports the latest release of the APIs, DirectX 10.0.

Because of this situation, the Upgrade Advisor application should be a permanent part of every desktop support technician's software toolkit. Upgrade Advisor runs on Windows Vista as well as Windows XP, so it can do double duty as a preinstallation tool and a postinstallation troubleshooting utility.

So, if your client has a video adapter that does not support Windows Aero and you are asked to find a replacement, the first thing you should do is consult the list of GPUs supporting Aero that Microsoft maintains on its Website at *http://technet.microsoft.com/en-us/windowsvista/aa905088.aspx*.

TAKE NOTE* You are initially looking for a graphics processor that supports Windows Aero, not a video adapter. There are relatively few GPU manufacturers in the video adapter marker, most of whom sell their processors to many different card manufacturers. You might find a dozen or more video adapters that use the same GPU. Some of the adapters might be fully compliant with Windows Aero; others might not.

Once you determine which GPUs are compliant with Windows Aero, you can start examining specific video adapter products. An adapter card might have an appropriate GPU, but the product might not work with Windows Aero. Make sure that there is a WDDM driver (or a driver specifically designed for Windows Vista) available for the adapter, and that the adapter has sufficient graphics memory to support the display the client intends to use with the computer.

Of course, the final test for a video adapter is to install it in a computer and run Upgrade Advisor again. Generally speaking, most of the higher-end video adapters on the market today should have an appropriate GPU and sufficient memory to run Windows Aero. However, there are many Windows users out there who are not hardcore gamers and who do not run graphics-intensive video editing or computer aided design (CAD) applications, but who still want the Windows Aero user experience without spending several hundred dollars on a video adapter.

It might be more difficult to find lower-priced adapters until manufacturers begin packaging and advertising them as suitable for use with Windows Vista. Until then, you might have to look at Websites with hardware reviews to confirm whether a particular adapter supports Aero. It's a good idea to identify a few low-priced, readily available video adapters that comply with the Vista hardware requirements so that when clients come to you with computers that can't run Aero because they have insufficient video hardware, you can offer them an economical solution.

Identifying Windows Aero

Many users running Windows Vista for the first time are unfamiliar with the appearance of Windows Aero and might be unable to tell whether their computers are running it.

Once users are familiar with Aero's appearance they recognize it immediately, but for first-time users, here is a list of ways to determine whether Aero is running:

- Translucent windows—The first positive indication the user sees that Aero is running is that all of the windows on the desktop have edges that are translucent, with a blurry image of whatever is behind them showing through. When you move a window around the desktop, the edges change to reflect the current background.

- 3D Flip—Pressing the Win+Tab key combination displays the 3D Flip screen, as shown in Figure 3-15, on which all of the windows for the programs currently running on the computer appear in a stacked display. Repeatedly pressing the Tab key while holding down the Win key causes the stack to flip each window to the front in turn. This is an effect that will be new and unique to any Windows user, providing positive confirmation that Windows Aero is running.

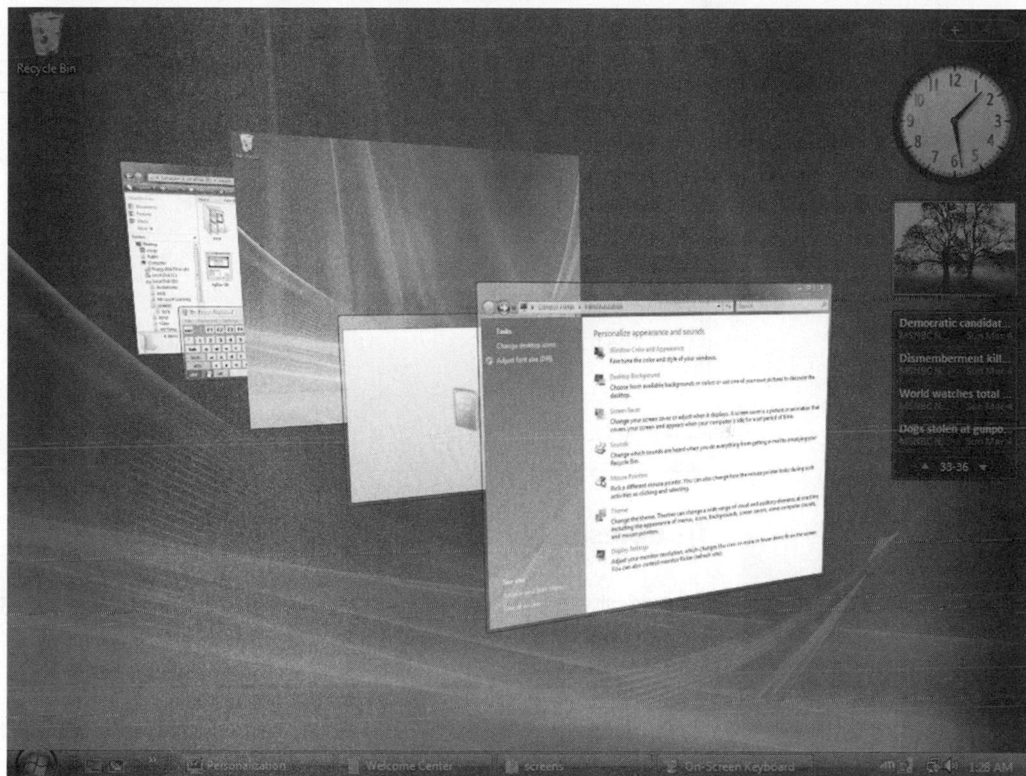

Figure 3-15

The 3D Flip display on a computer running Windows Aero

TAKE NOTE*

If the computer's keyboard does not have the Win key, you can use the On-Screen Keyboard to enter the key combination. Click **Start > Accessories > Ease Of Use > On-Screen Keyboard.**

- Live thumbnails—When Aero is running, passing the mouse cursor over a taskbar button representing a running program causes the current screen for that program to appear over the button, in a real-time display. The same live thumbnails appear in the task switcher display produced by pressing the Alt+Tab key combination, as shown in Figure 3-16.

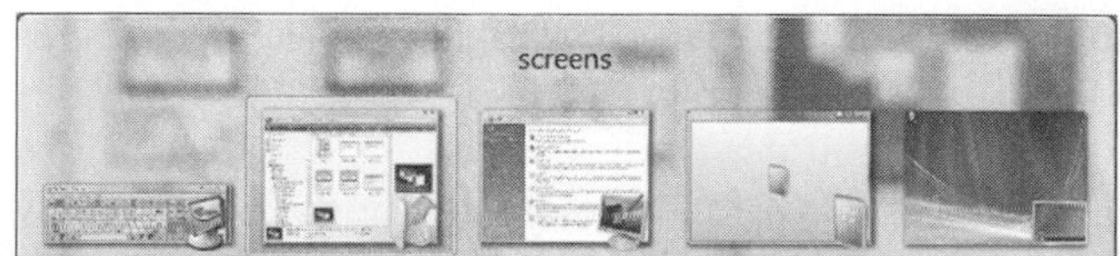

Figure 3-16

Live thumbnails in the Windows Aero task switcher

- Display settings—Open the Personalize Appearance And Sounds page and click **Windows Color and Appearance**. If the Windows Color and Appearance page appears, as shown in Figure 3-17, then Windows Aero is running. If the Appearance Settings dialog box appears, Windows Aero is not running.

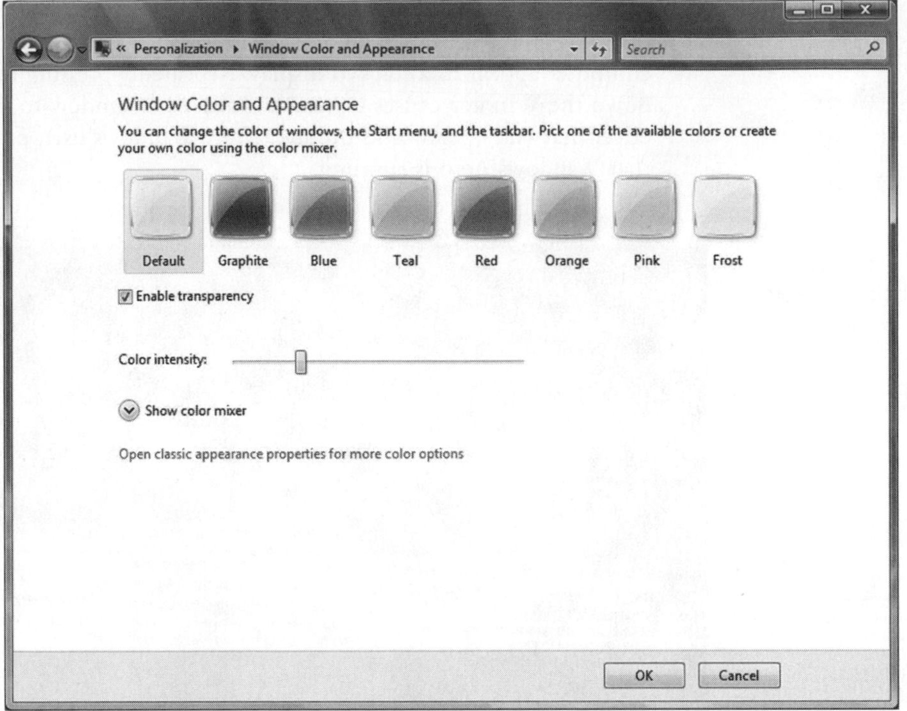

Figure 3-17

The Windows Color and Appearance page that appears only when Windows Aero is running

CERTIFICATION READY?
Configure and troubleshoot Windows Aero:
- Troubleshoot graphics card issues
- Identify WDDM drivers (using Win+Tab to check Aero is on)

2.2

Troubleshooting Video Adapter Issues

For desktop support technicians, the question of why a computer is not running Windows Aero is likely to be a common complaint.

Assuming that the computer meets the hardware requirements to run Windows Aero, there are a number of reasons why it might not be running it. The following sections cover these reasons.

CERTIFICATION READY?
Configure and troubleshoot Windows Aero: Configure Windows Genuine Advantage

2.2

Validating Windows

You must validate a Windows Vista installation before it can run Windows Aero, even if it has the proper hardware and the right edition of Windows Vista installed.

Validating a Windows installation generates what Microsoft calls the Windows Genuine Advantage. Without a Windows installation that has been proven to be genuine, users cannot manually download free updates from the Windows Update Website, obtain free downloads from the Microsoft Download Center, or use certain operating system features, including Windows Aero.

TAKE NOTE* Although you must validate a computer before you can use the Windows Update and Microsoft Update Websites manually, the Automatic Updates feature in Windows Vista enables computers to download system updates automatically, with no validation.

The Microsoft ***Windows Genuine Advantage*** program reduces the number of pirated Windows installations. Validation typically occurs the first time you attempt to use the Microsoft Download Center, Windows Update, or Microsoft Update Website. During the validation process, the Website prompts the user to download an ActiveX control that collects system information including the following:

- Computer make and model
- Operating system version information
- Region and language setting
- Globally Unique Identifier (GUID), a unique number assigned to the computer

WARNING Do not confuse validation with activation; they are two different procedures. Activation is a process that prevents multiple users from running Windows using the same product key. You must activate a copy of Microsoft Windows within a specified period of time (typically 30 days); failure to complete the activation causes the operating system to stop running. During the activation process, the computer creates a unique key based on its hardware configuration, and uploads it to Microsoft along with the product key specified during the Windows installation process. As long as the product key is not already associated with a different computer, the activation succeeds.

- Product ID and product key
- BIOS name, revision number, and revision date
- Volume serial number

The ActiveX control then uploads this information to a Microsoft server, which stores it in a database.

If the hardware/product key information does not already exist in the database, and if the information successfully passes a number of anti-counterfeiting checks, the system considers the computer to be validated and grants it access to the Website. If the database indicates that the product key is already associated with another computer, the system denies the validation and does not allow access to the Website.

If a client's computer fails to run Windows Aero because it has not been validated, either there is a problem preventing the validation process from completing or the copy of Windows running on the computer has been pirated. If the latter is the cause, the only solution is to install a genuine copy of Windows.

If you suspect that there is a malfunction inhibiting the validation process, you can test the computer's performance of the validation process using the Windows Genuine Advantage Diagnostic Site at *http://www.microsoft.com/genuine/diag/default.aspx*. Running the diagnostic routine at this site tests the following:

- If the computer is capable of executing scripts
- If the computer can display images correctly
- If the system date and time are relatively correct
- If the Microsoft Genuine Advantage ActiveX control loads correctly
- If the Microsoft Genuine Advantage ActiveX control is able to connect to the validation servers successfully

When the diagnostic routine is finished, the results appear on a page like the one shown in Figure 3-18. If the computer does not pass each test, the Web page displays information about the configuration settings you probably need to adjust to resolve the problem.

Figure 3-18

The Microsoft Genuine Advantage Diagnostic Results page

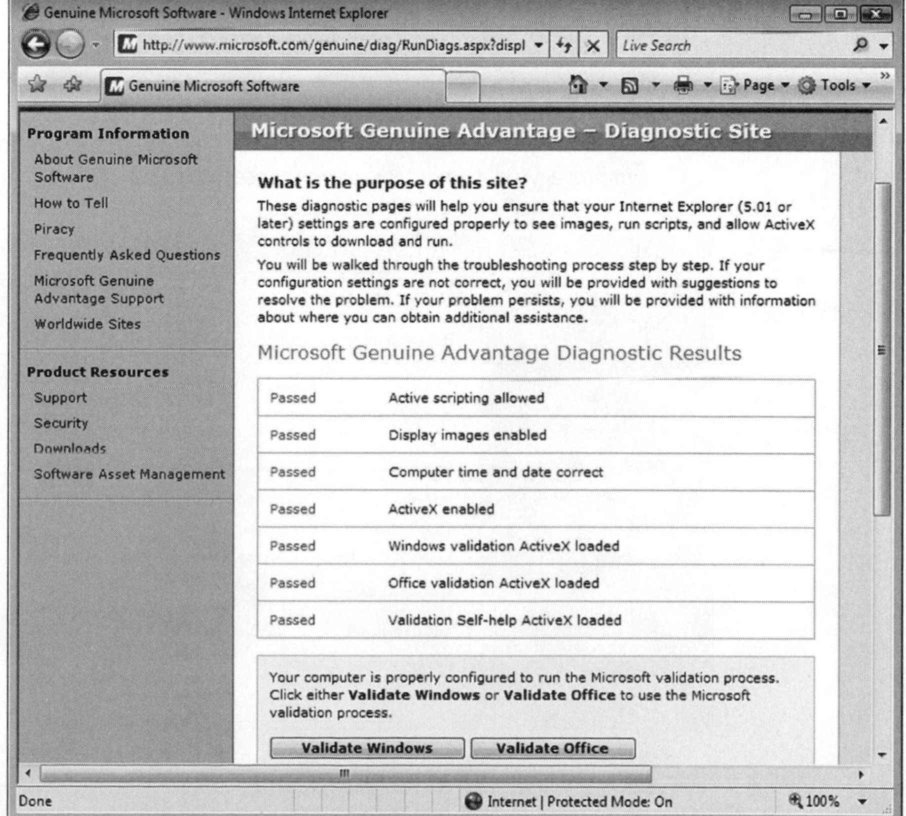

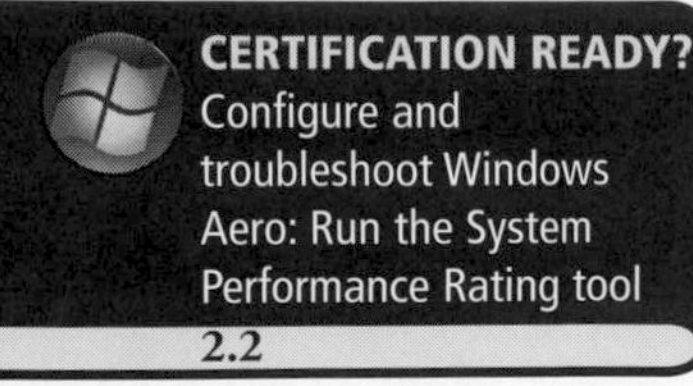

CERTIFICATION READY?
Configure and troubleshoot Windows Aero: Run the System Performance Rating tool
2.2

Running the System Performance Rating Tool

When troubleshooting problems with running Windows Aero, you can use the System Performance Rating Tool to get an overall picture of the computer's capabilities.

The System Performance Rating Tool quantifies the capabilities of a Windows Vista computer by breaking it down into categories and assigning each one a rating. To run the tool, use the following procedure:

RUN THE SYSTEM PERFORMANCE TOOL

GET READY. Turn on the computer and log on using one of the existing user accounts.

1. Click **Start**, and then click **Control Panel**. The Control Panel page appears on the desktop.
2. Click **System and Maintenance**. The System and Maintenance page appears.
3. Click **System**. The *View basic information about your computer* page appears, as shown in Figure 3-19.

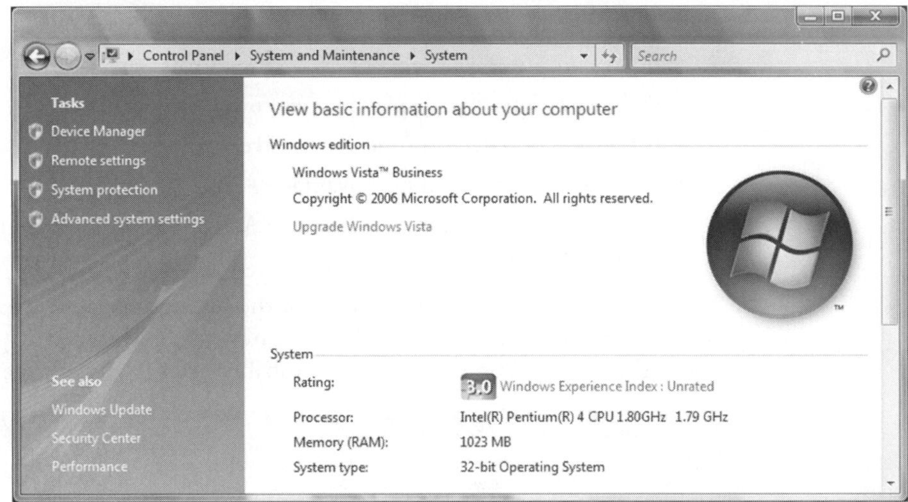

Figure 3-19

The View basic information about your computer page

4. In the System section, click the **Windows Experience Index** link. The *Rate and improve your computer's performance* page appears, as shown in Figure 3-20.

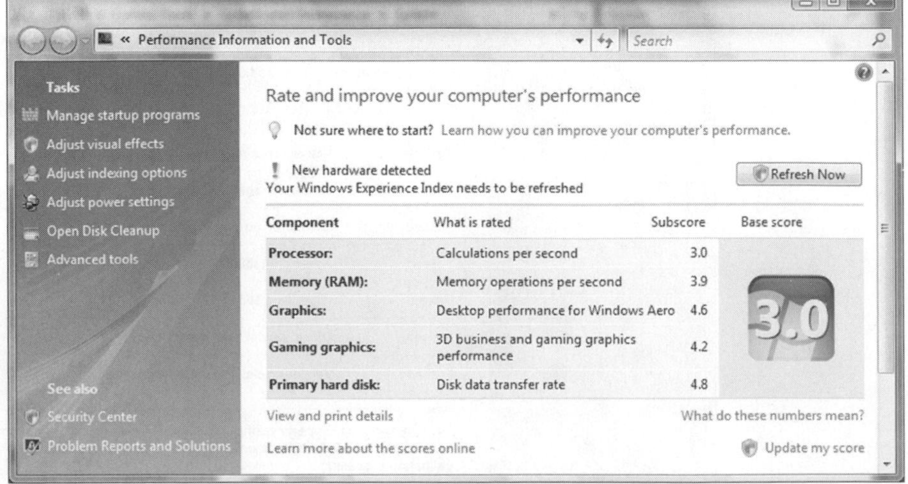

Figure 3-20

The Rate and improve your computer's performance page

5. Click the **View and print details** link.

The Performance Information and Tools page appears, as shown in Figure 3-21.

Figure 3-21

The Performance Information and Tools page

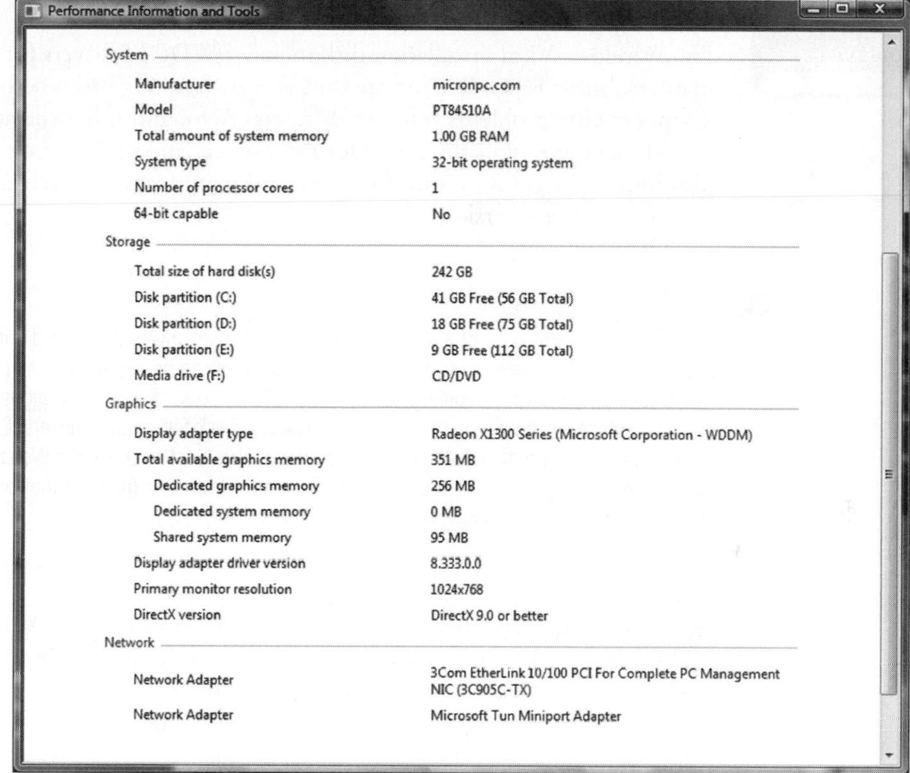

The System Performance Rating Tool breaks down the computer into the following five components:

- Processor
- Memory (RAM)
- Graphics
- Gaming graphics
- Primary hard disk

The tool assigns to each of these areas a numerical score that gauges its performance. The overall system performance rating for the computer, known as the *base score*, is the lowest of the component scores. As a general rule, computers with a base score under 3.0 are unable to run Windows Aero. A computer with a base score of 3.0 or more should be able to run Aero.

TAKE NOTE*

The base score for a computer, as specified in the System Performance Rating Tool, is the lowest of the component subscores, not the average of the subscores. This is because the least functional component acts as a bottleneck, preventing the other components from reaching their full potential.

In addition to the base score and subscores, the System Performance Rating Tool displays a variety of information about the hardware in the computer and the software running on it. For example, the Graphics section of the Performance Information and Tools page provides the following information:

- Display adapter type—Specifies the manufacturer of the GPU on the video adapter. This entry also specifies whether there is a WDDM driver installed on the system.
- Total available graphics memory—Specifies how much memory is installed on the video adapter and how much system memory is devoted to graphics tasks.
- Display adapter driver version—Specifies the version number of the display driver currently installed on the system.
- Primary monitor resolution—Specifies the primary resolution at which the computer's monitor is designed to run.
- DirectX version—Specifies the version of the DirectX APIs supported by the graphics hardware.

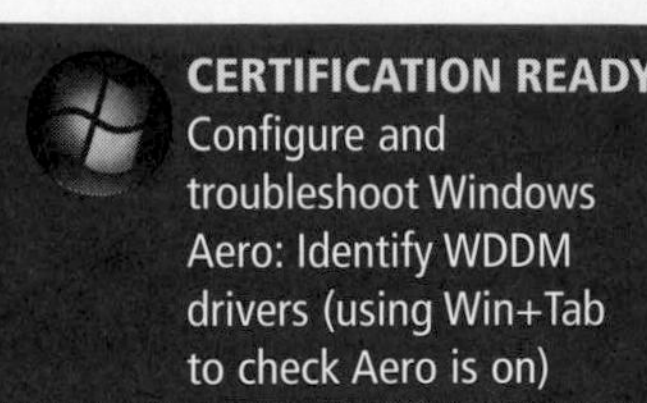

CERTIFICATION READY?
Configure and troubleshoot Windows Aero: Identify WDDM drivers (using Win+Tab to check Aero is on)
2.2

Updating Display Drivers

For a Windows Vista computer to run Windows Aero, it must have a WDDM driver for the video display adapter.

The Windows Vista installation disk includes WDDM drivers for a large number of video adapters, but it is possible for the card you are working on to be omitted. When a computer is experiencing problems running Windows Aero, and it has the appropriate hardware, you should make sure that the driver for the video adapter is based on the WDDM standard. In addition, it is a good idea to check the card manufacturer's Website to see if the computer is running the latest version of the driver.

MORE INFORMATION

Hardware manufacturers, not Microsoft, develop the display drivers distributed with Windows Vista (and all of the Microsoft operating systems). These manufacturers can be highly variant in their driver development capabilities and in their scheduling. Some of the drivers included with Vista might be rush jobs, completed just in time to make the operating system release. Always check for updated drivers if a Windows Vista computer is experiencing any type of display problem. You might also want to check the Website of the GPU manufacturer. Sometimes, the GPU manufacturer can provide generic drivers for the GPU that outperform the card-specific drivers released by the manufacturer of the adapter.

To check whether the currently installed display driver supports WDDM, use the System Performance Rating Tool or check the driver's version number in Device Manager and compare it with the versions available from the manufacturer's Website. If the site does not explicitly say that the driver supports WDDM, check to see whether it is a new version designed only for Windows Vista. If this is the case, then it is probably a WDDM driver.

CERTIFICATION READY?
Configure and troubleshoot Windows Aero: Change the desktop theme to Windows Aero
2.2

Enabling Aero Display Settings

When you install Windows Vista on a computer that meets the Premium Ready PC requirements, the Setup program activates the Windows Aero user experience unless some condition prevents it.

If a client's computer is not running Windows Aero, and you think you've corrected the condition that is preventing it from running, you can try enabling Aero by changing the display settings.

ENABLE AERO DISPLAY SETTINGS

GET READY. Turn on the computer and log on using one of the existing user accounts. Close any windows that appear on the desktop.

1. Right-click the desktop and then, from the context menu, select **Personalize**. The Personalize Appearance And Sounds page appears.
2. Click **Windows Color and Appearance**. The Appearance Settings dialog box appears, as shown in Figure 3-22.

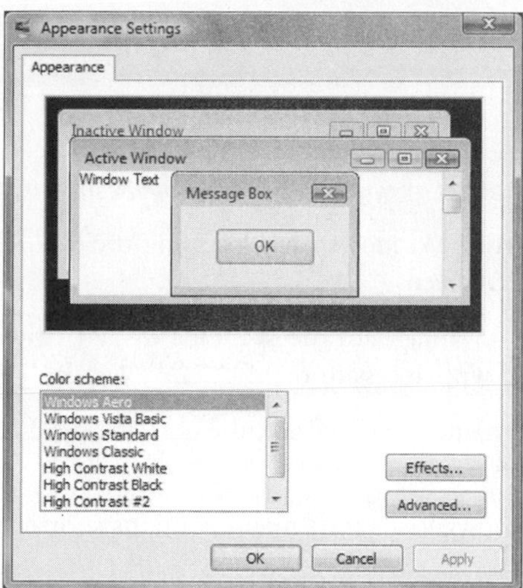

Figure 3-22

The Appearance Settings dialog box

3. In the *Color scheme* list, select **Windows Aero** and then click **OK.** The display changes to reflect the Windows Aero user experience. If the Window Aero does not appear in the *Color scheme* list, then there is some condition preventing the system from supporting Windows Aero.
4. Close the Personalize Appearance And Sounds page.
5. Press **Win+Tab** to display the Flip 3D screen, demonstrating that Windows Aero is running.

SUMMARY SKILL MATRIX

IN THIS LESSON YOU LEARNED:
It is possible to customize the Start menu by changing the number of icons displayed, whether the icons change or are permanent, and whether the system elements appear as links or as menus.
It is possible to customize the taskbar by changing its default behavior and adding any or all of six toolbars.
The Windows Sidebar contains gadgets, which are mini-applications that run on the Windows desktop.
There are graphics hardware requirements for a Windows Vista Premium Ready PC to be able to run the Windows Aero user experience.
Windows Vista introduces Windows Display Driver Model (WDDM), a new display driver model that enables the operating system to utilize the graphics processing unit to create 3D screen elements.
WDDM drivers run primarily in user mode (instead of kernel mode), so they are less likely to crash the entire system.
To run Windows Aero, a video adapter must have an appropriate GPU, sufficient graphics memory, and a WDDM driver.
To run Windows Aero, you must validate a Windows Vista computer.
The System Performance Rating Tool assigns a numerical rating to each of five components in the computer. The lowest of these ratings becomes the base score of the computer.

Knowledge Assessment

Fill in the Blank

Complete the following sentences by writing the correct word or words in the blanks provided.

1. On a computer running Windows Aero, pressing the Win+Tab key combination displays the ______________ screen.
2. One of the primary advantages of the WDDM display driver model is that it provides the operating system with access to the ______________.
3. In the System Performance Rating Tool, the ______________ is the lowest of the component subscores.
4. By default, the Windows Vista Start menu contains shortcuts for ______________ of your most often-used applications.
5. The component in Windows Vista that is responsible for drawing and updating windows is called ______________.
6. The mini-applications that run in the Windows Sidebar are called ______________.
7. Shortcut icons on the Start menu that do not change with the applications' popularity are known as ______________ icons.
8. If a computer is running Windows Aero, pressing the Alt+Tab key combination produces ______________.
9. It is still possible for a computer with a video adapter containing the right GPU and sufficient graphics memory to fail to run Windows Aero if it lacks ______________.
10. The part of the Windows taskbar where the clock display appears is called the ______________.

True / False

Circle T if the statement is true or F if the statement is false.

T | F 1. Any video adapter with an appropriate GPU will enable a computer to run the Windows Aero user experience.

T | F 2. WDDM display drivers are less likely to crash a Windows computer than GDI drivers.

T | F 3. To run Windows Aero, a computer must have a video adapter that supports the latest version of the DirectX APIs.

T | F 4. A Windows Vista computer must be validated to use Windows Aero.

T | F 5. WDDM 2.0 provides true multitasking for the graphics processing unit.

T | F 6. Enabling Windows Aero on a Windows Vista computer causes the base score generated by the System Performance Rating Tool to change.

T | F 7. A computer must be able to download and run ActiveX controls before it can be validated.

T | F 8. GDI drivers enable applications to share the graphics processing unit.

T | F 9. If the Appearance Settings dialog box appears when you select Windows Color and Appearance from the Personalize Appearance and Sounds page, then your computer is not running Windows Aero.

T | F 10. A single display driver that supports both Windows XP and Windows Vista cannot support Windows Aero.

Review Questions

1. Explain how Windows Display Driver Model (WDDM) drivers can improve overall system performance when compared to graphics display interface (GDI) drivers.
2. Name three ways to determine whether Windows Aero is running on a Windows Vista computer.

Case Scenarios

Scenario #1: Troubleshooting Windows Aero 1

Your client has just upgraded his computer from Windows XP to Windows Vista Home Basic, using a clean installation. According to Windows Upgrade Advisor, his computer should be able to run Windows Aero, but he cannot make it do so. What could be preventing Windows Aero from running?

Scenario #2: Troubleshooting Windows Aero 2

You have just installed Windows Vista Ultimate on a new computer for a client. The computer has 2 gigabytes of memory, a 3-gigahertz processor, a 250-gigabyte hard disk, and the latest model of video adapter from a major manufacturer. When the system restarts after the installation, the computer runs in Windows Vista Basic mode. What is the most likely cause for the computer not starting up in Windows Aero mode?

4 LESSON Working with Disks

OBJECTIVE DOMAIN MATRIX

Technology Skill	Objective Domain	Objective Number
Configuring Data Protection	Configure Data Protection	6.4
Using the Back Up Files Wizard	Configure Data Protection • Use Windows backup and restore	6.4
Using Complete PC	Configure Data Protection • Use Complete PC to create an image	6.4
Restoring Previous Versions	Configure Data Protection • Restore damaged or deleted files by using previous versions	6.4

KEY TERMS

access control entry (ACE)
access control list (ACL)
basic disk
dynamic disk
FAT (file allocation table)
GUID (globally unique identifier) partition table (GPT)
master boot record (MBR)
security principal
shadow copy
share permission
simple volume
spanned volume
striped volume
NTFS permission

■ Understanding Disk Management

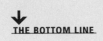

Hard disks are a personal computer's primary storage medium, but in many cases, desktop technicians must prepare a hard disk to store data by performing certain tasks before the computer can use it. Once you prepare the hard disk, you can keep the data stored on the disk secure with the tools and features that Windows Vista provides.

When you install Windows Vista on a computer, the setup program performs all of the preparation tasks for the hard disks in the computer automatically. However, a frequent client request is to add another disk, and after you install the hardware, you must perform the following tasks before the user can begin storing data on it:

- Select a partitioning style—A new feature in Windows Vista, two hard disk partition styles are available for both x86- and x64-based computers. The ***master boot record (MBR)*** partition style has been around as long as Windows, and is still the default partition style. ***GUID (globally unique identifier) partition table (GPT)*** has been around for a while also, but no x86 version of Windows prior to Vista supports it. (Windows XP Professional x64 Edition does support GPT.) You must choose one of these partition styles for a drive; you cannot use both.

- Select a disk type—Two disk types are available for Windows Vista: basic disks and dynamic disks. Both the MBR and the GPT partition styles support basic and dynamic disks. You cannot use both disk types on the same disk drive. You need to decide which is best for the client's computer.
- Divide the disk into partitions or volumes—Although many professionals use the terms *partition* and *volume* interchangeably, it is correct to refer to creating partitions on basic disks, and volumes on dynamic disks.
- Format the volumes with a file system—Because of the high capacities of the hard drives on the market today, NTFS is the preferred file system for Windows. The ***FAT (file allocation table)*** file system is also available, in the form of FAT32, but FAT32 is limited to a maximum volume size of 32 gigabytes and does not support several other important windows features.

Understanding Partition Styles

The term *partition style* refers to the method that Windows operating systems use to organize partitions on the disk.

There are two hard disk partition styles that you can use in Windows Vista:

- MBR—This is the default partition style for x86-based and x64-based computers.
- GPT—New to Windows Vista, you can now use the GPT partition style on x86-, as well as x64-based, computers.

Before Windows Vista, all x86-based computers used the MBR partition style only. Computers based on the x64 platform could use either the MBR or GPT partition style, as long as the GPT disk was not the boot disk.

MBR uses a partition table to point to the locations of the partitions on the disk. Windows selected this style automatically on x86-based workstation computers because, prior to Windows Vista, this was the only style available to them. The MBR disk partitioning style supports volumes up to 2 terabytes in size, and up to either four primary partitions or three primary partitions and one extended partition. Data critical to platform operations is stored in hidden (unpartitioned) sectors.

The following systems can use either the MBR or the GPT partition style for their disks:

- Itanium-based computers
- Windows Server 2003 SP1 (or later) x86-based machines
- Windows Server 2008
- Windows Vista x86-based computers
- x64-based computers

Bear in mind, however, that unless the computer's architecture provides support for an Extensible Firmware Interface (EFI)—based boot partition, it is not possible to boot from GPT disks. In this case, the operating system must reside on an MBR disk, and GPT must reside on an entirely separate, non-bootable disk, used for data storage only.

Itanium architecture–based computers do support EFI; in fact, developers created the EFI specification with Itanium's use in mind. The Itanium processor's main use is for driving applications larger than 4 GB of memory, such as enterprise databases.

One of the ways that GPT differs from MBR is that partitions, rather than hidden sectors, store data critical to platform operation. Additionally, GPT partitioned disks use redundant primary and backup partition tables for improved integrity. Although GPT specifications permit an unlimited number of partitions, the Windows implementation restricts partitions to 128 per disk. The GPT disk partitioning style supports volumes up to 18 exabytes in size (1 exabyte = 1 billion gigabytes, or 2^{60} bytes).

MORE INFORMATION

As far as the Windows Vista disk management tools are concerned, there is no difference between creating partitions or volumes in MBR and in GPT. You create partitions and volumes for both by using the same tools in the same ways.

Table 4-1 compares some of the characteristics of the MBR and GPT partition styles.

Table 4-1

MBR and GPT Partition Style Comparison

Master Boot Record (MBR)	GUID partition table (GPT)
Supports up to four primary partitions or three primary partitions and one extended partition, with unlimited logical drives on the extended partition	Supports up to 128 primary partitions
Supports volumes up to 2 terabytes in size	Supports volumes up to 18 exabytes in size
Supports volumes up to 2 terabytes in size	Supports volumes up to 18 exabytes in size
Replication and CRC are not features of MBR's partition table	Replication and cyclical redundancy check (CRC) protection of the partition table provide increased reliability

Understanding Disk Types

Windows Vista supports two disk types: basic disks and dynamic disks.

Most personal computers use ***basic disks*** because they are the easiest to manage. A basic disk uses primary partitions, extended partitions, and logical drives to organize data. A primary partition appears to the operating system as though it is a physically separate disk and can host an operating system. A primary partition that hosts an operating system is marked as the *active partition*.

During the operating system installation, the setup program creates a *system partition* and a *boot partition*. The system partition contains hardware-related files that the computer uses to start. The boot partition contains the operating system files, which are stored in the Windows file folder. In most cases, these two partitions are one and the same, and are stored on the active primary partition that Windows uses when starting. The active partition tells the computer which system partition and operating system it should use to start Windows.

When you use the Disk Management snap-in to work with basic disks, you can create up to three primary partitions. The fourth partition you create must be an extended partition, after which you can create as many logical drives as needed from the space in the extended partition. You can format and assign driver letters to logical drives, but they cannot host an operating system. Table 4-2 compares some of the characteristics of primary and extended partitions.

Table 4-2

Primary and Extended Partition Comparison

PRIMARY PARTITIONS	EXTENDED PARTITIONS
A primary partition functions as though it is a physically separate disk and can host an operating system.	Extended partitions cannot host an operating system.
A primary partition can be marked as an active partition. You can have only one active partition per hard disk. The system BIOS looks to the active partition for the boot files it uses to start the operating system.	You cannot mark an extended partition as an active partition.
You can create up to four primary partitions or three primary partitions and one extended partition.	A basic disk can contain only one extended partition, but unlimited logical partitions.
You format each primary partition and assign a unique drive letter.	You do not format the extended partition itself, but the logical drives it contains. You assign a unique drive letter to each of the logical drives.

When you attempt to create a fifth partition on a basic disk, a Disk Management warning box appears, as shown in Figure 4-1, prompting you to convert the basic disk to a dynamic disk. This is because a basic disk cannot hold more than four partitions.

Figure 4-1

A Disk Management warning box prompting you to convert a basic disk to a dynamic disk

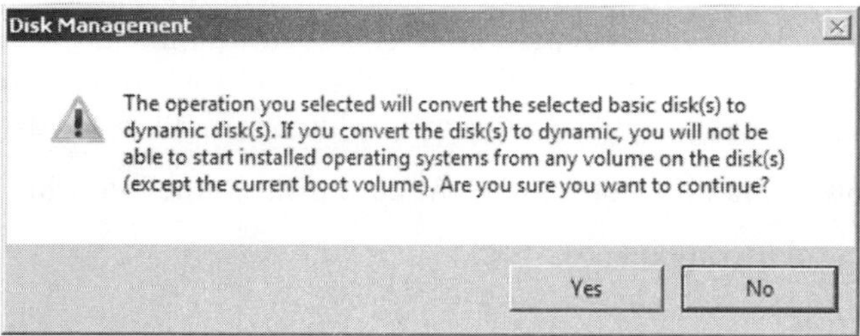

When you use DiskPart, a command-line utility included with Windows Vista, to manage basic disks, you can create up to four primary partitions or three primary partitions and one extended partition.

TAKE NOTE*

The DiskPart command-line utility contains a superset of the commands that the Disk Management snap-in supports. In other words, DiskPart can do everything Disk Management can do, and more. The Disk Management Snap-in prohibits you from unintentionally performing actions that may result in data loss. DiskPart does not have the built-in protections that Disk Management possesses, and so does not prohibit you from performing such actions. For this reason, Microsoft recommends that only advanced personnel use DiskPart and that they use it infrequently and with due caution because, unlike Disk Management, DiskPart provides absolute control over partitions and volumes.

The alternative to using a basic disk is to convert it to a ***dynamic disk***. The process of converting a basic disk to a dynamic disk creates a single partition that occupies the entire disk. You can then create an unlimited number of volumes out of the space in that partition. The advantage of using dynamic disks is that they support several different types of volumes, as described in the next section.

Understanding Volume Types

You can create five types of volumes on a dynamic disk: simple, spanned, striped, mirrored, and Redundant Array of Independent Disks-5 (RAID-5). Windows Vista supports only three of these volume types, however: simple, spanned, and striped.

A dynamic disk is able to contain an unlimited number of volumes that function like primary partitions on a basic disk, but you cannot mark an existing dynamic disk as active. When you create a volume on a dynamic disk in Windows Vista, you choose from the following three volume types:

- ***Simple volume***—Consists of space from a single disk. Once you have created a simple volume, you can later extend it to multiple disks to create a spanned or striped volume, as long as it is not a system volume or boot volume.
- ***Spanned volume***—Consists of space from 2 to 32 physical disks, all of which must be dynamic disks. A spanned volume is essentially a method for combining the space from multiple dynamic disks into a single large volume. Windows Vista writes to the spanned volume by filling all of the space on the first disk, and then proceeding to fill each of the additional disks in turn. You can extend a spanned volume at any time by adding additional disk space. Creating a spanned volume does not increase the read/write performance, nor does it provide fault tolerance. In fact, if a single physical disk in the spanned volume fails, all of the data in the entire volume is lost.
- ***Striped volume***—Consists of space from 2 to 32 physical disks, all of which must be dynamic disks. The difference between a striped volume and a spanned volume is that in a striped volume, the system writes data one stripe at a time to each successive disk in the volume. Striping provides improved performance because each disk drive in the array has time to seek the location of its next stripe while the other drives are writing. Striped volumes do not provide fault tolerance, and you cannot extend them after creation. If a single physical disk in the striped volume fails, all of the data in the entire volume is lost.

Windows Vista does not support dynamic disks in the following environments:

- portable computers
- removable disks
- detachable disks that use the Universal Serial Bus (USB) or IEEE 1394 (FireWire) interface
- disks connected to shared Small Computer System Interface (SCSI) buses

The type of disk configuration you choose for a computer depends on the client's needs. For most personal computers, basic disks are adequate. If the client's computer stores data that requires additional performance or protection against failure, dynamic disks can fill the bill.

Table 4-3 compares partition styles and disk storage types in the Windows Vista, Windows XP, Windows Server 2003, and Windows Server 2008 operating systems:

Table 4-3

Partition Styles and Disk Types Comparison Table

Operating System	Basic Volumes	Dynamic Volumes: Simple, Spanned, Striped	Dynamic Volumes: Mirrored and RAID-5	MBR Boot Volume	MBR Data Volume	GPT Boot Volume	GPT Data Volume
Windows Vista Home Basic and Home Premium	X			X	X		X
Windows Vista Business, Enterprise, and Ultimate	X	X		X	X		X
Windows Vista–all versions for EFI-based systems	X	X (Business, Enterprise, Ultimate only)			X	X	X
Windows XP Home Edition	X			X	X		
Windows XP Professional	X	X		X	X		
Windows XP Professional x64 Edition	X	X		X	X		X
Windows XP 64-bit Edition (Itanium)	X	X			X	X	X
Windows Server 2008	X	X	X	X	X		X
Windows Server 2008 for EFI-based systems	X	X	X		X	X	X
Windows Server 2003, Standard, Enterprise, and Datacenter Editions	X	X	X	X	X		
Windows Server 2003, Standard, Enterprise, and Datacenter Editions with Service Pack 1 and later	X	X	X	X	X		X
Windows Server 2003, Standard, Enterprise, and Datacenter x64 Editions	X	X	X	X	X		X
Windows Server 2003, Enterprise, and Datacenter Editions for Itanium-based Systems	X	X	X		X	X	X

Understanding File Systems

To organize and store data or programs on a hard drive, you must install a file system. A *file system* is the underlying disk drive structure that the enables you to store information on your computer. You install file systems by formatting a partition or volume on the hard disk.

In Windows Vista, there are three file system options to choose from: NTFS, FAT32, and FAT (also known as FAT16). NTFS is the preferred file system for Vista, the main benefits being improved support for larger hard drives and better security in the form of encryption and permissions that restrict access by unauthorized users.

Because the FAT file systems lack the security that NTFS provides, any user who gains access to your computer can read any file without restriction. Additionally, FAT file systems have disk size limitations: FAT32 cannot handle a partition greater than 32 GB, nor a file greater than 4 GB. FAT cannot handle a hard disk greater than 4 GB, nor a file greater than 2 GB. Because of these limitations, the only viable reason for using FAT16 or FAT32 is the need to dual boot the computer with a non-Windows operating system or a previous version of Windows that does not support NTFS.

■ Using the Disk Management Snap-in

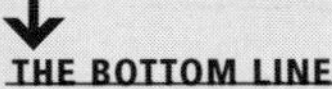

Disk Management is a Microsoft Management Console (MMC) snap-in.

Disk Management is a Microsoft Management Console (MMC) snap-in that you use to perform disk-related tasks, such as the following:

- Initializing disks
- Selecting a partition style
- Converting basic disks to dynamic disks
- Creating partitions and volumes
- Extending, shrinking, and deleting volumes
- Formatting partitions and volumes
- Assigning and changing driver letters and paths
- Examining and managing physical disk properties, such as disk quotas, folder sharing, and error-checking

You can also use command-line utilities, such as the DiskPart command, to perform Disk Management tasks.

Opening the Disk Management Snap-in

The Disk Management snap-in is a graphical tool you use to manage hard disks.

To access the Disk Management Snap-in, use the following procedure:

OPEN THE DISK MANAGEMENT SNAP-IN

GET READY. Log on to Windows Vista using an account with Administrator privileges. When the logon process is completed, close the Welcome Center window and any other windows that appear.

1. Click **Start**, and then click **Control Panel**. The Control Panel window appears.
2. Click **System and Maintenance**, and then click **Administrative Tools**. The Administrative Tools window appears, as shown in Figure 4-2.

Figure 4-2

The Administrative Tools window

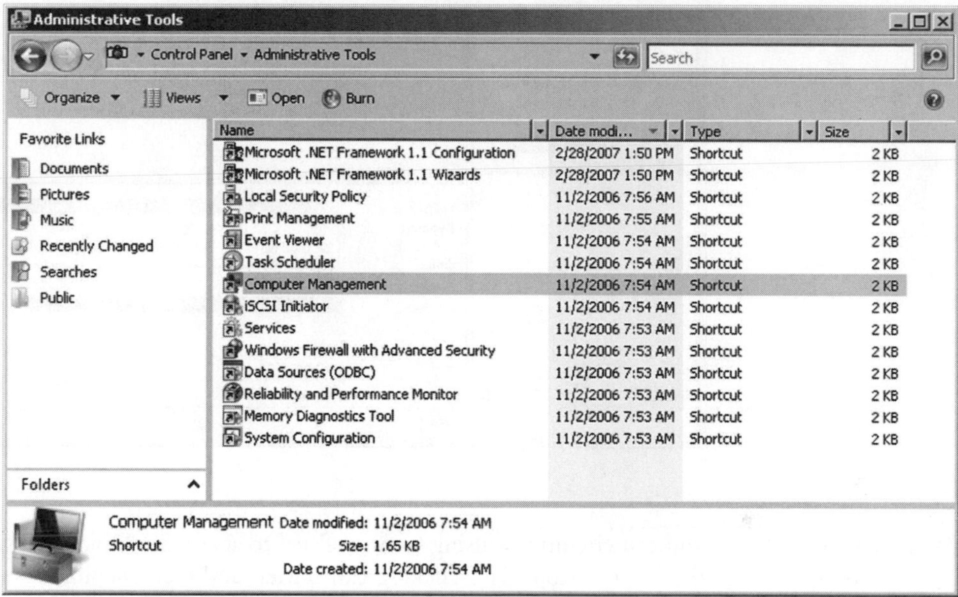

3. Double-click **Computer Management**, and then click **Continue** to confirm your access. The Computer Management console appears, as shown in Figure 4-3.

Figure 4-3

The Computer Management console

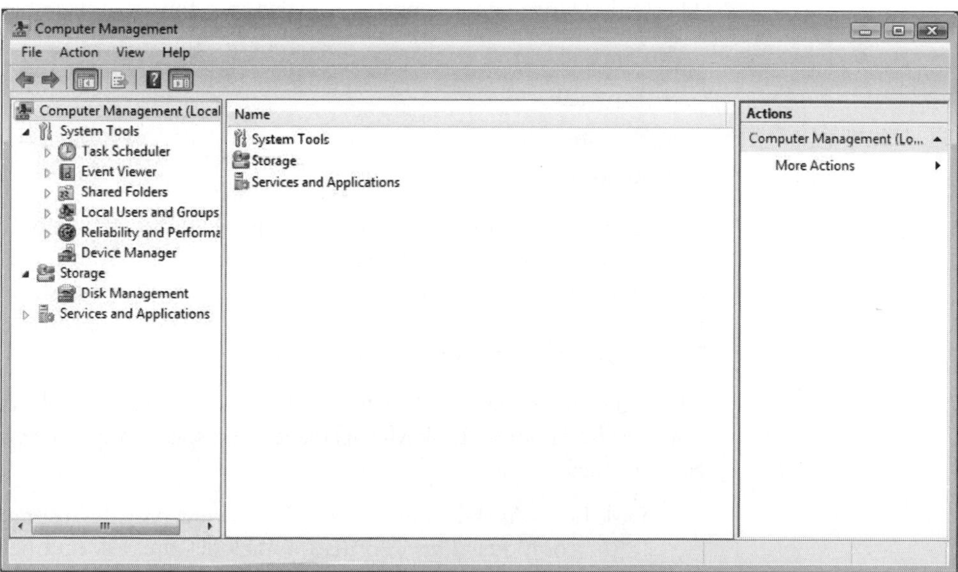

4. In the console tree, open the Storage node, and then click **Disk Management**.

The Disk Management console appears, as shown in Figure 4-4.

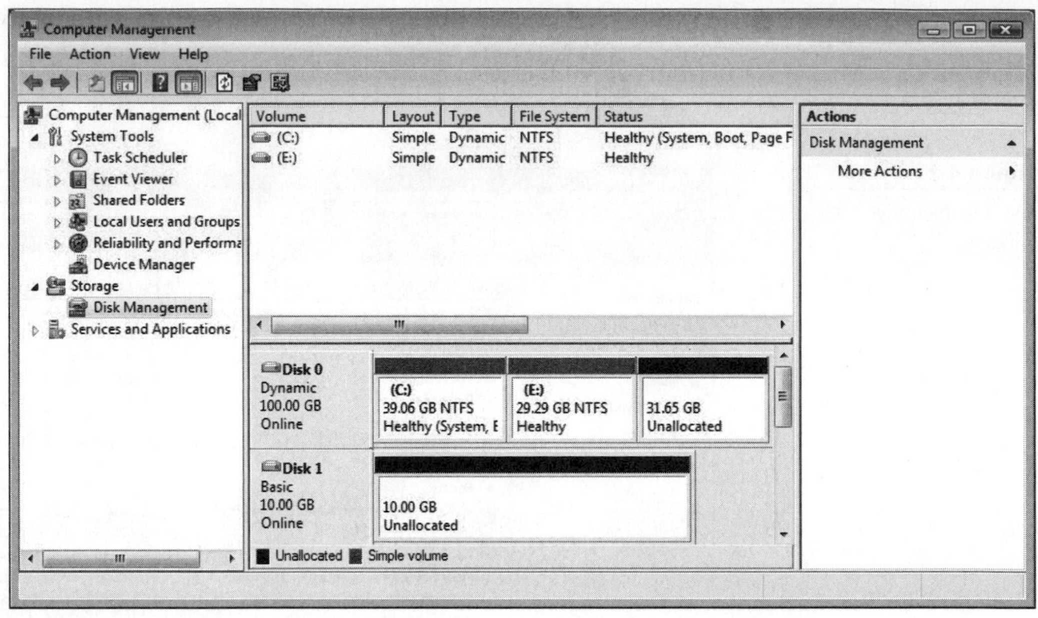

Figure 4-4

The Disk Management console

You can circumvent using Control Panel to access the Disk Management console by clicking the **Start** button, right-clicking **Computer**, and then clicking **Manage**. After confirming your access, click **Continue**. The Computer Management console appears. Under the Storage node, click **Disk Management**.

You can also click **Start**, and then use the Run dialog box to execute the compmgmt.msc file.

The Disk Management console is divided into four customizable panes:

- Console tree
- Top view
- Bottom view
- Actions pane

The console tree is located at the far left pane, and lists Computer Management's tool nodes: System Tools, Storage, and Services and Applications. You find Disk Management under the Storage node. Once you open the Disk Management window, you do not use the console tree to perform Disk Management tasks. To hide or show the console tree, you click the **Show/ Hide Console Tree** button in the toolbar.

The two center panes, the Top view and the Bottom view, display disk and volume information, respectively. Although Disk Management can display only two views at any one time, three views are available:

- Disk List—As shown in Figure 4-5, this view provides a summary about the physical drives in the computer. This information includes the disk number; disk type, such as basic or DVD; disk capacity; size of unallocated space; the status of the disk device, such as online, offline, or no media; the device type, such as small computer system interface (SCSI) or integrated device electronics (IDE); and the partition style, such as MBR or GPT.

Figure 4-5

Disk Management's Disk List view

Disk	Type	Capacity	Unallocated Space	Status	Device Type	Partition Style
Disk 0	Basic	37.27 GB	2 MB	Online	SCSI	MBR
Disk 1	Dynamic	93.04 GB	92.79 GB	Online	SCSI	GPT
CD-ROM 0	DVD (E:)	0 MB	0 MB	No Media	IDE	MBR
CD-ROM 1	CD-ROM (F:)	0 MB	0 MB	No Media	IDE	MBR

- Volume List—As shown in Figure 4-6, this view provides a more detailed summary of all the drives on the computer. This information includes the volume name; the volume layout, such as simple; the disk type, such as basic or dynamic; the file system in use,

Figure 4-6

Disk Management's Volume List view

Volume	Layout	Type	File System	Status	Capacity	Free Space	% Free	Fault Tolerance	Overhead
(C:)	Simple	Basic	NTFS	Healthy (System,...	37.07 GB	24.12 GB	65 %	No	0%
D (D:)	Simple	Basic	NTFS	Healthy (Primary...	200 MB	182 MB	91 %	No	0%
G (G:)	Simple	Dyna...	NTFS	Healthy	249 MB	227 MB	91 %	No	0%

such as NTFS or CDFS; the hard disk status, such as healthy, failed, or formatting; the disk capacity; the disk available free space; the percentage of the hard disk that is free; whether the hard disk is fault tolerant; and the disk overhead percentage.

- Graphical View—As shown in Figure 4-7, this view displays a graphical representation of all the physical disks, partitions, volumes, and logical drives available on the computer. The graphical view is divided into two columns: the disk status column (located on the left) and the volume status column (located on the right). Table 4-4 shows the information displayed in these columns and the commands available in the context menu produced by right-clicking them.

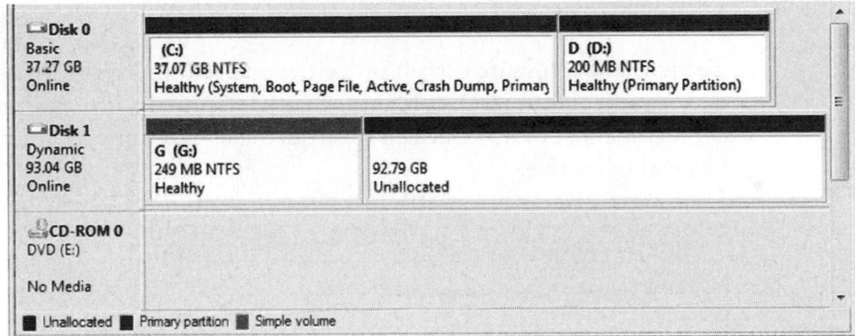

Figure 4-7

Disk Management's Graphical View

Table 4-4

Disk Management Graphical View Information

	DISK STATUS COLUMN	VOLUME STATUS COLUMN
Information displayed	• Disk number • Disk type • Disk capacity • Disk status	• Volume name • Volume size • File system • Volume status
Context menu commands	• Convert a basic disk to a dynamic disk • Convert an MBR disk to a GPT disk • Create a new spanned volume • Create a new striped volume • Open the Properties dialog box	For a mounted partition or volume: • Mark a basic disk as active • Change the drive letter and paths • Format the partition or volume • Extend the volume • Shrink the volume • Delete the volume • Open the Disk Properties dialog box For unallocated space: • Create a new simple volume • Create a new spanned volume • Create a new striped volume • Open the Properties dialog box

By default, the Top view pane depicts the Volume List view, and the Bottom view pane depicts the Graphical View. You can change the views of both the Top view and Bottom view to suit your purposes by clicking the **View** menu, selecting either Top or Bottom, and then selecting the desired view. You can hide the Bottom view by clicking the Hidden menu option.

The Action pane is new to Windows Vista. It is located on the right-hand side of the console. The purpose of the Action pane is to list available actions based on the currently selected item in the console tree or in the results panes, which in the case of Disk Management are the items in Top view or Bottom view. To hide or show the Action pane, you click the **Show/Hide Action Pane** button in the toolbar.

Viewing Physical Disk Properties

The Disk Management snap-in displays detailed information about each disk installed in the computer.

To view and configure certain properties and settings for the physical disk, right-click the disk status column in Disk Management's Graphical View and then select Properties from the context menu. A Disk Device Properties dialog box appears, as shown in Figure 4-8, with the General tab active.

Figure 4-8

Disk Management's Disk Device Properties dialog box with the General tab active

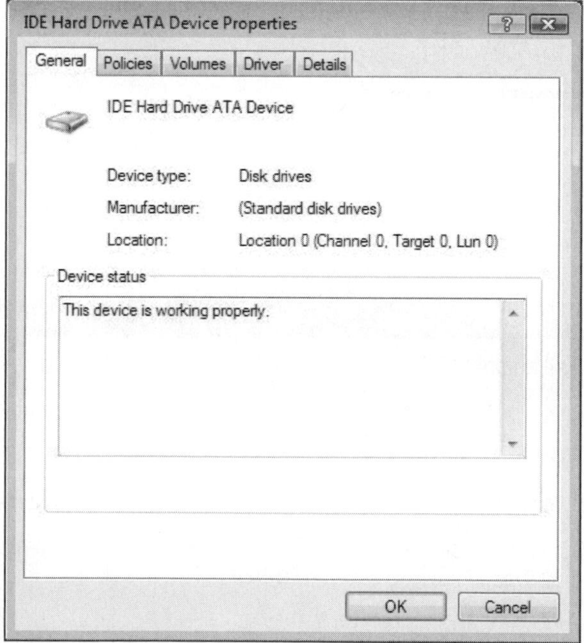

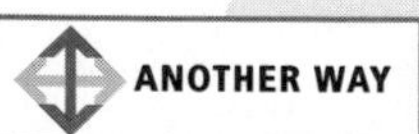

You can open the Disk Device Properties dialog box by right-clicking a drive in the Disk List view, and then clicking **Properties**.

The Disk Device Properties dialog box contains the following tabs:

- General—Lists the device type, drive manufacturer, device status, and physical location of the device, including the bus number or the SCSI identifier.
- Policies—Enables you to configure write caching and safe removal policies for the disk. Selecting Optimize for Quick Removal disables write caching on the disk and in Windows, so you can disconnect the device without using the Safe Removal icon.

Selecting Optimize for Performance enables write caching in Windows to improve disk performance, but a power outage or equipment failure might result in data loss or corruption. To disconnect this device from the computer, click the **Safely Remove Hardware** icon in the taskbar notification area.

- Volumes—Lists the volumes contained on the disk, as well as the disk number, disk type, status, partition style, capacity, unallocated space, and reserved space. If you highlight a volume in the Volumes list, you can click the **Properties** button to display the Properties dialog box for the partition or volume.
- Driver—Displays driver information, and enables you to update, roll back, disable, and uninstall the driver for this device.
- Details—Displays extensive information about driver properties.

Viewing Partition or Volume Properties

The Disk Management snap-in displays detailed information about each partition and volume on a disk.

To view or configure the properties of a partition or volume, right-click the volume status column in Disk Management's Graphical View and then select Properties from the context menu. The drive's Properties dialog box appears, as shown in Figure 4-9, with the General tab active.

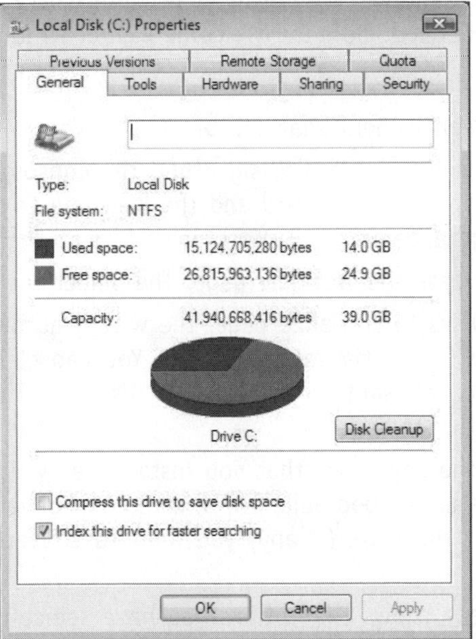

Figure 4-9

Disk Management's drive Properties dialog box with the General tab active

You can also open a drive's Properties dialog box by right-clicking a drive in the Volume List view, and then selecting Properties from the context menu.

The Properties dialog box for a partition or volume contains the following tabs:

- General—Lists the volume label, type of disk, file system, used space, and free space, and provides a graphical representation of the total disk capacity. For drives formatted with the NTFS file system, you can choose to compress the drive and to have the Indexing Service index the disk for faster file searching. Additionally, you can run the Disk Cleanup tool to delete unnecessary files, clearing up disk space.
- Tools—Enables you to check the partition or volume for errors and fragmentation, and to back up files on the volume.
- Hardware—Enables you to view properties for all of the disk drives on the computer, including their manufacturers, bus locations, and device status.
- Sharing—Enables you to share the drive or specific folder(s) on the drive, set permissions for the share, and specify the type of caching for the share.

- Security—Enables you to set NTFS permissions to secure files and folders by assigning permissions that allow or deny users or groups to perform specific actions on that object. (This appears only on NTFS drives and in the Business, Enterprise, and Ultimate editions of Windows Vista.)
- Previous Versions—Displays shadow copies that Windows automatically saves to your computer's hard disk as part of a restore point. A restore point represents a specific point in time of your computer's system files. You can use these previous versions of files to restore files that users have accidentally deleted or modified.
- Quota—Enables you to configure disk quota management on the computer, which limits the amount of disk space a user can consume. You must format the disk with the NTFS file system in order for this tab to be available.

Adding a New Disk

To add a new secondary disk, shut down your computer and install or attach the new physical disk per the manufacturer's instructions.

Use the following procedure to initialize the new disk:

ADD A NEW DISK

GET READY. Log on to Windows Vista using an account with Administrator privileges. When the logon process is completed, close the Welcome Center window and any other windows that appear.

1. Open the Disk Management snap-in.
2. If the disk does not have a disk signature, the console automatically starts the Initialize and Convert Disk wizard and the Welcome to the Initialize and Convert Disk Wizard page appears.
3. Click **Next** to bypass the Welcome page. The Select Disks to Initialize page appears.
4. On the Select Disks to Initialize page, the wizard automatically selects the uninitialized disks for the initialization process. You can clear the related option for any disk that you do not want to initialize at this time. Then, click **Next.** The Select Disks to Convert page appears.
5. This page lists the new disks that you installed as well as any disk that is a nonsystem disk and is not bootable. The wizard can convert these disks to a dynamic disk type. Select the disks (if any) you want to convert to a dynamic disk, and then click **Next.**
6. The summary page shows the options you have selected and the actions that the wizard will perform on each disk. If you agree with the summary, click **Finish.**

The wizard performs the designated tasks. During this final stage, the wizard writes a disk signature to each disk that you have chosen to initialize. Additionally, if you chose to convert a disk to a dynamic disk type, the wizard first writes the disk signature to it and then converts the disk to a dynamic disk. Otherwise, the wizard selects the default basic disk type.

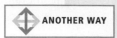

You do not have to use the wizard to initialize the disk. If you prefer to use Disk Management to initialize the disk manually, close the wizard when it appears. Using the Disk List view, find the disk marked with a red icon and an exclamation point. Disk Management should list the disk's status as Not Initialized. Right-click the disk's icon, and then select Initialize Disk from the pop-up menu. Make sure you that you have selected the correct disk, and then click **OK** to start the initialization process. Initializing the disk in this manner does not give you the option to convert the disk to a dynamic disk type. You will have to perform this task manually.

Choosing a Partition Style

Partition style refers to the method that Windows operating systems use to organize partitions on the disk. Starting with Windows Vista, x86-based computers can use either MBR or GPT partition styles.

If you are running an x86-based computer, Disk Management has most likely selected the MBR partition style by default. You can quickly check which partition style the hard disk is assigned by right-clicking the disk status column in Graphical View. If the context menu contains the Convert to GPT Disk menu item, then the disk is using the MBR partition style.

You can also check the volume's information by opening the Properties dialog box for the disk and then clicking the Volumes tab, as shown in Figure 4-10. This tab displays information such as disk type, disk status, and partition style.

Figure 4-10

The Volumes tab of a Disk Device Properties dialog box

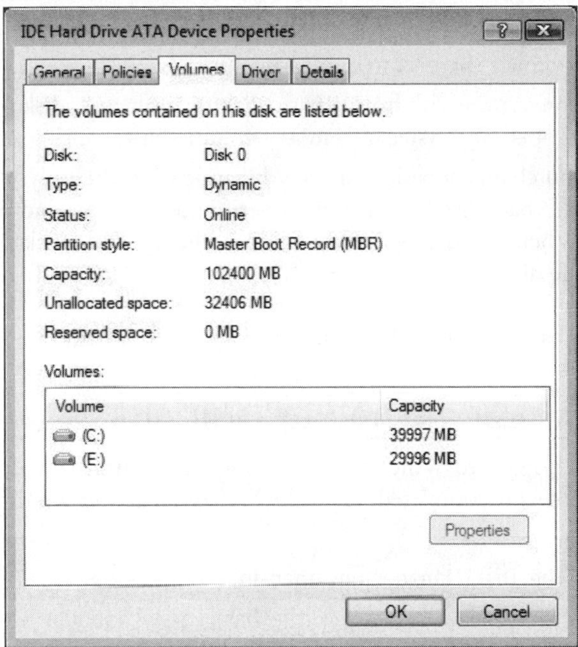

To convert the partition style for a disk, use the following procedure:

CONVERT THE DISK PARTITION STYLE

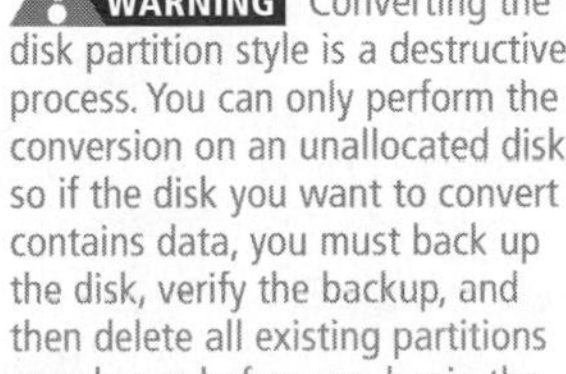

WARNING Converting the disk partition style is a destructive process. You can only perform the conversion on an unallocated disk, so if the disk you want to convert contains data, you must back up the disk, verify the backup, and then delete all existing partitions or volumes before you begin the process.

GET READY. Log on to Windows Vista using an account with Administrator privileges. When the logon process is completed, close the Welcome Center window and any other windows that appear.

1. Open the Disk Management snap-in.
2. Clear the disk of existing partitions or volumes (if any).
3. In Disk List view, right-click the disk you need to convert and then, from the context menu, select **Convert to GPT Disk** or **Convert to MBR Disk.**

The system proceeds with the conversion. The length of time this process takes depends on the size of the hard disk.

Converting a Basic Disk to a Dynamic Disk

You can convert a basic disk to a dynamic disk at any time, without affecting the data stored on the disk.

However, before you convert a basic disk to a dynamic disk, you must be aware of the following conditions:

- Make sure that you have enough hard disk space available for the conversion. The conversion will fail if the hard drive does not have at least 1 MB of free space at the end of the disk. The Disk Management console reserves this free space when creating partitions and volumes, but you cannot presume that other disk management tools that you might use also preserve that space.
- You should not convert a basic disk to a dynamic disk if you are dual booting. If you convert to a dynamic disk, you will not be able to start installed operating systems from any volume on the disk, except the current boot volume.
- You cannot convert removable media to dynamic disks. You can configure them only as basic disks with primary partitions.
- You cannot convert drives that use an allocation unit size (sector size) greater than 512 bytes unless you reformat the drive with a smaller sector size before upgrading.
- If the boot partition or system partition is part of a striped or spanned volume, you cannot convert the disk to a dynamic disk.
- If you convert the disk from a basic disk to a dynamic disk, you will not be able to start installed operating systems from any volume on the disk, except the current boot volume.
- Once you change a basic disk to a dynamic disk, the only way you can change it back again is to back up the entire disk, verify the backups, and delete the dynamic disk volumes. When you delete the last volume, the dynamic disk automatically converts back to a basic disk.

To convert a basic disk to a dynamic disk, use the following procedure:

CONVERT A BASIC DISK TO A DYNAMIC DISK

GET READY. Log on to Windows Vista using an account with Administrator privileges. When the logon process is completed, close the Welcome Center window and any other windows that appear.

1. Open the Disk Management snap-in.
2. In Disk List view, right-click the basic disk that you want to convert and then, from the context menu, select **Convert to Dynamic Disk**. The Convert to Dynamic Disk dialog box appears, as shown in Figure 4-11.

Figure 4-11

The Convert to Dynamic Disk dialog box

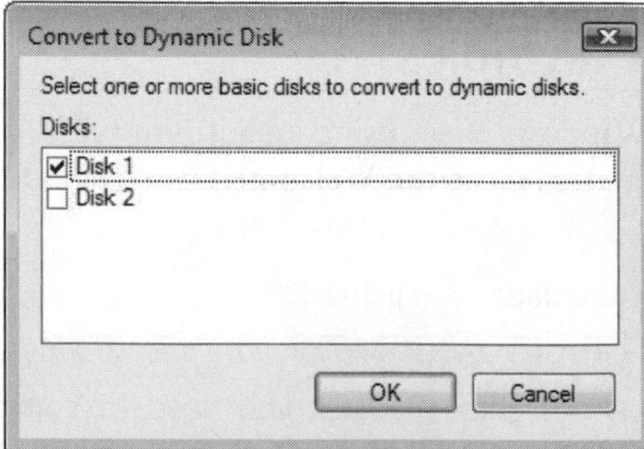

3. Select the checkboxes for the disks you want to convert, and then click **OK**. If the disks you selected do not contain formatted partitions, clicking OK immediately converts the disks, and you do not need to follow the remaining steps. If the disks you are converting to dynamic disks have formatted partitions, clicking **OK** displays the Disks to Convert dialog box, as shown in Figure 4-12, which means that you need to follow the remaining steps to complete the disk conversion.

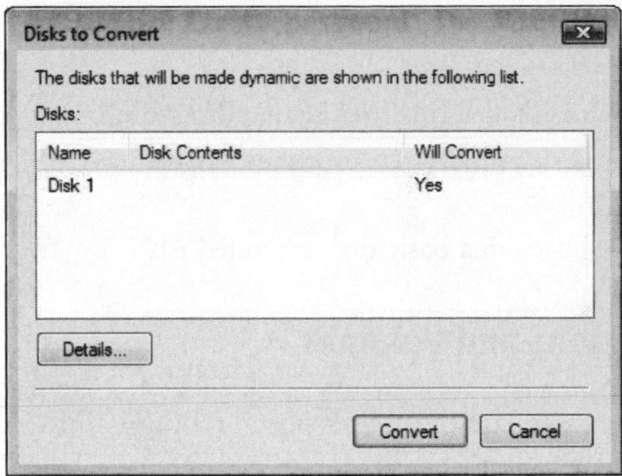

Figure 4-12

The Disks to Convert dialog box

4. The Disks to Convert dialog box lists the disks you chose for conversion for your confirmation. Check the value in the Will Convert column. It should be set to Yes for each of the disks that you are converting. If any of the disks have the value No, then they may not meet Windows conversion criteria.
5. Click **Details**. The Convert Details dialog box appears, as shown in Figure 4-13. This dialog box lists the partitions on the selected drives that Disk Management will convert.

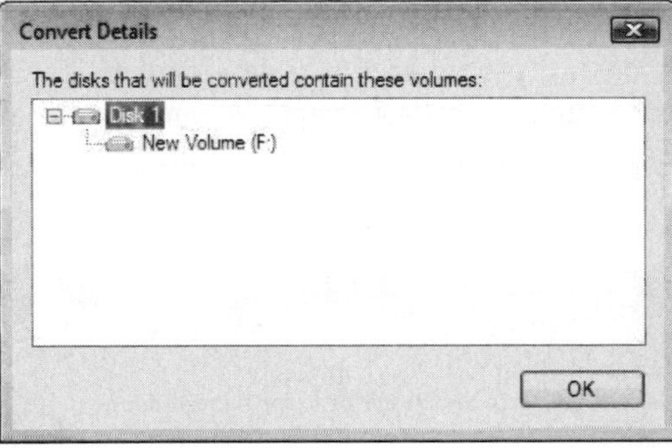

Figure 4-13

The Convert Details dialog box

6. Click **OK** when you are ready to continue with the conversion.
7. On the Disks to Convert dialog box, click **Convert** to start the conversion. A Disk Management information box, shown in Figure 4-14, appears to warn you that once you convert the disks to dynamic disks, you will not be able to boot installed operating systems from any volume other than the current boot volume.

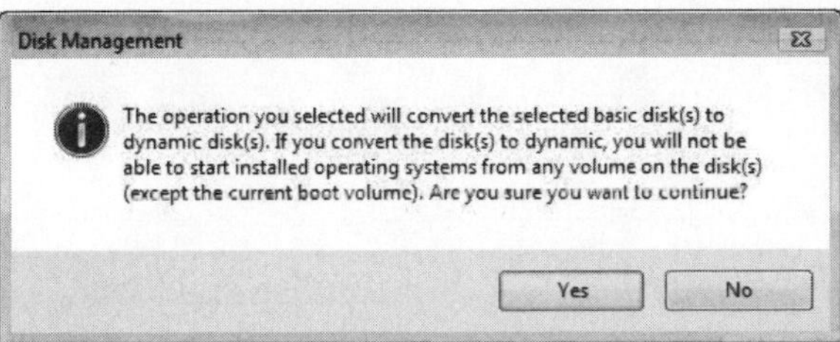

Figure 4-14

A Disk Management information box

8. If you are running a dual boot computer, Disk Management warns you that it will dismount the file systems on the disks you are converting, so they will be temporarily inaccessible. Click **Yes** to continue.

If a selected drive contains the boot partition, the system partition, or a partition that is in use, Disk Management prompts you to restart the computer.

When you convert from a basic disk to a dynamic disk, Disk Management performs the following tasks:

- Converts basic disk partitions to dynamic disk volumes of equal size.
- Converts basic disk primary partitions and logical drives in the extended partition to simple volumes.
- Marks any free space in a basic disk extended partition as unallocated.

Creating Partitions and Volumes

The Disk Management console creates both partitions and volumes with one set of dialog boxes and wizards.

To create a new partition on a basic disk, or a new volume on a dynamic disk, use the following procedure:

CREATE A PARTITION OR VOLUME

GET READY. Log on to Windows Vista using an account with Administrator privileges. When the logon process is completed, close the Welcome Center window and any other windows that appear.

1. Open the Disk Management snap-in.
2. In the Graphical View, right-click the unallocated area on the volume status column for the disk on which you want to create a partition or volume, and then click **New Simple Volume**. The New Simple Volume Wizard appears.
3. Click **Next**. The Specify Volume Size page appears, as shown in Figure 4-15.

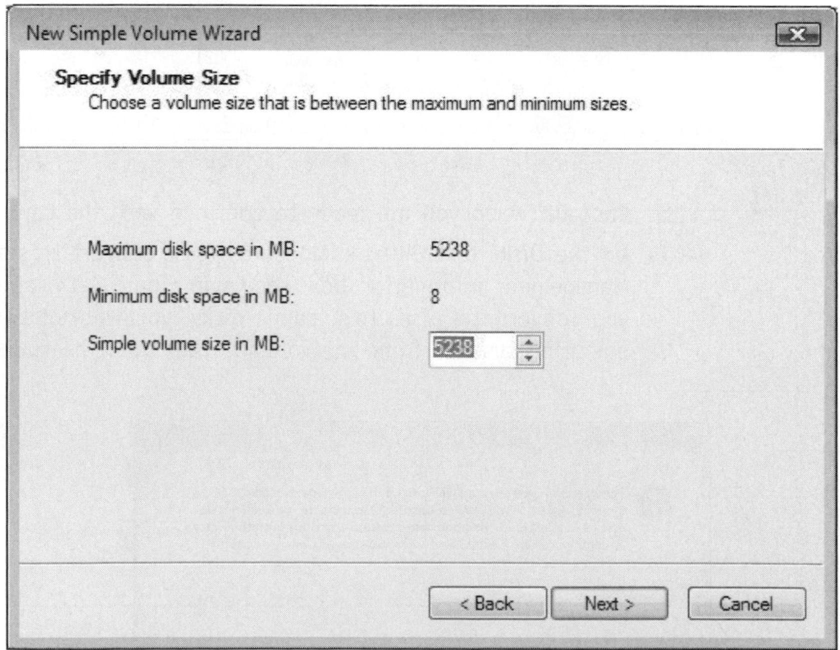

Figure 4-15
The Specify Volume Size page

4. Select the size for the new partition or volume, within the maximum and minimum limits stated on the page, using the *Simple volume size in MB* spin box, and then click **Next**. The Assign Drive Letter or Path page appears, as shown in Figure 4-16.

Figure 4-16

The Assign Drive Letter or Path page

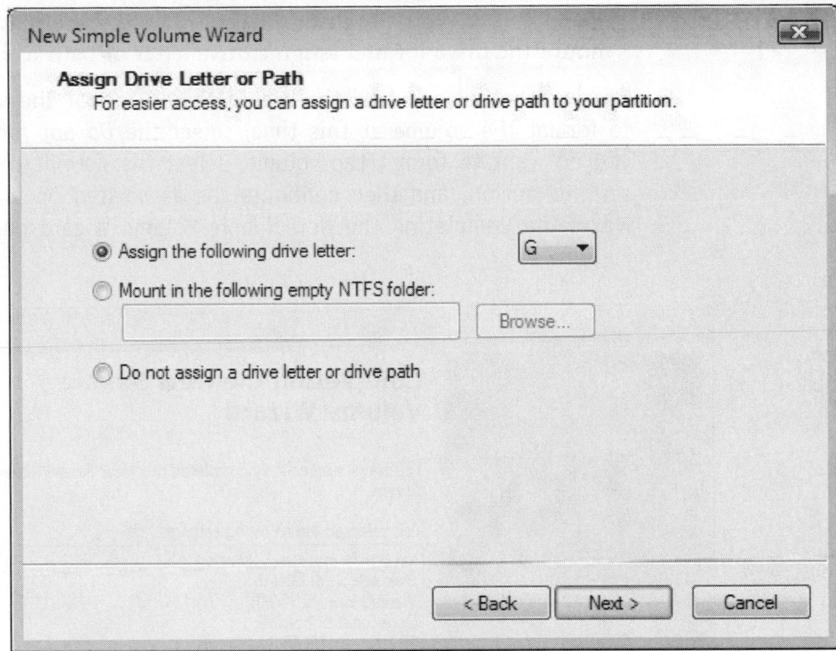

5. Configure one of the following three options, and then click **Next**. The Format Partition page appears, as shown in Figure 4-17.

Figure 4-17

The Format Partition page

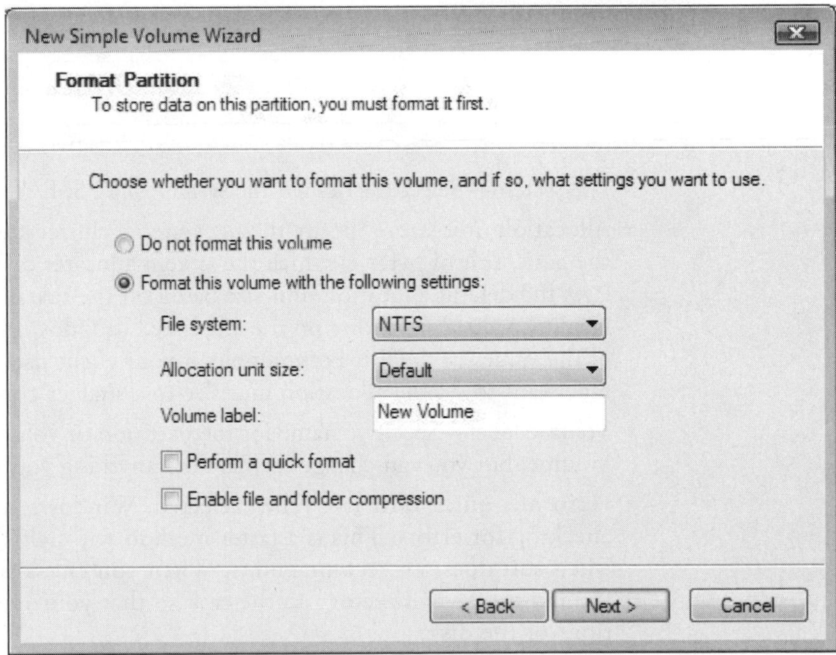

- Assign the following drive letter—If you select this option, click the associated dropdown list for a list of available drive letters, and then select the desired letter you want to assign to the drive.
- Mount in the following empty NTFS folder—If you select this option, either key the path to an existing NTFS folder or click **Browse** to search for or create a new folder. The entire contents of the new drive will appear in the folder you specify.
- Do not assign a drive letter or drive path—Select this option if you want to create the partition, but are not yet ready to use it. When you do not assign a volume a

drive letter or path, the drive is left unmounted and inaccessible. When you want to mount the drive for use, assign a drive letter or path to it.

6. Specify whether and how the wizard should format the volume. If you do not want to format the volume at this time, select the *Do not format this volume* option. If you do want to format the volume, select the *Format this volume with the following settings* option, and then configure the associated options, which follow. Then click **Next.** The Completing the New Simple Volume Wizard page appears, as shown in Figure 4-18.

Figure 4-18

The Completing the New Simple Volume Wizard page

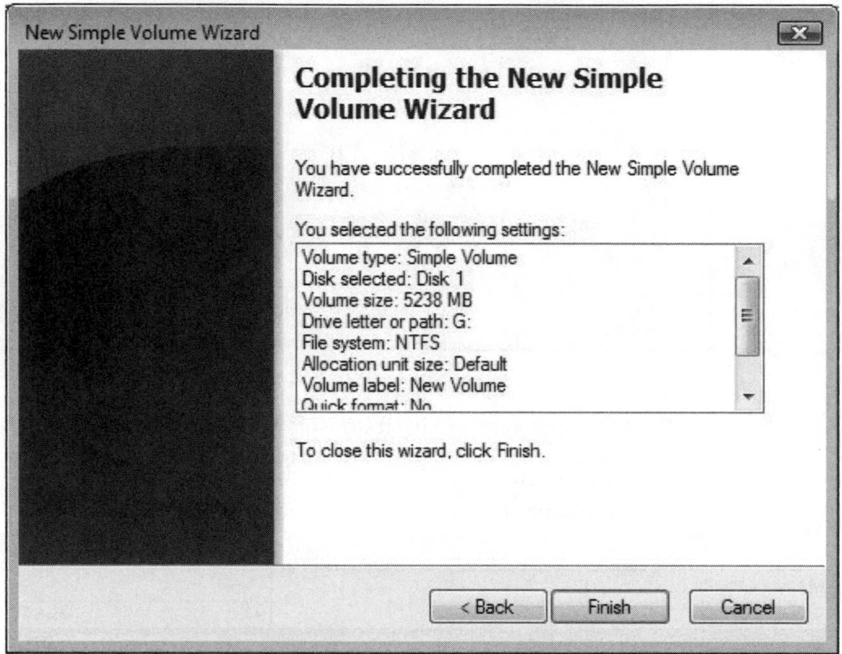

- File system—Select the desired file system: NTFS, FAT, or FAT32.
- Allocation unit size—Specify the file system's cluster size. The cluster size signifies the basic unit of bytes in which the system allocates disk space. The system calculates the default allocation unit size based on the size of the volume. You can override this value by clicking on the associated dropdown list and then selecting one of the values in the list. For example, if your client uses consistently small files, you may want to set the allocation unit size to a smaller cluster size.
- Volume label—Specify a name for the partition or volume. The default name is New Volume, but you can change the name to anything you want.
- Perform a quick format—When selected, Windows formats the disk without checking for errors. This is a faster method with which to format the drive, but Microsoft does not recommend it. When you check for errors, the system looks for and marks bad sectors on the disk so that your clients will not use those portions of the disk.
- Enable file and folder compression—Turns on folder compression for the disk. This option is available only for the NTFS file system.

7. Review the settings to confirm your options, and then click **Finish**. The wizard creates the volume according to your specifications.

Extending and Shrinking Partitions and Volumes

Shrinking and extending partitions and volumes are new Windows Vista features.

TAKE NOTE*

You must be a member of the Backup Operator or the Administrators group to extend or shrink any partition or volume.

To extend or shrink a partition or volume, you simply right-click a partition or volume and select Extend Volume or Shrink Volume from the context menu, or from the Action menu.

Vista extends existing primary partitions, logical drives, and simple volumes by expanding them into adjacent unallocated space on the same disk. When you extend a simple volume across multiple disks, the simple volume becomes a spanned volume. You cannot extend striped volumes.

To extend a partition on a basic disk, the system must meet the following requirements:

- A basic partition must be either unformatted or formatted with the NTFS file system.
- If you extend a logical drive, the console first consumes the contiguous free space remaining in the extended partition. If you attempt to extend the logical drive beyond the confines of its extended partition, the extended partition expands to any unallocated space left on the disk.
- You can extend the partition of logical drives, boot volumes, or system volumes only into contiguous space, and only if the hard disk can be upgraded to a dynamic disk. The operating system will permit you to extend other types of basic volumes into non-contiguous space, but will prompt you to convert the basic disk to a dynamic disk.

To extend a simple or spanned volume on a dynamic disk, the system must meet these requirements:

- When extending a simple volume, you can only use the available space on the same disk, if the volume is to remain simple.
- You can extend a simple volume across additional disks if it is not a system volume or a boot volume. However, once you expand a simple volume to another disk, it is no longer a simple volume but becomes a spanned volume.
- You can extend a simple or spanned volume if it does not have a file system (a raw volume) or if you formatted it using the NTFS file system. (You cannot extend FAT or FAT32 file systems.)

When shrinking partitions or volumes, the Disk Management console frees up space at the end of the volume, relocating the existing volume's files, if necessary. The console then converts that free space to new unallocated space on the disk. To shrink a basic disk partition or any kind of dynamic disk volume except for a striped volume, the system must meet the following requirements:

- The existing partition or volume must not be full and must contain the specified amount of available free space for shrinking.
- The partition or volume must not be a raw partition (one without a file system). Shrinking a raw partition that contains data might destroy the data.
- You can shrink a partition or volume only if you formatted it using the NTFS file system. (You cannot shrink FAT or FAT32 file systems.)

Creating Spanned and Striped Volumes

You must use dynamic disks to create spanned and striped volumes. When you create a spanned or striped volume, you create a single dynamic volume that extends across multiple physical disks.

To create a spanned or striped volume on dynamic disks, use the following procedure:

CREATE A SPANNED OR STRIPED VOLUME

GET READY. Log on to Windows Vista using an account with Administrator privileges. When the logon process is completed, close the Welcome Center window and any other windows that appear.

1. Open the Disk Management snap-in.
2. In the Graphical View, right-click an unallocated area on a dynamic disk and then, from the context menu, select **New Spanned Volume** or **New Striped Volume.**
3. Click **Next** to exit the Welcome page.
4. On the Select Disks page, under the Available standard list box, select each dynamic disk you want to use in the spanned or striped volume, and then click **Add.**
5. Specify the space you want to use on each disk by clicking the disk in the selected standard list box, and then using the *Select the amount of space in MB* spin box to specify the amount of disk space that you want to include in the spanned or striped volume.
6. Click **Next.** The Assign Drive Letter or Path page appears.
7. Specify whether you want to assign a drive letter or path, and then click **Next.** The Format Partition page appears.
8. Specify whether or how you want to format the volume, and then click **Next.** The Completing the New Simple Volume Wizard page appears.
9. Review the settings to confirm your options, and then click **Finish.**

The wizard creates the volume according to your specifications.

Managing Permissions

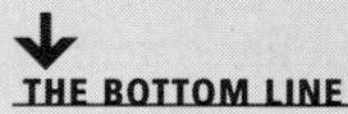

Everything you've learned so far in this lesson has been intended to help you prepare your hard disk drives so that you can store your files on them. You also learned about some Windows Vista technologies that prevent unauthorized users from accessing your files. However, locking people completely out is a lot easier than granting them partial access. To do this, Windows Vista uses *permissions.*

Permissions are privileges granted to specific system entities, such as users, groups, or computers, enabling them to perform a task or access a resource. For example, you can grant a specific user permission to read a file, while denying that same user the permissions needed to modify or delete the file.

Windows Vista has several sets of permissions, which operate independently of each other. As a Vista desktop technician, you should be familiar with the operation of the following four permission systems:

- ***NTFS permissions***—Control access to the files and folders stored on disk volumes formatted with the NTFS file system. To access a file, whether on the local system or over a network, a user must have the appropriate NTFS permissions.
- ***Share permissions***—Control access to folders over a network. To access a file over a network, a user must have appropriate share permissions and appropriate NTFS permissions.
- Registry permissions—Control access to specific parts of the Windows registry. An application that modifies registry settings or a user attempting to manually modify the registry must have the appropriate registry permissions.
- Active Directory permissions—Control access to specific parts of an Active Directory hierarchy. Although Windows Vista cannot host an Active Directory domain, desktop technicians might require these permissions when servicing computers that are members of a domain.

All of these permission systems operate independently of each other, and can conceivably combine to provide increased protection to a specific resource. For example, Alice might grant Ralph the NTFS permissions needed to access the budget spreadsheet stored on her computer.

If Ralph sits down at Alice's computer and logs on as himself, he will be able to access that spreadsheet. However, if Ralph is working at his own computer, he will not be able to access the spreadsheet until Alice creates a share containing the file and grants Ralph the proper share permissions.

TAKE NOTE*

While all of these permissions systems are operating all the time, desktop technicians do not necessarily have to work with them all on a regular basis. In fact, you might not ever have to manually alter a Registry or Active Directory permission. However, many technicians have to work with NTFS and share permissions on a daily basis.

Understanding the Windows Permission Architecture

Permissions protect files, folders, shares, registry keys, and Active Directory objects.

To store permissions, each of these elements has an ***access control list (ACL)***. An ACL is a collection of individual permissions, in the form of ***access control entries (ACEs)***. Each ACE consists of a ***security principal*** (that is, the name of the user, group, or computer being granted the permissions) and the specific permissions assigned to that security principal. When you manage permissions in any of the Windows Vista permission systems, you are actually creating and modifying the ACEs in an ACL.

It is crucial to understand that, in all of the Windows operating systems, permissions are stored as part of the element being protected, not the security principal being granted access. For example, when you grant a user the NTFS permissions needed to access a file, the ACE you create is stored in the file's ACL; it is not part of the user account. You can move the file to a different location, and its permissions go with it.

To manage permissions in Windows Vista, you use a Security tab in the element's Properties dialog box, like the one shown in Figure 4-19, with the security principals listed at the top and the permissions associated with them at the bottom. All of the Windows permission systems use the same interface, although the permissions themselves differ.

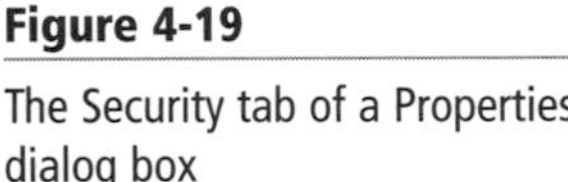

Figure 4-19

The Security tab of a Properties dialog box

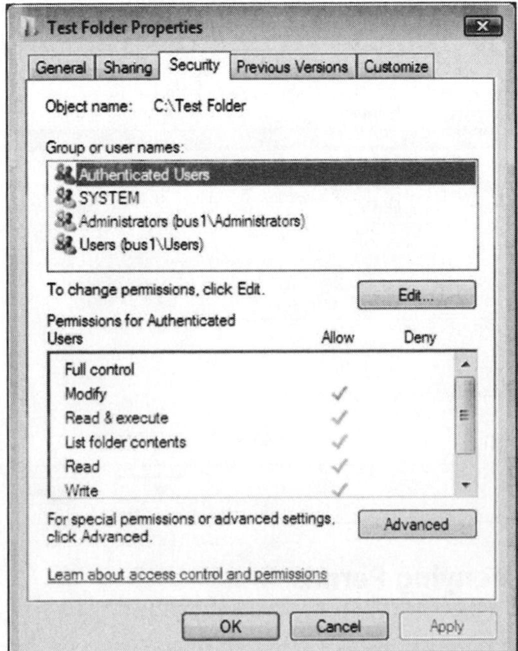

Understanding Standard and Special Permissions

The permissions protecting a particular system element are not like the keys to a lock, which provide either full access or no access at all. Permissions are designed to be granular, enabling you to grant specific degrees of access to security principals.

For example, you can use NTFS permissions to control not only who has access to Alice's spreadsheet, but also to what degree each user has access. You might grant Ralph permission to read the spreadsheet and also modify it, while Ed can only read it, and Trixie cannot see it at all.

To provide this granularity, each of the Windows permission systems has an assortment of permissions that you can assign to a security principal in any combination. Depending on the permission system you are working with, you might have literally dozens of different permissions available for a single system element.

If this is all starting to sound extremely complex, don't worry. Windows provides you with preconfigured permission combinations that are suitable for most common access control chores. When you open the Properties dialog box for a system element and look at its Security tab, the permissions you are seeing are called *standard permissions*. Standard permissions are actually combinations of *special permissions,* which provide the most granular control over the element.

For example, the NTFS permission system has 14 special permissions that you can assign to a folder or file. However, there are also 6 standard permissions, which are various combinations of the 14 special permissions. In most cases, you will only have to work with the standard permissions. Many technicians rarely, if ever, work directly with the special permissions.

If you do find it necessary to work with special permissions directly, Windows makes it possible. When you click the **Advanced** button on the Security tab of any Properties dialog box, an Advanced Security Settings dialog box appears, as shown in Figure 4-20, which enables you to access the ACEs for the selected system element directly.

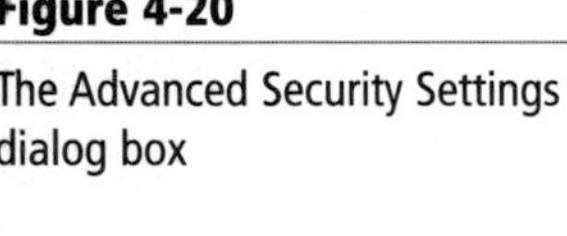

Figure 4-20

The Advanced Security Settings dialog box

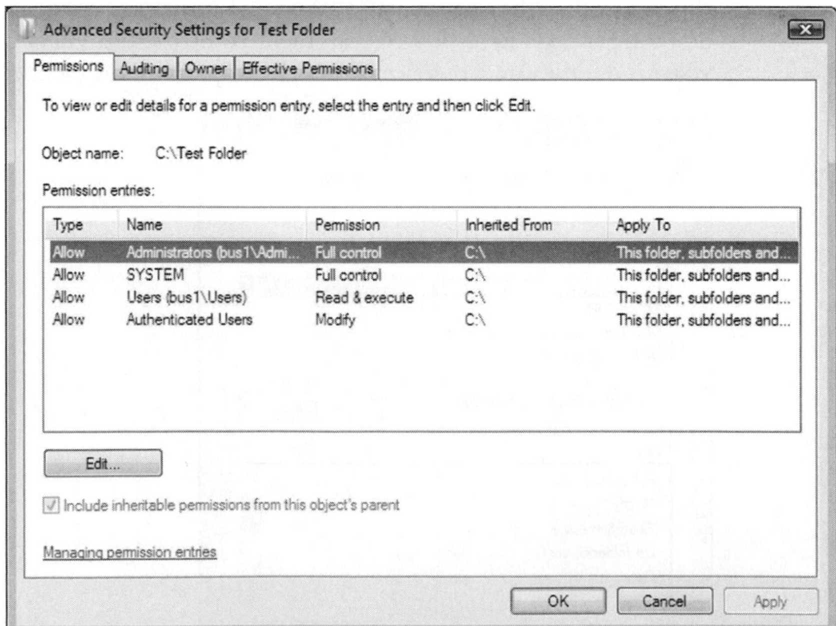

Allowing and Denying Permissions

When you assign permissions to a system element, you are, in effect, creating a new ACE in the element's ACL.

There are two basic types of ACEs: *Allow* and *Deny*. This makes it possible to approach permission management tasks from two directions:

- Additive—Start with no permissions and then grant Allow permissions to individual security principals to provide them with the access they need.
- Subtractive—Start by granting all possible Allow permissions to individual security principals, providing them with full control over the system element, and then grant them Deny permissions for the access you don't want them to have.

Most administrators prefer the additive approach, because Windows, by default, attempts to limit access to important system elements. In a properly designed permission hierarchy, the use of Deny permissions is often not needed at all. Many administrators frown on their use, because combining Allow and Deny permissions in the same hierarchy can make it difficult to determine the effective permissions for a specific system element.

Inheriting Permissions

The most important principle in permission management is that permissions tend to run downwards through a hierarchy.

This is called *permission inheritance*. Permission inheritance means that parent elements pass their permissions down to their subordinate elements. For example, when you grant Alice Allow permissions to access the root of the D: drive, all of the folders and subfolders on the D: drive inherit those permissions, and Alice can access them. The principle of inheritance simplifies the permission assignment process enormously. Without it, you would have to grant security principals individual Allow permissions for every file, folder, share, object, and key they need to access. With inheritance, you can grant access to an entire file system by creating one set of Allow permissions.

In most cases, whether they do it consciously or not, system administrators take inheritance into account when they design their file systems and Active Directory trees. The location of a system element in a hierarchy is often based on how the administrators plan to assign permissions. For example, the section of a directory tree shown in Figure 4-21 is intended to be a place where network users can temporarily store files that they want other users to access.

Figure 4-21

A sample xfer directory structure

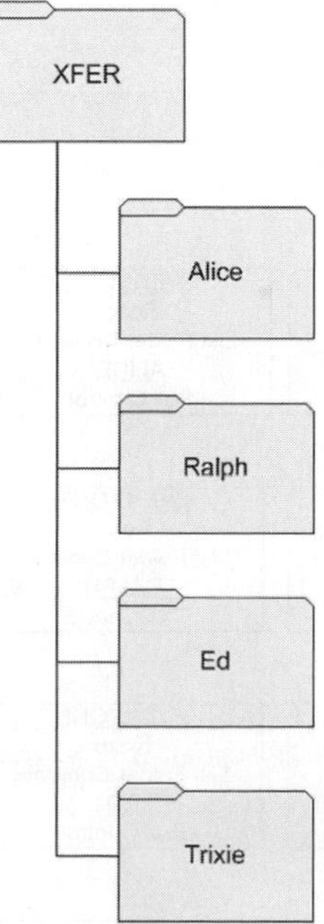

Because the administrator has assigned all users the Allow Read and Allow List Folder Contents standard permissions to the xfer folder, as shown in Figure 4-22, everyone is able to read the files in the xfer directory. Because the assigned permissions run downwards, all of the subfolders beneath xfer inherit those permissions, so all of the users can read the files in all of the subfolders as well.

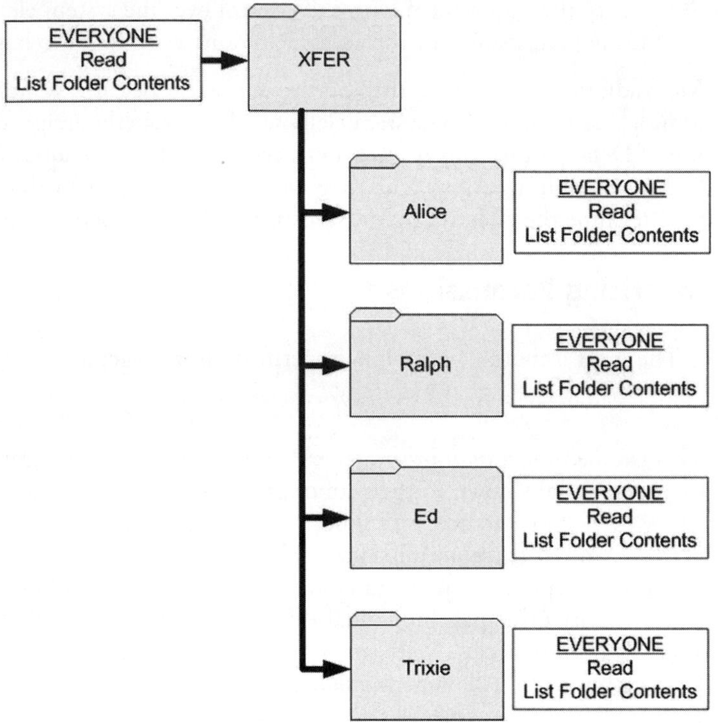

Figure 4-22

Granting Allow permissions to the xfer folder

The next step for the administrator is to assign each user the Allow Full Control permission to his or her own subfolder, as shown in Figure 4-23. This enables each user to create, modify, and delete files in his or her own folder, without compromising the security of the other users' folders. Because the user folders are at the bottom of the hierarchy, there are no subfolders to inherit the Full Control permissions.

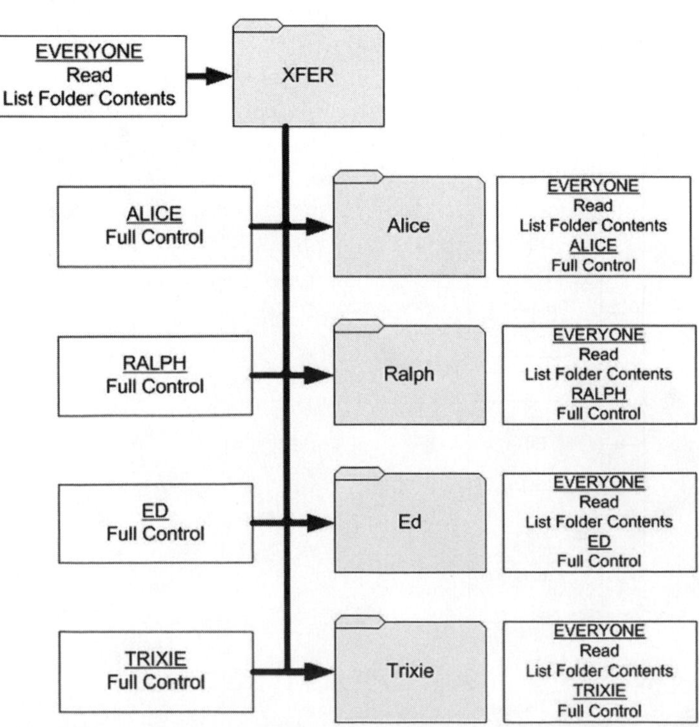

Figure 4-23

Granting Full Control to individual user folders

There are some situations in which an administrator might want to prevent subordinate elements from inheriting permissions from their parents. There are two ways to do this:

- Turn off inheritance—When you assign special permissions, you can configure an ACE not to pass its permissions down to its subordinate elements. This effectively blocks the inheritance process.
- Deny permissions—When you assign a Deny permission to a system element, it overrides any Allow permissions that the element might have inherited from its parent objects.

Understanding Effective Permissions

A security principal can receive permissions in many different ways, and it is important for an administrator to understand how these permissions interact.

Effective permissions are the combination of Allow permissions and Deny permissions that a security principal receives for a given system element, whether explicitly assigned, inherited, or received through a group membership. Because a security principal can receive permissions from so many sources, it is not unusual for those permissions to conflict, so there are rules defining how the permissions combine to form the effective permissions. These rules are as follows:

- Allow permissions are cumulative—When a security principal receives Allow permissions from more than one source, the permissions are combined to form the effective permissions. For example, if Alice receives the Allow Read and Allow List Folder Contents permissions for a particular folder by inheriting them from its parent folder, and receives the Allow Write and Allow Modify permissions to the same folder from a group membership, Alice's effective permissions for the folder is the combination of all four permissions. If you then explicitly grant Alice's user account the Allow Full Control permission, this fifth permission is combined with the other four.
- Deny permissions override Allow permissions—When a security principal receives Allow permissions, whether explicitly, by inheritance, or from a group, you can override those permissions by granting the principal Deny permissions of the same type. For example, if Alice receives the Allow Read and Allow List Folder Contents permissions for a particular folder by inheritance, and receives the Allow Write and Allow Modify permissions to the same folder from a group membership, explicitly granting her the Deny permissions to that folder prevents her from accessing it in any way.
- Explicit permissions take precedence over inherited permissions—When a security principal receives permissions by inheriting them from a parent or from group memberships, you can override those permissions by explicitly assigning contradicting permissions to the security principal itself. For example, if Alice inherits the Deny Full Access permission for a folder, explicitly assigning her user account the Allow Full Access permission to that folder overrides the denial.

Of course, instead of examining and evaluating all of the possible permission sources, you can just open the Advanced Security Settings dialog box and click the **Effective Permissions** tab, as shown in Figure 4-24, to display your current effective permissions for the selected file or folder.

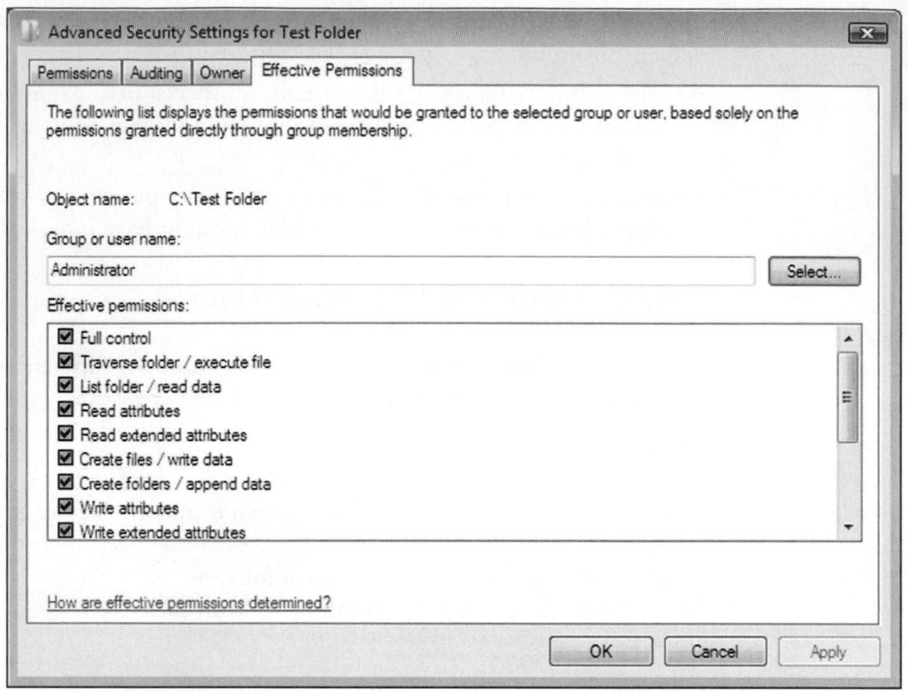

Figure 4-24

The Effective Permissions tab of the Advanced Security Settings dialog box

Managing NTFS Permissions

Windows Vista supports two file systems, NTFS and FAT, but the majority of Windows installations today use NTFS.

One of the main advantages of NTFS is that it supports permissions, which FAT does not. As described earlier in this lesson, every file and folder on an NTFS drive has an ACL that consists of ACEs, each of which contains a security principal and the permissions assigned to that principal.

MORE INFORMATION

The original 12-bit *file allocation table* file system (now referred to as FAT12) was severely limited in several ways. The FAT12 file system was the source of the 8.3 DOS filename limitation, and it originally imposed a volume size limitation of 32 megabytes. Subsequent enhancements to the file system increased its address space to 16 and eventually 32 bits. The resulting FAT32 file system now supports filenames up to 255 characters long and volumes up to 8 terabytes in size, but it still has no built-in permissions system. However, the versions of Windows supporting FAT32, including Windows Vista, impose a FAT32 volume size limit of 32 gigabytes, which is the primary reason why most Windows computers today use NTFS.

In the NTFS permission system, the security principals involved are users and groups, which Windows refers to as *security identifiers (SIDs)*. When a user attempts to access an NTFS file or folder, the system reads the user's *security access token*, which contains the SIDs for the user's account and all of the groups to which the user belongs. The system then compares these SIDs to those stored in the file or folder's ACEs to determine what access the user should have. This process is called *authorization*.

Assigning Standard NTFS Permissions

Most desktop technicians and Windows system administrators work with standard NTFS permissions almost exclusively. This is because there is no need to work directly with special permissions for most common access control tasks. To assign standard NTFS permissions, use the following procedure:

ASSIGN STANDARD NTFS PERMISSIONS

GET READY. Log on to Windows Vista using an account with Administrator privileges. When the logon process is completed, close the Welcome Center window and any other windows that appear.

> **TAKE NOTE***
> The Security tab only appears in Properties dialog boxes if you are running the Business, Enterprise, or Ultimate edition of Windows Vista. The Home Premium, Home Basic, and Starter editions do not support NTFS permissions.

1. Click **Start > All Programs > Accessories**, and then select **Windows Explorer**. A Windows Explorer window appears.
2. In the Folders pane, scroll down to the Computer container and expand it. Then, right-click the **Local Disk (C:)** drive and then, on the context menu, point to **New** and select **Folder**. Give the folder the name **Test Folder**.
3. Right-click the **Test Folder** folder you created and then, from the context menu, select **Properties**. The Test Folder Properties dialog box appears.
4. Click the **Security** tab. The top half of the resulting display lists all of the security principals currently possessing permissions to the Test Folder folder. The bottom half lists the permissions held by the selected security principal.
5. Click **Edit**, and then, when you are prompted for permission to continue, click **Continue**. The Permissions for Test Folder dialog box appears, as shown in Figure 4-25. The interface is the same as that of the previous dialog box, except that the permissions are now represented by checkboxes, indicating that you can modify their states.

Figure 4-25

The Permissions for Test Folder dialog box

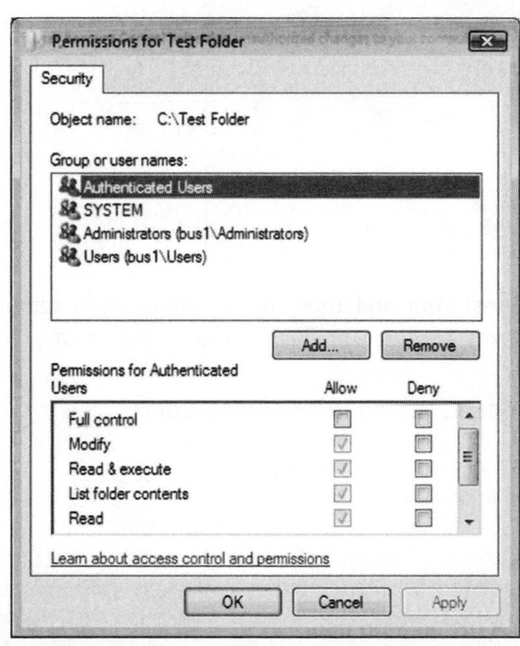

6. Click **Add**. The Select Users or Groups dialog box appears, as shown in Figure 4-26.

Figure 4-26

The Select Users or Groups dialog box

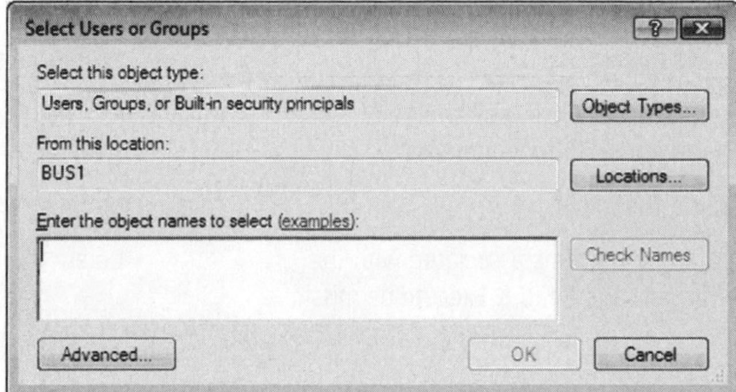

TAKE NOTE*

When you assign permissions on a standalone computer, you select local user and group accounts to be the security principals that receive the permissions. However, if the computer is a member of an Active Directory domain, you can also assign permissions to domain users, groups, and other objects.

7. In the *Enter the object names to select* text box, key **Guest** and then click **OK**. The Guest user account appears on the Permissions for Test Folder dialog box in the *Group or user names* list, as shown in Figure 4-27.

Figure 4-27

The Permissions for Test Folder dialog box, with the Guest user added

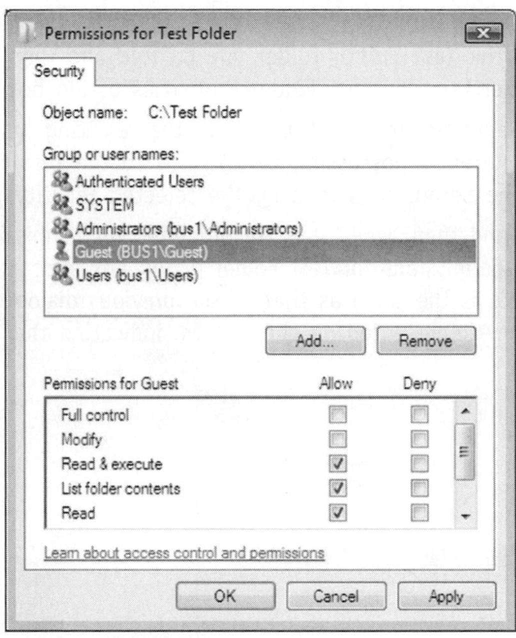

TAKE NOTE*

Assigning permissions to the single folder you created takes only a moment, but for a folder with a large number of files and subfolders subordinate to it the process can take a long time because the system must modify the ACL of each folder and file.

8. Click the **Guest** user and then, in the Permissions for Guest box, select or clear the checkboxes to Allow or Deny the user any of the standard permissions shown in Table 4-5.
9. Click **OK** twice to close the two dialog boxes.

Table 4-5

NTFS Standard Permissions

Standard Permission	When applied to a folder, enables a security principal to:	When applied to a file, enables a security principal to:
Full Control	• Modify the folder permissions. • Take ownership of the folder. • Delete subfolders and files contained in the folder. • Perform all actions associated with all of the other NTFS folder permissions.	• Modify the file permissions. • Take ownership of the file. • Perform all actions associated with all of the other NTFS file permissions.
Modify	• Delete the folder. • Perform all actions associated with the Write and the Read & Execute permissions.	• Modify the file. • Delete the file. • Perform all actions associated with the Write and the Read & Execute permissions.

(continued)

Table 4-5 (*continued*)

STANDARD PERMISSION	WHEN APPLIED TO A FOLDER, ENABLES A SECURITY PRINCIPAL TO:	WHEN APPLIED TO A FILE, ENABLES A SECURITY PRINCIPAL TO:
Read & Execute	• Navigate through restricted folders to reach other files and folders. • Perform all actions associated with the Read and List Folder Contents permissions.	Perform all actions associated with the Read permission. • Run applications.
List Folder Contents	• View the names of the files and subfolders contained in the folder.	• Not applicable
Read	• See the files and subfolders contained in the folder. • View the ownership, permissions, and attributes of the folder.	• Read the contents of the file. • View the ownership, permissions, and attributes of the file.
Write	• Create new files and subfolders inside the folder. • Modify the folder attributes. • View the ownership and permissions of the folder.	• Overwrite the file. • Modify the file attributes. • View the ownership and permissions of the file.

Assigning Special NTFS Permissions

If you ever have the need to work with special NTFS permissions directly, Windows Vista provides the tools to do so.

To view and manage the special NTFS permissions for a file or folder, use the following procedure:

ASSIGN SPECIAL NTFS PERMISSIONS

GET READY. Log on to Windows Vista using an account with Administrator privileges. When the logon process is completed, close the Welcome Center window and any other windows that appear.

1. Click **Start > All Programs > Accessories**, and then select **Windows Explorer**. A Windows Explorer window appears.
2. In the Folders pane, scroll down to the Computer container and expand it. Then, expand the **Local Disk (C:)** drive.
3. Right-click the **Test Folder** folder you created earlier and then, from the context menu, select **Properties.** The Test Folder Properties dialog box appears.
4. Click the **Security** tab, and then click **Advanced.** The Advanced Security Settings for Test Folder page appears. This dialog box is as close as the Windows graphical interface can come to displaying the contents of an ACL. Each of the lines in the *Permission entries* list is essentially an ACE, and includes the following information:
    - Type—Specifies whether the entry allows or denies the permission.
    - Name—Specifies the name of the security principal receiving the permission.
    - Permission—Specifies the name of the standard permission being assigned to the security principal. If the entry is used to assign special permissions, the word *Special* appears in this field.

- Inherited From—Specifies whether the permission is inherited and if so, where it is inherited from.
- Apply To—Specifies whether the permission is inherited by subordinate objects and if so, by which ones.

5. Click **Edit.** Another Advanced Security Settings for Test Folder dialog box appears, this one editable, as shown in Figure 4-28. This dialog box also contains the following two checkboxes:

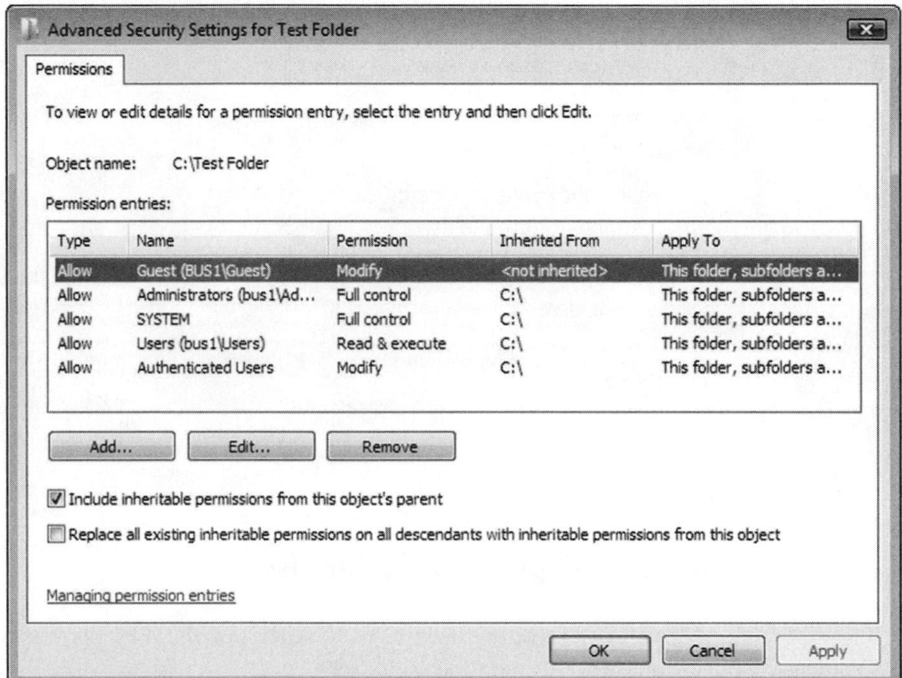

Figure 4-28

The editable Advanced Security Settings for Test Folder page

- Include inheritable permissions from this object's parent—Specifies whether the file or folder should inherit permissions from parent objects. This checkbox is selected by default. Deselecting it causes a Windows Security message box to appear, enabling you to choose whether to remove all of the inherited ACEs from the list or copy the inherited permissions from the parent to the file or folder. If you choose the latter, the effective permissions stay the same, but the file or folder is no longer dependent on the parent for permission inheritance. If you change the permissions on the parent objects, the file or folder remains unaffected.
- Replace all existing inheritable permissions on all descendents with inheritable permissions from this object—Causes subordinate objects to inherit permissions from this file or folder, to the exclusion of all permissions explicitly assigned to the subordinate objects.

6. Click **Add.** The Select Users or Groups dialog box appears.
7. In the *Enter the object names to select* text box, key **Guest** and click **OK.** The Permission Entry for Test Folder dialog box appears, as shown in Figure 4-29.

Figure 4-29

The Permission Entry for Test Folder dialog box

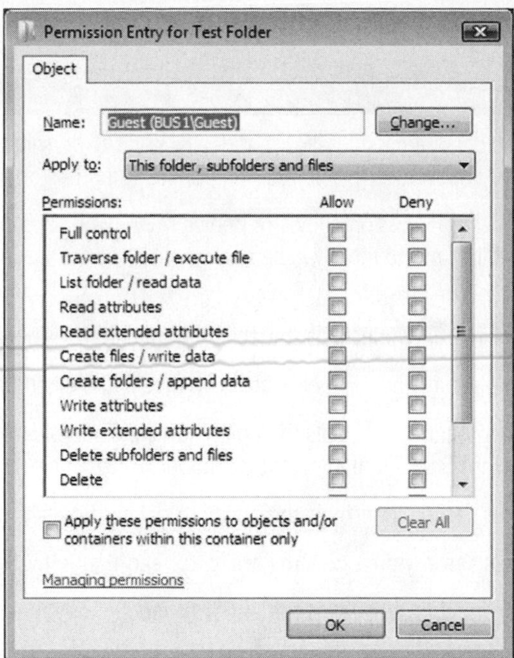

8. In the *Apply to* dropdown list, select which subordinate elements should receive the permissions you assign using this dialog box.
9. In the Permissions list, select or clear the checkboxes to Allow or Deny the user any of the special permissions shown in Table 4-6.

Table 4-6

NTFS Special Permissions

SPECIAL PERMISSION	FUNCTIONS
Traverse Folder/Execute File	• The Traverse Folder permission allows or denies security principals the ability to move through folders that they do not have permission to access, so as to reach files or folders that they do have permission to access. This permission applies to folders only. • The Execute File permission allows or denies security principals the ability to run program files. This permission applies to files only.
List Folder/Read Data	• The List Folder permission allows or denies security principals the ability to view the file and subfolder names within a folder. This permission applies to folders only. • The Read Data permission allows or denies security principals the ability to view the contents of a file. This permission applies to files only.
Read Attributes	Allows or denies security principals the ability to view the NTFS attributes of a file or folder.
Read Extended Attributes	Allows or denies security principals the ability to view the extended attributes of a file or folder.
Create Files/Write Data	• The Create Files permission allows or denies security principals the ability to create files within the folder. This permission applies to folders only.
	• The Write Data permission allows or denies security principals the ability to modify the file and overwrite existing content. This permission applies to files only.

(continued)

Table 4-6 (*continued*)

SPECIAL PERMISSION	FUNCTIONS
Create Folders/Append Data	• The Create Folders permission allows or denies security principals the ability to create subfolders within a folder. This permission applies to folders only. • The Append Data permission allows or denies security principals the ability to add data to the end of the file but not to modify, delete, or overwrite existing data in the file. This permission applies to files only.
Write Attributes	Allows or denies security principals the ability to modify the NTFS attributes of a file or folder.
Write Extended Attributes	Allows or denies security principals the ability to modify the extended attributes of a file or folder.
Delete Subfolders and Files	Allows or denies security principals the ability to delete subfolders and files, even if the Delete permission has not been granted on the subfolder or file.
Delete	Allows or denies security principals the ability to delete the file or folder.
Read Permissions	Allows or denies security principals the ability to read the permissions for the file or folder.
Change Permissions	Allows or denies security principals the ability to modify the permissions for the file or folder.
Take Ownership	Allows or denies security principals the ability to take ownership of the file or folder.
Synchronize	Allows or denies different threads of multithreaded, multiprocessor programs to wait on the handle for the file or folder and synchronize with another thread that might signal it.

10. Click **OK** repeatedly until you return to the Windows Explorer window.

As mentioned earlier in this lesson, standard permissions are combinations of special permissions designed to provide frequently needed access controls. Table 4-7 lists all of the standard permissions, and the special permissions that compose them.

Table 4-7

NTFS Standard Permissions and Their Special Permission Equivalents

STANDARD PERMISSION	SPECIAL PERMISSIONS
Read	• List Folder/Read Data • Read Attributes • Read Extended Attributes • Read Permissions • Synchronize
Read & Execute	• List Folder/Read Data • Read Attributes • Read Extended Attributes • Read Permissions • Synchronize • Traverse Folder/Execute File

(continued)

Table 4-7 (*continued*)

STANDARD PERMISSION	SPECIAL PERMISSIONS
Modify	• Create Files/Write Data • Create Folders/Append Data • Delete • List Folder/Read Data • Read Attributes • Read Extended Attributes • Read Permissions • Synchronize • Write Attributes • Write Extended Attributes
Write	• Create Files/Write Data • Create Folders/Append Data • Read Permissions • Synchronize • Write Attributes • Write Extended Attributes
List Folder Contents	• List Folder/Read Data • Read Attributes • Read Extended Attributes • Read Permissions • Synchronize • Traverse Folder/Execute File
Full Control	• Change Permissions • Create Files/Write Data • Create Folders/Append Data • Delete • Delete Subfolders and Files • List Folder/Read Data • Read Attributes • Read Extended Attributes • Read Permissions • Synchronize • Take Ownership • Write Attributes • Write Extended Attributes

Understanding Resource Ownership

As you study the NTFS permission system, it might occur to you that it seems possible to lock out a file or folder—that is, assign a combination of permissions that permits access to no one at all, leaving the file or folder inaccessible. In fact, this is true.

A user with administrative privileges can revoke his or her own permissions, as well as everyone else's, preventing them from accessing a resource. However, the NTFS permissions system includes a "back door" that prevents these orphaned files and folders from remaining permanently inaccessible.

Every file and folder on an NTFS drive has an owner, and the owner always has the ability to modify the permissions for the file or folder, even if the owner has no permissions him- or herself. By default, the owner of a file or folder is the user account that created it. However, any account possessing the Take Ownership special permission (or the Full Control standard permission) can take ownership of the file or folder.

The other purpose for file and folder ownership is to calculate disk quotas. When you set quotas specifying the maximum amount of disk space particular users can consume, Windows calculates a user's current disk consumption by adding up the sizes of all the files and folders that the user owns.

Sharing Files and Folders

On a standalone Windows Vista computer, the partitions and volumes you create on the hard disks provide a place to store applications and files. However, when you connect the computer to a network, they become a means to share files with other users.

Windows Vista is capable of functioning as both a client and a server on a network, meaning that users can access files on other computers, as well as share files and folders on their own computers with other network users. For network users to be able to access your files, you must first create a network share out of a specific drive or folder. Once you have created a share, users on the network can browse to it in Windows Explorer and access the files there, just as if they were on a local drive.

Understanding Folder Sharing in Windows Vista

When compared to previous versions of Windows, Vista provides additional methods for sharing files and folders, as well as additional security mechanisms to protect the computer from intrusion.

Windows Vista provides two basic methods for sharing the files and folders on the computer: any folder sharing and Public folder sharing. Table 4-8 lists the capabilities of each sharing method.

Table 4-8

Any folder sharing and Public folder sharing features

Any folder sharing	Public folder sharing
Shares files from any location	Places all shared files in a single location
Enables you to set different sharing permissions for individual network users	Uses the same sharing permissions for all network users
Access can be limited to network users with a user account and password on your computer	Access can be limited to network users with a user account and password on your computer
Individual users can be granted read-only or read/write access to the share	Can be configured as a read-only share or a read/write share
Shares files from their original locations	Requires you to copy or move files to be shared to the Public folder

The type of sharing method you elect to use depends on the size and formality of the network to which the computer is connected. For many home or small business networkers, Public folder sharing is the easiest method, one that users can easily maintain for themselves on a day-to-day basis. For larger networks, Windows domain networks, or any network with more elaborate security requirements, any folder sharing is preferable.

Sharing the Public Folder

Sharing files and folders using the Public folder is the simplest way to give your clients file sharing capability.

All you have to do to activate Public folder sharing is enable Network Discovery and Public Folder Sharing in the Network and Sharing Center. Once you have done that, any files and folders that the user copies to the Public folder are automatically shared. Users on other network computers can browse to the Public share on the client's computer and access any of the files placed there.

Depending on the setting you chose when you enabled Public folder sharing, network users are granted either read-only access or full read/write access with the ability to create new files. In addition, if Password protected sharing is turned on, only network users with local user accounts and passwords on your computer can access the Public share.

Windows Vista automatically enables or disables certain network settings, depending on the type of network the installer specified during the operating system installation. Before you can share files or folders with network users, you must open the Network and Sharing Center and be sure that Network Discovery and either File Sharing or Public Folder Sharing are enabled. For more information on enabling these options, see Lesson 7, "Configuring Network Connectivity."

Sharing a Folder

Public folder sharing is a new feature on Windows Vista that is designed to provide users a simplified way to share files and folders, without the need for network administrators.

The real power and flexibility of Windows Vista file sharing is found in the any folder sharing capability. With any folder sharing, you have full control over what material on the computer is shared, which users are permitted to access the shared material, and what degree of access each user is granted.

To share a folder on a Windows Vista computer, use the following procedure:

SHARE A FOLDER

GET READY. Log on to Windows Vista using an account with Administrator privileges. When the logon process is completed, close the Welcome Center window and any other windows that appear. Make sure that Network Discovery, File Sharing, and Password Protected Sharing are all turned on.

1. Click **Start > All Programs > Accessories**, and then select **Windows Explorer**. A Windows Explorer window appears.
2. In the Folders pane, scroll down to the Computer container and expand it. Then, expand the **Local Disk (C:)** drive.
3. If you have not done so already, create a new folder on the C: drive and call it **Test Folder**.

4. Right-click **Test Folder** and then, from the context menu, select **Properties**. The Test Folder Properties dialog box appears.
5. Click the **Sharing** tab to display the interface shown in Figure 4-30.

Figure 4-30

The Sharing tab of a folder's Properties dialog box

6. Click **Advanced Sharing**, and then click **Continue** to proceed. The Advanced Sharing dialog box appears, as shown in Figure 4-31.

Figure 4-31

The Advanced Sharing dialog box

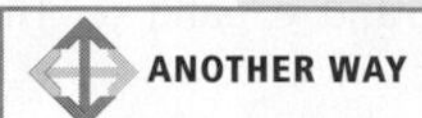

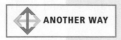

If you click **Share** on the Sharing tab, or if you right-click a folder and select Share from the context menu, Windows Vista takes you to the File Sharing Wizard, which is a simplified method for creating a share. The wizard is designed for end users and provides a limited set of features, as well as a means for informing network users that a new share is available. Desktop technicians and system administrators will usually want to use the Advanced Sharing interface. It is possible to disable the wizard entirely by clearing the Use Sharing Wizard checkbox on the View tab of the Folder Options control panel.

7. Select the *Share this folder* checkbox. By default, the name of the folder you selected appears as the name of the share, but you can change the name, if desired, without affecting the original folder. The number of users permitted to access the share simultaneously is 10, by default, which is the maximum number of user connections that Windows Vista permits. To conserve system resources and network bandwidth, you can reduce this number by adjusting the value in the *Limit the number of simultaneous users to* spin box.

MORE INFORMATION

It is possible to create a share that is invisible to users browsing the network simply by appending a dollar symbol ($) to the share name. For example, each drive in the computer has an administrative share that the setup program creates during the operating system installation, called C$, D$, and so on. These shares do not appear in Windows Explorer, but you can still access them by specifying the share name in a command line. Any hidden shares that you create are also accessible, though invisible.

8. Click **OK** to create the share.

If you open Windows Explorer and browse to the computer in the Network container, you can now see the shared folder there, as shown in Figure 4-32.

Figure 4-32

A Windows Explorer window displaying a new share

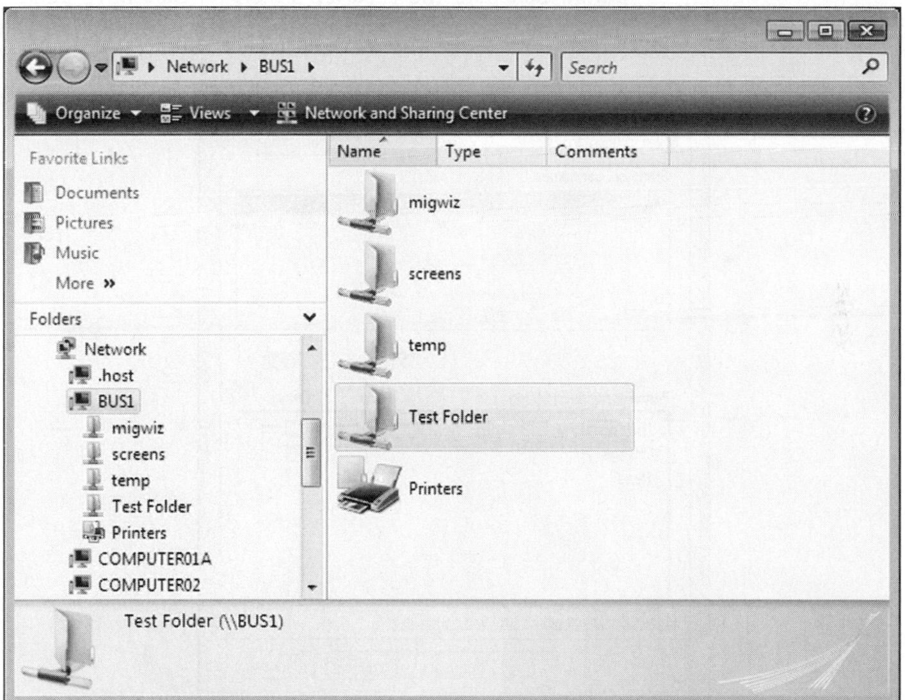

Managing Share Permissions

Windows Vista shares have their own permission system, which is completely independent from the other Windows permission systems.

For network users to access shares on a Windows Vista computer with Password protected sharing enabled, they must have user accounts on the sharing computer and you must grant them the appropriate permissions.

To set share permissions, use the following procedure:

SET SHARE PERMISSIONS

GET READY. Log on to Windows Vista using an account with Administrator privileges. When the logon process is completed, close the Welcome Center window and any other windows that appear. Make sure that Network Discovery, File Sharing, and Password Protected Sharing are all turned on.

1. Click **Start > All Programs > Accessories**, and then select **Windows Explorer**. A Windows Explorer window appears.
2. In the Folders pane, scroll down to the Computer container and expand it. Then, expand the **Local Disk (C:)** drive.
3. If you have not done so already, create a new folder on the C: drive and call it **Test Folder**.
4. Right-click **Test Folder** and then, from the context menu, select **Properties.** The Test Folder Properties dialog box appears.
5. Click the **Sharing** tab, click **Advanced Sharing**, and then click **Continue** to proceed. The Advanced Sharing dialog box appears.
6. Click **Permissions.** The Permissions for Test Folder dialog box appears, as shown in Figure 4-33. As with all of the Windows permission systems, the top half of the dialog box lists the security principals that have been granted permissions, and the bottom half displays the permissions granted to the selected principal.

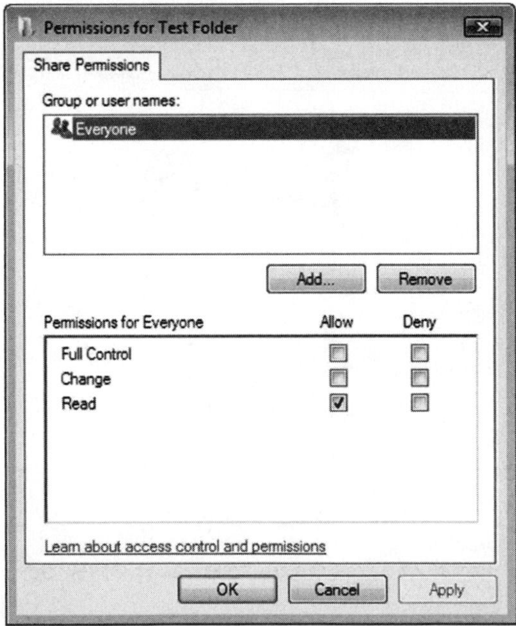

Figure 4-33

The Permissions for Test Folder dialog box

7. Click **Add.** The Select Users or Groups dialog box appears.
8. In the *Enter the object names to select* text box, key **Guest** and click **OK.** The Guest user account is added to the *Group or user names* list.
9. In the Permissions for Guest list, select or clear the checkboxes to Allow or Deny the user any of the permissions shown in Table 4-9.

Table 4-9

Share Permissions and Their Functions

SHARE PERMISSION	ALLOWS OR DENIES SECURITY PRINCIPALS THE ABILITY TO:
Read	• Display folder names, file names, file data, and attributes • Execute program files • Access other folders within the shared folder
Change	• Create folders • Add files to folders • Change data in files • Append data to files • Change file attributes • Delete folders and files • Perform all actions permitted by the Read permission
Full Control	• Change file permissions • Take ownership of files • Perform all tasks allowed by the Change permission

10. Click **OK** repeatedly until you return to the Windows Explorer window.

When assigning share permissions, be aware that they do not combine in the same way that NTFS permissions do. If you grant Alice the Allow Read and Allow Change permissions to the C:\Documents folder, and at a later time deny her all three permissions to the C:\ share, the Deny permissions prevent her from accessing any files on the C:\ share, but she can still access the C:\Documents share because of the Allow permissions. In other words, the C:\ Documents share does not inherit the Deny permissions from the C:\share.

Combining Share and NTFS Permissions

It is crucial for desktop technicians to understand that the NTFS and Share permission systems are completely separate from each other, and that for network users to access files on a shared NTFS drive, they must have both the correct NTFS and the correct share permissions.

The share permission system is the simplest of the Windows permission systems, and provides only basic protection for shared network resources. Share permissions provide only three levels of access, compared to the far more complex system of NTFS permissions. Generally speaking, network administrators prefer to use either NTFS or share permissions, but not both.

TAKE NOTE*

The Effective Permissions display in the Advanced Security Sailings dialog box shows only the effective NTFS permissions, not the share permissions that might also constrain the user's access.

Share permissions provide limited protection, but this might be sufficient on some small networks. Share permissions might also be the only alternative on a computer with FAT32 drives, because the FAT file system does not have its own permission system.

On networks already possessing a well-planned system of NTFS permissions, share permissions are not really necessary. In this case, you can safely grant the Full Control share permission to Everyone, and allow the NTFS permissions to provide security. Adding share permissions to the mix only complicates the administration process, without providing any additional security.

Configuring Data Protection

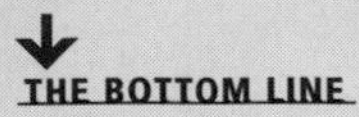

THE BOTTOM LINE

Protecting data from unauthorized access is important, but it is equally critical to protect it from accidental loss or deliberate destruction. To do this, you must create system backups at regular intervals.

CERTIFICATION READY? Configure Data Protection 6.4

Larger, and even some medium-sized, organizations have network-based backup systems that enable multiple workstations to transmit their data to a backup device on the network, usually a magnetic tape drive. Depending on the amount of data involved and the type of storage device, these network backup solutions can easily cost tens of thousands of dollars.

For standalone systems or small networks, Windows Vista includes backup tools that you can use to protect your data by copying it to a network drive, another hard disk drive, a USB flash drive, or a series of writable CDs or DVDs.

Using the Back Up Files Wizard

The Windows Vista Primary backup program enables users to easily set up a repeating regimen of backup jobs using a wizard-based interface.

CERTIFICATION READY? Configure Data Protection: Use Windows backup and restore 6.4

The backup program included with Windows XP and some other recent Windows versions was capable of getting the job done, but suffered from some serious drawbacks. The software was limited in the types of backup devices it could use, and scheduling repeated backup jobs was difficult.

The Windows Vista Back Up Files Wizard addresses both of these problems. Creating a repeating backup job is a simple matter of running the wizard, selecting the files to back up, and selecting the medium you want to use to store the backups. If anything, the Back Up Files Wizard is too simple; it backs up only document files, not application or operating system files, and there is no way to avoid the wizard and manually create a backup job. To perform a full backup of the entire system, you must use the Complete PC utility, covered later in this lesson.

To create a backup job with the Back Up Files Wizard, use the following procedure:

CREATE A BACKUP JOB

GET READY. Log on to Windows Vista using an account with Administrator privileges. When the logon process is completed, close the Welcome Center window and any other windows that appear.

1. Click **Start > All Programs > Accessories > System Tools**, and then select **Backup Status and Configuration.** The Backup Status and Configuration window appears, as shown in Figure 4-34.

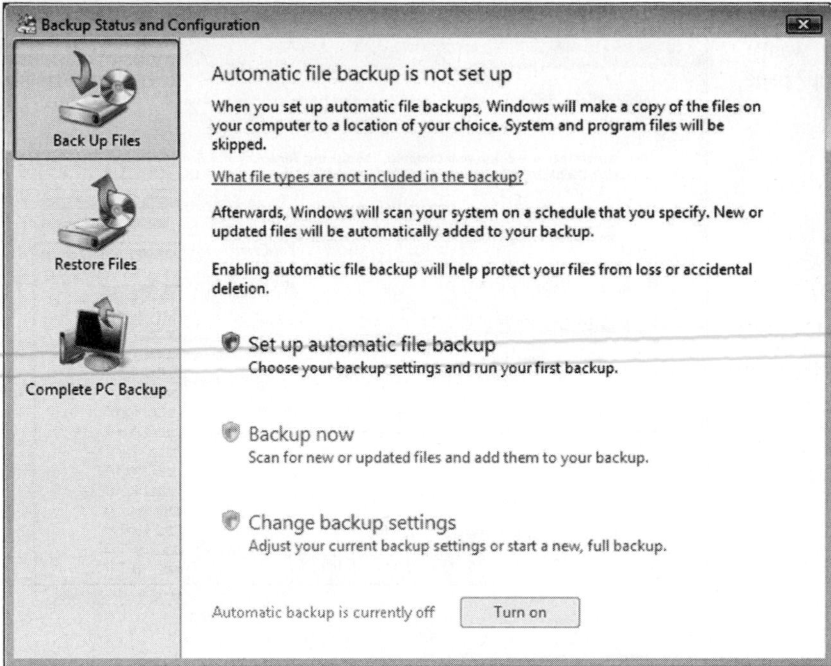

Figure 4-34

The Backup Status and Configuration window

2. In the left pane, make sure that Back Up Files is selected.
3. Click **Set up automatic file backup**. After you confirm your credentials, the program searches for backup devices and the *Where do you want to save your backup?* page appears, as shown in Figure 4-35.

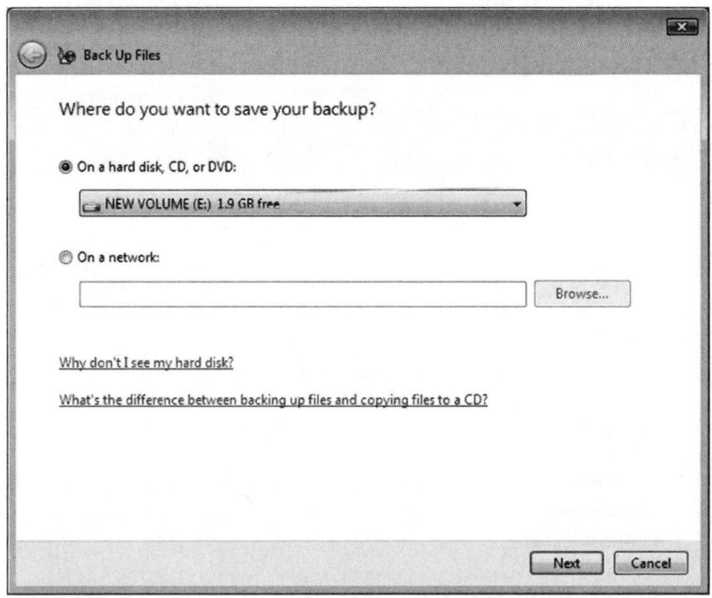

Figure 4-35

The Where do you want to save your backup? page

4. Select the appropriate radio button to choose whether you want to back up to a local or a network drive, and then specify the drive or network location. Then click **Next**. The *Which disks do you want to include in the backup?* page appears, as shown in Figure 4-36.

Figure 4-36

The Which disks do you want to include in the backup? page

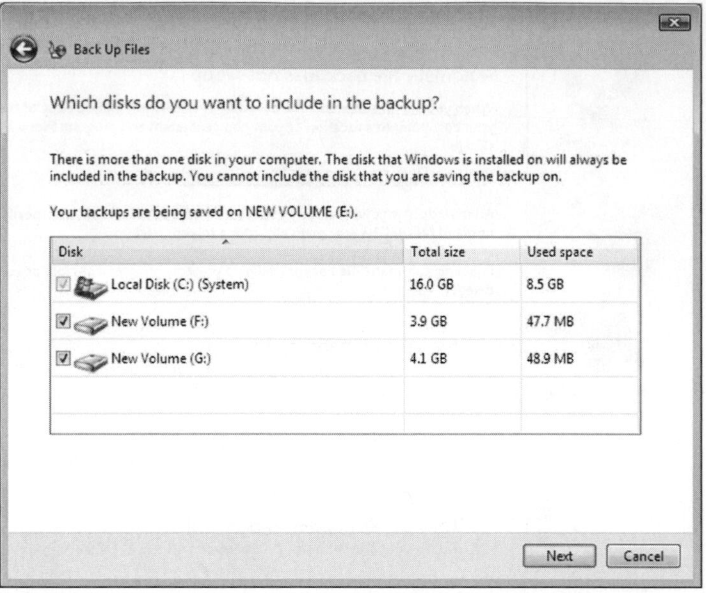

MORE INFORMATION

Although magnetic tape drives are the traditional backup medium of choice, the low prices, portability, and excellent performance of external hard drives are rapidly making them a popular backup medium.

5. Select or clear the checkboxes to indicate which drives you want to include in the backup job. The system drive is included by default, and cannot be deselected. Then click **Next** to continue. The *Which file types do you want to back up?* page appears, as shown in Figure 4-37.

Figure 4-37

The Which file types do you want to back up? page

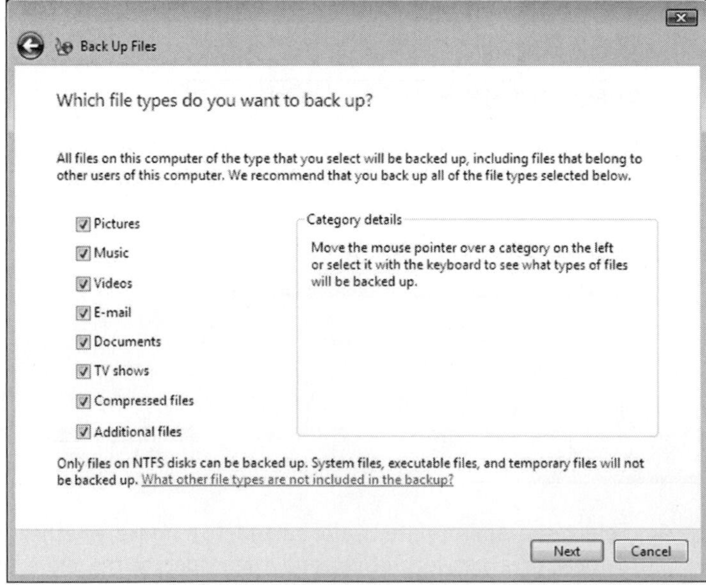

6. Select or clear the checkboxes to indicate which types of files you want to back up. Then click **Next.** The *How often do you want to create a backup?* page appears, as shown in Figure 4-38.

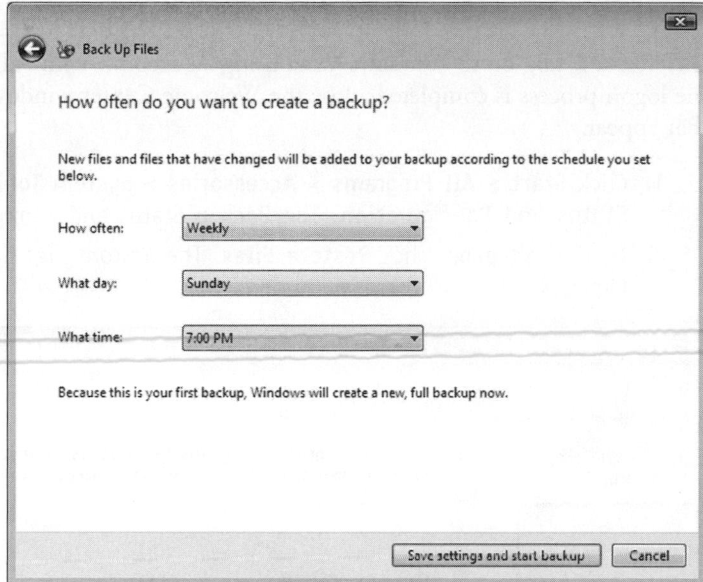
Back Up Files
How often do you want to create a backup?
New files and files that have changed will be added to your backup according to the schedule you set below.
How often:
Weekly
What day:
Sunday
What time:
7:00 PM
Because this is your first backup, Windows will create a new, full backup now.
Save settings and start backup
Cancel

Figure 4-38

The How often do you want to create a backup? page

7. Using the *How often*, *What day*, and *What time* dropdown lists, specify when and how often you want to back up your files. Then click **Save settings and start backup**. The program creates the backup job, executes it for the first time, and schedules it to repeat at the interval you selected.

The Backup Status and Configuration window now displays the status of the backup job, as shown in Figure 4-39.

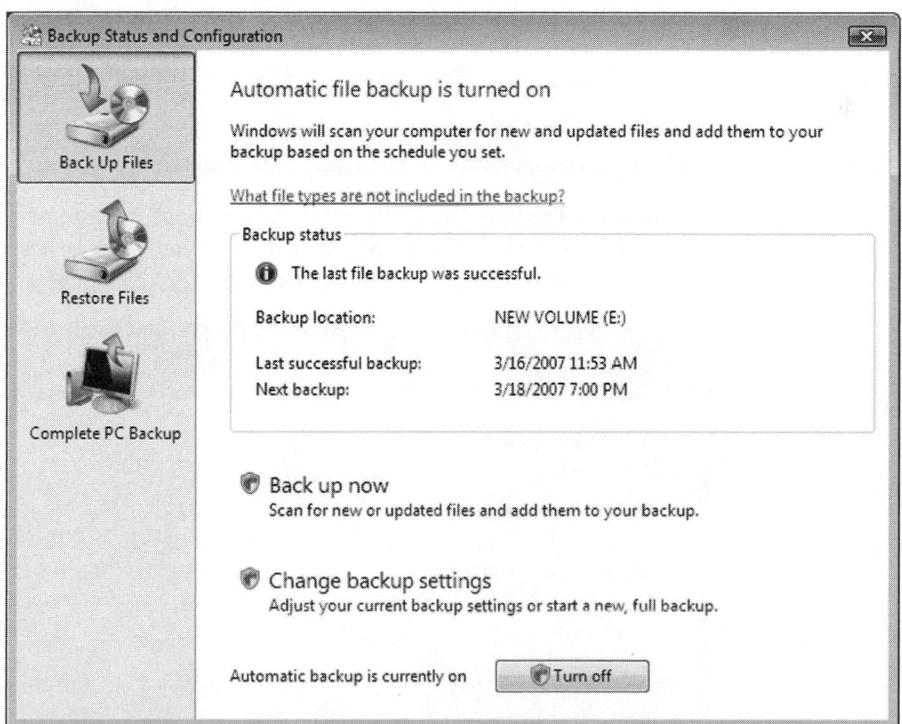
Backup Status and Configuration
Back Up Files
Restore Files
Complete PC Backup
Automatic file backup is turned on
Windows will scan your computer for new and updated files and add them to your backup based on the schedule you set.
What file types are not included in the backup?
Backup status
The last file backup was successful.
Backup location:
NEW VOLUME (E:)
Last successful backup:
3/16/2007 11:53 AM
Next backup:
3/18/2007 7:00 PM
Back up now
Scan for new or updated files and add them to your backup.
Change backup settings
Adjust your current backup settings or start a new, full backup.
Automatic backup is currently on
Turn off

Figure 4-39

The Backup Status And Configuration window, displaying the backup job status

Once you have completed a backup job, you can restore files from that job at any time. To perform a restore, use the following procedure:

RESTORE FILES

GET READY. Log on to Windows Vista using an account with Administrator privileges. When the logon process is completed, close the Welcome Center window and any other windows that appear.

1. Click **Start** > **All Programs** > **Accessories** > **System Tools**, and then select **Backup Status and Configuration**. The Backup Status and Configuration window appears.
2. In the left pane, click **Restore Files**. The *Restore files* page appears, as shown in Figure 4-40.

Figure 4-40

The Restore files page

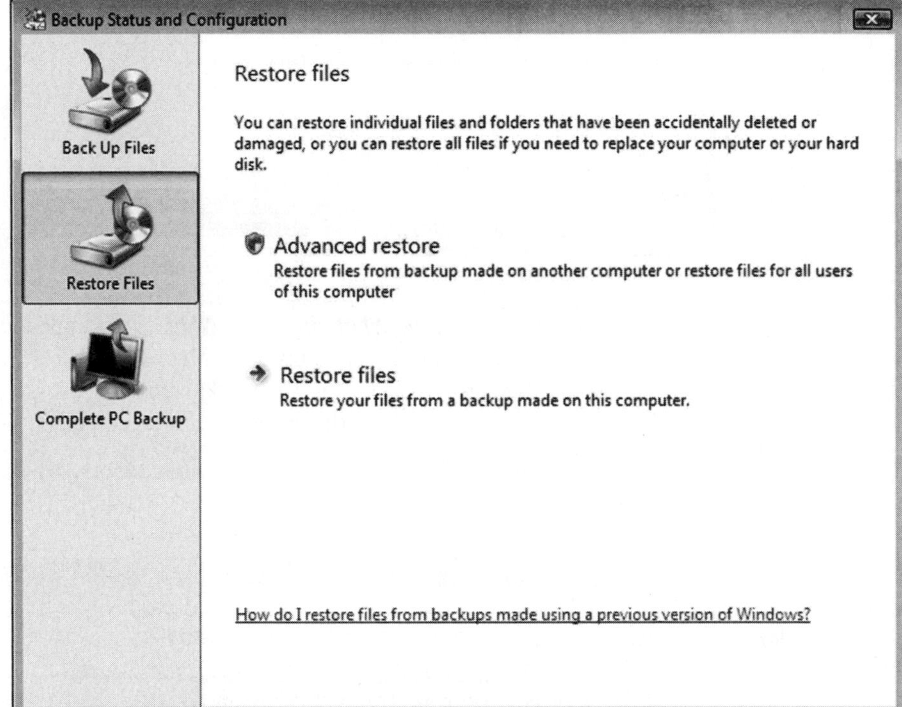

3. Click **Restore files**. The *What do you want to restore?* page appears, as shown in Figure 4-41. Click ***Advanced restore*** if you want to restore files from backups made by other computers or other users on this computer.

Figure 4-41

The What do you want to restore? page

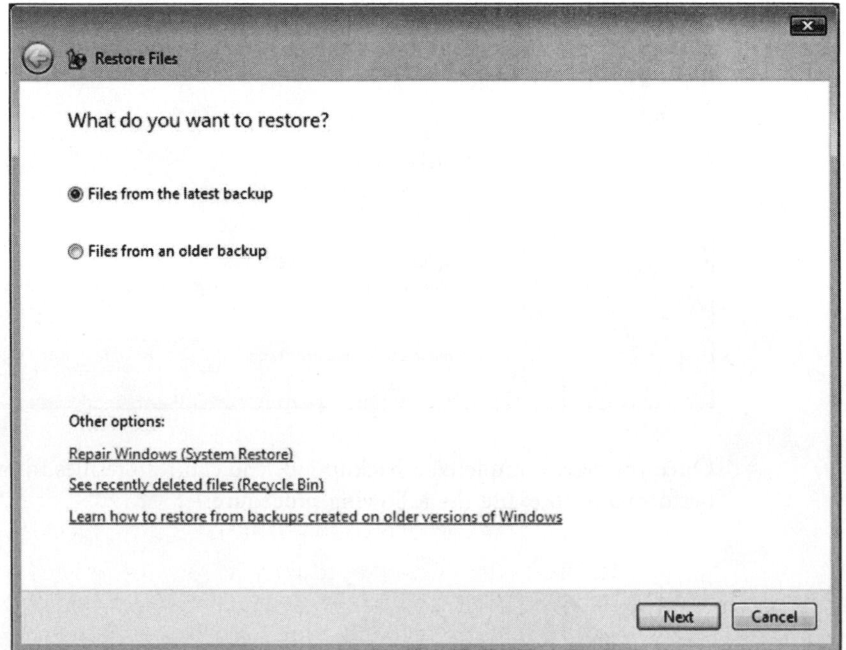

4. Select the **Files from the latest backup** radio button and then click **Next.** The *Select the files and folders to restore* page appears, as shown in Figure 4-42.

Figure 4-42

The Select the files and folders to restore page

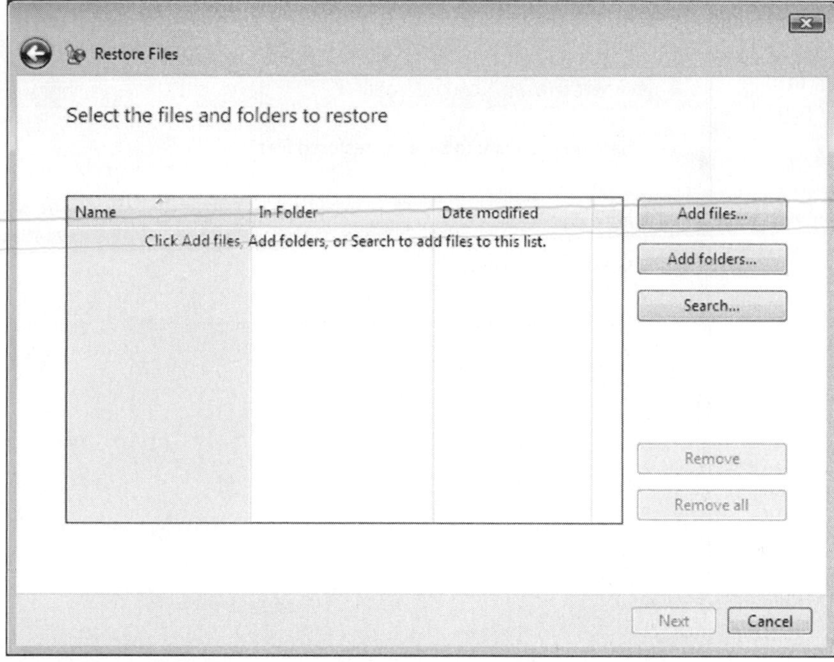

5. Click **Add files.** The *Add files to restore* dialog box appears, as shown in Figure 4-43.

Figure 4-43

The Add files to restore dialog box

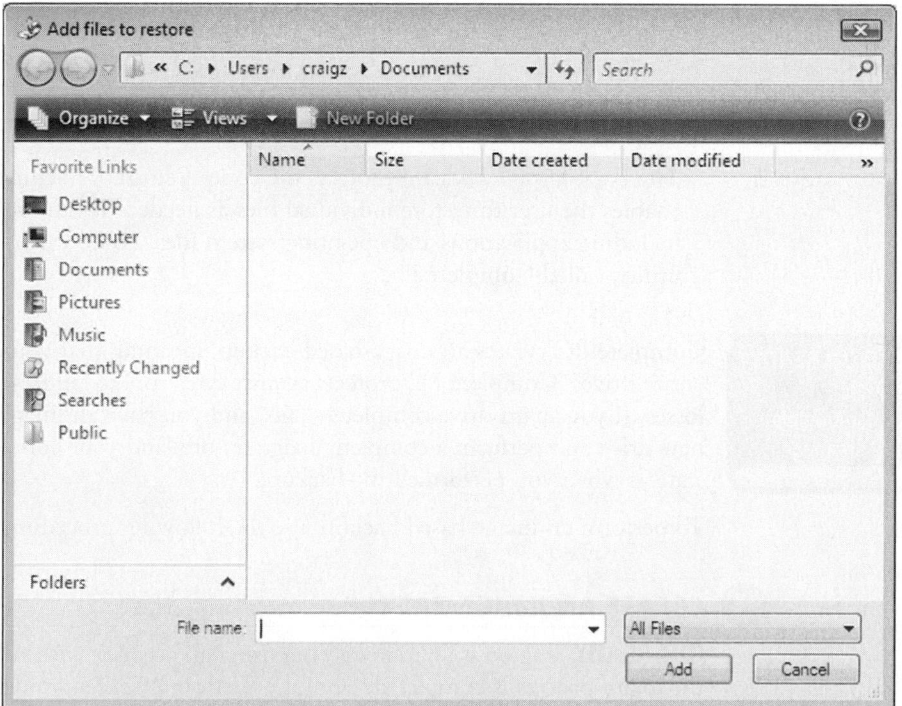

6. Browse to Computer > C: and select a file to restore. Then click **Add.** The file appears in the *Select the files and folders to restore* page. You can add or search for additional files and folders that you want to restore.

7. Click **Next.** The *Where do you want to save the restored files?* page appears, as shown in Figure 4-44. Select the **In the following location** radio button and then key **C:** in the text box. Select the *Restore the files to their original subfolders* checkbox if

you want the wizard to recreate the directory structure from the restored files' original locations. Select *Create a subfolder for the drive letter* to create an additional subfolder named for the drive where the restored file was originally stored.

Figure 4-44

The Where do you want to save the restored files? page

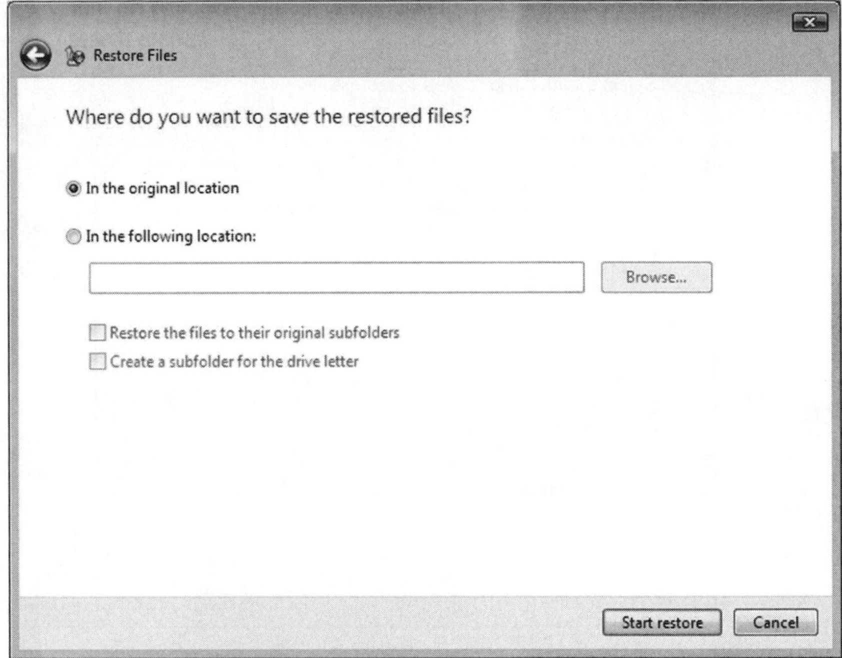

8. Click **Start restore**.

The wizard executes the restore job and displays a page indicating its success or failure.

Using Complete PC

The Back Up Files wizard protects the computer user's documents and data files, and enables the user to restore individual files as needed. It cannot back up the entire system, including applications and operating system files. To do this, you must use a separate utility, called Complete PC.

CERTIFICATION READY? Configure Data Protection: Use Complete PC to create an image 6.4

Complete PC creates an image-based backup, meaning that you can only back up and restore entire drives. Complete PC protects against catastrophic failures, such as complete hard drive losses. If your hard drive completely fails, and you have an image backup, you can install a new drive and perform a complete image restore, and your computer will be left in the same state as when you performed the backup.

To perform an image-based backup, use the following procedure:

CREATE AN IMAGE BACKUP

GET READY. Log on to Windows Vista using an account with Administrator privileges. When the logon process is completed, close the Welcome Center window and any other windows that appear.

1. Click **Start** > **All Programs** > **Accessories** > **System Tools**, and then select **Backup Status and Configuration**. The Backup Status and Configuration window appears.
2. In the left pane, select **Complete PC Backup**.
3. Click **Create a Backup Now**. After confirming your credentials, the program searches for devices with sufficient space for the backup and the *Where do you want to save your backup?* page appears, as shown in Figure 4-45.

Figure 4-45

The Where do you want to save your backup? page

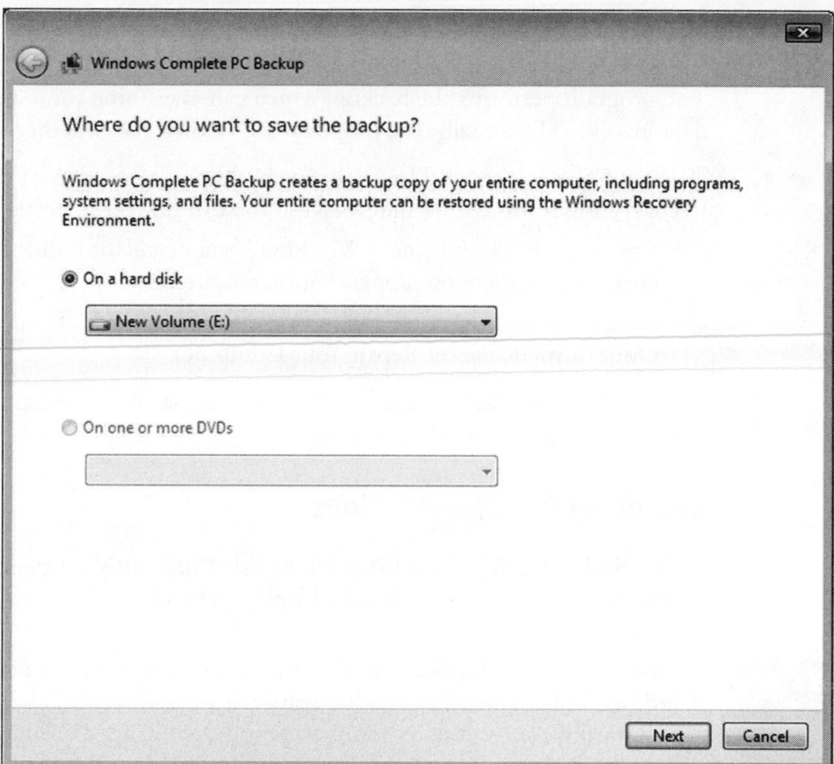

4. Select the appropriate radio button to choose whether you want to back up to a hard disk or DVDs, and then specify which drive or network location you want to use. Then click **Next**. The *Which disks do you want to include in the backup?* page appears.
5. Select or clear the checkboxes to indicate which drives you want to include in the backup job. The system drive is included by default, and cannot be deselected. Then click **Next** to continue. The *Confirm your backup settings* page appears, as shown in Figure 4-46.

Figure 4-46

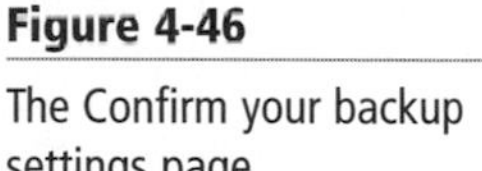

The Confirm your backup settings page

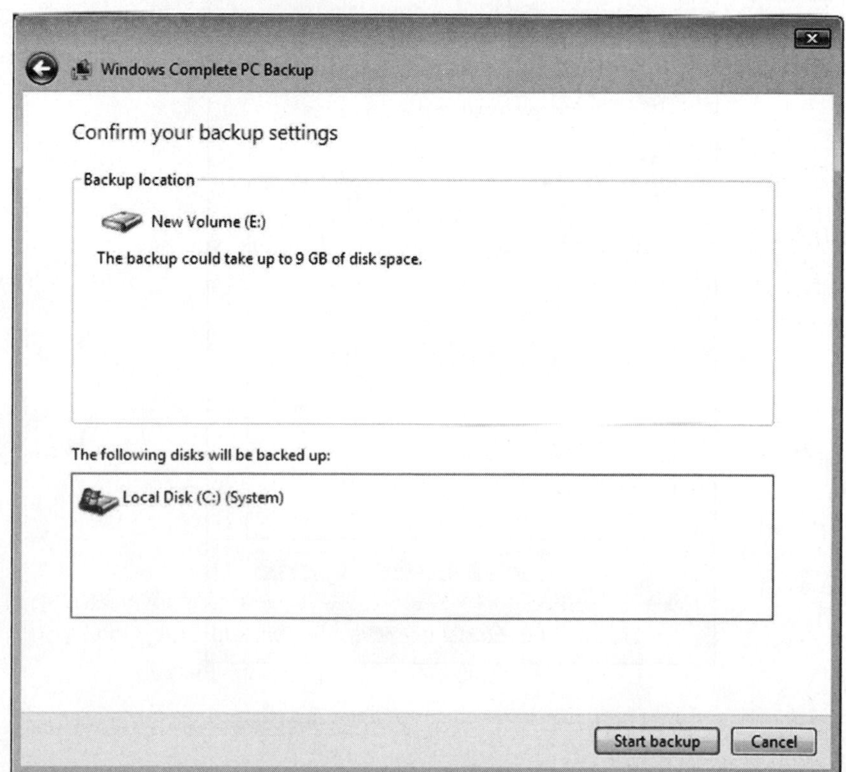

6. Click **Start backup**.

The program performs the backup, which can take some time, depending on the amount of data involved. Eventually, the program will inform you whether the backup was successful.

To restore the computer from an image backup, you must boot the system into the Windows Recovery Environment (Windows RE). You can do this in either of the following ways:

- Start the computer using a Windows Vista installation disk and, after selecting your language settings, choose Repair Your Computer.
- Restart the computer and press F8 as Windows loads. Then, from the Advanced Boot Options menu, select Repair Your Computer.

In either case, you will have to specify the location of the backup, and then you will be able to restore the system to the computer.

Restoring Previous Versions

The Back Up Files Wizard is one method Windows Vista has of saving previous versions of files; the other method is called shadow copies.

Shadow copies are duplicates of files that Windows creates as part of a restore point. If Windows Vista's System Protection feature is turned on (which it is by default), the system automatically creates restore points at periodic intervals. During the creation of a restore point, Windows creates shadow copies of files that have been added or modified and saves them in a cache.

If you should accidentally damage or delete one of the files that has been protected with either a backup or a shadow copy, you can restore one of the previous versions by opening its Properties dialog box (or that of its parent) and clicking the Previous Versions tab, as shown in Figure 4-47.

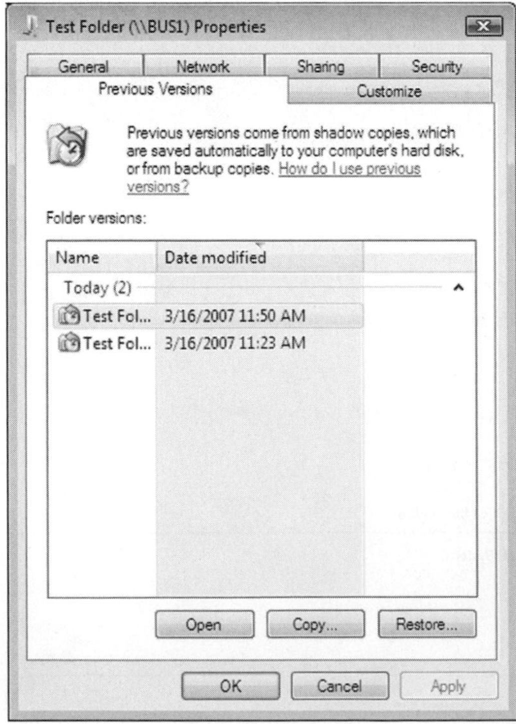

Figure 4-47

The Previous Versions tab of a Properties dialog box

SUMMARY SKILL MATRIX

IN THIS LESSON YOU LEARNED:
Windows Vista uses two hard disk partition styles: MBR and GPT.
Windows Vista supports two disk types: basic disks and dynamic disks.
Basic disks can have up to four partitions: three primary partitions and a fourth usually being an extended partition, on which you can create multiple logical drives.
Windows Vista supports three types of dynamic volumes: simple, spanned, and striped.
You use the Disk Management snap-in for MMC to manage disks.
Windows Vista has several sets of permissions, which operate independently of each other, including NTFS permissions, share permissions, registry permissions, and Active Directory permissions.
NTFS permissions enable you to control access to files and folders by specifying just what tasks individual users can perform on them.
Share permissions provide rudimentary access control for all of the files on a network share.
The Back Up Files Wizard protects users' document files and enables them to restore single files as needed.
The Complete PC utility creates image backups of the entire system, which the user can restore in the event of a catastrophic disk failure.

■ Knowledge Assessment

Fill in the Blank

Complete the following sentences by writing the correct word or words in the blanks provided.

1. If a user has the Deny Full Control permission for the root of the D: drive and the Allow Full Control permission for D:\Documents, then the user's effective permissions for D:\Documents will be ______________ Full Control.
2. The two sources for the files listed in the Previous Versions tab are ______________ and ______________.
3. To back up an entire Windows Vista system, including the operating system and application files, you must use the ______________ utility.
4. In the NTFS permission system, ______________ permissions are actually combinations of ______________ permissions.
5. In Windows, the ______________ file system is limited to volumes no larger than 32 gigabytes.
6. When no users have NTFS permissions to access a particular file, the only person who can regain access to it is the ______________.
7. To create a fourth primary partition on a basic disk, you must use the ______________ utility.
8. To extend or shrink a partition on a basic disk, you must be a member of the ______________ or ______________ group.
9. The default partition style used by Windows Vista on an x86 computer is ______________.
10. To create a share called DOCS and hide it from network users, you must assign it the name ______________.

True / False

Circle T if the statement is true or F if the statement is false.

T | F 1. There is no way to create a fourth primary partition on a basic disk in Windows.

T | F 2. Striped volumes provide greater fault tolerance than simple volumes.

T | F 3. All dynamic disks have only one partition on them.

T | F 4. A security principal is the person granting permissions to network users.

T | F 5. NTFS permissions always take precedence over share permissions.

T | F 6. All permissions are stored in the access control list of the element being protected.

T | F 7. When you have an image backup of a system made with Complete PC, you must use Windows RE to restore individual files.

T | F 8. You cannot convert an MBR disk to a GPT disk without erasing all data on the disk.

T | F 9. You cannot extend a striped volume unless it is on a dynamic disk.

T | F 10. To convert a dynamic disk to a basic disk, you must first delete all of the partitions.

Review Questions

1. Explain the difference between a spanned volume and a striped volume, and specify which (if any) provides increased performance and/or fault tolerance.
2. Explain the differences between the Back Up Files Wizard and the Complete PC backup utility.

Case Scenarios

Scenario #1: Assigning Permissions

You are working the help desk for a corporate network and you receive a call from a user named Leo, who is requesting access to the files for a new classified project called Trinity. The Trinity files are stored in a shared folder on a file server, which is locked in a secured underground data storage facility in New Mexico. After verifying that the user has the appropriate security clearance for the project, you create a new group on the file server called TRINITY_USERS and add Leo's user account to that group. Then, you add the TRINITY_USER group to the access control list for the Trinity folder on the file server, and assign the group the following NTFS permissions:

- Allow Modify
- Allow Read & Execute
- Allow List Folder Contents
- Allow Read
- Allow Write

Some time later, Leo calls you back to tell you that while he is able to access the Trinity folder and read the files stored there, he has been unable to save changes back to the server. What is the most likely cause of the problem?

Scenario #2: Lost File

Heidi, a junior desktop technician, approaches you, her supervisor, ashen-faced. A few minutes earlier, the president of the company called the help desk and asked Heidi to give his new assistant the permissions needed to access his personal budget spreadsheet. As she was attempting to assign the permissions, she accidentally deleted the BUDGET_USERS group from the spreadsheet's access control list. Heidi is now terrified because that group was the only entry in the file's ACL. Now, no one can access the spreadsheet file, not even the president or the Administrator account. Is there any way to gain access to the file, and if so, how?

Working with Users and Groups

LESSON 5

OBJECTIVE DOMAIN MATRIX

TECHNOLOGY SKILL	OBJECTIVE DOMAIN	OBJECTIVE NUMBER
Introducing User Account Control	Configure and troubleshoot User Account Control	3.1
Understanding User Account Control	Configure and troubleshoot User Account Control	3.1
Understanding Recommended UAC Practices	Configure and troubleshoot User Account Control • Configure user accounts to run as standard users	3.1
Performing Administrative Tasks with a Standard User Account	Configure and troubleshoot User Account Control • Elevate user privileges	3.1
Configuring User Account Control	Configure and troubleshoot User Account Control • Use local security policies to configure User Account Control • Disable Secure Desktop	3.1

KEY TERMS

Active Directory
Admin Approval Mode
authentication
authorization
credential prompt
Directory service
domain
domain controller
elevation prompt
group
mandatory user profile
roaming user profile
secure desktop
snap-in
special identity
User Account Control (UAC)
user rights
virtualization
workgroup

Working with Users and Groups

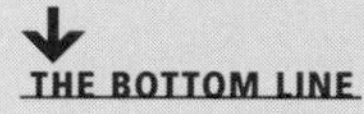

The user account is the fundamental unit of identity in the Windows operating systems. When referring to computers, the term *user* has two meanings: it can refer to the human being that is operating the computer, or it can be an operating system element that represents a single human user.

From a programming perspective, a user account is a relatively simple construct, no more than a collection of properties that apply to the human being or other entity that the user account represents. These properties can include information about the user, such as names and contact information, and identifying characteristics, such as passwords.

MORE INFORMATION

Most user accounts represent humans, but Windows also employs user accounts to provide system processes and applications with access to secured resources. These accounts are no different from standard user accounts structurally; the only difference is that they are created and managed automatically by the operating system or an application.

As an operating system element, the user account and its properties are vital components in two of the most important Windows functions:

- ***Authentication***–the process of verifying that the identity of the person operating the computer is the same as the user account the person is employing to gain access. Typically, to be authenticated, the human user must supply some piece of information associated with the user account, such as a password, demonstrate some personal characteristic, such as a fingerprint, or prove access to an identifying possession, such as a smart card.
- ***Authorization***–the process of granting an authenticated user a specific degree of access to specific computer or data resources. A user account includes permissions that grant the human user access to files and folders, printers, and other Windows resources.

The first thing a human user does with a Windows system is authenticate him- or herself, a process typically referred to as logging on. The human user specifies the name of a user account and supplies a password or other identifying token. Once the authentication is successful, the person is known by that user name throughout the Windows session, and the operating system grants access to specific resources using that name.

As the authenticated user begins working with the operating system, the authorization process occurs whenever the user attempts to access certain resources or perform specific tasks. All of the Windows permission systems, including NTFS, share, registry, and ***Active Directory*** permissions, are user-based. The access control list (ACL) for each permission-protected resource contains a list of users and the degree of access each user is granted to the resource.

Another user-based Windows element, completely separate from the permission systems, is called ***user rights***. User rights are specific operating system tasks, such as Shut Down the System or Allow Log On Through Terminal Services, which can only be performed by certain users designated by a system administrator.

A ***group*** is another type of entity that Windows uses to represent a collection of users. System administrators can create groups for any reason and with any name, and then use them just as they would a user account. Any permissions or user rights that an administrator assigns to a group are automatically inherited by all of the members of the group.

MORE INFORMATION

The concept of group inheritance is one of the fundamental principles of network administration. On all but the smallest networks, administrators typically assign permissions to groups, rather than individual users, and then control access by adjusting group memberships. For example, if a person performing a particular job needs access to a variety of different network resources, it might take an administrator some time to assign all of the rights and permissions that person needs to an individual user account. Later, if that job should be taken over by another person, the administrator has to go through the entire process again twice, once to remove the rights and permissions from the old user's account and once to grant the same rights and permissions to the new user. By creating a group to represent the job, the administrator only has to grant the rights and permissions to the group once. When someone new takes over the job, the administrator only has to remove the departed user from the group and add the new user.

Understanding Local and Domain Users

The concept of users and groups is complicated in Windows because there are two completely separate user account systems: local users and domain users. Which user account system a Windows computer uses depends on whether it is a member of a workgroup or an Active Directory domain.

Windows Vista supports two types of networks, workgroups and domains, as described in the following sections.

INTRODUCING THE WORKGROUP

A ***wo**rkgroup* is a collection of computers that are all peers. A peer network is one in which every computer can function as both a server, by sharing its resources with other computers, and a client, by accessing the shared resources on other computers.

On a workgroup network, each computer has its own set of users and groups that it uses to control access to its own resources. For example, if you want to use one computer to access resources on all four of the other computers on a five-node workgroup network, you must have a user account on each of those four computers. As you connect to each computer, you are authenticated and authorized by each one. If effect, you are logging on to each computer individually.

TAKE NOTE*

Although it is technically a separate authentication process every time a workgroup computer accesses another computer, this does not necessarily mean that users have to supply account names and passwords each time they connect to another computer. If a user has accounts with the same name and password on multiple workgroup computers, then the authentications occur automatically, with no user intervention. This is called ***passthrough authentication***. If the passwords for the accounts are different, however, a manual authentication is necessary for each one.

INTRODUCING THE DOMAIN

A ***domain*** is a collection of computers that all utilize a central directory service for authentication and authorization. A ***directory service*** is a collection of logical objects that represent various types of network resources, including computers, applications, users, and groups. Each object consists of attributes that contain information about the object.

TAKE NOTE*

Do not confuse an Active Directory domain with a Domain Name System (DNS) domain. An Active Directory domain is a collection of Windows computers that are all joined to the Windows directory service. A DNS domain is a collection of Internet host names used by computers that can be running any operating system.

To create a domain, you must have at least one Windows server with the Active Directory directory service installed. This server is called a ***domain controller***. Each of the workstation computers then joins the domain, and is represented by a computer object. In the same way, administrators create user objects that represent human users. The main difference between a domain and a workgroup is that users log on to the domain once, rather than each computer individually. When users attempt to access network resources, the individual computers hosting the resources send authorization requests to the domain controller, rather than handling the authorizations themselves.

DIFFERENTIATING LOCAL AND DOMAIN USERS

The primary advantage of a domain over a workgroup is that administrators only have to create one user account for each person, while workgroups can require many different user accounts for one person. If, on a workgroup network, a user's password is compromised, someone must change that password on every computer where that user has an account. On a domain, there is only one user account for each person, so only one password change is needed.

Windows Vista computers always have a need for local user accounts, if for no other reason than for administrative access to the system. For networking purposes, though, it is typical to use local user accounts or domain user accounts, but not both. Workgroup networks are typically small and informal, with each user administering his or her own computer. Domain networks are usually larger, and have dedicated network administrators responsible for managing user accounts and controlling access to network resources.

Local and domain users are different in several important ways. You use different tools to create and manage the two types of users, and the user accounts themselves are different in composition. As mentioned earlier, a user account consists of attributes, which contain information about the user. Domain users have many more attributes than local users, however.

As a demonstration of this, Figures 5-1 and 5-2 contain the Properties sheets of a local user account and a domain user account. Notice that the local user has only three tabs on its dialog box, while the domain user has 12. This means that the domain user account can store a great deal more information about the user, and can access many more different kinds of network resources.

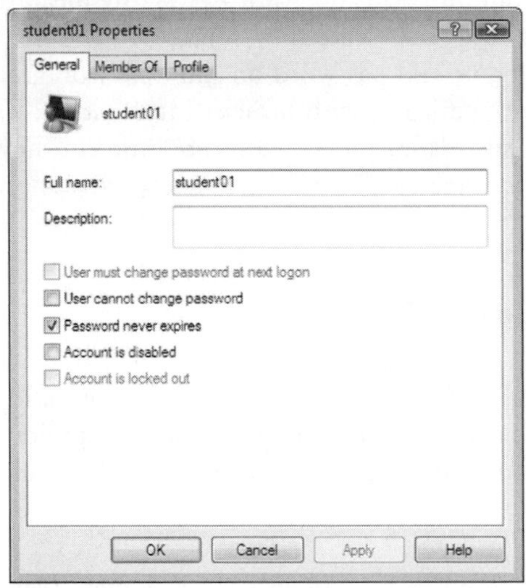

Figure 5-1

The Properties sheet for a local user

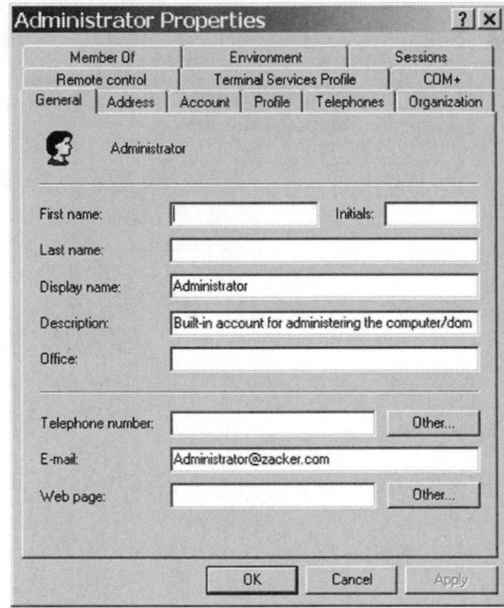

Figure 5-2

The Properties sheet for a domain user

Table 5-1 lists some of the other differences between local and domain users.

Table 5-1

Frequently Asked Questions About Local and Domain Users

	Local Users	Domain Users
What tools do you use to manage the user accounts?	The Local Users and Groups MMC snap-in or the User Accounts control panel	The Active Directory Users and Computers MMC snap-in (supplied with the Windows Active Directory server)
Where are the user accounts stored?	In the Security Account Manager (SAM) on the local computer	On the Active Directory domain controllers
What can you access with the user account?	Local computer resources only	All domain and network resources
What restrictions are there on the user name?	Each user name must be unique on the computer	Each user name must be unique in the directory

As a desktop technician, the type of user accounts you will work with depends on the nature of your clients and their security requirements. Home networks and small businesses are more likely to use workgroup networking, in which case you will be working with local user accounts. Depending on the Windows experience your clients have, you might have to set up all of the user accounts for all of the computers on the network, or you might be able to show the users how to create user accounts on their own computers. Local users are relatively simple to create and manage, and a workgroup network often is a casual affair.

If your client is a medium or large business, it is more likely to be running an Active Directory domain, in which case you will be working primarily with domain user accounts. The question of whether to host a Windows domain is a major decision that is usually made long before desktop technicians become involved in the picture. Hosting a Windows domain is a costly undertaking, both in terms of the additional hardware and software required, and in terms of the time and effort needed for planning and deployment. Desktop technicians are usually limited to implementing plans and policies created by more senior IT specialists.

Introducing Built-In Local Users

As mentioned earlier, Windows Vista (like the other Windows workstation operating systems) always has a need for local user accounts. When you install Vista, you are required to create one user account. In addition, the Setup program automatically creates a number of other user accounts.

The following user accounts are built-in on Windows Vista:

- Administrator–During a typical Windows Vista installation, the Setup program creates an Administrator account and makes it a member of the Administrators group, giving it complete access to all areas of the operating system. However, the Setup program leaves the account in a disabled state and does not assign it a password.
- New User Account–During the operating system installation process, the installer must specify the name for a new user account, to which the Setup program supplies membership in the Administrators group. This grants the new account full access to the operating system. Windows Vista uses this account for its initial logons.
- Guest–This account is designed for users that require only temporary access to the computer, and who do not need high levels of access. The Guest account is disabled, by default, and is a member only of the Guests group, which provides it with only the most rudimentary access to the system.

In addition to these accounts, Windows Vista also creates a number of system and service accounts, none of which you have to manipulate directly.

TAKE NOTE* After the Vista installation is completed, you might want to consider enabling the Administrator account and assigning it a strong password. This will provide you with administrative access to the system, even if your main user account becomes compromised.

Understanding Local and Domain Groups

Just as there are local and domain users, there are local and domain groups as well. Whether local or domain, a group is essentially just a collection of users and, in some cases, other groups. As mentioned earlier, by assigning rights and permissions to a group, you assign those rights and permissions to all of its members.

USING LOCAL GROUPS

When compared to domain groups, local groups are quite simple, and are defined more by what they cannot do than what they can do. Local groups are subject to the following restrictions:

- You can only use local groups on the computer where you create them.
- Only local users from the same computer can be members of local groups.
- When the computer is a member of an Active Directory domain, local groups can have domain users and domain global groups as members.
- Local groups cannot have other local groups as members.
- You can only assign permissions to local groups when you are controlling access to resources on the local computer.
- You cannot create local groups on a Windows server computer that is functioning as a domain controller.

INTRODUCING BUILT-IN LOCAL GROUPS

Windows Vista includes a number of built-in local groups that are already equipped with the permissions and rights needed to perform certain tasks. You can enable users to perform these tasks simply by adding them to the appropriate group. Table 5-2 lists the Windows Vista built-in local groups and the capabilities they provide to their members.

Table 5-2

Windows Vista Built-in Local Groups and Their Capabilities

Built-In Local Group	Group Function
Administrators	Members have full administrative access to the entire operating system. By default, the Administrator user and the user account created during the operating system installation are both members of this group.
Backup Operators	Members have user rights enabling them to override permissions, for the sole purpose of backing up and restoring files, folders, and other operating system elements.
Cryptographic Operators	Members are capable of performing cryptographic operations.
Distributed COM Users	Members are capable of launching, activating, and using Distributed COM objects.
Event Log Readers	Members can read the computer's event logs.
Guests	Members have no default user rights. By default, the Guest user account is a member of this group.
IIS_IUSRS	Group used to provide privileges to dedicated Internet Information Services users.
Network Configuration Operators	Members have privileges that enable them to modify the computer's network configuration settings.
Performance Log Users	Members have privileges that enable them to schedule the logging of performance counters, enable trace providers, and collect event traces on this computer, both locally and from remote locations.
Performance Monitor Users	Members have privileges that enable them to monitor performance counter data on the computer, both locally and from remote locations.

(*continued*)

Table 5-2 (*continued*)

Built-In Local Group	Group Function
Power Users	Members possess the same capabilities as the Users group, plus a limited number of administrative functions, including the ability to run uncertified applications, configure printers and some other system resources, and manage local users and groups.
Remote Desktop Users	Members can log on to the computer from remote locations, using Terminal Services or Remote Desktop.
Replicator	When the computer is joined to a domain, this group provides the access needed for file replication functions. The only member should be a user account dedicated solely to the replication process.
Users	Members can perform most common tasks, such as running applications, using local and network printers, and locking the server. However, members are prevented from making many system-wide configuration changes, whether they do so accidentally or deliberately.

TAKE NOTE*

Some of the built-in local groups in Windows Vista, such as Administrators, Backup Operators, and Remote Desktop Users, are created for the convenience of system administrators so that they can easily grant certain privileges to users. Other groups, such as IIS_USRS and Replicator, are designed to support automated functions that create their own system user accounts. There is no need to manually add users to these groups.

The built-in local groups in Windows Vista, although created by the operating system, are groups like any other. You can modify their properties, change their names, and assign new rights and permissions to them. However, it's a better idea to create your own groups and assign whatever additional rights and permissions you need to them. You can make a single user a member of multiple groups, and the permissions from all of the groups will be combined according to the rules specified in Lesson 4, "Working with Disks."

INTRODUCING SPECIAL IDENTITIES

Another type of element on Windows Vista (and all other Windows operating systems) is a special identity, which functions much like a group. A ***special identity*** is essentially a placeholder for a collection of users with a similar characteristic. For example, the Authenticated Users special identity represents all of the users that are logged on to the computer at a given instant. You can assign rights and permissions to a special identity just as you would to a group.

When the access control list (ACL) for a system resource contains a special identity in one of its access control entries (ACEs), the system substitutes the users that conform to the special identity at the moment the ACL is processed.

TAKE NOTE*

It's important to understand that the set of computers represented by a special identity can change from minute to minute. The Authenticated Users special identity changes every time a user logs on or off, for example. When you assign rights and permissions to a special identity, the users who receive those rights and permissions are not those who conform to the special identity at the time you make the assignment, but rather those who conform to the special identity at the time the special identity is read from the ACL.

Table 5-3 lists the special identities included in Windows Vista.

Table 5-3

Windows Vista Special Identities and Their Constituents

SPECIAL IDENTITY	FUNCTION
Anonymous Logon	Includes all users who have connected to the computer without authenticating.
Authenticated Users	Includes all users with a valid local user account whose identities have been authenticated. The Guest user is not included in the Authenticated Users special identity, even if it has a password.
Batch	Includes all users who are currently logged on through a batch facility such as a task scheduler job.
Creator Group	Includes the primary group of the user who created or most recently took ownership of the resource.
Creator Owner	Includes only the user who created or most recently took ownership of a resource.
Dialup	Includes all users who are currently logged on through a dial-up connection.
Everyone	Includes all members of the Authenticated Users special identity plus the Guest user account.
Interactive	Includes all users who are currently logged on locally or through a Remote Desktop connection.
Network	Includes all users who are currently logged on through a network connection.
Remote Interactive Logon	Includes all users who are currently logged on through a Remote Desktop connection.
Service	Includes all security principals that have logged on as a service.
Terminal Server Users	Includes all users who are currently logged on to a Terminal Services server that is in Terminal Services version 4.0 application compatibility mode.

Creating and Managing Users and Groups

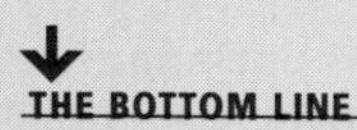

Windows Vista provides two separate interfaces for creating and managing local user accounts: the User Accounts control panel and the Local Users and Groups snap-in for the Microsoft Management Console (MMC). Both of these interfaces provide access to the same Security Account Manager (SAM) where the user and group information is stored, so any changes you make using one interface will appear in the other.

Microsoft designed the User Accounts control panel and the Local Users and Groups ***snap-in*** for computer users with different levels of expertise, and they provide different degrees of access to the Security Account Manager, as follows:

- User Accounts–Microsoft designed the User Accounts control panel for relatively inexperienced end users; it provides a simplified interface with extremely limited access to user accounts. With this interface, it is possible to create local user accounts and modify their basic attributes, but you cannot create groups or manage group memberships (except for the Administrators group).
- Local Users and Groups–Microsoft includes this MMC snap-in as part of the Computer Management console; it provides full access to local users and groups, as well as all of their attributes. Designed more for the desktop technician or system administrator, this interface is not difficult to use, but it does provide access to controls that beginning users generally do not need.

TAKE NOTE*

Both the User Accounts control panel and the Local Users and Groups snap-in are capable of working with local users and local groups only. You cannot create and manage domain users and groups using these tools. To work with domain users and groups, you must use a domain tool, such as Active Directory Users and Groups, which is supplied with the server operating system that is hosting the Active Directory domain.

Using the User Accounts Control Panel

As described earlier, the first local user account on a Windows Vista computer is the one created during the operating system installation process. The Setup program prompts the installer for an account name, and creates a new user account with administrative privileges. The program also creates the Administrator and Guest accounts, both of which are disabled by default.

When the Windows Vista installation process is completed, the system restarts. Because only one user account is available, the computer automatically logs on using that account. This account has administrative privileges, so at this point you can create additional user accounts or modify the existing ones.

CREATING A NEW USER ACCOUNT

To create a new user account with the User Accounts control panel, use the following procedure:

CREATE A NEW USER ACCOUNT

GET READY. Log on to Windows Vista using an account with Administrator privileges. When the logon process is completed, close the Welcome Center window and any other windows that appear.

1. Click **Start**, and then click **Control Panel**. The Control Panel window appears.
2. Click **User Accounts**. The User Accounts window appears, as shown in Figure 5-3.

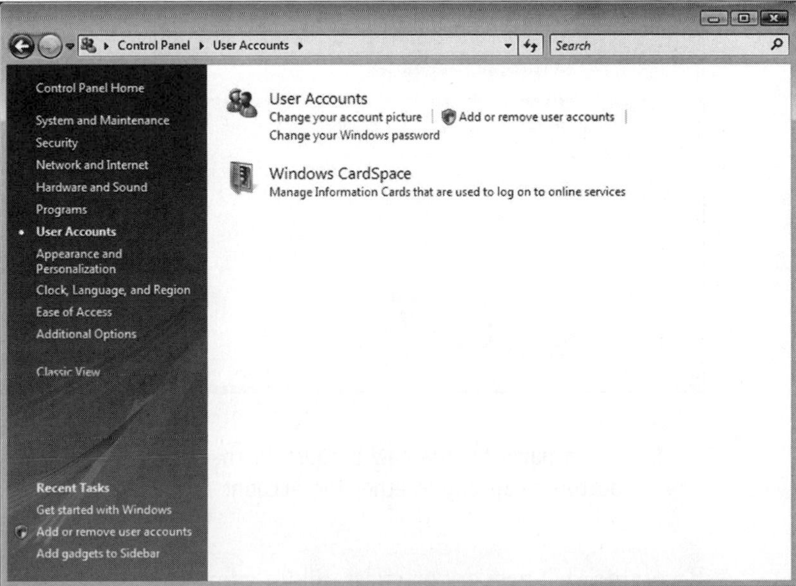

Figure 5-3
The User Accounts window

3. Click **Add or remove user accounts.** After confirming the action, the *Choose the account you would like to change* page appears, as shown in Figure 5-4.

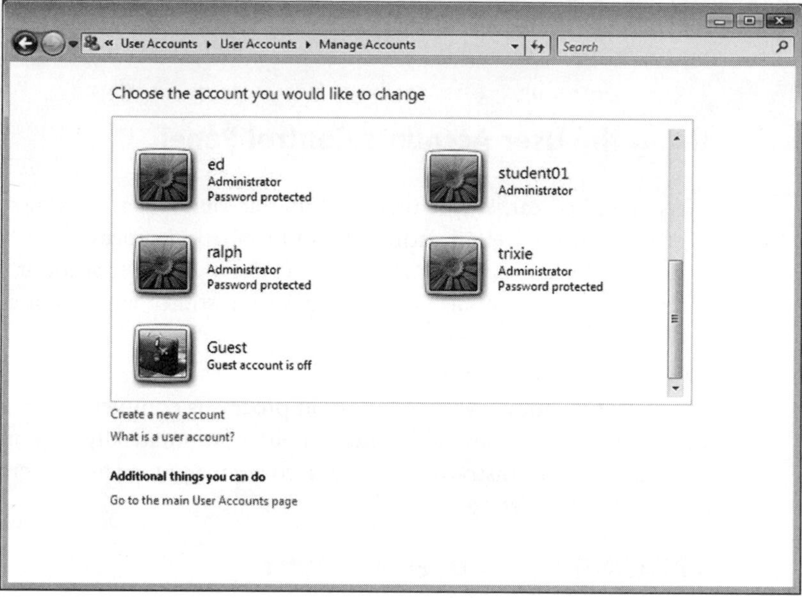

Figure 5-4

The Choose the account you would like to change page

4. Click **Create a new account.** The *Name the account and choose the account type* page appears, as shown in Figure 5-5.

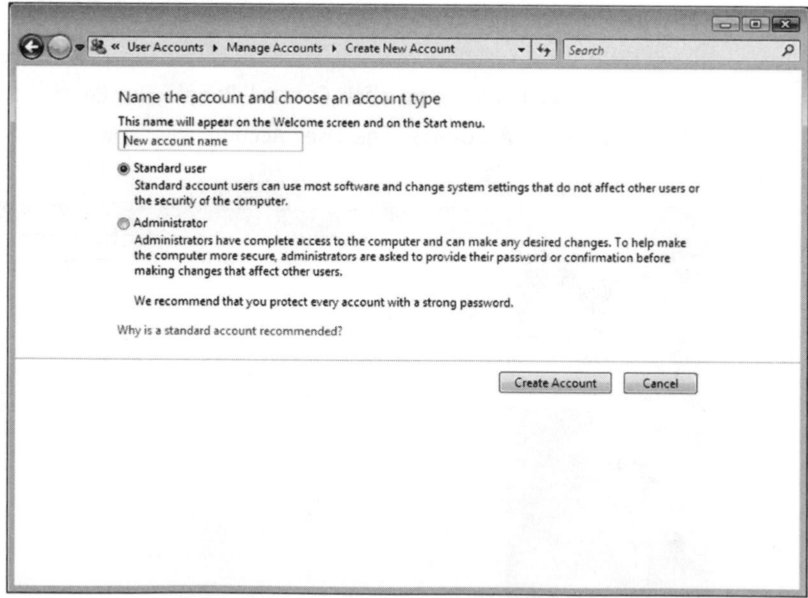

Figure 5-5

The Name the account and choose the account type page

5. Key a name for the new account in the text box, and then choose the appropriate radio button to specify whether the account should be a Standard user or an Administrator.

TAKE NOTE*

Recommended network practices call for administrators to use a standardized system for creating user account names. For example, smaller networks often use the first name followed by the first letter of the surname, such as JohnD. For larger networks with a greater chance of name duplication, use of the first initial plus the surname is common, such as JDoe. The purpose of standardizing user names in this way is to enable any administrator to determine the account name for any user.

WARNING Following this procedure creates an account that is capable of logging on to the system without supplying a password. For security purposes, In all but the most informal circumstances, you should assign a password to all user accounts immediately after creating them.

6. Click **Create Account.**

This procedure provides only the most rudimentary access to the user account attributes. Apart from supplying a name for the account, all you can do is specify the account type.

What the User Accounts control panel refers to as an account type is actually a group membership. Selecting the Standard user option adds the user account to the local Users group, while selecting the Administrator option adds the account to the Administrators group.

Most critically, when you create a new user account with this procedure, the account is not protected by a password. You must modify the account after creating it to specify a password or change any of its other attributes.

MANAGING A USER ACCOUNT

To modify an existing local user account with the User Accounts control panel, use the following procedure:

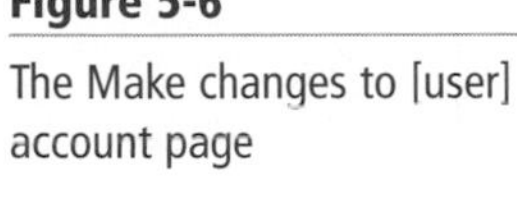

MANAGE USER ACCOUNTS

GET READY. Log on to Windows Vista using an account with Administrator privileges. When the logon process is completed, close the Welcome Center window and any other windows that appear.

1. Click **Start**, and then click **Control Panel.** The Control Panel window appears.
2. Click **User Accounts.** The User Accounts window appears.
3. Click **Add or remove user accounts.** After confirming the action, the *Choose the account you would like to change* page appears.
4. Click one of the existing accounts. The *Make changes to [user] account* page appears, as shown in Figure 5-6.

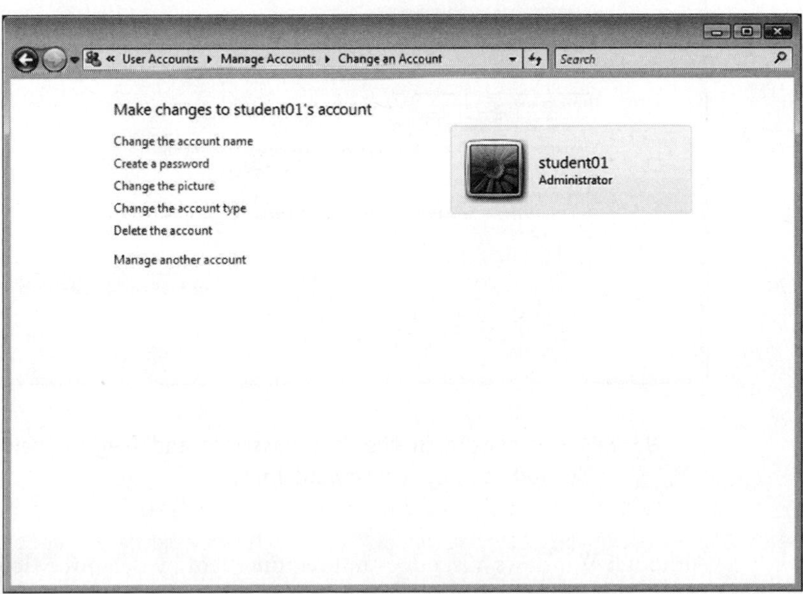

Figure 5-6

The Make changes to [user] account page

5. Click **Change the account name.** The *Type a new account name for [user] account* page appears, as shown in Figure 5-7.

Figure 5-7

The Type a new account name for [user] account page

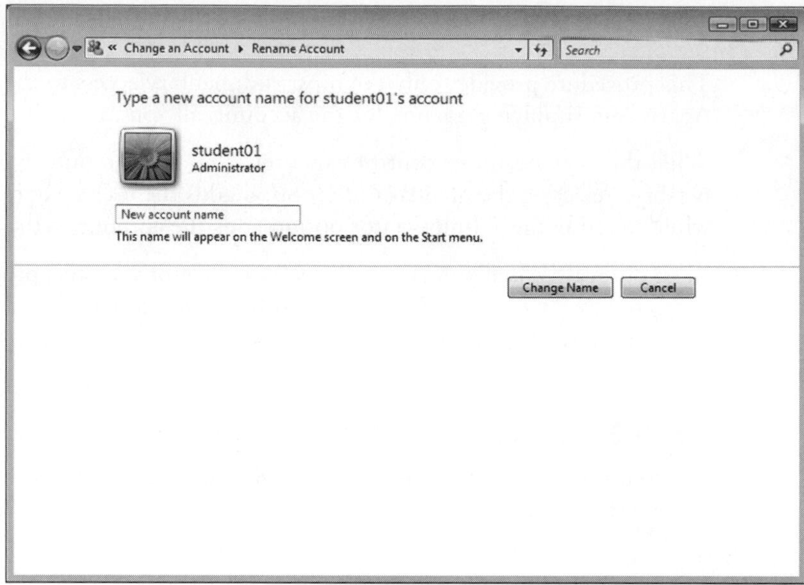

6. Key a new name for the account in the text box, and then click **Change Name**. The *Make changes to [user] account* page reappears.
7. Click **Create a password**. The *Create a password for [user] account* page appears, as shown in Figure 5-8.

Figure 5-8

The Create a password for [user] account page

8. Key a password in the *New password* and *Confirm new password* text boxes and, if desired, supply a password hint.

TAKE NOTE*

Although Windows Vista does not require them by default, Microsoft recommends that you use complex passwords for all user accounts. By the Windows definition, a complex password is one that is at least six characters long, does not contain any part of the user account name, and contains characters from three of the following four categories: uppercase letters, lowercase letters, numbers, and symbols. You can configure Windows Vista to require complex passwords by enabling the Password Must Meet Complexity Requirements policy in the Local System Policies snap-in. For more information, see "Working with Password Policies" later in this chapter.

9. Click **Create password.** The *Make changes to [user] account* page reappears, now with a *Remove the password* option added.

10. Click **Remove the password.** The *Remove a password* page appears, as shown in Figure 5-9.

Figure 5-9

The Remove a password page

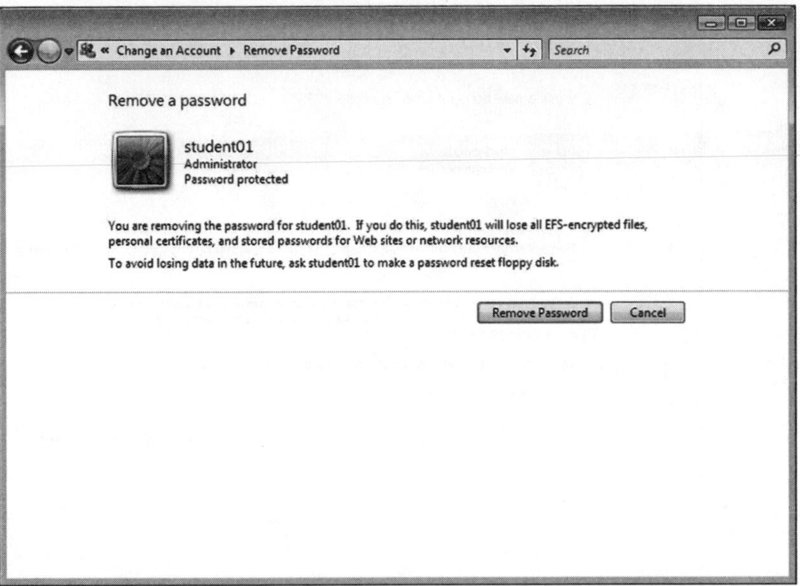

TAKE NOTE*

When an administrator adds, modifies, or removes a user account password, the user loses access to all existing Encrypting File System (EFS) files, personal certificates, and cached Internet and network passwords. Therefore, if you are going to use passwords on your network, administrators should always create them (or have users create them) before they perform any cryptographic activities with the account.

11. Click **Remove Password.** The *Make changes to [user] account* page reappears.

12. Click **Change the picture.** The *Choose a new picture for [user] account* page appears, as shown in Figure 5-10.

Figure 5-10

The Choose a new picture for [user] account page

13. Select a new picture for the account, or click **Browse for more pictures**, and then click **Change Picture**. The *Make changes to [user] account* page reappears.
14. Click **Change the account type**. The *Choose a new account type for [user]* page appears, as shown in Figure 5-11.

Figure 5-11

The Choose a new account type for [user] page

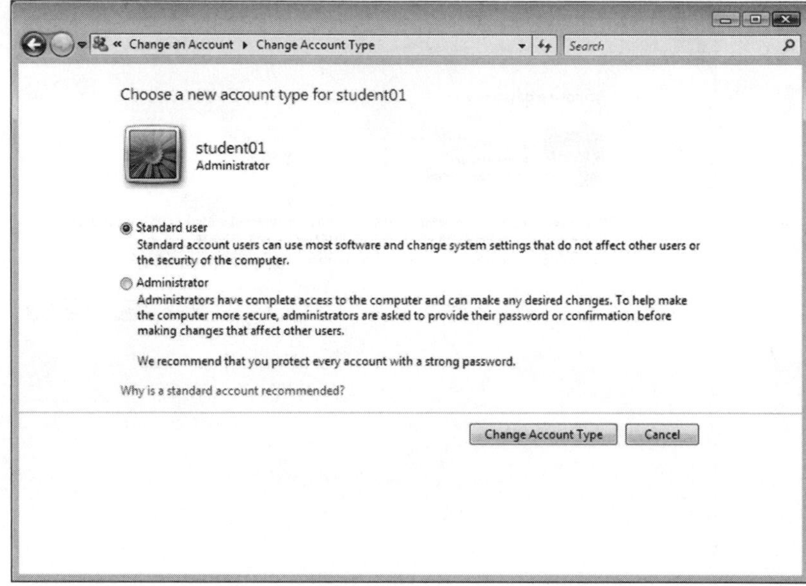

15. Select the **Standard user** or **Administrator** radio button, and then click **Change Account Type**. The *Make changes to [user] account* page reappears.
16. Click **Delete the account**. The *Do you want to keep [user's] files?* page appears, as shown in Figure 5-12.

Figure 5-12

The *Do you want to keep [user's] files?* page

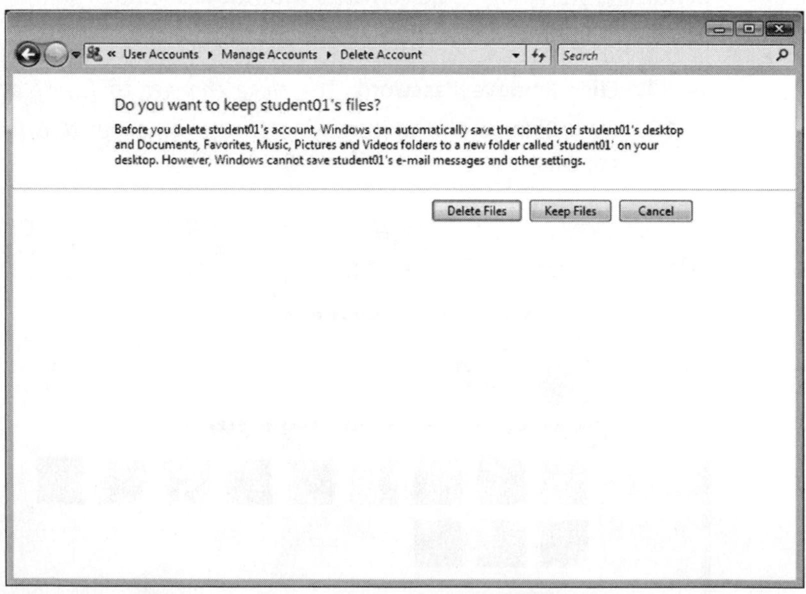

17. Click **Delete Files** to delete the user profile, or click **Keep Files** to save it to the desktop. The *Are you sure you want to delete [user's] account?* page appears, as shown in Figure 5-13.

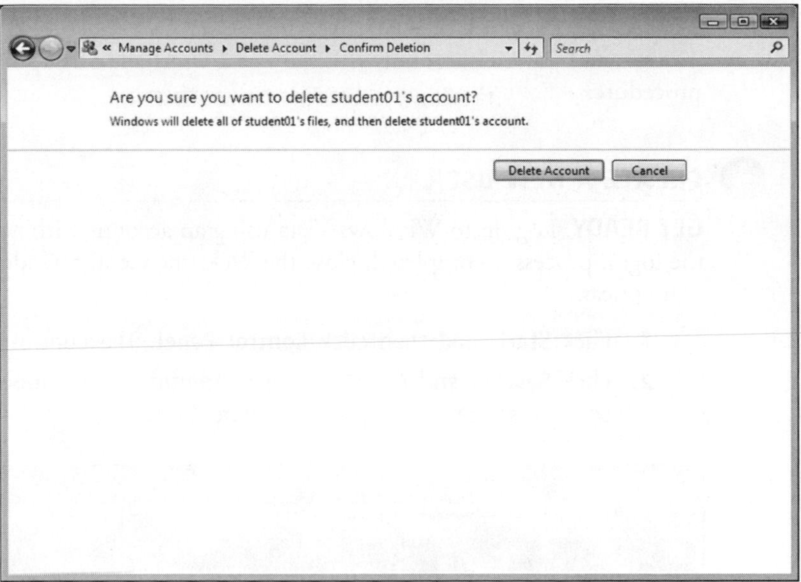

Figure 5-13

The *Are you sure you want to delete [user's] account?* page

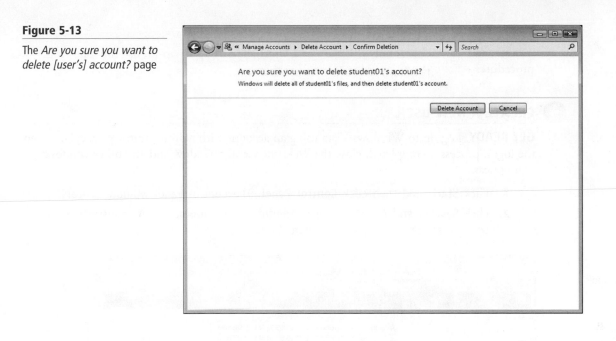

18. Click **Delete Account**. The *Choose the account you would like to change* page reappears.

    CLOSE the User Accounts control panel window.

Using the Local Users and Groups Snap-in

As you might have noticed in the previous sections, the User Accounts control panel provides only partial access to local user accounts, and no access to groups other than members of the Users and Administrators groups. The Local Users and Groups snap-in, on the other hand, provides full access to all of the local user and group accounts on the computer.

The *Microsoft Management Console (MMC)* is a shell application that runs software modules called snap-ins. A shell application has no functions of its own, other than the ability to load and run snap-ins. Many of Windows Vista's administrative tools take the form of MMC snap-ins.

MMC is capable of loading and running multiple snap-ins at once, to create what is called a console. By default, the Local Users and Groups snap-in is part of the Computer Management console. However, you can also load the snap-in by itself, or create your own console with any combination of snap-ins you wish.

OPENING THE LOCAL USERS AND GROUPS SNAP-IN

You can open the Local Users and Groups snap-in in one of three basic ways, as follows:

- Open the Computer Management console from the Administrative Tools control panel.
- Launch Microsoft Management Console (Mmc.exe), choose File > Add/Remove Snap-In, and then select the Local Users and Groups snap-in.
- Open the Run dialog box and then execute the Lusrmgr.msc snap-in file.

Each of these three methods provides access to the same snap-in and the same controls for creating, managing, and deleting local users and groups.

CREATING A LOCAL USER

To create a local user account with the Local Users and Groups snap-in, use the following procedure:

CREATE A NEW USER

GET READY. Log on to Windows Vista using an account with Administrator privileges. When the logon process is completed, close the Welcome Center window and any other windows that appear.

1. Click **Start**, and then click **Control Panel**. The Control Panel window appears.
2. Click **System and Maintenance > Administrative Tools**. The Administrative Tools window appears, as shown in Figure 5-14.

Figure 5-14

The Administrative Tools window

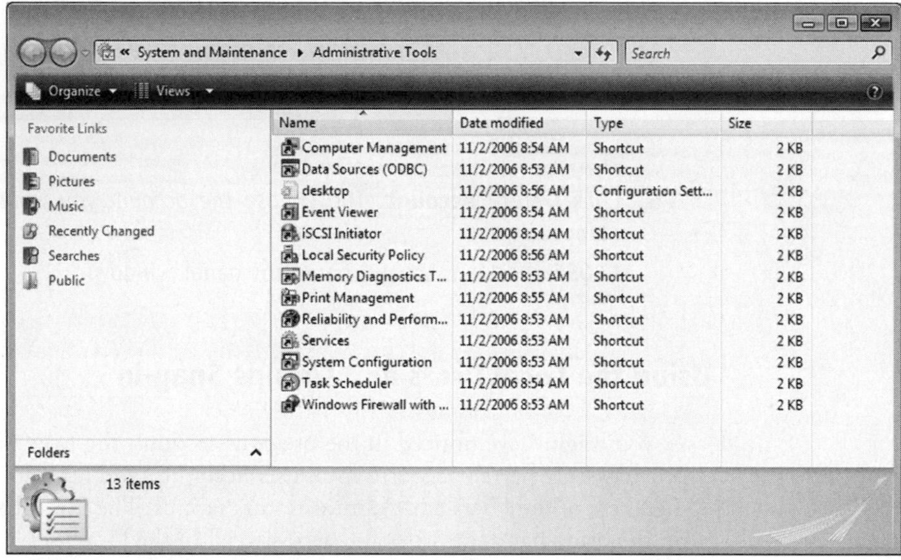

3. Double-click **Computer Management**. After confirming that you want to perform the task, the Computer Management window appears, as shown in Figure 5-15.

Figure 5-15

The Computer Management window

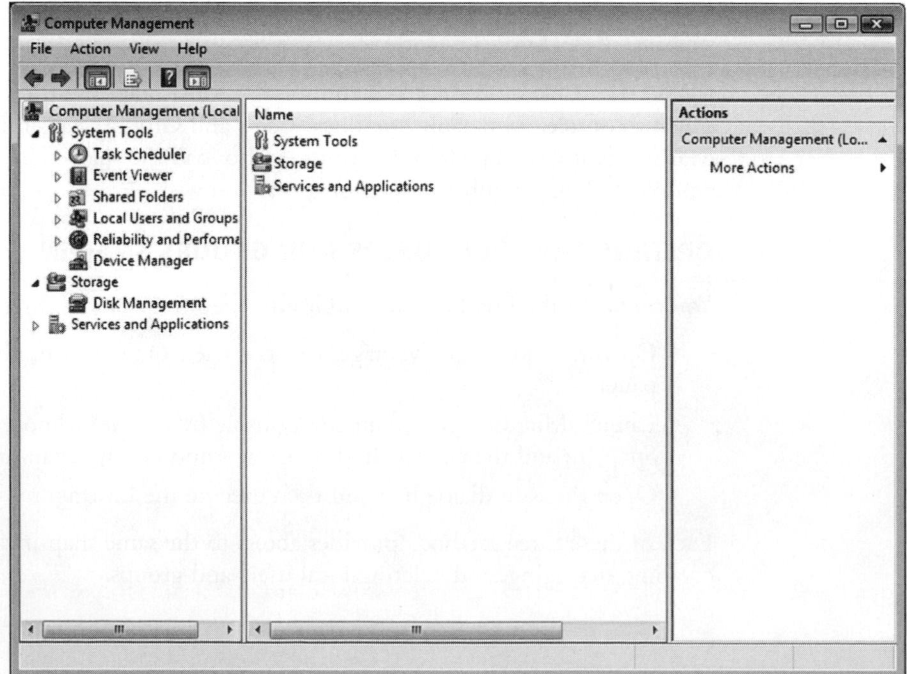

4. In the scope pane of the console (on the left side), expand the Local Users and Groups subheading and click **Users.** A list of the current local users appears in the details pane (in the middle), as shown in Figure 5-16.

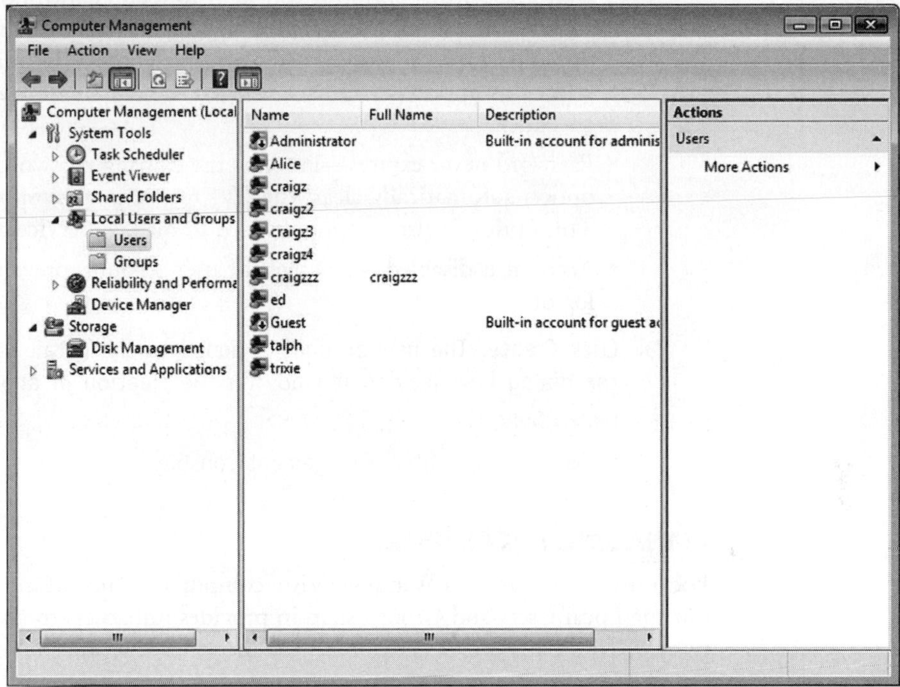

Figure 5-16

The Local Users and Groups snap-in

5. Right-click the **Users** folder and then, from the context menu, select **New User.** The New User dialog box appears, as shown in Figure 5-17.

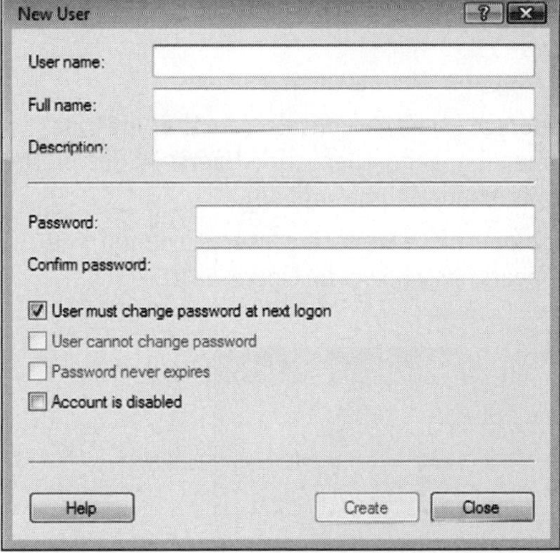

Figure 5-17

The New User dialog box

6. In the User name text box, key the name you want to assign to the user account. This is the only required field in the dialog box.
7. Specify a Full name and a Description for the account, if desired.
8. In the Password and Confirm password text boxes, key a password for the account, if desired.
9. Select or clear the four checkboxes to control the following functions:
   - User must change password at next logon—Forces the new user to change the password after logging on for the first time. Select this option if you want to assign an initial password and have users control their own passwords after the first logon. You

cannot select this option if you have selected the *Password never expires* checkbox. Selecting this option automatically clears the *User cannot change password* checkbox.

- User cannot change password—Prevents the user from changing the account password. Select this option if you want to retain control over the account password, such as when multiple users are logging on with the same user account. This option is also commonly used to manage service account passwords. You cannot select this option if you have selected the *User must change password at next logon* checkbox.
- Password never expires—Prevents the existing password from ever expiring. This option automatically clears the *User must change password at next logon* checkbox. This option is also commonly used to manage service account passwords.
- Account is disabled—Disables the user account, preventing anyone from using it to log on.

10. Click **Create.** The new account is added to the detail pane and the console clears the dialog box, leaving it ready for the creation of another user account.
11. Click **Close.**

CLOSE the Computer Management console.

MANAGING LOCAL USERS

Local user accounts on a Windows Vista computer are not nearly as complex as domain users, but the Local Users and Groups snap-in provides full access to all of the attributes they do possess. To modify a user's attributes, use the following procedure:

MANAGE A USER

GET READY. Log on to Windows Vista using an account with Administrator privileges. When the logon process is completed, close the Welcome Center window and any other windows that appear.

1. Open the Computer Management console.
2. In the scope pane of the console (on the left side), expand the Local Users and Groups subheading, and then click **Users.** A list of the current local users appears in the details pane (in the middle).
3. Double-click one of the existing user accounts. The Properties sheet for the user account appears, as shown in Figure 5-18.

Figure 5-18
A user's Properties sheet

4. If desired, modify the contents of the Full name and Description text boxes.
5. Select or clear any of the following checkboxes:
    - User must change password at next logon—Forces the new user to change the password after logging on for the first time. Select this option if you want to assign an initial password and have users control their own passwords after the first logon. You cannot select this option if you have selected the *Password never expires* checkbox. Selecting this option automatically clears the *User cannot change password* checkbox.
    - User cannot change password—Prevents the user from changing the account password. Select this option if you want to retain control over the account password, such as when multiple users are logging on with the same user account. This option is also commonly used to manage service account passwords. You cannot select this option if you have selected the *User must change password at next logon* checkbox.
    - Password never expires—Prevents the existing password from ever expiring. This option automatically clears the *User must change password at next logon* checkbox. This option is also commonly used to manage service account passwords.
    - Account is disabled—Disables the user account, preventing anyone from using it to log on.
    - Account is locked out—When selected, indicates that the account has been disabled because the number of unsuccessful attempts to log on specified in the local system policies has been exceeded.
6. Click the **Member Of** tab. The interface shown in Figure 5-19 appears.

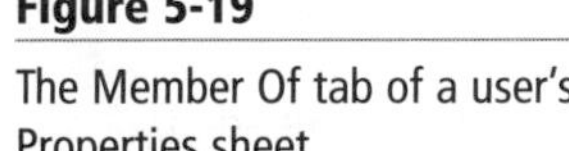

Figure 5-19

The Member Of tab of a user's Properties sheet

7. To add the user to a group, click the **Add** button. The Select Groups dialog box appears, as shown in Figure 5-20.

Figure 5-20

The Select Groups dialog box

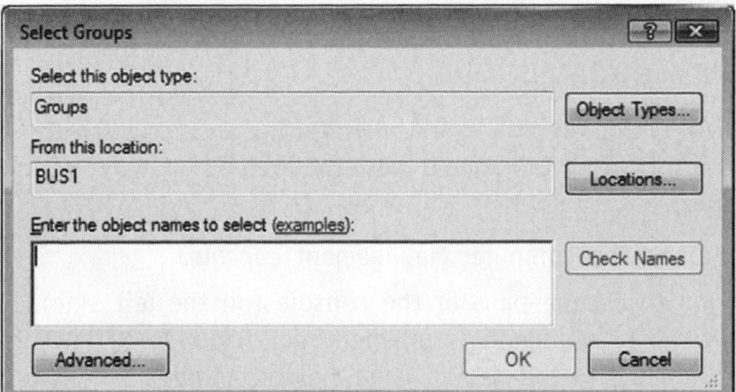

8. Key the name of the group to which you want to add the user in the text box, and then click **OK**. The group is added to the Member of list. You can also key part of the group name and click **Check Names** to complete the name or click **Advanced** to search for groups.
9. Click the **Profile** tab. The interface shown in Figure 5-21 appears.

Figure 5-21
The Profile tab of a user's Properties sheet

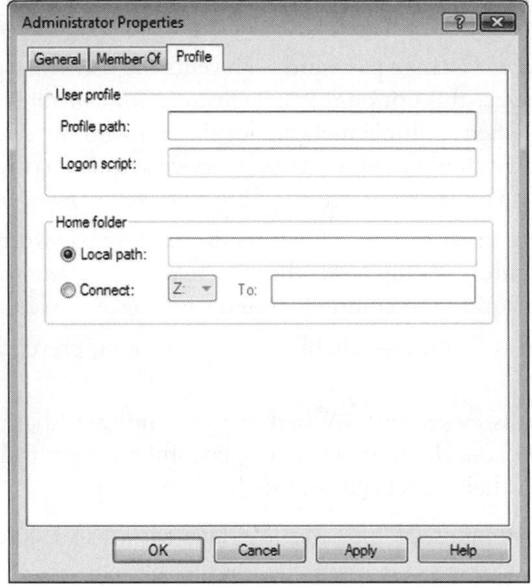

10. Key a path or file name into any of the following four text boxes as needed:
    - Profile path—To assign a roaming or mandatory user profile to the account, key the path to the profile stored on a network share using Universal Naming Convention (UNC) notation.
    - Logon script—Key the name of a script that you want to execute whenever the user logs on.
    - Local path—To create a home folder for the user on a local drive, specify the path in this text box.
    - Connect—To create a home folder for the user on a network drive, select an unused drive letter and key the path to a folder on a network share using Universal Naming Convention (UNC) notation.
11. Click **OK** to save your changes and close the Properties sheet.

CLOSE the Computer Management console.

X REF

For more information on roaming and mandatory user profiles, see "Understanding User Profiles" later in this lesson.

CREATING A LOCAL GROUP

To create a local group with the Local Users and Groups snap-in, use the following procedure:

CREATE A LOCAL GROUP

GET READY. Log on to Windows Vista using an account with Administrator privileges. When the logon process is completed, close the Welcome Center window and any other windows that appear.

1. Open the Computer Management console.
2. In the scope pane of the console (on the left side), expand the Local Users and Groups subheading, and then click **Groups**. A list of the current local groups appears in the details pane (in the middle).

3. Right-click the **Groups** folder and then, from the context menu, select **New Group**. The New Group dialog box appears, as shown in Figure 5-22.

Figure 5-22

The New Group dialog box

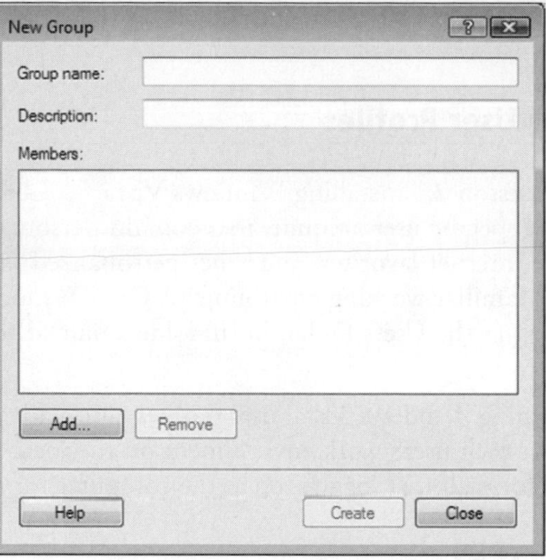

4. In the Group name text box, key the name you want to assign to the group. This is the only required field in the dialog box.
5. If desired, specify a Description for the group.
6. Click the **Add** button. The Select Users dialog box appears, as shown in Figure 5-23.

Figure 5-23

The Select Users dialog box

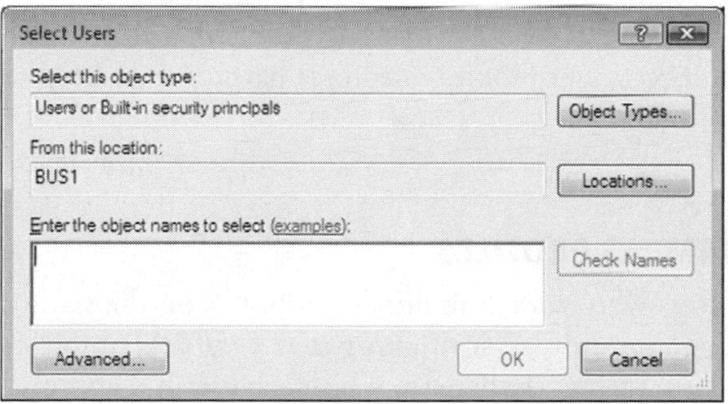

7. Key the names of the users that you want to add to the group, separated by semicolons, in the text box, and then click **OK**. The users are added to the Members list. You can also key part of a user name and click **Check Names** to complete the name or click **Advanced** to search for users.
8. Click **Create** to create the group and populate it with the user(s) you specified. The console then clears the dialog box, leaving it ready for the creation of another group.
9. Click **Close**.

   CLOSE the Computer Management console.

Local groups have no attributes other than a members list, so the only modifications you can make when you open an existing group are to add or remove members. As noted earlier in this lesson, local groups cannot have other local groups as members, but if the computer is a member of a Windows domain, a local group can have domain users and domain groups as members.

TAKE NOTE*

To add domain objects to a local group, you click the **Add** button on the group's Properties sheet and, when the Select Users dialog box appears, change the Object Types and Location settings to those of the domain. Then, you can select domain users and groups just as you did local users in the previous procedure.

Understanding User Profiles

As discussed in Lesson 2, "Installing Windows Vista," a *user profile* is a series of folders, associated with a specific user account, that contain personal documents, user-specific registry settings, Internet favorites, and other personalized information—everything that provides a user's familiar working environment. On a Windows Vista computer, user profiles are stored in the Users folder, in subfolders named for the user accounts.

On computers running Windows Vista, user profiles automatically create and maintain the desktop settings for each user's work environment on the local computer. The system creates a new user profile for each user logging on at the computer for the first time.

USER PROFILE TYPES

The three main types of user profiles are as follows:

- Local user profile—A profile that Windows Vista automatically creates for each user when he or she logs on at the computer for the first time. The local user profile is stored on the computer's local hard disk.
- Roaming user profile—A copy of a local user profile that is stored on a shared server drive, making it accessible from anywhere on the network.
- Mandatory user profile—A roaming profile that users cannot change. Administrators use mandatory user profiles to enforce particular desktop settings for individuals or for a group of users.

USING ROAMING PROFILES

To support users who work at multiple computers on the same network, administrators can create roaming user profiles. A ***roaming user profile*** is simply a copy of a local user profile that is stored on a network share (to which the user has appropriate permissions), so that the user can access it from any computer on the network. No matter which computer a user logs on from, he or she always receives the files and desktop settings from the profile stored on the server.

To enable a user to access a roaming user profile, rather than a local profile, you must open the user's Properties sheet to the Profile tab and specify the location of the roaming profile in the Profile Path field. Then, the next time the user logs on, Windows Vista accesses the roaming user profile in the following manner:

1. During the user's first logon, the computer copies the entire contents of the roaming profile to the appropriate subfolder in the Users folder on the local drive. Having the roaming user profile contents stored on the local drive enables the user access to the profile during later logons, even if the server containing the roaming profile is unavailable.
2. The computer applies the roaming user profile settings to the computer, making it the active profile.
3. As the user works, the system saves any changes he or she makes to the user profile to the copy on the local drive.
4. When the user logs off, the computer replicates any changes made to the local copy of the user profile back to the server where the roaming profile is stored.

WARNING When you create roaming profiles, you must be conscious of the Windows version running on your various network workstations. Windows Vista user profiles are not compatible with earlier versions of Windows, and in the same way, profiles from DOS-based Windows versions (such as Windows 98) are not compatible with Windows XP and other NT-based Windows versions.

5. The next time the user logs on at the same computer, the system compares the contents of the locally stored profile with the roaming profile stored on the server. The computer copies only the roaming profile components that have changed to the copy on the local drive, which makes the logon process shorter and more efficient.

You should create roaming user profiles on a file server that you back up frequently, so that you always have copies of your users' most recent profiles. To improve logon performance for a busy network, place the users' roaming profiles folder on a member server instead of a domain controller.

USING MANDATORY PROFILES

A ***mandatory user profile*** is simply a read-only roaming user profile. Users receive files and desktop settings from a server-based profile, just as they would with any roaming profile, and they can modify their desktop environments while they are logged on. However, because the profile is read-only, the system cannot save any profile changes back to the server when the users log off. The next time the user logs on, the server-based profile will be the same as during the previous logon. Windows Vista downloads the mandatory profile settings to the local computer each time the user logs on. You can assign one mandatory profile to multiple users who require the same desktop settings, such as a group of users who all do the same job. Because the profile never changes, you do not have to worry about one user making changes that affect all of the other users. Also, a mandatory profile makes it possible to modify the desktop environment for multiple users by changing only one profile.

To create a mandatory user profile, you rename the Ntuser.dat file in the folder containing the roaming profile to Ntuser.man. The Ntuser.dat file consists of the Windows Vista system registry settings that apply to the individual user account and contains the user environment settings, such as those controlling the appearance of the desktop. Renaming this file with a .man extension makes it read-only, preventing the client computers from saving changes to the profile when a user logs off.

Introducing User Account Control

One of the most common Windows security problems arises from the fact that many users perform their everyday computing tasks with more system access than they actually need. Logging on as Administrator or as a user that is a member of the Administrators group grants the user full access to all areas of the operating system. This degree of system access is not necessary to run many of the applications and perform many of the tasks users require every day; it is needed only for certain administrative functions, such as installing system-wide software or configuring system parameters.

For most users, logging on with administrative privileges all the time is simply a matter of convenience. Microsoft recommends logging on as a standard user, and using administrative privileges only when you need them. However, many users who do this frequently find themselves encountering situations in which they need administrative access. There is a surprisingly large number of common, and even mundane, Windows tasks that require administrative access, and the inability to perform those tasks can negatively affect a user's productivity.

The recommended practices when a user account has insufficient access to perform a task are as follows:

CERTIFICATION READY?
Configure and troubleshoot User Account Control
3.1

- Ask a user with the required access to perform the task.
- Log off the computer and log on again with an administrative account.
- Use the Run As feature to access a particular system function with administrative privileges.

Many users find these solutions are too much to ask, however, and they find themselves adding their standard user accounts to the Administrators group, just to avoid the repeated interruptions.

The two main problems with this practice are:

1. It grants users the ability to make system-wide configuration changes, install unauthorized software, and potentially compromise the security of the network. For a corporate installation, this can be a major difficulty. Allowing end users to configure their own systems makes it extremely difficult for desktop technicians to troubleshoot problems. Many organizations prefer to enforce strict control over desktop computers to maintain a standard system configuration throughout the enterprise.
2. A computer running with administrative privileges is left wide open to exploits by all kinds of malware (malicious software). If, for example, a user unknowingly downloads an infected file, the potential for damage to the system is far greater if the user is logged on as an administrator at the time, rather than if the user is logged on as a standard user. The same would be true if a burglar broke into the basement of a three-story building. The potential for loss is far greater if all of the floors are unlocked than if the burglar can access only the first floor.

Understanding User Account Control

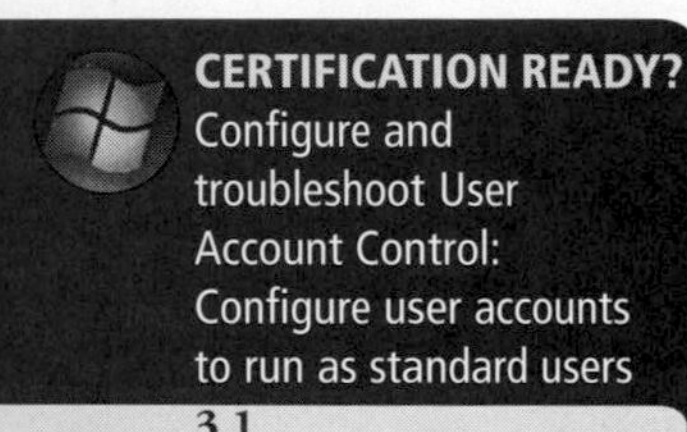

Microsoft decided to solve these problems by keeping all Windows Vista users from accessing the system using administrative privileges unless those privileges are required to perform the task at hand. The mechanism that does this is called ***User Account Control (UAC)***.

When a user logs on to Windows Vista, the system issues a token, which indicates the user's access level. Whenever the system authorizes the user to perform a particular activity, it consults the token to see if the user has the required privileges. In previous versions of Windows, standard users received standard user tokens and members of the Administrators group received administrative tokens. Every activity performed by an administrative user was therefore authorized using the administrative token, resulting in the problems described earlier.

On a Windows Vista computer running User Account Control (UAC), a standard user still receives a standard user token, but an administrative user receives two tokens: one for standard user access and one for administrative user access. By default, the standard and administrative users both run using the standard user token most of the time.

UNDERSTANDING RECOMMENDED UAC PRACTICES

Despite the introduction of UAC, Microsoft still recommends that all Windows users log on with a standard user account, except when they are logging on for administrative purposes only. As compared to earlier Windows versions, Vista and UAC simplify the process by which standard users can gain administrative access, making the user of standard user accounts less frustrating, even for system administrators.

PERFORMING ADMINISTRATIVE TASKS WITH A STANDARD USER ACCOUNT

When a standard user attempts to perform a task that requires administrative privileges, the system displays a ***credential prompt***, as shown in Figure 5-24, requesting that the user supply the name and password for an account with administrative privileges.

Figure 5-24

A UAC credential prompt

PERFORMING ADMINISTRATIVE TASKS WITH AN ADMINISTRATIVE ACCOUNT

When an administrator attempts to perform a task that requires administrative access, the system switches the account from the standard user token to the administrative token. This is known as ***Admin Approval Mode.***

MORE INFORMATION

The decision to run all users with a standard user token was not one that Microsoft made unilaterally. Part of the process of developing UAC involved working with the software developers both at Microsoft and at third-party companies to minimize the number and type of administrative-level access requests made by applications.

Before the system permits the user to employ the administrative token, it requires the human user to confirm that he or she is actually trying to perform an administrative task. To do this, the system generates an elevation prompt. An ***elevation prompt*** is the by-now familiar Allow or Cancel (or Continue or Cancel) message box shown in Figure 5-25. This confirmation prevents unauthorized processes, such as those initiated by malware, from accessing the system using administrative privileges.

Figure 5-25

A UAC elevation prompt

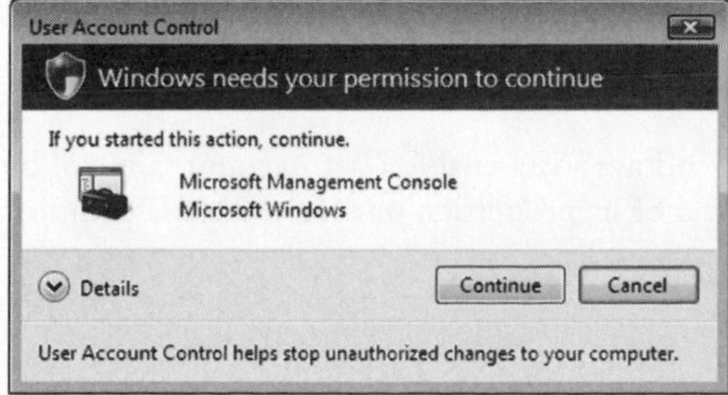

TAKE NOTE*

The system component that is responsible for recognizing the need for elevated privileges and generating elevation prompts is called the Application Information Service (AIS). AIS is a new Windows service that has to be running for UAC to function properly. Disabling this service prevents applications that require administrative access from launching, resulting in Access Denied errors.

Although many users do not notice, there are four elevation prompts that Windows Vista can display in response to a request for administrative access. When an application requests administrative access, Vista evaluates the potential threat the application poses by checking its publisher, and then displays one of the color-coded elevation prompts listed in Table 5-4.

Table 5-4

UAC Elevation Prompts

Color Scheme	Message	Meaning
Red background with an X on a red shield	This program has been blocked.	The application originates from a blocked publisher or has been blocked by Group Policy settings.
Blue/green background with a multicolored shield	Windows needs your permission to continue.	The application is a Windows Vista administrative application, such as a control panel.
Gray background with an exclamation point on a gold shield	A program needs your permission to continue.	The application has been Authenticode signed and is trusted by the local computer.
Yellow background with a question mark on a gold shield	An unidentified program wants access to your computer.	The application is unsigned or has been signed but is not yet trusted by the local computer.

USING SECURE DESKTOP

By default, whenever Windows Vista displays an elevation prompt or a credential prompt, it does so using the secure desktop. The ***secure desktop*** is an alternative to the interactive user desktop that Windows normally displays. When Vista generates an elevation or credential prompt, it switches to the secure desktop, suppressing the operation of all other desktop controls and permitting only Windows processes to interact with the prompt. The object of this is to prevent malware from automating a response to the elevation or credential prompt and bypassing the human reply.

WARNING It is still possible for a malware program to imitate the secure desktop and create its own artificial elevation or credential prompt, but an artificial prompt cannot provide the program with genuine access to administrative functions. The only possible danger is that a malware program could use an artificial credential prompt to harvest administrative account names and passwords from unsuspecting users.

Configuring User Account Control

All versions of Windows Vista enable User Account Control by default, but it is possible to configure several of its properties, or even disable it completely.

When Windows Vista starts, if the AIS service is not running and UAC is disabled, the Windows Security Center warns you of its absence and gives you the opportunity to turn it on. However, the most granular control over UAC properties is through Local Security Policy or, on an Active Directory network, Group Policy.

To configure UAC properties using Local Security Policy, use the following procedure:

CONFIGURE UAC LOCAL SECURITY POLICIES

GET READY. Log on to Windows Vista using an account with Administrator privileges. When the logon process is completed, close the Welcome Center window and any other windows that appear.

1. Click **Start**, and then click **Control Panel**. The Control Panel window appears.
2. Click **System and Maintenance > Administrative Tools**. The Administrative Tools window appears.
3. Double-click **Local Security Policy**. After confirming that you want to perform the task, the Local Security Policy console appears, as shown in Figure 5-26.

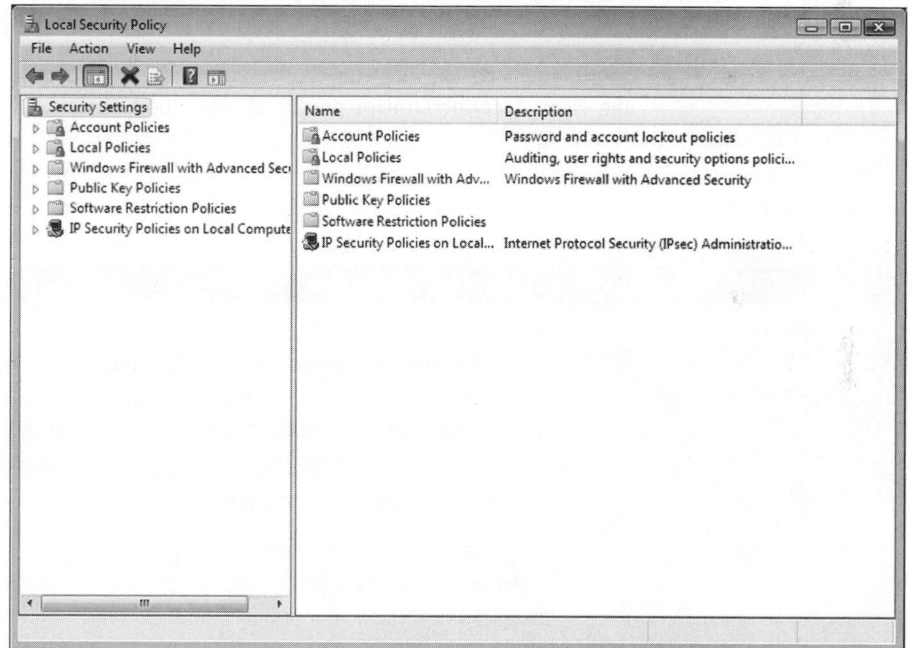

Figure 5-26
The Local Security Policy console

4. Expand the Local Policies header, and then click **Security Options**. A list of Security Options policies appears in the details pane, as shown in Figure 5-27.

Figure 5-27

The Security Options list

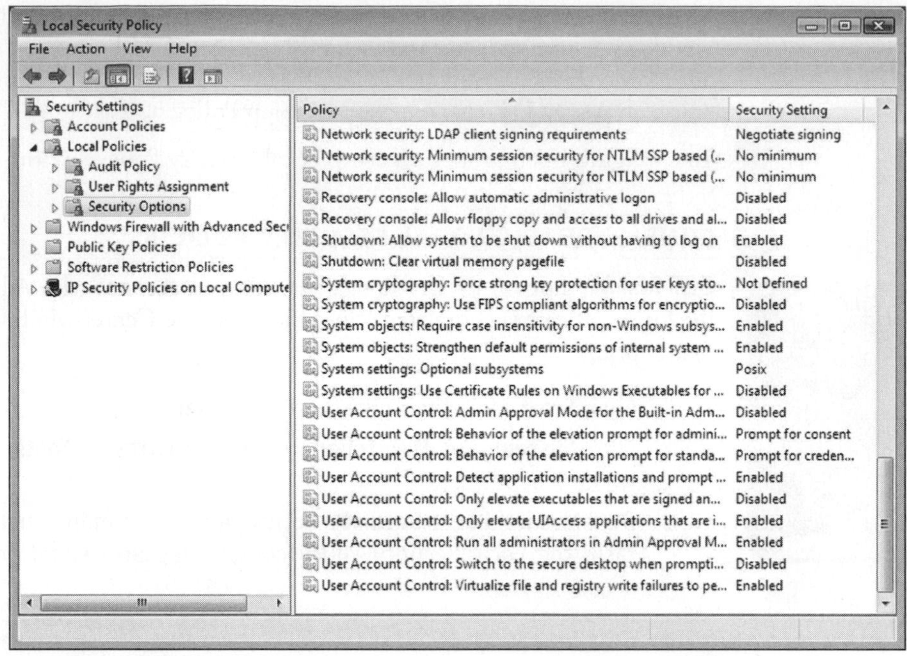

5. Scroll down to the bottom of the policy list until you see the nine policies with the User Account Control prefix, as described in Table 5-5.

Table 5-5

UAC Local Security Policy Settings

POLICY SETTING	VALUES AND FUNCTIONS
User Account Control: Admin Approval Mode for the Built-in Administrator Account	• When enabled, the built-in Administrator account is issued two tokens during logon and runs in Admin Approval Mode. This is the default setting, except in cases of upgrades from Windows XP systems in which the built-in Administrator account is the only active member of the Administrators group. • When disabled, the built-in Administrator account receives only an administrative token, and runs with full administrative access at all times.
User Account Control: Behavior of the Elevation Prompt for Administrators in Admin Approval Mode	• When set to No Prompt, administrative users are elevated to the administrative token with no consent or credentials from the human user. This setting, in effect, disables the security provided by UAC and is not recommended. • When set to Prompt for consent, administrative users are elevated to the administrative token only after the presentation of an elevation prompt and the consent of the human user. This is the default setting. • When set to Prompt for credentials, administrative users are elevated to the administrative token only after the presentation of a credential prompt, to which the user must supply a valid administrative account name and password, even if he or she is already logged on using such an account.
User Account Control: Behavior of the Elevation Prompt for Standard Users	• When set to No Prompt, suppresses the credential prompt and prevents standard users from being elevated to an administrative token. Standard users can perform administrative tasks only by using the Run As program or by logging on using an administrative account. This is the default setting for the Windows Vista Enterprise edition. • When set to Prompt for credentials, standard users attempting to perform an administrative function receive a credential prompt, to which the user must supply a valid administrative account name and password. This is the default setting for the Windows Vista Home Basic, Home Premium, Business, and Ultimate editions.

(continued)

Table 5-5 (*continued*)

POLICY SETTING	VALUES AND FUNCTIONS
User Account Control: Detect Application Installations and Prompt for Elevation	• When enabled, an attempt to install an application causes standard users to receive a credential prompt and administrative users to receive an elevation prompt. The user must supply authentication credentials or consent before the installation can proceed. This is the default setting. • When disabled, elevation and credential prompts are suppressed during application installations, and the installations will fail. This setting is for use on enterprise desktops that use an automated installation technology, such as Microsoft Systems Management Server.
User Account Control: Only Elevate Executables that are Signed and Validated	• When enabled, requires successful public key infrastructure (PKI) signature verifications on all interactive applications that request administrative access. Unsigned applications will not run. • When disabled, both signed and unsigned applications will run. This is the default setting.
User Account Control: Only Elevate UIAccess Applications that are Installed in Secure Locations	• When enabled, Windows Vista will provide access to the protected system user interface only if the executable is located in the Program Files or Windows folder on the system drive. If the executable is not located in one of these folders, access will be denied, despite a positive response to the elevation prompt. This is the default setting. • When disabled, the folder location checks are omitted, so any application can be granted access to the protected system user interface upon successful completion of the elevation prompt.
User Account Control: Run All Administrators in Admin Approval Mode	• When enabled, standard users receive credential prompts and administrative users receive elevation prompts, when either one requests administrative privileges. This policy essentially turns UAC on and off. A change in the value of this policy does not take effect until the system is restarted. This is the default setting. • When disabled, the AIS service is disabled and does not automatically start. This turns UAC off and prevents elevation and credential prompts from appearing. When the system starts, the Windows Security Center warns the user that operating system security is reduced and provides the ability to activate UAC.
User Account Control: Switch to the Secure Desktop when Prompting for Elevation	• When enabled, causes Windows Vista to display all elevation prompts on the secure desktop, which can receive messages only from Windows processes. This is the default setting. • When disabled, causes Windows Vista to display all elevation prompts on the interactive user desktop.
User Account Control: Virtualize File and Registry Write Failures to Per-user Locations	• When enabled, allows non-UAC-compliant applications to run by redirecting write requests to protected locations, such as the Program Files and Windows folders or the HKLM\Software registry key, to alternative locations in the registry and file system. This process is called ***virtualization***. This is the default setting. • When disabled, virtualization is disabled, and non-UAC-compliant applications attempting to write to protected locations will fail to run. This setting is recommended only when the system is running UAC-compliant applications exclusively.

6. Double-click one of the User Account Control policies. The Properties sheet for the policy appears, as shown in Figure 5-28.

Figure 5-28

The Properties sheet of a UAC policy

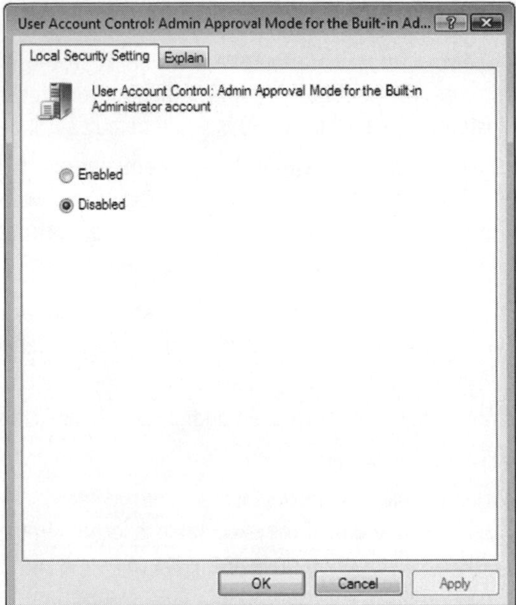

7. Select the radio button (or drop-down list option) for the setting you want the policy to use, and then click **OK**. The Properties sheet closes.
8. Repeat Steps 6 and 7 to configure other policies, if desired.

CLOSE the Local Security Policy console and the Administrative Tools window.

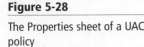

If you are working on an Active Directory network, you can configure the same UAC policies for multiple computers simultaneously by creating a Group Policy object and applying it to a domain, site, or organizational unit.

Securing User Accounts with Local Security Policies

THE BOTTOM LINE

Earlier in this lesson, you learned about user account attributes that you can set while creating or managing the accounts. It is also possible to configure certain aspects of user accounts using Local Security Policy on a standalone Windows Vista computer, or Group Policy on an Active Directory network.

Working with Password Policies

Some of the most common security breaches on Windows computers are directly related to users' password habits.

Password protection can be a highly secure means of protecting data, unless end users are lax in their password maintenance procedures. By enforcing certain password practices using Local Security Policy or Group Policy, you can ensure that your systems remain secure, even though the end users are responsible for their own passwords.

To control passwords using Local Security Policy, use the following procedure:

CONFIGURE PASSWORD POLICIES

GET READY. Log on to Windows Vista using an account with Administrator privileges. When the logon process is completed, close the Welcome Center window and any other windows that appear.

1. Click **Start**, and then click **Control Panel**. The Control Panel window appears.
2. Click **System and Maintenance > Administrative Tools**. The Administrative Tools window appears.
3. Double-click **Local Security Policy**. After confirming you want to perform the action, the Local Security Policy console appears.
4. Expand the Account Policies header, and then click **Password Policy**. A list of password policies appears in the details pane, as shown in Figure 5-29.

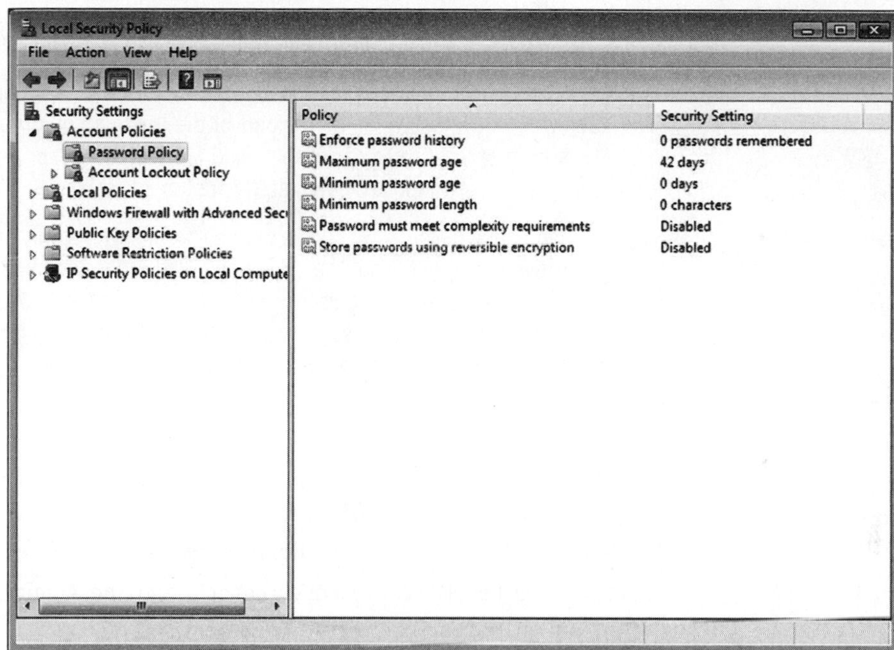

Figure 5-29

The Password Policy list

5. Double-click one of the password policies described in Table 5-6. The Properties sheet for the policy appears, as shown in Figure 5-30.

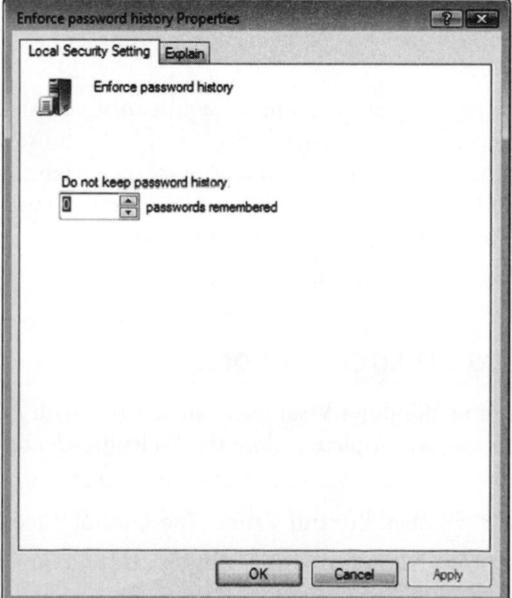

Figure 5-30

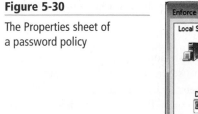

The Properties sheet of a password policy

Table 5-6

Password Policy Settings in Local Security Policy

Password Policy Settings	Values and Function
Enforce Password History	Specifies the number of unique passwords that users have to supply before Windows Vista permits them to reuse an old password. Possible values range from 0 to 24. The default value is 0.
Maximum Password Age	Specifies how long a single password can be used before Windows Vista forces the user to change it. Possible values range from 0 to 999. The default value is 42 days.
Minimum Password Age	Specifies how long a single password must be used before Windows Vista permits the user to change it. Possible values range from 0 to 998. The default value is 0 days.
Minimum Password Length	Specifies the minimum number of characters Windows Vista permits in user-supplied passwords. Possible values range from 0 to 14. The default value is 0.
Password Must Meet Complexity Requirements	When enabled, indicates that passwords supplied by users must be at least six characters long, with no duplication of any part of the user's account name; and must include characters from at least three of the following four categories: uppercase letters, lowercase letters, numbers, and symbols. By default, this policy is disabled.
Store Passwords Using Reversible Encryption	When enabled, causes Windows Vista to store user account passwords using a less effective encryption algorithm. This policy is designed to support authentication protocols that require access to the user's password, such as the Challenge Handshake Authentication Protocol (CHAP). From a security perspective, this policy is functionally equivalent to using plaintext passwords. The default value is disabled.

6. Configure the policy by setting a value using the spin box, radio button, or other control, and then click **OK**. The Properties sheet closes.
7. Repeat Steps 5 and 6 to configure other policies, if desired.

   CLOSE the Local Security Policy console and the Administrative Tools window.

Working with Account Lockout Policies

It is possible to penetrate any password-protected resource, given enough time and an unlimited number of access attempts. This "brute force" approach to password penetration is supported by programs designed to try thousands of different character combinations in an attempt to find the one that matches the password.

Windows Vista can protect against brute force password penetration techniques by limiting the number of unsuccessful logon attempts allowed by each user account. When a potential infiltrator exceeds the number of allowed attempts, the system locks the account for a set period of time. To impose these limits, you can use Local Security Policy for standalone computers, or Group Policy for Active Directory networks.

To set account lockout parameters using Local Security Policy, use the following procedure:

CONFIGURE ACCOUNT LOCKOUT POLICIES

GET READY. Log on to Windows Vista using an account with Administrator privileges. When the logon process is completed, close the Welcome Center window and any other windows that appear.

1. Click **Start**, then click **Control Panel**. The Control Panel window appears.
2. Click **System and Maintenance** > **Administrative Tools**. The Administrative Tools window appears.

3. Double-click **Local Security Policy.** After confirming you want to perform the action, the Local Security Policy console appears.
4. Expand the Account Policies header and click **Account Lockout Policy.** A list of policies appears in the details pane, as shown in Figure 5-31.

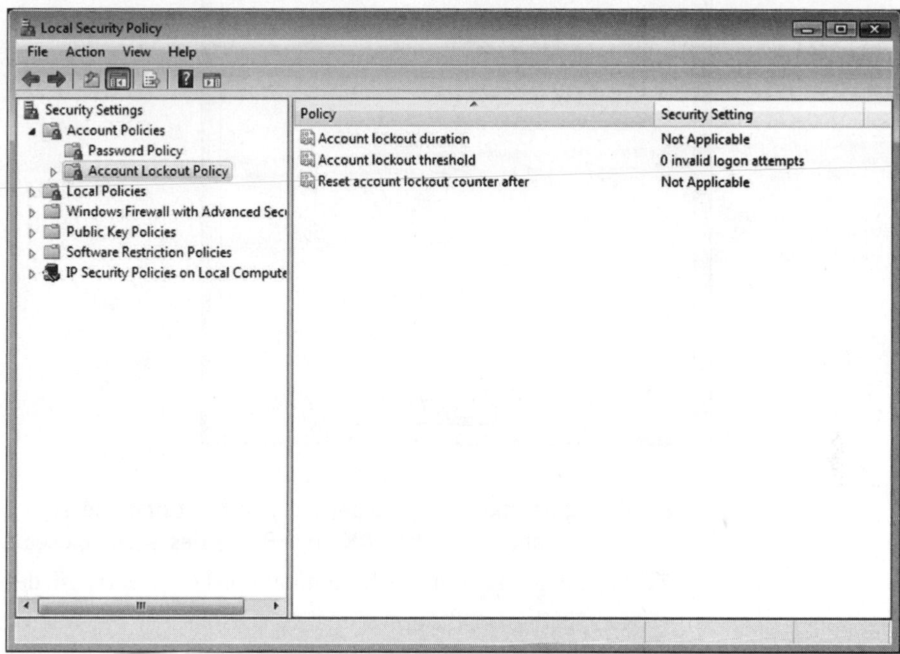

Figure 5-31
The Account Lockout Policy list

5. Double-click one of the policies described in Table 5-7. The Properties sheet for the policy appears, as shown in Figure 5-32.

Table 5-7
Account Lockout Policy Settings in Local Security Policy

Account Lockout Policy Setting	Values and Function
Account Lockout Duration	Determines the period of time that must pass after a lockout before Windows Vista will automatically unlock a user's account. The policy is not set by default, as it is viable only in conjunction with the Account Lockout Threshold policy. Possible values range from 0 to 99999 minutes (about 10 weeks). A low setting (5 to 15 minutes) is sufficient to reduce attacks significantly without unreasonably affecting legitimate users who are mistakenly locked out. A value of 0 requires the user to contact an administrator to unlock the account manually. When the Account Lockout Threshold policy is activated, this policy is activated as well and set to a default value of 30.
Account Lockout Threshold	Specifies the number of invalid logon attempts that will trigger an account lockout. Possible values range from 0 to 999. A value that is too low (as few as three, for example) may cause lockouts due to normal user error during logon. A value of 0 prevents accounts from ever being locked out. The default value is 0.
Reset Account Lockout Counter After	Specifies the period of time that must pass after an invalid logon attempt before the lockout counter resets to zero. Possible values range from 1 to 99999 minutes, and must be less than or equal to the account lockout duration. When the Account Lockout Threshold policy is activated, this policy is activated as well and set to a default value of 30.

Figure 5-32

The Properties sheet of an account lockout policy

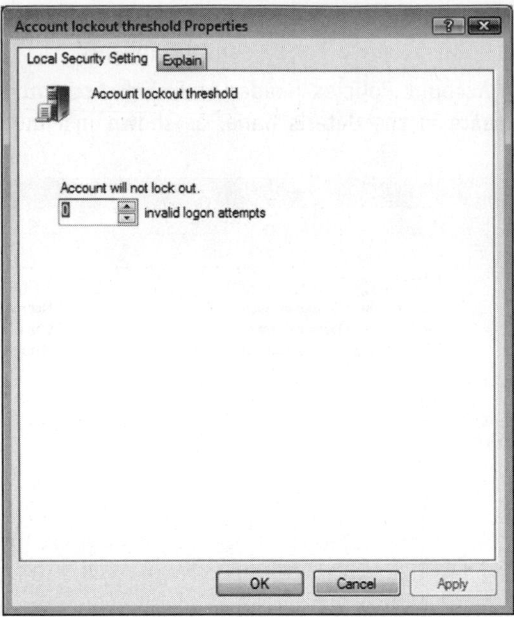

6. Configure the policy by setting a value using the spin box, radio button, or other control and then click **OK**. The Properties sheet closes.
7. Repeat Steps 5 and 6 to configure other policies, if desired.

CLOSE the Local Security Policy console and the Administrative Tools window.

SUMMARY SKILL MATRIX

IN THIS LESSON YOU LEARNED:
The user account is the fundamental unit of identity in the Windows operating systems.
A group is an identifying token that Windows uses to represent a collection of users.
A workgroup is a collection of computers that are all peers. A peer network is one in which every computer can function as both a server, by sharing its resources with other computers, and a client, by accessing the shared resources on other computers.
A domain is a collection of computers that all utilize a central directory service for authentication and authorization.
Windows Vista includes a number of built-in local groups that are already equipped with the permissions and rights needed to perform certain tasks.
A special identity is essentially a placeholder for a collection of users with a similar characteristic.
Windows Vista provides two separate interfaces for creating and managing local user accounts: the User Accounts control panel and the Local Users and Group snap-in for the Microsoft Management Console (MMC).
A roaming user profile is simply a copy of a local user profile that is stored on a network share, so that the user can access it from any computer on the network.
A mandatory user profile is simply a read-only roaming user profile.
On a Windows Vista computer running User Account Control (UAC), a standard user still receives a standard user token, but an administrative user receives two tokens: one for standard user access and one for administrative user access.

(continued)

SUMMARY SKILL MATRIX *(continued)*

IN THIS LESSON YOU LEARNED:
When a standard user attempts to perform a task that requires administrative privileges, the system displays a credential prompt, requesting that the user supply the name and password for an account with administrative privileges.
When an administrator attempts to perform a task that requires administrative access, the system switches the account from the standard user token to the administrative token. This is known as Admin Approval Mode.
Before the system permits the user to employ the administrative token, it requires the user to confirm that he or she is actually trying to perform an administrative task. To do this, the system generates an elevation prompt.
The secure desktop is an alternative to the interactive user desktop that Windows normally displays. When Vista generates an elevation or credential prompt, it switches to the secure desktop, suppressing the operation of all other desktop controls and permitting only Windows processes to interact with the prompt.
User Account Control is enabled by default in all Windows Vista installations, but it is possible to configure several of its properties, or even disable it completely, using Local Security Policy.

Knowledge Assessment

Fill in the Blank

Complete the following sentences by writing the correct word or words in the blanks provided.

1. The process by which a user's identity is verified by checking his or her user name and password is known as ______________.
2. The computer responsible for providing authentication and authorization services on an Active Directory network is called a(n) ______________.
3. A read-only copy of a user profile stored on a network share is called a(n) ______________ profile.
4. The Local Users and Groups snap-in is included by default in the ______________ console.
5. An elevation prompt with a(n) ______________ background indicates that the task you are attempting cannot be performed.
6. Specifying a high value for the Enforce Password History policy prevents users from ______________.
7. Microsoft Management Console is a shell application that runs individual program modules called ______________.
8. By default, Windows Vista user accounts with passwords must undergo password changes every ______________ days.
9. Roaming profiles enable a user to ______________.
10. When you create a new user account with the User Accounts control panel, you can only add it to the ______________ or ______________ group.

True / False

Circle T if the statement is true or F if the statement is false.

T | F 1. The Administrator account is disabled by default on a clean Windows Vista installation.

T | F 2. When User Account Control is functioning with its default settings on a Windows Vista computer, standard users are issued two tokens whenever they log on.

T | F 3. Under no circumstances can a local group have another local group as a member.

T | F 4. When you create a new user account with the User Accounts control panel, you have no control over the user account's group memberships.

T | F 5. If a user working on a Windows Vista computer is presented with an elevation prompt for no apparent reason, it is likely that some type of malware is trying to exercise administrative control over the system.

T | F 6. It is possible to turn User Account Control on from the Windows Security Center, but it is not possible to turn it off.

T | F 7. When you are specifying NTFS permissions for a folder on a Windows Vista computer, you can only add local users from that same computer to the access control list.

T | F 8. The User Accounts control panel is capable of creating new local user accounts and new local groups.

T | F 9. Storing passwords with reversible encryption is essentially the same as storing them in plain text.

T | F 10. User Account Control: Admin Approval Mode for the Built-in Administrator Account is the only UAC policy that requires a system restart to take effect.

Review Questions

1. Explain why it is recommended that administrators do not disable the User Account Control: Switch To The Secure Desktop When Prompting For Elevation policy.
2. Explain how a special identity differs from a local group.

Case Scenarios

Scenario #1: User Account Policies

You are working on a corporate network owned by a company with several government contracts to develop classified technology. You have been assigned the task to create a set of password and account policy settings that meet the following criteria:

- Users must change passwords every four weeks and cannot reuse the same passwords for one year.
- User passwords must be at least 12 characters long, case sensitive, and consist of letters, numbers, and symbols.
- Users are allowed no more than three unsuccessful logon attempts before the account is permanently locked down until released by an administrator.

In the following table, enter the values for the policies that will meet these requirements.

POLICY SETTING	VALUE
Enforce Password History	
Maximum Password Age	
Minimum Password Age	
Minimum Password Length	
Password Must Meet Complexity Requirements	
Store Passwords Using Reversible Encryption	
Account Lockout Threshold	
Account Lockout Duration	
Reset Account Lockout Counter After	

Scenario #2: User Account Policies

You are a system administrator for a company network running all Windows Vista workstations, and you rely on User Account Control to minimize the possibility of system infiltration by unauthorized software. Many of the department employees spend most of their time performing administrative tasks for the network and therefore require administrative access to their systems. The IS department for the company headquarters also uses an "open office" design, meaning that employees are constantly wandering around to each others' work areas, often leaving their workstations logged on.

You are concerned about the danger of unattended workstations being used to gain administrative access to the systems. What changes can you make to the UAC configuration to minimize this possibility? Explain how these changes would enhance the security of the systems.

Working with Drivers and Printers

OBJECTIVE DOMAIN MATRIX

Technology Skill	Objective Domain	Objective Number
Understanding Drivers and Devices	Install and configure Windows Vista drivers	1.6
Updating Drivers with Windows Update	Install and configure Windows Vista drivers • Use Windows Update to download current drivers	1.6
Using Device Manager	Install and configure Windows Vista drivers • Use Device Manager to install, update, and troubleshoot drivers	1.6
Updating Drivers	Install and configure Windows Vista drivers	1.6

KEY TERMS

device driver
driver signing
print device
print server
printer
Printer control language (PCL)
printer driver
printer pool

Understanding Drivers and Devices

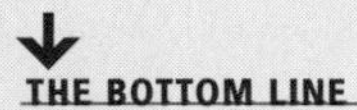

A computer is a collection of hardware devices, each of which requires a piece of software called a device driver in order to function. Windows Vista includes a large library of device drivers, but it is sometimes necessary to obtain them yourself.

CERTIFICATION READY?
Install and configure Windows Vista drivers
1.6

As most people know, a PC is a collection of hardware *devices*, all of which are connected together and installed in a single case. Drives, keyboards, mice, modems, and printers are all types of devices. To communicate with the operating system running on the computer, each device also requires a software element called a ***device driver***. The device driver provides the operating system with information about a specific device.

For example, when you use a word processing application to save a file to a hard disk, the application issues a generic WriteFile function call to the operating system. The application knows nothing specific about the disk drive hardware; it just issues an instruction to store a particular file there. When the operating system processes the function call, it accesses the device driver for the hard disk, which provides detailed information about how to communicate with the drive. If the user selects a different target location for the file, the operating system accesses the device driver for that location, whether it's a hard drive, a floppy drive, or USB flash drive.

In most cases the information the device driver provides is integrated into the Windows interface. For example, the Properties sheet for a printer includes generic system information, such as which port the printer is connected to and who is permitted to use it. Other tabs, and particularly the Device Settings tab, as shown in Figure 6-1, are based on hardware-specific information provided by the device driver.

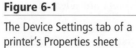

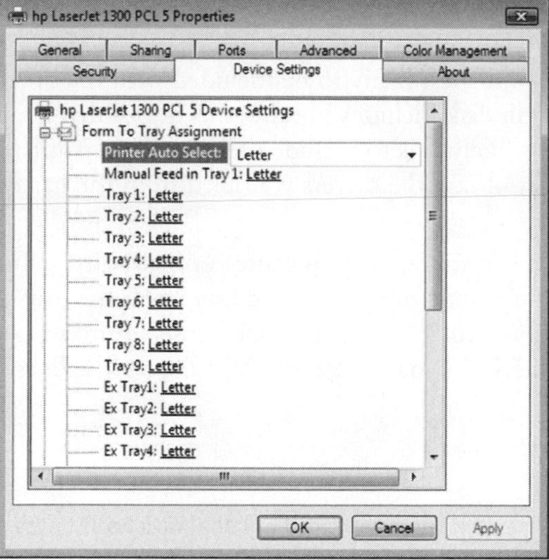

Figure 6-1

The Device Settings tab of a printer's Properties sheet

In addition to providing information about a device, drivers also permit the operating system to modify the hardware configuration settings of the device. For example, when you configure a printer to print a document in landscape mode instead of portrait mode, the printer device driver generates the appropriate command and sends it to the hardware.

Understanding Device Drivers

For virtually every hardware component in a computer, there must also be a software component. These software components are called device drivers. The process of installing a hardware device primarily consists of identifying the device and installing a device driver for it. This process can occur during the operating system installation or at a later time; the steps are fundamentally the same.

Generally speaking, a major part of the Windows Vista installation process consists of identifying the devices in the computer and installing the appropriate drivers for them. The Windows Vista installation package includes hundreds of drivers for many different devices, which is why many installations finish without any user intervention. Sometimes, however, you might have to supply device drivers yourself.

UNDERSTANDING DRIVER COMPLEXITY

Virtually every component in a PC requires a device driver, but they can vary greatly in complexity. Many computer devices are so standardized that their drivers operate virtually invisibly. When was the last time you had a problem with a keyboard driver, for example? Nearly every computer has a keyboard, and the generic keyboard driver included with Windows Vista functions properly in almost every case. If you have a keyboard with special features, you might need a special driver to access them, but the basic keyboard functions will still function.

At the other end of the scale are more complex drivers, such as those for video display adapters. Many of the video adapters on the market are self-contained computers in themselves, with their own processors and memory. The drivers for these complex devices are equally complex, and are often much more problematic than simple keyboard drivers, for the following reasons:

- The device driver is likely to be revised more often—Drivers that are required to do more are more likely to go wrong. Generic keyboard drivers can go for years without upgrades, because keyboards rarely change. New video display adapters are released often, however, and therefore require new drivers as well.
- The device driver is less likely to be included with the operating system—The Windows Vista installation disk includes hundreds of device drivers, but the older the operating system, the less likely it is to include the latest drivers for the newest devices. In these cases, you must obtain the drivers you need from the hardware manufacturer and install them yourself.
- The device driver is more likely to cause compatibility or functionality problems—New devices are often rushed to market, and as a result the drivers that ship with them might not be fully debugged. This is particularly true, again, with video display drivers. It is a good idea to check the manufacturer's Website for the latest drivers before installing new hardware.

MORE INFORMATION

With a few exceptions, the device drivers included with the Windows Vista operating system, as well as all other Windows versions, are supplied by the hardware manufacturers themselves, not by Microsoft. Therefore, if you experience driver problems for a specific device, you are much more likely to get help from the hardware manufacturer than from Microsoft.

DECIDING WHEN TO UPDATE DRIVERS

As a desktop technician, you will likely work with many different computers, each containing many devices. Keeping up with the drivers for all of these devices can be difficult, and you also must consider whether installing each driver update is necessary and, above all, safe.

There are two basic schools of thought when it comes to updating drivers. The "latest is the greatest" school advocates downloading and installing every new driver that is released, while the "if it ain't broke, don't fix it" school prefers to leave things as they are until they experience a problem. Both of these philosophies have their advantages and disadvantages, and unfortunately, this is not likely to be a question that is best answered with a hard and fast rule or a company policy.

The three main reasons why hardware manufacturers release new driver updates are:

- To address problems with the previous driver release(s)
- To implement new features
- To enhance performance of the device

The question of whether to update a driver is most easily answered for the first of these reasons. If you are experiencing the problem that the update is designed to address, then you should install it. Otherwise, you probably should not. As to the other two reasons, new features and enhanced performance are certainly desirable, but you should be sure that the driver update does not introduce new problems at the same time.

As a general rule, it is a good idea to test all driver updates before deploying them on clients' computers. Another good safety measure is to avoid installing driver updates as soon as they are released. Waiting at least a week gives the manufacturer time to address any major issues that arise.

Above all, the question of whether to install driver updates should depend on the hardware devices involved and the policies and reputation of the hardware manufacturer. Some manufacturers release driver updates frequently and haphazardly, while others are more careful.

Examining the manufacturer's support Website is a good way to ascertain how it deals with hardware problems and how often it releases driver updates.

INTRODUCING THE DRIVER STORE

The driver store, a new Windows Vista feature, enables administrators to exercise flexible control over the devices that standard users are allowed to install. Only administrators can add driver packages to the driver store, but any standard user can install the package once it has been added. Administrators can deliver device drivers to standard users in the following ways:

- An administrator can prepopulate the driver store on the local computer with drivers from trusted sources, so that standard users can install the device drivers as needed. This feature is especially helpful for users who travel with their laptops and might have to install a driver, such as a printer driver, while on the road.
- When an administrator installs a third-party driver on a local computer, Vista automatically copies the driver package to the driver store and then installs the driver from the store.
- An administrator can use Group Policy to grant standard users the permissions they need to install classes of devices, such as company-authorized flash drives and printers.

The Windows Vista driver store is essentially a cache of trusted inbox and third-party device drivers that is located on the hard drive of each computer. This makes it easy for standard users to install drivers without requiring administrative privileges or having to contact the help desk. When a user installs an authorized device, Vista checks the driver store for a compatible driver and then, if it finds one, automatically installs the device.

MORE INFORMATION

An *inbox driver* is a driver that Microsoft supplies on the Windows Vista installation media.

The device drivers are maintained in the file repository of the driver store located in the *%SystemRoot%*/System32/DriverStore/FileRepository folder. The DriverStore folder can contain additional subfolders for driver information. For example, the en-US subfolder contains localized U.S. English driver information.

MORE INFORMATION

Administrators use a command-line tool named PnPUtil.exe to manage the driver store. They use this tool to perform tasks such as adding and removing driver packages, or listing the driver packages that are in the store.

UNDERSTANDING DRIVER SIGNING

As with any other software, device drivers have the potential to damage a computer. Unscrupulous programmers could alter device drivers by adding their own malware, and the average user, downloading the driver from the Internet, would never know the difference. For that reason, Microsoft digitally signs the device drivers it has tested and approved.

A signed driver is a device driver that includes a digital signature. The signer uses a cryptographic algorithm to compute the digital signature value and then appends that value to the device driver. A *signer* is an organization, or publisher, that uses its private key to create the digital signature for the device driver. This process ensures that the device driver comes from the authentic publisher and that someone has not maliciously altered it.

MORE INFORMATION

Public key cryptography is an encryption method based on a pair of keys: the public key and the private key. As the names imply, the public key is freely available to anyone and the private key is kept secret by its owner. Any code that is digitally encrypted using the public key can be decrypted only by the holder of the private key. In the same way, any code that is encrypted using the private key can be decrypted only by the public key. It is the latter example that publishers use for driver signing. The signer encrypts the device driver using its private key. A user's ability to decrypt the driver using that signer's public key confirms that the software has not been modified.

Generally, the process the publisher uses to create the digital signature starts by running the device driver files through a hash algorithm and then using the publisher's private key to transform the hash result cryptographically. The resulting value is the digital signature of the device driver.

The digital signature value is a protected checksum. A protected checksum is the value of an algorithmic function that is dependant on the contents of the data object and that is stored together with the data object. Its purpose is to protect the data object against active attacks that attempt to change the checksum to match changes that a malicious individual has made to the data object. Thus, the properties of a cryptographic hash ensure that when a malicious individual attempts to change the data object, the digital signature no longer matches the object.

Previous versions of Windows used digital signatures to merely discourage users from installing untrusted device drivers. Vista goes a step further with new policies that make better use of digital signatures. These new policies include:

- Microsoft requires digital signatures for hardware-related drivers in its Windows Logo Program.
- Vista requires users to have administrative privileges to install unsigned kernel-mode components, such as device drivers and services.
- Administrators can control which device driver publishers Vista trusts. The result is that Vista automatically installs drivers from trusted publishers with no prompting, and does not install drivers from untrusted sources.
- When more than one compatible driver is available, Vista uses a ranking signature score to determine which driver is the best. By default, Microsoft digital signatures take priority over third-party digital signatures. However, administrators can configure the third-party drivers to be equivalent to Microsoft's digitally signed drivers, thus moving them up in rank for selection.
- Any packages or self-extracting executables that you download via Internet Explorer must contain the publisher's digital signature for the installation to occur on your computer.
- Windows Vista x64-based versions require Kernel Mode Code Signing (KMCS) to install any kernel-mode software.

If Vista perceives a problem with a digital signature of a device driver, it alerts you with one of the following messages during the installation attempt.

- Windows can't verify the publisher of this driver—Either a certification authority has not verified the digital signature or the driver does not contain a digital signature. Install this driver only if you obtained it from the original manufacturer's disk.
- This driver has been altered—A malicious individual has altered this driver after the verified publisher has digitally signed it. The driver package may now include malware that could harm your computer or steal information. Install this driver only if you obtained it from the original manufacturer's disk.
- Windows cannot install this driver—x64-based Vista versions cannot install a device driver that someone has altered after the verified publisher has digitally signed it nor one that lacks a valid digital signature altogether. This message appears only if you are running an x64-based version of Windows.

CONFIGURING DRIVER POLICIES

Windows Vista introduces new Group Policy settings that enable administrators to exercise control over device and driver installation. Users with the proper administrative privileges can configure these policy settings on an individual Vista computer using Local Group Policy or throughout an enterprise using Active Directory Group Policy.

You use the Group Policy Object Editor to configure and apply these policy settings in both instances. To use the Group Policy Object Editor, you must run Microsoft Management Console (MMC), and then add the Group Policy Object Editor snap-in, as in the following procedure.

CONFIGURE DRIVER POLICIES

GET READY. Log on to Windows Vista using an account with Administrator privileges. When the logon process is completed, close the Welcome Center window and any other windows that appear.

1. Click **Start,** key **mmc** in the Start Search text box, and then press **Enter**. After you confirm that you have performed the task, the Microsoft Management Console (MMC) console appears.
2. Click **File**, and then click **Add/Remove Snap-in**. The Add or Remove Snap-ins dialog box appears.
3. Scroll down the Available Snap-ins list box and select **Group Policy Object Editor**. Then, click **Add**. The Select Group Policy Object dialog box appears.
4. Ensure that Local Computer appears in the Group Policy Object text box, and then click **Finish**. The Add or Remove Snap-ins dialog box appears. Local Computer Policy should be listed in the Selected snap-ins list box.
5. Click **OK** to close the Add or Remove Snap-ins dialog box. The MMC console lists Local Computer Policy in both the scope (left) pane and the details pane.
6. In the console pane, expand **Local Computer Policy**. The Computer Configuration and User Configuration nodes appear.
7. Locate the policy you want to configure using the information in Tables 6-1 and 6-2 and modify them as needed.

CLOSE the MMC console.

Tables 6-1 and 6-2 contain brief descriptions of the driver installation and device installation policies.

Table 6-1

Driver Installation Policies

NODE LOCATION	POLICY	DESCRIPTION
Local Computer Policy > Computer Configuration > Administrative Templates > System > Driver Installation	Allow non-administrators to install drivers for these device setup classes	Enabling this policy allows members of the Users group to install drivers for the specified device setup classes that administrators have listed in this policy, providing that the drivers are included in the driver store. Disabling or not configuring this policy enables only members of the Administrators group to install new device drivers.

(continued)

Table 6-1 (*continued*)

NODE LOCATION	POLICY	DESCRIPTION
	Turn off Windows Update device driver search prompt	If you enable this policy, Vista will not prompt administrators to search Windows Update. If you disable or do not configure this policy, and if "Turn off Windows Update device driver searching" is disabled or not configured, Vista prompts the administrator for consent before going to Windows Update to search for device drivers. (*Turn off Windows Update device driver searching* is located at Computer Configuration > Administrative Templates > System > Internet Communication Management > Internet Communication settings.)
Local Computer Policy > User Configuration > Administrative Templates > System > Driver Installation	Configure driver search locations	This policy specifies the locations that Vista searches for drivers when it finds new hardware. By default, Vista searches the local installation, floppy drives, CD-ROM drives, and Windows Update. Enabling this setting removes the selected location(s) from the search algorithm. Disabling or not configuring this setting causes Windows to search the installation location, floppy drives, CD-ROM drives, and Windows Update. Note that you must also enable "Turn off Windows Update device driver searching" if you select the Windows Update checkbox.
	Turn off Windows Update device driver search prompt	If you enable this policy, Vista will not prompt administrators to search Windows Update. If you disable or do not configure this policy, and if "Turn off Windows Update device driver searching" is disabled or not configured, Vista prompts the administrator for consent before going to Windows Update to search for device drivers.
	Code signing for device drivers	This policy determines how the computer responds when a user attempts to install an unsigned device driver. There are three settings: • Ignore—This setting tells the computer to proceed with the installation, even if the driver is unsigned. • Warn—This setting is the default setting. It informs the user when files are not digitally signed and lets the user decide whether to abort or to proceed with the installation. • Block—This setting tells the computer to refuse to install unsigned drivers.

(*continued*)

Table 6-2

Device Installation Policies

NODE LOCATION	POLICY	DESCRIPTION
Local Computer Policy > Computer Configuration > Administrative Templates > System > Device Installation	Treat all digitally signed drivers equally in the driver ranking and selection process	Enabling this policy causes all valid Authenticode digital signatures (both third party and Windows Signing Authority) to be treated equally for the purpose of selecting the best device driver to install. Disabling or not configuring this policy causes Vista to select drivers that a Windows Signing Authority has signed over those that third parties have signed.
	Turn off "Found New Hardware" balloons during device installation	Enabling this policy causes the "Found New Hardware" balloons to appear. Disabling or not configuring this policy causes the "Found New Hardware" balloons to appear.
	Do not send a Windows Error Report when a generic driver is installed on a device	Enabling this policy prevents Vista from sending a Windows Error Report for a generic driver. Disabling or not configuring this policy causes Vista to send a Windows Error Report.
	Configuring device installation timeout	Enabling this policy causes the computer to wait the number of seconds the administrator has specified before forcibly aborting the installation. Disabling or not configuring this policy causes the computer to wait 300 seconds (5 minutes) for a device installation to complete before aborting the installation.
	Do not create system restore point when new device driver installed	Enabling this policy prevents Vista from creating system restore points when you install a new device driver or when you update a driver. Disabling or not configuring this policy causes a system restore point to be created whenever a new device driver is installed or when a driver is updated.
	Allow remote access to the PnP interface	Enabling this policy allows remote connections to the PnP interface. Disabling or not configuring this policy makes the PnP interface unavailable remotely.
Local Computer Policy > Computer Configuration > Administrative Templates > System > Device Installation > Device Installation Restrictions	Allow administrators to override Device Installation Restriction policies	By default, users who are members of the Administrators group can install any device on any computer. However, when they configure device policy settings on a computer, those settings affect all users of that computer. Administrators cannot apply these policies to specific groups or users. There is one exception to this rule. Administrators can enable this policy to exempt members of the local Administrators group from any device installation restrictions.

(continued)

Table 6-2 (*continued*)

NODE LOCATION	POLICY	DESCRIPTION
		Disabling or not configuring this setting makes administrators subject to all policies that restrict device installation.
	Allow installation of devices using drivers that match these device setup classes	Use this policy only when an administrator has enabled the "Prevent installation of devices not described by other policy settings" setting. Enabling this policy allows installation of any device with a compatible hardware ID that matches an ID in this policy's list, and updates its associated driver as long as no other policy prevents its installation or update. Disabling or not configuring this policy causes the "Prevent installation of devices not described by other policy settings" setting to determine whether you can install the device.
	Prevent installation of devices using drivers that match these device setup classes	Enabling this policy prevents new device installations and driver updates if they use drivers that belong to any of the listed device setup classes. Disabling or not configuring this policy does not prevent new device installations or existing driver updates. This policy takes precedence over any other policy that dictates whether you can install a device.
	Display a custom message when installation is prevented by policy (balloon text)	Enabling this setting allows the administrator to enter a text message that will display whenever policy prevents device installation. Disabling or not configuring this setting causes Vista to display the default message whenever policy prevents device installation.
	Allow installation of devices that match any of these device IDs	Use this policy only when you enable the "Prevent installation of devices not described by other policy settings" policy. Enabling this policy allows you to install any device with a compatible hardware ID that matches an ID in this setting's list and updates its driver as long as no other policy prevents its installation or update. Disabling or not configuring this policy causes the "Prevent installation of devices not described by other policy settings" setting to determine whether you can install the device.

(*continued*)

Table 6-2 (*continued*)

Node Location	Policy	Description
	Prevent installation of devices that match any of these device IDs	Enabling this policy prevents you from installing a device or updating its driver if its compatible hardware ID matches one in this setting's list. Disabling or not configuring this policy allows you to install new devices and to update existing device drivers, as permitted by other policy settings. This policy setting takes precedence over any other policy setting that dictates whether you can install a device.
	Prevent installation of removable devices	This policy considers a device to be removable when the drivers for the device indicate that the device is removable. Enabling this device prevents you from installing removable devices, and prevents you from updating drivers for existing removable devices. Disabling or not configuring this policy permits you to install removable devices and to update drivers.
	Prevent installation of devices not described by other policy settings	When you enable this policy, you cannot install any device nor update any driver not described by "Allow installation of devices for these device classes" or "Allow installation of devise that match these devices IDs." When you disable or do not configure this policy, you can install any device or update any driver that is not described by the "Prevent installation of removable devices," "Prevent installation of devices that match these devices IDs," or "Prevent installation of devices for these device classes" policy.

Understanding Automatic Device Driver Installation

Windows Vista can, in most cases, install the device drivers it needs automatically, using the processes described in this section.

Windows Vista is frequently capable of installing device drivers automatically, during the installation of either the operating system or a new hardware device. The following sections examine the processes by which these automatic driver installations occur.

SUPPLYING DRIVERS DURING VISTA INSTALLATION

As mentioned earlier, one of the primary functions of the Windows Vista installation program is to identify the hardware devices in the computer and install the appropriate device drivers for them. For most devices, this process occurs invisibly. However, sometimes the installation program fails to identify a device. When this occurs, one of three things happens:

- The installation program installs a generic driver instead—For devices that are essential to system operation, such as keyboards and video adapters, Windows Vista includes generic drivers that support nearly all hardware devices. If Vista does not include a driver for your specific video adapter, for example, it installs a generic VGA driver. This VGA driver won't support the esoteric features of your video adapter, but it will at least display an image on your screen, albeit a low-resolution one. After the operating system installation is completed, you can obtain a driver for your hardware and install it in place of the generic driver.
- The installation program leaves the device without a driver and completes the installation—If the hardware device is not essential to basic system operation, such as an audio adapter, Windows Vista leaves the hardware uninstalled and proceeds with the rest of the installation. When the installation is completed, the hardware appears in the device manager with a warning icon, indicating that it has no driver.
- The installation program permits you to supply an alternate driver or, failing that, halts—The sole exception to the preceding condition is when the installation program cannot access a disk drive with sufficient free space to install Windows Vista. When this happens, the setup program halts, unless you are able to supply the device driver for an unrecognized mass storage hardware device. For example, if your hard drives are connected to an interface card that Windows Vista does not recognize, you can click **Load Driver** on the installation program's *Where do you want to install Windows?* page, and specify the location of a driver for the interface card.

X REF

To install a device driver after the installation is complete, you must use the Device Manager utility, as described later in this lesson in "Using Device Manager."

INSTALLING PLUG AND PLAY DEVICES

Microsoft, Intel, and other leading manufacturers developed Plug and Play (PnP) standards to simplify the process of adding new hardware to computers. Vista PnP device driver installation requires that driver packages include a digitally signed catalog file. Because device drivers typically consist of multiple files, the catalog file contains the digital signature for the entire device driver package. Vista uses the package's digital signature to identify the driver's publisher, and to validate the driver files against the digital signature to ensure that malicious software has not altered any of the package's files.

Most of the hardware devices on the market today are Plug and Play compatible, which means that you install most devices in one of two ways:

- For USB and FireWire devices, you connect the device, and Vista detects the new hardware automatically.
- For non-USB or non-FireWire devices, you shut down the computer, connect the device, and then restart the computer so that Vista can automatically detect it.

This process sounds easy on the surface, but there is more going on behind the scenes. Vista performs the following tasks in the course of installing a Plug and Play device.

1. When Vista detects a new device, it checks the driver store for a compatible driver and then, if it finds one, examines the catalog file for a digital signature.
2. If the signature is present, Vista validates the package's files against the digital signature.
3. After validation, Vista places the device driver in one of the categories listed in Table 6-3.
4. After Vista has categorized the driver, it determines whether it should continue with the installation. This determination depends on whether the user is a standard user or a user with administrative privileges. Table 6-4 shows how Vista determines whether to continue with the driver installation.

Table 6-3

Plug and Play Device Driver Categories

DRIVER CATEGORY	DESCRIPTION
Signed by a Windows signing authority	These drivers are signed in one of three ways: • Windows Hardware Quality Labs (WHQL)—This Microsoft division tests and certifies third-party device drivers and hardware products to determine whether they meet the Windows operating systems compatibility requirements. • Windows Sustained Engineering—This Microsoft division consists of software design engineers, program managers, and testers. Once Microsoft releases a new version of Windows to manufacturing, this group is responsible for any further changes to the operating system, such as hotfixes, service packs, security patches, and all updates. • Inbox—An inbox driver is a driver that Microsoft supplies with the Windows installation disk.
Signed by a trusted publisher	A third-party publisher has digitally signed these drivers, and the user has explicitly chosen always to trust drivers from this publisher.
Signed by an untrusted publisher	A third-party publisher has digitally signed these drivers, and the user has explicitly chosen never to trust drivers from this publisher.
Signed by a publisher of unknown trust	A third-party publisher has digitally signed these drivers, but the user has not indicated whether to trust this publisher.
Altered	A Windows signing authority or a third party has signed these drivers, but Vista has detected that malicious software has altered at least one file in the driver package since the publisher has signed the package.
Unsigned	Either no publisher has signed these drivers, or the publisher has not signed the driver with a valid signature. Publishers must create a valid digital signature with a certificate that a trusted certificate authority has issued.

Table 6-4

Driver Installation Based on User Type

STANDARD AND NON-ADMINISTRATIVE USERS	ADMINISTRATIVE USERS
Vista automatically installs a Microsoft Windows signing authority or a trusted publisher's driver and silently refuses to install any other driver category.	If a Microsoft Windows signing authority or a trusted publisher has signed the driver, Vista automatically installs the driver without prompting the user. If an untrusted publisher has signed the driver, Vista will not install the driver. Windows does not prompt the user about the error in this case, but does log an error to the Setupapi.dev.log file. If a publisher of unknown trust signs the driver, Vista displays a Windows Security dialog box asking whether you want to install the driver. The dialog box also provides an *Always trust software from [publisher name]* checkbox. If you select this checkbox, Vista trusts all future drivers from this named publisher. If you do not select this checkbox, Vista keeps this publisher in the unknown trust category. If someone has altered the driver or if the driver lacks a valid digital signature, Vista prompts you with a Windows Security dialog box stating that it cannot verify the publisher and asks if you want to continue with the installation. If you choose to abort the installation, you must obtain a valid driver from the manufacturer before retrying the installation.

In some cases, for example, if Vista detects the new device but cannot locate the driver, it may start the Found New Hardware wizard. If this occurs, you can complete the installation using the following procedure:

USE THE FOUND NEW HARDWARE WIZARD

GET READY. This procedure assumes that you have already installed the new hardware device and logged on to Windows Vista using an account with Administrator privileges.

1. In the Found New Hardware wizard, click **Locate And Install Driver Software (Recommended)**. Vista searches for a preconfigured driver. If it cannot find one, Vista prompts you to insert the manufacturer's disk.
2. If you have the manufacturer's disk, insert the disk and then follow the prompts to complete the installation (these steps will vary depending on the device you are installing). You will not need to complete the remaining steps in this procedure.
3. If you do not have the manufacturer's disk, click **I don't have the disk. Show me other options**.
4. On the next page, click **Browse my computer for driver software**.
5. Click **Browse**. The Browse for Folder dialog box appears.
6. Select the start folder you want to use to begin your search, and then click **OK**.
7. Click **Next**. Vista searches the selected folder and all of its subfolders for an appropriate driver, and installs it if it finds one.

CERTIFICATION READY?
Install and configure Windows Vista drivers: Use Windows Update to download current drivers
1.6

If Vista cannot find the driver, obtain the device driver from the manufacturer and then use either Device Manager or the Add New Hardware wizard to install it.

UPDATING DRIVERS WITH WINDOWS UPDATE

The Windows Update Website was originally designed to provide users with operating system updates, but it now includes a large library of device driver updates as well. The drivers distributed through Windows Update have all undergone Windows Hardware Quality Labs (WHQL) testing and have received the Windows logo.

When you access the Windows Update Website manually, Windows Vista transmits a list of installed hardware and device version numbers to the site. If there are any updated drivers available for your hardware, the Website makes them available, usually as an optional download.

If Windows Vista is configured to use automatic updating, the system will download device drivers only for hardware that does not have a driver installed. If you use Device Manager to search for updated drivers, Vista examines the drivers that are available and downloads a new driver only if it is a better match for the device than the driver that is currently installed.

Using Device Manager

The primary Windows Vista tool for managing devices and their drivers is Device Manager. You can use Device Manager to get information about the devices installed in the computer, as well as to install, update, and troubleshoot device drivers.

CERTIFICATION READY?
Install and configure Windows Vista drivers: Use Device Manager to install, update, and troubleshoot drivers
1.6

Although it is not immediately apparent, Device Manager is snap-in for the Microsoft Management Console (MMC). This means that there are many ways that you can access Device Manager, including the following:

- Open the System control panel, and then click the **Device Manager** link.
- Open the Computer Management console from the Administrative Tools control panel, and then click Device Manager in the scope (left) pane.

- Run the Microsoft Management Console shell application (Mmc.exe), select File > Add/Remove Snap-in, and select Device Manager from the list of snap-ins provided.
- Open the Start menu, key the file name of the Device Manager snap-in (Devmgmt.msc) in the Start Search box, and then execute the resulting file.

Each of these procedures launches the Device Manager and displays a window like that shown in Figure 6-2.

Figure 6-2

The Windows Vista Device Manager

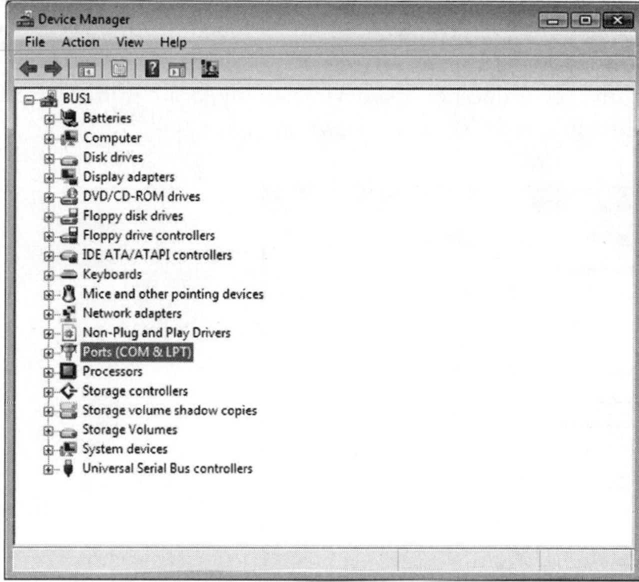

VIEWING DEVICE PROPERTIES

Device Manager can display information in the following four modes:

- Devices by type—Displays a list of device categories, which you can expand to show the devices in each category. This is the default Device Manager view, as shown in Figure 6-3.

Figure 6-3

Device Manager's devices by type display, expanded

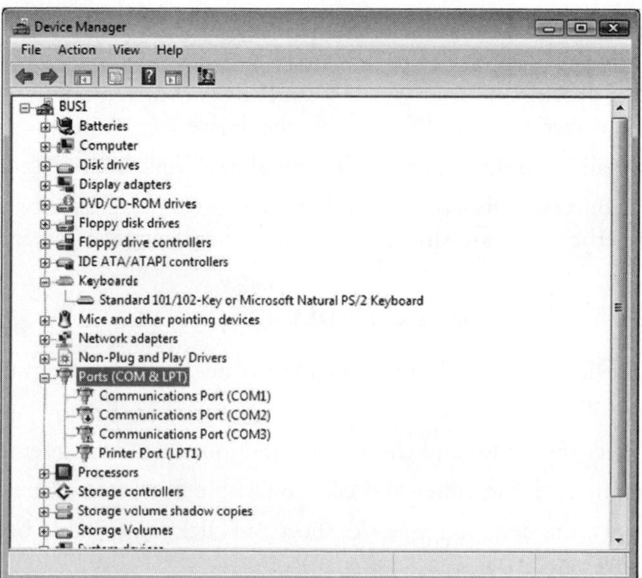

- Devices by connection—Displays a list of the interfaces that hardware devices use to communicate with the computer. Expanding a connection shows the devices using that connection.
- Resources by type—Displays a list of resource types, including Direct Memory Access (DMA), Input/Output (I/O), Interrupt Request (IRQ), and Memory, which you can expand to show the resources of each type and the devices that are using them.
- Resources by connection—Displays a list of resource types, including Direct Memory Access (DMA), Input/Output (I/O), Interrupt Request (IRQ), and Memory, which you can expand to show the connection associated with each individual resource and the device using each connection.

To examine the properties of a device, simply locate it in the tree display and double-click it to open its Properties sheet, as shown in Figure 6-4.

Figure 6-4

A Device Manager Properties sheet

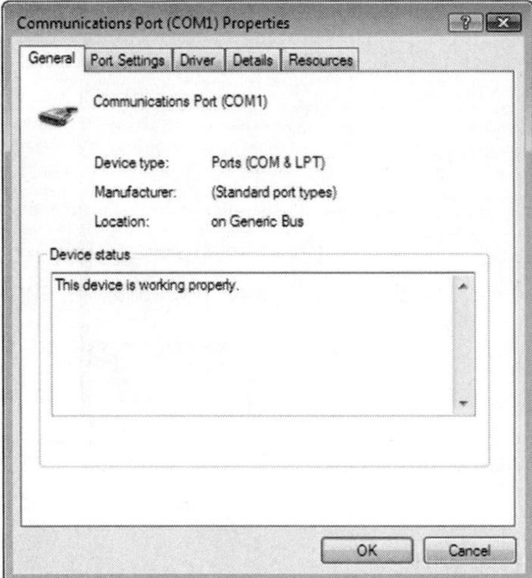

The tabs on the Properties sheet vary depending on the nature of the device you select, but virtually all devices have the following four tabs:

- General—Displays the name of the device, its type, manufacturer, and location in the system. The Device status box indicates whether the device is functioning and, if not, provides troubleshooting help.
- Driver—Displays the device driver's provider, date, version, and digital signer. The tab also provides buttons you can use to display driver details, update, roll back, or uninstall the driver, and enable or disable the device.
- Detail—Displays extensive information about the driver and its properties.
- Resources—Displays the hardware resources being used by the device and indicates whether there are any conflicts with other devices in the computer.

ENABLING AND DISABLING DEVICES

With Device Manager, you can disable any device in the computer, using any of the following procedures:

- Select the device and choose Disable from the Action menu.
- Right-click the device and choose Disable from the context menu.
- Open the device's Properties sheet and click the **Disable** button on the Driver tab.

Disabling a device does not affect the hardware in any way or uninstall the device driver, it simply renders the device inoperative until you enable it again. Obviously, you cannot disable devices that are necessary for the system to function, such as the processor, and some devices that are in use require you to restart the system before they can be disabled.

TAKE NOTE* Disabling a device releases the hardware resources it was using back to the operating system. If you restart the computer with the device disabled, Windows might reassign those hardware resources to other devices. If you re-enable the device, the computer might allocate different hardware resources to it than it had originally. This can affect the functionality of the devices.

UPDATING DRIVERS

When you update a driver using Device Manager, you can point to a location on your computer where you have already saved the new driver, or you can run a search of your computer and the Internet. To update a device driver, use the following procedure:

UPDATE A DEVICE DRIVER

CERTIFICATION READY? Install and configure Windows Vista drivers 1.6

GET READY. Log on to Windows Vista using an account with Administrator privileges. When the logon process is completed, close the Welcome Center window and any other windows that appear.

1. Open Device Manager and locate the device that you want to update.
2. Double-click the device you want to update, so that its Properties sheet appears.
3. Click the **Driver** tab, and then click the **Update Driver** button. The *How do you want to search for driver software?* page appears, as shown in Figure 6-5.

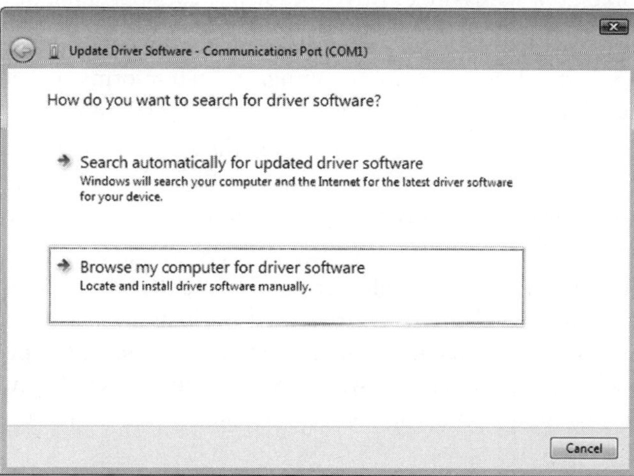
Update Driver Software - Communications Port (COM1)
How do you want to search for driver software?
Search automatically for updated driver software
Windows will search your computer and the Internet for the latest driver software for your device.
Browse my computer for driver software
Locate and install driver software manually.
Cancel

Figure 6-5
The How do you want to search for driver software? page

4. Click **Browse my computer for driver software** to specify a location for the driver or to select from a list of installed drivers, as shown in Figure 6-6. Click **Search automatically for updated driver software** to initiate a search for a driver.

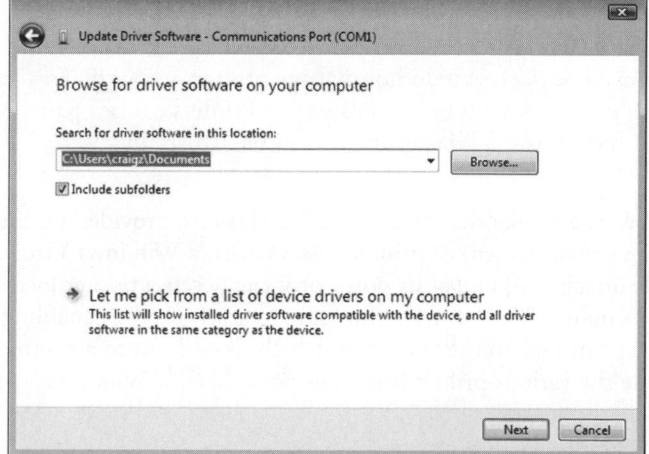
Update Driver Software - Communications Port (COM1)
Browse for driver software on your computer
Search for driver software in this location:
C:\Users\craigz\Documents
Browse...
Include subfolders
Let me pick from a list of device drivers on my computer
This list will show installed driver software compatible with the device, and all driver software in the same category as the device.
Next
Cancel

Figure 6-6
The Browse for driver software on your computer page

5. Click **Next** when you locate the driver you want to install. The *Windows has successfully updated your driver software* page appears.
6. Click **Close**.

CLOSE the Device Manager window.

ROLLING BACK DRIVERS

When you update a device driver in Windows Vista, the operating system does not discard the old driver completely. It is not uncommon for new drivers to cause more problems than they solve, and many users find that they would prefer to go back to the old version. Windows Vista makes this possible with the Roll Back feature, which you initiate by clicking the **Roll Back Driver** button on the Driver tab of the device's Properties sheet. This procedure uninstalls the current driver and reinstalls the previous version, returning the device to its state before you performed the most recent driver update.

TROUBLESHOOTING DRIVERS

Installing a new hardware device or a new device driver is a risky undertaking. There is always the possibility of a problem that, depending on the devices involved, could be trivial or catastrophic. For a peripheral device, such as a printer, a hardware misconfiguration or faulty driver would probably just cause the new device to malfunction. However, if the device involved is a video display adapter, a bad driver could prevent the system from functioning.

To troubleshoot hardware or driver problems, consider some of the following techniques:

- Open the Properties sheet for the device and check the Device status box on the General tab. If the device is malfunctioning, this tab informs you of its status and enables you to launch a troubleshooter.
- Open the Device Manager and delete the device entirely. Then restart the system and allow Windows Vista to detect and install the device over again. This process will cause Vista to reallocate hardware resources to the device, which could resolve the problem if it was caused by a hardware resource conflict.
- If the device or driver malfunction prevents the system from running properly, as in the case of a bad video display driver that prevents an image from appearing on the screen, you can start the computer in Safe Mode by pressing the F8 key as the system starts. Safe Mode loads the operating system with a minimal set of generic devices drivers, bypassing the troublesome ones, so you can uninstall or troubleshoot them.

Working with Printers

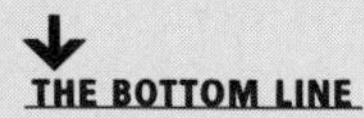

The printer is one of the most common external devices you find connected to a PC, but unlike most devices, you do not manage printers using the Device Manager application. Instead, you work with printers using the Printers control panel or the Print Management snap-in for Microsoft Management Console (MMC).

Windows Vista, like the other Windows versions, provides a great deal of flexibility in its handling and management of printers. As a client, a Windows Vista computer can have a printer directly attached to one of its ports, or it can access a printer located elsewhere on the network. Windows Vista can also function as a print server, enabling other users on the network to send print jobs to the computer, which feeds them to a printer. The following sections examine the various printer functions possible with Windows Vista.

Understanding the Windows Print Architecture

Printing in the Windows environment involves a number of different roles and components, and the names used to refer to these roles and components can sometimes be confusing. You can avoid confusion by making sure that you understand the terms used for the print components and how they work together.

Printing in Microsoft Windows typically involves the following four components:

- Print device—A ***print device*** is the actual hardware that produces hard copy documents on paper or other print media. Windows Vista supports both *local print devices*, which are directly attached to the computer's parallel, serial, Universal Serial Bus (USB), or IEEE 1394 (FireWire) ports, or *network interface print devices*, which are connected to the network, either directly or through another computer.
- Printer—In Windows parlance, a ***printer*** is the software interface through which a computer communicates with a print device. Windows Vista supports numerous interfaces, including parallel (LPT), serial (COM), USB, IEEE 1394, Infrared Data Access (IrDA), and Bluetooth ports, and network printing services such as lpr, Internet Printing Protocol (IPP), and standard TCP/IP ports.

TAKE NOTE*

The most common misuse of the Windows printing vocabulary is the confusion of the terms printer and print device. Many sources use the term printer to refer to the printing hardware, but in Windows, the two are not equivalent. For example, you can add a printer to a Windows Vista computer without a physical print device being present. The computer can then host the printer, print server, and printer driver. These three components enable the computer to process the print jobs and store them in a print queue until the print device is actually available.

- Print server—A ***print server*** is a computer (or standalone device) that receives print jobs from clients and sends them to print devices that are either locally attached or connected to the network.
- Printer driver—A ***printer driver*** is a device driver that converts the print jobs generated by applications into an appropriate string of commands for a specific print device. Printer drivers are designed for a specific print device and provide applications with access to all of the print device's features.

UNDERSTANDING WINDOWS PRINTING

These four components work together to process the print jobs produced by Windows applications and turn them into hard copy documents, as shown in Figure 6-7.

Figure 6-7

The Windows print architecture

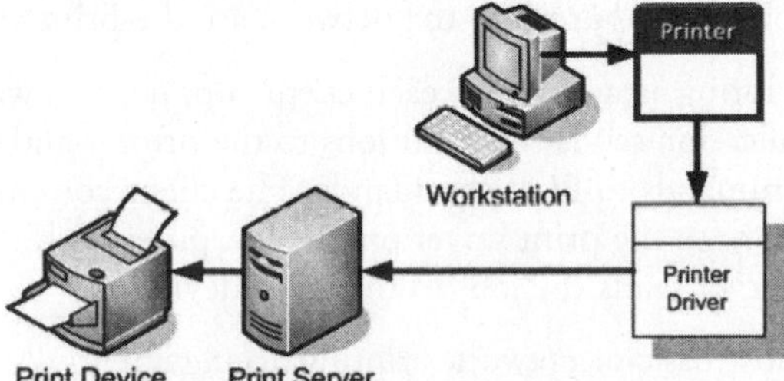

Before you can print documents in Windows, you must install at least one printer. To install a printer in Windows, you must do the following:

- Select a specific manufacturer and model of print device.
- Specify the port (or other interface) the computer will use to access the print device.
- Supply a printer driver specifically created for that print device.

When you print a document in an application, you select the printer that will be the destination for the print job.

The printer is associated with a printer driver that takes the commands generated by the application and converts them into a language understood by the printer, which is called a ***printer control language (PCL)***. PCLs can be standardized, as in the case of the PostScript language, or they can be proprietary languages developed by the print device manager.

The printer driver enables you to configure the print job to use the various capabilities of the print device. These capabilities are typically incorporated into the printer's Properties dialog box, like the one shown in Figure 6-8.

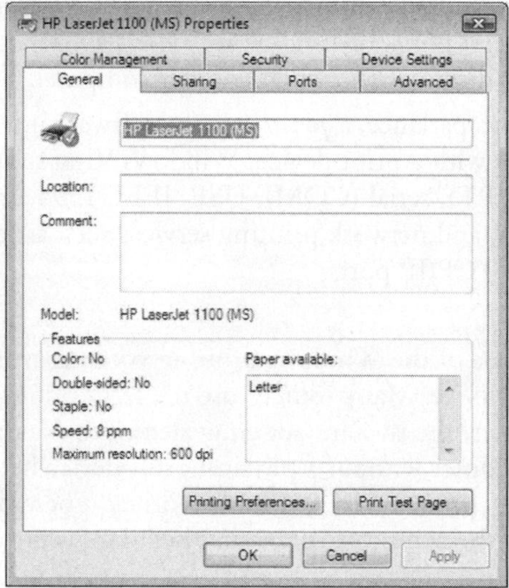

Figure 6-8

A Windows printer's Properties dialog box

Once the computer converts the print job into the appropriate PCL, it stores the job in a print queue. The print queue then sends the job to the print device when the device is ready to receive it. If there are other jobs waiting to be printed, a new job might wait in the print queue for some time. When the server sends the job to the print device, the device reads the PCL commands and produces the hard copy document.

WINDOWS PRINTING FLEXIBILITY

The flexibility of the Windows print architecture manifests itself in how the roles of these components can be performed by a single computer, or distributed around a network.

When you connect a print device to a standalone Windows Vista computer, for example, the computer supplies the printer, printer driver, and print server functions. However, you can also connect the computer to a local area network (LAN) and share the printer with other users. In this arrangement, the computer with the print device attached to it functions as a print server. The other computers on the network are the print clients.

In this network printing arrangement, each client supplies its own printer and printer driver. As before, the application sends the print jobs to the printer and the printer driver converts the application commands to PCL commands. The client computer then sends the PCL print jobs over the network to the print server on the computer with the attached print device. Finally, the print server sends the jobs to the print device.

This is only the most basic of network printing arrangements. A multitude of possible variations exist to enable you to create a network printing architecture that supports your organization's printing needs. Some of the more advanced possibilities are as follows:

- Print devices do not necessarily have to be connected to computers. Many print devices have integrated network interfaces that enable them to connect directly to the LAN and function as their own print servers. You can also purchase standalone print server devices that connect a print device to a network. In these cases, print devices have their own IP addresses, which clients use to communicate with the devices.

- You can connect a single print server to multiple print devices. This is called a ***printer pool.*** On a busy network with many print clients, the print server can distribute large numbers of incoming jobs among several identical print devices to provide timely service. Alternatively, you can connect print devices that support different forms and paper sizes to a single print server, which will distribute jobs with different requirements to the appropriate print devices.
- You can connect multiple print servers to a single print device. By creating multiple print servers, you can configure different priorities, security settings, auditing, and monitoring parameters for different users. For example, you can create a high-priority print server for company executives, while junior users send their jobs to a lower priority server. This ensures that the executives' jobs get printed first, even if the servers are both connected to the same print device.

Adding a Local Printer

Local printers are used by most home and small business users.

The most common configuration for home and small business users is to connect a print device directly to a computer running Windows Vista or another version of Windows, and then add a printer and printer driver. This enables local users to print their own jobs, and it also makes it possible to share the printer with other network users.

To add a local printer to a Windows Vista computer, user the following procedure:

TAKE NOTE*

This procedure is necessary only if the print device is connected (or will be connected) to the computer by a parallel (LPT) port or serial (COM) port interface. This is because these interfaces are not capable of automatically detecting connected devices. If your print device connects to the computer using USB, IEEE 1394, IrDA, Bluetooth, or any other auto-detecting technology, simply connecting the print device will cause the computer to detect it and install it automatically.

ADD A LOCAL PRINTER

GET READY. Log on to Windows Vista using an account with Administrator privileges. When the logon process is completed, close the Welcome Center window and any other windows that appear.

1. Click **Start**, and then click **Control Panel**. The Control Panel window appears.
2. Click **Hardware and Sound**, and then click **Printers**. The Printers window appears, as shown in Figure 6-9.

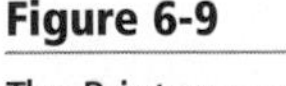

Figure 6-9

The Printers control panel

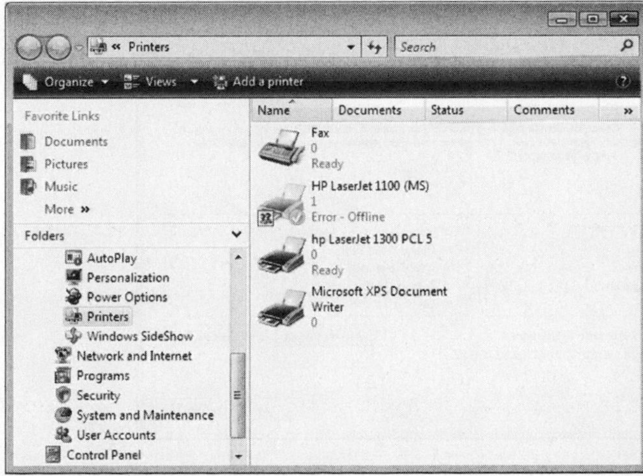

3. Click **Add a printer**. The *Choose a local or network printer* page appears, as shown in Figure 6-10.

Figure 6-10

The Choose a local or network printer page

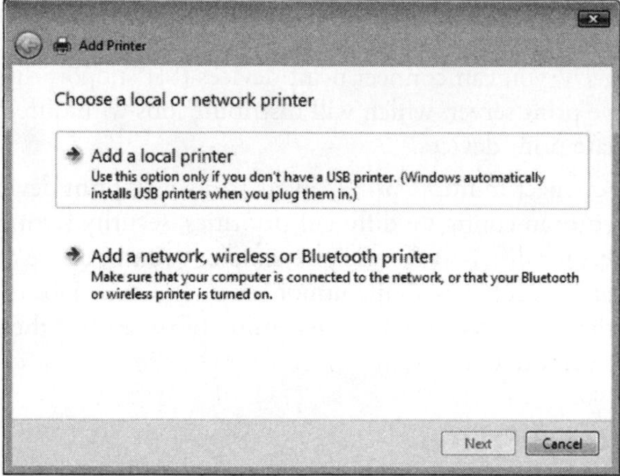

4. Click **Add a local printer**. The **Choose a printer port** page appears, as shown in Figure 6-11.

Figure 6-11

The Choose a printer port page

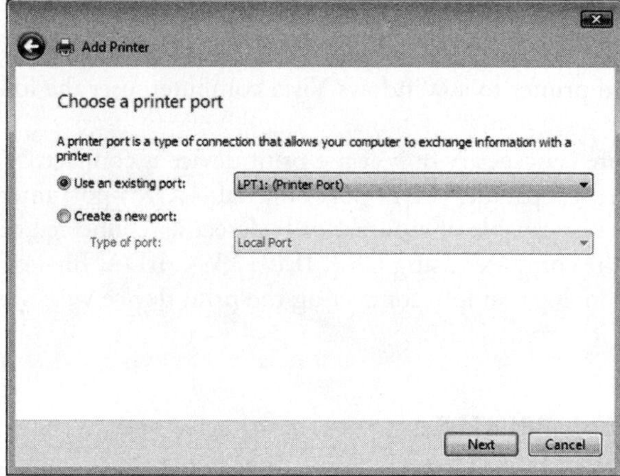

5. Select the **Use an existing port** radio button, and then select the LPT or COM port to which the print device is connected.
6. Click **Next** to continue. The *Install the printer driver* page appears, as shown in Figure 6-12.

Figure 6-12

The Install the printer driver page

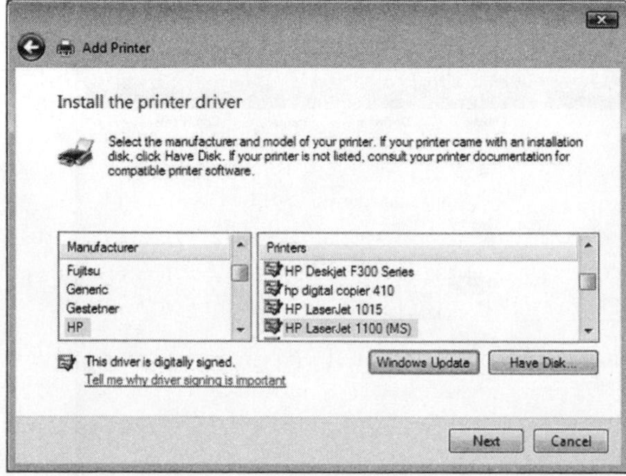

7. In the Manufacturer column, scroll down and select the manufacturer of your print device. Then, in the Printers column, select the specific model of print device you want to install. If your print device does not appear in the list, you must either click **Have Disk**, to supply a driver you downloaded or that came with the print device, or Windows Update, to display a selection of drivers available from the Windows Update Website.
8. Click **Next** to continue. The Type a printer name page appears, as shown in Figure 6-13.

Figure 6-13

The Type a printer name page

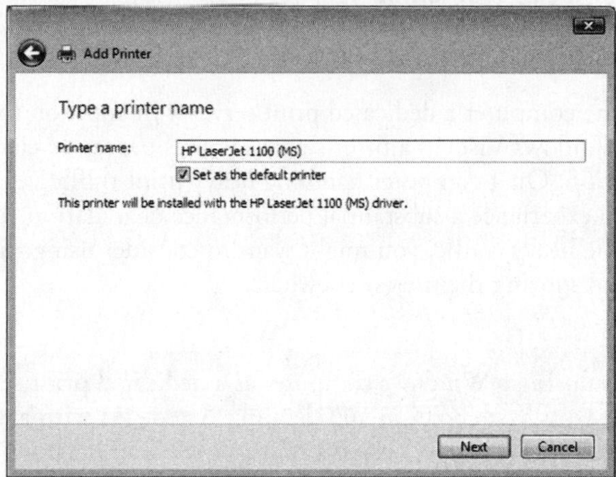

9. Key a name for the printer in the Printer name text box and, if desired, select the **Set as the default printer** checkbox.
10. Click **Next** to continue. After a few moments, the *You've successfully added [printer name]* page appears. If desired, and if the printer is connected and ready to use, click the ***Print a test page*** button.
11. Click **Finish**. The printer appears in the Printers control panel.

CLOSE the Control Panel window.

At this point, the printer is ready to receive jobs from applications, but this does not necessarily mean that the print device is ready. As stated earlier, you can complete this entire procedure without the print device being attached to the computer, or turned on, or loaded with paper. Jobs that users send to the printer are processed and remain in the print queue until the print device is available for use.

Sharing a Printer

A local printer is, of course, available for use by anyone working at the computer to which it is attached. However, you can also share the printer with other users on either a workgroup or a domain network. When you share a printer connected to a Windows Vista computer, you are essentially using Windows Vista as a print server.

Using Windows Vista as a print server can be a simple or a complex matter, depending on how many clients the server has to support and how much printing they do. For a home or small business network, in which a handful of users need occasional access to the printer, no special preparation is necessary. However, if the computer must support heavy printer use, any or all of the following hardware upgrades might be needed:

- Additional system memory—Processing print jobs requires system memory, just like any other application. If you plan to run heavy print traffic on a Windows Vista computer, in addition to regular applications, you might want to install extra system memory.

- Additional disk space—When a print device is busy, any additional print jobs that arrive at the print server must be stored temporarily on a hard drive until the print device is free to receive them. Depending on the amount of print traffic involved, the print server might require a substantial amount of temporary storage for this purpose.

TAKE NOTE*

When in PCL format, print jobs can often be much larger than the document files from which they were generated, especially if they contain graphics. When estimating the amount of disk space required for a print server, be sure that you consider the size of the PCL files, not the application files.

- Make the computer a dedicated print server—In addition to memory and disk space, using Windows Vista as a print server requires processor clock cycles, just like any other application. On a computer handling heavy print traffic, standard user applications are likely to experience a substantial performance degradation. If you need a print server to handle heavy traffic, you might want to consider using the computer to print server tasks and moving the user(s) elsewhere.

TAKE NOTE*

If you plan on using a Windows computer as a dedicated print server, Windows Vista might not be your best choice as an operating system. As with all of the workstation versions of Windows, Windows Vista is limited to ten simultaneous network connections, so no more than ten clients can print at any one time. If you need a print server that can handle more than ten connections, you must use a server operating system, such as Windows Server 2003.

To share a printer on a Windows Vista computer, you must enable the appropriate settings in the Network and Sharing Center, just as you have to do to share files and folders. To share printers, the following Sharing and Discovery settings must be turned on:

- Network Discovery
- Printer Sharing

In addition, if the Password Protected Sharing setting is turned on, users must be logged on and have appropriate permissions to use the printer.

To share a printer that is already installed on a Windows Vista computer, use the following procedure:

SHARE A PRINTER

GET READY. Log on to Windows Vista using an account with Administrator privileges. When the logon process is completed, close the Welcome Center window and any other windows that appear.

1. Click **Start**, and then click **Control Panel**. The Control Panel window appears.
2. Click **Hardware and Sound**, and then click **Printers**. The Printers window appears.
3. Right-click one of the printer icons in the window and then, from the context menu, select **Sharing**. The printer's Properties sheet appears, with the Sharing tab selected, as shown in Figure 6-14.

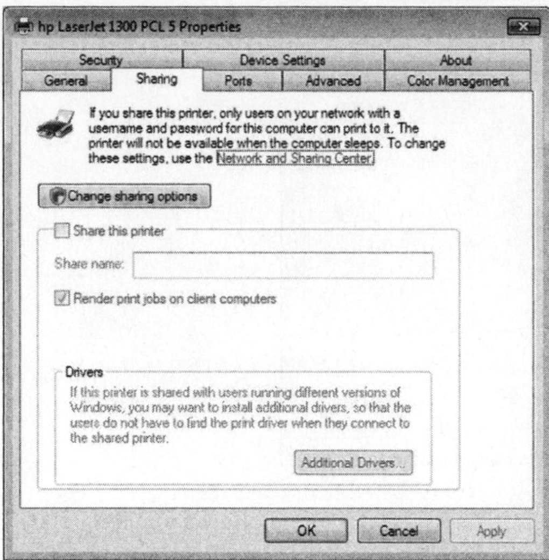

Figure 6-14

The Properties sheet for a printer

4. Click **Change sharing options**. After confirming that you want to perform the task, the Sharing tab appears with all of its controls activated, as shown in Figure 6-15.

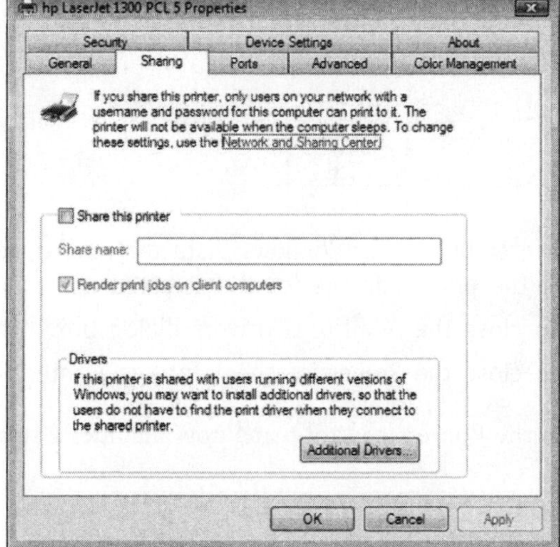

Figure 6-15

The Sharing tab of a printer's Properties sheet

5. Select the **Share this printer** checkbox. The printer name appears in the Share name text box. You can accept the default name or supply one of your own. Select the *Render print jobs on client computers* checkbox if you want to use the printer drivers on the individual client computers. Leaving this box unchecked will force the print server on the computer hosting the printer to process all of the jobs.

TAKE NOTE*

If the computer is a member of an Active Directory domain, an additional *List printer in the directory* checkbox appears in this dialog box. Selecting this checkbox creates a new printer object in the Active Directory database, which enables domain users to locate the printer by searching the directory.

6. Click **Additional Drivers**. The Additional Drivers dialog box appears, as shown in Figure 6-16. This dialog box enables you to load printer drivers for other operating system versions, so that clients installing the printer do not have to locate the drivers themselves.

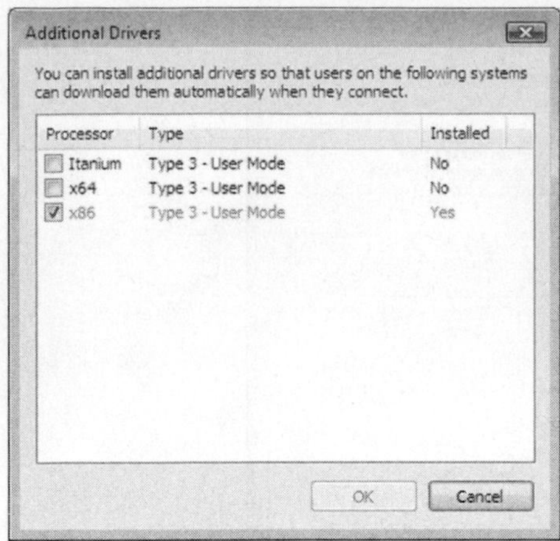

Figure 6-16

The Additional Drivers dialog box

7. Select any combination of the available checkboxes and click **OK.** For each checkbox you selected, Windows Vista displays a Printer Drivers for Windows Vista dialog box, as shown in Figure 6-17.

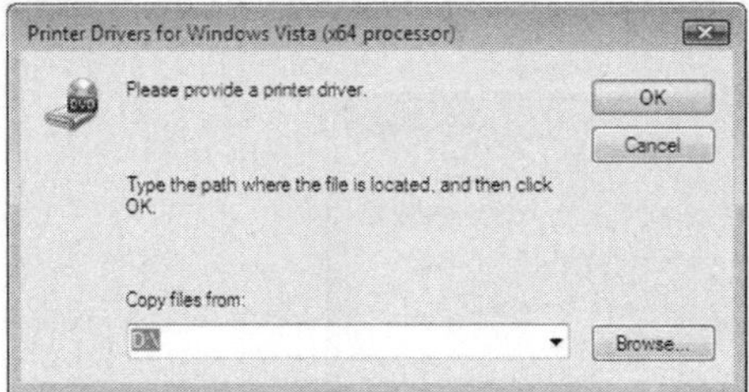

Figure 6-17

The Printer Drivers for Windows Vista dialog box

8. In each Printer Drivers for Windows Vista dialog box, key or browse to the location of the printer drivers for the selected operating system and click **OK.**
9. Click **OK** to close the Additional Drivers dialog box.
10. Click **OK** to close the Properties sheet for the printer.

The printer icon in the Printers control panel now includes a symbol indicating that it has been shared.

Configuring Printer Security

Just like NTFS files and folders, Windows printers have their own permissions, which enable you to control who has access to the printer and to what degree.

When Password Protected Sharing is turned on in the Windows Vista Network and Sharing Center, users must log on to the computer with a user account that requires a password before they can access a shared printer. In addition, the user account must have the appropriate permissions to use the printer.

Printer permissions are much simpler than NTFS permissions; they basically dictate whether users are allowed to merely use the printer, manage documents submitted to the printer, or manage the properties of the printer itself. To assign permissions for a printer, use the following procedure:

ASSIGN PRINTER PERMISSIONS

GET READY. Log on to Windows Vista using an account with Administrator privileges. When the logon process is completed, close the Welcome Center window and any other windows that appear.

1. Click **Start**, and then click **Control Panel**. The Control Panel window appears.
2. Click **Hardware and Sound**, and then click **Printers**. The Printers window appears.
3. Right-click one of the printer icons in the window and, from the context menu, select **Properties**. When the printer's Properties sheet appears, click the **Security** tab, as shown in Figure 6-18. The top half of the display lists all of the security principals currently possessing permissions to the selected printer. The bottom half lists the permissions held by the selected security principal.

Figure 6-18

The Security tab of a printer's Properties sheet

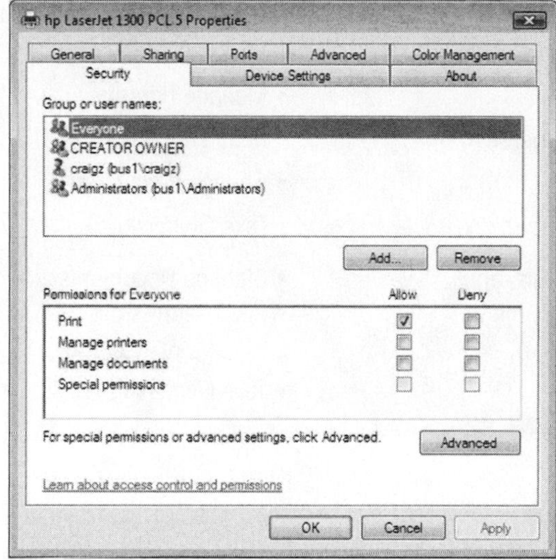

4. Click **Add**. The Select Users or Groups dialog box appears, as shown in Figure 6-19.

Figure 6-19

The Select Users or Groups dialog box

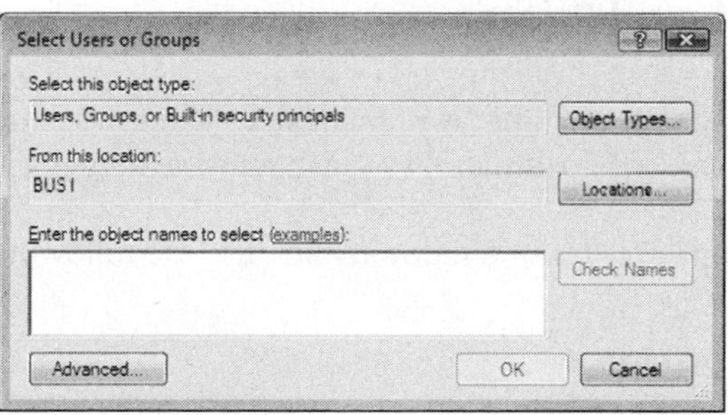

TAKE NOTE*

When you assign permissions on a standalone computer, you select local user and group accounts to be the security principals that receive the permissions. However, if the computer is a member of an Active Directory domain, you can also assign permissions to domain users, groups, and other objects.

5. In the *Enter the object names to select* text box, key a user or group name, and then click **OK**. The user or group appears in the *Group or user names* list.
6. Select the user or group you added, and select or clear the checkboxes in the bottom half of the display to Allow or Deny the user any of the standard permissions shown in Table 6-5.
7. Click **OK** to close the Properties sheet.

Table 6-5

Standard Printer Permissions

Permission	Capabilities	Special Permissions	Default Assignments
Print	• Connect to a printer • Print documents • Pause, resume, restart, and cancel the user's own documents	• Print • Read Permissions	Assigned to the Everyone special identity
Manage Printers	• Cancel all documents • Share a printer • Change printer properties • Delete a printer • Change printer permissions	• Print • Manage Printers • Read Permissions • Change Permissions • Take Ownership	Assigned to the Administrators group
Manage Documents	• Pause, resume, restart, and cancel all users' documents • Control job settings for all documents	• Manage Documents • Read Permissions • Change Permissions • Take Ownership	Assigned to the Creator Owner special identity

TAKE NOTE As with NTFS permissions, there are two types of printer permissions: standard permissions and special permissions. Each of the three standard permissions consists of a combination of special permissions.

Accessing a Shared Printer

Once you have shared a printer, it is available to all network users with the appropriate permissions, just as a shared folder is available to the network.

To access a shared printer from Windows Vista, use the following procedure:

ADD A LOCAL PRINTER

GET READY. Log on to Windows Vista using any user account. When the logon process is completed, close the Welcome Center window and any other windows that appear.

1. Click **Start**, and then click **Control Panel**. The Control Panel window appears.
2. Click **Hardware and Sound**, and then click **Printers**. The Printers window appears.
3. Click **Add a printer**. The *Choose a local or network printer* page appears.
4. Click ***Add a network, wireless, or Bluetooth printer***. The *Searching for available printers* page appears, as shown in Figure 6-20.

Figure 6-20

The Searching for available printers page

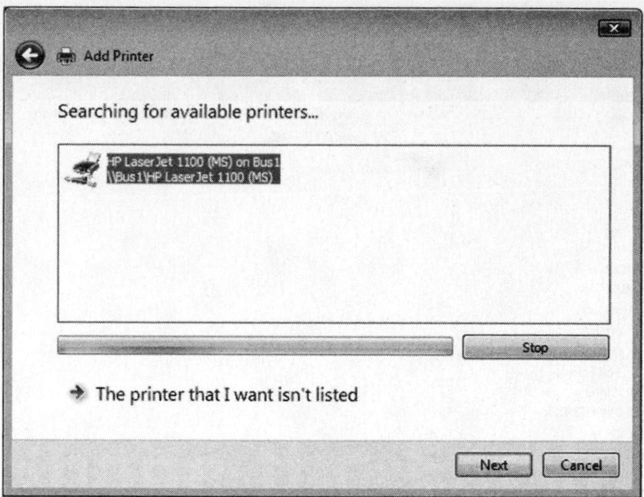

5. Select one of the listed printers and click **Next.** The *Type a printer name* page appears. If the printer you want does not appear, click **The printer that I want isn't listed**, and the *Find a printer by name or TCP/IP address* page appears, as shown in Figure 6-21. Select the proper radio button to browse for a network printer, key a UNC name or URL for a printer, or enter a printer's IP address or hostname. Then click **Next.** When you have selected a printer, the *Type a printer name* page appears.

Figure 6-21

The Find a printer by name or TCP/IP address page

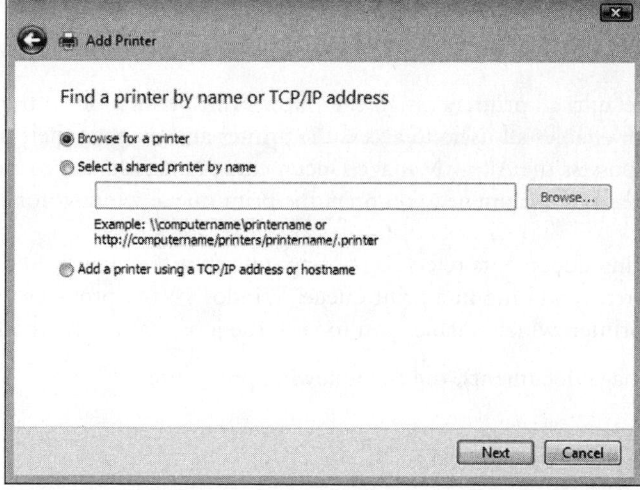

6. Key a name for the printer in the Printer name text box and then, if desired, select the *Set as the default printer* checkbox.
7. Click **Next** to continue. After a few moments, the *You've successfully added [printer name]* page appears. If desired, and if the printer is connected and ready to use, click the ***Print a test page*** button.
8. Click **Finish.** The printer appears in the Printers control panel.

CLOSE the Control Panel window.

In addition to using the Add Printer wizard, there are several other ways to access shared network printers. When browsing the network in Windows Explorer, you can see the shared printers for each computer on the network, as shown in Figure 6-22. By right-clicking a printer in any Windows Explorer window and selecting Connect from the context menu, you can access any printer for which you have the appropriate permissions. Any other Windows Vista mechanism that can display the shared printers on the network provides access to them in the same way.

Figure 6-22

Viewing printers in Windows Explorer

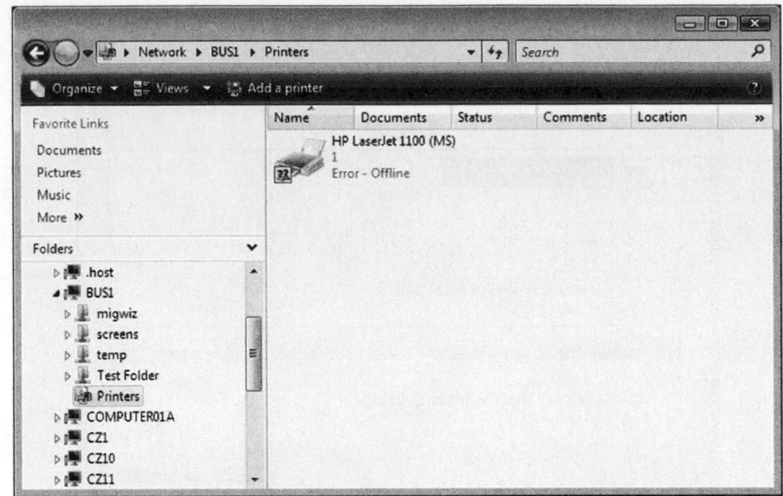

When the computer hosting the printer is a member of an Active Directory domain, the ability to locate shared printers is enhanced even further. Opting to list the printer in the Active Directory database creates an object for the printer, and in this object you can specify a lot of information about the print device, including its location and its capabilities.

Recording this information in the printer object makes it possible for users to locate printers by searching the directory for specific characteristics. For example, if a user on a large corporate network needs to find a color duplex printer on the third floor, running a directory search with the appropriate keywords will enable the user to locate the required printer.

Managing Documents

By default, all printers assign the Allow Print permission to the Everyone special identity, which enables all users to access the printer and manage their own documents. Users that possess the Allow Manage Documents permission can manage any users' documents. To manage documents, you open the print queue window for the printer.

Managing documents refers to pausing, resuming, restarting, and cancelling documents that are currently waiting in a print queue. Windows Vista provides a print queue window for every printer, which enables you to view the jobs that are currently waiting to be printed.

To manage documents, use the following procedure:

MANAGE DOCUMENTS

GET READY. Log on to Windows Vista using any user account. When the logon process is completed, close the Welcome Center window and any other windows that appear.

1. Click **Start**, and then click **Control Panel**. The Control Panel window appears.
2. Click **Hardware and Sound**, and then click **Printers**. The Printers window appears.
3. Double-click one of the printer icons. A print queue window named for the printer appears, as shown in Figure 6-23.

Figure 6-23

A Windows Vista print queue window

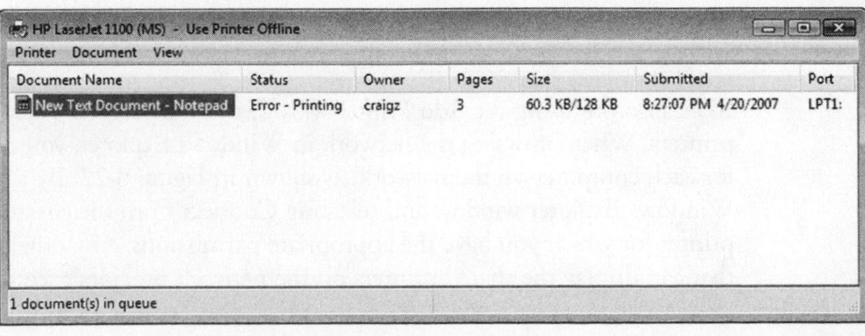

4. Select one of the menu items listed in Table 6-6 to perform the associated function. **CLOSE** the print queue window.

Table 6-6

Document Management Menu Commands

MENU ITEM	FUNCTION
Printer > Pause Printing	Causes the print server to stop sending jobs to the print device until you resume it by selecting the same menu item again. All pending jobs remain in the queue.
Printer > Cancel All Documents	Removes all pending jobs from the queue. Jobs that are in progress complete normally.
Printer > Use Printer Offline	Enables users to send jobs to the printer, where they remain in the queue, unprocessed, until you select the same menu item again.
Printer > Properties	Opens the Properties sheet for the printer.
Document > Pause	Pauses the selected document, preventing the print server from sending the job to the print device.
Document > Resume	Causes the print server to resume processing a selected document that has previously been paused.
Document > Restart	Causes the print server to discard the current job and restart printing the selected document from the beginning.
Document > Cancel	Causes the print server to remove the selected document from the queue.
Document > Properties	Opens the Properties sheet for the selected job.

TAKE NOTE*

When managing documents, keep in mind that the commands accessible from the print queue window affect only the jobs waiting in the queue, not those currently being processed. For example, a job that is partially transmitted to the print device cannot be completely cancelled. The data already in the print device's memory will be printed, even though the remainder of the job was removed from the queue. To stop a job that is currently printing, you must clear the print device's memory (by power cycling the unit), as well as clear the job from the queue.

Managing Printers

Users with the Allow Manage Printers permission can go beyond just manipulating queued documents and reconfigure the printer itself. Managing a printer refers to altering the operational parameters that affect all users and controlling access to the printer.

Generally speaking, most of the software-based tasks that fall under the category of managing a printer are those you perform once, while setting up the printer for the first time. Day-to-day printer management is more likely to involve clearing print jams, reloading paper, and changing toner or ribbon cartridges. However, the following sections examine some of the printer configuration tasks that typically are the responsibility of a printer manager.

SETTING PRINTER PRIORITIES

In some cases, you might want to give certain users in your organization priority access to a print device so that when a print device is busy, their jobs are processed before those of other users. To do this, you must create multiple printers, associate them with the same print device, and then modify their priorities, as described in the following procedure:

SETTING A PRINTER'S PRIORITY

GET READY. Log on to Windows Vista using an account with the Manage Printer permission. When the logon process is completed, close the Welcome Center window and any other windows that appear.

1. Click **Start**, and then click **Control Panel**. The Control Panel window appears.
2. Click **Hardware and Sound**, and then click **Printers**. The Printers window appears.
3. Right-click one of the printer icons and then, from the context menu, select **Properties**. The Properties sheet for the printer appears.
4. Click the **Advanced** tab, as shown in Figure 6-24.

Figure 6-24

The Advanced tab of a printer's Properties sheet

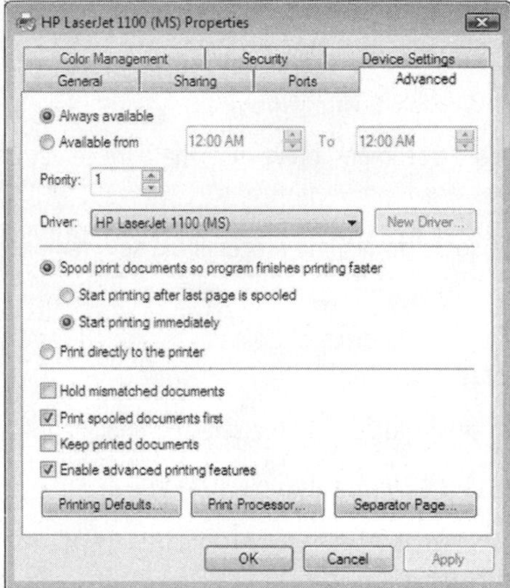

5. Set the Priority spin box to a number representing the highest priority you want to set for the printer. Higher numbers represent higher priorities. The highest possible priority is 99.

TAKE NOTE*

The values of the Priority spin box do not have any absolute significance; they are pertinent only in relation to each other. As long as one printer has a higher priority value than another, its print jobs will be processed first. In other words, it doesn't matter if the high-priority value is 9 or 99, as long as the low-priority value is less than 9.

6. Click the **Security** tab.
7. Add the users or groups that you want to provide with high-priority access to the printer and assign them the Allow Print permission.
8. Revoke the Allow Print permission from the Everyone special identity.
9. Click **OK** to close the Properties sheet.
10. Create an identical printer using the same printer driver and pointing to the same print device. Leave the Priority setting to its default value of 1 and leave the default permissions in place.
11. Rename the printers, specifying the priority assigned to each one.

Inform the privileged users that they should send their jobs to the high-priority printer. All jobs sent to that printer will be processed before those sent to the other, low-priority printer.

SCHEDULING PRINTER ACCESS

Sometimes, you might want to limit certain users' access to a printer to specific times of the day or night. For example, your organization might have a color laser printer that the company's graphic designers use during business hours, but which you permit other employees to use after 5:00 PM. To do this, you associate multiple printers with a single print device, much as you did to set different printer priorities.

After creating two printers, both pointing to the same print device, you configure their scheduling using the following procedure:

CONFIGURING A PRINTER'S SCHEDULE

GET READY. Log on to Windows Vista using an account with the Manage Printer permission. When the logon process is completed, close the Welcome Center window and any other windows that appear.

1. Click **Start**, and then click **Control Panel**. The Control Panel window appears.
2. Click **Hardware and Sound**, and then click **Printers**. The Printers window appears.
3. Right-click one of the printer icons and then, from the context menu, select **Properties**. The Properties sheet for the printer appears.
4. Click the **Advanced** tab.
5. Select the **Available from** radio button and then, in the two spin boxes provided, select the range of hours you want the printer to be available.
6. Click the **Security** tab.
7. Add the users or groups that you want to provide with access to the printer during the hours you selected and grant them the Allow Print permission.
8. Revoke the Allow Print permission from the Everyone special identity.
9. Click **OK** to close the Properties sheet.

CREATING A PRINTER POOL

As mentioned earlier, a printer pool is an arrangement that increases the production capability of a single printer by connecting it to multiple print devices. When you create a printer pool, the print server sends each incoming job to the first print device it finds that is not busy. This effectively distributes the jobs among the available print devices, providing users with more rapid service.

To create a printer pool, you must have at least two identical print devices, or at least print devices that use the same printer driver. The print devices must be in the same location, because there is no way to tell which print device will process a given document. You must also connect all of the print devices in the pool to the same print server. If the print server is a Windows Vista computer, you can connect the print devices to any viable ports.

To configure a printer pool, use the following procedure:

CREATE A PRINTER POOL

GET READY. Log on to Windows Vista using an account with the Manage Printer permission. When the logon process is completed, close the Welcome Center window and any other windows that appear.

1. Click **Start**, and then click **Control Panel**. The Control Panel window appears.
2. Click **Hardware and Sound**, and then click **Printers**. The Printers window appears.

3. Right-click one of the printer icons and then, from the context menu, select **Properties**. The Properties sheet for the printer appears.
4. Click the **Ports** tab, and then select all of the ports to which the print devices are connected.
5. Select the **Enable printer pooling** checkbox, and then click **OK**.

SUMMARY SKILL MATRIX

IN THIS LESSON YOU LEARNED:
Device drivers are software components that enable applications and operating systems to communicate with specific hardware devices. Every hardware device you install in a computer must have a corresponding driver.
Plug and Play is a standard that enables computers to detect and identify hardware devices, and then install and configure drivers for those devices. PnP dynamically assigns hardware resources to each device, and can reconfigure devices at will to accommodate each component's special needs.
The drivers included with Windows Vista have all been digitally signed to ensure that they have not been modified since they were published.
Device Manager is an MMC snap-in that lists all hardware devices in the computer and indicates problems with hardware identification or driver configuration. Using Device Manager, you can enable and disable devices, update and roll back drivers, and manage device and device driver properties.
Many hardware manufacturers periodically release driver updates, and it is up to system administrators to decide whether to install the updates.
The printing architecture in Windows is modular, consisting of the print device, a printer, a print server, and a printer driver.
A local printer is one that supports a print device directly attached to the computer or attached to the network. A network printer connects to a shared printer hosted by another computer.
To install a printer, you run the Add Printer wizard and specify the printer driver and port to use.
A single printer can direct jobs to more than one port, creating a printer pool.
A single print device can be served by multiple printers, each of which can have unique properties, drivers, settings, permissions, or monitoring characteristics.
The print queue window enables you to monitor printers for potential signs of trouble.

Knowledge Assessment

Fill in the Blank

Complete the following sentences by writing the correct word or words in the blanks provided.

1. By default, Windows Vista standard users are permitted to install Plug and Play devices only if their drivers are ________________.
2. A user calls the help desk and asks you why she cannot send print jobs to a shared printer that is using Windows Vista as a print server. You determine that the problem is related to the printer permissions. The user cannot send jobs to the printer because she only has the ________________ permission for the printer.

3. To share a printer with network users, you must first open the Network and Sharing Center and turn on ______________ and ______________.
4. In the Windows printing architecture, the two hardware components are called the ______________ and the ______________.
5. Jack has the Allow Print, Allow Manage Documents, and Allow Manage Printers permissions to a printer with a priority of 1. Jill has the Allow Print permission to a printer with a priority of 10, connected to the same print device. If Jack and Jill both submit a print job at exactly the same time, ______________'s print job will be processed first.
6. The primary function of a printer driver is to take printer commands generated by applications and convert them into ______________ commands.
7. The three main reasons why manufacturers release driver updates are to ______________, ______________, and ______________.
8. The digital signature of a driver consists of a(n) ______________ that is appended to the driver itself before publication.
9. To share a printer, you must be a member of the ______________ group.
10. All digitally signed drivers have undergone ______________ testing.

True / False

Circle T if the statement is true or F if the statement is false.

T | F 1. Granting users the Manage Printers permissions enables them to submit jobs to the printer.

T | F 2. By default, all device drivers must be digitally signed to be installed on a Windows Vista computer.

T | F 3. Windows Update dynamically updates device drivers only when a hardware device has no driver installed.

T | F 4. To create a printer pool, you must create a separate printer for each print device.

T | F 5. Granting someone the Allow Manage Printers permission enables them to submit jobs to the printer.

T | F 6. The x64-based versions of Windows Vista do not permit the installation of unsigned drivers under any circumstances.

T | F 7. To assign different printer priorities to two different groups, you must create two printers.

T | F 8. Disabling a device in Device Manager causes its device driver to be uninstalled.

T | F 9. When you install a printer for a print device connected to a Windows Vista computer's USB port, you must specify the print device's manufacturer and model.

T | F 10. When you open a print queue window and cancel the document that is currently printing, the print device stops immediately.

Review Questions

1. You are the administrator of a network with several print devices, all of which are hosted by Windows Vista computers and shared with all of the users on the network. One of the print devices is malfunctioning and must be sent out for repair. What is the most practical way to prevent network users from sending jobs to that printer while the print device is unavailable?
2. A standard user wants to install a USB printer connected to her computer. The drivers for the printer are included with Windows Vista. Can the user install the printer without help from an administrator? Why or why not?

Case Scenarios

Scenario #1: Troubleshooting Display Drivers

A client asks you to troubleshoot his Windows Vista computer, which is behaving erratically. He has recently purchased and installed a new video display adapter, and ever since then, he sees occasional wavy lines in the display. You run Device Manager on the system and note the manufacturer, model, and driver version of the video adapter. Then, you check the video adapter manufacturer's Website and discover that there is a new driver available for the adapter. After downloading and installing the driver update, you restart the system. The system appears to start normally, except that the graphical interface has been replaced by incomprehensible noise. Because you can't see the display, you can't work with the system. What should you do return the computer to an operational state?

Scenario #2: Enhancing Print Performance

You are a desktop support technician for a law firm with a group of ten legal secretaries who provide administrative support to the attorneys. All of the secretaries use a single, shared, high-speed laser printer that is connected to a dedicated Windows Vista print server. The secretaries print multiple copies of large documents on a regular basis, and although the laser printer is fast, it is kept running almost constantly. Sometimes the secretaries have to wait 20 minutes or more after submitting a print job for their documents to reach the top of the queue. The office manager has offered to purchase additional printers for the department. However, the secretaries are accustomed to simply clicking the **Print** button, and don't like the idea of having to examine multiple print queues to determine which one has the fewest jobs before submitting a document. What can you do to provide the department with a printing solution that will enable the secretaries to utilize additional printers most efficiently?

Configuring Network Connectivity

LESSON 7

OBJECTIVE DOMAIN MATRIX

Technology Skill	Objective Domain	Objective Number
Using the Network and Sharing Center	Use the Network and Sharing Center to configure networking	4.1
Understanding Network Discovery	Troubleshoot connectivity issues • Configure network settings in Windows Firewall • Apply Public vs. Private settings to network connections	4.2
Running Network Diagnostics	Troubleshoot connectivity issues: • Troubleshoot wireless network settings • Use the Diagnose Internet Connection tool to troubleshoot connectivity issues	4.2
Managing Local Area Network Connections	Manage network connections	4.1
Creating a New Network Connection	Manage network connections • Connect to a network • Set up a connection for a network	4.1

KEY TERMS

connectionless protocol
connection-oriented protocol
firewall
IP address
subnet masks
OSI reference model
packet-switching network
ports
protocols
router
sockets

Understanding Windows Networking

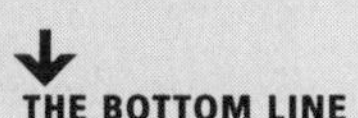

The networking modifications introduced in Windows Vista are the most significant changes to the networking engine since it was first incorporated into the operating system in Windows 95. Windows Vista includes a revamped TCP/IP stack and a variety of new tools that simplify the networking process for both users and administrators.

Networking is one of the primary functions of Windows Vista. Most Windows computers are connected to either a private local area network (LAN) or to the Internet, and many are connected to both. These connections provide users with access to remotely stored data, shared resources, network-attached hardware, and the virtually unlimited information and services available on the Internet. Most Windows users are unaware of how computer networks function or even of when they are accessing network, as opposed to local, resources. Users expect Windows to provide a seamless network experience wherever they happen to be located, and Windows Vista includes many new networking features that help to provide this experience.

Networking Basics

Computer networks are, for the most part, based on independent standards. The networking capabilities built into Windows Vista are implementations of those standards. Before you work directly with the Vista networking tools, it is important to have a firm grasp of the underlying principles on which they were designed.

Computer networking is a highly complex process, but most of the technology operates invisibly, both to the user and the administrator. Computers on a network communicate using ***protocols***, which are nothing more than languages that all of the computers understand. These protocols operate on different levels, forming what is commonly known as a networking stack or protocol stack. The most common method for illustrating the operations of the networking stack is the ***OSI*** (Open Systems Interconnection) ***reference model***, which consists of seven layers, as shown in Figure 7-1.

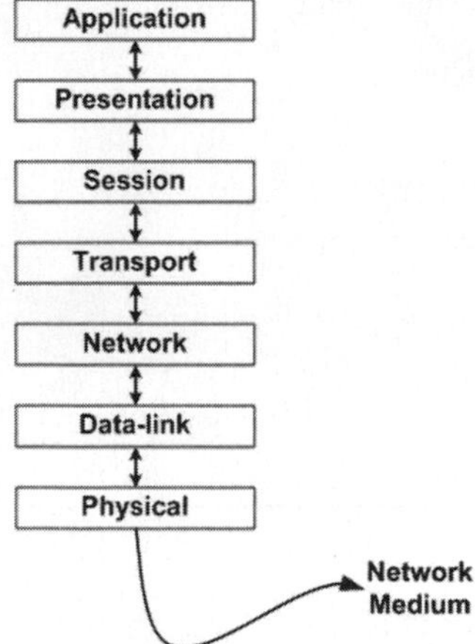

Figure 7-1

The OSI reference model

THE PHYSICAL LAYER

At the bottom of the OSI model is the physical layer, which represents the hardware that forms the network. This consists of the cable or radio signals that carry data from one system to another and the network interface adapters, which are the hardware components in the computers that provide the connection to the physical network.

Most cabled networks use a type of cable called unshielded twisted pair, which is similar to telephone cable except that it contains four twisted pairs of wires instead of two. The RJ-45 connectors the network cables use are also similar to the RJ-11 connectors used by telephones.

A network interface adapter is the component that provides the connection to the network. Most of the computers manufactured today have Ethernet network interface adapters integrated into their motherboards, but the adapter can also take the form of an expansion card that you install into the computer or an external device that connects to a Universal Serial Bus (USB) port. For wireless networking, the cable connectors are replaced by radio transceivers that transmit the same data using a different kind of signal.

THE DATA-LINK LAYER

As you move up beyond the physical layer, the subsequent layers of the OSI model are realized in software, as protocols that provide different types of communications. Most Windows networks use a protocol called Ethernet at the data-link layer. Local area networks are sometimes described as ***packet-switching networks***, which means that the messages generated by each computer are divided into many pieces called packets, which are transmitted separately over the network. A single file might be divided into hundreds or thousands of packets, each of which is transmitted separately. The packets might take different routes to the destination, and might even arrive there in a different order. The receiving computer is then responsible for putting the pieces back together to reassemble the file.

MORE INFORMATION

The cable on a packet-switching network, at any given moment, can be carrying packets generated by dozens of different computers. The alternative to a packet-switching network is a circuit-switching network, in which two systems establish a dedicated connection that they use exclusively until their transaction is completed. The most common example of a circuit-switching network is the telephone system.

For the packets to reach their destination, they must know where they are going. Therefore, they require an address. Just like the letters mailed in the post office, each packet needs an address identifying the destination computer. Ethernet is the protocol responsible for addressing the packets, which it does by surrounding the data it receives from the network layer just above it with a header and footer, as shown in Figure 7-2. This header and footer, and the data between them, are collectively called a *frame,* and the process of applying it is called *data encapsulation*. The header and footer perform the same functions as an envelope does to a letter, protecting the contents and displaying the address of the recipient.

Figure 7-2

Data-link layer data encapsulation

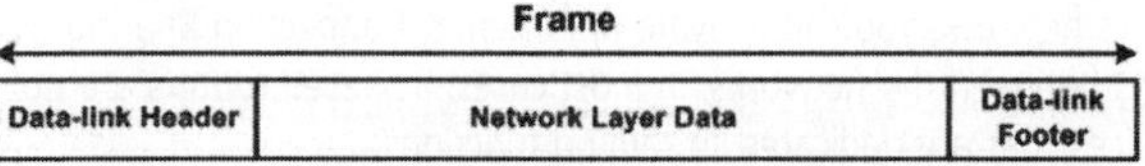

TAKE NOTE

Other data-link layer protocols, such as Token Ring, are available, but the vast majority of LANs use Ethernet. Two computers must both be running the same protocol in order to communicate.

The addresses computers use at the data-link layer are six-byte hexadecimal sequences, hard-coded into each network interface adapter by the manufacturer. These sequences are called hardware addresses or media access control (MAC) addresses. The first three bytes of a hardware address identify the manufacturer of the network interface adapter, and the last three bytes identify the adapter itself.

MORE INFORMATION

The standards on which Ethernet networks are based are published by the Institute of Electrical and Electronics Engineers (IEEE) and are known as IEEE 802.3, which refers to the number of the working group that produced the standards. The IEEE 802.3 standard defines three elements of an Ethernet network: a frame format for the packets transmitted over the network, a media access control mechanism called Carrier Sense Multiple Access with Collision Detection (CSMA/CD), and a series of physical layer specifications that describe the types of cables and other media that can be used to build an Ethernet network.

In addition to addresses, the Ethernet header contains other information that helps to direct and protect the data in the packet. Each Ethernet frame contains a code that identifies the network-layer protocol that generated the data in the packet, and a checksum that the receiving system will use to confirm that the packet has not been altered in transit.

THE NETWORK LAYER

The protocols that Windows uses by default at the network and transport layers are collectively called TCP/IP. TCP is the Transmission Control Protocol and IP is the Internet Protocol. Early versions of Windows used a different protocol called NetBIOS, but TCP/IP is the native protocol of the Internet, and the explosive growth in the Internet's popularity eventually led the developers of all network operating systems to adopt TCP/IP as their default protocol.

IP is the network layer protocol that performs many important networking functions. These functions are described in the following sections.

TAKE NOTE*

There are other network layer protocols that perform functions similar to those of IP, such as Internetwork Packet Exchange (IPX), a proprietary protocol developed by Novell for use with its NetWare operating system. However, the ubiquity of TCP/IP on the Internet has led to the almost universal adoption of IP at the network layer.

IP ROUTING

The term internet (with a lowercase "i") literally means a network of networks. The Internet as we know it (with a capital "I") is a huge conglomeration of networks, all connected by devices called routers. A ***router*** is simply a device that connects one network to another. When you install a LAN in a home or office and connect it to the Internet, you are actually installing a router that connects your network with another network, that of an Internet service provider (ISP).

MORE INFORMATION

Windows Vista itself can function as a router. When a Vista computer is connected to two networks, such as a LAN and an ISP's network, you can activate the Internet Connection Sharing (ICS) feature, which enables Vista to route packets between the networks. In most cases, however, routers are not general-purpose computers, but specialized devices that are dedicated to routing functions.

IP is the primary end-to-end protocol used on most data networks. Data-link layer protocols like Ethernet are actually LAN protocols; they are designed to send packets from one system to another system on the same local network. An *end-to-end protocol* like IP is responsible for the complete transmission of a packet from its source to its final destination on another network.

To get to that final destination, packets must be passed from router to router, through many different networks. A single packet might pass through dozens of routers before it reaches its destination network. The IP protocol is responsible for this routing process. Every TCP/IP system maintains a routing table that functions as the road map to other networks. By examining the destination address on each packet, and comparing it with the information in the routing table, IP decides which router to send the packet to next. The next router to receive the packet does the same thing, and step by step, the packet makes its way to the destination. Actually, each router the packet passes through is called a *hop*, so it is really a hop-by-hop process.

Of course, this process occurs much more quickly than this text can describe it. When you key a URL into your Web browser and press the Enter key, in the time it takes for the Web page to begin appearing on your screen, dozens of packets have traveled back and forth through dozens of routers to and from a destination that might be in another state or another country.

MORE INFORMATION

To see how many routers there are between your Windows Vista computer and a destination on the Internet, open a Command Prompt window and key *tracert destination*, where *destination* is the name of a server on the Internet, such as www.microsoft.com. The Tracert.exe program will gradually compile a list of the routers as they process the packets on the way to the destination.

IPv4 ADDRESSING

IP has its own addressing system, which it uses to identify all of the devices on a network. Every network interface in a computer, and every device that is directly connected to a TCP/IP network, must have an ***IP address***. IP addresses are independent of the hardware addresses assigned to network interface adapters. A Windows Vista computer that is connected to a LAN has both a hardware address and an IP address.

As mentioned earlier, data-link layer protocols like Ethernet are LAN protocols; their addresses are used only to transmit packets to other systems on the same local network. The IP address in a given packet, on the other hand, always identifies the packet's final destination, even if it is on another network. This is why IP is called an end-to-end protocol. When you use your Web browser to connect to a site on the Internet, the packets your computer generates contain the IP address of the destination site, but at the data-link layer they carry the hardware address of a router on the local network that they can use to access the Internet. Thus, the data-link layer and the network layer both have their own addresses, but they do not have to point to the same destination.

The current standard for IP is version 4 (IPv4), which calls for 32-bit IP addresses. Each address is split into two parts:

- Network identifier—As the name implies, specifies the network on which a particular system is located.
- Host identifier—Specifies a particular network interface (also called a *host*) on the network.

Unlike hardware addresses, however, which always use three bytes for the network and three bytes for the interface, IP addresses can have variable numbers of network and host bits. To locate the division between the network identifier and the host identifier, TCP/IP systems use a mechanism called a ***subnet mask***.

MORE INFORMATION

The TCP/IP protocols are defined by public domain documents that are published by a body called the Internet Engineering Task Force (IETF). When they are first published, these documents are known as Requests For Comments (RFC). They then proceed through a lengthy ratification process before being declared Internet standards. The original IP standard, published as RFC 791, "Internet Protocol: DARPA Internet Program Protocol Specification" in September 1981, is a relatively short document that concentrates largely on IPv4 addressing. There are numerous other RFCs that define other aspects of the IP protocol, all of which are available from the IETF Website at http://www.ietf.org.

IPv4 addresses are expressed in dotted decimal notation, that is, four eight-bit numbers, separated by dots (or periods), such as 192.168.3.64. An eight-bit binary number, when expressed in decimal form, can have any value from 0 to 255. A subnet mask is also a 32-bit number, expressed in dotted decimal notation, such as 255.255.255.0. The difference between a subnet mask and an IPv4 address is that a subnet mask consists, in binary form, of a series of consecutive ones followed by a series of consecutive zeroes. When you compare the subnet mask to the IPv4 address, the one bits in the mask represent the network identifier, while the zero bits represent the host identifier.

For example, a Windows Vista computer might be configured with the following IPv4 address and subnet mask:

- IP address: 192.168.3.64
- Subnet mask: 255.255.255.0

The concept of the subnet mask is easier to understand if you convert both values from decimal to binary, as follows:

- IP address: 11000000 10101000 00000011 100000000
- Subnet mask: 11111111 11111111 11111111 00000000

In binary form, you can see that the first 24 bits of the subnet mask are ones. Therefore, the first 24 bits of the IPv4 address form the network identifier. The last eight bits of the mask are zeroes, so the last eight bits of the address are the host identifier. As a result, in decimal form, the network identifier is 192.168.3 and the host identifier is 64.

The IP standard defines three classes of IP addresses, based on the byte divisions of their subnet masks. Table 7-1 shows these classes and their characteristics.

Table 7-1

IPv4 Address Classes

	Class A	Class B	Class C
Subnet mask	255.0.0.0	255.255.0.0	255.255.255.0
First bit values (binary)	0	10	110
First byte value (decimal)	0–127	128–191	192–223
Number of network identifier bits	8	16	24
Number of host identifier bits	24	16	8
Number of possible networks	126	16,384	2,097,152
Number of possible hosts	16,777,214	65,534	254

The division between the network identifier and the host identifier can fall anywhere in an IPv4 address; it does not have to fall on one of the eight-bit divisions. For example, a subnet mask of 255.255.240.0 translates into a binary value of 11111111 11111111 11110000 00000000, meaning that the network identifier is 20 bits long and the host identifier is 12 bits.

Networks that are connected directly to the Internet must use IPv4 addresses that are registered with the Internet Assigned Numbers Authority (IANA). This prevents the duplication of IP addresses on the Internet. The IANA assigns blocks of network identifiers to ISPs, who in turn assign them to their customers. Once an organization is assigned a network identifier, it is up to the network administrators to assign a unique host identifier to each computer on the network. Private LANs do not need registered addresses, so they can use network identifiers from three special ranges of private addresses that are reserved for that purpose. Table 7-2 shows the three private address ranges.

Table 7-2

IPv4 Private Addresses

Address Class	IPv4 Private Address Range	Subnet Mask
Class A	10.0.0.0 through 10.255.255.255	255.0.0.0
Class B	172.16.0.0 through 172.31.255.255	255.255.0.0
Class C	192.168.0.0 through 192.168.255.255	255.255.255.0

Although it is possible to manually assign IP addresses and configure computers to use them, most networks use the Dynamic Host Configuration Protocol (DHCP) to dynamically assign addresses. Windows Vista includes a DHCP client, which it uses by default. The Windows server products all include a full-featured DHCP server, which you can configure to assign any range of addresses in a variety of ways. Windows Vista includes a DHCP server, which is incorporated into the ICS feature, but it has only rudimentary capabilities and is not configurable.

IPv6 ADDRESSING

When the IP protocol was first being developed in the late 1970s, the Internet was an experimental network used only by a few hundred engineers and scientists. At that time, the 32-bit address space defined in the IPv4 standard seemed enormous. No one could have foreseen the explosive growth of the Internet that began in the 1990s, and which threatened to deplete the existing IP address space.

> **TAKE NOTE***
> In hexadecimal (or base 16) notation, each digit can have a value from 0 to 9 or A to F, for a total of 16 possible values. Remember, an eight-bit (one-byte) number can have 256 possible values. If each hexadecimal digit can have 16 values, two digits are required to express the 256 possible values for each byte of the address (16^2 = 256). This is why some of the two-byte values in the sample IPv6 address require four digits.

To address this situation, work began in the 1990s on a new revision of the IP protocol, known as Internet Protocol Version 6, or IPv6. IPv6 expands the address space from 32 to 128 bits, which is large enough to provide a more than sufficient number of addresses for our foreseeable needs.

Unlike IPv4 addresses, which use decimal notation, IPv6 addresses use hexadecimal notation, in the form of eight two-byte values, separated by colons, as follows:

XX : XX : XX : XX : XX : XX : XX : XX

Each X is a hexadecimal value for one byte, resulting in a total of 16 bytes, or 128 bits. An example of an IPv6 would be as follows:

FDC0 : 0 : 0 : 02BD : FF : BECB : FEF4 : 961D

To simplify IPv6 notation, you can eliminate the zero blocks from an address and replace them with a double colon, as follows:

FDC0 : : 02BD : FF : BECB : FEF4 : 961D

IPv4 is still the IP addressing standard used on most networks and on the Internet. However, the inclusion of IPv6 support in Windows Vista makes the operating system ready for the transition when it occurs. Windows Vista, by default, installs support for both IPv4 and IPv6 addressing when it detects a network interface adapter in the computer, as shown in Figure 7-3. Microsoft refers to this as Vista's *dual IP stack*.

Figure 7-3

Windows Vista support for IPv4 and IPv6

In addition, the DHCP server applications in Windows Server 2003 and Windows Server 2008 support both addressing standards, so when a Vista computer requests an IP address, the DHCP server supplies two, one IPv4 and one IPv6, as shown in the Ipconfig.exe display in Figure 7-4.

Figure 7-4

Windows DHCP servers supply both IPv4 and IPv6 addresses

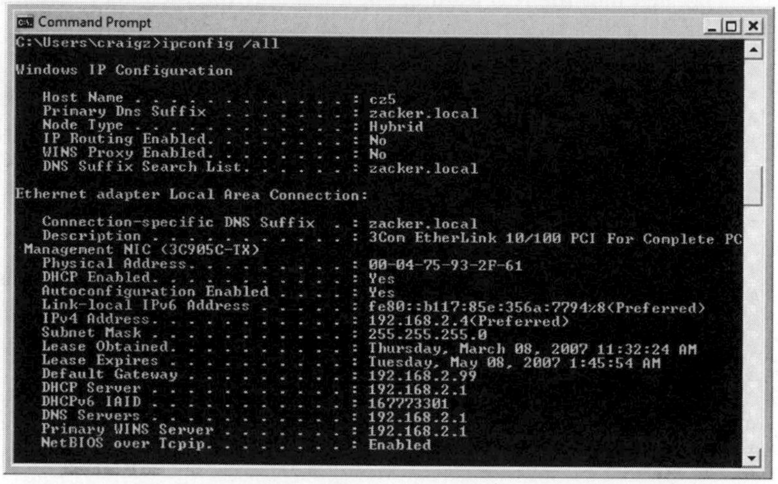

```
Command Prompt
C:\Users\craigz>ipconfig /all

Windows IP Configuration

   Host Name . . . . . . . . . . . . : cz5
   Primary Dns Suffix  . . . . . . . : zacker.local
   Node Type . . . . . . . . . . . . : Hybrid
   IP Routing Enabled. . . . . . . . : No
   WINS Proxy Enabled. . . . . . . . : No
   DNS Suffix Search List. . . . . . : zacker.local

Ethernet adapter Local Area Connection:

   Connection-specific DNS Suffix  . : zacker.local
   Description . . . . . . . . . . . : 3Com EtherLink 10/100 PCI For Complete PC
 Management NIC (3C905C-TX)
   Physical Address. . . . . . . . . : 00-04-75-93-2F-61
   DHCP Enabled. . . . . . . . . . . : Yes
   Autoconfiguration Enabled . . . . : Yes
   Link-local IPv6 Address . . . . . : fe80::b117:85e:356a:7794%8(Preferred)
   IPv4 Address. . . . . . . . . . . : 192.168.2.4(Preferred)
   Subnet Mask . . . . . . . . . . . : 255.255.255.0
   Lease Obtained. . . . . . . . . . : Thursday, March 08, 2007 11:32:24 AM
   Lease Expires . . . . . . . . . . : Tuesday, May 08, 2007 1:45:54 AM
   Default Gateway . . . . . . . . . : 192.168.2.99
   DHCP Server . . . . . . . . . . . : 192.168.2.1
   DHCPv6 IAID . . . . . . . . . . . : 167773301
   DNS Servers . . . . . . . . . . . : 192.168.2.1
   Primary WINS Server . . . . . . . : 192.168.2.1
   NetBIOS over Tcpip. . . . . . . . : Enabled
```

Windows Vista applications that are capable of using IPv6 do so by default; otherwise, applications revert to IPv4.

DATA ENCAPSULATION

Earlier in this lesson, you learned how data-link layer protocols encapsulate data for transmission, much as an envelope encapsulates a letter for mailing. IP encapsulates data as well, so that it can provide the address of the system that is the packet's final destination. In fact, IP performs its encapsulation first, by adding a header to the data it receives from the transport layer protocol. This header includes the packet's source and destination IP addresses, as well as other information that facilitates the transmission of the packet.

After IP adds its header, it sends the packet down to the data-link layer, where Ethernet adds its own header and footer to the packet. Thus, the data-link layer packet that gets transmitted over the network consists of transport layer data, encapsulated within an IP packet, which is called a *datagram*, which is in turn encapsulated within an Ethernet frame, as shown in Figure 7-5.

Figure 7-5

IP data encapsulation

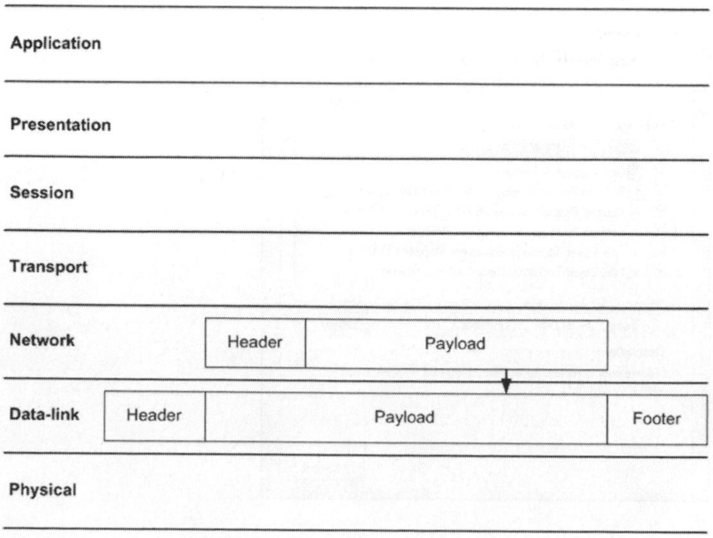

Application
Presentation
Session
Transport
Network
Header
Payload
Data-link
Header
Payload
Footer
Physical

As with Ethernet, one of the functions of the IP header is to identify the protocol that generated the data in the datagram. The Protocol field in the IP header uses codes standardized by the IANA to specify the transport layer protocol that created the packet.

THE TRANSPORT LAYER

The OSI reference model calls for the network and transport layers to provide a flexible quality of service, so that applications can operate at peak efficiency. Two types of protocols operate at these layers:

- Connection-oriented—A ***connection-oriented protocol*** is one in which two communicating systems establish a connection before they transmit any data. Once the connection is established, the computers exchange packets with complex headers designed to provide error detection and correction. A connection-oriented protocol ensures bit-perfect data transmissions, but at the price of greatly increased overhead.
- Connectionless—A ***connectionless protocol*** does not require the establishment of a connection, nor does it perform error detection or correction. Systems simply transmit their packets to the destination, without knowing if the destination system is ready to accept data, or if it even exists. Connectionless protocols do not guarantee delivery of their data, but they operate with a very low overhead that conserves network bandwidth.

IP, at the network layer, is a connectionless protocol, and there is no connection-oriented alternative at that layer. At the transport layer, TCP is the connection-oriented protocol, and the connectionless alternative is the User Datagram Protocol (UDP).

CONNECTION-ORIENTED PROTOCOLS

Applications that use TCP require every bit of data they transmit to be received properly at the destination. For example, if you download a service pack from the Microsoft Website, a single garbled bit could render the package useless. Using TCP/IP guarantees that every packet arrives intact. If a packet is damaged or lost, the systems retransmit it. However, to use TCP, the systems must exchange extra packets to establish a connection and append a 20-byte header to each packet. This adds up to a lot of extra data that has to be transmitted over the network.

CONNECTIONLESS PROTOCOLS

Applications that use UDP are not terribly concerned if a packet goes astray. There are two reasons why this can be so. Either the messages are so small that the systems can easily retransmit them if they do not receive a response, or the data transmitted by the application is of a type that can tolerate the loss of an occasional packet.

An example of the former reason is the Domain Name System (DNS) communications that are a part of every Internet transaction. When you key a URL into your Web browser, the first thing the system does is send a UDP message to a DNS server requesting the IP address corresponding to the domain name in the URL. This is a tiny message that fits in a single packet, so it's not worth transmitting several additional packets to establish a TCP connection. It's more economical just to retransmit the DNS request if no response if forthcoming.

A good example of the latter reason is streaming video. A video stream consists of large amounts of data, but unlike a file transfer, a few missing bits will not cause a catastrophic failure. A few packets lost from a video stream due to damaged UDP packets might mean a few lost frames, but that would hardly be noticeable to the viewer. The alternative, using TCP to transmit all of the packets, would provide a perfect viewing experience for the user, but at the cost of vastly increased bandwidth.

PORTS AND SOCKETS

Just like the network and data-link layers, transport layer protocols encapsulate the data they receive from the layer above by appending a header to each packet, as shown in Figure 7-6. Unlike the lower layers, however, transport layer protocols are not concerned with addressing packets to the correct system. This addressing is performed by IP and Ethernet, so there is no need for it here. However, transport layer protocols are concerned with identifying the applications that created the packet and to which the packet will ultimately be delivered.

Figure 7-6

Transport layer data encapsulation

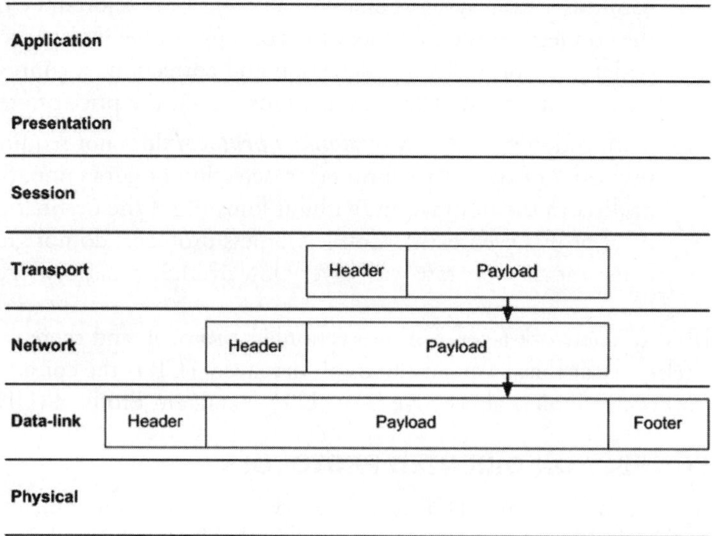

As with the protocol codes included in IP headers, the TCP and UDP headers both contain codes that identify specific applications running on the system. The codes, called ***ports***, are again published by the IANA, and the combination of an IP address and a port number is called a ***socket***. For example, the standard port number for the Hypertext Transfer Protocol (HTTP), the application layer protocol used for Web communications, is 80. If your Web browser is sending an HTTP request to a Web server with the IP address 192.168.87.33, the Web server application on that computer can be identified by the socket 192.168.87.33:80.

The two basic types of port numbers are *well-known port numbers*, which are numbers permanently assigned to specific applications, and *ephemeral port numbers*, which are created automatically by client applications. In the previous example, the Web browser is using the well-known HTTP port 80 as the destination for its packets, but the source port would be an ephemeral port number created by the system running the browser.

This system works because the client is initiating contact with the server. The client has to know the port number to use in its messages to the server, so it uses a well-known port. There is no need for the client to have a well-known port number because the server will be able to discover the client's ephemeral port number from its incoming messages.

Table 7-3 lists some of the most common well-known port numbers.

Table 7-3

Well-Known Port Numbers Used by TCP and UDP

SERVICE NAME	PORT NUMBER	PROTOCOL	FUNCTION
ftp-data	20	TCP	FTP data channel; used for transmitting files between systems
ftp	21	TCP	FTP control channel; used by FTP-connected systems for exchanging commands and responses
ssh	22	TCP and UDP	SSH (Secure Shell) Remote Login Protocol; used to securely log on to a computer from another computer on the same network and execute commands
telnet	23	TCP	Telnet; used to execute commands on network-connected systems
smtp	25	TCP	Simple Mail Transport Protocol (SMTP); used to send e-mail messages
domain	53	TCP and UDP	DNS; used to receive host name resolution requests from clients
bootps	67	TCP and UDP	Bootstrap Protocol (BOOTP) and DHCP servers; used to receive TCP/IP configuration requests from clients
bootpc	68	TCP and UDP	BOOTP and DHCP clients; used to send TCP/IP configuration requests to servers
http	80	TCP	HTTP; used by Web servers to receive requests from client browsers
pop3	110	TCP	Post Office Protocol 3 (POP3); used to retrieve e-mail requests from clients
nntp	119	TCP and UDP	Network News Transfer Protocol (NNTP); used to post and distribute messages to, and retrieve them from, Usenet servers on the Internet
ntp	123	TCP and UDP	Network Time Protocol (NTP); used to exchange time signals for the purpose of synchronizing the clocks in network computers
imap	143	TCP and UDP	Internet Message Access Protocol version 4 (IMAP4); used by e-mail client programs to retrieve messages from a mail server
snmp	161	TCP and UDP	Simple Network Management Protocol (SNMP); used by SNMP agents to transmit status information to a network management console
https	443	TCP and UDP	Hypertext Transfer Protocol Over TLS/SSL; used to provide secure transmission of data between web browsers and servers.

DATA ENCAPSULATION

The headers that the TCP and UDP protocols add to the data they receive from the application layer are vastly different in size and complexity. The headers for both protocols contain source and destination port numbers. The UDP header includes little else, except for a checksum used to check for errors in the header. The TCP header, on the other hand, includes a multitude of fields that implement additional services, including the following:

- Packet acknowledgment—Informs the sender which packets have been delivered successfully.
- Error correction—Informs the sender which packets must be retransmitted.
- Flow control—Regulates the rate at which the sending system transmits its data.

THE UPPER LAYERS

The application layer is the top of the networking stack, and as such, it provides the entrance point for programs running on a computer. Windows applications themselves have no networking capabilities. They simply make function calls to application layer protocols, which in turn initiate the entire network communications process.

TAKE NOTE*

The session and presentation layers typically do not have individual protocols dedicated to them. In most cases, application layer protocols include functions attributed to all of the top three layers.

For example, Microsoft Mail is a client program that enables you to send messages to users on other computers, but the Mail program knows nothing about the nature of your network. When you send an e-mail message, Microsoft Mail takes the message and the address of the intended recipient and packages it using an application layer protocol called Simple Mail Transport Protocol (SMTP). SMTP creates a properly formatted e-mail message and passes it down to the next lower layer in the networking stack, which for this application is TCP.

TCP then adds its header and passes the packet down to IP, which encapsulates it and passes it down to Ethernet, which adds its frame and transmits it over the network. Thus, by the time the e-mail message reaches the network, it has been encapsulated four times, by SMTP, TCP, IP, and Ethernet, as shown in Figure 7-7.

Figure 7-7

Application layer data encapsulation

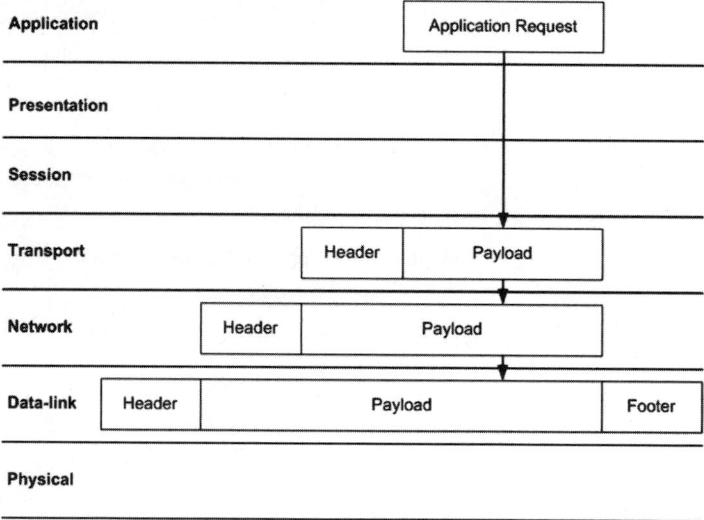

When the packet arrives at its final destination, the networking stack on the receiving computer performs the same steps in reverse. The system passes the incoming packets up through the layers, with each one removing its header and using the header information in it to pass the contents to the correct protocol at the next higher layer. Finally, the packet arrives at its final terminus, which is an application running on the destination computer, in this case an e-mail server.

What's New in Windows Vista Networking?

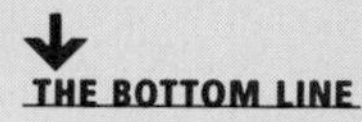

The networking capabilities in Windows Vista minimize the threat of intrusion from outside, while providing users with a simple and reliable networking experience. The following sections examine some of the new networking tools and concepts introduced in Windows Vista.

Networking provides Windows Vista with an open door to a virtually unlimited array of resources, but an open door can let things in as easily as it lets things out. This makes security a primary concern for Windows Vista administrators. Windows Vista includes a variety of new tools and features that enable users and administrators to manage the operating system's networking capabilities and help to protect it against unauthorized access. Many of these new features lie "under the hood," and operate invisibly to both users and administrators.

However, some of the new tools that desktop technicians must use regularly are as follows:

- Network and Sharing Center—Provides a centralized access point for Windows Vista networking administration features, including security controls, mapping, and diagnostics.
- Network Map—Provides a graphical display of the computer on the network and the connections between them.
- Network Diagnostics—Provides automated troubleshooting for Internet connections.

The following sections examine these tools and the concepts that they support.

Installing Network Support

Windows Vista usually is able to detect a network interface adapter in a computer and automatically install and configure the networking client.

The installation of Windows Vista's networking support is usually automatic. When the operating system detects a network interface adapter in the computer, either during the initial installation or afterwards, it installs a device driver for the adapter as well as the components of the default networking stack, which are as follows:

- Client for Microsoft Networks—Provides application layer services that enable programs to access shared files and printers on the network.
- QoS Packet Scheduler—Enables the network client to prioritize network traffic based on bandwidth availability and changing network conditions.
- File and Printer Sharing for Microsoft Networks—Enables the computer to share its files and printers with other users on the network.
- Internet Protocol Version 6 (TCP/IPv6)—Provides support for the IPv6 network layer protocol, including 128-bit IP addresses.
- Internet Protocol Version 4 (TCP/IPv4)—Provides support for the IPv4 network layer protocol, including 32-bit IP addresses.
- Link Layer Topology Discovery Mapper I/O Driver and Link Layer Topology Discovery Responder—Implements the protocol that enables Windows Vista to compile a map of the computers on the network.

The first time that the computer connects to a network, Vista presents the user with a selection of three network locations. These selections are actually combinations of network discovery and file sharing settings, which determine how much access the workstation user will have to the network and how much access network users will have to the workstation.

The three network location options are as follows:

- Home—Indicates that the computer is connected to a private workgroup network and not directly connected to the Internet. This means that it is safe for the computer to share its files and discover other computers.
- Work—Indicates that the computer is connected to a Windows domain network. This means that it is safe for the computer to share its files and discover other computers.
- Public—Indicates that the computer is connected to a network in a public place, such as an airport or coffee shop "hot spot" for wireless computers. This means that the computer and its shares cannot be seen or accessed from the network. In addition, some applications might not be able to access the network.

TAKE NOTE*

When a Windows Vista computer is set to use the Home or Public network location, the user can modify the setting manually from the Network and Sharing Center. When the network location is set to Work, the setting is controlled by domain policy and is not manually configurable. See "Changing the Network Location" later in this lesson for more information.

Using the Network and Sharing Center

The Network and Sharing Center is a centralized console that provides system technicians and administrators with access to most of the major networking tools included with Windows Vista.

CERTIFICATION READY?
Use the Network and Sharing Center to configure networking
4.1

Many of the common network configuration and administration tasks that technicians perform on Windows Vista computers start by opening the Network and Sharing Center. As with many Windows tools, there are several ways to open the Network and Sharing Center, some of which are as follows:

- Click **Start > Control Panel > Network and Internet > Network and Sharing Center**
- Click **Start > Network > Network and Sharing Center**
- Click **Start > Search for "Network" > Network and Sharing Center**

When the Network and Sharing Center appears, you see a window like the one shown in Figure 7-8.

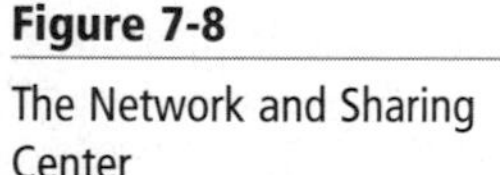

Figure 7-8

The Network and Sharing Center

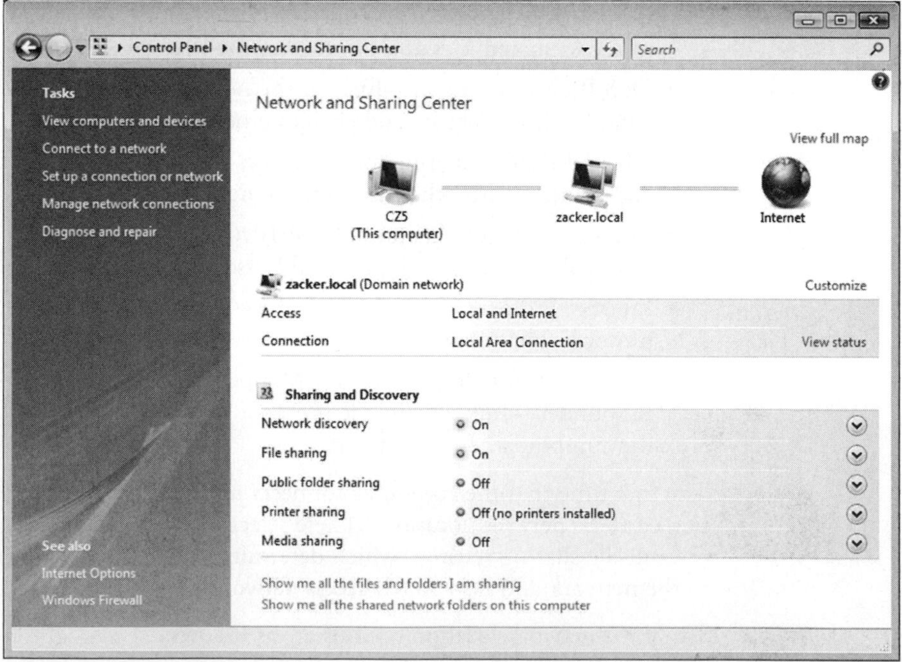

The Network and Sharing Center main window consists of the following elements:

- Task list (left pane)—Contains links that enable you to create and manage network connections and diagnose Internet connection problems.
- Summary network map (top right)—Provides a graphical representation of the computers and networks in the immediate vicinity of the workstation and their connections. The computers and networks are represented by icons, with lines representing their connections. A link also provides access to a complete map of the entire network.

- Network details (middle right)—Displays the name of the network and other information, such as the network location (private, domain, or public); whether the workstation is connected to a local network, the Internet, or both; and the name of the local area connection the system is using to access the network. There are also links that enable you to customize the network display and view the current status of the local area connection.
- Sharing and discovery (bottom right)—Contains switches that enable you to control the sharing and discovery behavior of the network.

UNDERSTANDING NETWORK DISCOVERY

Network Discovery is one of the most important new security concepts introduced in Windows Vista, because it enables users to control critical network firewall controls with a single switch. Windows Firewall is a feature that was first introduced in the Windows XP Service Pack 2 release, and is now included in Windows Vista as well.

A ***firewall*** is a software routine that acts as a virtual barrier between a computer and the network to which it is attached. A firewall is essentially a filter that enables certain types of incoming and outgoing traffic to pass through the barrier, while blocking other types.

Firewalls typically base their filtering on the TCP/IP characteristics at the network, transport, and application layers, as follows:

- IP addresses—Represent specific computers on the network.
- Protocol numbers—Identify the transport layer protocol being used by the packets.
- Port numbers—Identify specific application running on the computer.

If, for example, you want to prevent all computers on the network from accessing your system using the Telnet protocol, you would configure the firewall to block the traffic from all IP addresses using TCP port number 23.

Configuring a firewall manually can be an extremely complex task. You must be conscious of all the protocols and port numbers used by specific operating system functions and applications. Network Discovery is a Windows Vista feature that simplifies the task of firewall configuration by enabling you to block or allow the protocols and ports need for the computer to browse and access the network.

The Network Discovery switch in the Network and Sharing Center controls two functions:

- Whether the computer can see and be seen by the other systems on the network.
- Whether the computer can share its resources and access shared resources on the network.

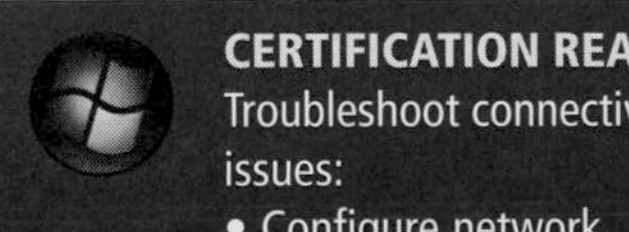

CERTIFICATION READY?
Troubleshoot connectivity issues:
- Configure network settings in Windows Firewall
- Apply Public vs. Private settings to network connections

4.2

It is critical to understand that this switch works in both directions. When a Windows Vista computer has Network Discovery turned off, it cannot browse the other computers on the network or access their shares. At the same time, the other computers on the network cannot browse to the Vista computer or access its shares.

The default state of the Network Discovery switch is dependent on the network location, as set manually by the user or automatically by the computer. Private and domain computers have Network Discovery turned on, and public computers have it turned off.

If it is necessary to manually change the Network Discovery setting, use the following procedure:

CONTROL NETWORK DISCOVERY

GET READY. Log on to Windows Vista using an account with administrative capabilities. When the logon process is completed, close the Welcome Center window and any other windows that appear.

1. Click **Start**, then click **Control Panel**. The Control Panel window appears.
2. Click **Network and Internet**, and then click **Network and Sharing Center**. The Network and Sharing Center window appears.
3. In the Sharing and Discovery section, click the **down arrow** to expand the Network discovery option, as shown in Figure 7-9.

Figure 7-9

The Network Discovery option

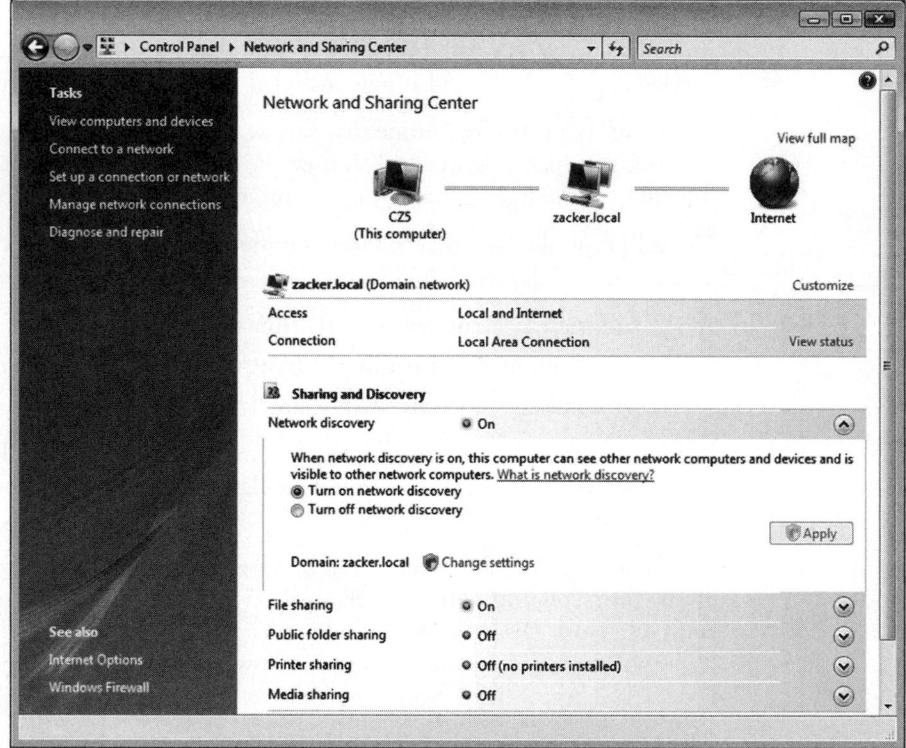

4. Click the appropriate radio button to turn Network Discovery on or off. Then click **Apply**.
5. After confirming that you are making the change, the Network Discovery status indicator changes to reflect the new state.

CLOSE the Network and Sharing Center.

CONTROLLING SHARING

In addition to Network Discovery, the Network and Sharing Center also enables you to exercise individual control over the computer's ability to share various types of resources. In the Sharing and Discovery section, beneath the Network discovery switch, are four additional switches:

- File sharing—Enables the computer to share files in any folder that the user designates as a share.
- Public folder sharing—Shares the contents of the public folder with network users.
- Printer sharing—Enables the computer to share any printer that the user designates as a share.
- Media sharing—Enables the computer to share media files with computers and digital media players on the network.

Before you can share resources on the computer, you must turn Network Discovery on and also activate one or more of these options. The general procedure for enabling and disabling these options is as follows:

CONTROL SHARING

GET READY. Log on to Windows Vista using an account with administrative capabilities. When the logon process is completed, close the Welcome Center window and any other windows that appear.

1. Open the Network and Sharing Center. The Network and Sharing Center window appears.
2. In the Sharing and Discovery section, click the **down arrow** to expand the option you want to modify.
3. Click the appropriate radio button to turn the option on or off. Then click **Apply**.
4. After you confirm that you are making the change, the Network Discovery status indicator changes to reflect the new state.

CLOSE the Network and Sharing Center.

TAKE NOTE* Another option in the Sharing and Discovery section, called Password Protected Sharing, enables access to the workstation's shares only when the network user logs on using a local user account with a password. This option does not appear when the computer is a member of a Windows domain.

CHANGING THE NETWORK LOCATION

After you select the initial network location during the network interface adapter installation, Windows Vista attempts to detect the type of location whenever you connect to a different network. If, for example, you selected Home when you installed Windows Vista on your laptop computer, and you later take the computer to a coffee shop with a wireless network, Vista will most likely detect the change and alter the network location to Public. This turns the Network Discovery and file sharing options off, for greater security.

TAKE NOTE* Public is also the default location Windows Vista uses when it cannot detect the network type, because the operating system would prefer to err on the side of caution.

If for any reason the computer fails to detect a network change and you want to manually alter the location setting, you can do so by performing the following procedure:

CHANGE THE NETWORK LOCATION

GET READY. Log on to Windows Vista using an account with administrative capabilities. When the logon process is completed, close the Welcome Center window and any other windows that appear.

1. Open the Network and Sharing Center. The Network and Sharing Center window appears.
2. In the network details section, click **Customize.** The Set Network Location page appears, as shown in Figure 7-10.

Figure 7-10

The Set Network Location page

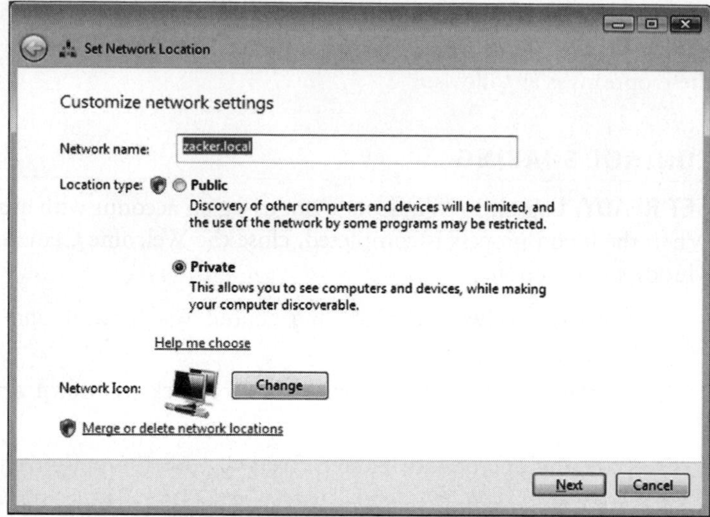

3. After you confirm that you are making the change, click the appropriate radio button to select the network Location type, and then click **Next.** The Successfully Set Network Settings page appears.
4. Click **Close.**

   CLOSE the Network and Sharing Center.

Using Network Map

Network Map is an administration and diagnostics tool that displays a graphical map of the computers on the network and the connections between them.

Network Map is a tool that is new to Windows Vista, but which is in the process of being deployed on all of the Windows operating systems. Network Map automatically compiles a graphical representation of the network, including icons representing the computers, printers, and other devices attached to it, and lines representing the connections between these elements.

Network Map uses a new protocol called Link Layer Topology Discovery (LLTD) to discover information about the network and the devices attached to it. LLTD devices called *enumerators* transmit requests for information over the network, and other computers, called *responders*, reply with the requested information. This protocol not only enables the computer to discover the existence of other systems on the network, it also tests the connections between them.

DISPLAYING A NETWORK MAP

The Network and Sharing Center displays a summary map on its main window, but to display a complete map of the network you must click the **View Full Map** link to open the window shown in Figure 7-11. For Windows Vista to display a full map of the network, the following conditions must be met:

- Network Discovery must be turned on.
- If the computer is a member of a Windows domain, group policy must be configured to permit network mapping.
- Any Windows XP computers on the network must have the LLTD Responder software installed.

Figure 7-11

The Network Map page

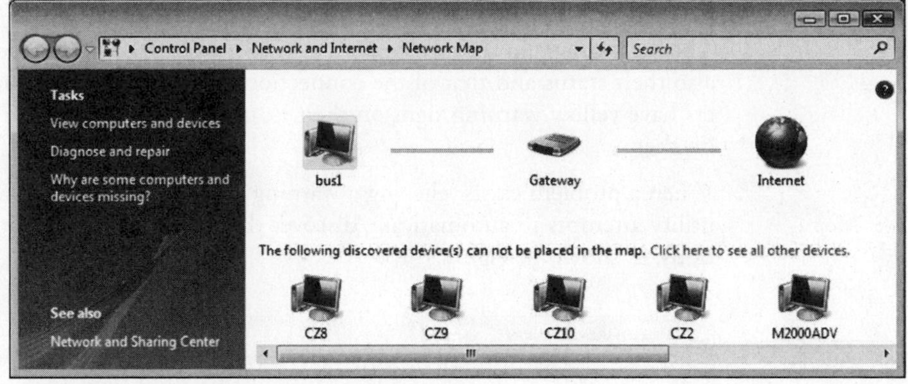

TAKE NOTE

Windows Vista computers have the LLTD networking components installed by default. However, Windows XP computers do not. To download the Windows XP version of the LLTD Responder software, see http://www.microsoft.com/downloads/details.aspx?FamilyID=4f01a31d-ee46-481e-ba11-37f485fa34ea or KnowledgeBase article KB922120.

From a security standpoint, it is not a good idea to allow just anyone to access a map of your network. As a result, when a Windows Vista computer is a member of a Windows domain, network mapping is disabled by the default group policy settings. To control network mapping with group policy, you must use the Group Policy Management Console to open an appropriate group policy object (GPO) and navigate to the Computer Configuration > Administrative Templates > Network > Link Layer Topology Discovery container. There you will find the following two policies:

- Turn on Mapper I/O (LLTDIO) driver—Enables a computer to map other systems on the network.
- Turn on Responder (RSPNDR) driver—Enables a computer to be mapped by other systems on the network.

Enabling these policies, as shown in Figure 7-12, allows you to control whether mapping can occur on domain, public, and private networks.

Figure 7-12

Controlling Network Map with Group Policy

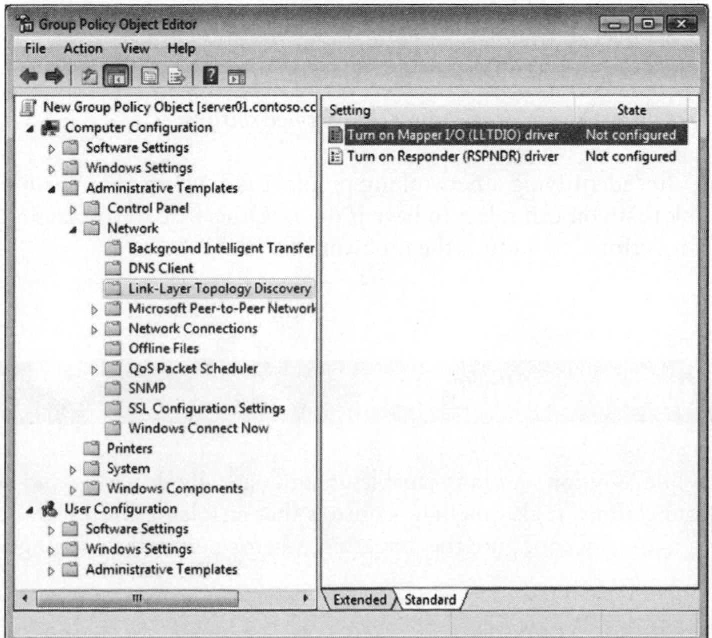

RUNNING NETWORK DIAGNOSTICS

The Network Map display shows not only the existence of the devices on the network, but also their status and that of the connections between them. Improperly configured computers have yellow warning signs on their icons and nonfunctioning connections have red X's on them.

When a problem exists, clicking a warning icon launches Windows Network diagnostics. This utility attempts to automatically discover the cause of the problem and displays possible solutions, as shown in Figure 7-13.

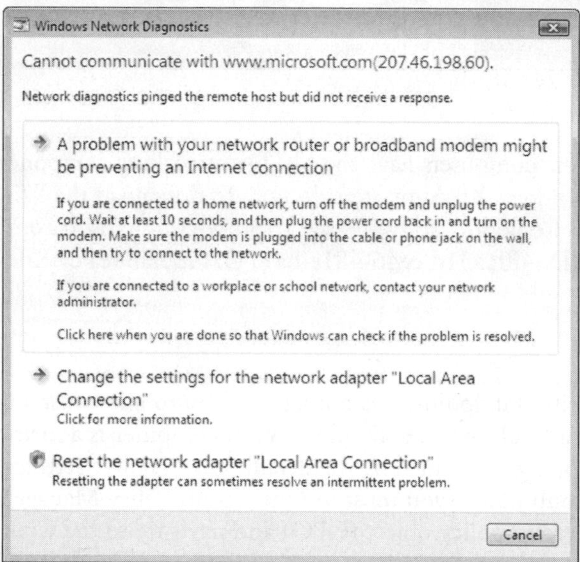

Figure 7-13
Running Windows Network Diagnostics

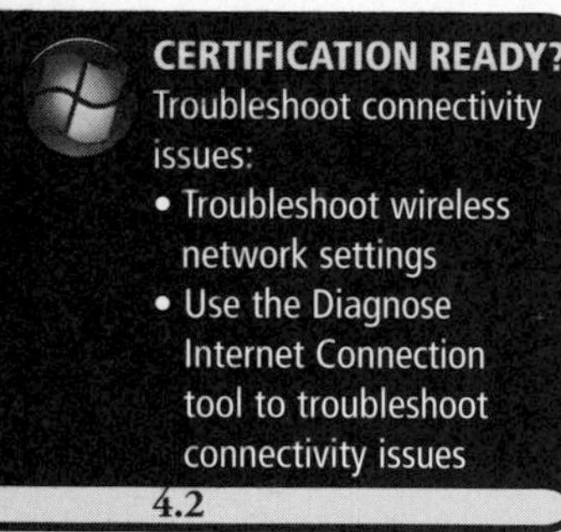

CERTIFICATION READY?
Troubleshoot connectivity issues:
• Troubleshoot wireless network settings
• Use the Diagnose Internet Connection tool to troubleshoot connectivity issues
4.2

Unlike previous troubleshooting tools, Network Diagnostics does not just display error messages; it tells you in clear language what might be wrong and what you have to do to repair the problem. The Network Diagnostics Framework (NDF) includes troubleshooting routines for wireless as well as wired networks. Problems that the system can diagnose include the following:

- Broken or detached cable connections
- IP address and subnet mask problems
- Default gateway problems
- DNS and DHCP configuration problems
- Networking hardware configuration problems
- Internet server addresses and service settings

If after identifying a networking problem the system can repair it automatically, it provides a link that you can select to have it do so. Otherwise, it displays a list of manual fixes that you can perform to address the problem.

Configuring Network Connections

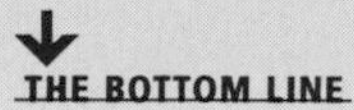

While Windows Vista is capable of automatically detecting and configuring network connections, it also includes controls that enable desktop technicians and administrators to manually configure the operating system's networking settings.

The Windows Vista Network and Sharing Center provides a central access point for all of the network connections on the computer. The following sections examine the procedures for creating and managing the network connection types that Vista supports.

Managing Local Area Network Connections

Windows Vista creates and configures local area connections automatically, but you can also manage and modify the properties of the connections manually.

CERTIFICATION READY? Manage network connections 4.1

When Vista detects a network interface adapter, it creates a network connection automatically, installs the TCP/IP networking components, and configures it to use DHCP to obtain IP addresses and other network configuration settings. To view and modify the Properties of local area connection, use the procedures in the following sections.

VIEWING A CONNECTION'S STATUS

Each local area connection on a Windows Vista system has a status dialog box that displays real-time information about the connection. To view the status of a connection, use the following procedure:

VIEW CONNECTION STATUS

GET READY. Log on to Windows Vista using an account with administrative capabilities. When the logon process is completed, close the Welcome Center window and any other windows that appear.

1. Click **Start**, then click **Control Panel.** The Control Panel window appears.
2. Click **Network and Internet**, and then click **Network and Sharing Center.** The Network and Sharing Center window appears.
3. In the network details section, click **View Status.** The Local Area Connection Status dialog box appears, as shown in Figure 7-14.

Figure 7-14

The Local Area Connection Status dialog box

4. Click **Details.** The Network Connection Details page appears, as shown in Figure 7-15.

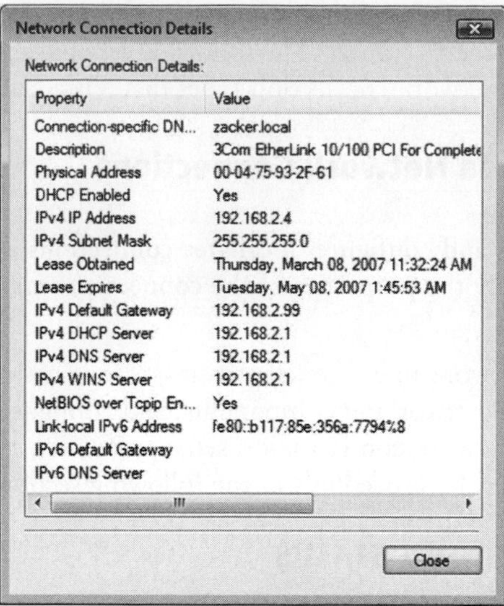

Network Connection Details
Network Connection Details:
Property	Value
Connection-specific DN...	zacker.local
Description	3Com EtherLink 10/100 PCI For Complete
Physical Address	00-04-75-93-2F-61
DHCP Enabled	Yes
IPv4 IP Address	192.168.2.4
IPv4 Subnet Mask	255.255.255.0
Lease Obtained	Thursday, March 08, 2007 11:32:24 AM
Lease Expires	Tuesday, May 08, 2007 1:45:53 AM
IPv4 Default Gateway	192.168.2.99
IPv4 DHCP Server	192.168.2.1
IPv4 DNS Server	192.168.2.1
IPv4 WINS Server	192.168.2.1
NetBIOS over Tcpip En...	Yes
Link-local IPv6 Address	fe80::b117:85e:356a:7794%8
IPv6 Default Gateway
IPv6 DNS Server
Close

Figure 7-15

The Network Connection Details page

The Local Area Connection Status dialog box displays basic information about the connection, such as its speed, which version(s) of IP it is using, and how long the computer has been connected. In the Activity area, you can see the number of bytes that the computer has sent and received in a real-time display, so you can tell if the network connection is currently functional.

At the bottom of the dialog box are buttons that enable you to perform the following tasks:

- Properties—Open the Properties sheet for the network connection.
- Disable/Enable—Toggle the operational status of the network connection.
- Diagnose—Start Windows Network Diagnostics and attempt to detect any problems affecting the network connection.

TAKE NOTE*

Disabling a network connection does not affect its configuration settings in any way. The networking hardware is still installed and configured and the TCP/IP settings remain intact. The connection is simply turned off until you turn it back on again, which renders it immediately operational.

The Network Connection Details page displays the configuration settings for the network connection, including the TCP/IP settings obtained using DHCP.

MANUALLY CONFIGURING TCP/IP SETTINGS

Most networks today use DHCP to configure the TCP/IP configuration settings of their workstations. DHCP automates the configuration process and prevents the duplication of IP addresses. However, there are still some situations in which it is desirable or necessary to configure the Windows TCP/IP client manually. To do this, use the following procedure:

MANUALLY CONFIGURE TCP/IP

GET READY. Log on to Windows Vista using an account with administrative capabilities. When the logon process is completed, close the Welcome Center window and any other windows that appear.

1. Click **Start**, and then click **Control Panel.** The Control Panel window appears.
2. Click **Network and Internet**, and then click **Network and Sharing Center.** The Network and Sharing Center window appears.
3. Click **Manage network connections.** The Network Connections window appears, as shown in Figure 7-16.

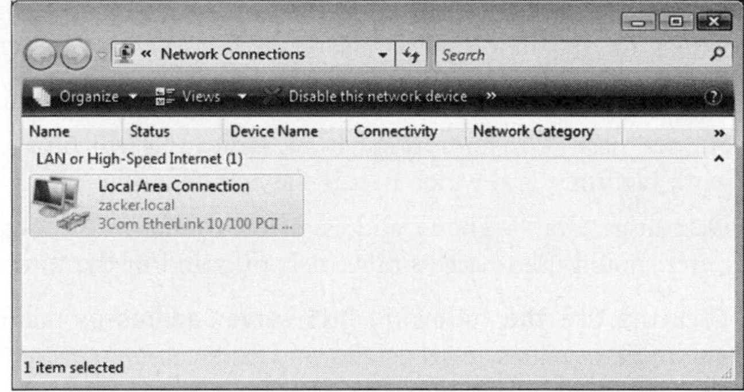

Figure 7-16

The Network Connections window

4. Right-click the connection you want to manage and then, from the context menu, select **Properties.** After confirming that you performed the action, the connection's Properties sheet appears, as shown in Figure 7-17.

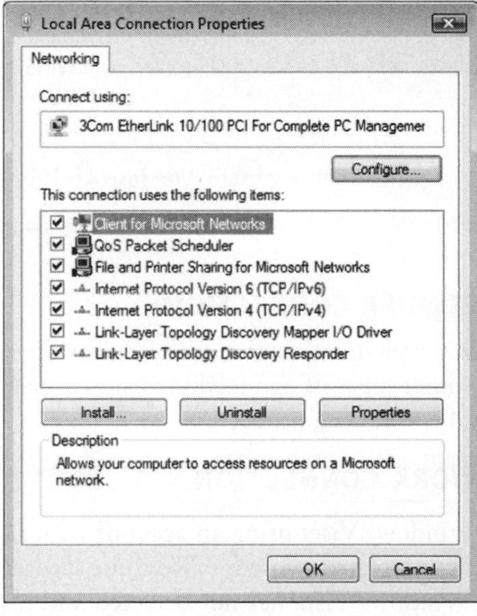

Figure 7-17

A network connection's Properties sheet

TAKE NOTE*

You can click the **Configure** button on the connection's Properties sheet to open the Properties sheet for the network interface adapter hardware. From this sheet, you can configure advanced networking settings, as well as the adapter's hardware resource settings.

5. Select **Internet Protocol Version 4 (TCP/IPv4)**, and then click **Properties.** The Internet Protocol Version 4 (TCP/IPv4) Properties sheet appears, as shown in Figure 7-18.

Figure 7-18

The Internet Protocol Version 4 (TCP/IPv4) Properties sheet

6. Click the **Use the following IP address** radio button, and then enter appropriate values for the following parameters:
   - IP address—A 32-bit IPv4 address, in dotted decimal notation.
   - Subnet mask—An appropriate mask indicating which part of the IP address is the network identifier and which part is the host identifier.
   - Default gateway—The IP address of the router on the local network that the computer should use to access other networks and/or the Internet.
7. Click the **Use the following DNS server addresses** radio button, and then enter appropriate values for the following parameters:
   - Preferred DNS server—The IP address of the DNS server the computer should use to resolve host and domain names into IP addresses.
   - Alternate DNS server—The IP address of a DNS server that the computer should use if the preferred DNS server is unavailable.

Clicking the Advanced button opens the Advanced TCP/IP Settings dialog box, in which you can configure multiple IP addresses, subnet masks, default gateways, DNS servers, and WINS servers for client computers with special requirements.

8. Click **OK** to close the Internet Protocol Version 4 (TCP/IPv4) Properties sheet.
9. Click **Close** to close the connection's Properties sheet.

CERTIFICATION READY?
Manage network connections:
• Connect to a network
• Set up a connection for a network
4.1

CREATING A NEW NETWORK CONNECTION

Windows Vista creates local area network connections automatically, but desktop technicians frequently have to create other types of connections manually, such as dial-up Internet connections. To do this, use the following procedure:

CREATE A NEW NETWORK CONNECTION

GET READY. Log on to Windows Vista using an account with administrative capabilities. When the logon process is completed, close the Welcome Center window and any other windows that appear. If Windows Vista has not detected and installed your modem, you must install it yourself using the Add New Hardware Wizard.

1. Click **Start**, and then click **Control Panel**. The Control Panel window appears.
2. Click **Network and Internet**, and then click **Network and Sharing Center**. The Network and Sharing Center window appears.
3. Click **Set up a connection or network**. The *Choose a connection option* page appears, as shown in Figure 7-19.

Figure 7-19

The Choose a connection option page

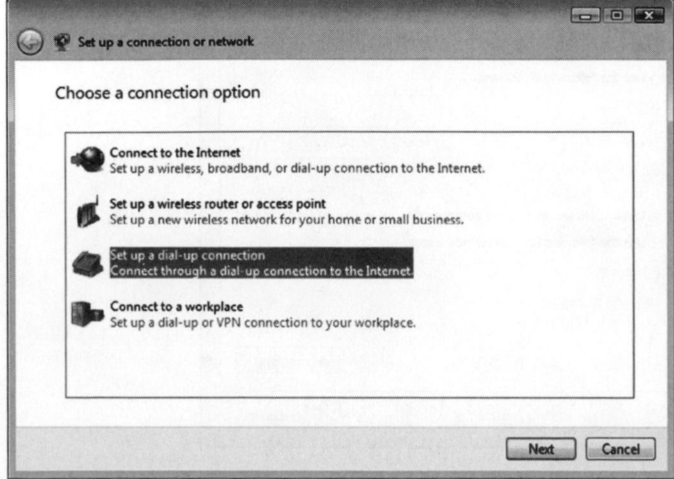

4. Click **Set up a dial-up connection**, and then click **Next**. The *Type the information from your Internet service provider (ISP)* page appears, as shown in Figure 7-20.

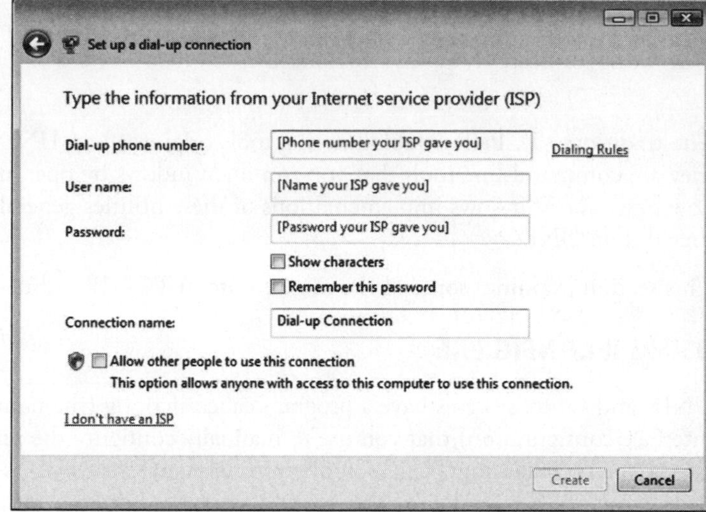

Figure 7-20

The Type the information from your Internet service provider (ISP) page appears

5. Enter the Dial-up phone number, User name, and Password supplied by your ISP. Click the **Remember this password** checkbox if you want to avoid typing the password each time you connect to the ISP.
6. Click **Create**. The system activates the modem, dials the number you supplied, and attempts to connect to the ISP. If the attempt succeeds, the connection is established and communication with the ISP commences. In virtually all cases, the ISP's server supplies the TCP/IP settings for the connection, so no further configuration is needed. If the connection attempt does not succeed, a The Internet Connectivity Test Was Unsuccessful page appears.
7. To create the dial-up connection without actually connecting to the ISP, click **Set Up The Connection Anyway**. A The Connection To The Internet Is Ready To Use page appears.
8. Click **Close**.

Once you have created the dial-up connection, you can open its Properties sheet, just as you did earlier with the local area connection. However, a dial-up connection's Properties sheet, as shown in Figure 7-21, has additional controls for dialing behavior and sharing, as well as the standard network configuration controls.

Figure 7-21

A dial-up connection's Properties sheet

Using TCP/IP Tools

Virtually all network operating systems today include support for the TCP/IP protocols, and TCP/IP traditionally includes some basic tools that you can use to troubleshoot network connectivity problems yourself.

The traditional TCP/IP troubleshooting tools originated on UNIX systems, and as a result they are command-line tools that you run on Windows by opening a Command Prompt window first. The Windows implementations of these utilities generally use the same syntax as they did on UNIX.

This section examines some of the most common TCP/IP utilities and their purposes.

USING IPCONFIG.EXE

UNIX and Linux systems have a program called ifconfig (the name is derived from the words interface configuration) that you use to manually configure the properties of network interface adapters, including TCP/IP configuration parameters such as IP addresses. Running ifconfig on a UNIX system with just the name of an interface displays the current configuration information for that interface.

All Windows operating systems, including Windows Vista, have a graphical interface for configuring network connections, but the configuration display capabilities of ifconfig have been retained in a command-line tool called Ipconfig.exe.

When you run Ipconfig.exe with the /all parameter at the Windows Vista command prompt, you see a display like the following:

```
Windows IP Configuration
    Host Name.......................................... : cz5
    Primary DNS Suffix................................. : zacker.local
    Node Type.......................................... : Hybrid
    IP Routing Enabled................................. : No
    WINS Proxy Enabled................................. : No
    DNS Suffix Search List............................. : zacker.local
Ethernet adapter Local Area Connection:
    Connection-specific DNS Suffix..................... : zacker.local
    Description........................................ : 3Com EtherLink 10/100 PCI For
                                                          Complete
PC Management NIC (3C905C-TX)
    Physical Address................................... : 00-04-75-93-2F-61
    DHCP Enabled....................................... : Yes
    Autoconfiguration Enabled.......................... : Yes
    Link-local IPv6 Address............................ : fe80::b117:85e:356a:7794%8(Preferred)
    IPv4 Address....................................... : 192.168.2.4(Preferred)
    Subnet Mask........................................ : 255.255.255.0
    Lease Obtained..................................... : Thursday, March 08, 2007 11:32:24 AM
```

```
    Lease Expires. . . . . . . . . . . . . . . . . . . . . . . . . . . . : Tuesday, May 08, 2007 1:45:53 AM
    Default Gateway. . . . . . . . . . . . . . . . . . . . . . . . . . . : 192.168.2.99
    DHCP Server. . . . . . . . . . . . . . . . . . . . . . . . . . . . . : 192.168.2.1
    DHCPv6 IAID. . . . . . . . . . . . . . . . . . . . . . . . . . . . . : 167773301
    DNS Servers. . . . . . . . . . . . . . . . . . . . . . . . . . . . . : 192.168.2.1
    Primary WINS Server. . . . . . . . . . . . . . . . . . . . . . . . . : 192.168.2.1
    NetBIOS over Tcpip. . . . . . . . . . . . . . . . . . . . . . . . . . : Enabled
Tunnel adapter Local Area Connection* 6:
    Connection-specific DNS Suffix. . . . . . . . . . . . . . . . . . . : zacker.local
    Description. . . . . . . . . . . . . . . . . . . . . . . . . . . . . : isatap.zacker.local
    Physical Address. . . . . . . . . . . . . . . . . . . . . . . . . . : 00-00-00-00-00-00-00-E0
    DHCP Enabled. . . . . . . . . . . . . . . . . . . . . . . . . . . . : No
    Autoconfiguration Enabled. . . . . . . . . . . . . . . . . . . . . : Yes
    Link-local IPv6 Address. . . . . . . . . . . . . . . . . . . . . . : fe80::5efe:192.168.2.4%10(Preferred)
Default Gateway.........:
    DNS Servers. . . . . . . . . . . . . . . . . . . . . . . . . . . . . : 192.168.2.1
    NetBIOS over Tcpip. . . . . . . . . . . . . . . . . . . . . . . . . . : Disabled
Tunnel adapter Local Area Connection* 7:
Connection-specific DNS Suffix.:
    Description. . . . . . . . . . . . . . . . . . . . . . . . . . . . . : Teredo Tunneling Pseudo-Interface
    Physical Address. . . . . . . . . . . . . . . . . . . . . . . . . . : 02-00-54-55-4E-01
    DHCP Enabled. . . . . . . . . . . . . . . . . . . . . . . . . . . . : No
    Autoconfiguration Enabled. . . . . . . . . . . . . . . . . . . . . : Yes
    IPv6 Address. . . . . . . . . . . . . . . . . . . . . . . . . . . . : 2001:0:4136:e37c:869:ae3:3f57:
                                                                            fdfb(Preferred)
    Link-local IPv6 Address. . . . . . . . . . . . . . . . . . . . . . : fe80::869:ae3:3f57:fdfb%9(Preferred)
Default Gateway.........:::
NetBIOS over Tcpip........: Disabled
```

The value of Ipconfig.exe is particularly apparent when a Windows Vista computer uses DHCP to obtain its IP address and other TCP/IP configuration parameters. A DHCP-configured computer does not display any configuration information in the Local Area Connection Properties sheet; it just shows that the DHCP client is activated. One of the few ways to see what settings the DHCP server has assigned to the computer (without examining the DHCP server itself) is to use Ipconfig.exe.

In addition to displaying the DHCP-obtained configuration settings, Ipconfig.exe also enables you to manually release the IP address the system obtained from the DHCP server and renew existing address leases. By running Ipconfig.exe with the /release and /renew command-line parameters, you can release or renew the IP address assignment of one of the network interfaces in the computer or for all of the interfaces at once.

USING PING

Ping is the most basic of TCP/IP utilities, and is included in some form with every TCP/IP implementation. On Windows Vista systems, the program is called Ping.exe.

Ping.exe can tell you if the TCP/IP stack of another system on the network is functioning normally. The Ping.exe program generates a series of Echo Request messages using the Internet Control Message Protocol (ICMP) and transmits them to the computer whose name or IP address you specify on the command line. The basic syntax of the Ping program is as follows:

```
ping target
```

The *target* variable contains the IP address or name of any computer on the network. Because Ping.exe is a TCP/IP utility, the target computer can be running any operating system, not just Windows. You can use DNS host and domain names or Windows NetBIOS names in Ping commands. Ping resolves the name into an IP address before sending the Echo Request messages, and it then displays the address in its output.

TCP/IP computers respond to any Echo Request messages they receive that are addressed to them by generating Echo Reply messages and transmitting them back to the sender. When the pinging computer receives the Echo Reply messages, it produces a display like the following:

```
Pinging cz1 [192.168.2.10] with 32 bytes of data:

Reply from 192.168.2.10: bytes=32 time<10ms TTL=128
Reply from 192.168.2.10: bytes=32 time<10ms TTL=128
Reply from 192.168.2.10: bytes=32 time<10ms TTL=128
Reply from 192.168.2.10: bytes=32 time<10ms TTL=128

Ping statistics for 192.168.2.10:

Packets: Sent = 4, Received = 4, Lost = 0 (0% loss),

Approximate round trip times in milli-seconds:

Minimum = 0ms, Maximum = 0ms, Average = 0ms
```

In Windows Vista's Ping.exe implementation, the display shows the IP address of the computer receiving the Echo Requests, the number of bytes of data included with each request, the elapsed time between the transmission of each request and the receipt of each reply, and the value of the Time To Live (TTL) field in the IP header.

In this example, the target computer was on the same local area network (LAN), so the time measurement is very short—less than 10 milliseconds. When pinging a computer on the Internet, the interval is likely to be longer. A successful Ping result like this one indicates that the target computer's networking hardware is functioning properly, as are its TCP/IP protocols, at least as high as the network layer of the OSI model. If a Ping test fails, there is a problem in one or both of the computers or in the network medium connecting them.

Ping.exe also has a series of command-line switches that you can use to modify the operational parameters of the program, such as the number of Echo Request messages it generates and the amount of data in each message. To display the syntax of the program, key *ping /?* At the command prompt.

USING TRACERT.EXE

Traceroute is another UNIX program that displays the path that TCP/IP packets take to their final destination. Traceroute is implemented in Windows Vista as Tracert.exe. Because of the nature of IP routing, the path from a packet's source to its destination on another network can change from minute to minute, especially on the Internet. Tracert.exe displays a list of the routers that are currently forwarding packets to a particular destination.

Tracert.exe is a variation on Ping.exe. The program uses ICMP Echo Request and Echo Reply messages just like Ping, but it modifies the messages by changing the value of the TTL field in the IP header. The values in the TTL field prevent packets from getting caught in router loops that keep them circulating endlessly around the internetwork. On a Windows Vista computer, the default value for the TTL field is relatively high, 128. Each time a packet passes from one network to another, the router connecting the networks reduces the TTL value by 1. If the TTL value ever reaches 0, the router processing the packet discards it and transmits an ICMP error message back to the original sender.

Tracert.exe works by modifying the TTL values in the successive Ping.exe packets that it transmits to a target computer. When you run Tracert.exe from the command prompt with a target parameter, the program generates its first set of Echo Request messages with TTL values of 1. When the messages arrive at the first router on their path to the destination, the router decrements the TTL values to 0, discards the packets, and reports the errors to the sender. The error messages contain the router's address, which Tracert.exe displays as the first hop in the path to the destination.

Tracert.exe's second set of Echo Request messages use a TTL value of 2, causing the second router on the path to discard the packets and generate error messages. The Echo Request messages in the third set have a TTL value of 3, and so on. Each set of packets travels one hop farther than the previous set before causing a router to return error messages to the source. The list of routers displayed by the program as the path to the destination is the result of these error messages.

The following is an example of a Tracert.exe display:

```
Tracing route to www.fineartschool.co.uk [173.146.1.1] over a maximum of 30 hops:
  1  <10 ms  1   ms  <10 ms  192.168.2.99

  2  105 ms  92  ms  98  ms  qrvl-67terminal01.cpandl.com [131.107.24.67.3]

  3  101 ms  110 ms  98  ms  qrvl.cpandl.com [131.107.67.1]

  4  123 ms  109 ms  118 ms  svcr03-7b.cpandl.com [131.107.103.125]

  5  123 ms  112 ms  114 ms  clsm02-2.cpandl.com [131.107.88.26]

  6  136 ms  130 ms  133 ms  sl-gw19-pen-6-1-0-T3.fabrikam.com [157.54.116.5]

  7  143 ms  126 ms  138 ms  sl-bb10-pen-4-3.fabrikam.com [157.54.5.117]

  8  146 ms  129 ms  133 ms  sl-bb20-pen-12-0.fabrikam.com [157.54.5.1]

  9  131 ms  128 ms  139 ms  sl-bb20-nyc-13-0.fabrikam.com [157.54.18.38]

 10  130 ms  134 ms  134 ms  sl-gw9-nyc-8-0.fabrikam.com [157.54.7.94]

 11  147 ms  149 ms  152 ms  sl-demon-1-0.fabrikam.com [157.54.173.10]

 12  154 ms  146 ms  145 ms  ny2-backbone-1-ge021.router.fabrikam.com[157.54.173.121]

 13  230 ms  225 ms  226 ms  tele-backbone-1-ge023.router.adatum.co.uk [157.60.173.12]

 14  233 ms  220 ms  226 ms  tele-core-3-fxp1.router.adatum.co.uk [157.60.252.56]
```

```
   15  223  ms  224  ms  224  ms  tele-access-1-14.router.adatum.co.uk [157.60.254.245]

   16  236  ms  221  ms  226  ms  tele-service-2-165.router.adatum.co.uk [157.60.36.149]

   17  220  ms  224  ms  210  ms  www.fineartschool.co.uk [206.73.118.65]

Trace complete.
```

In this example, Tracert.exe displays the path between a computer in Pennsylvania and one in the United Kingdom. Each of the hops contains the elapsed times between the transmission and reception of three sets of Echo Request and Echo Reply packets. In this trace, you can clearly see the point at which the packets begin traveling across the Atlantic Ocean. At hop 13, the elapsed times increase from approximately 150 to 230 milliseconds (ms) and stay in that range for the subsequent hops. This additional delay of only 80 ms is the time it takes the packets to travel the thousands of miles across the Atlantic Ocean.

Ping.exe simply tells you whether two TCP/IP systems are having trouble communicating. It can't pinpoint the location of the problem. A failure to contact a remote computer could be due to a problem in your workstation, in the remote computer, or in any of the routers in between. Tracert.exe can tell you how far your packets are going before they run into the problem.

TAKE NOTE*

Because the configuration of the Internet is constantly changing, there is no guarantee that the route displayed by Tracert.exe is completely accurate. The ICMP messages that execute each step of the Tracert.exe process could be taking different routes to the same destination, resulting in the display of a composite route between two points that does not actually exist. There is also no way of knowing what path the packets are taking as they return to the source.

In addition, routers typically deprioritize ICMP processing in favor of packet forwarding and other more critical router tasks. When a router is busy, it might delay the processing of an Echo Request or Echo Reply packet. The resulting latency numbers will be higher than the delay experienced by actual data packets crossing the network.

USING NSLOOKUP

The Nslookup.exe command-line utility enables you to generate DNS request messages and transmit them to specific DNS servers on the network. The advantage of Nslookup.exe is that you can test the functionality and the quality of the information on a specific DNS server by specifying it on the command line.

The basic command-line syntax of Nslookup.exe is as follows:

nslookup *DNSname DNSserver*

- *DNSname* — Specifies the DNS name that you want to resolve.
- *DNSserver* — Specifies the DNS name or IP address of the DNS server that you want to query for the name specified in the *DNSname* variable.

There are also many additional parameters that you can include on the command line to control the server query process. The output generated by Nslookup.exe in Windows Vista looks like the following:

```
C:\>nslookup www.microsoft.com 206.73.118.54
Server: ns1-dlls.cpandl.com
Address: 206.73.118.54
Non-authoritative answer:
Name: www2.microsoft.net
Addresses: 207.46.156.252, 207.46.244.188, 207.46.245.92, 207.46.249.29
Aliases:     www.microsoft.com, www.microsoft.net
```

The Nslookup.exe utility has two operational modes: command-line and interactive. When you run Nslookup.exe with no command-line parameters, the program displays its own prompt from which you can issue commands to specify the default DNS server to query, resolve multiple names, and configure many other aspects of the program's functionality.

SUMMARY SKILL MATRIX

In this lesson you learned:
The networking stack used on Windows Vista computers corresponds roughly to the seven-layer OSI reference model.
The OSI (Open Systems Interconnection) reference model consists of seven layers: physical, data-link, network, transport, session, presentation, and application.
Ethernet, the data-link layer protocol used on most LANs, consists of physical layer specifications, a frame format, and a MAC mechanism.
The network and transport layer protocols work together to provide an end-to-end communication service that achieves the quality of service required by the application requesting network services.
The functions of the session, presentation, and application layers are often combined into a single application layer protocol.
Windows Vista includes support for both the IPv4 and IPv6 protocols.
Network Discovery is a Windows Vista feature that simplifies the task of firewall configuration by enabling you to block or allow the protocols and ports need for the computer to browse and access the network.
The Network Map utility uses the Link Layer Discovery Protocol (LLTD) to detect network devices and connections.
Most networks use DHCP to configure their TCP/IP clients, but it is still possible to configure them manually.
Windows Vista includes a variety of command line TCP/IP tools, including Ipconfig.exe, Ping.exe, Tracert.exe, and Nslookup.exe.

Knowledge Assessment

Fill in the Blank

Complete the following sentences by writing the correct word or words in the blanks provided.

1. A software routine, which also acts as a filter that blocks certain type of incoming and outgoing traffic while enabling other types, is called a(n) ______________.
2. The ______________ provides a central access point for all of the network connections on the computer.
3. A device that connects one network to another is called a(n) ______________.
4. The most common method for illustrating the operations of a networking stack is the ______________, which consists of ______________ layers.
5. Protocols that do not guarantee delivery of their data but do operate with a very low overhead that conserve network bandwidth are called ______________.
6. The command-line utility that tells you if the TCP/IP stack of another system on the network is functioning normally is called ______________.
7. The command-line utility that enables you to generate DNS request messages and then transmit them to specific DNS servers on the network is called ______________.
8. Most networks use the ______________ to dynamically assign addresses and configure computers to use them.
9. The utility that displays a list of the routers currently forwarding packets to a particular destination is called ______________.
10. The top and bottom layers of the OSI model are called the ______________ and ______________ layers.

True / False

Circle T if the statement is true or F if the statement is false.

T | F 1. The purpose of Network Diagnostics is to display error messages only.

T | F 2. Transport layer protocols are not concerned with addressing packets to the correct system.

T | F 3. The Network Map utility uses a new protocol call Link Layer Topology Discovery (LLTD) to discover information about the network and the devices attached to it.

T | F 4. The protocols that Windows uses by default at the network and transport layers are collectively called TCP/IP.

T | F 5. Private and domain computers have Network Discovery turned off, and public computers have it turned on.

T | F 6. There are two basic types of port numbers: ephemeral port numbers and well-known port numbers.

T | F 7. A Windows Vista computer that is connected to a LAN has a hardware address and one that is connected to the Internet has an IP address.

T | F 8. The only two layers of the OSI reference model that do not have individual protocols associated with them are the transport layer and the session layer.

T | F 9. Because the configuration of the Internet is constantly changing, the only way you can know for certain what route packets are taking to a specific destination is to use Tracert.exe.

T | F 10. The addresses computers use at the data-link layer are six-byte hexadecimal sequences, hard-coded into each network interface adapter by the manufacturer.

Review Questions

1. What is the difference between a hardware address and an IP address?
2. Explain how the process of data encapsulation works on a TCP/IP network when an application sends a message to another computer on the Internet.

Case Scenarios

Scenario #1: Configuring TCP/IP Clients

Mark is setting up a small Ethernet network in his home by installing network adapters in three computers running Windows Vista and connecting them to a switch. Mark only uses one of the computers to access the Internet with a dial-up modem, but he wants to be able to access files and his printer from any one of the three systems. After he installs the network interface adapters, he notes that the default networking components have been installed on all three systems, and he sets about configuring their TCP/IP configuration parameters manually. Of the settings on the Internet Protocol Version 4 (TCP/IPv4) Properties sheet, which must Mark configure to provide the network connectivity he desires, and which can he leave blank?

Scenario #2: Using Port Numbers

While you are installing an Internet Web server on a client's network, the owner of the company tells you that he also wants to build a Web server for internal use by the company's employees. This intranet Web server will not contain confidential information, but it should not be accessible from the company's Internet Website. To do this, you create a second site on the Web server. The Internet site uses the well-known port number for Web servers, which is 80. For the intranet site, you select the port number 283. Assuming that the Web server's IP address on the internal network is 10.54.3.145, what should the users on the company network do to access the intranet Website with Microsoft Internet Explorer?

Configuring Windows Vista Security

OBJECTIVE DOMAIN MATRIX

Technology Skill	Objective Domain	Objective Number
Configuring Windows Firewall Settings	Configure security settings in Windows Firewall	3.4
Configure Exceptions and Ports	Configure security settings in Windows Firewall • Configure rules and exceptions	3.4
Introducing Windows Defender	Configure Windows Defender • Configure custom scans	3.2
Configuring Windows Defender	Configure Windows Defender	3.2
Using Software Explorer	Configure Windows Defender • Manage applications by using Software Explorer	3.2
Updating Definitions	Configure Windows Defender • Troubleshoot definition update issues	3.2
Setting Up Users	Configure and troubleshoot parental controls • Set up users and system access	2.3
Setting Up Parental Controls	Configure and troubleshoot parental controls • Troubleshoot Web browsing issues • Troubleshoot gaming issues	2.3

KEY TERMS

filters	**private key**	**rules**
malware	**public key**	**spyware**

Defending against Malware

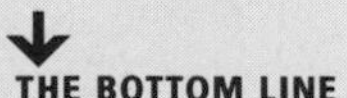

Malware is one of the primary threats to Windows Vista security, and the operating system includes a variety of tools that you can use to combat it. The following sections examine these tools and how to implement and configure them.

Windows Vista holds security as one of its primary goals. Beginning with the Windows XP Service Pack 2 release, Windows has monitored the state of the security mechanisms included with the operating system and warns the user if any components are misconfigured, outdated, or not functioning.

Chief among the threats to Windows Vista computers is malicious software created specifically for the purpose of infiltrating or damaging a computer system without the user's knowledge or consent. This type of software includes a variety of technologies, including viruses, Trojan horses, worms, spyware, and adware. The term most commonly used to collectively refer to these malicious software technologies is ***malware***.

The types of malware to which Vista is susceptible range from the relatively innocuous to the extremely destructive. The effects they can have on a Windows Vista computer include the following:

- Collect usage information about the computer user and transmit to an Internet server
- Display advertisements on the user's system
- Use the system's e-mail address book to send spam
- Attach code to document files that spreads to other files on any system opening the document
- Install and run a program that enables a remote user to take control of the system
- Damage or destroy the files stored on the computer
- Infiltrate the computer's boot sector and spread to other systems

Malware is, in most cases, introduced onto a computer by a deliberate action on the part of a user. Someone opens an e-mail attachment, installs an infected program, or accesses a dangerous Website, and the malicious code is introduced to the system. Windows Vista includes a variety of tools that attempt to prevent users from inadvertently infecting their computers and also attempt to block the activities of malicious software programs once they are present.

Security is a pervasive concern throughout the Windows Vista operating system, and as a result there are some Vista security mechanisms that are discussed elsewhere in this text:

- In Lesson 5, "Working with Users and Groups," you learn how User Account Control helps to prevent malware from obtaining administrative privileges.
- In Lesson 9, "Configuring Windows Vista Applications," you learn about the security features included in Internet Explorer.
- In Lesson 12, "Working with Mobile Computers," you learn about the security features specifically designed for use on mobile and wireless computers.

Introducing Windows Security Center

The Windows Vista Security Center ensures that your system is protected by malware intrusion if any of the Vista security mechanisms are not running properly.

Like the Network and Sharing Center, the Security Center is a centralized console that enables users and administrators to access, monitor, and configure the various Windows Vista security mechanisms. The primary function of the Security Center is to provide an automatic notification system that alerts users when the system is vulnerable.

Security Center is a service that starts automatically and runs continuously on Windows Vista computers, by default. The service constantly monitors the different security mechanisms running on the computer. If Security Center detects a mechanism that is not functioning properly for any of several reasons, it displays an icon in the notification area (formerly known as the taskbar tray) to inform the user of the condition.

TAKE NOTE*

The Windows Vista Security Center is not limited to monitoring Microsoft security solutions. The service can also monitor third-party programs for their currency and operational status.

ACCESSING SECURITY CENTER

When the user clicks the icon to open the Security Center window (or clicks **Start > Control Panel > Security > Security Center**), the system displays links to vendors that can help to solve the problem. For example, if an antivirus program is out of date, Security Center can often provide a link to a site where the user can purchase an upgraded version.

When you open Security Center, as shown in Figure 8-1, the main window is divided into five sections:

- Links–Provides hyperlinks to the other Windows security tools and to the Security Center notification controls.
- Firewall–Specifies whether the computer is being protected by Windows Firewall and/or a third-party firewall.
- Automatic updating–Specifies whether the computer is configured to automatically download and install operating system updates.
- Malware protection–Specifies whether the computer is being protected from malware infiltration by Windows Defender and antivirus software.
- Other security settings–Specifies whether the Internet Explorer configuration meets security recommendations and whether User Account Control is operating.

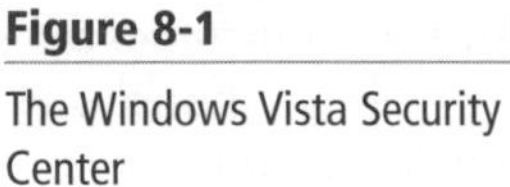

Figure 8-1

The Windows Vista Security Center

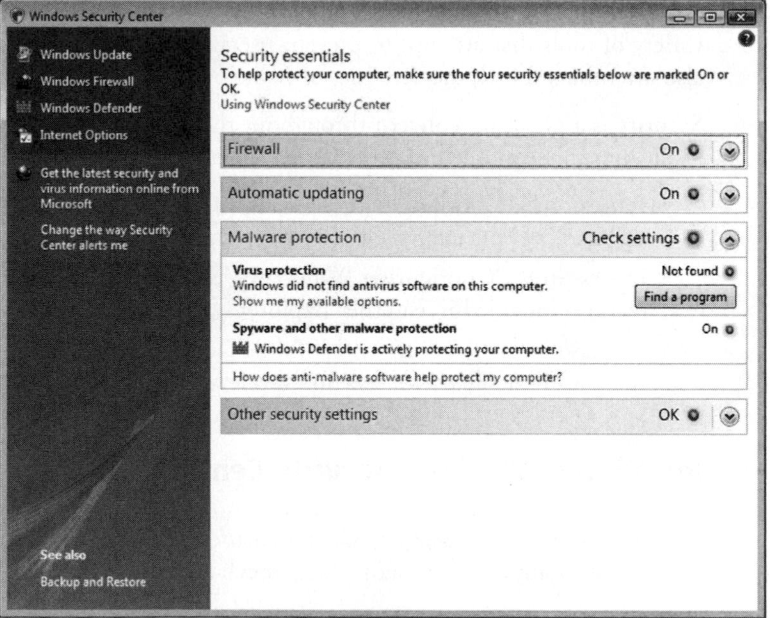

In addition to monitoring the computer's security status, Security Center provides users with a single point of access to information about Vista security. The hyperlinks scattered about the window provide quick access to the various Windows security tools and access to help pages that describe the roles of Vista's various security mechanisms.

SECURITY CENTER AND WINDOWS DOMAINS

Security Center is an end-user tool that provides critical notifications to people who have no other security infrastructure to protect them and who are unaware of the security hazards to which Windows Vista is prone. However, in a Windows domain environment, Microsoft assumes that there are domain-wide security mechanisms in place, supervised by an administrator. Therefore, when a Windows Vista computer is a member of a domain, Security Center is deactivated by a Group Policy setting.

The Group Policy setting that controls Security Center on domain workstations is called Turn On Security Center (Domain PCs Only), and is located in the Computer Configuration\Administrative Templates\Windows Components\Security Center node of a group policy object. When you set the policy value to Enabled, domain computers have the Security Center service turned on.

Introducing Windows Firewall

Windows Firewall protects Windows Vista computers by blocking dangerous traffic, both incoming and outgoing.

As discussed in Lesson 7, "Configuring Network Connectivity," a firewall is a software program that protects a computer by allowing certain types of network traffic in and out of the system while blocking others. Firewalls are essentially packet filters that examine the contents of packets and the traffic patterns to and from the network to determine which packets should be allowed passage through the filter.

Network connections are all but ubiquitous in the computing world these days. All business computers are networked, and virtually all home computers have an Internet connection. Many homes have local area networks as well. Network connections provide Windows Vista users with access to virtually unlimited resources, but any door that allows data out can also allow data in. Some of the hazards that firewalls protect against are as follows:

- Trojan horse applications that users inadvertently download and run can open a connection to a computer on the Internet, enabling an attacker on the outside to run programs or store data on the system.
- A mobile computer can be compromised while connected to a public network and then brought onto a private network, compromising the resources there in turn.
- Network scanner applications can probe systems for unguarded ports, which are essentially unlocked doors that attackers can use to gain access to the system.
- Attackers that obtain passwords by illicit means, such as social engineering, can use remote access technologies to log on to a computer from another location and compromise its data and programming.

MONITORING WINDOWS FIREWALL

Windows Vista includes a firewall program called Windows Firewall, which is activated by default on all Windows Vista systems. Windows Firewall is one of the programs monitored by the Security Center service. The main Security Center window indicates whether Windows Firewall is running, and also whether any third-party firewall products are running.

When you click the Windows Firewall link in the left column, a new Windows Firewall window appears, displaying the firewall's status in greater detail, as shown in Figure 8-2.

Figure 8-2

The Windows Firewall window

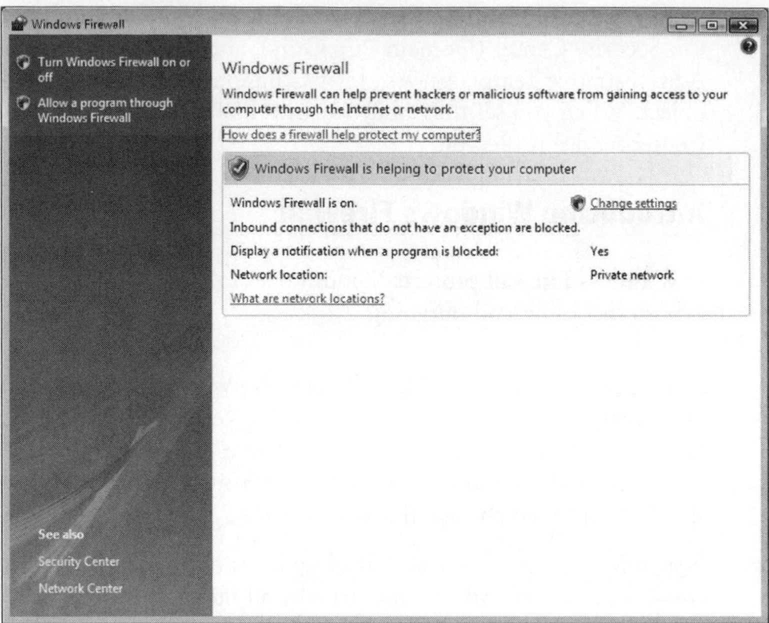

The Windows Firewall window contains the following information:

- Whether the Windows Firewall service is currently turned on or off
- Whether inbound and outbound connections are blocked
- Whether users are notified when a program is blocked
- Whether the computer is connected to a domain, private, or public network

On the left side of the window are two links: one that enables you to turn Windows Firewall on and off, and one that enables you to configure Windows Firewall to allow a specific program through its barrier. This second link opens the Windows Firewall Settings dialog box, as shown in Figure 8-3.

Figure 8-3

The Windows Firewall Settings dialog box

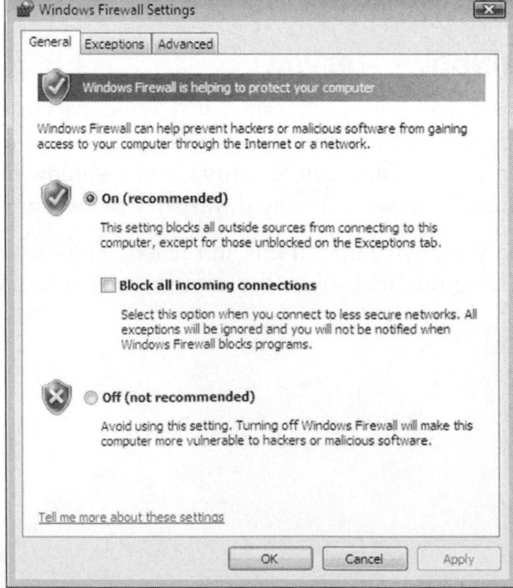

CONFIGURING WINDOWS FIREWALL SETTINGS

Firewalls typically base their filtering on the TCP/IP characteristics at the network, transport, and application layers, as follows:

- IP addresses–Represent specific computers on the network.
- Protocol numbers–Identify the transport layer protocol being used by the packets.
- Port numbers–Identify specific applications running on the computer.

CERTIFICATION READY?
Configure security settings in Windows Firewall
3.4

To filter traffic, firewalls use ***rules***, which specify which packets are allowed to pass through the firewall and which are blocked. Firewalls can work in two ways, as follows:

- Admit all traffic, except that which conforms to the applied rules
- Block all traffic, except that which conforms to the applied rules

Generally speaking, blocking all traffic by default is the more secure arrangement. From the firewall administrator's standpoint, you start with a completely blocked system, and then start testing your applications. When an application fails to function properly because network access is blocked, you create a rule that opens up the ports the application needs to communicate.

CERTIFICATION READY?
Configure security settings in Windows Firewall: Configure rules and exceptions
3.4

This is the method that Windows Firewall uses by default for incoming network traffic. The default rules preconfigured into the firewall are designed to admit the traffic used by standard Windows networking functions, such as file and printer sharing. For outgoing network traffic, Windows Firewall uses the other method, allowing all traffic to pass except that which conforms to a rule.

BLOCKING INCOMING CONNECTIONS

On the General page of the Windows Firewall Settings dialog box, a *Block all incoming connections* checkbox enables you to increase the security of your system by blocking all unsolicited attempts to connect to your computer. Note, however, that this does not prevent you from performing common networking tasks, such as accessing Websites and sending or receiving e-mails. These activities are not unsolicited connection attempts; they begin with the client contacting the server first. When the firewall detects the outgoing traffic from your Web browser to a Web server on the Internet, for example, it knows that it should admit the incoming response from the server.

Users might want to modify the firewall settings in other ways also, typically because a specific application requires access to a port not anticipated by the firewall's preconfigured rules. To do this, use the Exceptions tab of the Windows Firewall Settings dialog box, shown in Figure 8-4.

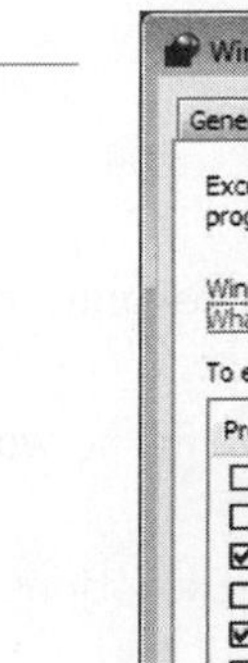

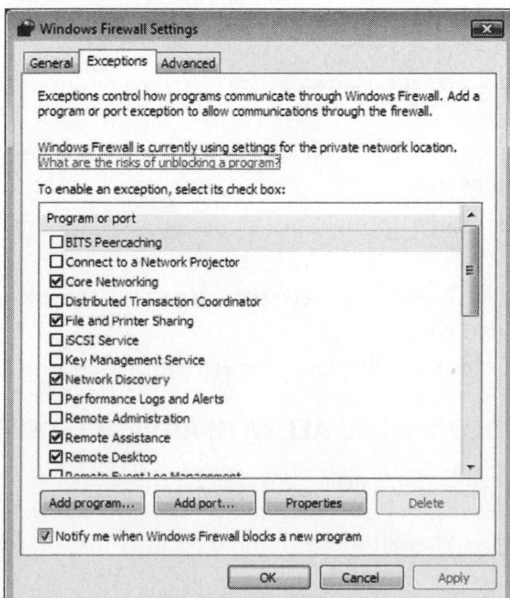

Figure 8-4

The Exceptions tab of the Windows Firewall Settings dialog box

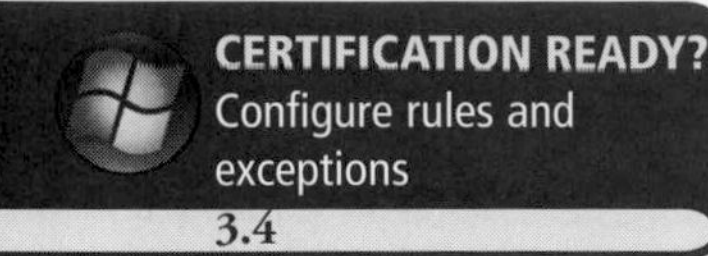
CERTIFICATION READY?
Configure rules and exceptions
3.4

Opening a port in your firewall is an inherently dangerous activity. The more holes you make in a wall, the greater the likelihood that intruders will get in. The two basic methods for opening a hole in your firewall are opening a port and creating a program exception. The latter is more desirable, because when you open a port, it stays open permanently. When you create a program exception, the specified port is open only while the program is running. When you terminate the program, the firewall closes the port.

To modify the Windows Firewall rules, use the following procedure:

CREATE A FIREWALL EXCEPTION

GET READY. Log on to Windows Vista using an account with administrative capabilities. When the logon process is completed, close the Welcome Center window and any other windows that appear.

1. Click **Start**, and then click **Control Panel**. The Control Panel window appears.
2. Click **Allow a program through Windows Firewall**. After confirming that you performed the action, the Windows Firewall Settings dialog box appears, opened to the Exceptions tab.
3. Click **Add program**. The Add a Program dialog box appears, as shown in Figure 8-5. Alternatively, you can click **Add port** to specify a TCP or UDP port that you want to open.

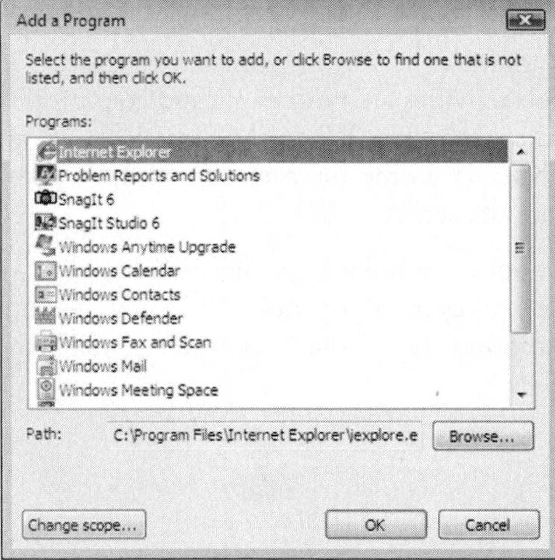

Figure 8-5

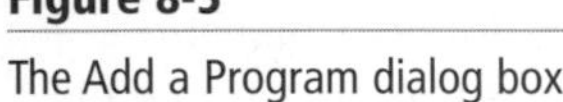
The Add a Program dialog box

4. Select the program for which you want to create an exception or click **Browse** to locate the program.
5. Click **Change scope** to limit the exception to a specific network or specific addresses.
6. Click **OK**. The program you selected appears in the Exceptions list, with its checkbox selected.
7. Click **OK** to close the Windows Firewall Settings dialog box.

USING THE WINDOWS FIREWALL WITH ADVANCED SECURITY CONSOLE

The Windows Firewall Settings dialog box enables end users to create exceptions in the current firewall settings as needed. For full access to the Windows Firewall configuration settings, you must use the Windows Firewall with Advanced Security snap-in for the Microsoft Management Console.

To create a Windows Firewall with Advanced Security console, use the following procedure:

CREATE A WINDOWS FIREWALL WITH ADVANCED SECURITY CONSOLE

GET READY. Log on to Windows Vista using an account with administrative capabilities. When the logon process is completed, close the Welcome Center window and any other windows that appear.

1. Click **Start**, key **mmc** in the Start Search box, and then press **Enter**. After confirming that you are performing the action, a blank MMC console appears.
2. Click **File** > **Add/Remove Snap-In**. The Add or Remove Snap-ins dialog box appears, as shown in Figure 8-6.

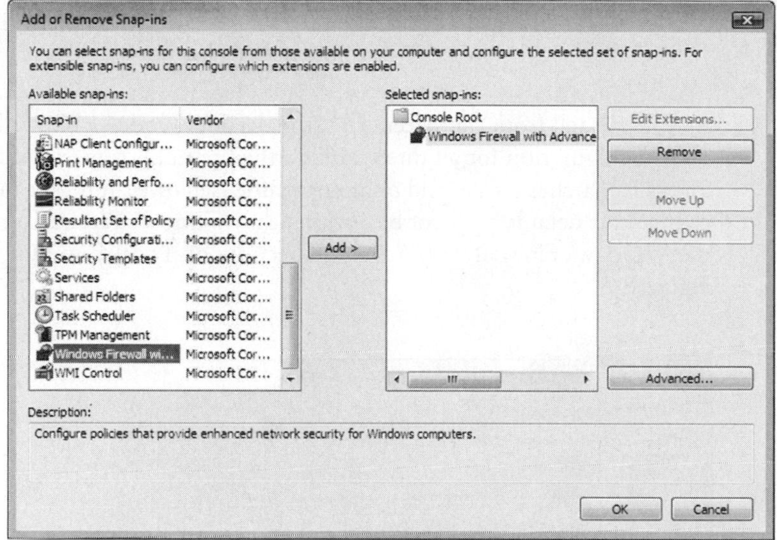

Figure 8-6

The Add or Remove Snap-ins dialog box

3. Scroll down in the Available snap-ins list, select **Windows Firewall with Advanced Security**, and then click **Add**. The Select Computer dialog box appears.
4. Click **Finish** to accept the default Local Computer option. The Windows Firewall with Advanced Security snap-in moves to the Selected Snap-ins list.
5. Click **OK.** The Windows Firewall with Advanced Security snap-in appears in the console, as shown in Figure 8-7.

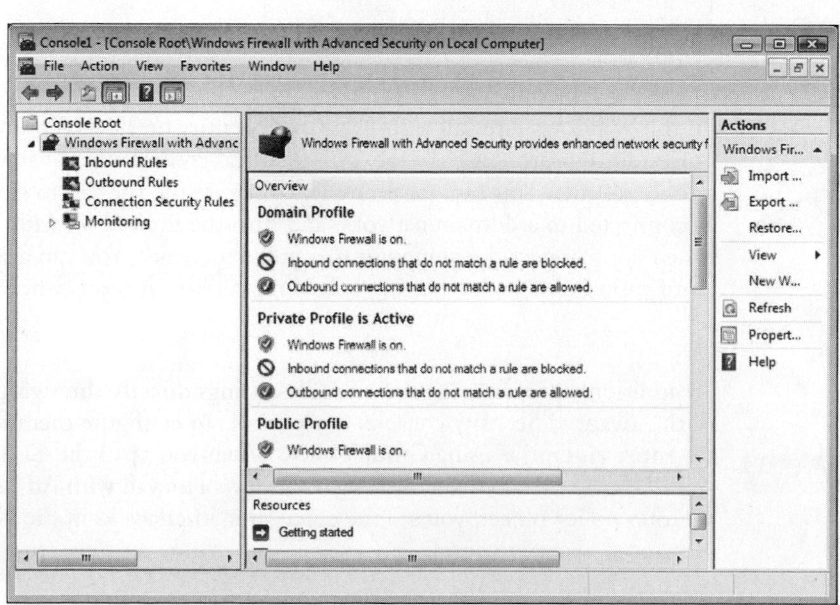

Figure 8-7

The Windows Firewall with Advanced Security console

CONFIGURING PROFILE SETTINGS

At the top of the details pane, in the Overview section, are status displays for the computer's three possible network locations. Windows Firewall maintains separate profiles for each of the three possible network locations: domain, private, and public. If you connect the computer to a different network, as in the case of a mobile laptop computer that you bring to an Internet "hot spot" in a coffee shop, Windows Firewall loads a different configuration for that profile and a different set of rules.

For more information about network location settings, see the discussion of the Network Discovery feature in Lesson 7, "Configuring Network Connectivity."

As you can tell from the screen shot, the default Windows Firewall settings call for the same basic configuration for all three profiles: the firewall is turned on, incoming traffic is blocked unless it matches a rule, and outgoing traffic is allowed unless it matches a rule. You can change this default behavior by clicking the **Windows Firewall Properties** link, which displays the Windows Firewall with Advanced Security on Local Computer dialog box, as shown in Figure 8-8.

Figure 8-8

The Windows Firewall with Advanced Security on Local Computer dialog box

In the Windows Firewall with Advanced Security on Local Computer dialog box, each of the three location profiles has a tab with identical controls that enables you to modify the default profile settings. You can, for example, configure the firewall to shut down completely when it is connected to a domain network, and turn the firewall on with its most protective settings when you connect the computer to a public network. You can also configure the firewall's notification options, its logging behavior, and how it reacts when rules conflict.

TAKE NOTE*

In addition to configuring these profile settings directly through the Windows Firewall with Advanced Security console, it is possible to configure them for a local computer or an entire enterprise using Group Policy. When you open the Computer Configuration\Windows Settings\Security Settings\Windows Firewall with Advanced Security folder in a group policy object, you see the exact same interface as in the Windows Firewall with Advanced Security console.

CREATING RULES

The exceptions and ports that you can create in the Windows Firewall Settings dialog box are a relatively friendly method for working with firewall rules. In the Windows Firewall with Advanced Security console, you can work with the rules in their raw form. Selecting either Inbound Rules or Outbound Rules in the scope pane displays a list of all the rules operating in that direction, as shown in Figure 8-9. The rules that are currently operational have a checkmark in a green circle, while the rules not in force are grayed out.

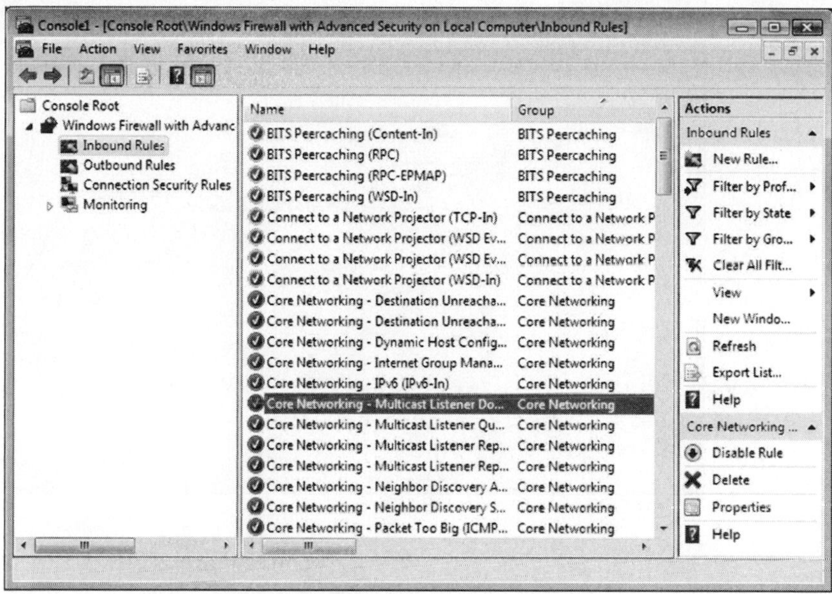

Figure 8-9

The Inbound Rules list in the Windows Firewall with Advanced Security console

TAKE NOTE*

It is important to remember that in the Windows Firewall with Advanced Security console, you are always working with a complete list of rules for all of the profiles, while in the Windows Firewall Settings dialog box, you are working only with the rules that apply to the currently active profile.

Creating new rules with this interface provides a great deal more flexibility than the Windows Firewall Settings dialog box. When you right-click the Inbound Rules or Outbound Rules node and select New Rule from the context menu, the New Rule Wizard, shown in Figure 8-10, takes you through the process of configuring the following sets of parameters:

- Rule Type–Specifies whether you want to create a program rule, a port rule, a variant on one of the predefined rules, or a custom rule. This selection determines which of the following pages the wizard displays.
- Program–Specifies whether the rule applies to all programs, to one specific program, or to a specific service.
- Protocol and Ports–Specifies the protocol and the local and remote ports to which the rule applies. This enables you to specify the exact types of traffic that the rule should block or allow.
- Scope–Specifies the IP addresses of the local and remote systems to which the rule applies. This enables you to block or allow traffic between specific computers.
- Action–Specifies the action the firewall should take when a packet matches the rule. You configure the rule to allow traffic if it is blocked by default, or block traffic if it is allowed by default. You can also configure the rule to allow traffic only when the connection between the communicating computers is secured using IPsec.

- Profile–Specifies the profile(s) to which the rule should apply: domain, private, and/or public.
- Name–Specifies a name and (optionally) a description for the rule.

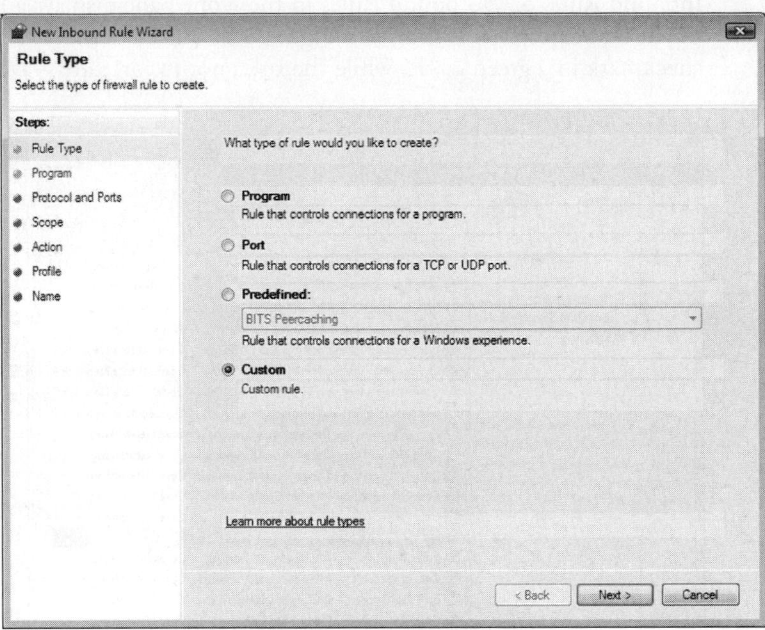

Figure 8-10

The New Inbound Rule Wizard

The rules you can create using the New Rule Wizard range from simple program rules, just like those you can create in the Windows Firewall Settings dialog box, to highly complex and specific rules that block or allow only specific types of traffic between specific computers. The more complicated the rules become, however, the more you have to know about TCP/IP communications in general and the specific behavior of your applications. Modifying the default firewall settings to accommodate some special applications is relatively simple, but creating an entirely new firewall configuration is a formidable task.

USING FILTERS

Although what a firewall does is sometimes referred to as packet filtering, in the Windows Firewall with Advanced Security console, the term ***filter*** is used to refer to a feature that enables you to display rules according to the profile they apply to, their current state, or the group to which they belong.

For example, to display only the rules that apply to the public profile, click **Action > Filter By Profile > Filter By Public Profile**. The display changes to show only the rules that apply to the public profile. In the same way, you can apply a filter that causes the console to display only the rules that are currently turned on, or the rules that belong to a particular group. Click **Action > Clear All Filters** to return to the default display showing all of the rules.

CREATING CONNECTION SECURITY RULES

Windows Vista adds a new feature to Windows Firewall that incorporates IPsec data protection into the Windows Firewall. The IP Security (IPsec) standards are a collection of documents that define a method for securing data while it is in transit over a TCP/IP network. IPsec includes a connection establishment routine, during which computers authenticate each other before transmitting data, and a technique called *tunneling*, in which data packets are encapsulated within other packets for their protection.

MORE INFORMATION

Data protection technologies such as the Windows Vista Encrypting File System (EFS) and BitLocker protect data while it is stored on a drive. However, they do nothing to protect data while it is being transmitted over the network, because they both decrypt the data before sending it. IPsec is the only technology included in Windows Vista that can protect data while it is in transit.

In addition to inbound and outbound rules, the Windows Firewall with Advanced Security console enables you to create connection security rules, using the New Connection Security Rule Wizard. Connection security rules defines the type of protection you want to apply to the communications that conform to Windows Firewall rules.

When you right-click the Connection Security Rules node and select New Rule from the context menu, the New Connection Security Rule Wizard, shown in Figure 8-11, takes you through the process of configuring the following sets of parameters:

- Rule Type–Specifies the basic function of the rule, such as to isolate computers based on authentication criteria, to exempt certain computers (such as infrastructure servers) from authentication, to authenticate two specific computers or groups of computers, or to tunnel communications between two computers. You can also create custom rules combining these functions.
- Endpoints–Specifies the IP addresses of the computer that will establish a secured connection before transmitting any data.
- Requirements–Specifies whether authentication between two computers should be requested or required in each direction.
- Authentication Method–Specifies the type of authentication the computers should use when establishing a connection.
- Profile–Specifies the profile(s) to which the rule should apply: domain, private, and/or public.
- Name–Specifies a name and (optionally) a description for the rule.

Figure 8-11

The New Connection Security Rule Wizard

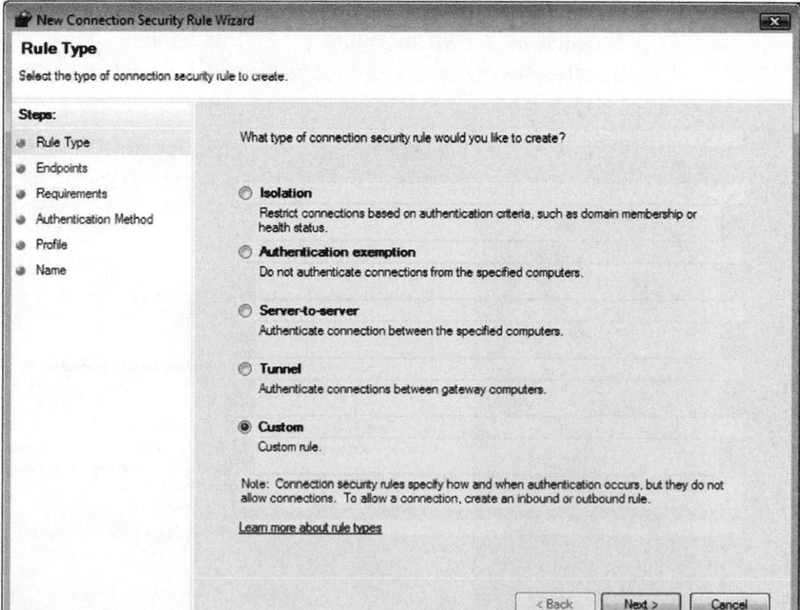

Using Automatic Updates

Automatic Updates is a Windows Vista features that enables users to keep their computers current, with no manual intervention.

Microsoft typically releases operating system updates on the 12th of each month, or, in special circumstances, more frequently. The majority of the operating system updates, and especially those released in special circumstances, address security issues. Keeping Windows computers updated should therefore be an important part of your regular maintenance regimen.

Microsoft maintains a Windows Update Website that provides authorized Windows Vista users with access to the latest update releases. Users can access the Website from a shortcut on the Start menu (Start > All Programs > Windows Update). However, Windows Vista also makes it possible to automate the update process by scheduling the downloading and installation of updates to occur at regular intervals, with no user intervention, if desired.

TAKE NOTE*

On Windows domain networks, updates are usually managed by network administrators, who download and test all new releases before distributing them to workstations. In these situations, Windows Vista workstations still use Automatic Updates, but they download the updates from a Windows Server Update Services (WSUS) server on their corporate network, instead of from the Internet. Administrators modify the behavior of the Automatic Updates feature using Group Policy settings, so the process is invisible to the end user.

By default, Automatic Updates is turned off in Windows Vista. To configure Windows Vista to perform Automatic Updates, use the following procedure:

CONFIGURE AUTOMATIC UPDATES

GET READY. Log on to Windows Vista using an account with administrative capabilities. When the logon process is completed, close the Welcome Center window and any other windows that appear.

1. Click **Start**, and then click **Control Panel**. The Control Panel window appears.
2. Click **System and Maintenance > Windows Update**. The Windows Update window appears, as shown in Figure 8-12. This window shows the current status of Automatic Updates, whether the service is turned on, and if so, its configuration settings.

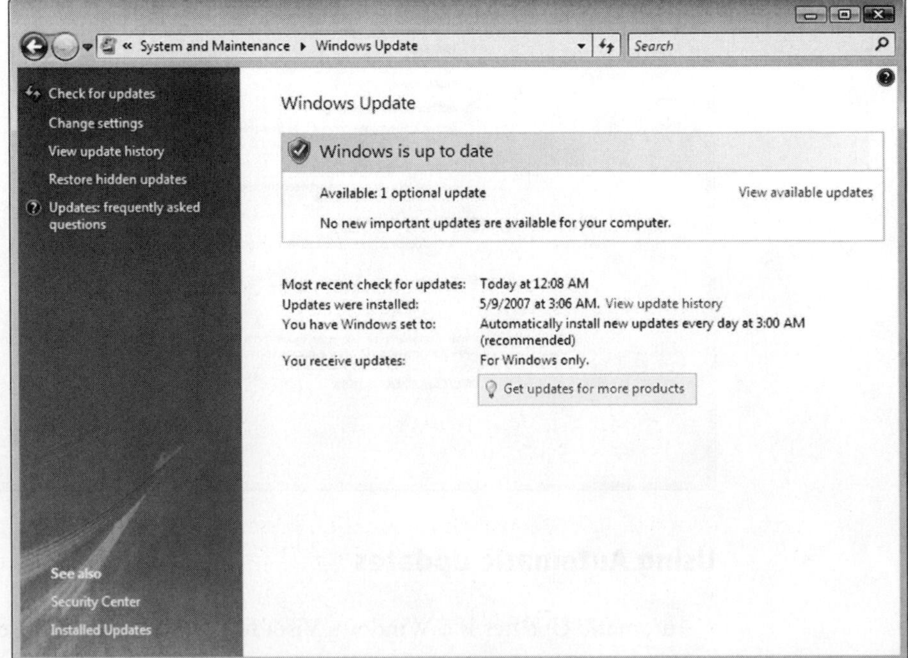

Figure 8-12

The Windows Update window

3. Click **Change settings**. The *Choose how Windows can install updates* page appears, as shown in Figure 8-13.

Figure 8-13
The Choose how Windows can install updates page

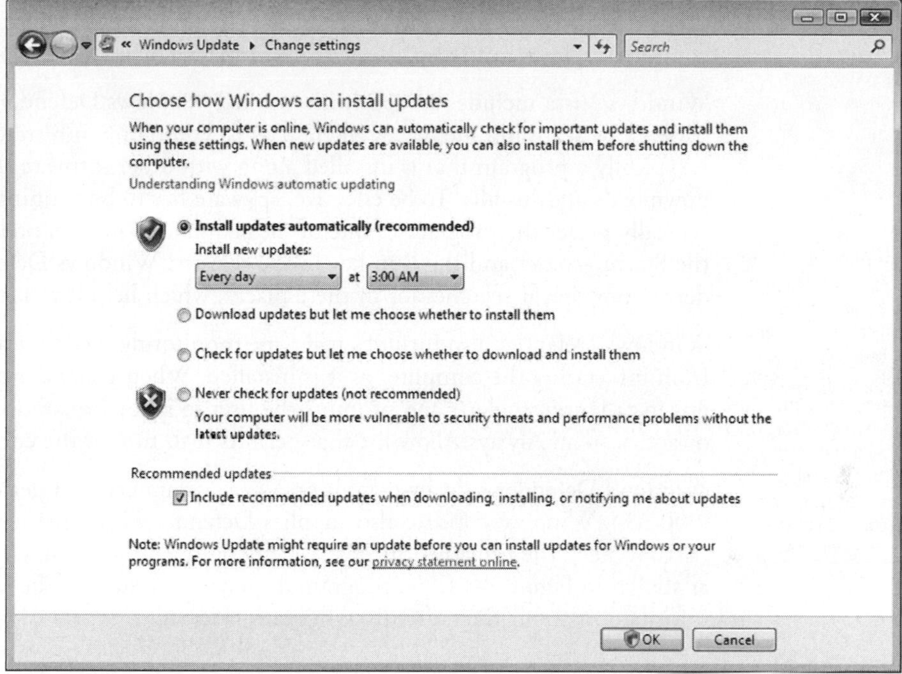

4. To enable Automatic Updates, select the **Install updates automatically** radio button. You can also opt to download updates but not install them until you say so, or check for updates without downloading or installing them.
5. In the *Install new updates* spin boxes, specify the frequency and the time of day you want the system to check for updates. Select the **Include recommended updates...** checkbox, if you want the system to download and install recommended, as well as critical, updates. Then, click **OK**.

MORE INFORMATION

Microsoft classifies its operating system updates as critical, recommended, or optional. Automatic Updates downloads and installs only the critical updates, unless you instruct it to install the recommended updates as well. Most of the security updates are classified as critical, so that Automatic Updates will download and install them as soon as possible.

6. After confirming that you performed the action, Vista applies your configuration changes and performs its first check for updates.

CLOSE the Windows Update window.

Introducing Windows Defender

Windows Defender is a new Windows Vista application that prevents the infiltration of spyware into the system.

Originally, the people who created and disseminated viruses and other types of malware did so purely out of gratuitous vandalism. Today, the primary motive is profit, and this has led to the development of new kinds of malware. ***Spyware***, for example, is a type of software that gathers information about users and transmits it back to the attacker.

The type of information spyware can gather ranges from the trivial to the critical. Some programs simply collect information about users' Web surfing habits, the better to target potential customers with their marketing efforts. Others collect personal and confidential information about the computer's users, including passwords and account numbers, which attackers can use for identity theft and other crimes. In addition to compromising the security of a computer, spyware can also affect its performance by consuming system resources.

Windows Vista includes an application called Windows Defender that helps to defend against spyware by scanning the places where it most commonly infiltrates a computer. Spyware is typically a program that is installed along with other software that the user deliberately downloads and installs. To be effective, spyware has to be running all the time, so the installer typically places the program in one of the standard Windows preloading mechanisms, such as the Startup folder and the Run key in the registry. Windows Defender has a set of predefined definitions that it searches for in these places, which help it to identify specific threats.

WARNING Windows Defender is not a full-featured antivirus program, as it cannot detect or remove true viruses, Trojans, and other types of malware. Windows Vista does not include a comprehensive antivirus solution, and Microsoft recommends that you purchase and install a third-party antivirus product. In fact, Windows Security Center monitors the computer for the presence of antivirus software and warns users when it fails to find it, even when Windows Defender is present and running.

Windows Defender also includes real-time monitoring, which attempts to prevent spyware from infiltrating the computer as it is installed. When Defender detects a potentially dangerous installation, it alerts and prompts the user to ignore, quarantine, or remove the program, or add it to an Always Allow list that permits it to run on the computer.

Windows Defender runs by default on Vista computers, and performs a scan every day at 2:00 AM. Windows Update also supplies Defender with signature updates on a regular basis, to keep the program current. When you open the main Windows Defender window, as shown in Figure 8-14, the program displays the results of the most recent scan, as well as information about the current configuration settings.

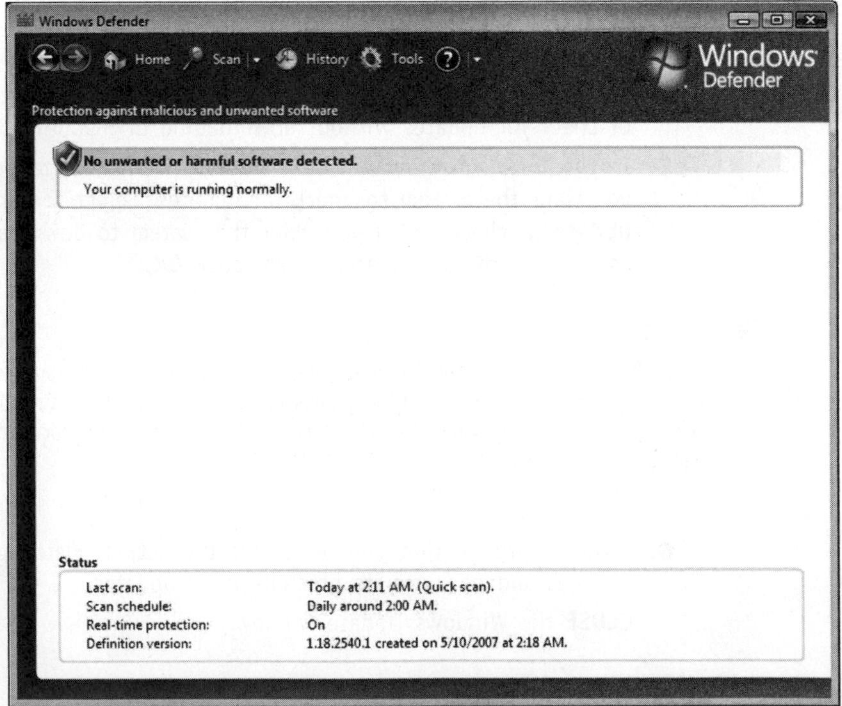

Figure 8-14

The Windows Defender window

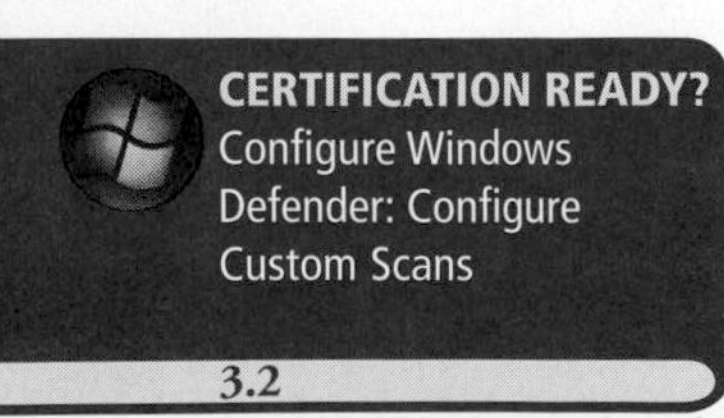

CERTIFICATION READY?
Configure Windows Defender: Configure Custom Scans
3.2

To perform an additional scan at any time, simply click the **Scan** link at the top of the window, and the program starts running.

CONFIGURING WINDOWS DEFENDER

You can modify the configuration of Windows Defender by using the following procedure:

CONFIGURE WINDOWS DEFENDER

GET READY. Log on to Windows Vista using an account with administrative capabilities. When the logon process is completed, close the Welcome Center window and any other windows that appear.

1. Click **Start**, and then click **Control Panel**. The Control Panel window appears.
2. Click **Security** > **Windows Defender**. The Windows Defender window appears. This window shows the current status of Windows Defender, and indicates whether the program has detected any unwanted or harmful software.
3. Click **Tools**. The Tools and Settings page appears, as shown in Figure 8-15.

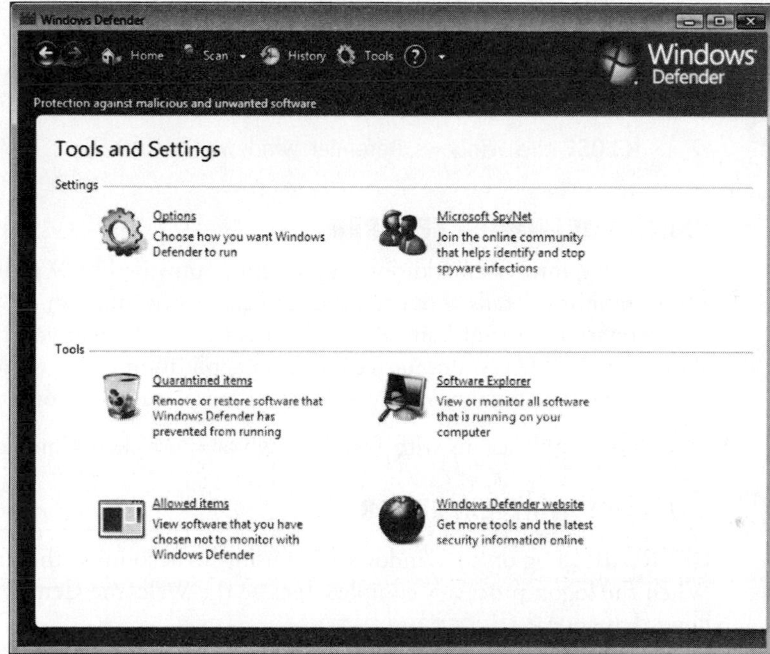

Figure 8-15

The Windows Defender Tools and Settings page

4. Click **Options**. The Options page appears, as shown in Figure 8-16.

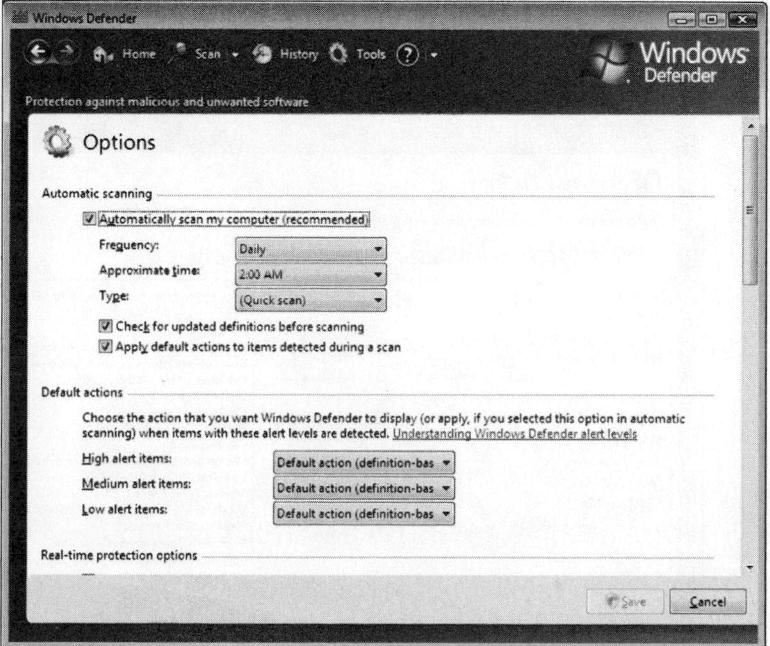

Figure 8-16

The Windows Defender Options page

5. After confirming your action, modify the configuration settings for any of the following items and click **Save**.
   - Automatic scanning–Specifies if, when, and how often Defender should scan the system. You can also configure the program to download updated definitions before scanning.
   - Default actions–Specifies what action Defender should take when it detects items at each of the three alert levels.
   - Real-time protection options–Specifies whether Defender should provide real-time protection and enables you to specify which types of real-time protection Defender should provide.
   - Advanced options–Enables you to configure Defender to scan within archives, create a restore point before applying actions, and specify files that Defender should avoid scanning.
   - Administrator options–Enables you to configure Defender to alert all users if it detects spyware and to allow all users to initiate Defender scans.

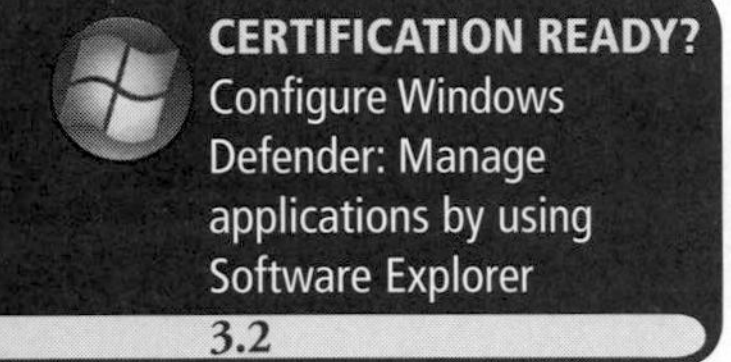

CERTIFICATION READY?
Configure Windows Defender: Manage applications by using Software Explorer
3.2

CLOSE the Windows Defender window.

USING SOFTWARE EXPLORER

Software Explorer is an additional application, provided by Windows Defender, that enables you to monitor details about specific applications running on a Windows Vista computer. The primary benefit of Software Explorer is that it can help you to find spyware running on your computer. If you do not recognize an application or the company that created it you should investigate it thoroughly as it might be spyware, or worse.

To monitor applications with Software Explorer, use the following procedure.

USE SOFTWARE EXPLORER

GET READY. Log on to Windows Vista using an account with administrative capabilities. When the logon process is completed, close the Welcome Center window and any other windows that appear.

1. Click **Start**, and then click **Control Panel**. The Control Panel window appears.
2. Click **Security** > **Windows Defender** > **Tools** > **Software Explorer**. The Software Explorer page appears, as shown in Figure 8-17.

Figure 8-17

The Software Explorer page

3. In the Category dropdown list, select one of the following four categories:
   - Startup Programs–There are a number of mechanisms that Windows Vista can use to automatically load applications when the computer starts. This categories includes all of them, and even displays the method used to launch the program. This is a good way to detect applications running on your system without your knowledge.
   - Currently Running Programs–This category includes all of the programs that are currently running on the computer, on the screen or in the background, whether explicitly launched by a user or by another process.
   - Network Connected Programs–This category includes all applications that are capable of accessing the network. You should recognize the programs that access the network, and question those that you do not recognize.
   - Winsock Service Providers–This category lists all of the programs that perform low-level networking functions. Most of the applications listed here should be part of the operating system. Any others might be suspicious, and you should examine them carefully.
4. Select an application in the left pane to display details about it in the right pane. If desired, click **Show for all users** to display the Startup Programs for all of the user accounts on the system.
5. If you select an application that appears suspicious, you can remove or disable it using the buttons provided.

CLOSE the Software Explorer window.

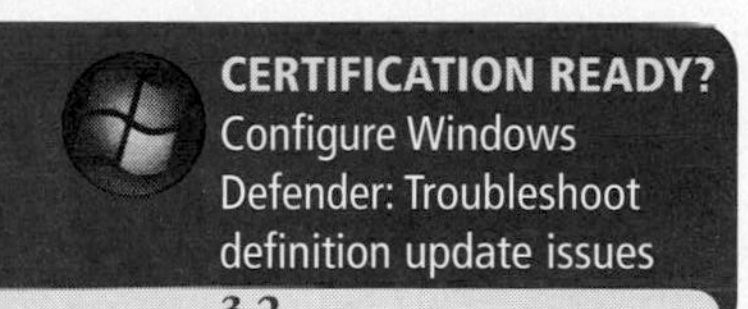

CERTIFICATION READY?
Configure Windows Defender: Troubleshoot definition update issues
3.2

UPDATING DEFINITIONS

Protecting Windows Vista computers against malware is a constant struggle between the attackers who create the malicious software and the people who design protective software for them. As a result, Windows Defender relies on continual updates to its definitions, which determine what the program should scan and how. Windows Defender definition updates are included in the software that is downloaded and installed by the Automatic Updates feature on a regular basis.

Using the Malicious Software Removal Tool

The Malicious Software Removal Tool is a one-time virus scanner program that Microsoft distributes with its monthly updates.

As stated earlier, Windows Vista does not include a full-featured antivirus program, and Microsoft strongly recommends that users obtain and install one. However, Microsoft does provide the Malicious Software Removal Tool, which can serve as a substitute or a backup to third-party antivirus products.

The Malicious Software Removal Tool is a single user virus scanner that Microsoft supplies in each of its monthly operating system updates. The tool scans the system for viruses and other forms of malware immediately after its installation, and removes any potentially damaging software that it finds. Because the tool is designed for a single use only, there are no controls, and it is not permanently installed in the operating system.

For systems with no other antivirus protection, the Malicious Software Removal Tool can function as a substitute until you obtain one. For systems that already have antivirus software, the tool functions as an effective backup. There are types of malware that are capable of disabling well-known virus scanners, and the Malicious Software Removal Tool can provide an effective scan in the event that the main software is not functioning.

Protecting Sensitive Data

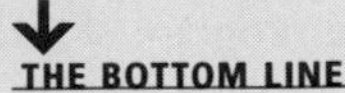

Windows Vista includes tools like BitLocker and the Encrypting File System (EFS), which make it possible to prevent data theft using cryptography.

Malware is not the only threat to the security of a Windows Vista computer. The primary reason for having security tools such as Windows Firewall and Windows Defender is to protect the data on a computer. However, tools like these can do nothing to prevent simple, old-fashioned attacks, such as when someone sits down at a computer while the user is at lunch and copies their data, or if someone simply steals the entire computer.

Windows Vista includes other tools that you can use to protect your clients' data from more direct attacks, such as those discussed in the following sections.

Using the Encrypting File System

The Encrypting File System (EFS) protects users' data by encrypting and decrypting it on the fly as the user works.

TAKE NOTE*

Only the Business, Enterprise, and Ultimate editions of Windows Vista support EFS. The Home Basic and Home Premium editions do not support EFS.

The Encrypting File System (EFS) is a feature of NTFS that encodes the files on a computer so that even if an intruder can obtain a file, he or she will be unable to read it. The entire system is keyed to a specific user account, using the public and private keys that are the basis of Windows public key infrastructure (PKI). The user who creates a file is the only person who can read it.

As the user works, EFS encrypts the files he or she creates using a key generated from the user's ***public key***. Data encrypted with this key can be decrypted only by the user's personal encryption certificate, which is generated using his or her ***private key***.

When the user logs on to the computer, the system gains access to the keys that are necessary to encrypt and decrypt the EFS-protected data. To that user, the encryption process is completely invisible, and usually does not have a major impact on system performance. The user creates, accesses, and saves files in the normal manner, unaware that the cryptographic processes are taking place.

If another user logs on to the computer, he or she has no access to the other user's private key, and therefore cannot decrypt the encrypted files. An attacker can conceivably sit down at the computer and try to copy the files off to a flash drive, but he or she will receive an "Access Denied" error message, just as if he or she lacked the appropriate NTFS permissions for the files.

There are two main restrictions when implementing EFS:

- EFS is a feature of the NTFS file system, so you cannot use EFS on FAT drives.
- You cannot use EFS to encrypt files that have already been compressed using NTFS compression.

WHAT'S NEW IN WINDOWS VISTA EFS

In previous versions of Windows, the effectiveness of EFS has been compromised by some of the other standard Windows features. Windows Vista includes some refinements to address these shortcomings, including the following:

- Smart cards–It is now possible to store the user keys required for access to EFS-encrypted files on a smart card, which is essentially a credit card with a chip that stores data. On a system so equipped, EFS-encrypted data is accessed by inserting the correct card and supplying a personal identification number (PIN) or password.

- Paging file–Windows uses a paging file on the system drive to store information when it runs out of available memory. After working with EFS-protected files, it is possible for all or part of a file to be left inside the paging file in its unencrypted form. Although it would be very difficult to locate specific data that could be anywhere in a huge paging file, this could still be considered a serious problem if the data is sensitive. Windows Vista makes it possible to encrypt the Windows paging file, using a key that is generated when the system starts and destroyed when the system shuts down.
- Offline Files cache–Windows' Offline Files feature enables the system to store copies of network files in a cache on a local drive. If access to the network files is interrupted, the system continues work using the cached copy. When the network becomes available again, the system synchronizes the cached copy with the network copy. Because the cached copy of an EFS-protected file would normally be unencrypted, leaving copies of sensitive files available to anyone, Windows Vista makes it possible to use Group Policy to configure EFS to encrypt the Offline Files cache with the user's key rather than a system key. This limits each cached file's access to the user that created it.

ENCRYPTING A FOLDER WITH EFS

In Windows Vista, you can use Windows Explorer to encrypt or disable EFS on any individual files or folders, as long as they are on an NTFS drive. To encrypt a file or folder, use the following procedure:

ENCRYPT A FOLDER

GET READY. Log on to Windows Vista using an account with administrative capabilities. When the logon process is completed, close the Welcome Center window and any other windows that appear.

1. Click **Start**, and then click **All Programs** > **Accessories** > **Windows Explorer.** The Windows Explorer window appears.
2. Right-click a file or folder and then, from the context menu, select **Properties.** The Properties sheet for the file or folder appears, as shown in Figure 8-18.

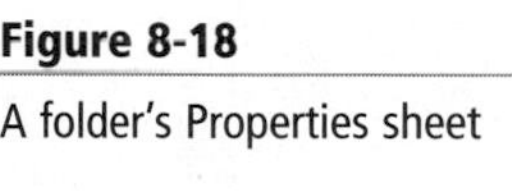

Figure 8-18

A folder's Properties sheet

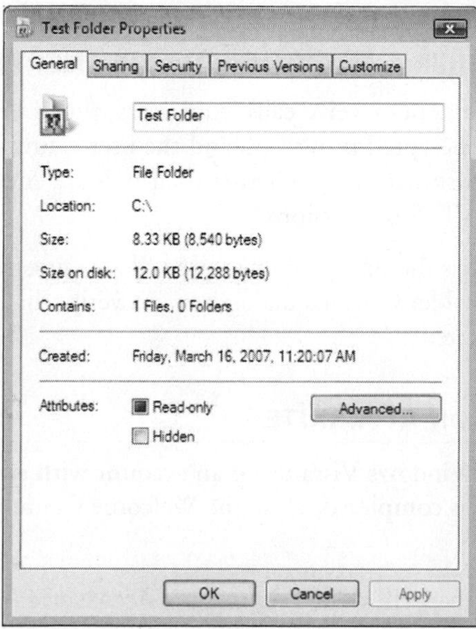

3. On the General tab, click **Advanced.** The Advanced Attributes dialog box appears, as shown in Figure 8-19.

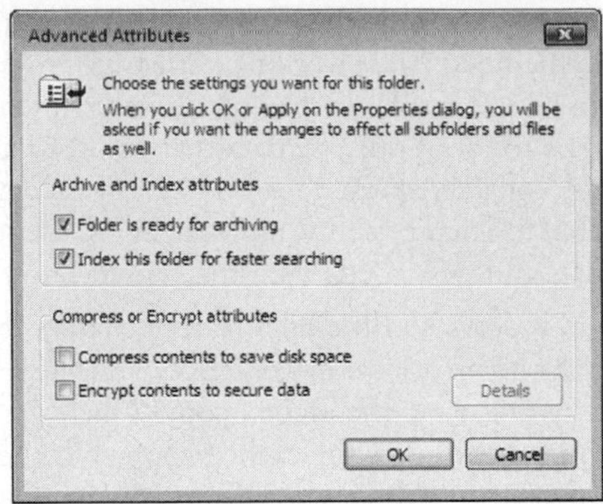

Figure 8-19

The Advanced Attributes dialog box

4. Select the **Encrypt contents to secure data** checkbox, and then click **OK**.
5. Click **OK** to close the Properties sheet. If you selected a folder that contains files or subfolders, a Confirm Attribute Changes dialog box appears, as shown in Figure 8-20, asking you to choose whether to apply changes to the folder only, or to the folder and all of its subfolders and files.

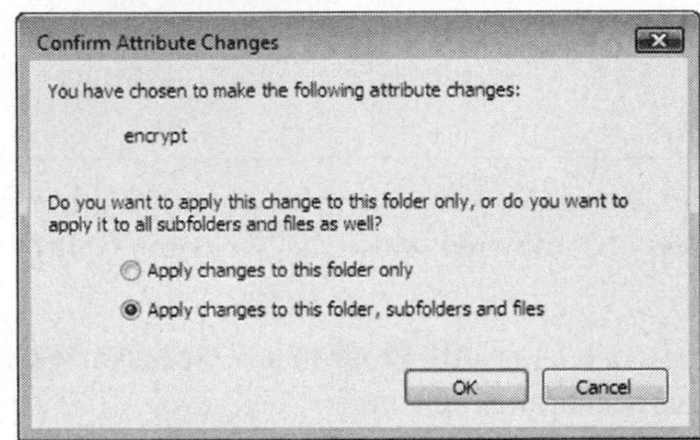

Figure 8-20

A Confirm Attribute Changes dialog box

TAKE NOTE*

If you elect to apply changes to the selected folder only, EFS does not encrypt any of the files that are currently in the folder. However, any files that you create, copy, or move to the folder after you enable EFS will be encrypted.

6. Select a confirmation option and click **OK**. Depending on how many files and folders there are to be encrypted, the process could take several minutes.

DETERMINING WHETHER A FILE OR FOLDER IS ENCRYPTED

Desktop technicians commonly receive calls from users who are unable to access their files because they have been encrypted using EFS and the user is unaware of this fact. To resolve the problem, you must first determine whether their files are encrypted or not, and whether the user has the proper NTFS permissions.

Windows Explorer displays the names of encrypted files in green, by default, but this setting is easily changed in the Folder Options dialog box. To verify that a folder or file is encrypted, use the following procedure:

VIEW THE ENCRYPTION ATTRIBUTE

GET READY. Log on to Windows Vista using an account with administrative capabilities. When the logon process is completed, close the Welcome Center window and any other windows that appear.

1. Click **Start**, and then click **All Programs > Accessories > Windows Explorer**. The Windows Explorer window appears.
2. Right-click a file or folder and then, from the context menu, select **Properties.** The Properties sheet for the file or folder appears.
3. On the General tab, click **Advanced.** The Advanced Attributes dialog box appears. If the *Encrypt contents to secure data* checkbox is selected, the file or folder is encrypted.

4. Click **OK** to close the Advanced Attributes dialog box.
5. Click **OK** to close the Properties sheet.

Configuring Parental Controls

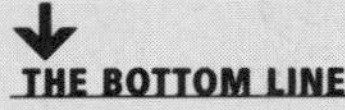

Parental control enables parents to limit their children's access to specific Internet sites, games, and applications.

Just as parents often want to control what their children watch on television, they also might want to control their computing habits. Windows Vista, in its Home Basic, Home Premium, and Ultimate editions (but not in the Business or Enterprise editions), includes parental controls that you can use to exercise the following restrictions:

- Filter the Websites users are allowed to access
- Limit downloads from Internet sites
- Enforce time limits for computer use
- Restrict access to games by rating, content, or title
- Allow or block specific applications

Setting Up Users

Parental controls are based on user accounts, so parents must create accounts for all family members and enforce their use.

Windows Vista Parental Controls are keyed to user accounts, so the first thing parents have to do is create separate accounts for their children and make sure the family becomes accustomed to logging on and off of their accounts whenever they use the computer. In many cases, this is the most difficult part of the process. Many families are accustomed to using a single account, often one with administrative privileges, and leaving it logged on at all times. This obviously poses dangers both to the operating system and to the parents' ideas of what children should and should not be permitted to see.

For more information on creating user accounts, see Lesson 5, "Working with Users and Groups."

In addition to creating user accounts for everyone in the family, parents must make sure that all of the accounts on the computer have passwords and that the passwords remain secure. If an account with administrative privileges does not have a password, then a child can simply log on using that account and modify or turn off the parental controls.

Setting Up Parental Controls

CERTIFICATION READY?
Configure and troubleshoot parental controls
2.3

After creating user accounts, you can then impose restrictions on those accounts.

Once you have created user accounts for the children whose access you want to restrict, use the following procedure to configure Parental Controls:

SET UP PARENTAL CONTROLS

GET READY. Log on to Windows Vista using an account with administrative capabilities. When the logon process is completed, close the Welcome Center window and any other windows that appear.

1. Click **Start**, and then click **Control Panel**. The Control Panel window appears.
2. Click **User Accounts and Family Safety > Parental Controls**. The *Choose a user and set up Parental Controls* page appears, as shown in Figure 8-21.

Figure 8-21

The Choose a user and set up Parental Controls page

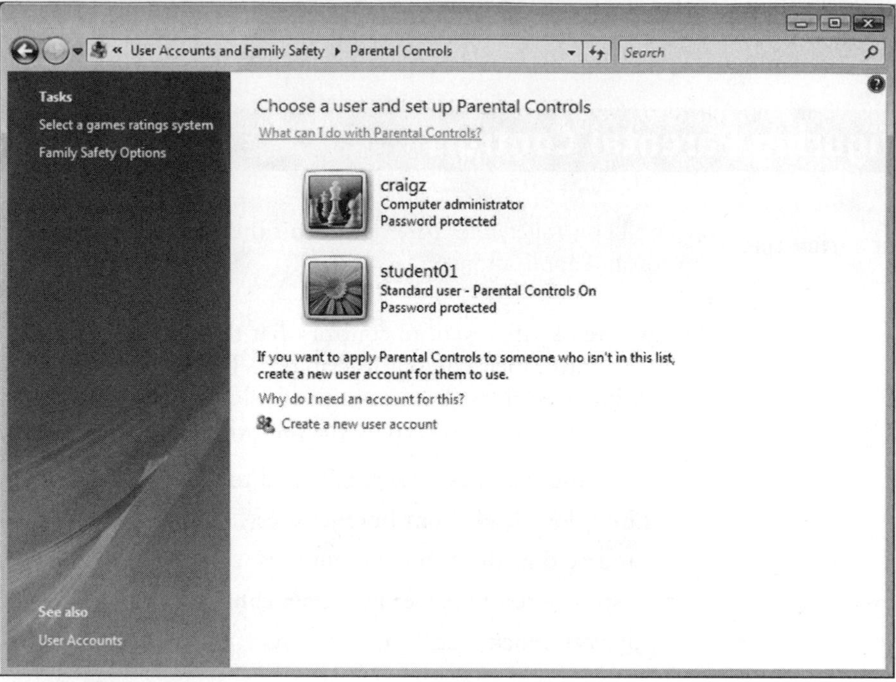

3. Select the account for which you want to configure parental controls. The User Controls page appears, as shown in Figure 8-22.

Figure 8-22

The User Controls page

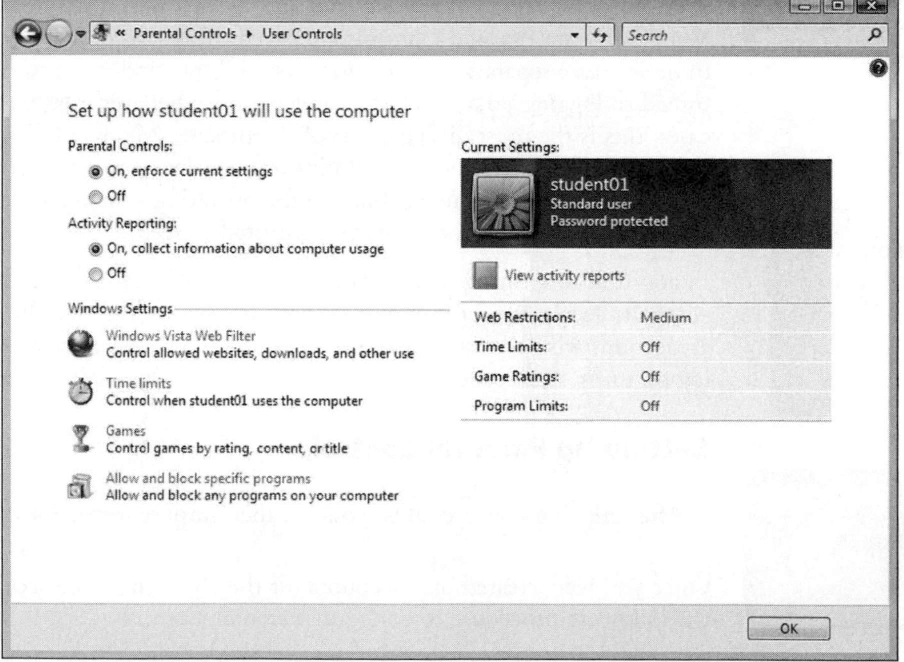

4. Click the **On, enforce current settings** radio button to enforce the current setting. By default, the Parental Control engine compiles activity reports about the accounts under its protection, but you can turn them off by clicking the **Off** radio button under Activity Reporting.
5. To restrict Internet access, under Windows Settings, click **Windows Vista Web Filter.** On the Web Restrictions page, shown in Figure 8-23, you can do the following:
   - Specify whether to block some Websites or content
   - Create a list of Websites to be allowed or blocked

- Block Web content according to ratings
- Block Internet file downloads

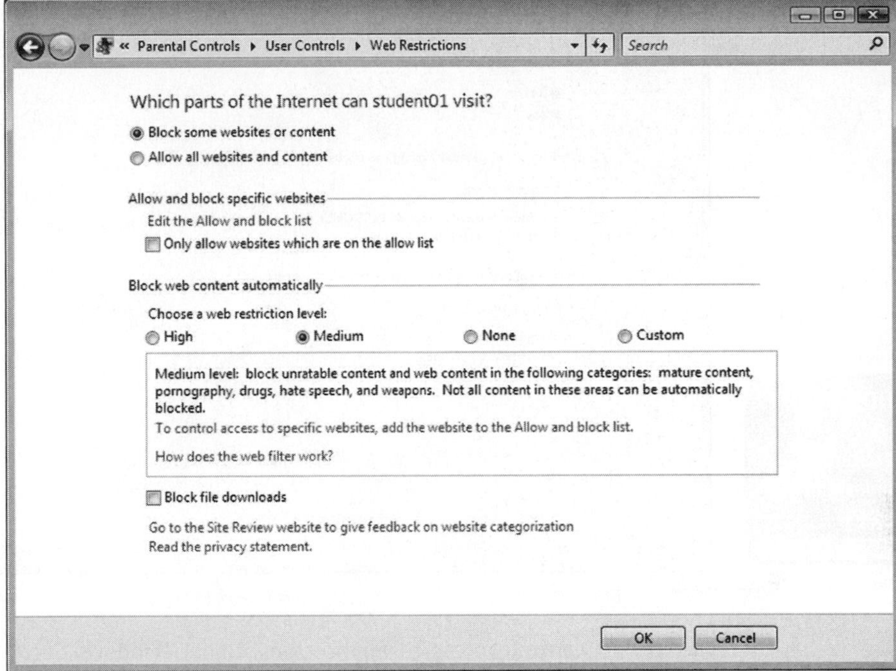

Figure 8-23

The Web Restrictions page

CERTIFICATION READY?
Configure and troubleshoot parental controls: Troubleshoot Web browsing issues
2.3

6. To impose computer time limits, under Windows Settings, click **Time limits.** The Time Restrictions page appears, as shown in Figure 8-24, where you can specify in a grid what hours of the day the user is permitted access to the computer.

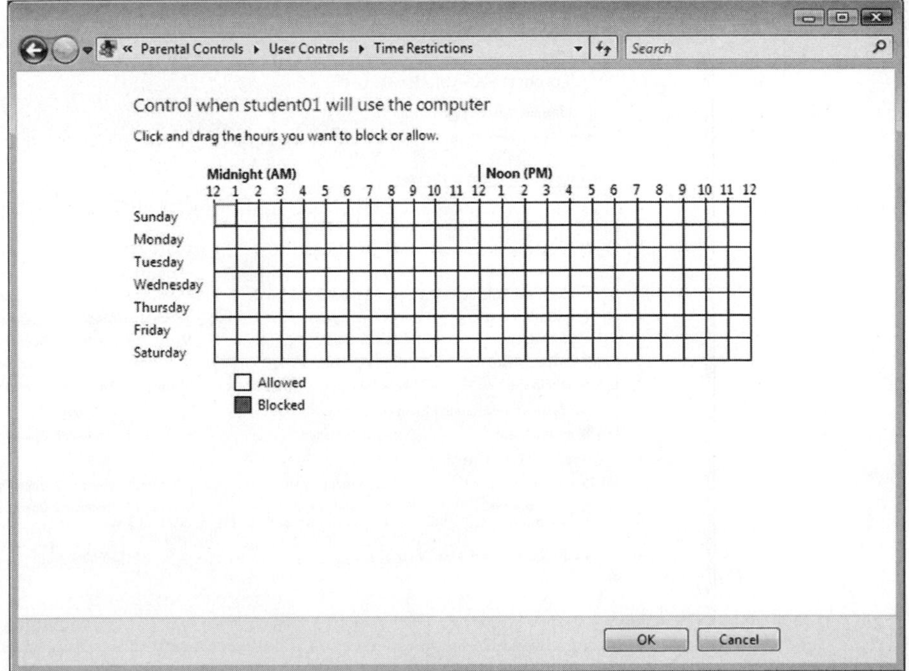

Figure 8-24

The Time Restrictions page

7. To control access to games, under Windows Settings, click **Games.** The Game Controls page appears, as shown in Figure 8-25, where you can do the following:

- Specify whether the user can play games
- Allow and block games according to ratings
- Create a list of games to be allowed or blocked

Figure 8-25

The Game Controls page

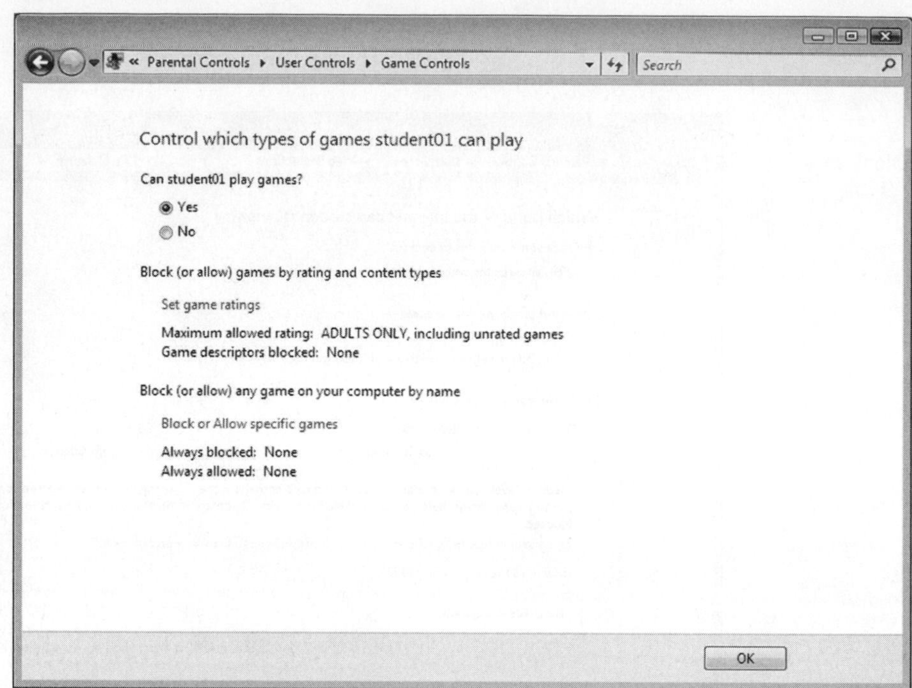

8. To control access to applications, under Windows Settings, click **Allow and block specific programs.** The Application Restrictions page appears, as shown in Figure 8-26, on which you can create a list of the only applications the user is permitted to run.

Figure 8-26

The Application Restrictions page

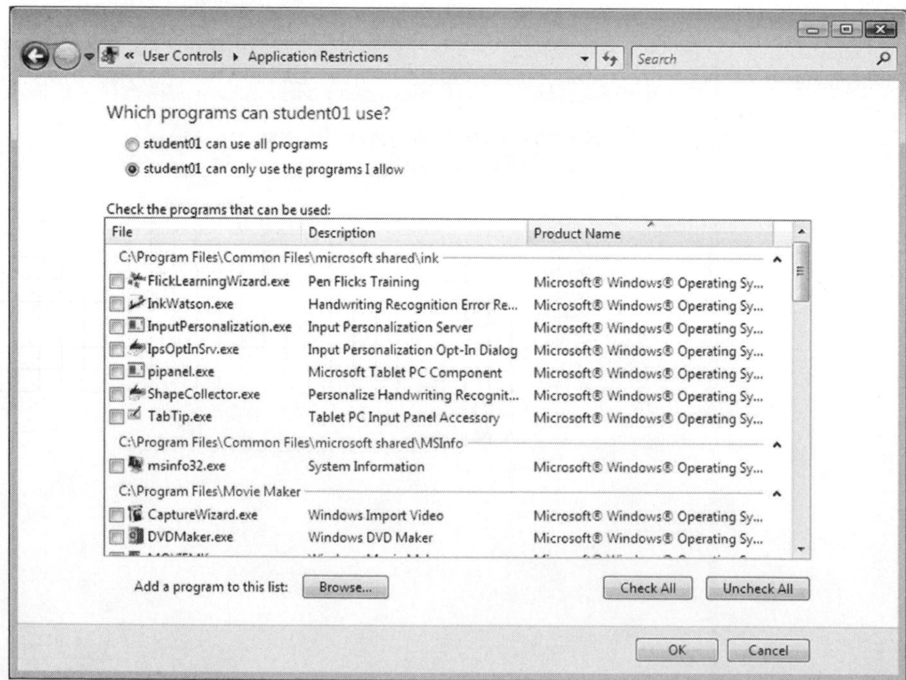

9. Click **OK** after configuring each page, and then click **OK** again to close the User Controls page.

Repeat the entire procedure for any other user accounts you want to control.

SUMMARY SKILL MATRIX

IN THIS LESSON YOU LEARNED:
Malware is malicious software created specifically for the purpose of infiltrating or damaging a computer system without the user's knowledge or consent. This type of software includes a variety of technologies, including viruses, Trojan horses, worms, spyware, and adware.
Security Center is a centralized console that enables users and administrators to access, monitor, and configure the various Windows Vista security mechanisms.
Windows Firewall is a software program that protects a computer by allowing certain types of network traffic in and out of the system while blocking others.
You configure Windows Firewall by creating rules that specify what types of traffic to block and/or allow.
Automatic Updates makes it possible to automate the operating system update process by scheduling the downloading and installation of updates to occur at regular intervals, with no user intervention.
Windows Defender helps to defend against spyware by scanning the places where it most commonly infiltrates a computer.
Software Explorer is an application that enables you to monitor details about specific applications running on a Windows Vista computer.
The Malicious Software Removal Tool is a single user virus scanner that Microsoft supplies in each of its monthly operating system updates.
The Encrypting File System (EFS) is a feature of NTFS that encodes the files on a computer so that even if an intruder can obtain a file, he or she will be unable to read it.
Windows Vista, in its Home Basic, Home Premium, and Ultimate editions, includes parental controls that you can use to exercise restrictions over other users' computing habits.

Knowledge Assessment

Fill in the Blank

Complete the following sentences by writing the correct word or words in the blanks provided.

1. A type of malware specifically designed to gather information about the computer user and send it to an attacker is called ________________.
2. A file cannot be encrypted with EFS if it is already ________________ by NTFS.
3. To create a Windows Firewall rule and apply it to all three network locations in one procedure, you must use the ________________.
4. Connection Security rules use ________________ to secure the authentication process between two computers.
5. The only true virus scanner that Microsoft supplies to Vista users free of charge is called ________________.
6. Windows Vista has improved the capabilities of EFS by making it possible to encrypt the ________________ and the ________________.

7. Windows Firewall maintains three sets of rules called ______________.

8. The Windows Vista version of Windows Firewall enables you to create rules that call for the use of IPsec to encapsulate data packets within other packets. This process is called ______________.

9. When Security Center detects that there is no antivirus software installed on a Windows Vista computer, it displays an icon in the ______________.

10. Files encrypted by EFS appear ______________ in Windows Explorer.

True / False

Circle T if the statement is true or F if the statement is false.

T | F 1. Windows Firewall eliminates the need for antivirus software.

T | F 2. Security Center was first introduced in Windows Vista.

T | F 3. Windows Defender uses rules that you create to control its scans.

T | F 4. The exceptions you create in the Windows Firewall Settings dialog box apply only to the currently operating profile.

T | F 5. Windows Firewall blocks inbound traffic by default.

T | F 6. Windows Defender can detect spyware that is already present on the system, but it cannot prevent the infiltration of new spyware.

T | F 7. Parental Controls are only supplied in the Home Basic and Home Premium editions of Windows Vista.

T | F 8. Windows Defender requires definition updates that are supplied free with the regularly scheduled Vista operating system updates.

T | F 9. Windows Security Center does not run by default on computers that are members of a domain.

T | F 10. Windows Security Center can monitor third-party security products, as well as those provided by Microsoft.

Review Questions

1. Explain why opening a program exception in Windows Firewall is inherently less dangerous than opening a port.

2. Explain how monitoring the applications in Software Explorer's Startup category can help you avoid the consequences of malware.

Case Scenarios

Scenario #1: Using Parental Controls

Mark has three children, all of whom share a single computer with a broadband Internet connection. Mark originally purchased the computer for the children to do homework, but it has now become a hub of their social activities as well. Their increasing need for computer time has resulted in frequent arguments, and Mark is also concerned about the amount of unsupervised Web surfing the children are doing. Mark decides to implement the Parental Controls feature in Windows Vista to address these problems. List the basic tasks that Mark must perform to successfully implement Parental Controls on the children's computer and solve the problems described here.

Scenario #2: Configuring Windows Firewall

You are a desktop technician in the IT department of a small corporation. Today is the day of the company picnic and, as the junior member of the department, you have been left in charge of the entire corporate network while everyone else is out of the office. Shortly after 2:00 PM, an e-mail arrives from the company's biggest customer, complaining that they can't access the Web server they use to place their orders. After checking the Web server logs, it seems clear that the server is undergoing a denial-of-service attack, because there are suddenly hundreds of Internet computers repeatedly trying to access it. What temporary modifications could you make to Windows Firewall on the Windows Vista computer that stands between the Web server and the Internet that would allow customers to access the Web server while blocking the attackers?

LESSON 9 Configuring Windows Vista Applications

OBJECTIVE DOMAIN MATRIX

TECHNOLOGY SKILL	OBJECTIVE DOMAIN	OBJECTIVE NUMBER
Configuring Internet Explorer 7	Configure Windows Internet Explorer 7+ • Configure RSS feeds • Manage subscriptions • Configure feed updates • Configure the Search bar and Search providers • Configure print and viewing controls • Troubleshoot Print Preview issues	2.4
Securing Internet Explorer 7	Configure Dynamic Security for Internet Explorer 7+ • Resolve Protected Mode issues • Configure the Phishing Service • Configure Pop-up Blocker • Configure Security Zones • Configure Privacy Settings • Manage Add-Ons	3.3
Using Windows Mail	Configure Windows Mail	5.2
Configuring the Inbox	Configure Windows Mail • Configure Inbox	5.2
Using Windows Contacts	Configure Windows Mail • Configure Contacts	5.2
Using Newsgroups	Configure Windows Mail • Configure Newsgroups	5.2
Using Windows Meeting Space	Configure Windows Meeting Space • Configure people near me • Create and manage meetings • Share files	5.3
Using Windows Calendar	Configure Windows Calendar • Troubleshoot shared calendar issues	5.4
Using Windows Fax and Scan	Configure Windows Fax and Scan	5.5
Working with Media Applications	Configure and Troubleshoot Media Applications	5.1

KEY TERMS

Instant Search
Network News Transfer Protocol (NNTP)
phishing
Post Office Protocol 3 (POP3)
protected mode
Quick Tabs
RSS feed
security zones
social engineering
Simple Mail Transfer Protocol (SMTP)
Usenet

Using Internet Explorer 7

Desktop technicians must be familiar with the extensive changes made to Internet Explorer for the Windows Vista release.

Windows Vista includes the latest version of the Internet Explorer Web browser, Version 7, which includes some important upgrades. For desktop technicians, this is likely to result in an increasing number of "user error" calls as users become accustomed to the new tools and the changes to the interface. Internet Explorer 7 also includes new security tools that you must know how to configure for maximum effectiveness.

What's New in Internet Explorer 7

Internet Explorer 7 includes a variety of new features that can streamline users' Web browsing tasks.

Users accustomed to Internet Explorer 6 (IE6) will find that while the basic functionality of the browser is intact in Internet Explorer 7 (IE7), there are a variety of new refinements and capabilities that can enhance user productivity. Some of these refinements are as follows.

- Modified interface
- Tabbed browsing
- Quick tabs
- Tab groups
- Page zoom
- Instant Search
- Enhanced printing
- RSS feeds

The following sections examine these improvements in greater depth.

USING THE IE7 INTERFACE

One of the changes in IE7 that should be most immediately obvious to IE6 users is that the control area at the top of the window is reduced, leaving more room for the content displayed in the browser. Previous versions of Internet Explorer had three rows of controls, a row of menus, a toolbar, and an address bar. IE7 reduces this to two.

The top row contains the Back and Forward buttons, the Address bar, and a new Live Search box, as shown in Figure 9-1. The second row contains tabs for the currently displayed Web pages, plus toolbar buttons that perform most of the functions from the menu bar, which has now been eliminated from the default configuration.

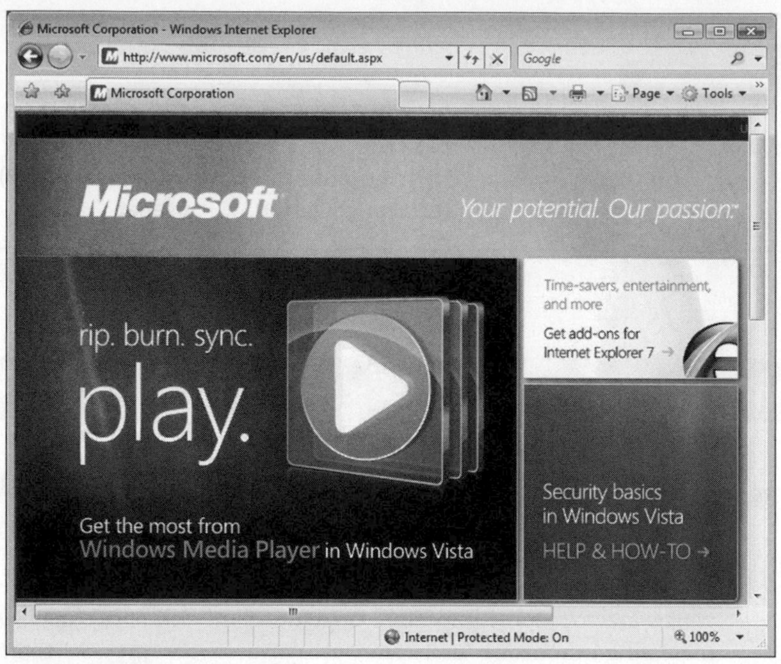

Figure 9-1

The Internet Explorer 7 interface

As with Windows Explorer, the menu bar no longer appears in the interface by default, but users can display it simply by pressing the Alt key at any time.

MORE INFORMATION

It is possible to permanently restore the display of the menu bar. One method is for users to right-click the toolbar and select Menu Bar from the context menu. Another is for administrators to use Group Policy to enable the Turn On Menu Bar By Default settings, which is found in the Computer Configuration > Administrative Templates > Windows Components > Internet Explorer container in a group policy object.

USING TABBED BROWSING

Tabbed browsing is the new IE7 feature that most people think of first. When you open a second Web page in IE7, it appears not in a separate window, but in a new layer in the same window. Each of the two layers is accessible by clicking a tab on the toolbar, as shown in Figure 9-2. As you open additional pages, you add more tabs.

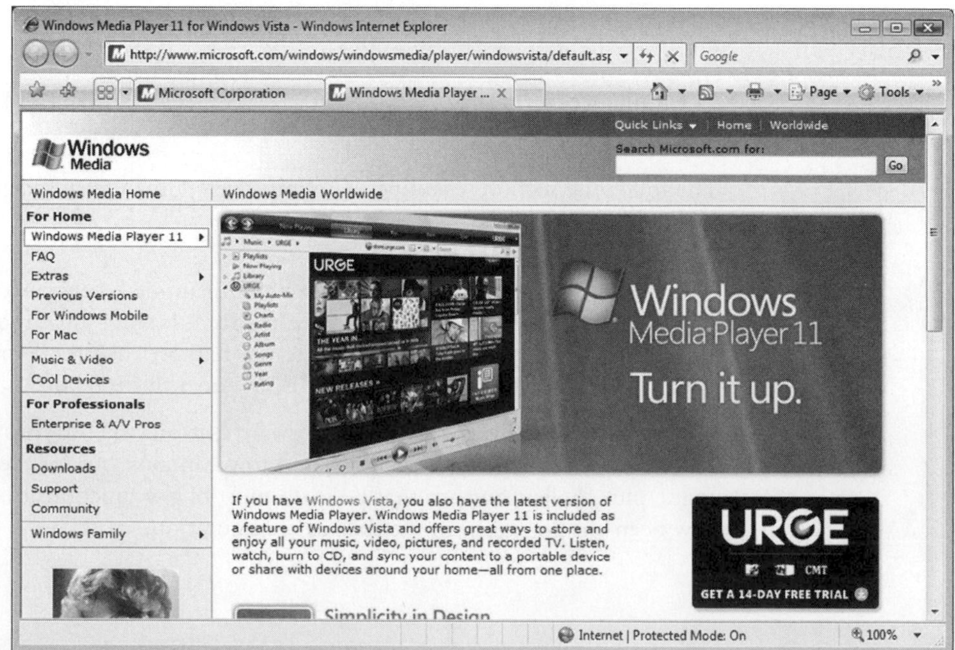

Figure 9-2

The Internet Explorer 7 tabbed interface

The advantage of the tabs is that you can switch between open pages quickly without clogging up the taskbar. Once you have multiple tabbed Web pages open, you can manipulate the order of the tabs (and their attached pages) by dragging and dropping them. You can also right-click a tab, which displays a context menu where you can refresh the tab, close it, or refresh and close all of the tabs at once.

TAKE NOTE*

The tabs in IE7 do not replace the traditional method of using multiple browser windows; they simply augment it. With IE7, users accustomed to working with many Web pages open simultaneously can now arrange those pages into organized sequences by opening multiple browser windows and creating tabs in each one.

USING TAB GROUPS

As in earlier versions of Internet Explorer, you use favorites to store the URLs for Web pages you visit frequently. IE7 adds a Favorites button and an Add to Favorites button to the toolbar, just under the Back and Forward buttons, which provides for convenient access. In addition, when you click the **Favorites** button, the list of favorites appears superimposed over the left side of the browser window, rather than displacing the window as it used to.

IE7 also adds a new facility for working with your favorites. As always, you can save your favorites in folders, as shown in Figure 9-3. However, IE7 now treats those folders as groups. By displaying the Favorites menu and clicking on a group, you can see the individual URLs saved within the group and select the one you want to open.

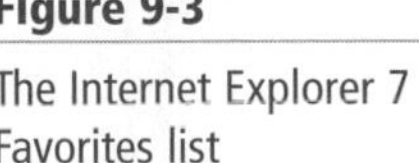

Figure 9-3

The Internet Explorer 7 Favorites list

However, you can now also click the arrow to the right of the group name (or select the group and press Ctrl+Enter) and all of the URLs in the group open as tabs in a single browser window. If you have several Web pages that you need to work with on a project, for example, you can place them in a group and open them all with one click of the mouse.

USING QUICK TABS

IE 7 also can display the contents of multiple tabbed Web pages as thumbnails called ***Quick Tabs***. When you click the **Quick Tabs** button (or press Ctrl+Q), a page appears containing thumbnail views of all the tabbed pages on the current browser window, as shown in Figure 9-4. These thumbnails are real-time images of the Web pages, so you can use this feature to monitor the states of several Web pages at once.

Figure 9-4

The Internet Explorer 7 Quick Tabs page

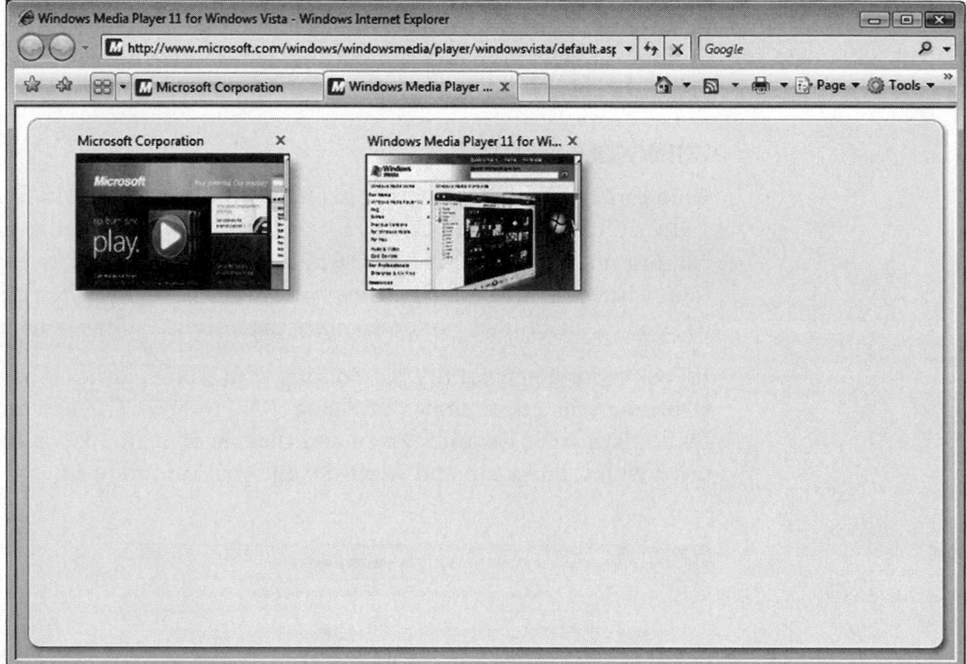

This is a particularly useful tool for technicians and administrators who have to monitor network devices that have Web-based interfaces. After you create favorites for the addresses of all the devices and put them in the same favorites subfolder, you can open them all at once as a tab group, as described in the previous section, and then click the **Quick Tabs** button to display them. Then, when necessary, clicking one of the thumbnails takes you to that page.

USING PAGE ZOOM

One of the most common problems users face in earlier versions of Internet Explorer, especially viewers with poor eyesight, is the variance in the type sizes found on Websites. Recent versions of Internet Explorer have included the ability to adjust the type size of a Web page, but the controls function only on page that use straight HTML code to control the typography. Internet Explorer 7 introduces a Page Zoom capability that enables users to increase or decrease the size of an entire page, both text and graphics, to suit their level of viewing comfort.

To adjust the size of a page, click **Page**, point to Zoom, and select a zoom factor from the menu, as illustrated in Figure 9-5. You can also press Ctrl+ or Ctrl– to enlarge or reduce the page.

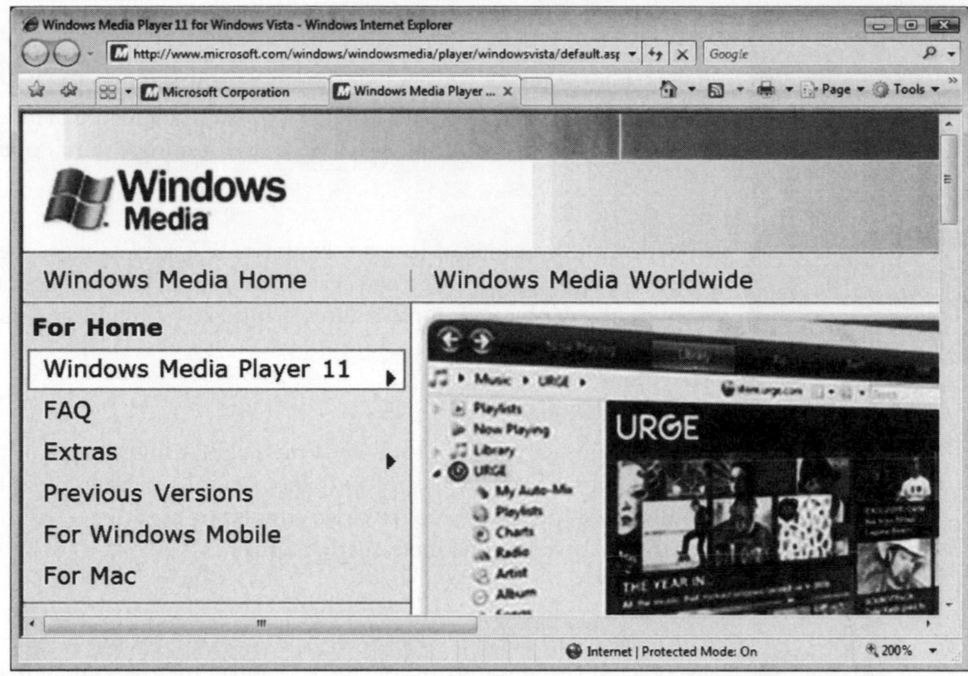

Figure 9-5

The Internet Explorer 7 Page Zoom feature

PRINTING WITH IE7

Printing is another aspect of Internet Explorer that has been problematic for some time. Users often find that pages that look as though they will print properly come out of the printer with some lines of text cut off at the right. Also, it is common for what looks like a single page to print out with a second page containing an orphan, that is, the last line or two of text.

Internet Explorer 7 has improved printing capabilities. By default, IE7 now reduces each page in size enough so that all of the content shown in the print preview page fits on the printed page, both from left to right and top to bottom.

USING INSTANT SEARCH

In previous versions of Internet Explorer, users could perform searches directly from the Address box by preceding the search string with a question mark. IE would then search for the term using the default search engine or one previously selected as the default by the user. In IE7, a separate ***Instant Search*** box to the right of the address box performs the same function, except that in this case the user can key a search string and then select a search provider from a configurable dropdown list. Network administrators can even configure the dropdown list to include internal search providers, such as Microsoft SharePoint servers.

USING RSS FEEDS

Many Websites that provide frequently changing content, such as news sites and blogs, support a push technology called ***RSS feed***, which simplifies the process of delivering updated content to designated users. IE7 includes an integrated RSS reader so users can subscribe to their favorite feeds and have updated content delivered to their browsers on a regular basis.

Configuring Internet Explorer 7

While most users accept the default options of Internet Explorer 7, there are some new features in this program that users may wish to configure. Those elements that a user may want to adjust include: RSS feeds, feed settings, search options, and printing.

CERTIFICATION READY?
Configure Windows
Internet Explorer 7+:
Configure RSS feeds
2.4

As with earlier versions of Internet Explorer, IE7 satisfies most users' needs with no adjustment. However, some of the new features in IE7 require configuration. The following sections examine the configuration procedures that desktop technicians might have to perform for their clients.

CONFIGURING RSS FEEDS

As mentioned earlier, RSS feeds are a means of pushing frequently changing content to Internet subscribers. News sites and blogs typically maintain text-based feeds, but an RSS feed can also push images, audio, or video content to users. For example, audio feeds, also known as *podcasts,* have become increasingly popular.

The initials RSS are most commonly said to stand for Really Simple Syndication, but several competing standards for the technology use the same initials, including Rich Site Summary and RDF Site Summary.

The whole point of an RSS feed is to eliminate the need for users to open multiple Websites and browse for new content. With an RSS feed, the RSS client automatically retrieves new content from the content provider, enabling users to browse only the new information from their favorite sites.

Before you can receive RSS feeds with IE7, however, you must subscribe to them. Subscription is the term used to refer to the process of configuring the RSS client to receive transmissions from a particular site. At the present time, most RSS feeds are available for subscription free of charge, but it is likely that future incarnations of the technology will take the form of services for which you pay a fee to the content provider.

SUBSCRIBING TO RSS FEEDS

When you access a Web page, IE7 automatically searches for RSS feeds. If IE7 locates feeds as part of the page, the RSS button changes its color to red and a sound plays. To subscribe to a feed, use the following procedure:

SUBSCRIBE TO AN RSS FEED

GET READY. Log on to Windows Vista. When the logon process is completed, close the Welcome Center window and any other windows that appear.

1. Click **Start**, and then click **Internet Explorer**. The Internet Explorer window appears.
2. Browse to the Website providing the feed to which you want to subscribe. When IE7 detects a feed, the Feeds button in the toolbar turns red.
3. Click the **Feeds** button. If there is more than one feed associated with the page, select one from the Feeds submenu. The feed page appears, as shown in Figure 9-6. You can always read the current contents of the feed on this page, whether you are subscribed or not.

Figure 9-6

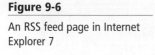

An RSS feed page in Internet Explorer 7

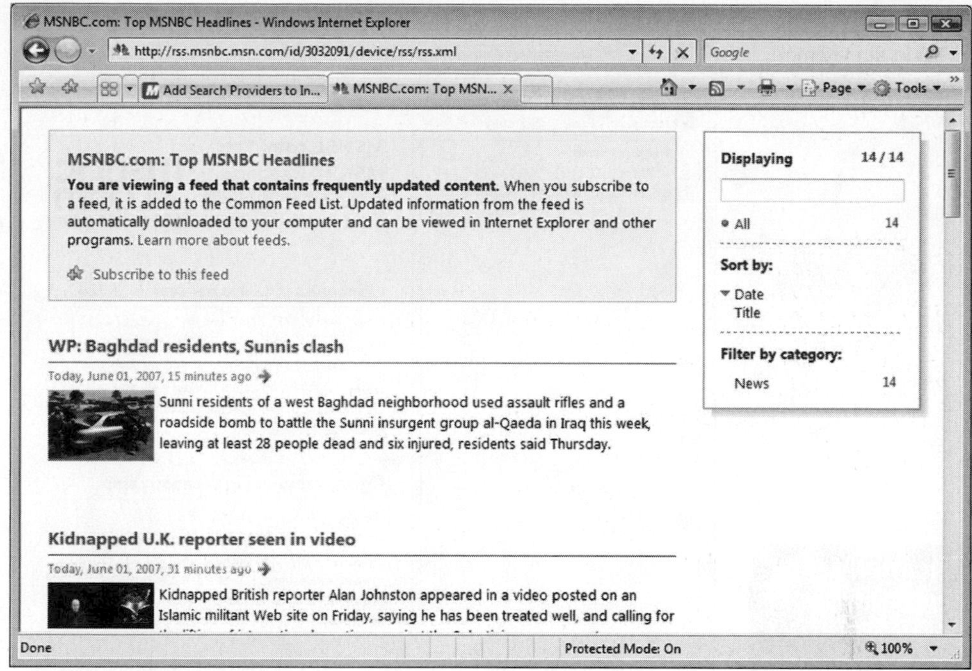

4. Click the **Subscribe to this feed** link. A Subscribe to this Feed dialog box appears, as shown in Figure 9-7.

Figure 9-7

An Internet Explorer 7 Subscribe to this Feed dialog box

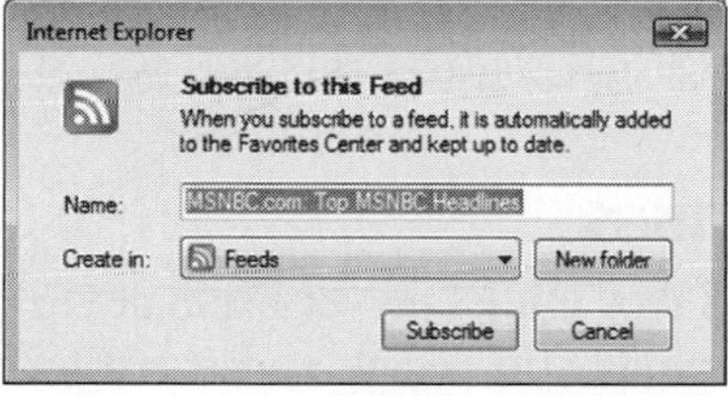

5. In the Name text box, key a name you want to assign to the feed (if it differs from the default).
6. Select the folder to which you want to add the feed, or click **New folder** to create one. Then click **Subscribe.** The feed page changes to indicate that you have successfully subscribed to the feed.

VIEWING RSS FEEDS

Once you have subscribed to RSS feeds, you can view their contents at any time by using the following procedure:

VIEW RSS FEEDS

GET READY. Log on to Windows Vista. When the logon process is completed, close the Welcome Center window and any other windows that appear.

1. Click **Start**, and then click **Internet Explorer**. The Internet Explorer window appears.
2. Click the **Favorites Center** button. The Favorites Center menu appears.
3. In the Favorites Center, click the **Feeds** button. The Favorites Center displays a list of your currently subscribed feeds, as shown in Figure 9-8. To leave the Favorites Center open so you can browse through a list of subscriptions, click the **Pin the Favorites Center** button, on the right side of the Favorites Center menu bar.

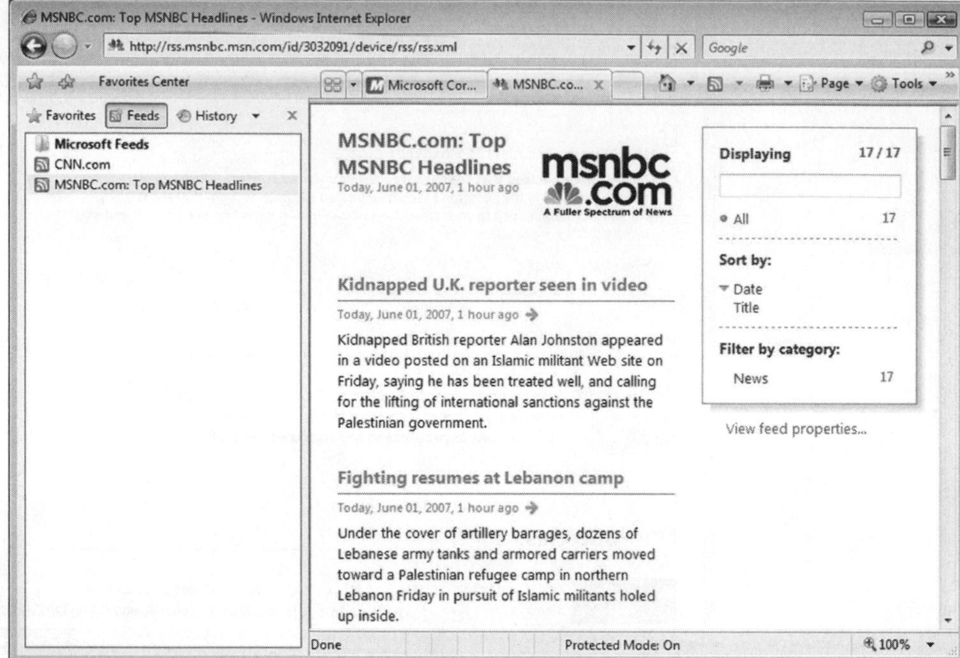

Figure 9-8

The Feeds list in the Internet Explorer 7 Favorites Center

CERTIFICATION READY?
Configure Windows Internet Explorer 7+:
- Manage subscriptions
- Configure feed updates

2.4

4. Click one of your subscribed feeds to display its contents in the main IE7 window.

MORE INFORMATION

The Feed Headlines gadget that Windows Vista places in the Windows Sidebar display by default is also an RSS feed client. You can use this gadget to display the contents of any feed you subscribe to using Internet Explorer 7.

CONFIGURING FEED SETTINGS

When you subscribe to an RSS feed using Internet Explorer 7, the content is updated once every day, by default. You can modify the default update setting for all feeds or for individual feeds. To update the default setting for all feeds, use the following procedure:

CONFIGURE DEFAULT FEED SETTINGS

GET READY. Log on to Windows Vista. When the logon process is completed, close the Welcome Center window and any other windows that appear.

1. Click **Start**, and then click **Internet Explorer**. The Internet Explorer window appears.
2. Click the **Tools** button, and then select **Internet Options**. The Internet Options dialog box appears.
3. Click the **Content** tab and then, in the Feeds section, click **Settings**. The Feed Settings dialog box appears, as shown in Figure 9-9.

Figure 9-9

The Feed Settings dialog box

4. In the Every dropdown list, specify the interval at which IE7 should check the subscribed RSS feeds for updates. Then click **OK** to close the Feed Settings dialog box.
5. Click **OK** to close the Internet Options dialog box.

To configure the settings for an individual feed, use the following procedure:

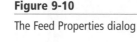

CONFIGURE INDIVIDUAL FEED SETTINGS

GET READY. Log on to Windows Vista. When the logon process is completed, close the Welcome Center window and any other windows that appear.

1. Click **Start**, and then click **Internet Explorer**. The Internet Explorer window appears.
2. Click the **Favorites Center** button. The Favorites Center menu appears.
3. In the Favorites Center, click the **Feeds** button. The Favorites Center displays a list of your currently subscribed feeds.
4. Right-click one of your feed subscriptions and then, from the context menu, select **Properties**. The Feed Properties dialog box appears, as shown in Figure 9-10.

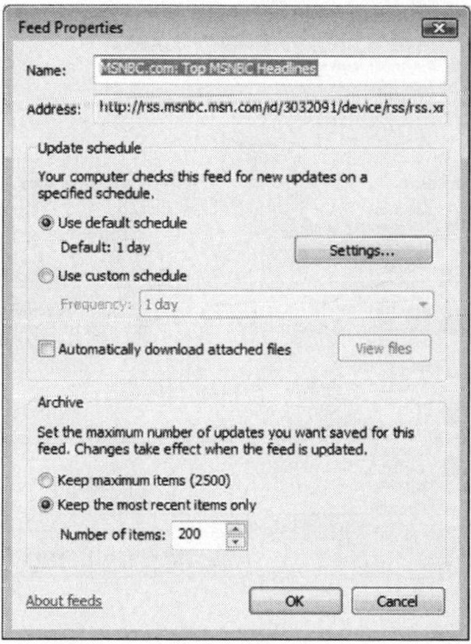

Figure 9-10

The Feed Properties dialog box

CERTIFICATION READY?
Configure Windows Internet Explorer 7+: Configure the Search bar and Search providers
2.4

5. To change the update schedule, select the **Use custom schedule** radio button and then, in the Frequency dropdown list, select the desired interval.
6. When subscribing to an RSS feed that includes podcasts, you must also select the **Automatically download attached files** checkbox.
7. To change the Archive settings for the feed, change the *Number of items* spin box to specify the number of new content items you want to retain in the feed window, or select the **Keep maximum items** radio button.
8. Click **OK** to close the Feed Properties dialog box.

CONFIGURING SEARCH OPTIONS

By default, the Instant Search box found in Internet Explorer 7 enables users to perform searches using Microsoft's Live Search engine. To use other search engines, you must first add them to the list of search providers. IE7 supports virtually any type of search provider, not just the well-known Web search engines such as Google. You can also add search providers for specific topics or sites, such as Amazon.com's internal search engine. Finally, you can add internal search engines of your own design, so that users can search your corporate intranet.

ADDING SEARCH PROVIDERS

To add search providers to the Instant Search list, use the following procedure:

ADD A SEARCH PROVIDER

GET READY. Log on to Windows Vista. When the logon process is completed, close the Welcome Center window and any other windows that appear.

1. Click **Start**, and then click **Internet Explorer**. The Internet Explorer window appears.
2. Click the down arrow on the right side of the Instant Search box and then, from the context menu, select **Find More Providers.** The Add Search Providers to Internet Explorer 7 page appears, as shown in Figure 9-11.

Figure 9-11

The Add Search Providers to Internet Explorer 7 page

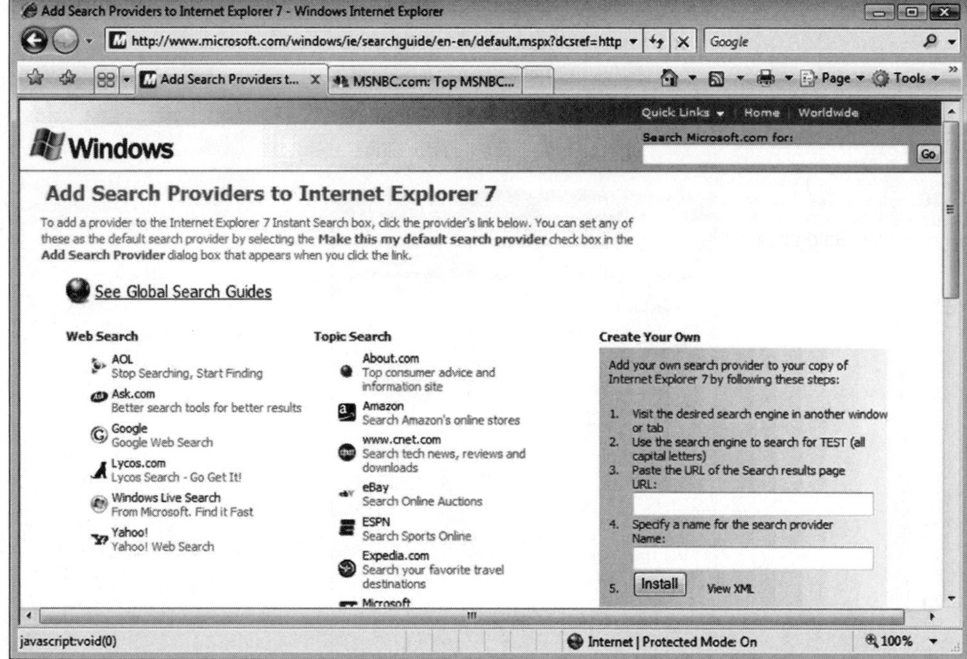

3. Select one of the Web Search or Topic Search providers. An Add Search Provider dialog box appears, as shown in Figure 9-12.

Figure 9-12

The Add Search Provider dialog box

MORE INFORMATION

To add international search providers in other languages, click the See Global Search Guides link, select a country, and then select one of the search providers for that country.

4. Click **Add Provider** to add the selected search engine to the Instant Search list.
5. To add a search provider that does not appear on the page, follow the steps in the Create Your Own box to capture the provider's URL syntax for a search.

SPECIFYING A DEFAULT SEARCH PROVIDER

When you first open an Internet Explorer 7 window, the Instant Search box displays the name of the default search provider, which initially is *Live Search*. Once you have added search providers to the Instant Search list, you can specify a different default provider, using the following procedure:

SPECIFY A DEFAULT SEARCH PROVIDER

GET READY. Log on to Windows Vista. When the logon process is completed, close the Welcome Center window and any other windows that appear.

1. Click **Start**, and then click **Internet Explorer**. The Internet Explorer window appears.
2. Click the down arrow on the right side of the Instant Search box and then, from the context menu, select **Change Search Defaults.** The Change Search Defaults dialog box appears.
3. In the Search Providers list, select the entry you want to set as the default, click **Set Default**, and then click **OK.** The Instant Search box changes to reflect the new default search provider.

PRINTING WITH IE7

As mentioned earlier in this lesson, Internet Explorer has had some long-standing problems with the printing of Web pages that are finally addressed in the IE7 release. Prior to IE7, it was common for Web pages to print with some text cut off in portrait mode. The only work-around was to switch to landscape mode, which printed all of the text but wasted a lot of paper and provided an awkward reading experience.

IE7 has redesigned the Print Preview page, as shown in Figure 9-13, to provide users with greater flexibility, both in viewing and formatting the pages to be printed. For example, IE7 adds a default Shrink To Fit setting that reduces each Web page to the point that it will fit on a single sheet of paper. No longer is text cut off on the right, and there are no more orphaned lines that print on a second page.

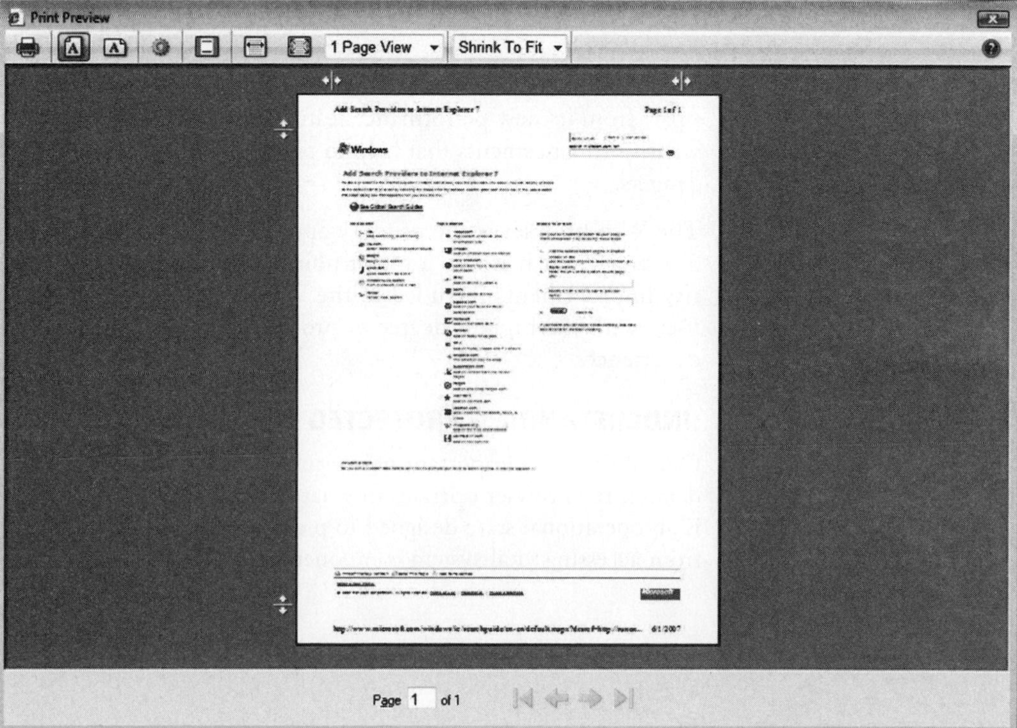

Figure 9-13

The Internet Explorer 7 Print Preview dialog box

In addition to shrinking Web pages to fit the printed page size, you can also make pages larger or smaller by adjusting the sizes using percentages. This enables you to print enlarged pages for easier reading or reduce the size to print multiple Web pages on a single sheet of paper.

When you click the down arrow next to the Print button on the toolbar, you can choose from the following options.

- Print—The Print dialog box, shown in Figure 9-14, enables you to select a printer, choose the pages you want to print, print multiple copies, and, on the Options tab, print specific frames from a Web page.

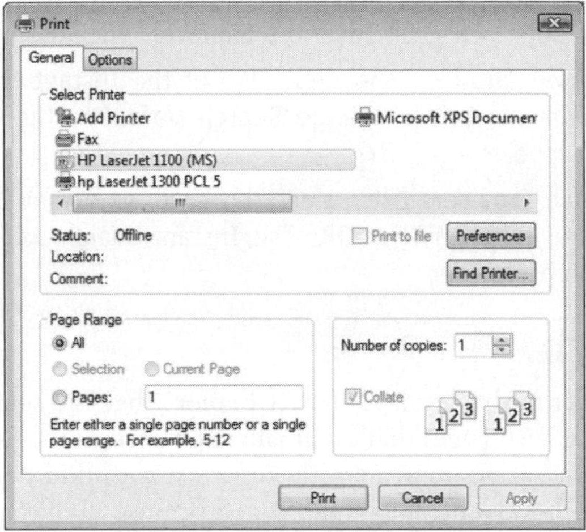

Figure 9-14

The Internet Explorer 7 Print dialog box

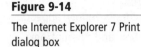

- Print Preview—The Print Preview window enables you to view the current Web page at various sizes, select the page orientation (portrait or landscape), specify the size at which the Web page should print, and dynamically adjust the margins.
- Page Setup—The Page Setup dialog box enables you to select a paper size, source tray, and orientation; modify the default header and footer that will print on each page; and adjust the margins numerically.

SECURING INTERNET EXPLORER 7

Apart from its new performance features, Internet Explorer 7 includes a number of important security enhancements that help to protect users from malware incursions and other Internet dangers.

The Web browser is the primary application that most people use to access the Internet, and as a result it is also a major point of weakness from a security perspective. The security improvements included in the Windows Vista release of Internet Explorer 7 provide users with the highest degree of protection possible without compromising their Internet experiences.

UNDERSTANDING PROTECTED MODE

One of the most important new security features found in Internet Explorer 7 is that, by default, the browser operates in what Microsoft refers to as ***protected mode***. Protected mode is an operational state designed to prevent attackers that do penetrate the computer's defenses from accessing vital system components.

Protected mode is essentially a way to run Internet Explorer 7 with highly reduced privileges. Windows Vista includes a security feature called Mandatory Integrity Control (MIC), which assigns various integrity access levels to processes running on the computer. These integrity access levels control what system resources the process is allowed to access. Table 9-1 shows the integrity levels assigned by MIC.

Table 9-1

Mandatory Integrity Control

Integrity Access Level	Privilege Level	Privileges
High	Administrator	The process is granted full access to the system, including write access to the Program Files folder and the HKEY_LOCAL_MACHINE registry key.
Medium	User	The process is granted limited access to the system, including write access to user-specific areas, such as the user's Documents folder and the HKEY_CURRENT_USER registry key. All processes that are not explicitly assigned an integrity access level receive this level of access.
Low	Untrusted	The process is granted minimal access to the system, including write access only to the Temporary Internet Files\Low folder and the HKEY_CURRENT_USER\Software\Microsoft\Internet Explorer/LowRegistry registry key.

In Windows Vista, Internet Explorer 7's protected mode means that it runs as a low-integrity procedure. The browser application can therefore write to only low-integrity disk locations, such as the Temporary Internet Files folder and the standard IE storage areas, including the History, Cookies, and Favorites folders.

TAKE NOTE*

Mandatory Integrity Control is a Windows Vista feature that is not present in Windows XP. As a result, when you install Internet Explorer 7 on a Windows XP system, it does not run in protected mode.

What this means is that even if attackers manage to gain access to the computer through a Web browser connection, there is little they can do to damage the system because they do not have access to vital system areas. For example, even if an attacker manages to upload a destructive application to the system, he or she cannot force it to load each time the system starts by installing it into the Startup group.

When a process requires a higher level of access to the system, the user is required to confirm the allocation of greater privileges by means of a standard User Account Control (UAC) message box. As always, if users are presented with UAC prompts that they did not instigate, they should not allow the process to obtain the additional privileges it is requesting.

Protected mode is not a complete defense against malware in itself. IE7 and Windows Vista have many other security mechanisms that work in combination. Protected mode is designed to limit the damage that attackers can do if they manage to penetrate the other security measures.

DETECTING PROTECTED MODE INCOMPATIBILITIES

Because IE7 on Windows Vista runs in protected mode by default, it is possible that Web-based applications designed to run on IE6 or earlier versions might not run properly on IE7. These applications might be designed to write to a disk area that is inaccessible while in protected mode, or they might not know how to handle the new prompts in IE7.

Comprehensive testing of all Web-based applications should be an essential part of every Windows Vista or IE7 deployment. To gather information about application incompatibilities, enable Compatibility Logging using the following procedure:

ENABLE COMPATIBILITY LOGGING USING GROUP POLICY

GET READY. Log on to Windows Vista using an account with administrative capabilities. When the logon process is completed, close the Welcome Center window and any other windows that appear.

1. Click **Start**, key **mmc** in the Start Search box, and then press **Enter**. After confirming that you are performing the action, a blank MMC console appears.
2. Click **File > Add/Remove Snap-In**. The Add or Remove Snap-ins dialog box appears.
3. In the Available Snap-ins list, select **Group Policy Object Editor**, and then click **Add**. The Select Group Policy Object page appears.
4. Click **Finish** to select the default Local Computer object.
5. Click **OK** to close the Add or Remove Snap-ins dialog box.
6. Open the Computer Configuration\Administrative Templates\Windows Components\Internet Explorer folder or the User Configuration\Administrative Templates\Windows Components\Internet Explorer folder, as shown in Figure 9-15.

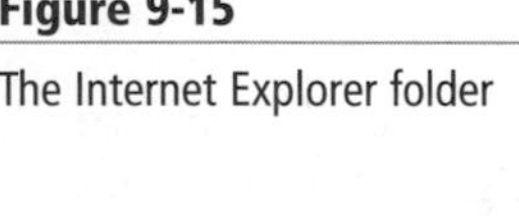

Figure 9-15

The Internet Explorer folder

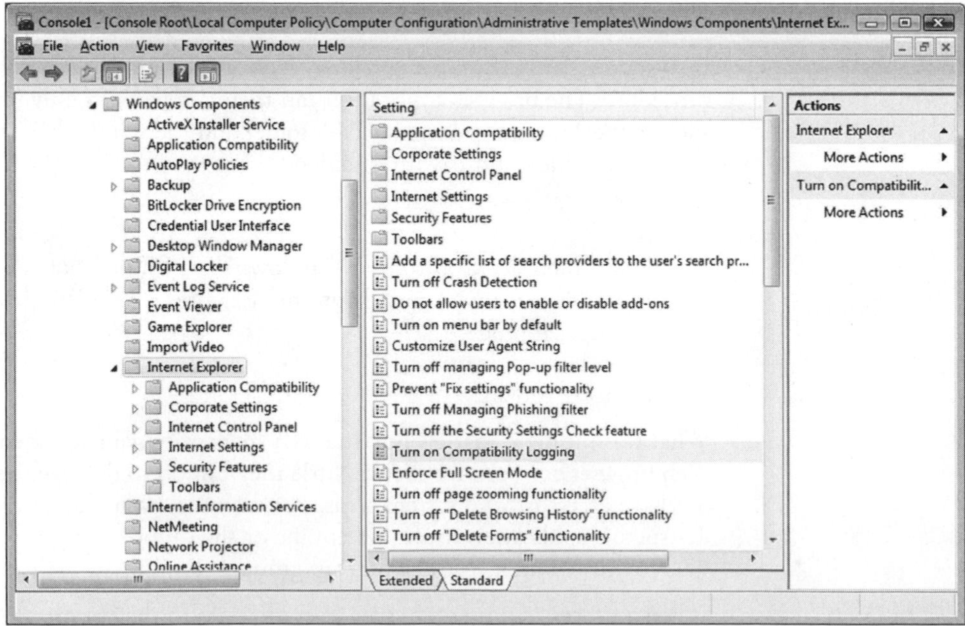

7. Double-click the **Turn on Compatibility Logging** policy. The Turn on Compatibility Logging Properties sheet appears, as shown in Figure 9-16.

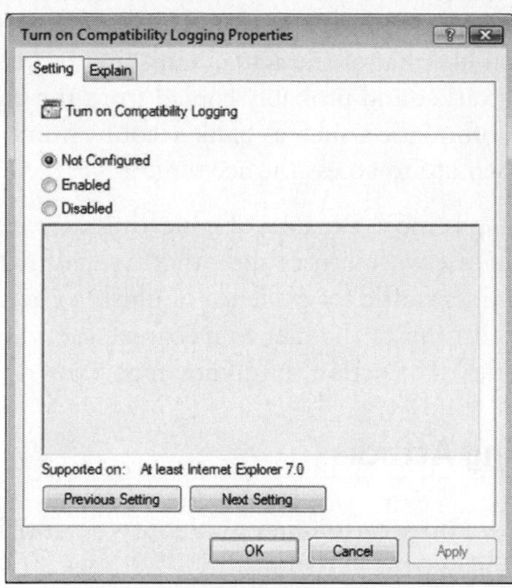

Figure 9-16
The Turn on Compatibility Logging Properties sheet

CERTIFICATION READY?
Configure Dynamic Security for Internet Explorer 7+: Resolve Protected Mode issues
3.3

8. Select the **Enabled** radio button, and then click **OK**.
9. Close the Group Policy Object Editor console.

Once you enable the Turn on Compatibility Logging policy, Windows Vista begins logging all information blocked by the Internet Explorer security settings. The logged data appears in the Windows Event Viewer console in the Internet Explorer application log.

RESOLVING PROTECTED MODE INCOMPATIBILITIES

Once you have determined the exact source of your application's incompatibility, you can use the following techniques to try to resolve the problem.

- Move the site to the Trusted Sites zone—IE maintains different security zones that provide applications with different levels of privileges. Sites in the Internet zone run in protected mode, with minimal privileges, but if you move them to the Trusted Sites zone, they do not run in protected mode, and receive elevated privileges.
- Disable protected mode in IE7—Although Microsoft does not recommend this practice, you can disable protected mode by selecting a zone and clearing the Enable Protected Mode checkbox. Disabling protected mode causes IE to apply the medium integrity access level to the zone.
- Modify the application—Probably the most difficult and time-consuming option, you can also modify the application itself so that it can run properly using the minimal privileges provided by protected mode.

CERTIFICATION READY?
Configure Dynamic Security for Internet Explorer 7+: Configure the Phishing Service
3.3

CONFIGURING THE PHISHING FILTER

Social engineering is a term that describes any attempt to penetrate the security of a system by convincing people to disclose secret information. Many would-be attackers have realized that discovering a user's password with an elaborate software procedure is a lot more difficult than simply calling the user up and asking for it. When asked for information by an authoritative-sounding person purporting to work for the IT department, most people are eager to help and are all too willing to give out information that should be kept confidential.

Phishing is a technique that takes social engineering to a mass scale. Instead of convincing-sounding telephone callers, phishing uses convincing-looking Websites that urge users to supply personal information, such as passwords and account numbers.

For example, an attacker might send out thousands of e-mail messages directed at customers of a particular bank, urging them to update their account information or risk having their accounts closed. Unsuspecting users click the hyperlink in the e-mail and are taken to a Web page that looks very much like that of the actual bank site, but it isn't. The page is part of a bogus site set up by the attacker and probably copied from the bank site. This false site proceeds to ask the user for information such as bank account numbers, PINs, and passwords, which the attacker can then use to access the account.

Defending against phishing is more a matter of educating users than competing in a technological arms race, as is the case with viruses and other types of malware. Internet Explorer 7 includes a filter that examines traffic for evidence of phishing activity and displays a warning to the user if it finds any. It is up to the user to recognize the warning signs and to refrain from supplying confidential information to unknown parties.

Filtering For Phishing Attacks

The IE7 phishing filter uses three techniques to identify potential phishing Websites. These techniques are as follows.

- Compare with legitimate address list—IE7 compiles a list of legitimate Websites on the computer's local drive; if a user attempts to access a URL on this list, the browser assumes the site to be genuine and performs no further checking.
- Onsite analysis—IE7 examines the code of each Web page as the system downloads it for patterns and phrases indicative of a phishing attempt. This technique provides a means to detect phishing sites that have not yet been positively identified and reported as such. If the scan indicates that the site might include a phishing attempt, IE7 displays a yellow Suspicious Website warning in the Address bar. Clicking the warning button displays more detail about the suspicion, but the user can also ignore the warning and proceed.
- Online lookup of phishing sites—Microsoft maintains a list of known phishing sites that it updates several times every hour. When a user attempts to access a Website, IE7 transmits the URL, along with other nonconfidential system information, to a Microsoft server, which compares it with the phishing site list. If the online lookup process determines that a Website is a known phishing site, IE7 displays a warning page and turns the status bar red. However, the user can continue to the site, if desired.

Configuring the Phishing Filter

The phishing filter in Internet Explorer 7 can be configured to perform only one or two of the three site checks, or it can be turned off completely. Phishing sites present no danger other than the temptation to reply to requests for confidential information. It is possible to turn the phishing filter off and remain safe from phishing attempts, as long as you follow one simple rule: Don't trust hyperlinks. Never supply a password or any other confidential information to a Website unless you key the URL yourself and you are sure that it is correct.

Most successful phishing attempts occur when a user clicks a hyperlink in an e-mail or another Website. It is a simple matter to create a hyperlink that looks like http://www.woodgrovebank.com, but which actually points to a server run by an evil attacker in another domain. However, as long as you yourself key www.woodgrovebank.com in the browser's Address bar, you are assured of accessing the true Website of Woodgrove Bank.

To configure the phishing filter, use the following procedure:

CONFIGURE THE PHISHING FILTER

GET READY. Log on to Windows Vista. When the logon process is completed, close the Welcome Center window and any other windows that appear.

1. Click **Start**, and then click **Control Panel**. The Control Panel window appears.
2. Select **Network and Internet > Internet Options**. The Internet Properties sheet appears.
3. Click the **Advanced** tab.
4. Scroll down in the Settings list and locate the Security section, as shown in Figure 9-17.

Figure 9-17

The Advanced tab of the Internet Options control panel

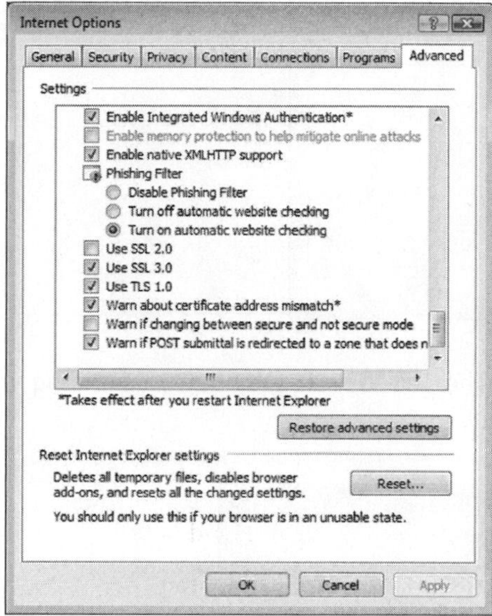

CERTIFICATION READY?
Configure Dynamic Security for Internet Explorer 7«Xtags error: Missing font: tag f+: Configure Pop-up Blocker
3.3

5. Find the Phishing Filter option and select one of the following three options:
   - Disable Phishing Filter—Renders all three phishing filter mechanisms inoperative.
   - Turn off automatic Website checking—Disables the online lookup of phishing sites, but IE7 still performs the onsite analysis.
   - Turn on automatic Website checking—Enables all three phishing filter mechanisms. This is the default setting.
6. Click **OK** to save your changes and close the Internet Properties sheet.

Configuring the Pop-Up Blocker

Pop-up windows are now a fact of Internet Web browsing. Some pop-ups are useful Website controls, most are simply annoying advertisements, and a few can even be dangerous sources of spyware or other malicious programs. Internet Explorer 7 includes a pop-up blocker that you can configure to suppress some or all pop-ups. To configure the pop-up blocker, use the following procedure:

CONFIGURE THE POP-UP BLOCKER

GET READY. Log on to Windows Vista. When the logon process is completed, close the Welcome Center window and any other windows that appear.

1. Click **Start**, and then click **Control Panel**. The Control Panel window appears.
2. Select **Network and Internet > Internet Options**. The Internet Properties sheet appears.
3. Click the **Privacy** tab, as shown in Figure 9-18.

Figure 9-18

The Privacy tab of the Internet Properties sheet

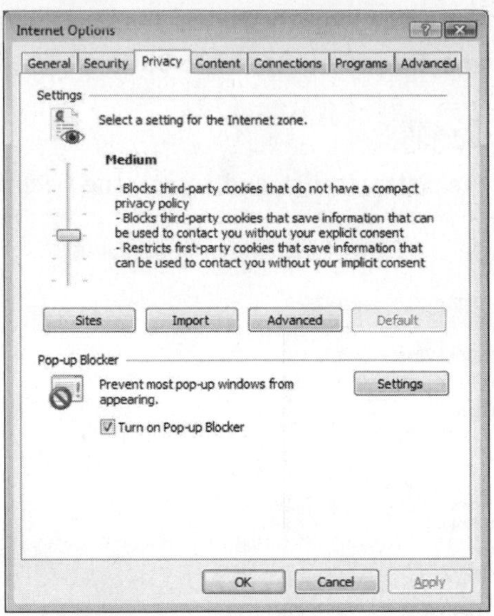

4. Click **Settings**. The Pop-Up Blocker Settings dialog box appears, as shown in Figure 9-19.

Figure 9-19

The Pop-Up Blocker Settings dialog box

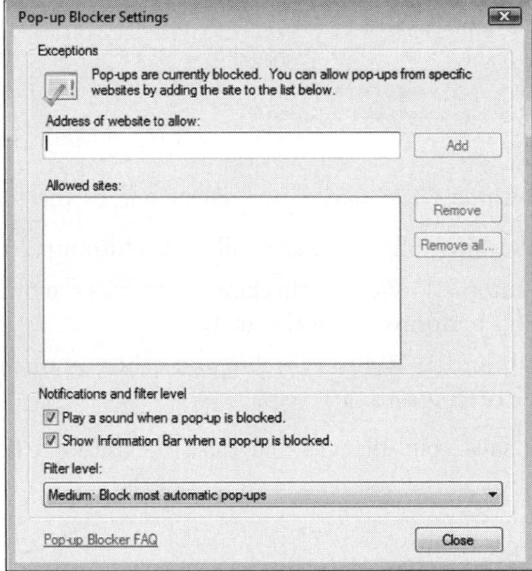

5. To allow pop-ups from a specific Website, key the URL of the site in the *Address of Website to allow* text box, and then click **Add**. Repeat the process to add additional sites to the *Allowed sites* list.

MORE INFORMATION

Some Websites use pop-ups for legitimate reasons. If you are aware of any that your users visit frequently, it is a good idea to add them to the *Allowed sites* list. This is particularly true if your organization runs intranet sites that use pop-ups.

6. Adjust the *Filter level* dropdown list to one of the following settings:
   - High: Block all pop-ups
   - Medium: Block most automatic pop-ups
   - Low: Allow pop-ups from secure sites
7. Click **Close** to close the Pop-Up Blocker Settings dialog box.
8. Click **OK** to close the Internet Properties sheet.

Configuring Security Zones

With the appropriate development tools and programming expertise, Web-based applications can do virtually anything that traditional software applications do, which can be either a good or a bad thing. For companies developing their own in-house software, Web browsers provide a stable, proven technological base. However, a Web-based intranet application is likely to require extensive access to system resources. An intranet application might have to install software on the computer, for example, or change system configuration settings.

CERTIFICATION READY?
Configure Dynamic Security for Internet Explorer 7+: Configure Security Zones
3.3

Granting this type of access is acceptable for an internal application, but you could not grant the same privileges to an Internet Website. Imagine what it would be like to surf the Internet if every site you accessed had the ability to install any software it wanted on your computer, or modify any of your system configuration settings. Your computer would likely be rendered inoperative within a matter of hours.

To provide different levels of access to specific applications, Internet Explorer 7 divides the addresses accessible with the Web browser into several different ***security zones***, each of which has a different set of privileges. The four zones are as follows:

- Internet—All Websites that are not listed in the other three zones fall into this zone. Sites in the Internet zone run in protected mode and have minimal access to the computer's drives and configuration settings.
- Local Intranet—IE7 automatically detects sites that originate from the local intranet and places them in this zone. Sites in this zone have significant access to the system, including the ability to run certain scripts, ActiveX controls, and plug-ins.
- Trusted Sites—This zone provides the most elevated set of privileges and is intended for sites that you can trust not to damage the computer. By default, there are no sites in this zone; you must add them manually.
- Restricted Sites—This zone has the most reduced set of privileges and runs in protected mode. It is intended for Websites that are known to be malicious, but which users still must access for some reason. As with the Trusted Sites zone, this zone is empty by default.

There are two ways to modify the default zone settings in IE7. You can assign Websites to specific zones, or you can modify the security settings of the zones themselves. These two procedures are described in the following sections.

Adding Sites to a Security Zone

The easiest way to modify the security settings that Internet Explorer 7 imposes on a specific Website is to manually add the site to a different security zone. The typical procedure is to add a site to the Trusted Sites zone, to increase its privileges, or add it to the Restricted Sites zone, to reduce its privileges. To do this, use the following procedure:

ADD A SITE TO A SECURITY ZONE

GET READY. Log on to Windows Vista. When the logon process is completed, close the Welcome Center window and any other windows that appear.

1. Click **Start**, and then click **Control Panel**. The Control Panel window appears.
2. Select **Network and Internet > Internet Options**. The Internet Properties sheet appears.
3. Click the **Security** tab, as shown in Figure 9-20.

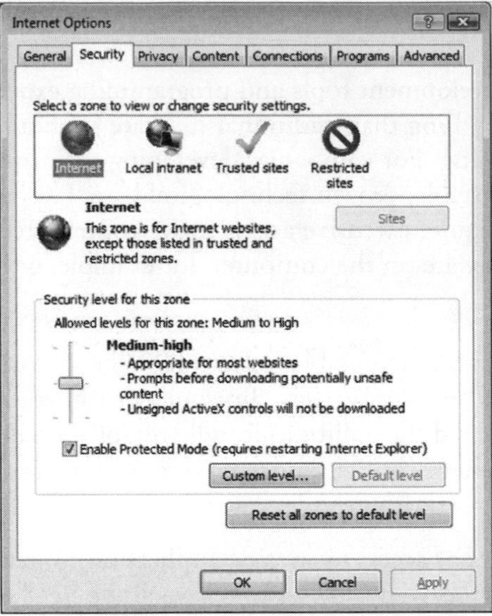

Figure 9-20

The Security tab of the Internet Properties sheet

4. Select the zone, either Trusted sites or Restricted sites, to which you want to add a site.
5. Click **Sites**. The *Trusted sites* or *Restricted sites* dialog box appears, as shown in Figure 9-21.

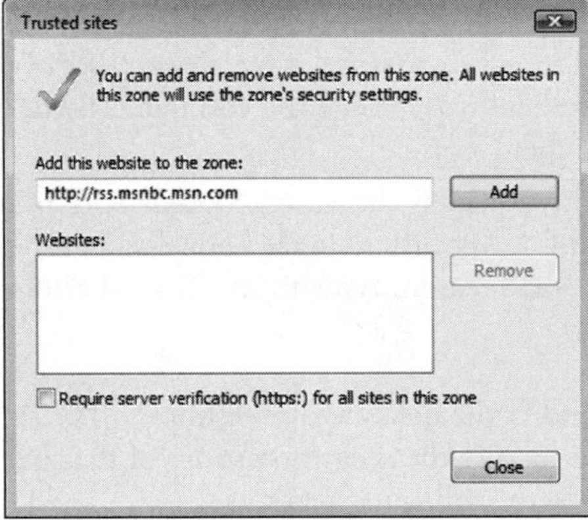

Figure 9-21

The Trusted sites dialog box

6. Key the URL of the Website you want to add to the zone into the *Add this Website to the zone* text box, and then click **Add**. The URL appears in the Websites list.
7. Click **Close** to close the *Trusted sites* or *Restricted sites* dialog box.
8. Click **OK** to close the Internet Properties sheet.

Configuring Zone Security

In addition to placing sites into zones, it is also possible to modify the properties of the zones themselves. Before you do this, however, you should consider that changing a zone's security properties will affect all of the sites in that zone. Decreasing the privileges allocated to a zone could prevent some sites in that zone from functioning properly. Increasing the privileges of a zone could open up security holes that attackers might be able to exploit.

To modify the security properties of a zone, use the following procedure:

MODIFY SECURITY ZONE SETTINGS

GET READY. Log on to Windows Vista. When the logon process is completed, close the Welcome Center window and any other windows that appear.

1. Click **Start**, and then click **Control Panel**. The Control Panel window appears.
2. Select **Network and Internet > Internet Options**. The Internet Properties sheet appears.
3. Click the **Security** tab.
4. Select the zone for which you want to modify the security settings.
5. In the *Security level for this zone* box, adjust the slider to increase or decrease the security level for the zone. Moving the slider up increases the protection for the zone and moving the slider down decreases it.
6. Select or clear the **Enable protected mode** checkbox, if desired,
7. To exercise more precise control over the zone's security settings, click **Custom level**. The Security Settings dialog box for the zone appears, as shown in Figure 9-22.

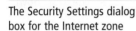

Figure 9-22

The Security Settings dialog box for the Internet zone

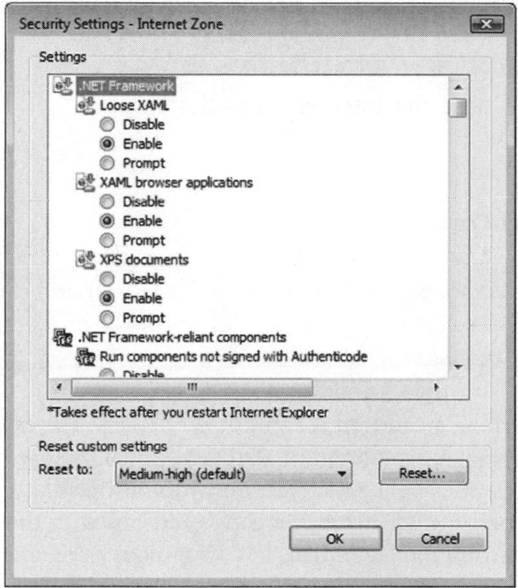

CERTIFICATION READY?
Configure Dynamic Security for Internet Explorer 7+: Configure Privacy Settings
3.3

8. Select radio buttons for the individual settings in each of the security categories. The radio buttons typically make it possible to enable a setting, disable it, or prompt the user before enabling it.
9. Click **OK** to close the Security Settings dialog box.
10. Click **OK** to close the Internet Properties sheet.

Configuring Privacy Settings

Earlier in this lesson, you learned how to prevent pop-up windows from invading your privacy. The other big privacy issue in Internet Explorer is cookies. Although the term has other applications in computer networking, in the context of Internet Explorer, a *cookie* is a file containing information about you or your Web-surfing habits that a Website maintains on your computer.

In some cases, cookies are extremely useful. They can save you keystrokes and remember who you are from one visit at a Website to the next. In other cases, however, Websites use cookies to track your Web surfing habits for the purpose of targeting you with specific ad campaigns. Many users resent the idea of outside parties saving data on their local drives and using it for their own purposes. IE7 includes a variety of privacy settings you can use to limit the ability of Websites to create cookies on a Windows Vista computer.

To configure these settings, use the following procedure:

CONFIGURE PRIVACY SETTINGS

GET READY. Log on to Windows Vista. When the logon process is completed, close the Welcome Center window and any other windows that appear.

1. Click **Start**, and then click **Control Panel**. The Control Panel window appears.
2. Select **Network and Internet > Internet Options**. The Internet Properties sheet appears.
3. Click the **Privacy** tab.
4. Adjust the slider up or down to configure the cookie settings for the Internet zone. Moving the slider all the way up blocks all cookies and moving it all the way down allows all cookies.
5. Click **OK** to close the Internet Properties sheet.

Managing Add-Ons

Internet Explorer 7 is an extensible application. Microsoft and third-party developers can create add-on modules that extend the capabilities of the browser by adding toolbars, alternative mouse cursors, and other elements.

In most cases, installing an add-on is an optional process. For example, you might install an application that gives you the option of adding a special toolbar to Internet Explorer that enables you to access the application's features without opening a separate window. Some application developers include other company's add-ons with their software, while presumably accepting a distribution fee. Other, less scrupulous developers might even install add-ons without informing you or giving you the option to avoid them.

Because you might have browser add-ons installed that you don't want, IE7 provides controls that enable you to view the add-ons installed on a Windows Vista computer and enable or disable them as needed. To manage the add-ons in Internet Explorer, use the following procedure:

MANAGE ADD-ONS

GET READY. Log on to Windows Vista. When the logon process is completed, close the Welcome Center window and any other windows that appear.

1. Click **Start**, and then click Internet. The **Internet Explorer** window appears.
2. Click the **Tools** button, point to **Manage Add-ons**, and then select **Enable or Disable Add-ons**. The Manage Add-ons dialog box appears, as shown in Figure 9-23.

Figure 9-23

The Manage Add-ons dialog box

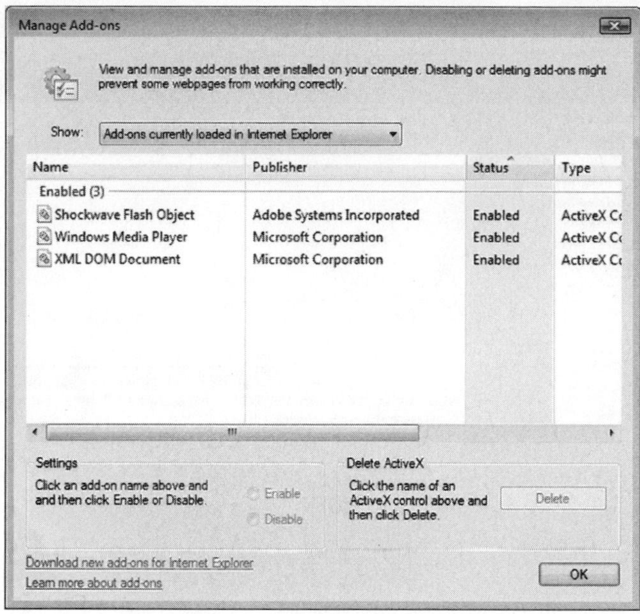

3. To view the Internet Explorer add-ons installed on the computer, select one of the options in the Show dropdown list. A list of add-ons appears, including the publisher, status, and type of each one.
4. To enable or disable an add-on, select it in the list and click the **Enable** or **Disable** radio button. Disabling an add-on does not remove it from the system; it simply stops it from functioning until you manually enable it again.

MORE INFORMATION

There will nearly always be a number of add-ons installed on your computer that you did not explicitly approve. These are pre-approved, digitally signed add-ons that might come from Microsoft or the computer manufacturer. However, if add-ons are present from publishers you do not recognize, or that you feel are causing problems on your computer, you can disable them until you are sure of their origins.

5. To delete an ActiveX control, select it in the list and click **Delete**. You can only delete ActiveX controls that you downloaded and installed.
6. Click **OK** to close the Manage Add-ons dialog box.

Using Windows Mail

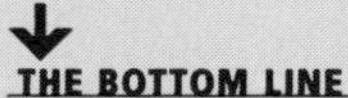
THE BOTTOM LINE

Windows Mail is an e-mail and news client that enables users to access their Internet e-mail accounts and browse through newsgroups.

CERTIFICATION READY?
Configure Windows Mail
5.2

Windows Mail, shown in Figure 9-24, is the standard e-mail and news client included with Windows Vista, replacing the Outlook Express application of previous versions. Windows Mail is quite similar to Outlook Express, but it includes some important new features such as the following:

Figure 9-24

The Windows Mail Inbox

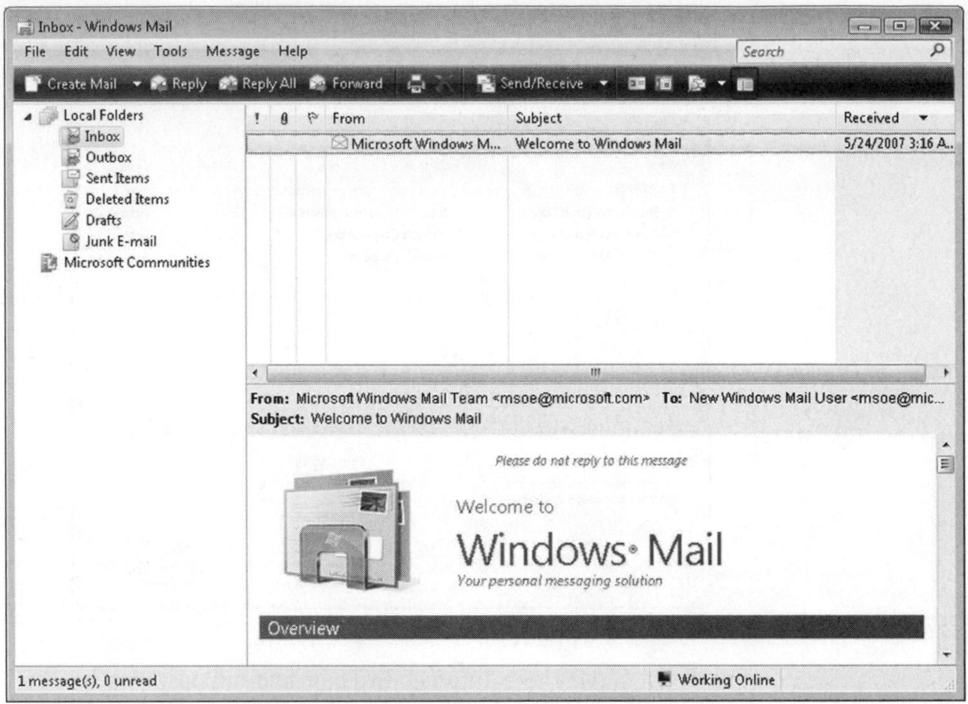

- Instant Search—Windows Mail includes a built-in Instant Search field that functions exactly like the one included in the Windows Vista operating system. You can search through your mail directly through Windows Mail, or by using the Instant Search field on the Start menu. The Search Explorer in Windows Vista integrates with Windows Mail, which means that when you search your PC's hard drive for a specific subject, it lists e-mail messages relevant to the subject along with other files and documents.
- Junk Mail Filter—Microsoft recognizes that unwanted junk e-mail (spam) has become a major issue. Spam forces you to wade through unsolicited, irrelevant, and often offensive messages to find the important e-mail in your inbox. The built-in Junk Mail Filter in Windows Mail automatically screens e-mail to identify and separate spam and place it in the default Junk E-mail folder. There is no need to train the filter. Windows Mail identifies and separates spam from the first time you use it, without any special configuration on your part. In addition, Windows Mail includes options to add a sender's e-mail address or domain to a Safe Senders or Blocked Senders list.

MORE INFORMATION

You add e-mail to the Safe Senders or Blocked Senders list by clicking Message, pointing to Junk E-mail, and then selecting the option you desire. Additionally, this menu contains options to unblock or mark an e-mail message as not junk.

- Phishing Filter—As discussed earlier in this lesson, phishing is a practice by which unscrupulous individuals attempt to obtain personal information by trickery. Phishing attempts in e-mail typically consist of messages impersonating a valid financial organization, threatening some sort of terrible penalty if the user does not click through to a Website and provide personal information, such as passwords or bank account data. The link included in the e-mail invariable points to a fraudulent Website designed to gather your information. Windows Mail now includes a phishing filter that automatically analyzes e-mail as it enters your inbox in an effort to detect most of these fraudulent links.
- More reliable e-mail data files—Microsoft Outlook Express often experienced issues when users attempted to open large e-mail data files. Microsoft uses new technology for storing e-mail and so provides a significant improvement in reliability, especially when using large e-mail data files.

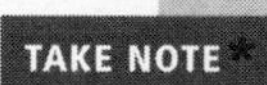

Windows Mail is an Internet e-mail client only. Users can configure the application to retrieve e-mail from multiple Internet accounts, but it cannot retrieve mail from a Microsoft Exchange server. To do this, you must use the Outlook client provided with Microsoft Office or Microsoft Exchange.

Configuring the Inbox

CERTIFICATION READY?
Configure Windows Mail:
Configure Inbox
5.2

To use Windows Mail to retrieve Internet e-mail, you must first configure the application with account information.

When you run Windows Mail for the first time, the Internet Connection Wizard launches automatically and leads you through the process of setting up an e-mail account. This process proceeds as follows:

CONFIGURE THE INBOX

GET READY. Log on to Windows Vista. When the logon process is completed, close the Welcome Center window and any other windows that appear.

MORE INFORMATION

If the Internet Connection wizard does not start when you open Windows Mail, you can set up your e-mail account by selecting Tools > Accounts from the menu bar. In the Internet Accounts dialog box, click Add to begin the Internet Connection wizard. On the Select Account Type page, double-click E-mail Account to create an e-mail account.

1. Click **Start**, and then click **All Programs > Windows Mail**. The Windows Mail window appears and the Internet Connection wizard launches. The Your Name page appears, as shown in Figure 9-25.

Figure 9-25

The Your Name page

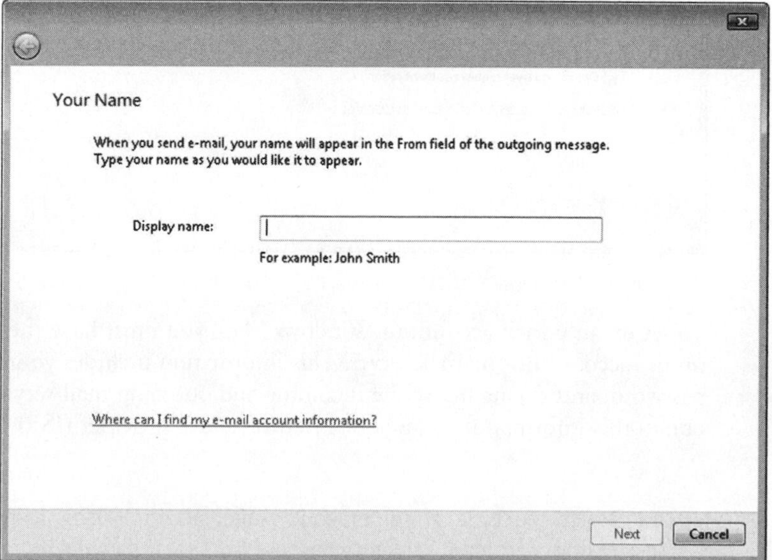

2. In the *Display name* text box, key your name as you would like it to appear in the From field of your outgoing messages, and then click **Next**. The Internet E-mail Address page appears, as shown in Figure 9-26.

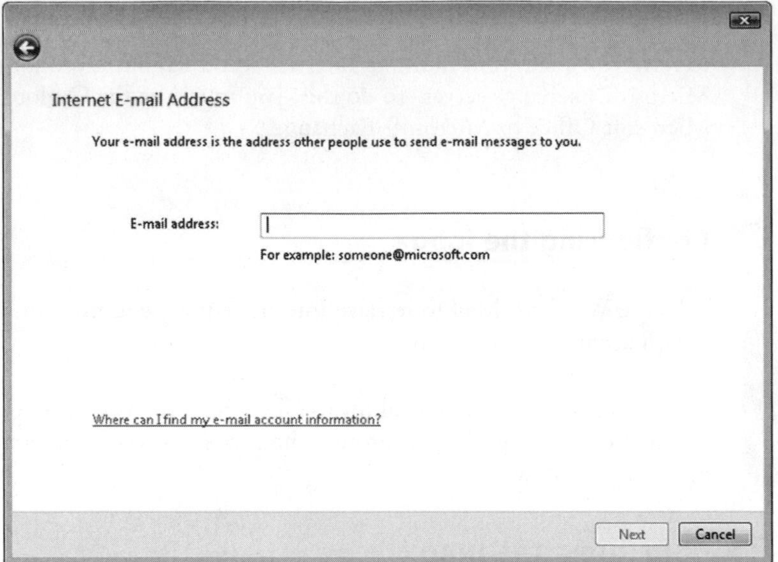

Figure 9-26

The Internet E-mail Address page

3. In the *E-mail address* text box, enter your e-mail address, and then click **Next**. Either you choose the e-mail address, or your ISP or administrator provides it for you. The *Set up e-mail servers* page appears, as shown in Figure 9-27.

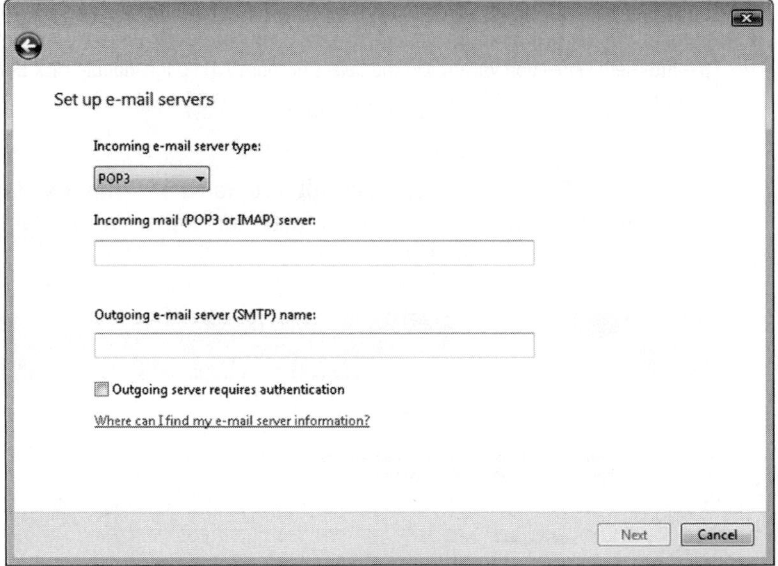

Figure 9-27

The Set up e-mail servers page

TAKE NOTE*

To set up an e-mail account in Windows Mail, you must have the information used to set up the account on the mail server. This information includes your e-mail address, user name, password, and the names of the incoming and outgoing mail servers you should use. You obtain this information from your Internet service provider (ISP) or network administrator.

4. Select the type of server your e-mail account uses. Windows Mail supports two incoming e-mail server types, but in the *Incoming e-mail server type* dropdown list, there are three types listed:
   - POP3—Post Office Protocol 3 (POP3) is the most popular type of e-mail server. The server holds your e-mail messages until you transfer them to your computer, after which the server deletes them.
   - IMAP—Internet Message Access Protocol (IMAP) is more popular with business e-mail accounts. The server stores your messages on its drives and lets you

preview, delete, and organize them directly without downloading them to your computer first.

- HTTP—Microsoft lists this option in the dropdown list only to inform you that Windows Mail no longer supports Hypertext Transfer Protocol (HTTP) servers that Web-based e-mail providers, such as Hotmail, use.

MORE INFORMATION

Microsoft has released a separate application called Windows Live Hotmail that you can use to access HTTP-based e-mail accounts on your Windows Vista computer. For more information, see http://get.live.com/general/http.

5. In the *Incoming mail (POP3 or IMAP) server* text box, enter the server name provided by your ISP or network administrator.
6. In the *Outgoing e-mail server (SMTP) name* text box, enter the ***Simple Mail Transfer Protocol (SMTP)*** server name provided by your ISP or network administrator. SMTP is the Transmission Control Protocol/Internet Protocol (TCP/IP) protocol that systems use to transmit e-mail messages between servers.
7. Select the **Outgoing server requires authentication** checkbox if your server requires you to log on before sending outgoing mail, and then click **Next**. The Internet Mail Logon page appears, as shown in Figure 9-28.

Figure 9-28

The Internet Mail Logon page

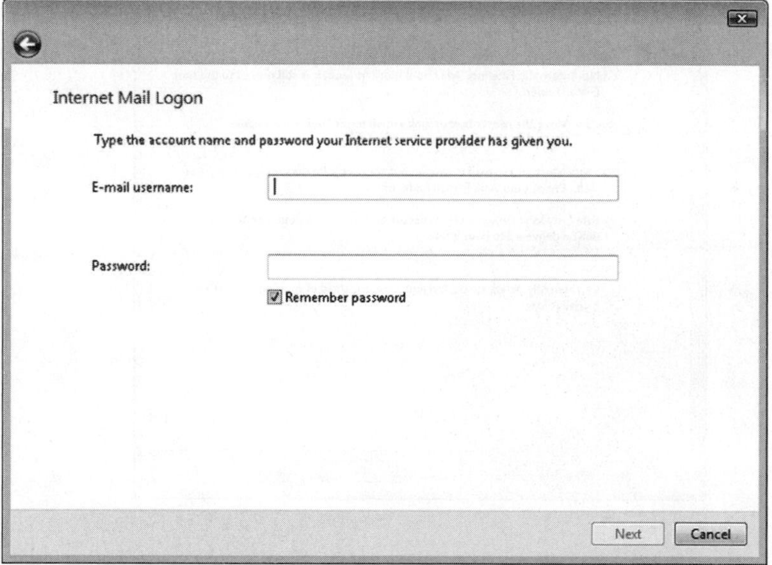

8. In the *E-mail username* text box, key the account name you will use to sign on to the e-mail server.
9. In the Password text box, key the password associated with your e-mail account.
10. Select the **Remember password** checkbox if you want Windows Mail to remember your password for future logons, and then click **Next**. The Congratulations page appears.
11. Click **Finish** to save your settings and to download your e-mail. The Internet Accounts window appears. Your newly created e-mail account is listed under the Mail section.
12. Click **Close**.

At this point, you can run the wizard again to create additional accounts, or begin working with your e-mail messages.

Filtering Junk Mail

Configuring the junk mail filter enables you to create a balance between junk mail that makes it into your inbox and legitimate mail that ends up in the junk mail folder.

The junk mail filter in Windows Mail is operational by default, but you can configure its settings to your own preferences, using the following procedure:

CONFIGURE JUNK MAIL OPTIONS

GET READY. Log on to Windows Vista. When the logon process is completed, close the Welcome Center window and any other windows that appear.

1. Click **Start**, click **All Programs**, and then click **Windows Mail**. The Inbox-Windows Mail window appears.
2. Click **Tools**, and then click **Junk E-mail Options**. The Junk E-mail Options dialog box appears with the Options tab active, as shown in Figure 9-29.

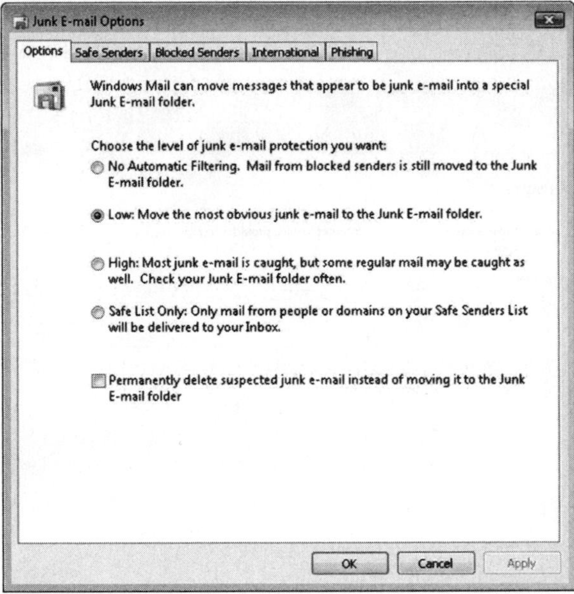

Figure 9-29
The Options tab in the Junk E-mail Options dialog box

3. On the Options tab, select the radio button for the level of junk e-mail protection you want, choosing from the following options:
   - No Automatic Filtering—Mail from blocked senders is still moved to the Junk E-mail folder.
   - Low—Move the most obvious junk e-mail to the Junk E-mail folder. This is the default setting.
   - High—Most junk e-mail is caught, but some regular mail may be caught as well. Check your Junk E-mail folder often.
   - Safe List Only—Only mail from people or domains on your Safe Senders List will be delivered to your inbox.
4. If you want Windows Mail to deleted suspected junk e-mail as it arrives, select the **Permanently delete suspected junk e-mail instead of moving it to the Junk E-mail folder** checkbox.
5. Click **Apply** to apply any changes you made, and then click the **Safe Senders** tab, as shown in Figure 9-30.

Figure 9-30

The Safe Senders tab in the Junk E-mail Options dialog box

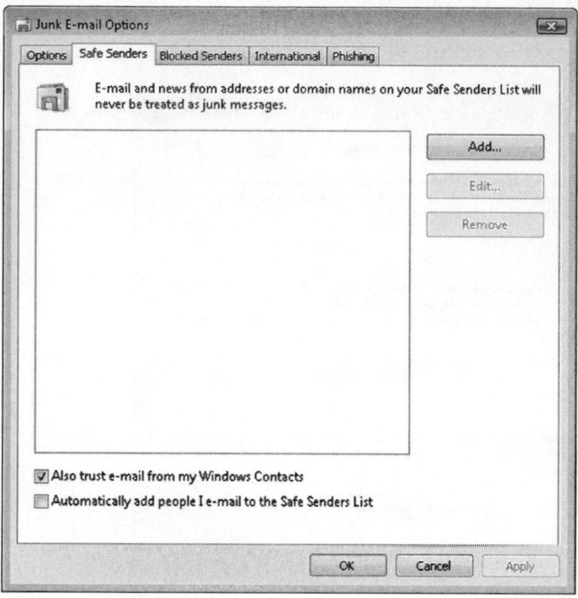

On the Safe Senders tab, you can enter e-mail addresses or domain names that you trust. Windows Mail does not treat incoming items conforming to this list as spam. You maintain the list using the following options:

- Add—Click to include a trusted address or domain in the list box.
- Edit—Click to modify a trusted address or domain already included in the list box.
- Remove—Click to delete an address or domain that you no longer trust.

6. Select the **Also trust e-mail from my Windows Contacts** checkbox if you trust all the contacts in your Contacts list.
7. Select the **Automatically add people I e-mail to the Safe Senders List** checkbox if you always send e-mail only to people you trust.
8. Click **Apply** to save your changes, and then click the **Blocked Senders** tab, as shown in Figure 9-31. On the Blocked Senders tab, you can enter e-mail addresses or domain names that you do not trust. Windows Mail always treats items in this list as spam. This tab includes the same Add, Edit, and Remove options as the Safe Senders tab.

Figure 9-31

The Blocked Senders tab in the Junk E-mail Options dialog box

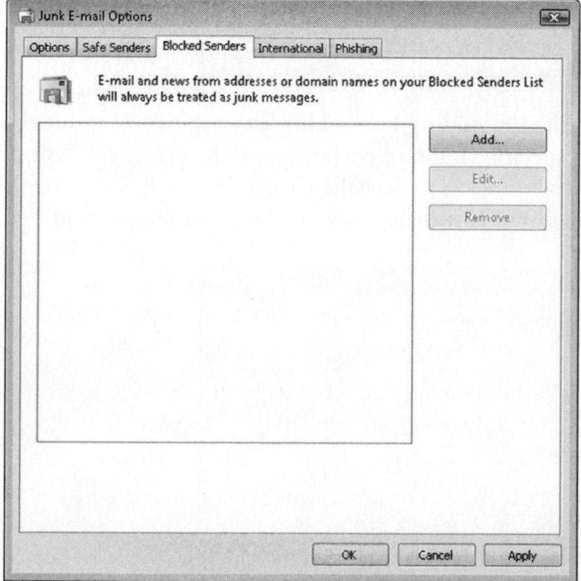

9. Click **Apply** to apply any changes you made, and then click the **International** tab, as shown in Figure 9-32.

Figure 9-32

The International tab in the Junk E-mail Options dialog box

The controls on this tab enable you to block messages written in languages you don't read. You maintain these lists with the following options:

- Blocked Top-Level Domain List—The sender's e-mail address in different countries/regions can end with top-level country code, such as .ca, .mx, or .ux. The Blocked Top-Level Domain List enables you to block all messages sent from an address ending with a specific top-level domain. You can select all countries/regions, clear all countries/regions, or select the checkboxes of specific countries or regions from the Blocked Top-Level Domain List dialog box, as shown in Figure 9-33.

Figure 9-33

The Blocked Top-Level Domain List dialog box

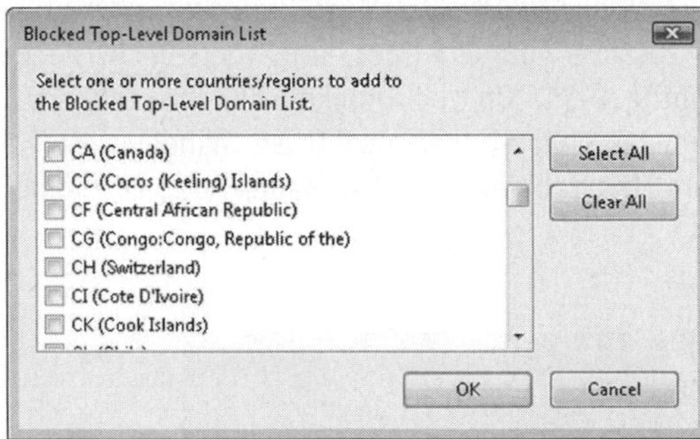

- Blocked Encoding List—This list enables you to block e-mail messages containing specific language encodings or character sets. You can select all encodings, clear all encodings, or select the checkboxes of specific encodings from the Blocked Encodings List dialog box, as shown in Figure 9-34.

Figure 9-34

The Blocked Encodings List dialog box

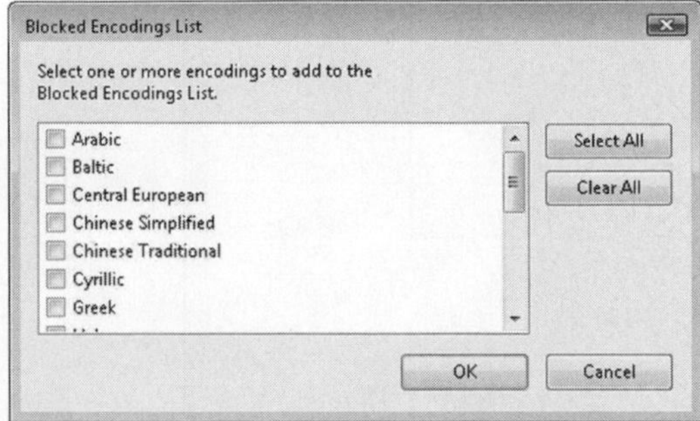

10. Click **Apply** to apply any changes you made, and then click the **Phishing** tab, as shown in Figure 9-35.

Figure 9-35

The Phishing tab in the Junk E-mail Options dialog box

11. Windows Mail selects the **Protect my Inbox from messages with potential Phishing links** checkbox by default. Microsoft recommends leaving this checkbox selected. You can optionally move the potential phishing e-mail to the Junk Mail folder by selecting the **Move phishing E-mail to the Junk Mail folder** checkbox.
12. Click **Apply** to save any changes you made, and then click **OK** to close the Junk E-mail Options dialog box.

CERTIFICATION READY?
Configure Windows Mail: Configure Contacts

5.2

Using Windows Contacts

Windows Contacts is a versatile application where you can store information about the people you communicate with on a regular basis.

Windows Mail uses the Windows Contacts application as its address book. By maintaining names and e-mail addresses in Windows Contacts, users can simply select a contact when composing e-mails, and the application inserts the e-mail address into the appropriate field. To create a contact, use the following procedure:

CREATE A CONTACT

GET READY. Log on to Windows Vista. When the logon process is completed, close the Welcome Center window and any other windows that appear.

1. Click **Start**, click **All Programs**, and then click **Windows Contacts**. The Contacts window appears, as shown in Figure 9-36.

Figure 9-36

The Contacts window

2. Click **New Contact.** An empty contact Properties sheet appears, as shown in Figure 9-37.

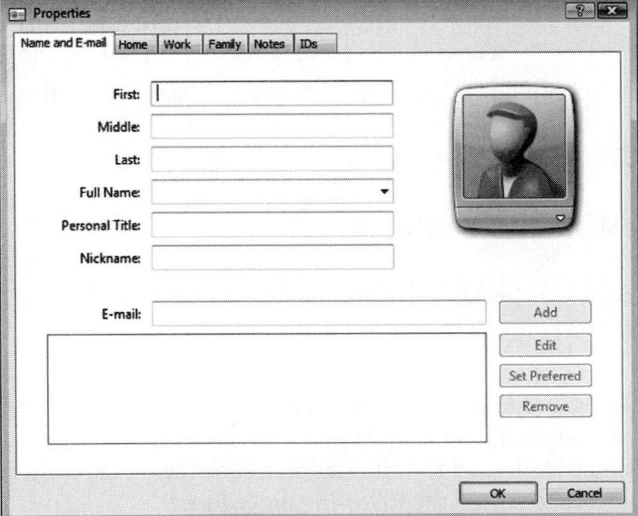

Figure 9-37

An empty contact Properties sheet

3. Key the first and last names of the person you want to add in the appropriate text boxes. The person's entire name appears in the Full Name field and in the title bar.
4. Key the user's e-mail address in the E-mail text box, and then click **Add.** If the contact has more than one e-mail address, you can add them individually, select the one you want to be the default, and then click **Set Preferred.** The Properties sheet for a contact contains additional tabs, with many additional fields where you can enter information about the person. Windows Mail does not use this information, but Windows Contact stores it for use by other applications.
5. Click **OK** to create the contact.

In addition to creating single contacts, Windows Contact enables you to create contact groups, which in Windows Mail function as mailing lists. Addressing an e-mail message to a contact group causes Windows Mail to send the message to all of the contacts in the group simultaneously. To create a contact group, use the following procedure:

CREATE A CONTACT GROUP

GET READY. Log on to Windows Vista. When the logon process is completed, close the Welcome Center window and any other windows that appear.

1. Click **Start**, click **All Programs**, and then click **Windows Contacts.** The Contacts window appears.
2. Click **New Contact Group.** An empty contact group Properties sheet appears, as shown in Figure 9-38.

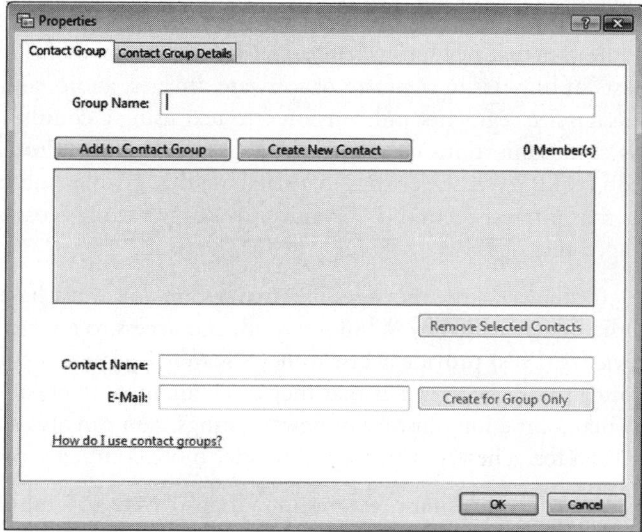

Figure 9-38

An empty contact group Properties sheet

3. Key a name for the group in the Group Name text box.
4. Click **Add to Contact Group.** The Add Members to Contact Group dialog box appears, as shown in Figure 9-39.

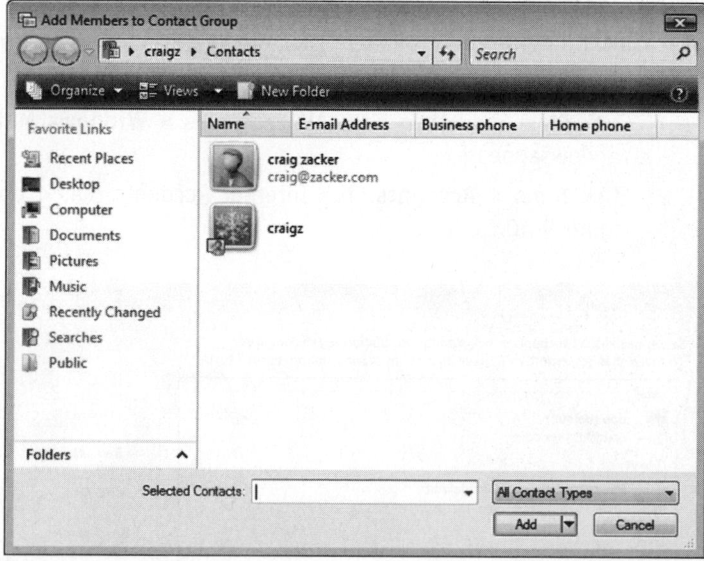

Figure 9-39

The Add Members to Contact Group dialog box

5. Select one or more contacts from the list, and then click **Add.** The program adds the contacts to the group. Alternatively, you can click **Create New Contact** to create a new single-user contact and add it to the group, or key your information into the Contact Name and E-Mail address text boxes provided and click **Create for Group Only.** This adds the contact to the group, but does not create a single-user contact at the same time.
6. Click **OK** to create the contact group.

CERTIFICATION READY?
Configure Windows Mail: Configure Newsgroups
5.2

Using Newsgroups

Newsgroups are distributed discussion forums that are freely available to users around the world.

Internet newsgroups, known collectively as ***Usenet***, are text-based messaging forums that participants around the world use to discuss topics of interest such as operating systems, television shows, software, politics, sex, religion, and virtually every other conceivable subject. Nearly all newsgroups are unmoderated and uncensored. Anyone who has a computer can read newsgroup entries and post their own in response.

Despite the fact that newsgroups are a text-based service, by far the vast majority of news traffic consists of binaries in the form of software, images, audio, and video. The binaries are split into message-size segments and converted to text using a coding scheme such as Uuencode. All news communications use the ***Network News Transfer Protocol (NNTP)***. Architects designed NNTP to store postings in a database that enables subscribers to read only those postings that interest them. NNTP also provides indexing, cross-referencing, and the expiration of aged messages.

Before you can access the messages in a newsgroup you must have a newsreader program, such as the one provided by Windows Mail, and access to a news server. Many Internet service providers (ISPs) provide access to news servers for their customers' use. The downside of using your ISP's news servers is that they often are incomplete and might not have the disk space to maintain a long history of news postings. You can also subscribe to third-party news services for a fee. These services typically offer more complete feeds and longer histories.

Windows Vista includes new features in Windows Mail to simplify the process of posting questions and answers to newsgroups and to rate the usefulness of information posted by others. However, before you can access newsgroups, you must set up an account. To create a newsgroup account, use the following procedure:

CREATE A NEWSGROUP ACCOUNT

GET READY. Log on to Windows Vista. When the logon process is completed, close the Welcome Center window and any other windows that appear.

1. Click **Start**, and then click **All Programs > Windows Mail.** The Windows Mail window appears.
2. Click **Tools > Accounts**. The Internet Accounts dialog box appears, as shown in Figure 9-40.

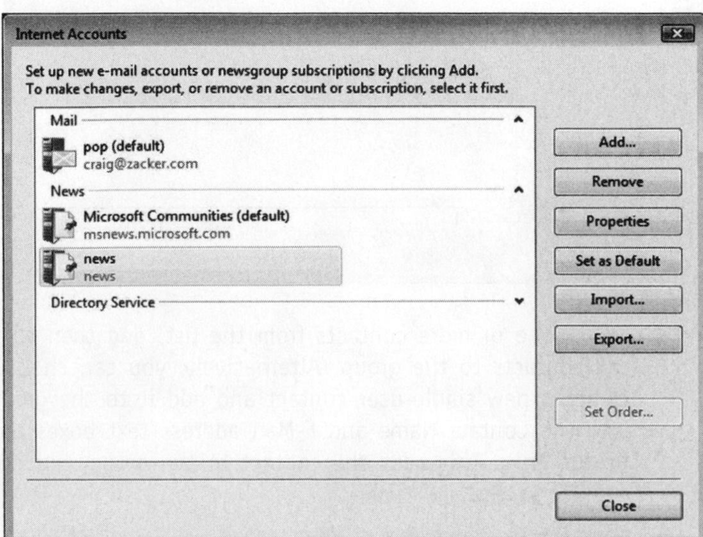

Figure 9-40

The Internet Accounts dialog box

3. Click **Add**. The Select Account Type page appears, as shown in Figure 9-41.

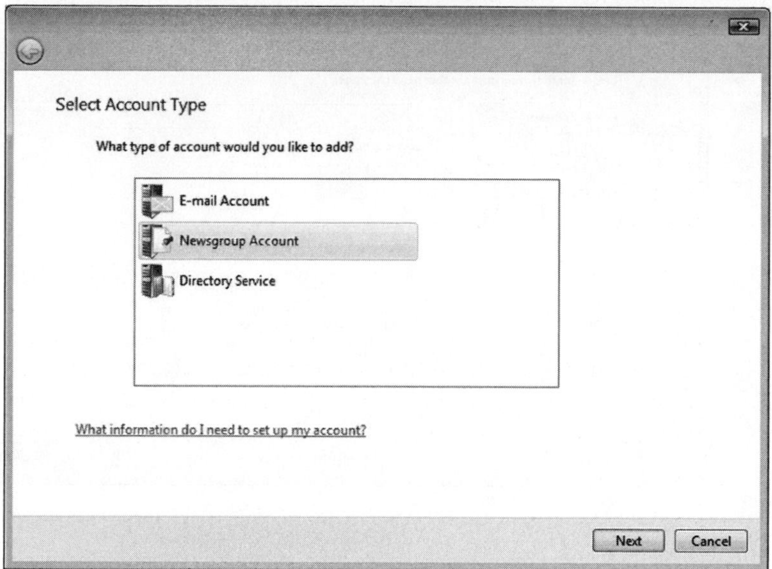

Figure 9-41

The Select Account Type page

4. Select **Newsgroup Account**, and then click **Next**. The Your Name page appears, as shown in Figure 9-42.

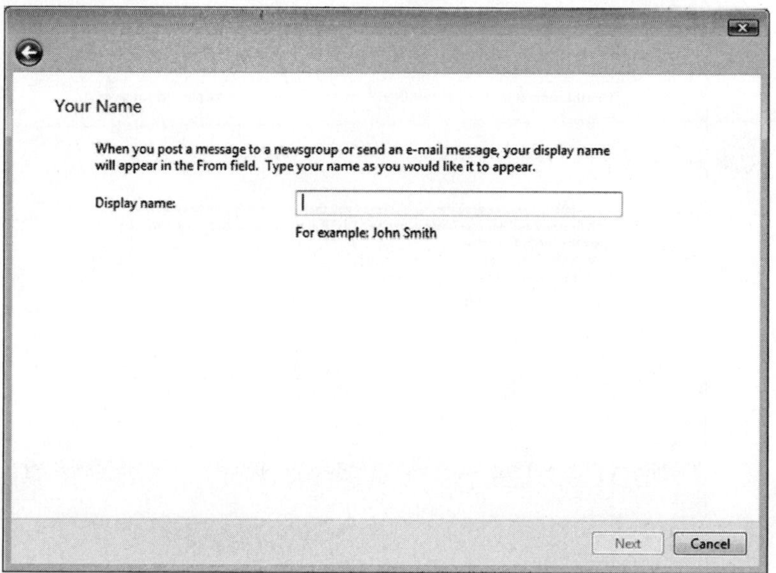

Figure 9-42

The Your Name page

5. In the *Display name* text box, key the name you want to use for newsgroup communications. Then click **Next**. The Internet News E-mail Address page appears, as shown in Figure 9-43.

Figure 9-43

The Internet News E-mail Address page

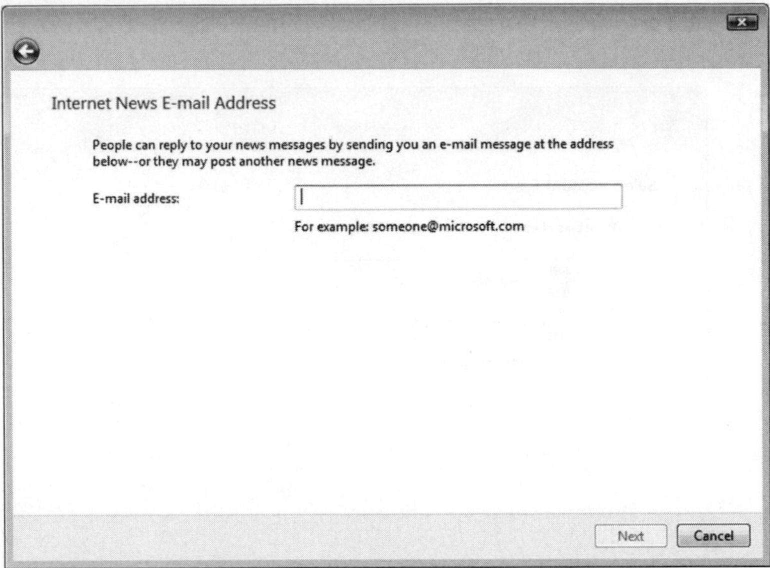

6. In the *E-mail address* text box, key the e-mail address you want to use when communicating offline with newsgroup participants. Then click **Next**. The Internet News Server Name page appears, as shown in Figure 9-44.

Figure 9-44

The Internet News Server Name page

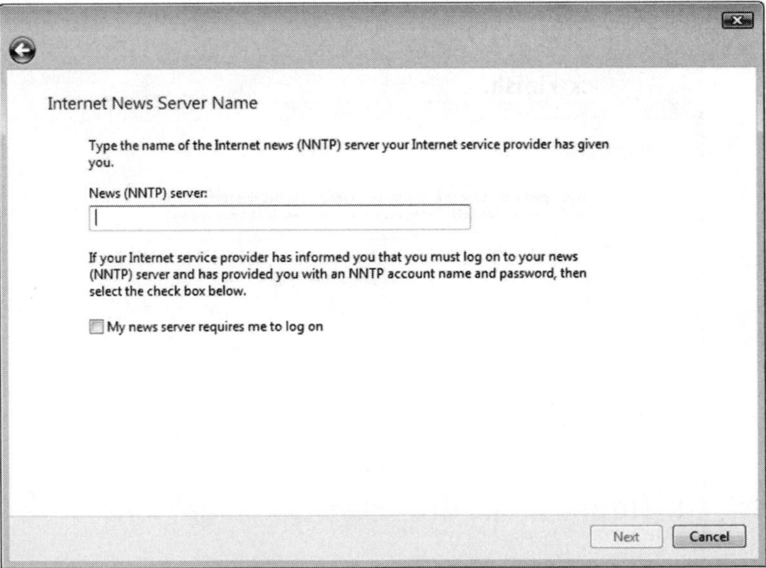

7. In the News (NNTP) server text box, key the name of your news server and select the *My news server requires me to log on* checkbox. Then click **Next**. The Internet News Server Logon page appears, as shown in Figure 9-45.

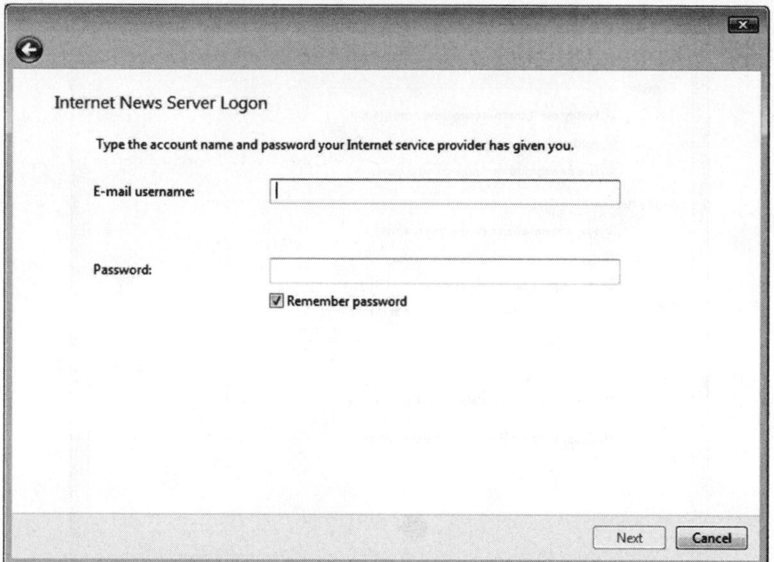

Figure 9-45

The Internet News Server Logon page

TAKE NOTE* Most news servers require users to log on, and the account credentials are often different from those you use to log on to your e-mail server. Be sure to obtain the correct news server name and credentials from your ISP or network administrator.

8. In the *E-mail username* and *Password* fields, key the credentials needed to log on to the news server, and then click **Next.** The Congratulations page appears.
9. Click **Finish.**
10. Click **Close** to close the Internet Accounts dialog box.

Configuring Mail and Newsgroup Options

Desktop technicians should be familiar with the configuration settings in Windows Mail.

Windows Mail has a large number of optional settings with which desktop technicians should be familiar. The following procedure examines a large number of these settings, more than you are likely to have to adjust in any one session.

CONFIGURE MAIL AND NEWSGROUP OPTIONS

GET READY. Log on to Windows Vista. When the logon process is completed, close the Welcome Center window and any other windows that appear.

1. Click **Start**, click **All Programs**, and then click **Windows Mail.** The Inbox-Windows Mail console appears.
2. Click **Tools**, and then click **Options.** The Options dialog box appears with the General tab active, as shown in Figure 9-46.

Figure 9-46

The General tab in the Options dialog box

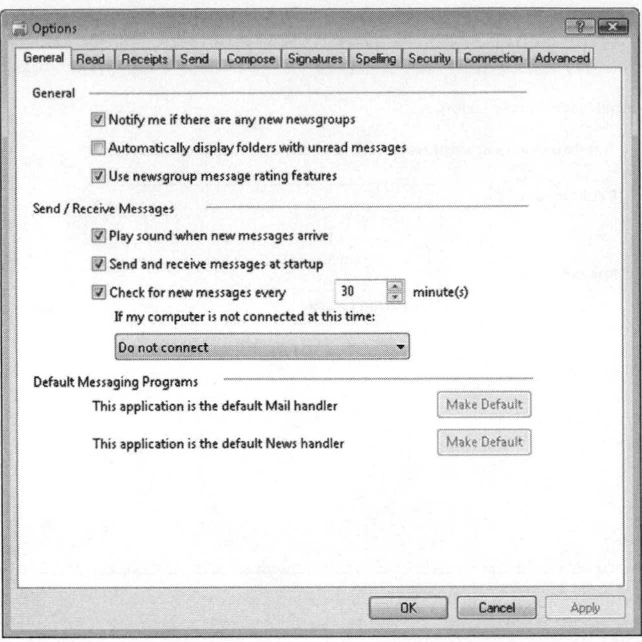

In the General section, three options are available:

- Notify me if there are any new newsgroups—Causes Windows Mail to alert you about new newsgroups when you connect to your news server.
- Automatically display folders with unread messages—Causes Windows Mail to assign priority viewing to messages that have not been read.
- Use newsgroup message rating features—Enables users to view and leave feedback about the usefulness of newsgroup messages.

In the Send/Receive Messages section, these options are available:

- Play sound when new messages arrive—Causes Windows Mail to notify you audibly each time a new message arrives in your inbox. Windows Mail must be running for this option to function.
- Send and receive messages at startup—Causes Windows Mail to automatically check for new messages and to send any pending e-mail in your outbox every time you start the program.
- Check for new messages every [x] minute(s)—Causes Windows Mail to checks for new messages at the time interval that you specify.

3. In the *If my computer is not connected at this time* dropdown list, select one of the following options:
   - Do not connect
   - Connect only when not working offline
   - Connect even when working offline
4. In the Default Messaging Programs section, select which applications you want to be the default Mail handler and the default News handler.
5. Click **Apply** to apply any changes you made, and then click the **Read** tab, as shown in Figure 9-47. The Reading Messages section options relate to how Windows Mail displays messages.

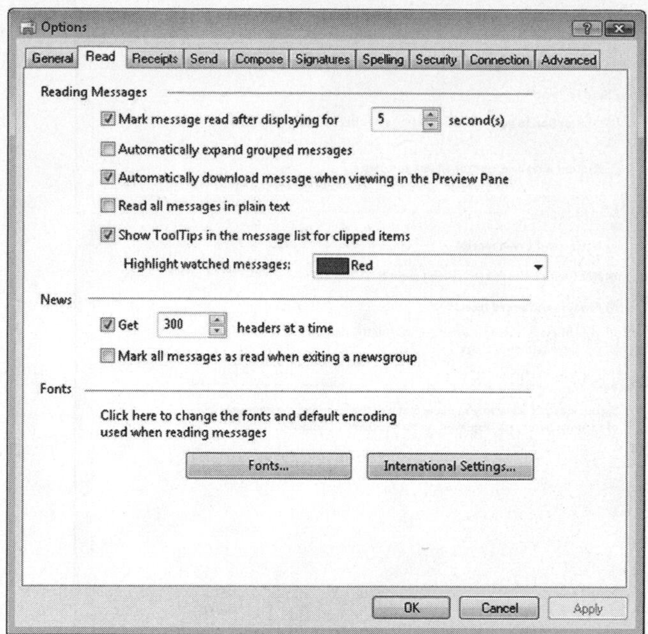

Figure 9-47

The Read tab in the Options dialog box

- Mark message read after displaying for [x] second(s)—The default is 5 seconds. Change the number of seconds in the second(s) spin box. The values you can choose range from 0 to 60. If you clear this checkbox, Windows Mail will not mark messages as read when you view them in the preview pane.
- Automatically expand grouped messages—Selecting this checkbox automatically expands messages when you are using the Group Messages by Conversation view.
- Automatically download message when viewing in the Preview Pane—Select this checkbox when you have chosen to display the preview pane and are only retrieving message headers when checking e-mail, but want to automatically download a message and display it when you select it in the message list.
- Read all messages in plain text—Selecting this checkbox disables the display of custom fonts and graphics when you read your e-mail messages.
- Show ToolTips in the message list for clipped items—Select this checkbox when you want a tooltip to display the entire text of an item in the message list when the column is too short to display the entire text.
- Highlight watched messages—Click this dropdown list when you want to change the color in which watched messages are displayed.

The News section options relate to how Windows Mail retrieves and manages newsgroup messages.

- Get [x] headers at a time—To change the number of messages that Windows Mail automatically downloads when you open a newsgroup, select this checkbox, and then change the number in the *headers at a time* spin box.
- Mark all messages as read when exiting a newsgroup—If you don't want unread messages to appear as new messages the next time that you open a newsgroup, select this checkbox.

The Fonts section options relate to how messages are displayed when you read them.

- Fonts—This option allows you to choose the font and size Windows Mail uses when you read messages.
- International Settings—This option allows you to change the default language encoding Windows Mail uses for message display.

6. Click **Apply** to apply any changes you made, and then click the **Receipts** tab, as shown in Figure 9-48.

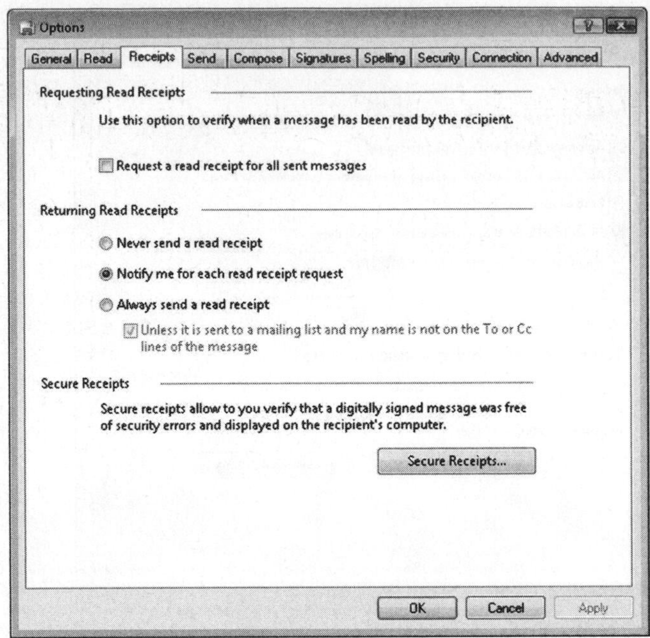

Figure 9-48

The Receipts tab in the Options dialog box

7. In the Requesting Read Receipts section, select the *Request a read receipt for all sent messages* checkbox if you want to verify when recipients have read the messages you sent. (Selecting this checkbox does not guarantee that you will receive the receipts because most e-mail programs allow the recipients to choose whether they want the receipt sent to you.)
8. These options are available in the Returning Read Receipts section:
   - Never send a read receipt—Select this option when you never want to send read receipts to the e-mail sender.
   - Notify me for each read receipt request—Select this option if you want to decide whether you want to send a receipt on each occasion that someone requests one.
   - Always send a read receipt—Select this option if you always want to send a requested read receipt whenever you read the message. Microsoft does not recommend using this option because it could alert spammers that you have read their messages.
9. In the Secure Receipts section, click **Secure Receipts** to display the Secure Receipt Options dialog box, as shown in Figure 9-49, where you can choose whether you want to request read receipts when you send digitally signed messages, and to set your options for responding to requests for digital signatures.

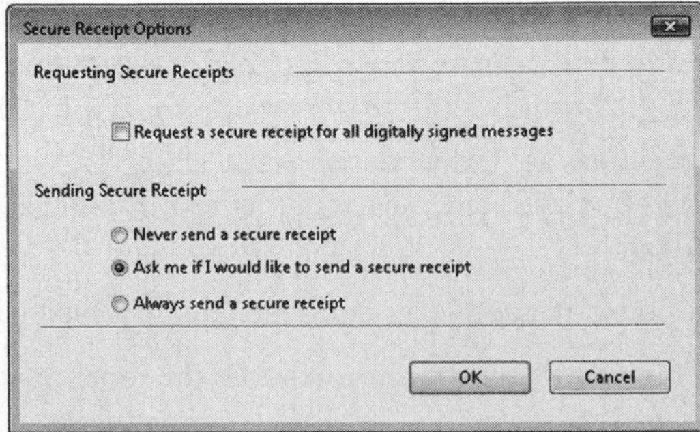

Figure 9-49

The Secure Receipt Options dialog box

10. Click **Apply** to apply any changes you made, and then click the **Send** tab, as shown in Figure 9-50. In the Sending section, you choose options for telling Windows Mail how to handle messages that you create.

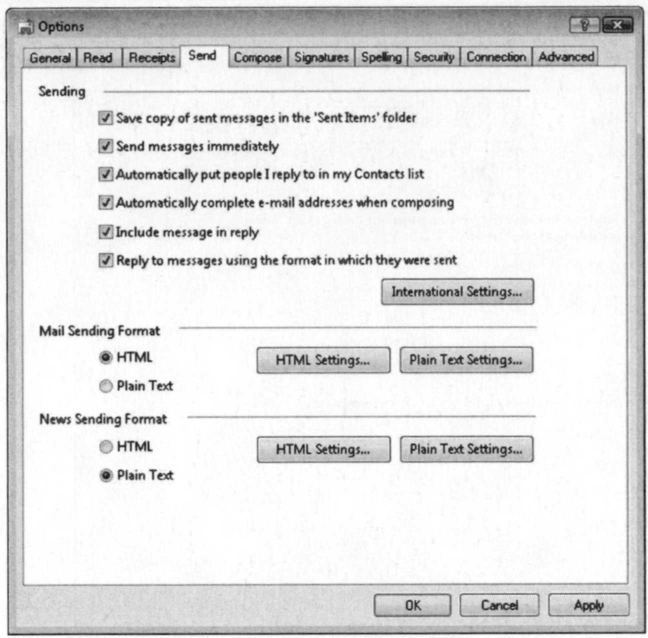

Figure 9-50

The Send tab in the Options dialog box

- Save copy of sent messages in the 'Sent Items' folder—Causes Windows Mail to retain a copy of all sent messages.
- Send messages immediately—Causes Windows Mail to send your messages immediately when you click **Send**, instead of waiting for you to click **Send/Receive**.
- Automatically put people I reply to in my Contacts list—Causes Windows Mail to create a new contact for the addressee of every e-mail you reply to, if the address is not already in Windows Contacts.
- Automatically complete e-mail addresses when composing—Causes Windows Mail to try to complete partially keyed names using the e-mail addresses stored in Windows Contacts.
- Include message in reply—Causes Windows Mail to include the original message sent to you in your reply.
- Reply to messages using the format in which they were sent—Causes Windows Mail to automatically choose plain text or Hypertext Markup Language (HTML), depending on the format of the original message.
- International Settings—Sets the default encoding for outgoing messages.

11. In the Mail Sending Format section, choose whether to send HTML or plain text messages by default. You can also adjust settings for the format you select.
12. In the News Sending Format section, choose whether to send HTML or plain text messages by default. You can also adjust settings for the format you select.
13. Click **Apply** to apply any changes you made, and then click the **Compose** tab, as shown in Figure 9-51.

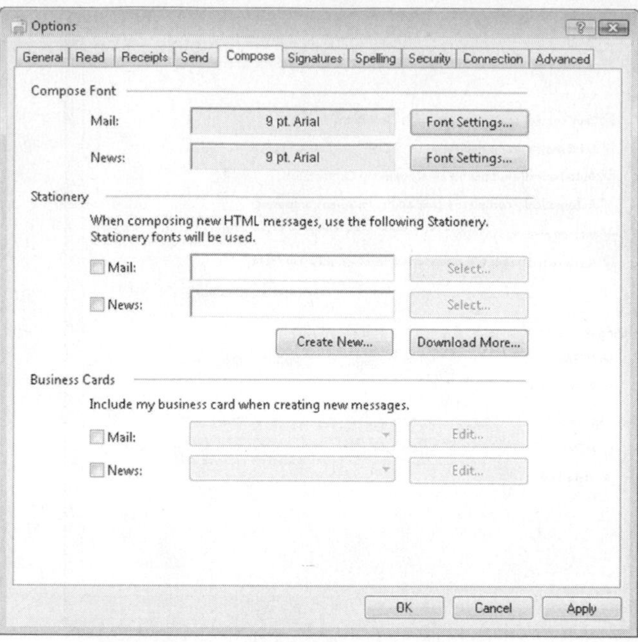

Figure 9-51

The Compose tab in the Options dialog box

14. In the Compose Font section, choose the fonts you use for creating e-mail and newsgroup messages. Windows Mail uses custom fonts only for messages you create in the HTML format. Plain text is typically used for messages sent to newsgroups.
15. In the Stationery section, select the default stationery you want to use for e-mail and newsgroup messages.
16. In the Business Cards section, choose to include a default contact card as an attachment to e-mail or newsgroup messages you send. (Microsoft advises that you do not include a default contact card for newsgroup postings because this information becomes available to anyone who reads that newsgroup.)
17. Click **Apply** to apply any changes you made, and then click the **Signatures** tab, as shown in Figure 9-52.

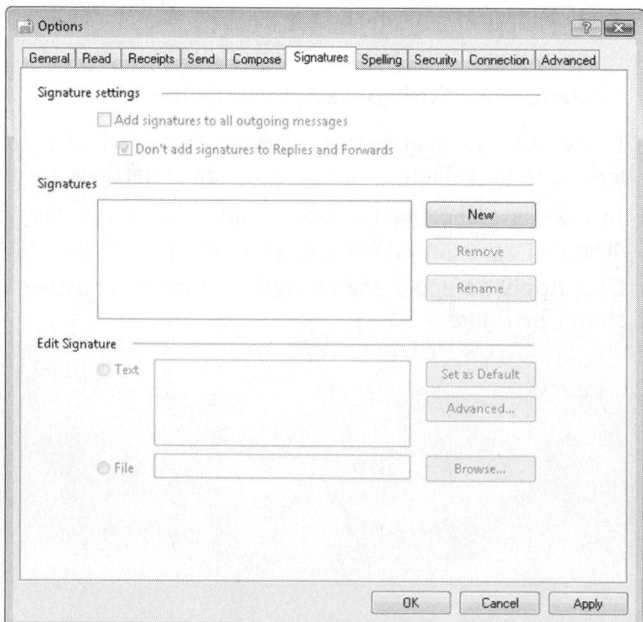

Figure 9-52

The Signatures tab in the Options dialog box

18. The Signatures tab enables you to add signatures to all outgoing messages, as well as to replies and forwards. The signature for business mail usually consists of the sender's title, address, phone number, and e-mail address.
19. Click **Apply** to apply any changes you made, and then click the **Spelling** tab, as shown in Figure 9-53.

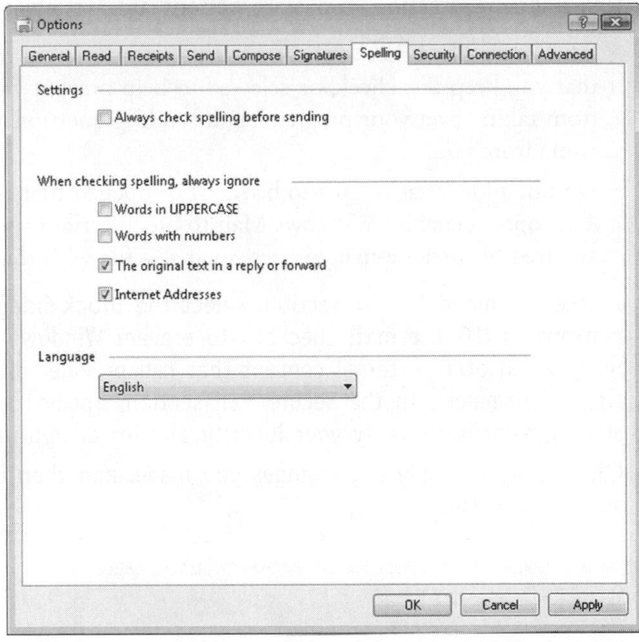

Figure 9-53

The Spelling tab in the Options dialog box

20. The Spelling tab enables you to always check spelling before sending an e-mail message. When checking spelling, you can choose to ignore:
    - Words in uppercase
    - Words with numbers
    - The original text in a reply or forward
    - Internet addresses
21. In the Language section, you can change the language for which you want to check spelling.
22. Click **Apply** to apply any changes you made, and then click the **Security** tab, as shown in Figure 9-54.

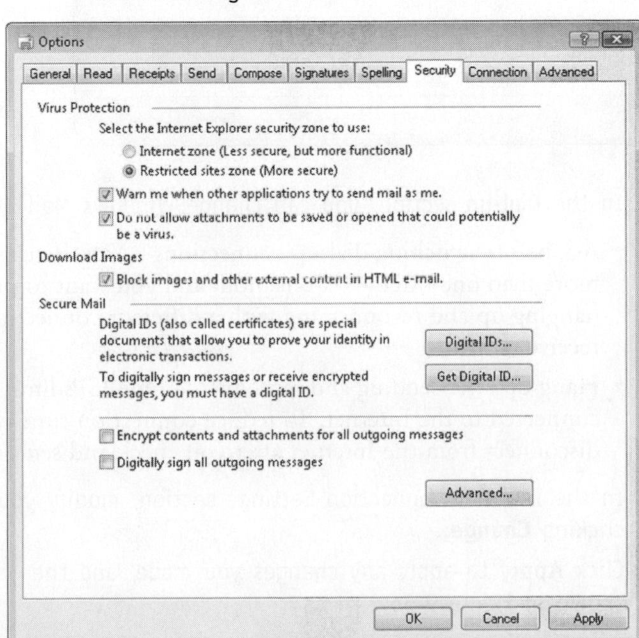

Figure 9-54

The Security tab in the Options dialog box

In the Virus Protection section, you specify the Internet Explorer security zone that Windows Mail should use from the following:

- Internet zone (Less secure, but more functional)
- Restricted sites zone (More secure)

Under Virus Protection, two more options are available:

- Warn me when other applications try to send mail as me—Microsoft recommends that you keep this checkbox selected to help prevent viruses or malicious intruders from taking over your programs and sending questionable e-mail that appears to come from you.
- Do not allow attachments to be saved or opened that could potentially be a virus—This option enables Windows Mail to block certain types of file attachments that are used to spread e-mail viruses, such as a file with the extension exe.

23. In the Download Images section, select the **Block images and other external content in HTML e-mail** checkbox to prevent Windows Mail from downloading images and other external content that can provide information about your identity to spammers. In the Secure Mail section, options are available for digitally signing e-mails to verify your identity and for encrypting confidential e-mails.
24. Click **Apply** to apply any changes you made, and then click the **Connection** tab, as shown in Figure 9-55.

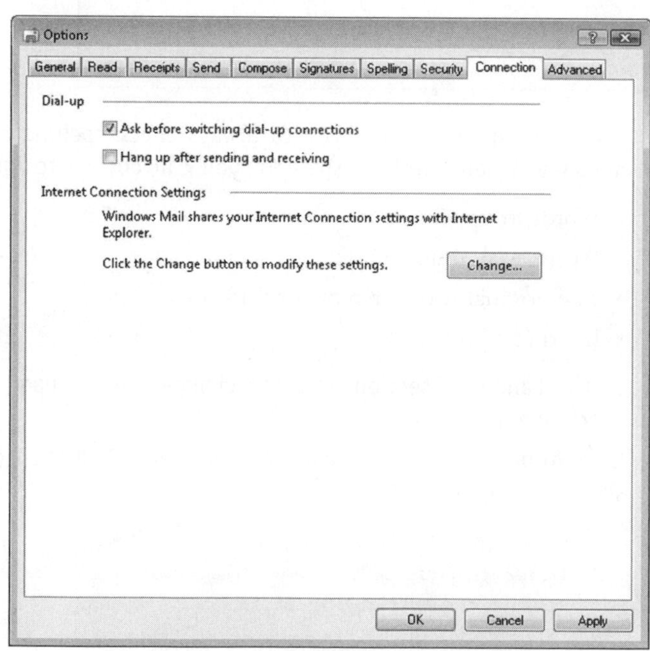

Figure 9-55

The Connection tab in the Options dialog box

In the Dial-up section, you can change Windows Mail dial-up settings:

- Ask before switching dial-up connections—You use this option when you have more than one Internet connection, and you want to prevent Windows Mail from hanging up and reconnecting with a different connection when you send and receive e-mail.
- Hang up after sending and receiving—Some ISPs limit the time that you spend connected to the Internet. To reduce connection time, you can select this option to disconnect from the Internet after you check and send e-mail.

25. In the Internet Connection Settings section, modify your connection settings by clicking **Change.**
26. Click **Apply** to apply any changes you made, and then click the **Advanced** tab, as shown in Figure 9-56.

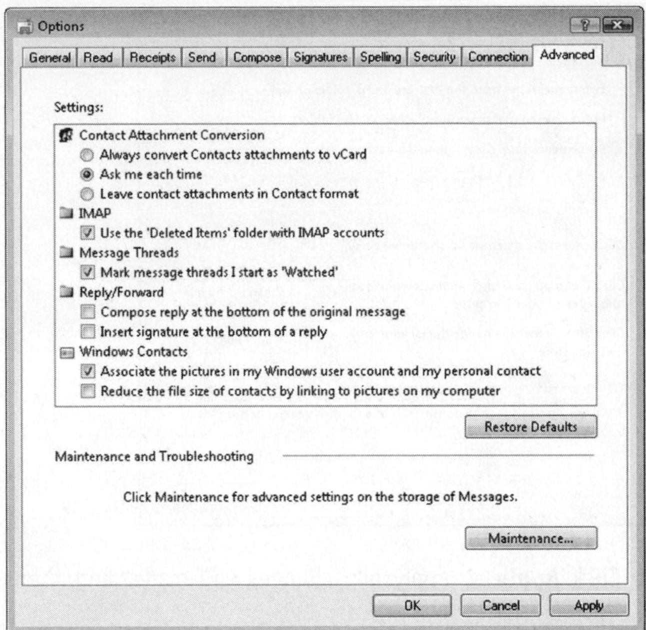

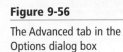

Figure 9-56

The Advanced tab in the Options dialog box

Under Contact Attachment Conversion, you can choose one of the following options:

- Always convert Contacts attachments to vCard—Select this option to automatically convert Windows Contacts e-mail attachments to vCards when you save them.
- Ask me each time—Select this option if you want to decide which format to save the Windows Contacts attachments in each time you receive an attachment.
- Leave contact attachments in Contact format—Select this option if you want to always leave the contact attachments in the Windows Contacts format.

27. Windows Mail marks IMAP messages as deleted but does not remove them from your message list until you remove the messages from the IMAP server. In the IMAP section, you can resolve this potential problem by selecting the **Use the 'Deleted Items' folder with IMAP accounts** checkbox if you want to remove IMAP messages from your message list as you delete them.

28. Under Message Threads, select the **Mark message threads I start as 'Watched'** checkbox if you want to watch any conversation that you start in a newsgroup automatically. Under Reply/Forward, you can choose from the following options:

    - Compose reply at the bottom of the original message—Select this option when you want to add your reply text at the bottom of a message you are replying to, instead of at the top of the message.
    - Insert signature at the bottom of a reply—This option will insert your signature automatically when you reply to a message. The default is that Windows Mail inserts the signature (if you have created one) when you create a new message.

    In the Windows Contacts section, you can choose these options:

    - Associate the pictures in my Windows user account and my personal contact
    - Reduce the file size of contacts by linking to pictures on my computer

29. Click **Maintenance** to open the Maintenance dialog box, as shown in Figure 9-57. Use this dialog box to adjust settings such as how long Windows Mail stores messages, when it should compact the e-mail database, and what information it should log for troubleshooting purposes.

Figure 9-57

The Maintenance dialog box

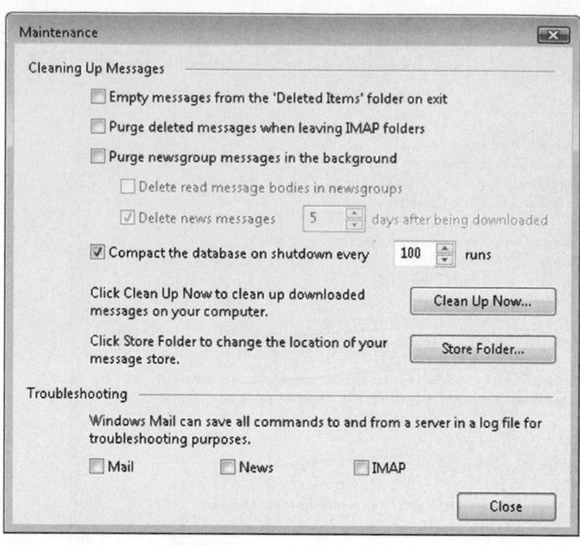
Maintenance
Cleaning Up Messages
Empty messages from the 'Deleted Items' folder on exit
Purge deleted messages when leaving IMAP folders
Purge newsgroup messages in the background
Delete read message bodies in newsgroups
Delete news messages 5 days after being downloaded
Compact the database on shutdown every 100 runs
Click Clean Up Now to clean up downloaded messages on your computer.
Clean Up Now...
Click Store Folder to change the location of your message store.
Store Folder...
Troubleshooting
Windows Mail can save all commands to and from a server in a log file for troubleshooting purposes.
Mail
News
IMAP
Close

30. Click **Apply** to apply any changes you made, and then click **OK** to close the Options dialog box.

■ Using Windows Meeting Space

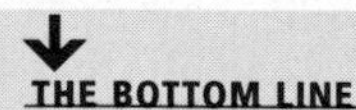
THE BOTTOM LINE

Windows Meeting Space is a collaboration tool that people at distant locations can use to conduct a discussion or work on a single document.

TAKE NOTE* Windows Meeting Space is not compatible with NetMeeting or any other collaboration tool. The users participating in a meeting must all be running Windows Vista.

Windows Meeting Space is the Windows Vista collaboration tool that replaces the NetMeeting application in previous Windows versions. With Windows Meeting Space, you can collaborate on a single document with up to ten users at remote locations, or perform real-time demonstrations by sharing your desktop with remote users.

Before a user can start or join a meeting with Windows Meeting Space, the following setup procedure must occur:

SET UP WINDOWS MEETING SPACE

CERTIFICATION READY?
Configure Windows Meeting Space
5.3

GET READY. Log on to Windows Vista using an account with administrative privileges. When the logon process is completed, close the Welcome Center window and any other windows that appear.

1. Click **Start**, point to **All Programs**, and then click **Windows Meeting Space**. The Windows Meeting Space Setup wizard appears and displays the *Ready to set up Windows Meeting Space?* page, as shown in Figure 9-58.

Figure 9-58

The Ready to set up Windows Meeting Space? page

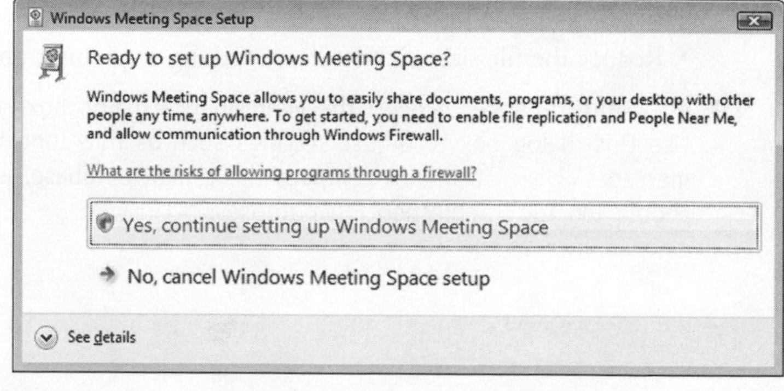
Windows Meeting Space Setup
Ready to set up Windows Meeting Space?
Windows Meeting Space allows you to easily share documents, programs, or your desktop with other people any time, anywhere. To get started, you need to enable file replication and People Near Me, and allow communication through Windows Firewall.
What are the risks of allowing programs through a firewall?
Yes, continue setting up Windows Meeting Space
No, cancel Windows Meeting Space setup
See details

2. Click **Yes, continue setting up Windows Meeting Space**. After confirming that you are performing the action, the People Near Me dialog box appears, as shown in Figure 9-59.

Figure 9-59

The People Near Me dialog box

3. In the *Your display name* text box, key the name you want to use when in a meeting.
4. If you want to restrict meeting invitations, use the *Allow invitations from* dropdown list to modify the default ("Anyone") setting.

TAKE NOTE 

During the Windows Meeting Space setup process, the wizard creates an exception in Windows Firewall, which enables the Windows Meeting Space traffic to pass to and from the network.

5. Click **OK**. The Windows Meeting Space window appears. At this point, the user can create a new meeting or join an existing meeting.

To initiate a meeting using Windows Meeting Space, use the following procedure:

CREATE A MEETING

GET READY. Log on to Windows Vista. When the logon process is completed, close the Welcome Center window and any other windows that appear.

1. Click **Start**, point to **All Programs**, and then click **Windows Meeting Space**. The Windows Meeting Space window appears.
2. Click **Start a new meeting**.
3. In the *Meeting name* text box, key an alternative name for the meeting, if desired.
4. In the Password text box, key a password at least eight characters long.
5. Click the right arrow button. The meeting launches and a meeting window appears, as shown in Figure 9-60.

Figure 9-60

An active meeting window

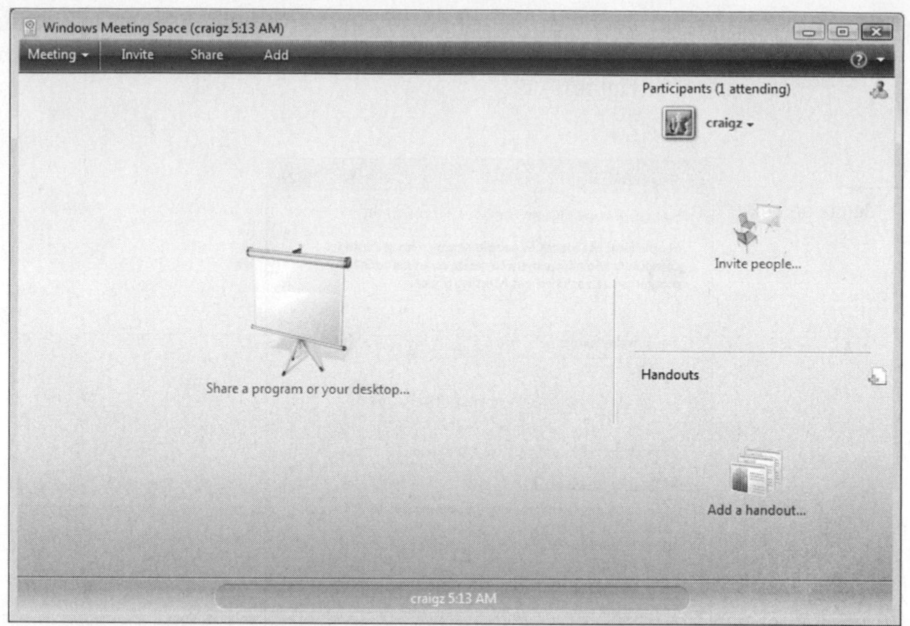
Windows Meeting Space (craigz 5:13 AM)
Meeting
Invite
Share
Add
Participants (1 attending)
craigz
Invite people...
Share a program or your desktop...
Handouts
Add a handout...
craigz 5:13 AM

Once you have launched a meeting, you can invite other people to join by clicking the *Invite people* button and selecting the names of others who have signed on to People Near Me. Users with the appropriate password can also join the meeting without an invitation by running Windows Meeting Space and selecting *Join a meeting*.

Once all of the participants have joined a meeting, you can share your entire desktop, or select a single document to share, using the following procedure:

SHARE A FILE

CERTIFICATION READY? Configure Windows Meeting Space: Share files
5.3

GET READY. Log on to Windows Vista. When the logon process is completed, close the Welcome Center window and any other windows that appear.

1. Click **Start**, point to **All Programs**, and then click **Windows Meeting Space**. The Windows Meeting Space window appears.
2. Start a new meeting or join an existing one.
3. Click **Share**. A Windows Meeting Space message box appears, asking if you want to share your entire desktop.
4. Click **OK**. The *Start a shared session* dialog box appears, as shown in Figure 9-61.

Figure 9-61

The Start a shared session dialog box

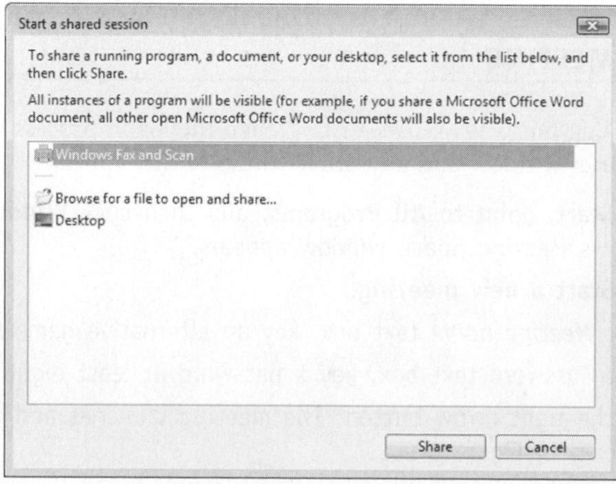
Start a shared session
To share a running program, a document, or your desktop, select it from the list below, and then click Share.
All instances of a program will be visible (for example, if you share a Microsoft Office Word document, all other open Microsoft Office Word documents will also be visible).
Windows Fax and Scan
Browse for a file to open and share...
Desktop
Share
Cancel

5. Select **Browse for a file to open and share**, and then click **Share**. An Open dialog box appears.

6. Browse to the document file you want to share, select it, and click **Open**.
7. The file opens on your desktop and is shared with all of the other users in the meeting.

Only one user in the meeting at a time can control (that is, edit) the shared document. To relinquish control to another user, click the **Give Control** button in the toolbar and select one of the other users in the meeting.

■ Using Windows Calendar

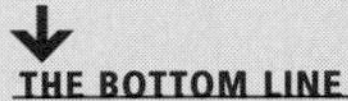

Windows Calendar is a simple scheduling program that can also share its data with other users on a network.

At first glance, Windows Calendar is a simple, though useful, application that enables users to keep track of their appointments, create task lists, and view their calendar information in various formats. However, the application takes on greater value when you consider its capabilities as a collaboration tool. By sharing information with other users, Windows Calendar becomes a valuable communications tool for both personal and business users.

Windows Calendar supports a variety of views, but by default it displays a monthly calendar, an hourly schedule for the selected day, and a details pane for a selected appointment or task, as shown in Figure 9-62. Creating appointments in Windows Calendar is simply a matter of clicking the New Appointment button and filling in the desired information in the details pane.

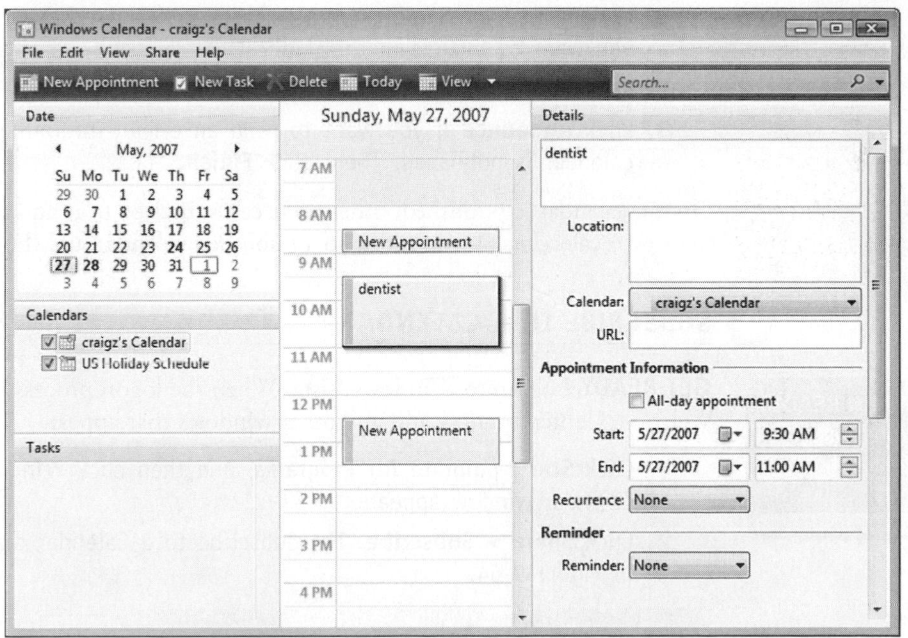

Figure 9-62

The main Windows Calendar window

To use Windows Calendar as a collaboration tool, you must first publish your calendar information. To publish a calendar, use the following procedure:

PUBLISH A CALENDAR

GET READY. Log on to Windows Vista. When the logon process is completed, close the Welcome Center window and any other windows that appear.

1. Click **Start**, point to **All Programs**, and then click **Windows Calendar**. The Windows Calendar window appears.
2. Click **Share > Publish.** The Publish Calendar dialog box appears, as shown in Figure 9-63.

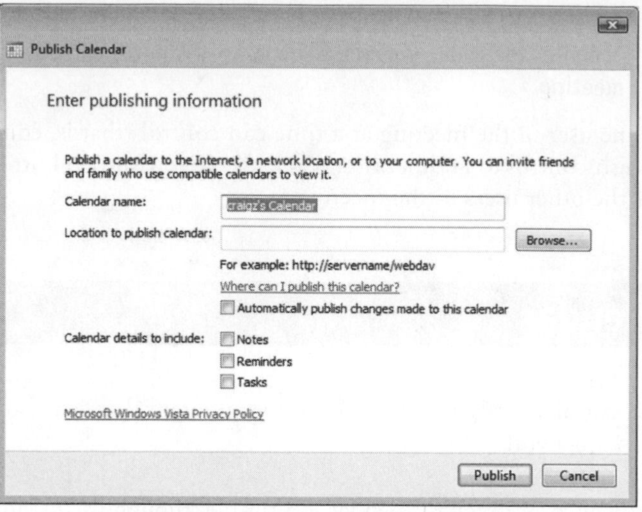

Figure 9-63

The Publish Calendar dialog box

TAKE NOTE 

To publish your calendar to an Internet Website, you must find an ISP that provides this service and obtain the appropriate URL and logon credentials from them.

3. In the *Calendar name* text box, key an alternative name for the calendar, if desired.
4. In the *Location to publish calendar* text box, key the name of or browse to the location where you want to publish the calendar. This could be a folder on a local drive, a shared drive on the network using UNC notation (\\server\share), or the URL of a Website on the Internet.
5. Select the **Automatically publish changes made to this calendar** checkbox if you want the program to update your published file each time you make changes to the calendar.
6. Under *Calendar details to include*, select the checkboxes for the calendar elements you want to include in the publication.
7. Click **Publish**. The Your Calendar Has Been Successfully Published page appears.
8. Click **Announce** if you want to send an e-mail informing other users that your calendar is published. Then, click **Finish**.

Once a calendar is published, other users can subscribe to it and integrate its information into their own calendars. To subscribe to a published calendar, use the following procedure:

SUBSCRIBE TO A CALENDAR

CERTIFICATION READY?
Configure Windows Calendar: Troubleshoot shared calendar issues
5.4

GET READY. Log on to Windows Vista. When the logon process is completed, close the Welcome Center window and any other windows that appear.

1. Click **Start**, point to **All Programs**, and then click **Windows Calendar**. The Windows Calendar window appears.
2. Click **Share > Subscribe**. The Subscribe to a Calendar dialog box appears, as shown in Figure 9-64.

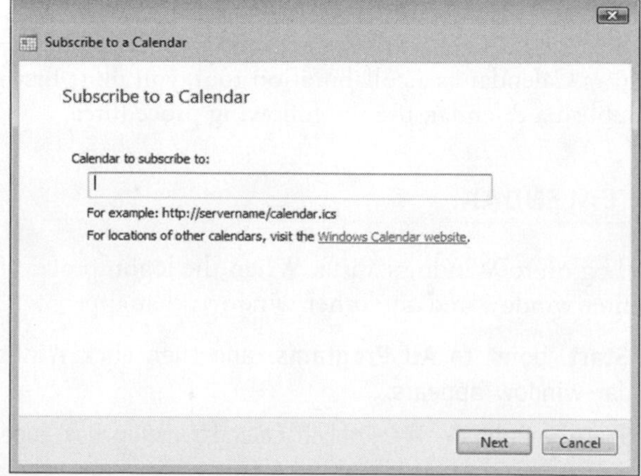

Figure 9-64

The Subscribe to a Calendar dialog box

3. In the *Calendar to subscribe to* text box, key the full path and name of the published calendar file to which you want to subscribe, using drive letter, UNC, or URL notation.
4. Click **Next**. The Calendar Subscription Settings page appears.
5. Key an alternative name for the calendar to which you have subscribed, if desired.
6. In the *Update interval* dropdown list, specify how often you want your calendar to update itself with information from the published calendar.
7. Select the checkboxes to specify whether you want to import the reminders and tasks from the published calendar.
8. Click **Finish**. The appointments from the subscribed calendar now appear in your calendar.

Using Windows Fax and Scan

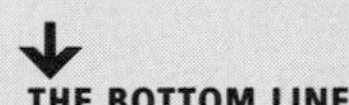

The Windows Fax and Scan program appears much like Windows Mail, with an inbox and an outbox, and can be used to compose text faxes or to scan documents for faxing.

Windows Fax and Scan is a Windows Vista application that enables you to send and receive faxes using a scanner and a modem with faxing capabilities. Windows Fax and Scan is similar in appearance to Windows Mail. Incoming faxes go to an inbox and outgoing ones are queued in an outbox until they can be transmitted by the modem.

Faxing is an option in Windows XP, but it is treated as standard equipment in Windows Vista. The basis for the outgoing communications in the Windows Fax and Scan application is a printer driver that sends documents to a fax modem instead of to a printer. As a result, you can fax from any Windows application simply by using the print function, or you can use the Windows Fax and Scan program to compose simple text faxes or scan documents for faxing.

When you attempt to fax a document for the first time, using Windows Fax and Scan or any other application, the Fax Setup wizard appears. The wizard will help you associate the fax driver with a fax modem, either installed in the local machine or managed by a network fax server. This setup procedure is as follows:

SETTING UP WINDOWS FAX

GET READY. Log on to Windows Vista. When the logon process is completed, close the Welcome Center window and any other windows that appear.

1. Click **Start**, point to **All Programs**, and then click **Windows Fax and Scan**. The Windows Fax and Scan window appears, as shown in Figure 9-65.

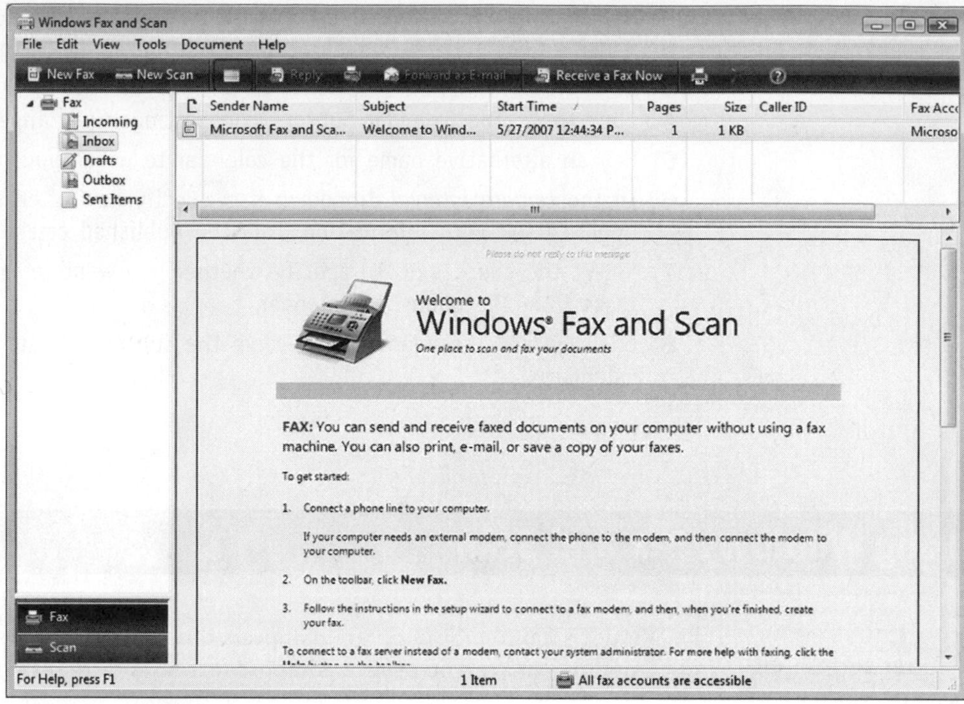

Figure 9-65

The Windows Fax and Scan window

2. Click **New Fax.** The Fax Setup Wizard launches and the Choose a Fax Modem or Server page appears.
3. Click **Connect to a fax modem.** The Choose a Modem Name page appears.
4. In the Name text box, key an alternative name for the fax modem, if desired. Then click **Next.** The Choose How to Receive Faxes page appears.
5. Select whether you want the modem to answer incoming calls automatically, to notify you of incoming calls, or to ignore them for now.

After confirming that you are performing the action, a Windows Security Alert message box appears, seeking your permission to unblock the ports in Windows Firewall needed to receive incoming network connections. A New Fax window appears in which you can compose and send a fax message.

Working with Media Applications

Windows Vista includes a variety of multimedia applications. Desktop technicians, especially those servicing home users, should be familiar with the setup and configuration tasks these applications require.

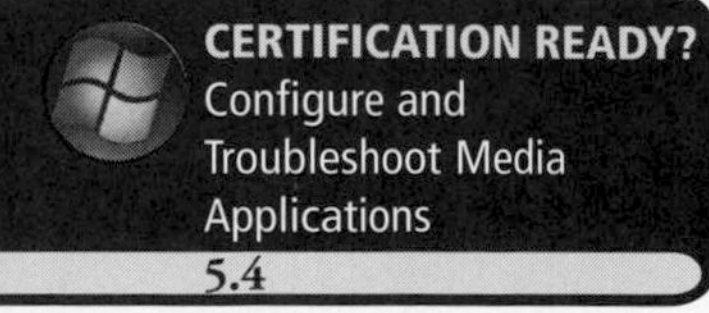

CERTIFICATION READY?
Configure and Troubleshoot Media Applications
5.4

The ever-increasing use of personal computers to work with audio and video files has led to an increased emphasis on multimedia applications, even by the most elementary computer users. Beginners might not concern themselves with producing or editing multimedia files, but they certainly are consumers of them, and applications that store, organize, and play multimedia files are all but ubiquitous.

All Windows Vista editions include some multimedia applications, but how many and which ones depends on the edition. All of the editions include Windows Media Player, which provides basic media library and playback functions. However, the Home Premium and Ultimate editions include additional applications, such as Windows Media Center, which provide more advanced multimedia functions.

Working with Windows Media Player

Windows Media Player is capable of enhancing the user experience with content downloaded from the Internet, but you must first configure its privacy options.

Windows Media Player version 11, which is included in all editions of Windows Vista, is a multifaceted application that you can use to play many different types of audio and video files. In addition to playing CDs and certain DVDs, the application can search the computer's drives for media files and maintain a library from which a user can select files to play. Media Player can also enhance the library by automatically downloading information about the media files from the Internet, such as album cover images and track lists.

Configuring Windows Media Player

When users run Windows Media player for the first time, they have to configure the application. Most users can simply choose the Express Settings option, but desktop technicians should be familiar with the various settings, as described in the following configuration procedure:

CONFIGURE MEDIA PLAYER

GET READY. Log on to Windows Vista. When the logon process is completed, close the Welcome Center window and any other windows that appear.

1. Click **Start**, point to **All Programs**, and then click **Windows Media Player.** The Welcome to Windows Media Player 11 for Windows Vista page appears, as shown in Figure 9-66.

Figure 9-66

The Welcome to Windows Media Player 11 for Windows Vista page

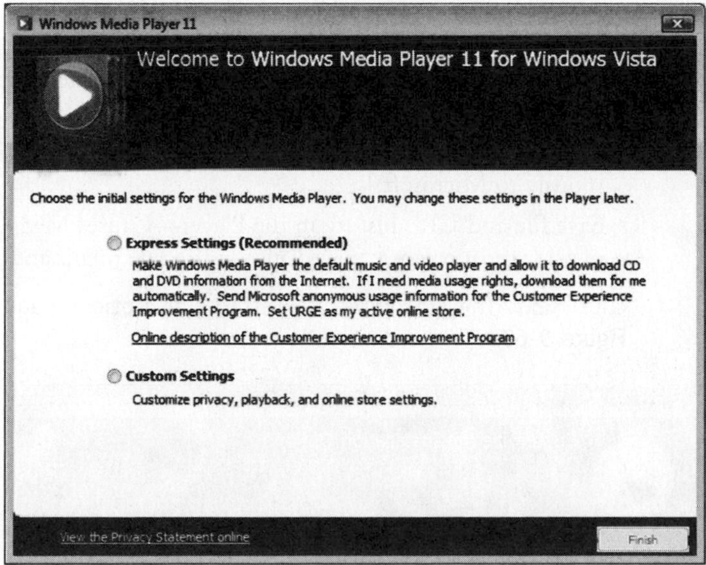

2. Select the **Custom Settings** option, and then click **Next.** The Select Privacy Options page appears, as shown in Figure 9-67.

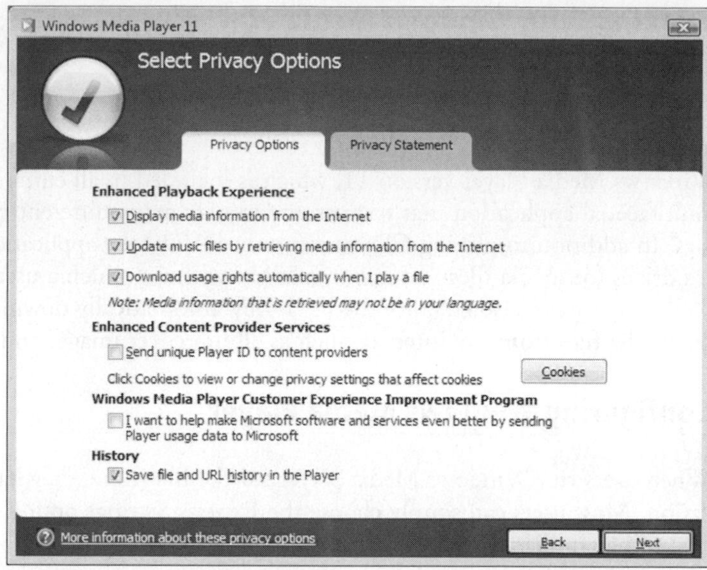

Figure 9-67

The Select Privacy Options page

3. Select the corresponding checkboxes to activate the following settings, if desired.
   - Display media information from the Internet—Causes Media Player to send the CD or DVD identifier for the disk you are playing to a server on the Internet, from which it can download media information.
   - Update music files by retrieving media information from the Internet—Causes Media Player to update the music files in the library with media information downloaded from the Internet, when available.
   - Download usage rights automatically when I play a file—Causes Media Player to automatically download media usage rights from the Internet when you play or synchronize a protected file that doesn't have the appropriate rights.
   - Send unique Player ID to content providers—Causes Media Player to generate a unique identifier and send it to Internet servers from which you are streaming data.
   - I want to help make Microsoft software and services even better by sending Player usage data to Microsoft—Causes Media Player to send usage information anonymously to Microsoft.
   - Save file and URL history in the Player—Causes Media Player to retain the names of your most recently played files in the File menu and the Open dialog box.
4. Click **Next.** The Customize the Installation Options page appears, as shown in Figure 9-68.

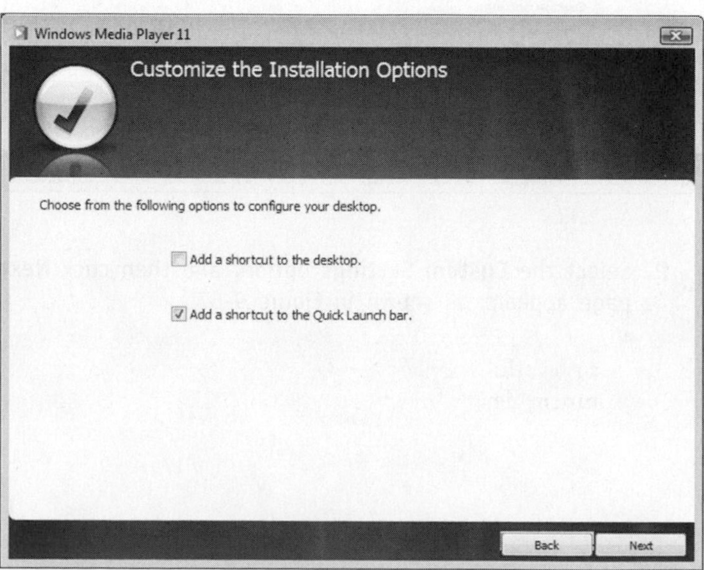

Figure 9-68

The Customize the Installation Options page

5. Specify whether you want a Media Player icon on the desktop, in the Quick Launch toolbar, both, or neither. Then click **Next.** The Select the Default Music and Video Player page appears, as shown in Figure 9-69.

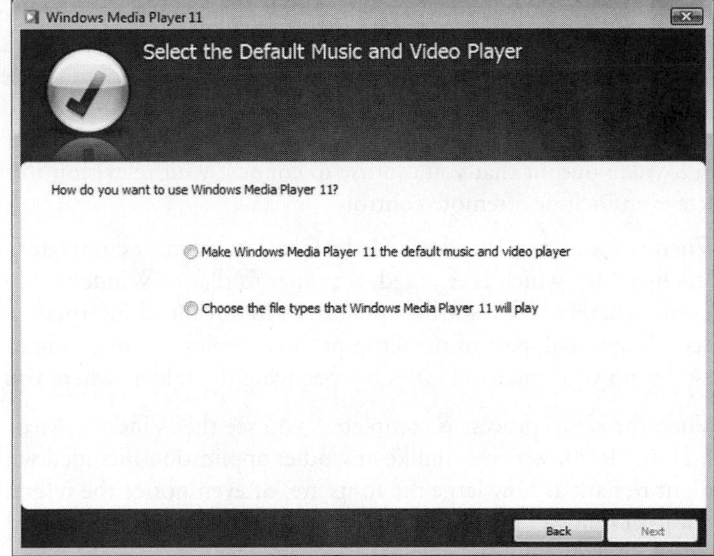

Figure 9-69

The Select the Default Music and Video Player page

6. Select whether Media Player should be the default application for all audio and video files or whether you want to select the file types that should default to Media Player. Then click **Next.** The Choose an Online Store page appears.

If you choose to select the file types for Media Player, a Set Program Associations dialog box appears in which you can choose from a list of file types.

7. Specify whether you want to configure Media Player to access an online store or not, and then click **Next.** Media Player searches the computer's local drives for media files, adds them to the library, and then displays the contents in the Library screen.
8. Close Media Player.

Understanding Digital Rights Management

Digital right management (DRM) is a method that media providers use to ensure that the media files they rent or sell are not misused. For example, when you purchase a song from an online music store, you might be paying only for the right to save the song in your library and play it on your computer. Once Media Player downloads the appropriate rights from the content provider, it will play the song, but it won't allow you to burn the song to an audio CD or copy it to your MP3 player unless you have also purchased the rights to perform those tasks.

Configuring Windows Media Center

Microsoft designed Windows Media Center to replace other home entertainment appliances, such as digital video recorders, but it requires specialized hardware to reach its full potential.

While all editions of Windows Vista include the Windows Media Player Application, only the Home Premium and Ultimate editions include Windows Media Center. Windows Media Center is a powerful application that can perform the same functions as most of the electronic entertainment devices in the average home. With the right hardware, Media Center can do all of the following tasks:

- Play CDs and DVDs
- Play digital audio and video files

TAKE NOTE*

In addition to this specialized hardware, a computer should have sufficient processor speed, memory, and especially hard disk space for Media Center to run properly. Video files can be enormously large, and the computer must have the resources to handle them properly.

- Send video output to your television set
- Record and play back television programs, just like a digital video recorder
- Burn recorded video files to DVDs

To take full advantage of Media Center's capabilities, the Windows Vista computer must have some specialized hardware. Obviously, a DVD burner is required to burn recorded or downloaded video files to disks. To use Media Center's digital video recording capabilities, the computer must have a digital cable tuner with a connection to a television provider. Digital cable tuners are available in the form of expansion cards and USB devices, and many include an S-video output that you can use to connect your television to the computer. Some products even include a remote control.

When you first run Windows Media Center, you must complete a two-part setup procedure. The first part, which is required, is similar to that of Windows Media Player, in which you specify whether you want the application to download information about your media files. The second, optional, part of the setup process enables you to configure and test your hardware and also set up your media libraries by specifying the folders where you store your media files.

When the setup process is completed, you see the Windows Media Center interface, shown in Figure 9-70, which is unlike any other application included with Windows Vista. You might remark at how large the fonts are, or even notice the resemblance to the menu screen of a DVD movie. In fact, the application is designed to be viewed from across the room, and navigated with the cursor buttons on a standard remote control.

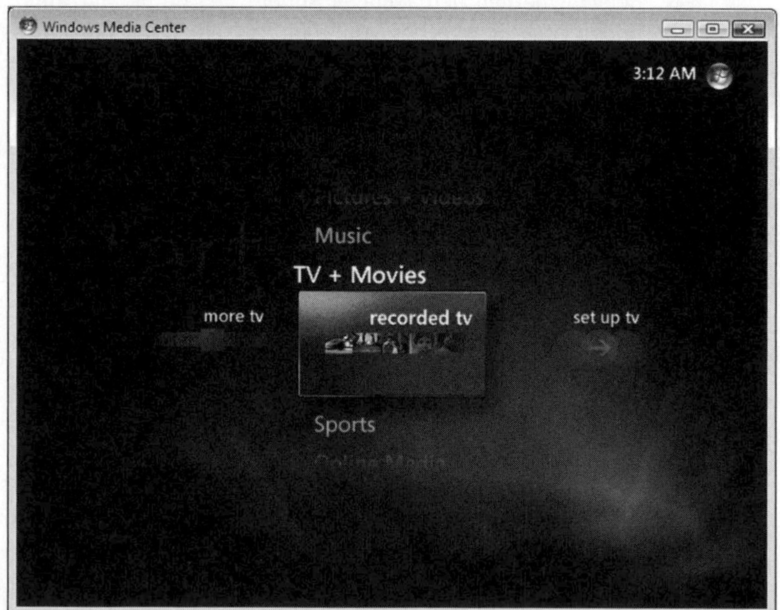

Figure 9-70

The Windows Media Center interface

TAKE NOTE*

If Media Center fails to locate a TV signal, the problem is most likely hardware related. Make sure that the tuner is installed properly and that the connection to the TV provider is functioning. Then retry the procedure.

Installing a Digital Cable Tuner

The options you see during the second phase of the setup process depend on the hardware that Media Center detects in the computer. If there is a digital cable tuner installed in the computer, the Optional Setup page contains a Configure Tuners, TV Signal, and Guide selection. Configuring the tuner hardware is usually a simple, largely automated, process. After selecting the region in which you are located, the system downloads the appropriate settings for the location and offers to configure the TV signal automatically.

When you choose this option, Media Center uses the tuner to scan for a TV signal from whatever device is providing it: an antenna, a direct cable connection, a set-top cable box, or a satellite dish. After you confirm the results of the scan, Media Center proceeds to set up the TV signal and download TV guide listings for your location and service. This enables you to select programs from the onscreen display.

Installing an Extender

You can use Media Center to watch programs on a television set, but in many cases, it might not be convenient to connect the TV directly to the computer. There is an alternative, however, and your users might even already own it. A device called a *media center extender* connects to a standard computer network, either wired or wireless, and also to a TV set. This enables Media Center, running on a computer placed in any location with network access, to send signals to the television.

WARNING Media center extenders designed for use with Windows XP Media Center Edition are not compatible with the Windows Vista Media Center application, with the sole exception of Xbox 360. When shopping for hardware, be sure to select products designed for use with Windows Vista.

The Microsoft Xbox 360 game console includes an integrated media center extender, and there are also stand-alone extenders on the market. Some high-definition televisions and DVD players have extenders built into them as well.

To install an extender in Media Center, select Tasks > Add Extender. The Extender Setup wizard appears. The primary function of the extender setup process is to provide Media Center with exclusive access to the extender hardware. To do this, the wizard prompts you to enter an eight-digit setup key that you must obtain from the extender device itself or the documentation supplied with it. This authentication prevents anyone else from accessing the Media Center signals, which is especially important if the network is wireless.

SUMMARY SKILL MATRIX

In this lesson you learned:
Windows Vista includes the latest version of the Internet Explorer Web browser, Version 7, which includes some important upgrades, including tabbed browsing, tabbed groups, quick tabs, and page zoom.
Many Websites that provide frequently changing content, such as news sites and blogs, support a push technology called RSS, which simplifies the process of delivering updated content to designated users.
By default, the Instant Search box found in all Internet Explorer 7 windows enables users to perform searches using Microsoft's Live Search engine. To use other search engines, you must first add them to the list of search providers.
IE7 has redesigned the Print Preview page to provide users with greater flexibility, both in viewing and formatting the pages to be printed. For example, IE7 adds a default Shrink To Fit setting that reduces each Web page to the point that it will fit on a single sheet of paper.
Protected mode is a way to run Internet Explorer 7 with highly reduced privileges. Windows Vista includes a security feature called Mandatory Integrity Control (MIC), which assigns various integrity access levels to processes running on the computer. These integrity access levels control what system resources the process is allowed to access.
Phishing is a technique that takes social engineering to a mass scale. Instead of convincing-sounding telephone callers, phishing uses convincing-looking Websites that urge users to supply personal information, such as passwords and account numbers. Internet Explorer 7 includes a filter that examines traffic for evidence of phishing activity and displays a warning to the user if it finds any.
To provide different levels of access to specific applications, Internet Explorer 7 divides the addresses accessible with the Web browser into several different security zones, each of which has a different set of privileges.
In the context of Internet Explorer, a cookie is a file containing information about you or your Web-surfing habits that a Website maintains on your computer. IE7 includes a variety of privacy settings you can use to limit the ability of Websites to create cookies on a Windows Vista computer.

(continued)

Windows Mail is the standard e-mail and news client included with Windows Vista, replacing the Outlook Express application of previous versions. Windows Mail includes some important new features, such as Instant Search, a junk mail filter, and a phishing filter.

Configuring the junk mail filter enables you to create a balance between junk mail that makes it into your inbox and legitimate mail that ends up in the junk mail folder.

Windows Contacts is a versatile application where you can store information about the people you communicate with on a regular basis.

Internet newsgroups are text-based messaging forums that participants around the world use to discuss topics of interest such as operating systems, television shows, software, politics, sex, religion, and virtually every other conceivable subject. Before you can access the messages in a newsgroup, you must have a newsreader program, such as the one provided by Windows Mail, and access to a news server.

Windows Meeting Space is the Windows Vista collaboration tool that replaces the NetMeeting application in previous Windows versions. With Windows Meeting Space, you can collaborate on a single document with up to ten users at remote locations, or perform real-time demonstrations by sharing your desktop with remote users.

Windows Calendar is a simple scheduling program that can share its data with other users on a network.

Windows Fax and Scan is a Windows Vista application that enables you to send and receive faxes using a scanner and a modem with faxing capabilities.

All Windows Vista editions include Windows Media Player, which provides basic media library and playback functions. The Home Premium and Ultimate editions include Windows Media Center, which provides more advanced multimedia functions.

Knowledge Assessment

Fill in the Blank

Complete the following sentences by writing the correct word or words in the blanks provided.

1. A podcast is a type of ______________.
2. A(n) ______________ server stores all of your e-mail messages on the server permanently.
3. The two security zones in Internet Explorer 7 that have no sites in them by default are ______________ and ______________.
4. The server that you use to send outgoing e-mail messages is called a(n) ______________ server.
5. Newsgroups use the ______________ protocol for communications between servers.
6. The only Internet Explorer 7 security zone that runs in protected mode is the ______________ zone.
7. Faxing in Windows Vista is accomplished by sending documents to a special ______________ driver.
8. In Windows Vista, the Windows Meeting Space application replaces the ______________ application from Windows XP.
9. Windows Mail no longer supports the ______________ mail server previously supported by Outlook Express.
10. Media files protected by ______________ can only be used in ways specified by the content provider.

True / False

Circle T if the statement is true or F if the statement is false.

T | F 1. Quick tabs are real-time thumbnails of all the Web pages open in a single Internet Explorer window.

T | F 2. To subscribe to an RSS feed, you must pay a fee to the Internet Engineering Task Force.

T | F 3. Phishing is a method for extracting personal information from the data packets transmitted by Internet Explorer.

T | F 4. Windows Mail can use POP3 servers to retrieve incoming mail.

T | F 5. Windows Meeting Space enables two users at different locations to edit the same document at the same time.

T | F 6. To publish a calendar with Windows Calendar, you must have an ISP with a Web server that supports the application.

T | F 7. The fact that Internet Explorer 7 runs in protected mode means that it has a low integrity access level.

T | F 8. Windows Mail is able to access newsgroups, but only if you have access to a news server.

T | F 9. The phishing mail filter in Windows Mail enables you to block all mail originating from a specific top-level domain.

T | F 10. To use Windows Media Center, you must have a television set connected to your Windows Vista computer.

Review Questions

1. Describe the process by which binary files are distributed through Internet newsgroups.
2. List the three ways that you can resolve a Web-based application's incompatibility with Internet Explorer 7's protected mode.

Case Scenarios

Scenario #1: Preventing Phishing Attempts

Several employees at the company you work for have recently been victims of identity theft. These incidents were the result of e-mails received by the victims requesting that they supply personal bank account information to a Website or risk having their accounts closed. The Website was, of course, bogus, and attackers used the information collected there to transfer funds from the victims' accounts. The company has recently upgraded all of the company workstations to Windows Vista, and you are examining the capabilities of the phishing filter in the new Internet Explorer 7 browser. Your superiors have told you that you can use any of the new IE7 security features for the company workstations, as long as they do not consume any additional Internet bandwidth.

Explain to your supervisor the various methods IE7 uses to protect against phishing attacks, and specify which ones you intend to use for the company workstations.

Scenario #2: Configuring Windows Mail

You are working in the service department of a retail computer store, and a customer comes in with a laptop computer. He wants you to configure Windows Mail to access his Internet e-mail. You tell the customer that you will be glad to do this, but first he must obtain some information from his Internet service provider. Make a list of all the information he must obtain for you to configure Windows Mail for him.

Optimizing Windows Vista Performance

OBJECTIVE DOMAIN MATRIX

Technology Skill	Objective Domain	Objective Number
Using the Windows Update Client	Configure Windows Update	6.3
Applying Updates	Configure Windows Update • Restore hidden updates • View Update History • Configure Update settings	6.3
Using Event Viewer	Troubleshoot reliability issues by using built-in diagnostic tools • Event Log	6.2
Using Performance Information and Tools	Troubleshoot performance issues • Use the Performance Center to troubleshoot performance issues	6.1
	Troubleshoot reliability issues by using built-in diagnostic tools • System Performance Rating tool	6.2
Introducing ReadyBoost	Troubleshoot performance issues • Implement ReadyBoost	6.1
Using ReadyBoost	Troubleshoot performance issues • Configure USB device for ReadyBoost • Page File vs. Solid State hard drive	6.1
Using Reliability Monitor	Troubleshoot reliability issues by using built-in diagnostic tools	6.2
Using the Reliability and Performance Monitor Console	Troubleshoot performance issues	6.1

KEY TERMS

Background Intelligent Transfer Service (BITS)
channel
events
ReadyBoost
SuperFetch
Systems Management Server (SMS)
Windows Server Update Services (WSUS)

■ Updating Windows Vista

THE BOTTOM LINE

Keeping Windows Vista systems updated with the latest software is one of the primary tasks of the desktop technician, and you should be familiar with types of update releases and the methods for deploying updates.

The process by which software is designed and developed has evolved over the years, not only in the tools and languages used to do the job, but also in the release strategies. At one time, software products were small enough and simple enough to be distributed on a few floppy disks. Today, a Windows operating system release consists of gigabytes of data; this increase in size is a reflection of the software's increased complexity.

One of the results of this complexity is that it is no longer practical to issue occasional updates for applications and operating systems. An operating system such as Windows consists of so many elements that, from a developmental standpoint, it is always a work-in-progress, constantly being updated to correct errors, enhance performance, and add features. Keeping the operating system updated is no longer an optional element of Windows Vista maintenance, justified by the belief that "if it ain't broke, don't fix it." The regular application of operating system updates is imperative, for reasons of compatibility, performance, and most importantly, security. There is no better way to protect a Windows Vista computer than to make sure to apply all of the latest security updates.

Understanding Update Types

Microsoft updates its operating systems frequently by issuing software updates in several forms.

Microsoft releases operating system updates on the 12th of each month, with occasional, additional releases when an issue (typically involving security) requires an immediate response. The updates that Microsoft releases typically take one of the following forms:

- Hotfixes—A hotfix is an update consisting of one or more files designed to address a specific problem or issue with the operating system. Some hotfixes are intended for all Windows users, and are released using the Windows Update Website, while others are intended for special circumstances and are released only to users experiencing a particular problem.
- Security Updates—A security update is a hotfix designed to address a particular vulnerability in Windows Vista security. In addition to the software itself, security updates include a security bulletin and a Knowledge Base article that discuss the nature and severity of the problem.
- Cumulative Updates (or Rollups)—Over time, Microsoft releases a large number of updates, and a cumulative update is a distribution method that consolidates all of the updates for a particular operating system element or application, such as Internet Explorer or Internet Information Services. Downloading and installing a single rollup is far easier than applying many different updates. Rollups typically undergo more testing than individual hotfixes, and because they are always installed together they provide a more stable platform than individually installed hotfixes.
- Service Packs—A service pack is a cumulative set of all updates for a particular operating system version since its original release. Unlike updates, service packs can contain new or enhanced features. More than any other type of update, service packs are extensively tested until Microsoft is confident that all users can safely apply them. To a certain degree, service packs are an extension of the operating system release itself. Once a service pack is released, Microsoft and original equipment manufacturer (OEM) providers typically distribute Windows with the service pack integrated into the installation.

In addition to these release types, Microsoft classifies updates using the following categories:

- Critical Updates—Updates that address important issues that require immediate attention and which all users should install. The Windows Update application always downloads all available critical updates by default.
- Recommended Updates—Updates that address less important issues or that apply only to certain users. You can configure Windows Update to download recommended updates along with critical updates, or ignore them.
- Optional Updates—Updates that contain enhancements or new features that are not essential for the proper functioning of the operating system.
- Device Drivers—Microsoft uses Windows Update to distribute fully tested and digitally signed device drivers for some hardware products.

Evaluating Updates

Despite all of the update testing that Microsoft performs, incompatibilities can occur, and individual testing is strongly recommended.

As mentioned earlier, Microsoft tests its update releases with varying degrees of thoroughness, depending on the complexity of the update and the time factor involved. Service packs can go through months of testing, including an extensive beta testing program, while some security updates are rushed to release because they address a time-critical vulnerability. No matter how much testing Microsoft does, however, it cannot possibly test every combination of hardware and software installed on millions of Windows computers, and incompatibilities do occur.

For this reason, network administrators should perform their own testing before deploying any updates to production computers. The testing methodology is usually dependent on the size of the network and the resources available to its administrators. For a large organization, it is a good idea to perform test deployments on an isolated lab network. This is not practical for most small businesses, though, so they might have to simply install the update on a single production computer and let it run for a while before performing a deployment to the rest of the network.

TAKE NOTE*

Home users often have no choice but to install updates on their computers, and then see if any problems occur. Fortunately, virtually all Windows updates have uninstall capabilities that enable you to roll a system back to its previous state.

If you are a desktop technician for a large organization, you are more likely to be involved in the actual update testing process than in the creation of the company or departmental policy defining the testing methodology. However, if you service individual customers, you might be forced to decide whether to recommend specific updates for your clients. In this case, it is up to you to remain informed about issues involving the latest update releases. For example, some technicians deliberately avoid installing new service pack releases for several weeks or months, to make sure that major compatibility issues do not appear.

Applying Updates

The Windows Update client facilitates the automatic downloading and installation of operating system updates.

Although it is possible to manually update Windows Vista computers by connecting to the Windows Update Website, the Windows Update client included with Vista makes it possible to configure computers to automatically download and install Windows updates as needed. Because Microsoft digitally signs all of its operating system update releases, any user can install them without the need for administrative privileges. This means that the entire process

TAKE NOTE*

Windows XP, Windows Server 2003, and Windows 2000 all include a client called Automatic Updates. For Windows Vista, Microsoft redesigned the client and called it Windows Update.

of downloading and installing updates can occur during non-production hours without user intervention.

Unlike the Automatic Updates client in Windows XP, the Windows Update client in Windows Vista is an independent application that can download updates from any of the following three locations:

- Windows Update—For individual computers and small networks, it is practical to use the default setting, which causes Windows Update to download its updates directly from Microsoft's Windows Update servers on the Internet.
- ***Windows Server Update Services (WSUS)***—For medium to large networks, WSUS is a free product that conserves bandwidth by downloading updates from the Internet once and then providing them to Windows Update clients on the local network. WSUS also enables administrators to select the updates they want to release to the clients, thus giving them the opportunity to evaluate and test the updates first, and then schedule the deployment.
- ***Systems Management Server (SMS)***—For large enterprise networks, SMS is a comprehensive network management tool that administrators can use to deploy all types of software products, including operating system updates. SMS is by far the most advanced and customizable method of deploying updates, but it is a paid product that must be licensed for the appropriate number of clients on the network.

TAKE NOTE*

The Windows Update client connects to the Microsoft Update servers on the Internet by default. To use an alternative SMS or WSUS server on your local network as the source for updates, you must configure the client using local or domain Group Policy settings, as discussed later in this lesson.

Using the Windows Update Client

The Windows Update client included in Windows Vista is a service that launches shortly after the computer starts. Windows Update is a pull client that periodically checks a designated server for the availability of updates. The update process consists of three basic stages, as follows:

CERTIFICATION READY?
Configure Windows Update
6.3

- Detection—At scheduled times, the Windows Update client connects to a designated server, either on the Internet or the company network, downloads the server's list of available updates, and compares the list with the computer's current configuration. The client then flags all of the updates that have not yet been installed on the system for download.

TAKE NOTE*

The Windows Update client can activate a computer that is on standby when it is time to check for updates. If the computer is turned off at the time of a scheduled update, the detection process will begin the next time the computer starts.

- Download—After determining which updates it needs, the client initiates a download using the ***Background Intelligent Transfer Service (BITS)***. BITS is an HTTP-based file transfer service that downloads files using only the network's idle bandwidth. This enables Windows Update to perform downloads without affecting other applications that are using the network. BITS downloads are also resumable, in the event they are interrupted.

TAKE NOTE*

BITS uses whatever idle network bandwidth is available when performing downloads, but it will not initiate a connection on a computer that uses dial-up access to the Internet. In this case, the download process will not start until the user initiates a network connection.

- Installation—By default, the Windows Update client installs updates immediately after downloading them. However, you can also configure the client to hold the updates until the user manually triggers the installation.

When you install Windows Vista, the Setup program displays the screen shown in Figure 10-1, which prompts you to specify whether you want the client to install all updates automatically, install only important updates, or do nothing and prompt you again later.

Figure 10-1

The Windows Update window

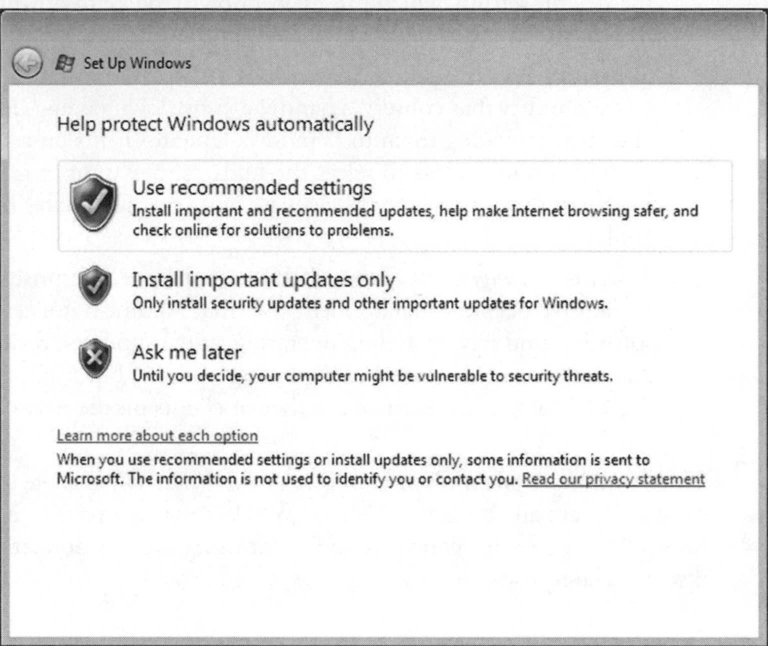

This screen provides only limited access to the Windows Update client. For example, you cannot choose to download updates and select the ones you want to install. Even if you are planning to reconfigure the client later, you might want to select the *Use recommended settings* option.

When you activate the client during the Windows installation, the computer performs an update as soon as it detects a connection to the Internet. This minimizes the system's potential vulnerability by applying the latest security updates as soon as possible after the installation. In addition, Windows Update downloads and installs drivers for hardware devices that have no driver installed or that are using generic drivers.

Once the operating system is fully installed, you can reconfigure the Windows Update client to make full use of its capabilities. The procedures for using and configuring the Windows Update client are discussed in the following sections.

Triggering an Update

Although the real benefit of the Windows Update client is the ability to automate the update process, it is also possible to manually trigger an update. To trigger an update, use the following procedure:

TRIGGER AN UPDATE

GET READY. Log on to Windows Vista using an account with administrative privileges. When the logon process is completed, close the Welcome Center window and any other windows that appear.

1. Click **Start**, and then click **Control Panel**. The Control Panel window appears.
2. Click **System and Maintenance > Windows Update**. The Windows Update window appears, as shown in Figure 10-2.

Figure 10-2

The Windows Update window

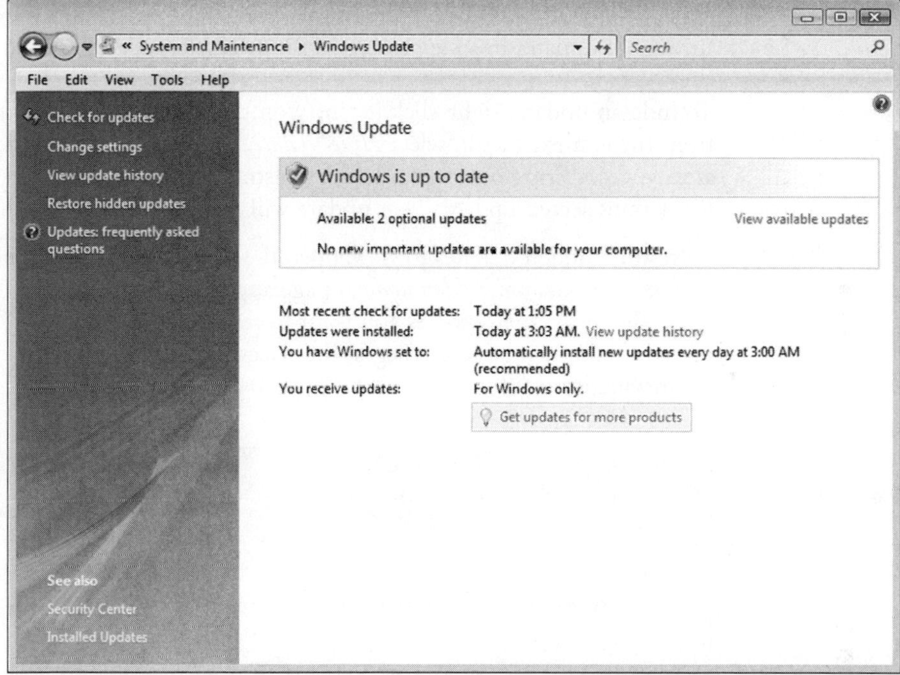

3. Click **Check for updates.** The client connects to the source server and determines whether there are any updates that need to be installed.
4. If the client finds and downloads any updates, click **View available updates.** The *Choose the updates you want to install* page appears, as shown in Figure 10-3.

Figure 10-3

The Choose the updates you want to install page

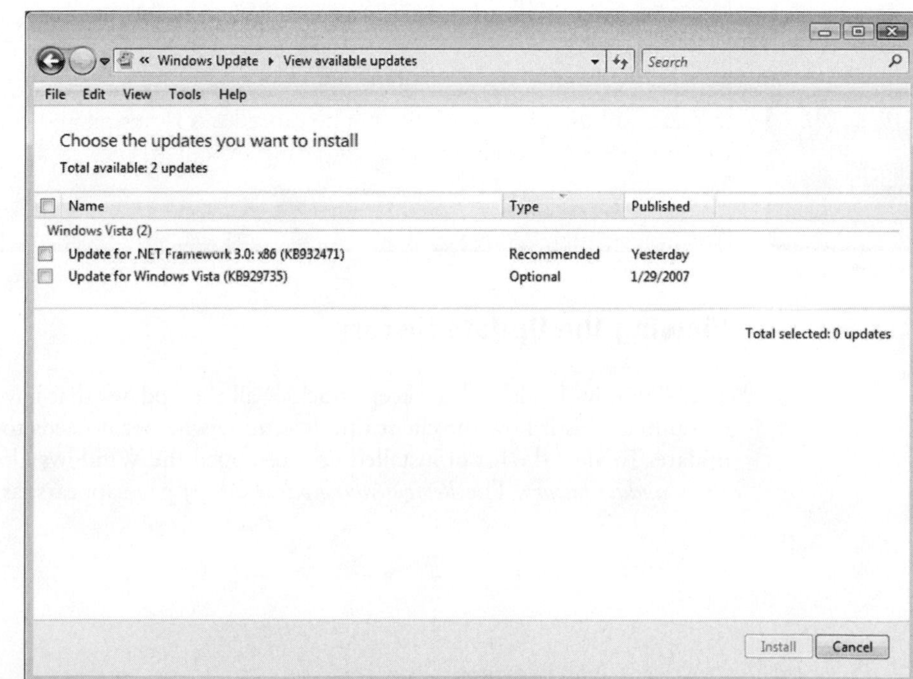

5. Double-click each update to display information about its function and links to associated articles on the Internet.
6. Select the checkbox for each update you want to install and click **Install**. The client installs the selected updates.

Hiding Updates

In some cases, there might be updates that you do not want to install on a particular computer. You might have discovered an incompatibility or other problem, or the update might simply not apply to the computer's role or configuration. In this event, you can prevent the unwanted updates from appearing in the available updates list.

To hide an update, right-click its entry on the *Choose the updates you want to install* page and, from the context menu, select *Hide update*. This action requires administrative privileges, so after you confirm your role as an administrator or supply administrative credentials, the client hides the selected update. That update will no longer appear in the list.

To restore hidden updates to view, open the Windows Update window and click *Restore hidden updates*. The *Restore hidden updates* page appears, as shown in Figure 10-4, in which you can select the individual updates you want to restore. Click **Restore**, and after once again invoking your administrative privileges, the selected items will appear in the list of updates available for installation.

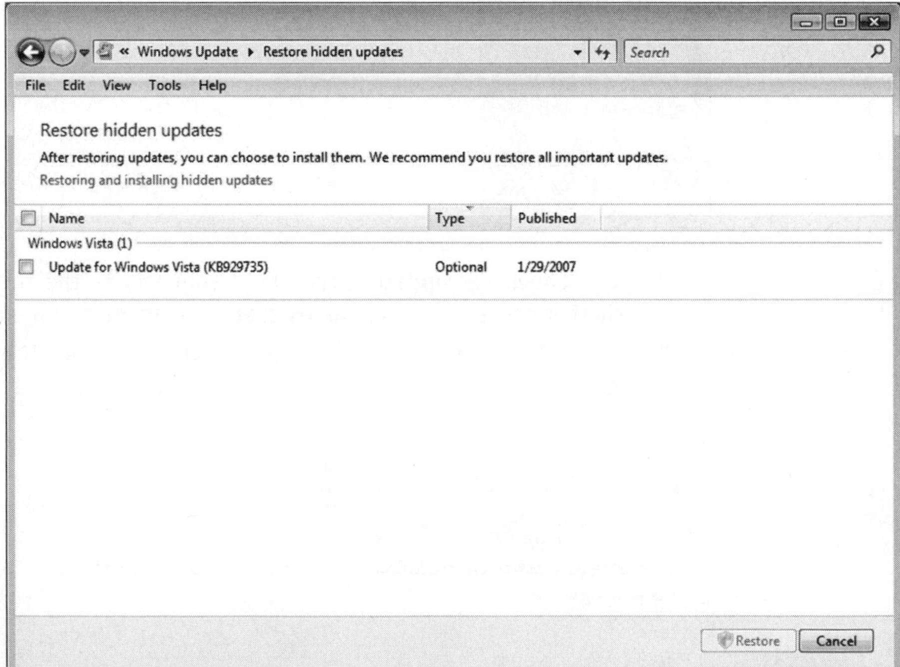

Figure 10-4

The Restore hidden updates page

Viewing the Update History

The Windows Update client keeps track of all the updates that have been installed on the computer. This is how the client can determine whether it needs to download a particular update. To view the list of installed updates, open the Windows Update window and click *View update history*. The *Review your update history* page appears, as shown in Figure 10-5.

Figure 10-5

The Review your update history page

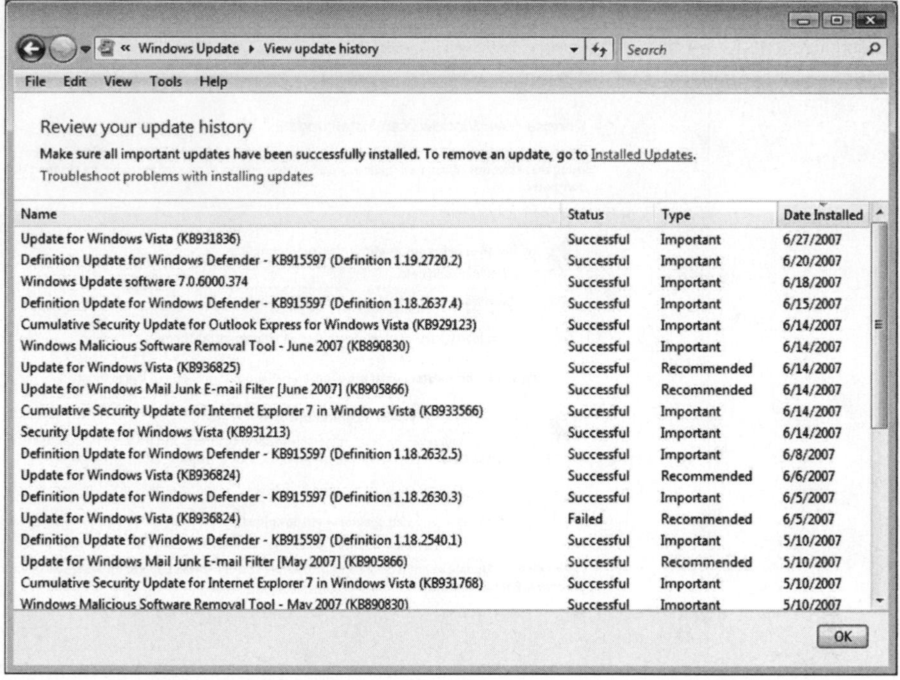

« Windows Update ▸ View update history
Search
File Edit View Tools Help
Review your update history
Make sure all important updates have been successfully installed. To remove an update, go to Installed Updates.
Troubleshoot problems with installing updates
Name Status Type Date Installed
Update for Windows Vista (KB931836) Successful Important 6/27/2007
Definition Update for Windows Defender - KB915597 (Definition 1.19.2720.2) Successful Important 6/20/2007
Windows Update software 7.0.6000.374 Successful Important 6/18/2007
Definition Update for Windows Defender - KB915597 (Definition 1.18.2637.4) Successful Important 6/15/2007
Cumulative Security Update for Outlook Express for Windows Vista (KB929123) Successful Important 6/14/2007
Windows Malicious Software Removal Tool - June 2007 (KB890830) Successful Important 6/14/2007
Update for Windows Vista (KB936825) Successful Recommended 6/14/2007
Update for Windows Mail Junk E-mail Filter [June 2007] (KB905866) Successful Recommended 6/14/2007
Cumulative Security Update for Internet Explorer 7 in Windows Vista (KB933566) Successful Important 6/14/2007
Security Update for Windows Vista (KB931213) Successful Important 6/14/2007
Definition Update for Windows Defender - KB915597 (Definition 1.18.2632.5) Successful Important 6/8/2007
Update for Windows Vista (KB936824) Successful Recommended 6/6/2007
Definition Update for Windows Defender - KB915597 (Definition 1.18.2630.3) Successful Important 6/5/2007
Update for Windows Vista (KB936824) Failed Recommended 6/5/2007
Definition Update for Windows Defender - KB915597 (Definition 1.18.2540.1) Successful Important 5/10/2007
Update for Windows Mail Junk E-mail Filter [May 2007] (KB905866) Successful Recommended 5/10/2007
Cumulative Security Update for Internet Explorer 7 in Windows Vista (KB931768) Successful Important 5/10/2007
Windows Malicious Software Removal Tool - May 2007 (KB890830) Successful Important 5/10/2007
OK

On the *Review your update history* page, each entry specifies the update type, whether it was installed successfully, and the date it was installed. To uninstall an update, click **Installed Updates**.

Configuring the Windows Update Client

Although it is possible to use the Windows Update client interactivity, its real usefulness is evident when you configure it to take the update process out of the user's hands by automatically downloading and installing operating system updates. There are two methods for configuring the client. You can use the Windows Update control panel or you can use Group Policy settings. Group Policy provides a great deal more flexibility, but for home and small business users, the options found in the control panel are usually sufficient.

To configure the Windows Update client with the control panel, use the following procedure:

CONFIGURE WINDOWS UPDATE

GET READY. Log on to Windows Vista using an account with administrative privileges. When the logon process is completed, close the Welcome Center window and any other windows that appear.

1. Click **Start**, and then click **Control Panel**. The Control Panel window appears.
2. Click **System and Maintenance > Windows Update**. The Windows Update window appears.
3. Click **Change settings**. The *Choose how Windows can install updates* page appears, as shown in Figure 10-6.

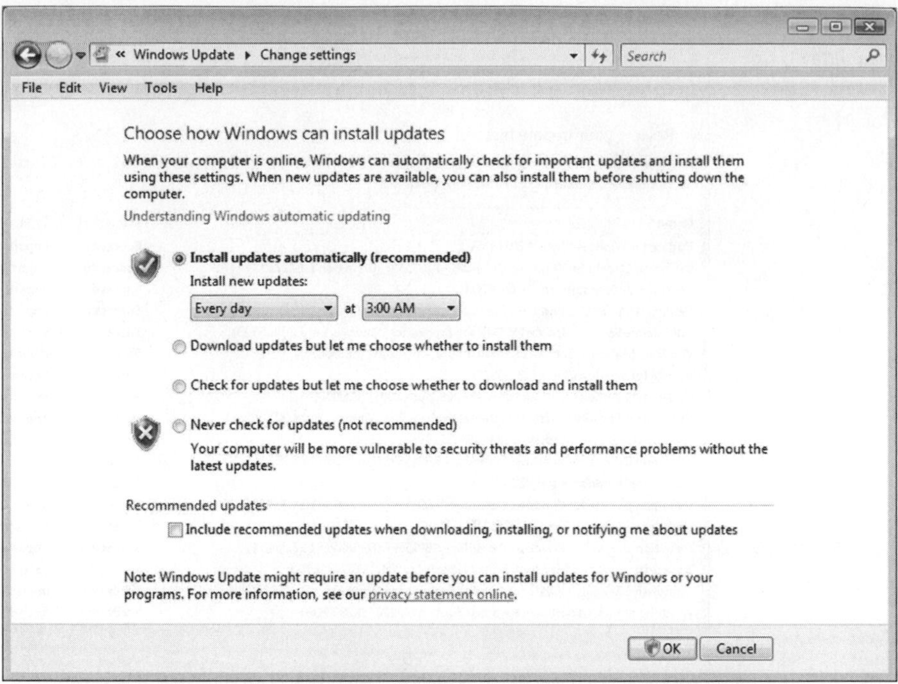

Figure 10-6

The Choose how Windows can install updates page

4. If you did not activate the windows Update client during the Windows Vista installation, do so now by selecting the **Install updates automatically** radio button.
5. Use the *Install new updates* dropdown lists to specify how often and at what time of day you want the client to check for new updates.
6. Select the **Download updates but let me choose whether to install them** option to prevent the client from performing the installation phase of the process. Select the **Check for updates but let me choose whether to download and install them** option to prevent the client from performing both the download and installation phases. Select the **Include recommended updates when downloading, installing, or notifying me about updates** checkbox to force the client to download recommended, as well as critical, updates.
7. Click **OK.** After you confirm your administrative credentials, the system configures the client for automatic updating.

Configuring Windows Update Using Group Policy

In addition to the control panel interface, it is possible to configure the Windows Update client using Group Policy settings. You can use local Group Policy settings to configure the client, but system administrators more commonly distribute the settings using the Active Directory directory service.

Group Policy is the only way to configure the client to check for updates on a local server rather than the Microsoft servers on the Internet. There are also other client options that are not accessible through the standard interface.

To configure the Windows Update client using Group Policy, you must open a group policy object (GPO) using the Group Policy Object Editor snap-in for Microsoft Management Console, as shown in Figure 10-7. On a stand-alone Windows Vista computer, you can apply the GPO to the local system. If you are using an Active Directory network, you must link the GPO to a domain, organizational unit, or site.

Figure 10-7

Windows Update policies in the Group Policy Object Editor

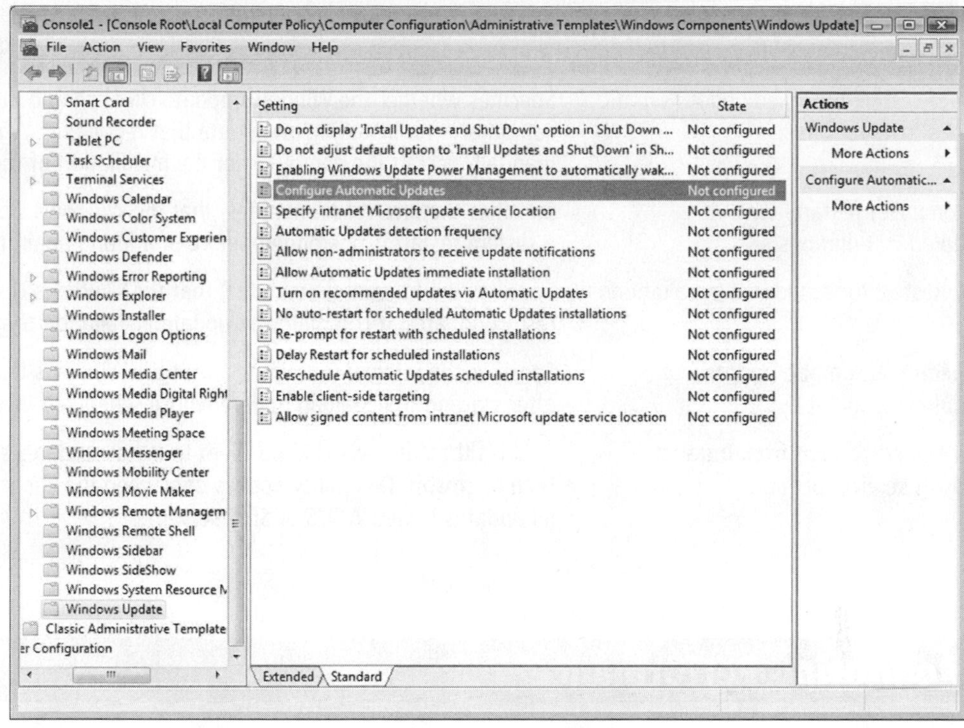

The policies that configure the Windows Update client are found in the Computer Configuration > Administrative Templates > Windows Components > Windows Update container of the GPO. Table 10-1 lists the most important Windows Update policies and their functions.

Table 10-1

Group Policy Settings for the Windows Updates Client

GROUP POLICY SETTING	FUNCTION
Configure Automatic Updates	Activates the Windows Update client and specifies when and how the client should apply updates. This policy performs the same basic functions as the *Choose how windows can install updates* page in the Windows Update control panel.
Specify intranet Microsoft update service location	Enables you to specify an alternative source for Windows updates. By default, the Windows Update client connects to Microsoft servers on the Internet. To configure clients to check a local WSUS or SMS server for updates, you must enable this policy and specify the name of the server.
Automatic Updates detection frequency	Specifies the interval (in hours) that Windows Update clients will wait before checking for updates.
Allow non-administrators to receive update notifications	Specifies whether the notifications that the Windows Update client is configured to generate should be displayed to users without administrative privileges.
Allow Automatic Updates immediate installation	Specifies whether the Windows Update client should install updates that do not require a system restart immediately after downloading them.
Turn on recommended updates via Automatic Updates	Specifies whether the Windows Update client should download recommended, as well as important, updates. This policy performs the same function as the Include Recommended Updates checkbox on the *Choose how Windows can install updates* page in the Windows Update control panel.

(*continued*)

Group Policy Setting	Function
No auto-restart for scheduled Automatic Updates installations	Specifies whether the Windows update client should automatically restart the computer after installing an update that requires it. When disabled, a user must manually restart the computer for the installation of the update to be completed.
Re-prompt for restarts with scheduled installations	Specifies the interval (in minutes) that the Windows Update client will wait after a system restart is postponed before prompting again for a restart.
Delay Restart for scheduled installations	Specifies the interval (in minutes) that the Windows Update client will wait before restarting, after it completes an update installation that requires a restart.
Reschedule Automatic Updates scheduled installations	Specifies the interval (in minutes) that the Windows Update client should wait after starting to install an update whose scheduled installation was missed.
Allow signed content from intranet Microsoft service location	Enables the Windows Update client to install updates signed by entities other than Microsoft. This policy applies only when the client is configured to download its updates from a WSUS or SMS server.

Monitoring Performance

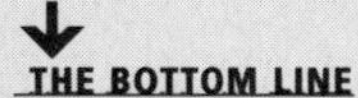

For a computer to perform well, all of its components must be individually efficient. Windows Vista includes a variety of tools that enable you to locate components whose performance is below par.

A computer's level of performance is based on a combination of factors, any of which can function as a bottleneck that slows down the entire system. For example, a Windows Vista computer might have an extremely fast processor, but if it is lacking in memory, it will have to page data to the swap file on the hard drive more often, slowing down the system. In the same way, a computer might have a fast processor and plenty of memory, but if its hard drive is slow, the faster components can't run at peak efficiency.

Hardware problems are not the only cause of performance degradations. Software incompatibilities and resource depletion can also affect performance. In essence, the task of optimizing the performance of a Windows Vista computer consists of locating the bottlenecks and eliminating them. This might require a hardware upgrade or a reexamination of the computer's suitability to its role. Whatever the solution, the first step in determining what factors are negatively affecting the computer's performance is to quantify that performance and monitor its fluctuations.

The following sections examine some of the tools provided by Windows Vista, which enable you to gather information about the computer's ongoing performance levels.

Using Event Viewer

The Event Viewer console has been enhanced in Windows Vista to provide easier access to a more comprehensive array of event logs.

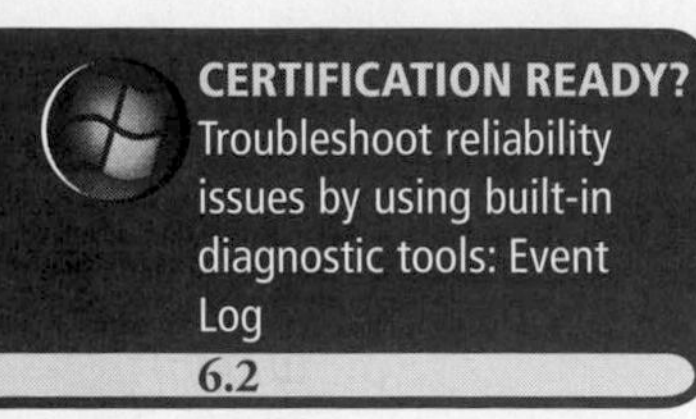

CERTIFICATION READY?
Troubleshoot reliability issues by using built-in diagnostic tools: Event Log
6.2

Windows has maintained the same three basic logs throughout several versions: Software developers commonly use logs as a means of tracking the activities of particular algorithms, routines, and applications. A log is a list of events, which can track the activity of the software, document errors, and provide analytical information to administrators. Logs are traditionally text files, but the Windows operating systems have long used a graphical application called Event Viewer to display the log information gathered by the operating system.

Windows has maintained the same three basic logs throughout several versions: a System log, a Security log, and an Application log. Servers performing certain roles have additional logs, such as those tracking DNS and File Replication activities. The format of these logs has remained consistent, although the Event Viewer has undergone some changes. In Windows Server 2003 and Windows XP, Event Viewer first took the form of an MMC snap-in, rather than an independent application.

Windows Vista and Windows Server 2008 represent the most comprehensive overhaul of the Windows Eventing engine in many years. Windows Eventing 6.0 includes the following enhancements:

- The addition of a Setup log documenting the operating system's installation and configuration history
- New logs for key applications and services, including DFS Replication and the Key Management Service
- Individual logs for Windows components
- Enhanced querying capabilities that simplify the process of locating specific events
- The ability to create subscriptions that enable administrators to collect and store specific types of events from other computers on the network

Launching the Event Viewer Console

The primary function of the Windows Eventing engine is to record information about system activities as they occur and package that information in individual units called ***events***. The application you use to view the events is an MMC snap-in called Event Viewer. As with all MMC snap-ins, you can launch the Event Viewer console in a variety of ways, including the following:

- Click Start, then click Control Panel > System and Maintenance > Administrative Tools > Event Viewer.
- Open a blank MMC console and add the Event Viewer snap-in.
- Open the Run dialog box or a Command Prompt window and key Eventvwr.msc.
- Open the Computer Management console and expand the Event Viewer node.

Using the Overview and Summary Display

When the Event Viewer console appears, you see the Overview and Summary display shown in Figure 10-8.

Figure 10-8

The Overview and Summary screen in the Event Viewer console

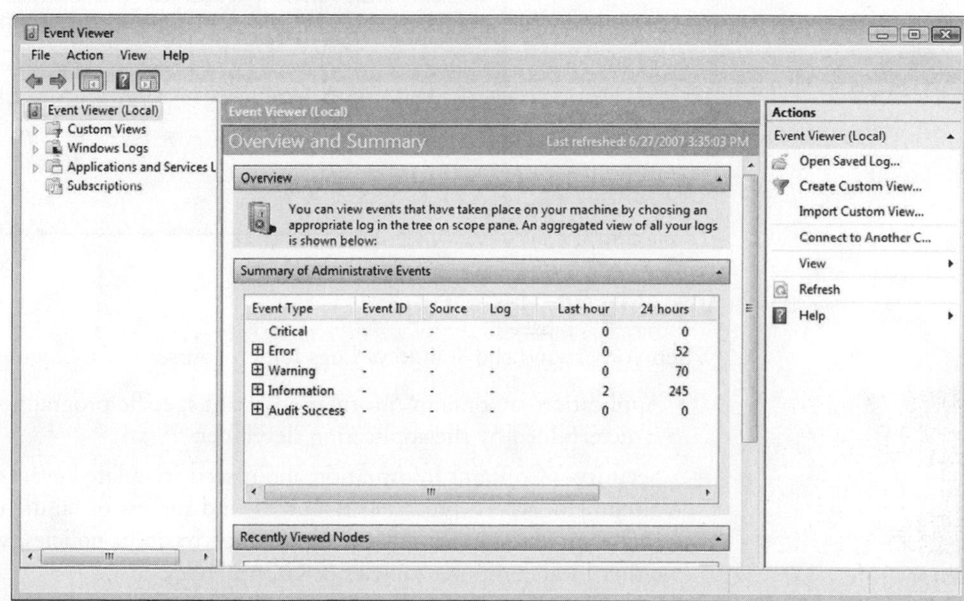

The Summary of Administrative Events displays the total number of events recorded in the last hour, day, and week, sorted by event type. When you expand an event type, the list is broken down by event ID, as shown in Figure 10-9.

Figure 10-9

The Event ID breakdown in the Event Viewer console

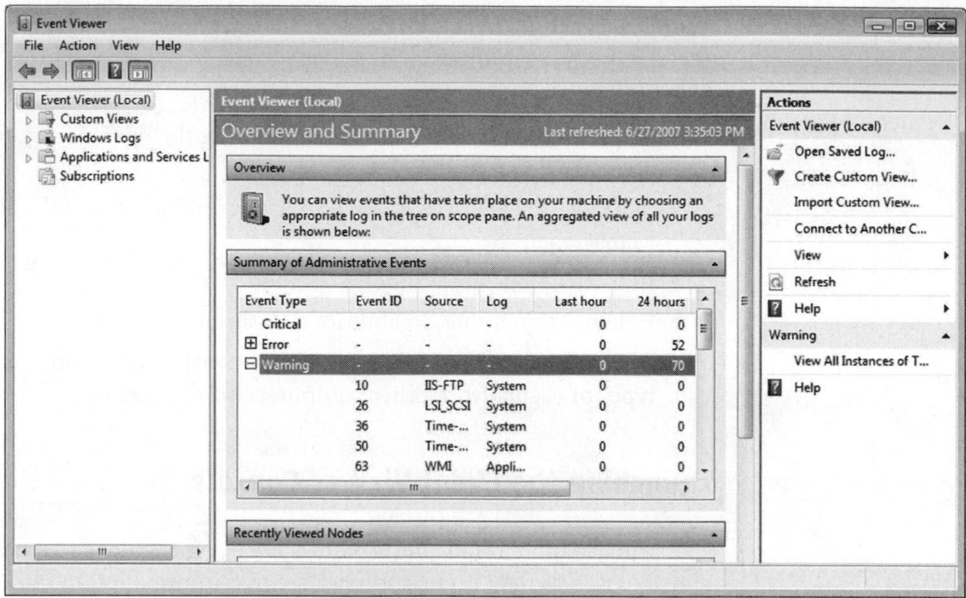

When you double-click one of the event IDs, the console creates a filtered custom view that displays only the events having that ID, as shown in Figure 10-10.

Figure 10-10

A custom view in the Event Viewer console

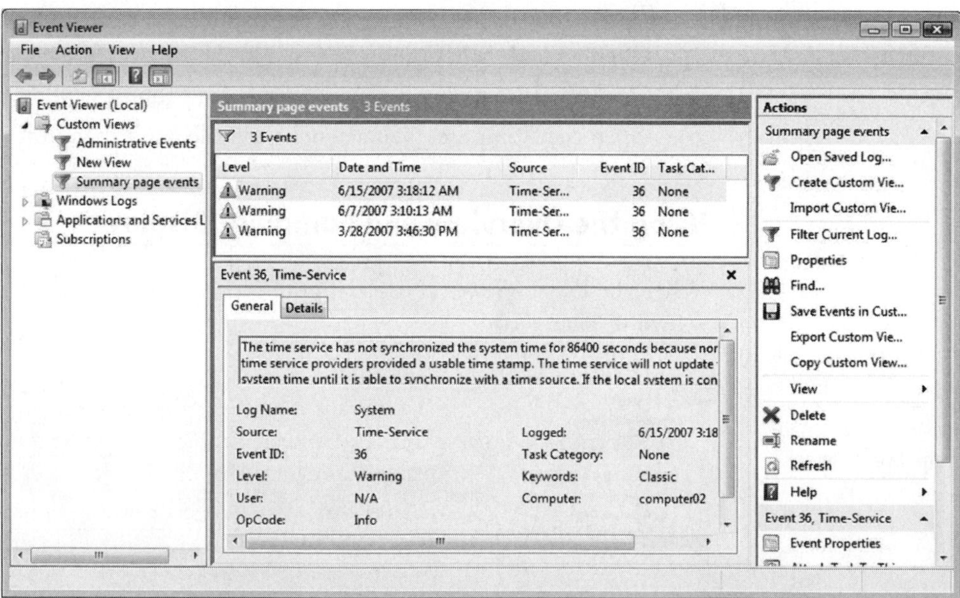

Viewing Windows Logs

When you expand the Windows Logs folder, you see the following logs:

- Application—Contains information about specific programs running on the computer, as determined by the application developer.
- Security—Contains information about security-related events, such as failed logons, attempts to access protected resources, and success or failure of audited events. The events recorded in this log are determined by audit policies, which you can enable using either local computer policies or Group Policy.

- Setup—Contains information about the operating system installation and setup history.
- System—Contains information about events generated by the operating system, such as services and device drivers. For example, a failure of a service to start or a driver to load during system startup is recorded in the System log.
- Forwarded Events—Contains events received from other computers on the network via subscriptions.

TAKE NOTE*

The System log is the primary Windows Vista operational log. You should always view this log first when looking for general information about system problems.

Selecting one of the logs causes a list of the events it contains to appear in the details pane, in reverse chronological order, as shown in Figure 10-11.

Figure 10-11

Contents of a log in the Event Viewer console

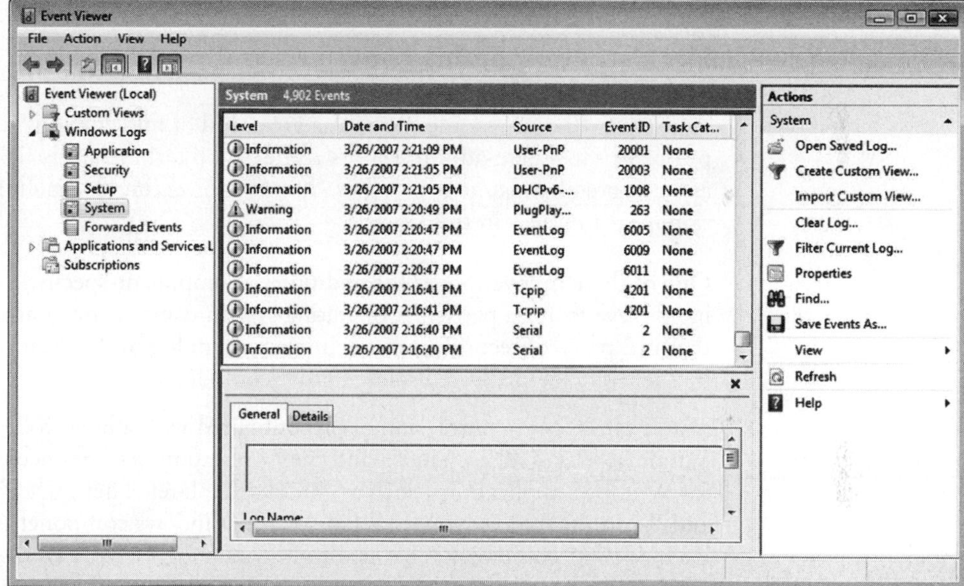

The Windows event logs contain different types of events, which are identified by icons. The four event types are as follows:

- Information—An event that describes a change in the state of a component or process as part of a normal operation.
- Error—An event that warns of a problem that is not likely to affect the performance of the component or process where the problem occurred, but that could affect the performance of other components or processes on the system.
- Warning—An event that warns of a service degradation or an occurrence that can potentially cause a service degradation in the near future, unless you take steps to prevent it.
- Critical—An event that warns that an incident resulting in a catastrophic loss of functionality or data in a component or process has occurred.

When you select one of the events in the list of events, its properties appear in the preview pane at the bottom of the list. You can also double-click an event to display a separate Event Properties dialog box, as shown in Figure 10-12.

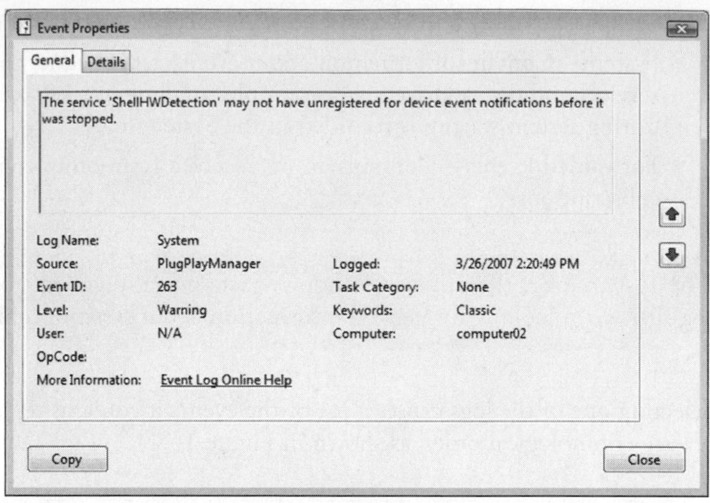

Figure 10-12

An Event Properties dialog box

Viewing Component Logs

The Event Viewer console contains a great deal of information, and one of the traditional problems for system administrators and desktop technicians is finding the events they need amidst an embarrassment of riches. Windows Eventing 6.0 includes a number of innovations that can help in this regard.

One of these innovations is the addition of component-specific logs that enable you to examine the events for a particular operating system component or application. Any component that is capable of recording events in the System log or Application log can also record events in a separate log dedicated solely to that component.

The Event Viewer console comes preconfigured with a large collection of component logs for Windows Vista. When you expand the Applications and Services Logs folder, you see logs for Windows applications, such as Internet Explorer. Then, when you expand the Microsoft and Windows folders, you see a long list of Windows components, as shown in Figure 10-13. Each of these components has its own separate log, called a ***channel***.

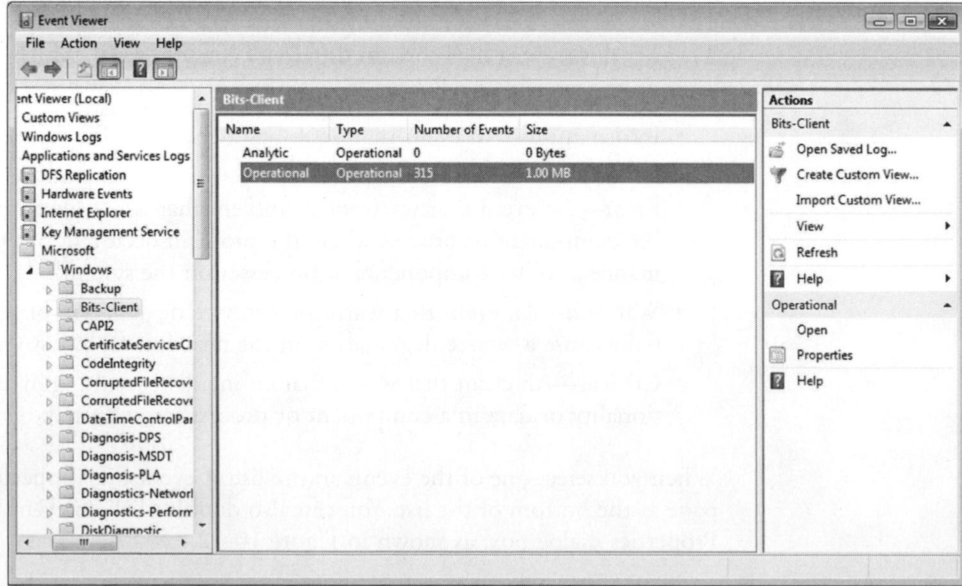

Figure 10-13

Windows component logs in the Event Viewer console

In most cases, the events in the component logs are non-administrative, meaning that they are not indicative of problems or errors. The components continue to save the administrative events to the System log or Application log. The events in the component logs are operational, analytic, or debug events, which means that they are more descriptive entries that document the ongoing activities of the component. The component logs are intended more for use in troubleshooting long-term problems and for software developers seeking debugging information.

Creating Custom Views

Another means of locating and isolating information about specific events is to use custom views. A custom view is essentially a filtered version of a particular log, configured to display only certain events. The Event Viewer console now has a Custom Views folder in which you can create filtered views and save them for later use.

To create a custom view, use the following procedure:

CREATE A CUSTOM VIEW

GET READY. Log on to Windows Vista. When the logon process is completed, close the Welcome Center window and any other windows that appear.

1. Click **Start**, and then click **Control Panel > System and Maintenance > Administrative Tools > Event Viewer**. After you confirm your action, the Event Viewer console appears.
2. Right-click the **Custom Views** folder and then, from the context menu, select **Create Custom View**. The Create Custom View dialog box appears, as shown in Figure 10-14.

Figure 10-14

The Create Custom View dialog box

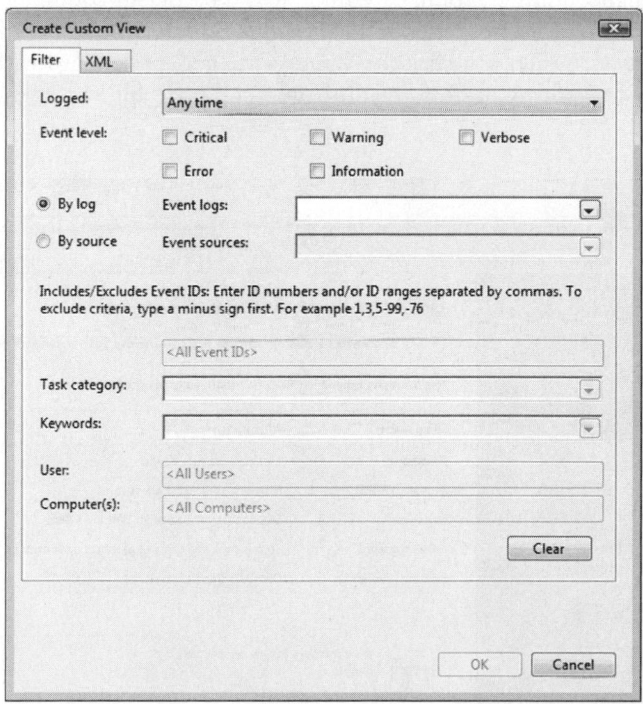

3. From the Logged dropdown list, select the time interval from which you want to display events.
4. In the *Event level* area, select the checkboxes for the types of events you want to display.
5. From the *By log* dropdown list, select the log(s) from which you want to display events. Alternatively, from the *By source* list select the source(s) from which you want to display events.
6. Optionally, you can specify event ID numbers, task categories, keywords, and user credentials to narrow your search.
7. Click **OK**. The Save Filter to Custom View dialog box appears, as shown in Figure 10-15.

Figure 10-15

The Save Filter to Custom View dialog box

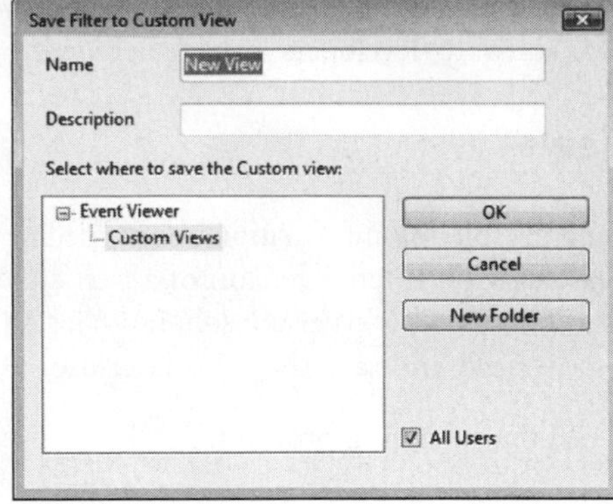

CERTIFICATION READY?
Troubleshoot performance issues: Use the Performance Center to troubleshoot performance issues
Troubleshoot reliability issues by using built-in diagnostic tools: System Performance Rating tool
6.1, 6.2

8. Key a name for the view in the Name text box, a description if desired, and select the folder in which you want to create your custom view. Then click **OK**. The console adds your view to the folder you selected and displays the view in the detail pane.

Using Performance Information and Tools

In Lesson 3, "Configuring System Settings," you learned how to run the System Performance Rating Tool to determine why a particular computer is unable to run the Windows Aero user experience. However, the underlying technology of this tool has other uses as well. When you click the Windows Experience Index link in the System control panel, the Performance Information and Tools page appears, as shown in Figure 10-16.

Figure 10-16

The Performance Information and Tools page

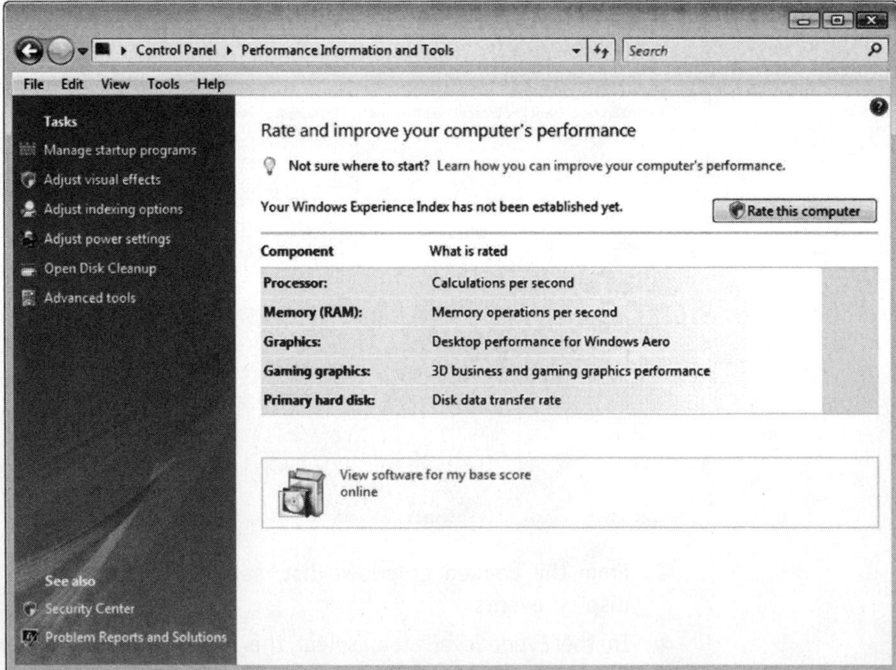

If you have not done so already, click the ***Rate this computer*** button to generate a score for each of the listed components. The component with the lowest number is responsible for the computer's base score. This is a perfect illustration of the bottleneck concept mentioned earlier. It is the slowest component on the computer that dictates its overall performance level. In the same way that one component can prevent the computer from running Windows Aero, it can also cause a general degradation of performance.

One of the best ways to improve the performance of your computer is to try to raise the system's base score. This usually means a hardware upgrade, such as installing additional memory, replacing a graphics adapter, or installing a faster hard drive. However, there are often less invasive (and less expensive) ways to improve performance. Clicking the *Learn how you can improve your computer's performance* link opens a help page that contains a number of tips that can help you to conserve system resources, thereby enhancing performance.

Using the Reliability and Performance Monitor Console

A computer's performance level is constantly changing as it performs different combinations of tasks. Monitoring the performance of the various components over a period of time is the only way to get a true picture of the system's capabilities.

While the Performance Information and Tools page provides a snapshot of your computer's performance at a single moment in time, the Reliability and Performance Monitor console enables you to view much of the same information, but on a continuous, real-time basis. Like Event Viewer, the Reliability and Performance Monitor console is an MMC snap-in that you can launch in a variety of ways, including the following:

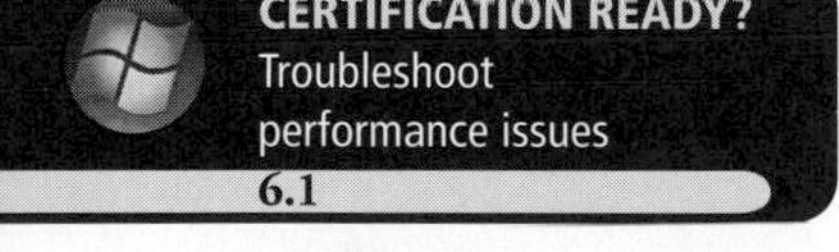

CERTIFICATION READY?
Troubleshoot performance issues

6.1

- Click Start, then click Control Panel > System and Maintenance > Administrative Tools > Reliability and Performance Monitor.
- Open a blank MMC console and add the Reliability and Performance Monitor snap-in.
- Open the Run dialog box or a Command Prompt window and key Perfmon.msc.
- Open the Computer Management console and expand the Reliability and Performance Monitor node.

Using Resource Overview

When you launch the Reliability and Performance Monitor, you see the Resource Overview screen, as shown in Figure 10-17. This screen contains four real-time line graphs that display information about four of the main system hardware components. Each of the four components also has a separate, expandable section below the graphs, displaying more detailed information in text form, such as the resources being utilized by individual applications and processes. Table 10-2 lists the statistics displayed by the graphs and the text sections.

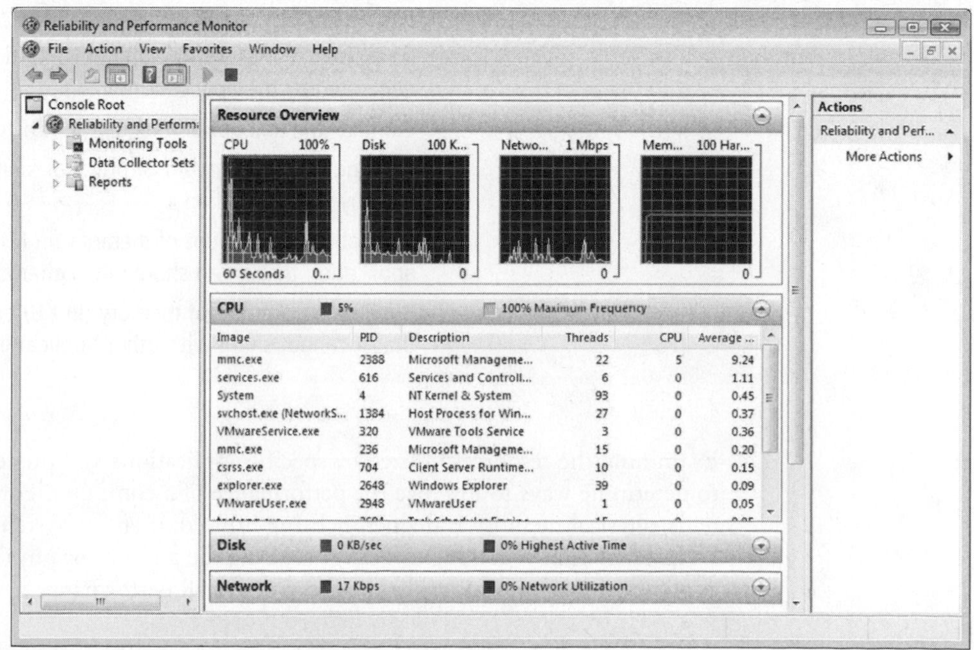

Figure 10-17

The Resource Overview page

Table 10-2

Resource Overview Line Graph Statistics

Component	Line graph statistics	Text statistics
CPU	Overall CPU utilization (%)	• Image–The application using CPU resources • PID–The Process ID of the application • Threads–The number of active threads generated by the application • CPU–The number of CPU cycles currently being used by the application • Average CPU–The percentage of the total CPU capacity being used by the application
Disk	Total current disk I/O rate (in KB/sec)	• Image–The application using disk resources • PID–The Process ID of the application • File–The file currently being read or written by the application • Read–The speed of the current read operation (in bytes/min) • Write–The speed of the current write operation (in bytes/min) • I/O Priority–The priority of the I/O task currently being performed by the application • Response Time–The interval between the issuance of a command to the disk and its response (in milliseconds)
Network	Current total network traffic (in KB/sec)	• Image–The application using network resources • PID–The Process ID of the application • Address–The network address or computer name of the system with which the computer is communicating • Send–The speed of the current network send operation (in bytes/min) • Receive–The speed of the current network receive operation (in bytes/min) • Total–The combined bandwidth of the current network send and receive processes (in bytes/min)
Memory	Current hard faults per second Percentage of physical memory currently in use (%)	• Image–The application using memory resources • PID–The Process ID of the application • Hard Faults Per Min–The number of hard faults currently being generated by the application • Commit–The amount of memory (in KB) committed by the application • Working Set–The amount of physical memory (in KB) currently being used by the application • Shareable–The amount of memory (in KB) being used by the application that it can share with other applications • Private–The amount of memory (in KB) being used by the application that it cannot share with other applications

Examining the resources utilized by specific applications and processes over time can help you to determine ways to improve the performance of a computer. For example, if all of the system's physical memory is frequently being utilized, then the system is probably being slowed by large amount of paging to disk. Increasing the amount of physical memory or reducing the application load will probably improve the overall performance level of the computer.

Using Performance Monitor

Performance Monitor (called System Monitor in previous versions of Windows) is another tool you can use to display system performance statistics in real time. The difference between the Performance Monitor and Resource Overview tools is that Performance Monitor can display hundreds of different statistics (called performance counters) and you can create a customized graph containing any statistics you choose.

When you select the Performance Monitor node, the detail pane of the snap-in contains a line graph, updated in real time, showing the current level for the % Processor Time performance counter, as shown in Figure 10-18.

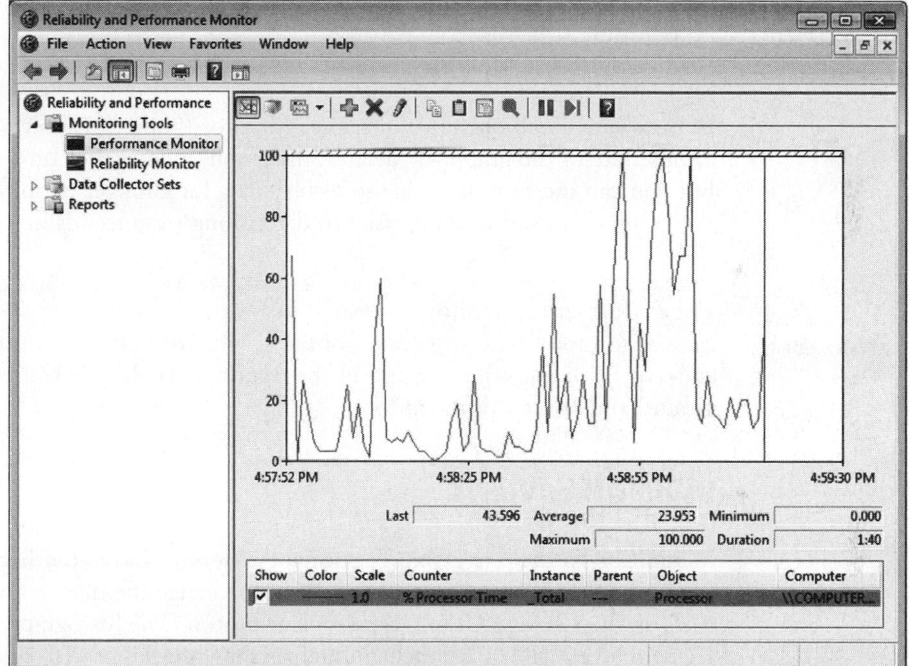

Figure 10-18

The default Performance Monitor display

Modifying the Graph View

The legend beneath the graph specifies the line color for the counter, the scale of values for the counter, and other identifying information. When you select a counter in the legend, its current values appear in numerical form at the bottom of the graph. Click the **Highlight** button in the toolbar (or press Ctrl+H) to change the selected counter to a broad line that is easier to distinguish in the graph.

If your computer is otherwise idle, you will probably notice that the line in the default graph is hovering near the bottom of the scale, making it difficult to see its value. You can address this problem by modifying the scale of the graph's Y (that is, vertical) axis. Click the **Properties** button in the toolbar (or press Ctrl+Q) to display the Performance Monitor Properties sheet box and click the Graph tab (see Figure 10-19). In the *Vertical scale* box, you can reduce the maximum value for the Y axis, thereby using more of the graph to display the counter data.

Figure 10-19

The Performance Monitor Properties sheet

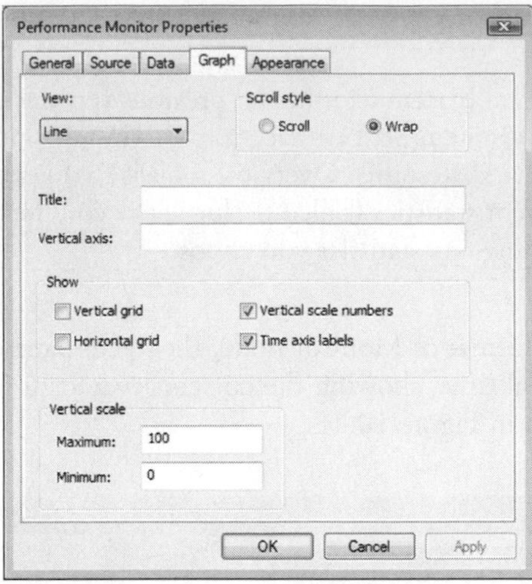

In the General tab of the Performance Monitor Properties sheet, you can also modify the sample rate of the graph. By default, the graph updates the counter values every one second, but you can increase this value to display data for a longer period of time on a single page of the graph. This can make it easier to detect long-term trends in counter values.

TAKE NOTE*

The Performance Monitor Properties sheet contains a number of other controls that you can use to modify the appearance of the graph. For example, on the Graph tab, you can add axis titles and gridlines, and in the Appearance tab, you can control the graph's background and select a different font.

Using Other Views

In addition to the line graph, Performance Monitor has two other views of the same data, a histogram view and a report view. You can change the display to one of these views by clicking the **Change Graph Type** toolbar button. The histogram view is a bar graph with a separate vertical bar for each counter, as shown in Figure 10-20. In this view, it is easier to monitor large numbers of counters, because the lines do not overlap.

Figure 10-20

The Performance Monitor histogram view

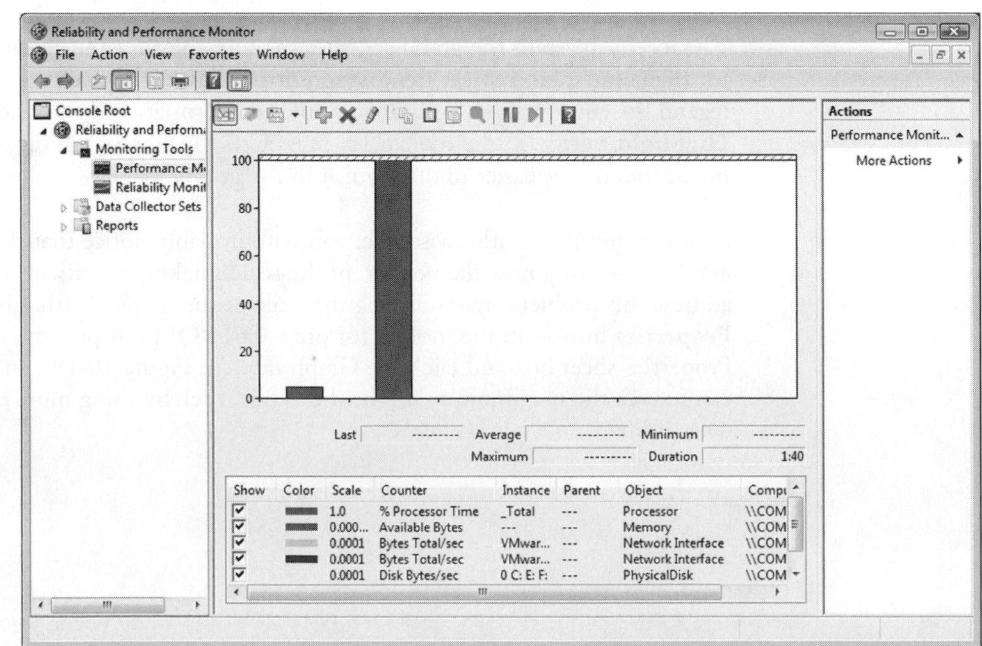

The report view (see Figure 10-21) displays the numerical value for each of the performance counters.

Figure 10-21

The Performance Monitor report view

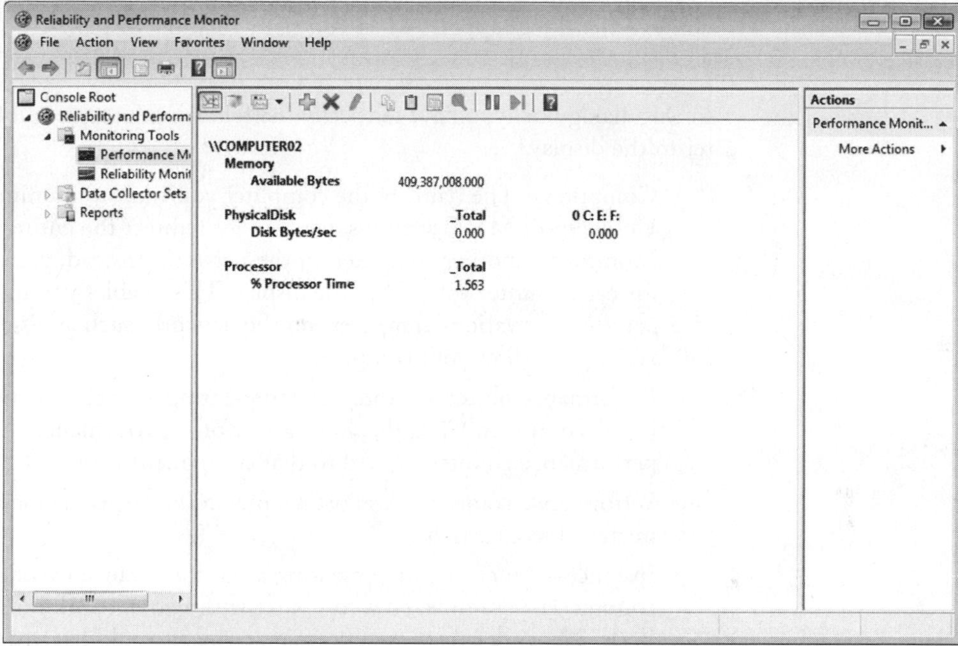

As with the line graph, the histogram and report views both update their counter values at the interval specified in the General tab of the Performance Monitor Properties sheet. The main drawback of these two views, however, is that they do not display a history of the counter values, only the current value. Each new sampling overwrites the previous one in the display, unlike the line graph, which displays the previous values as well.

Adding Counters

The performance counter that appears in Performance Monitor by default is a useful gauge of the computer's performance, but the snap-in includes dozens of other counters that you can add to the display. To add counters to the Performance Monitor display click the **Add** button in the toolbar, or press Ctrl+I to display the Add Counters dialog box (see Figure 10-22).

Figure 10-22

The Add Counters dialog box

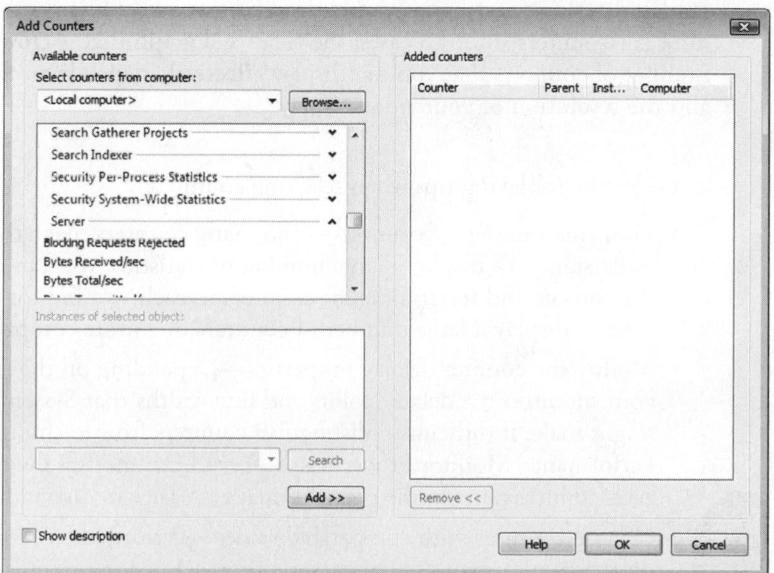

TAKE NOTE*

Unlike most MMC snap-ins, Performance Monitor does not insert its most commonly used functions into the MMC console's Action menu. The only methods for accessing Performance Monitor functions are the toolbar buttons, hotkey combinations, and the context menu that appears when you right-click the display.

In this dialog box, you have to specify the following four pieces of information to add a counter to the display:

- Computer—The name of the computer you want to monitor with the selected counter. Unlike most MMC snap-ins, you cannot redirect the entire focus of Performance Monitor to another computer on the network. Instead, you specify a computer name for each counter you add to the display. This enables you to create a display showing counters for various computers on the network, such as a single graph of processor activity for all of your computers.
- Performance object—A category representing a specific hardware or software component in the computer. Click the down arrow on a performance object to display a selection of performance counters related to that component.
- Performance counter—A statistic representing a specific aspect of the selected performance object's activities.
- Instance—An element representing a specific occurrence of the selected performance counter. For example, on a computer with two network interface adapters, each counter in the Network Interface performance object would have two instances, one for each adapter, enabling you to track the performance of each adapter individually. Some counters also have instances such as Total or Average, enabling you to track the performance of all instances combined or the median value of all instances.

TAKE NOTE*

Select the *Show description* checkbox to display a detailed explanation of the selected performance counter.

Once you have selected a computer name, a performance object, a performance counter in that object, and an instance of that counter, click **Add** to add the counter to the Added Counters list. The dialog box remains open so that you can add more counters. Click **OK** when you are finished to update the graph with your selected counters.

The performance objects, performance counters, and instances that appear in the Add Counters dialog box depend on the computer's hardware configuration, the software installed on the computer, and the computer's role on the network.

Creating an Effective Display

In most cases, when users first discover Performance Monitor, they see the hundreds of available performance counters and proceed to create a line graph containing dozens of different counters. In most cases, the result is a graph that is crowded and incoherent. The number of counters that you can display effectively depends on the size of your monitor and the resolution of your video display.

Consider the following tips when selecting counters:

- Limit the number of counters—Too many counters make the graph more difficult to understand. To display a large number of statistics, you can display multiple windows in the console and select different counters in each window, or use the histogram or report view to display a large number of counters in a more compact form.
- Modify the counter display properties—Depending on the size and capabilities of your monitor, the default colors and line widths that System Monitor uses in its graph might make it difficult to distinguish counters from each other. In the Data tab in the Performance Monitor Properties sheet, you can modify the color, style, and width of each counter's line in the graph to make it easier to distinguish.
- Choose counters with comparable values—Performance Monitor imposes no limitations on the combinations of counters you can select for a single graph, but some statistics are

not practical to display together because of their disparate values. When a graph contains a counter with a typical value that is under twenty and another counter with a value in the hundreds, it is difficult to arrange the display so that both counters are readable. Choose counters with values that are reasonably comparable so that you can display them legibly. If you must display counters with different value ranges, you might prefer to use the report view instead of the graph view.

Saving a System Monitor Console

Once you are satisfied with the display you have created, you can save it as a console file by selecting Save As from the File menu and specifying a filename with an .msc extension. Launching this console file will open the Reliability and Performance Monitor console and display the Performance Monitor snap-in with all of the counters and display properties you configured before saving it.

Using Reliability Monitor

Reliability Monitor is a new addition to Windows Vista that automatically tracks events that can have a negative effect on system stability and uses them to calculate a stability index. The default display when you click the Reliability Monitor node contains a System Stability Chart for the most recent 28 days and a System Stability Report, as shown in Figure 10-23. The interface includes a scroll bar and calendar in the form of a dropdown list, either of which you can use to display the reliability information for any 28-day period in the last year.

Figure 10-23

The Reliability Monitor display

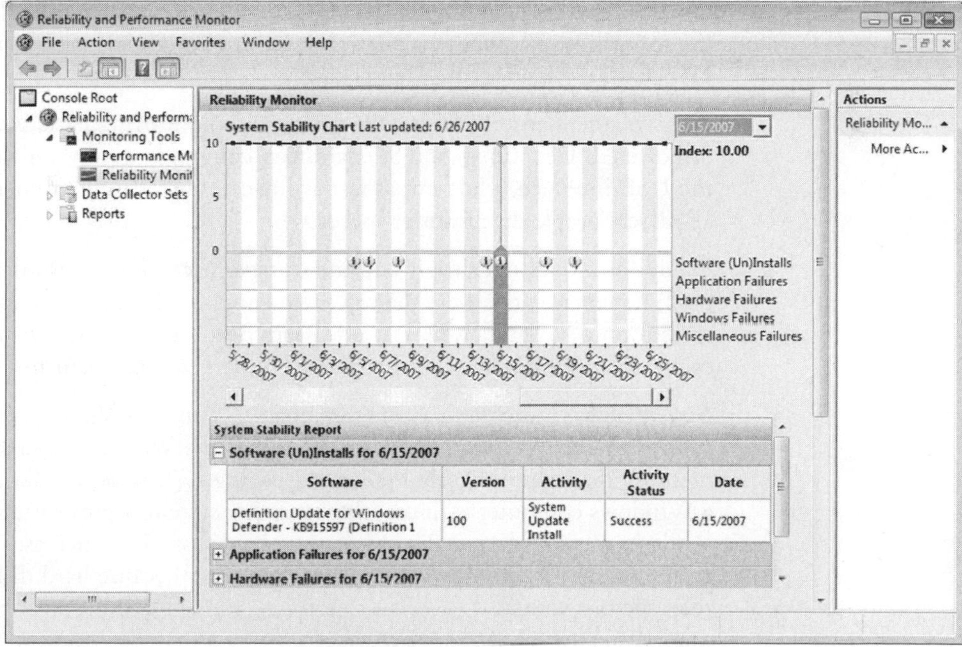

Reliability Monitor gathers information using a hidden scheduled task called Reliability Access Component Agent (RACAgent). The agent collects data from the event logs every hour and updates the Reliability Monitor display every 24 hours. The stability index is a number from 0 to 10 (with 0 representing the least and 10 the most stability) that is calculated using information about the following types of events:

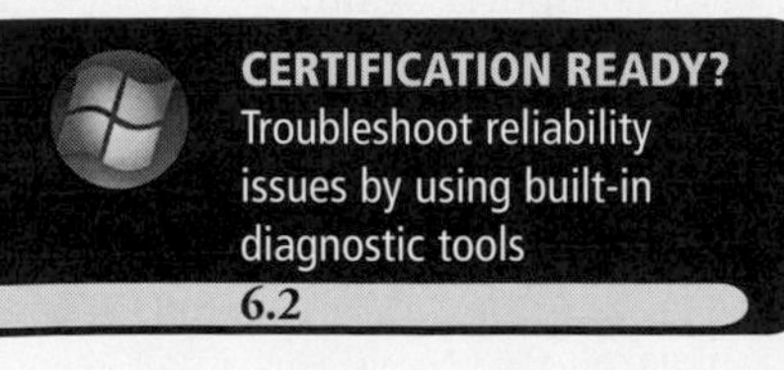

CERTIFICATION READY?
Troubleshoot reliability issues by using built-in diagnostic tools
6.2

- Software (Un)Installs—Includes software installations, uninstallations, updates, and configurations for the operating system, applications, and device drivers
- Application Failures—Includes application hangs, crashes, and terminations of non-responding applications

- Hardware Failures—Includes disk and memory failures
- Windows Failures—Includes boot failures, operating system crashes, and sleep failures
- Miscellaneous Failures—Includes unrequested system shutdowns
- System Clock Changes—Includes all significant clock time changes. This entry appears only when a significant clock time change has occurred recently

Pertinent events appear in the System Stability Chart as data points. Clicking one of the points displays information about it in the System Stability Report.

The Reliability Monitor snap-in doesn't actually do anything except present event log information in a new way. It is not possible to configure the snap-in or alter the criteria it uses to evaluate a computer's reliability. If you ever notice that the stability index has decreased, you should check the events that caused the reduction and evaluate for yourself how serious the situation is and what actions you should take, if any.

Introducing ReadyBoost

ReadyBoost is a new Windows Vista feature that enables you to use the storage space on a USB flash drive to free up system memory for other uses.

CERTIFICATION READY?
Troubleshoot performance issues: Implement ReadyBoost
6.1

Every desktop technician should know that one of the easiest ways to improve the performance of a Windows computer is to install more system memory. However, in many cases this is not possible. A computer might already have the maximum amount of RAM the motherboard can support, or it might not be economically feasible to purchase more memory. In cases like these, Windows Vista includes a new feature called ***ReadyBoost***, which you can use to increase a computer's memory capacity using non-volatile memory in the form of a USB flash drive or Secure Digital card.

Non-volatile memory is a storage device with no moving parts that retains its data, even when unpowered. USB drives and SD cards can contain large amounts of non-volatile memory, and the USB interface, while not as fast as the computer's internal memory bus, is fast enough to allow serviceable data transfer speeds.

ReadyBoost does not simply add the storage space on the flash drive to the system memory pool, however. If this were the case, removing the drive at the wrong time could cause a catastrophic system failure. Instead, ReadyBoost uses the non-volatile memory for a memory cache, in coordination with the system's SuperFetch mechanism.

SuperFetch is a caching routine that enables Windows Vista to restore user access to applications much faster than Windows XP. All of the Windows operating systems use a virtual memory management technique called paging. When nearly all of the physical memory in a Windows computer is in use, the operating system begins swapping some of the data currently in memory to a paging file on the hard disk. This increases the memory capacity of the computer, but it also slows down some processes because hard disks transfer data much slower than memory chips.

When your computer is, to all appearances, idle, there are usually a variety of tasks occurring in the background. Backups, updates, and virus scans are just a few of the various types of tasks that wait until the system is idle before they run. These background tasks require system memory also, and while they are running, the idle applications that you have open are swapped to the paging file on your hard drive. The result is that when you attempt to use your computer again, there is a delay as the applications are swapped from the paging file back into system memory.

MORE INFORMATION

You can easily compare the difference in speed between memory chips and hard disk drives simply by examining their access rates. Hard disk drive access rates are measured in milliseconds, that is, thousandths of a second. By comparison, the access rates of DRAM memory chips are measured in nanoseconds, that is, billionths of a second.

SuperFetch addresses this problem by storing copies of your most frequently used applications in a cache in system memory. With this information in cache memory, the system can recall it almost instantaneously when you try to start working at your idle computer again. The paging delay is eliminated.

USB storage devices are not as fast as system memory, but they are faster than hard drives. Therefore, when you use a USB flash drive, ReadyBoost stores the SuperFetch cache on the flash drive, rather than in system memory. This frees up the area of system memory that was formerly used for the cache, and still provides quick access to the cached applications. ReadyBoost is also completely safe, because even if you yank the flash drive out of the system with no warning, you are removing only a copy of the cached information. The same data is also available from the paging file on the hard drive.

Using ReadyBoost

When you insert a flash drive into a USB slot, Windows Vista automatically tests the speed of the drive and offers to use it for ReadyBoost, if it qualifies.

CERTIFICATION READY?
Troubleshoot performance issues: Configure USB device for ReadyBoost
6.1

ReadyBoost requires a computer with a USB 2.0 interface and a 256 MB or larger flash drive or SD card that is fast enough to be useful. When you insert the drive into a USB slot, Vista tests the speed of the device and, if it's fast enough, gives you the option of using it for ReadyBoost.

You can also manually configure a flash drive to use ReadyBoost by opening its Properties sheet and clicking the **ReadyBoost** tab. Using this interface, you can specify how much of the storage space on the device you want to devote to memory caching.

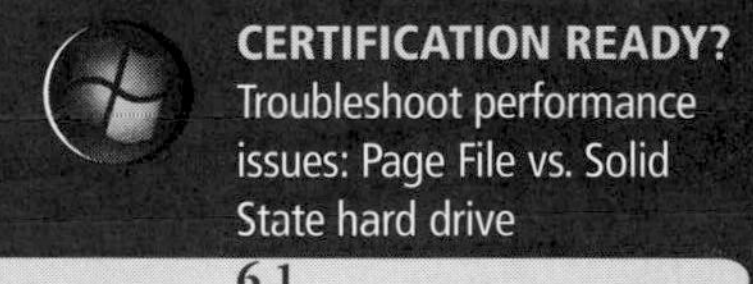

CERTIFICATION READY?
Troubleshoot performance issues: Page File vs. Solid State hard drive
6.1

Another way to take advantage of non-volatile memory with Windows Vista is to use hard drives that have flash memory integrated into them. Some hard drives have a traditional disk mechanism plus a small amount of flash memory for use as a cache. Others are completely solid state, with no moving parts at all. ReadyDrive is a variation of ReadyBoost that can use these drives to store data from the paging file, proving an even greater increase in performance.

SUMMARY SKILL MATRIX

IN THIS LESSON YOU LEARNED:
Microsoft releases operating system updates on the 12th of each month, with occasional, additional releases when an issue requires an immediate response.
Microsoft classifies updates using the following categories: Critical Updates, Recommended Updates, Optional Updates, and Device Drivers.
The Windows Update client included with Vista makes it possible to configure computers to automatically download and install Windows updates as needed.
In addition to the control panel interface, it is possible to configure the Windows Update client using Group Policy settings.
Windows uses a graphical application called Event Viewer to display the log information gathered by the operating system.
While the Performance Information and Tools page provides a snapshot of your computer's performance at a single moment in time, the Reliability and Performance Monitor console enables you to view much of the same information, but on a continuous, real-time basis.
The Resource Overview screen contains four real-time line graphs that display information about four of the main system hardware components. Each component also has a separate, expandable section, displaying more detailed information in text form, such as the resources being utilized by individual applications and processes.

(continued)

Performance Monitor can display hundreds of different statistics (called performance counters). You can create a customized graph containing any statistics you choose.

Reliability Monitor is a new Windows Vista tool that automatically tracks events that can have a negative effect on system stability and uses them to calculate a stability index.

ReadyBoost is a new Windows Vista feature that enables you to use the storage space on a USB flash drive to free up system memory for other uses.

Knowledge Assessment

Fill in the Blank

Complete the following sentences by writing the correct word or words in the blanks provided.

1. Windows Vistas ReadyBoost feature uses USB flash drives to store data cached by the Windows ______________ feature.
2. For a large organization, it is a good idea to perform test deployments on an ______________ network.
3. Performance Monitor can display hundreds of different statistics called ______________.
4. The Windows Update ______________ keeps track of all the updates that have been installed on the computer.
5. In Performance Monitor, the ______________ view is a bar graph with a separate vertical bar for each counter.
6. A ______________ is a cumulative set of all updates for a particular operating system version since its original release.
7. ______________ is a new addition to Windows Vista that automatically tracks events that can have a negative effect on system stability and uses them to calculate a stability index.
8. You can manually trigger an update by using ______________.
9. A storage device with no moving parts that retains its data, even when unpowered, uses ______________ memory.
10. In the Event Viewer console, you use ______________ as a means of locating, isolating, and displaying information about specific events.

True / False

Circle T if the statement is true or F if the statement is false.

T | F 1. ReadyBoost requires a computer with a USB 1.0 interface or higher and a 256 MB or larger flash drive or SD card that is fast enough to be useful.

T | F 2. USB storage devices are not as fast as system memory or hard drives.

T | F 3. The Windows Update client connects to the Microsoft Update servers on the Internet by default.

T | F 4. Hardware problems are the only cause of performance degradations.

T | F 5. Microsoft releases operating system updates on the 12th of each month, with occasional, additional releases when an issue (typically involving security) requires an immediate response.

T | F 6. ReadyBoost uses the non-volatile memory for a memory cache, in coordination with the system's SuperFetch mechanism.

T | F 7. The difference between the Performance Monitor and Resource Overview tools is that Resource Overview tools can display hundreds of different statistics and you can create a customized graph containing any statistics you choose.

T | F 8. Microsoft classifies updates using the following categories: Critical Updates, Recommended Updates, Optional Updates, and Security Updates.

T | F 9. SuperFetch stores copies of your most frequently used applications in a cache in system memory, thus virtually eliminating paging delays.

T | F 10. In addition to the control panel interface, it is possible to configure the Windows Update client using Group Policy settings.

Review Questions

1. Explain why Performance Monitor counters sometime have multiple instances.
2. The Windows Vista computers on a company network are configured to download and install updates every day at 3:00 AM. However, the company is currently running three shifts, and there are workers using the computers 24 hours a day. Explain why the update downloads will not interfere with the users' activities.

■ Case Scenarios

Scenario #1: Configuring the Windows Update Client

You are a newly hired desktop technician at a company with a network of Windows Vista computers. You have been given the task of configuring several new computers to automatically download and install updates on a nightly basis. The company has recently installed a server running Windows Server Update Services (WSUS), which the IT director wants all of the workstations to use to retrieve their updates. The director plans to install Active Directory servers on the network in the near future, but they are not yet available. Describe the procedure you must perform to configure the Windows update client on the computers.

Scenario #2: Eliminating a Bottleneck

You are a desktop technician who has been given the task of determining why a particular Windows Vista computer on a 10Base-T local area network is performing poorly. You must also implement a remedy for the problem. The computer is functioning as a file and print server for a small department of eight graphic designers. After monitoring the computer's performance using the Performance Monitor tool, you have determined that the network itself is the bottleneck preventing peak performance. The graphic designers routinely work with very large files, saturating the network with traffic. Give two possible solutions that will remedy the problem and increase the performance level of the computer in question.

LESSON 11 Troubleshooting Windows Vista

OBJECTIVE DOMAIN MATRIX

TECHNOLOGY SKILL	OBJECTIVE DOMAIN	OBJECTIVE NUMBER
Understanding Troubleshooting Practices	Troubleshoot post-installation configuration issues	2.1
Using Troubleshooting Tools	Troubleshoot reliability issues by using built-in diagnostic tools	6.2
Using Remote Access Technologies	Configure remote access	4.3
Troubleshooting Installation and Startup Issues	Troubleshoot installation issues	1.5

KEY TERMS

Boot Configuration Data (BCD)
Power on self-test (POST)
Remote Desktop Protocol (RDP)
Watson Feedback Platform (WFP)
Windows Error Reporting (WER)

Understanding Troubleshooting Practices

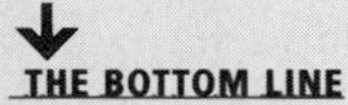

Troubleshooting is a primary function of the Windows Vista desktop technician. Clients call for help because something doesn't work or they've done something wrong, and it is up to you to determine what the problem is and how to fix it.

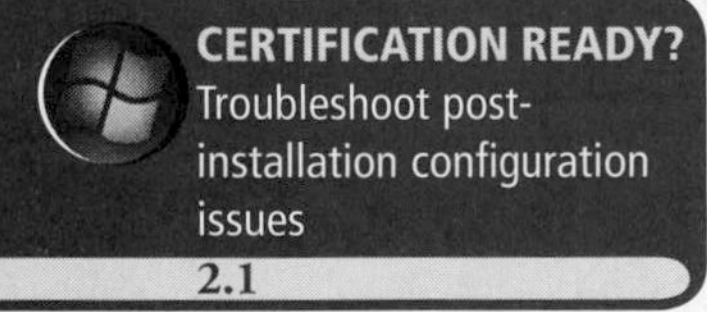

CERTIFICATION READY?
Troubleshoot post-installation configuration issues
2.1

Many desktop technicians have troubleshooting skills that are largely intuitive, and this is fine. However, when troubleshooting a problem in a professional environment, whether it's a corporate enterprise network, a help desk in a retail store, or a freelance consultancy, it is important to have a set troubleshooting procedure. This will enable you to explain to the client what you've done, share your findings with your colleagues, and account for your time and effort.

Many troubleshooting calls stem from user error, that is, people who are improperly using the software of hardware. These can often be cleared up immediately with some remedial user training. When you are faced with what appears to be a serious problem, however, you should follow a set troubleshooting procedure that consists of steps similar to the following:

1. Establish the symptoms.
2. Identify the affected area.
3. Establish what has changed.

4. Select the most probable cause.
5. Implement a solution.
6. Test the result.
7. Document the solution.

Various desktop technicians might use slightly different steps or perform them in a slightly different order, but the overall process should be similar. The following sections examine each of these steps.

Establishing the Symptoms

Have the user explain the problem and assign it a priority.

The first step in troubleshooting any problem is to determine exactly what is going wrong. Depending on the situation, you might also have to note the effects of the problem so that you can assign it a priority. In a business environment, the support staff often receives more calls for help than they can handle at one time. In these cases, it is essential to establish a system of priorities that dictates which calls are addressed first. As in the emergency department of a hospital, the priorities should not necessarily be based on who is first in line. The severity of the problem and its potential for wide-reaching effects should determine who receives attention first. However, it is also not wise to ignore the political reality that senior management problems are often addressed before those of the rank and file.

Some of the guidelines you might use to establish service priorities are as follows:

- Shared resources take precedence over individual resources—A problem with a computer that prevents other users from performing their jobs should take precedence over one that affects only a single user.
- Network-wide problems take precedence over workgroup or departmental problems—A problem with a computer that provides services to the entire network, such as a file or print server, should take precedence over a problem with a departmental resource.
- Departmental issues should be rated according to the function of the department—A problem with a computer belonging to a department that is critical to the organization, such as order entry or a customer service call center, should take precedence over a problem with a computer belonging to a department that can better tolerate a period of down time, such as research and development.
- System-wide problems take precedence over application problems—A problem that puts an entire computer out of commission and prevents a user from getting any work done should take precedence over a problem a user is experiencing with a single device or application.

It sometimes can be difficult to determine the exact nature of a problem from a description supplied by a relatively inexperienced user. Part of the process of narrowing down the cause of a problem involves obtaining accurate information about what has occurred. Users are often vague about what they were doing when they experienced the problem, or even what the indications of the problem were. For example, in many cases, users call for help because they received an error message, but they neglect to write down the exact wording of the message. Training users in the proper procedures for documenting and reporting problems is often part of the desktop technician's job. It might not be any help now, but it can help the next time a user receives an error.

Begin by asking the user questions like the following:

- What exactly were you doing when the problem occurred?
- What were you doing just before the problem occurred?
- Were you ever able to complete the task you were performing successfully? If so, what has changed?

- Have you had any other problems with your computer lately?
- Was the computer behaving normally just before the problem occurred?
- Has any hardware or software been installed, removed, or reconfigured recently?
- Did you or anyone else do anything to try to resolve the problem?

Identifying the Affected Area

Isolate the hardware or software component that is the source of the problem.

The next step in troubleshooting a network problem is to see whether it can be duplicated. Computer problems that can be reproduced are far easier to fix, primarily because you can easily test to see whether a solution was successful. However, many problems are intermittent or might occur for only a short period of time. In these cases, you might have to leave the incident open until the problem occurs again. In some instances, having the user reproduce the problem can lead to a solution. User error is a common cause of problems that might at first seem to be hardware-related.

If you can duplicate a problem, you can set about finding the source of the difficulty. For example, if a user has trouble opening a file in a word processing application, the difficulty might lie in the file itself, in the application, or in the disk drive where the file is stored. The process of isolating the location of the problem consists of logically and methodically eliminating elements that are not the cause.

If you can duplicate the problem, you can begin to isolate the cause by reproducing the conditions under which the problem occurred. To do this, use a procedure like the following:

1. Have the user reproduce the problem on the computer repeatedly, to determine whether the user's actions are causing the error.
2. If possible, sit at the computer yourself and perform the same task. If the problem does not occur, the cause might lie in how the user is performing a particular task. Watch the user carefully to see if he or she is doing something wrong. It is possible that you and the user are performing the same task in different ways and that the user's method is exposing a problem that yours does not.
3. If the problem recurs when you perform the task, log off from the user's account, log on using a different account, and repeat the task. If the problem does not recur, the user is probably lacking the rights or permissions needed to perform the task.
4. If the problem recurs, and the computer is connected to a network, try to perform the same task on a similarly equipped computer connected to the same network. If you cannot reproduce the problem on another computer, you know that the cause lies in the user's computer. If the problem occurs on another computer, then there is likely to be a network problem that is affecting both computers.

Establishing What Has Changed

Ask the user if the computer has recently been upgraded or reconfigured.

When a computer that used to work properly now does not, it stands to reason that some change has occurred. When a user reports a problem, it is important to determine how the computing environment changed immediately before the malfunction. Unfortunately, getting this information from the user often can be difficult. The response to the question "Has anything changed on the computer recently?" is nearly always "No." Only later will the user remember to mention that a major hardware or software upgrade was performed just before the problem occurred. In an organization with properly established maintenance and documentation procedures, you should be able to determine whether the user's computer has been upgraded or modified recently. IT or departmental records are the first place to look for information like this.

Major changes, such as the installation of new hardware or software, are obvious possible sources of the problem, but you must be aware of causes produced by more subtle changes as well. Tracking down the source of a networking problem can often be a form of detective work, and learning to "interrogate" your "suspects" properly can be an important part of the troubleshooting process.

Selecting the Most Probable Cause

Look for the simplest possible causes of the problem first.

Once you have narrowed down the possible sources of the problem, you can begin to compile a list of possible causes. Almost any computer problem can have many possible causes, and it is up to you to determine which is the most likely culprit.

There's an old medical school axiom that says when you hear hoofbeats, think horses, not zebras. In the context of computer troubleshooting, this means that when you look for the possible causes of a problem, start with the obvious first. For example, if a computer fails to print a document, do not start by checking the drivers and the printer configuration; check the simple things first, such as whether the printer is plugged in and connected to the computer. You also must work methodically and document everything so that you do not duplicate your efforts.

Implementing a Solution

Try different solutions until the problem is solved.

After you isolate the problem, try to determine whether hardware or software is the culprit. If it is a hardware problem, you might replace the unit that is at fault or use an alternative that you know is functioning properly. Printing problems, for example, might force you to replace the printer cable. If the problem is inside the computer, you might need to replace components, such as hard drives, until the defective component is found. If you determine that the problem is caused by software, try reinstalling the application.

In some cases, the process of isolating the source of a problem includes resolving the problem. For example, if you determine that a printer cable is bad by replacing it with a new one, then the replacement resolves the problem. In other cases, however, the resolution might be more involved, such as one that requires reinstalling an application or even the operating system. Because the user might need to use the computer to complete important tasks, you might have to wait to resolve the problem until a later time, when the computer is not in use and after you have had a chance to back up its data. Sometimes you can use an interim solution, such as a substitute computer, until you can definitively resolve the problem.

Testing the Results

Try to recreate the problem to make sure that the solution is effective.

After implementing a resolution to the problem, you should return to the beginning of the process and repeat the task that originally caused the problem. If the problem no longer occurs, you should test any other functions related to the changes you made to ensure that solving one problem has not created another. At this point, the time you have spent documenting the troubleshooting process becomes worthwhile. Repeat the procedures used to duplicate the problem exactly to ensure that the trouble the user originally experienced has been completely eliminated, and not just temporarily masked. If the problem was intermittent to begin with, it might take some time to ascertain whether the solution has been effective. It might be necessary to check with the user several times to make sure that the problem is not recurring.

Documenting the Solution

Keep a complete record of the entire troubleshooting process.

Although it is presented here as a separate step, the process of documenting all of the actions you perform should begin as soon as the user calls for help. A well-organized technical support organization should have a system in place in which each problem call is registered as a trouble ticket that eventually contains a complete record of the problem and the steps taken to isolate and resolve it. In many cases, a technical support organization operates using tiers, which are groups of technicians with different skill levels. Calls come in to the first tier, and if the problem is sufficiently complex or the first-tier technician cannot resolve it, the call is escalated to the second tier, which is composed of senior technicians. As long as all who are involved in the process document their activities, there should be no problem when one technician hands off the trouble ticket to another. In addition, keeping careful notes prevents people from duplicating one another's efforts.

CERTIFICATION READY?
Troubleshoot reliability issues by using built-in diagnostic tools.
6.2

The final phase of the troubleshooting process is to explain to the user what happened and why. Of course, the average computer user is probably not interested in hearing all the technical details, but it is a good idea to let users know whether their actions caused the problem, exacerbated it, or made it more difficult to resolve. Educating users can lead to a quicker resolution next time or can even prevent a problem from occurring altogether.

Using Troubleshooting Tools

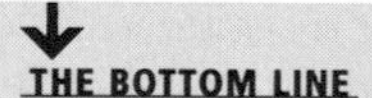

Repairing anything requires the right tools and the ability to use them properly.

Windows Vista includes a variety of tools that can aid in the troubleshooting process, some of which were discussed earlier in this book. Table 11-1 lists these tools, along with the location of their coverage.

Table 11-1

Windows Vista Troubleshooting Tools

Tool	Function	Location
Upgrade Advisor	Determines whether a computer can run Windows Vista and identifies components that could be upgraded to provide better performance	Lesson 1
Windows PE	Provides a pre-installation environment from which you can use command-line tools to work with drivers, disks, and network resources	Lesson 2
Windows Easy Transfer	Enables you to back up and restore user profile information. In the event of a catastrophic malfunction that requires a reinstallation of the operating system, you can use this tool to preserve the user's personalized working environment	Lesson 2
System Performance Rating Tool	Assigns a numerical score to each of the computer's main components, enabling you to identify bottlenecks that affect system performance	Lesson 3, 10
Disk Management snap-in	Displays information about the storage devices installed in the computer and provides tools for managing partitions and volumes	Lesson 4
Properties sheets	Shares, disk drives, and most other components in a Windows computer have a Properties sheet that contains a Security tab, which is where you work with the permissions that control access to the component	Lesson 4

Table 11-1 ***(continued)***

TOOL	FUNCTION	LOCATION
Backup Files Wizard	Performs backups of selected document files. Before performing any major procedure on a client's computer, you should perform a backup of important files	Lesson 4
Complete PC	Performs image backups of complete disks, enabling you to restore a computer to its exact former state	Lesson 4
User Accounts control panel	Enables you to create and manage local user accounts	Lesson 5
Local Users and Groups snap-in	Provides comprehensive control over local users and groups	Lesson 5
Local Security Policies console	Provides access to granular controls that enable you to set system security policies and regulate access to specific system functions	Lesson 5
Group Policy Object Editor	Provides access to controls that enable you to configure an extensive collection of local and Active Directory policies for specific Windows features and components	Lesson 6
Device Manager	Enables you to view information about and manage the drivers for all of the hardware devices installed in the computer	Lesson 6
Network and Sharing Center	Provides a central point of access for most of Windows Vista's networking components and tools	Lesson 7
Network Map	Provides a graphical depiction of the network topology	Lesson 7
Network Diagnostics	Displays networking error messages, and specifies in plain language what might be wrong and how to repair the problem	Lesson 7
Ipconfig.exe	Displays configuration data for all of the network interfaces in the computer	Lesson 7
Ping.exe	Tests network connections to other TCP/IP systems	Lesson 7
Tracert.exe	Displays the names of the routers on the path taken by packets to a specific destination	Lesson 7
Nslookup.exe	Enables you to send customized DNS requests to a specific DNS server	Lesson 7
Windows Security Center	Provides a central point of access for most of Windows Vista's security components and tools	Lesson 8
Windows Firewall	Enables you to control what types of network traffic are permitted to enter and leave a computer	Lesson 8
Windows Update	Enables you to configure a computer to automatically download and install operating system updates	Lesson 8, 10
Windows Defender	Prevents the infiltration of spyware into a Windows Vista system	Lesson 8
Software Explorer	Displays information about the applications running on the computer, for the purpose of detecting spyware	Lesson 8
Malicious Software Removal Tool	A single use virus scanner that Microsoft updates monthly	Lesson 8
Parental Controls	Enables you to limit the system access granted to specific users	Lesson 8
Event Viewer	Displays log information about operating system components	Lesson 10
Reliability and Performance Monitor console	Displays continuous real-time information about the performance of specific system hardware and software components	Lesson 10

Using Remote Access Technologies

Remote access technologies enable a user on one computer to effectively take control of another computer on the network. For desktop technicians, this capability can save many hours of travel time.

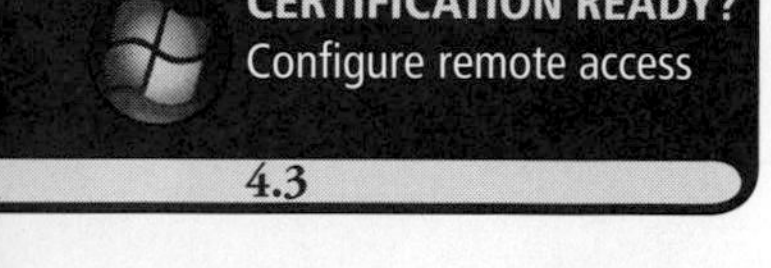

A main objective for desktop technicians working on large corporate networks is to minimize the amount of travel from site to site to work on individual computers. Some of the troubleshooting tools included with Windows Vista are capable of managing services on remote computers as well as on the local system. For example, most MMC snap-ins have this capability, enabling technicians to work on systems throughout the enterprise without traveling. However, most snap-ins are specialized tools used only for certain administration tasks. For comprehensive access to a remote computer, Windows Vista includes two tools that are extremely useful to the desktop technician: Remote Assistance and Remote Desktop.

Using Remote Assistance

Remote Assistance is a Windows Vista feature that enables an administrator, trainer, or desktop technician at one location to connect to a distant user's computer, chat with the user, and either view all of the user's activities or take complete control of the system. Remote Assistance eliminates the need for administrative personnel to travel to a user's location for any of the following reasons:

TAKE NOTE*

In Microsoft interfaces and documentation, the person connecting to a client using Remote Assistance is referred to as an expert or a helper.

- Technical support—A desktop technician can use Remote Assistance to connect to a remote computer to modify configuration parameters, install new software, or troubleshoot user problems.
- Troubleshooting—By connecting in read-only mode, an expert can observe a remote user's activities and determine whether improper procedures are the source of problems the user is experiencing. The expert can also connect in interactive mode to try to recreate the problem or to modify system settings to resolve it. This is far more efficient than trying to give instructions to inexperienced users over the telephone.
- Training—Trainers and help desk personnel can demonstrate procedures to users right on their systems, without having to travel to their locations.

To receive remote assistance, the computer running Windows Vista must be configured to use the Remote Assistance feature in one of the following ways:

- Using Control Panel—Open the System control panel and click **Remote Settings**. After confirming your action, select the *Allow Remote Assistance connections to this computer* checkbox, as shown in Figure 11-1. By clicking the **Advanced** button, the user can specify whether the expert can take control of the computer or simply view activities on the computer. The user can also specify the amount of time that the invitation for remote assistance remains valid.

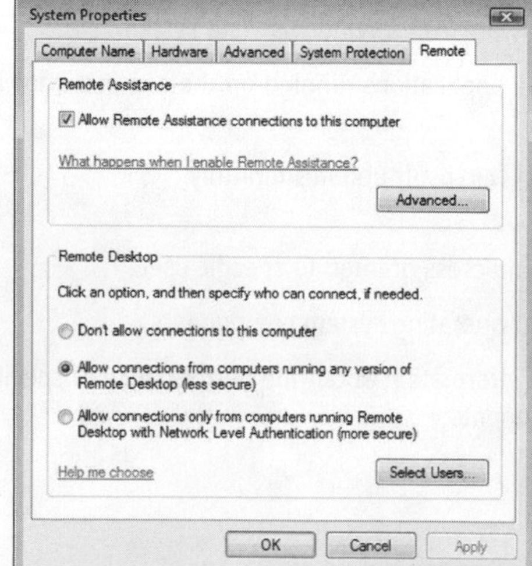

Figure 11-1

The Remote tab of the System Properties sheet

- Using Group Policies—Use the Group Policy Object Editor console to access the computer's local Group Policy settings or to open a group policy object (GPO) for an Active Directory domain, site, or organizational unit object containing the computer. Browse to the Computer Configuration > Administrative Templates > System > Remote Assistance container and enable the Solicited Remote Assistance policy, as shown in Figure 11-2. The Solicited Remote Assistance policy also enables you to specify the degree of control the expert receives over the client computer, the duration of the invitation, and the method for sending e-mail invitations. The Offer Remote Assistance policy enables you to specify the names of users or groups that can function as experts, and whether those experts can perform tasks or just observe.

Figure 11-2

The Solicited Remote Assistance policy in the Group Policy Object Editor console

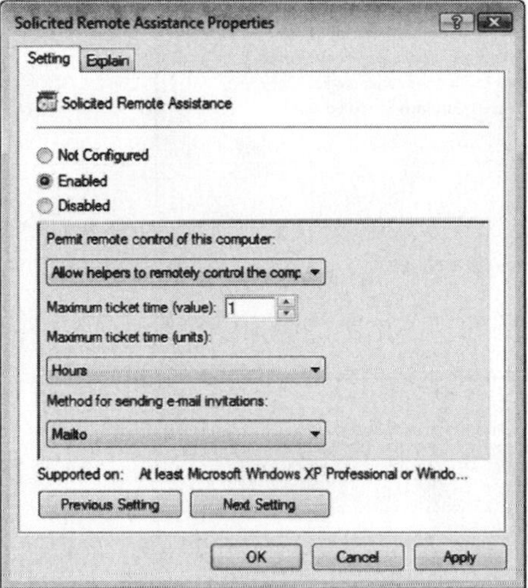

Creating an Invitation

To request a Remote Assistance session, a client must issue an invitation and send it to a particular expert. The client can send the invitation using e-mail, or save it as a file to be sent to the expert in some other manner. To create an invitation, use the following procedure:

TAKE NOTE*

It is also possible for an expert to initiate a Remote Assistance connection to the client by specifying the client's computer name or IP address. However, Vista cannot establish the session unless the client approves the connection.

CREATE AN INVITATION

GET READY. Log on to Windows Vista. When the logon process is completed, close the Welcome Center window and any other windows that appear.

1. Click **Start**, and then click **Help and Support**. The Windows Help and Support window appears, as shown in Figure 11-3.

Figure 11-3
The Windows Help And Support Center window

2. Click **Windows Remote Assistance.** The Windows Remote Assistance wizard loads and displays the *Do you want to ask for or offer help?* page, as shown in Figure 11-4.

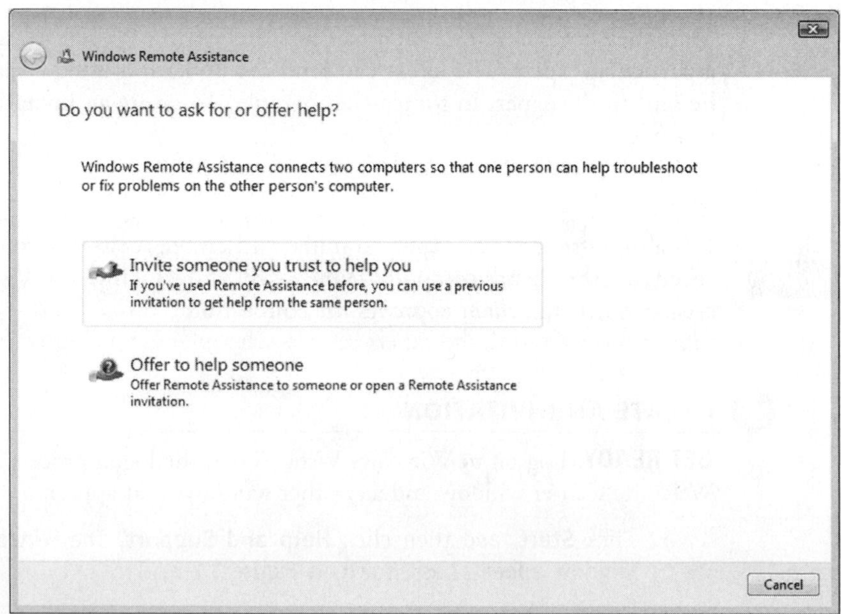

Figure 11-4
The Do you want to ask for or offer help? page in the Windows Remote Assistance wizard

3. Click **Invite someone you trust to help you.** The How do you want to invite someone to help you? page appears, as shown in Figure 11-5.

Figure 11-5

The How do you want to invite someone to help you? page

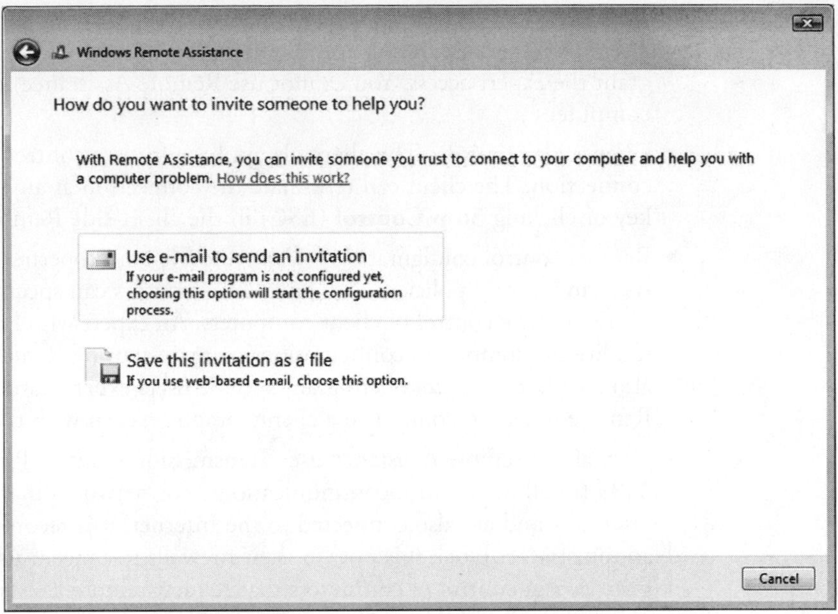

4. Select whether you want to send the invitation in an e-mail or save it as a file. The next page in the wizard appears.
5. Specify a password for the invitation and confirm it. If you chose to save the invitation as a file, you must also specify the folder in which the wizard should create the invitation.
6. Click **Finish** to complete the procedure if you are saving the invitation to a file. If you are sending it in an e-mail, click **Next** to open your e-mail program, which you can use to select a recipient and send the message.

MORE INFORMATION

When users create Remote Assistance invitations, they can specify a password that the expert must supply to connect to their computers. You should urge your users to always require passwords for Remote Assistance connections, and instruct them to supply the expert with the correct password using a different medium than the one they are using to send the invitation.

Once the expert receives the invitation, invoking it launches the Remote Assistance application, which enables the expert to connect to the remote computer. Using this interface, the user and the expert can talk or key messages to each other and, by default, the expert can see everything that the user is doing on the computer. If the client computer is configured to allow remote control, the expert can also click the **Take Control** button and operate the client computer interactively.

Securing Remote Assistance

Because an expert offering remote assistance to another user can perform virtually any activity on the remote computer that the local user can, this feature can be a significant security hazard. An unauthorized user who takes control of a computer using Remote Assistance can cause almost unlimited damage. However, Remote Assistance is designed to minimize the dangers. Some of the protective features of Remote Assistance are as follows:

- Invitations—No person can connect to another computer using Remote Assistance unless that person has received an invitation from the client. Clients can configure the effective lifespan of their invitations in minutes, hours, or days to prevent experts from attempting to connect to the computer later.

- Interactive connectivity—When an expert accepts an invitation from a client and attempts to connect to the computer, a user must be present at the client console to grant the expert access. You cannot use Remote Assistance to connect to an unattended computer.
- Client-side control—The client always has ultimate control over a Remote Assistance connection. The client can terminate the connection at any time, by pressing the ESC key or clicking **Stop Control** (ESC) in the client-side Remote Assistance page.
- Remote control configuration—Using the System Properties sheet or the Remote Assistance group policies, users and administrators can specify whether experts are permitted to take control of client computers. An expert who has read-only access cannot modify the computer's configuration in any way using Remote Access. The group policies also enable administrators to grant specific users expert status, so that no one else can use Remote Access to connect to a client computer, even with the client's permission.
- Firewalls—Remote Assistance uses Transmission Control Protocol (TCP) port number 3389 for all its network communications. For networks that use Remote Assistance internally and are also connected to the Internet, it is recommended that network administrators block this port in their firewalls to prevent users outside the network from taking control of computers that request remote assistance. However, it is also possible to provide remote assistance to clients over the Internet, which would require leaving port 3389 open.

Using Remote Desktop

While Remote Assistance is intended to enable users to obtain interactive help from other users, Remote Desktop is an administrative feature that enables users to access computers from remote locations, with no interaction required at the remote site. Remote Desktop is essentially a remote control program for Windows computers; there are no invitations and no read-only capabilities. When you connect to a computer using Remote Desktop, you can operate the remote computer as though you were sitting at the console and perform most configuration and application tasks.

MORE INFORMATION

One of the most useful application of Remote Desktop is to connect to servers, such as those in a locked closet or data center, that are not otherwise easily accessible. In fact, some administrators run their servers without monitors or input devices once the initial installation and configuration of the computer is complete, relying solely on Remote Desktop access for everyday monitoring and maintenance.

Remote Desktop is essentially an implementation of the Terminal Services technology built into the Windows server operating systems. When you use Terminal Services on a server to host a large number of clients, you must purchase licenses for them. However, Windows Vista allows up to two simultaneous Remote Desktop connections without the need for a separate license.

The Remote Desktop client communicates with a host computer using the ***Remote Desktop Protocol (RDP)***. This protocol essentially transmits screen information, keystrokes, and mouse movements between the two computers. Any applications you launch in the client are still running on the remote computer, using its processor and memory resources.

When you connect to a computer using Remote Desktop, the system creates a separate session for you, independent of the console session. This means that even someone working at the console cannot see what you are doing. You must log on when connecting using Remote Desktop, just as you would if you were sitting at the console, meaning that you must have a user account and the appropriate privileges to access the host system. After you log on, the system displays the desktop configuration associated with your user account, and you can then proceed to work as you normally would.

Activating Remote Desktop

By default, the Terminal Services service that powers the server side of Remote Desktop is disabled on computers running Windows Vista. Before you can connect to a distant computer using Remote Desktop, you must enable it using the controls on the Remote tab of the System Properties sheet, accessed from the Control Panel. Select one of the Allow Connections options, depending on your security needs, and click **OK**.

TAKE NOTE*

Because Remote Desktop requires a standard logon, it is inherently more secure than Remote Assistance, and needs no special security measures such as invitations and session passwords. However, you can also click **Select Remote Users** in the Remote tab to display a Remote Desktop Users dialog box, in which you can specify the names of the users or groups that are permitted to access the computer using Remote Desktop. All users with Administrator privileges are granted access by default.

Using the Remote Desktop Client

In addition to the Terminal Services service, Windows Vista includes the Remote Desktop Connection client program needed to connect to a host computer. To connect to a remote computer with the client, use the following procedure:

RUN THE REMOTE DESKTOP CLIENT

GET READY. Log on to Windows Vista. When the logon process is completed, close the Welcome Center window and any other windows that appear.

1. Click **Start**, and then click **All Programs** > **Accessories** > **Remote Desktop Connection.** The Remote Desktop Connection dialog box appears, as shown in Figure 11-6.

Figure 11-6

The Remote Desktop Connection dialog box

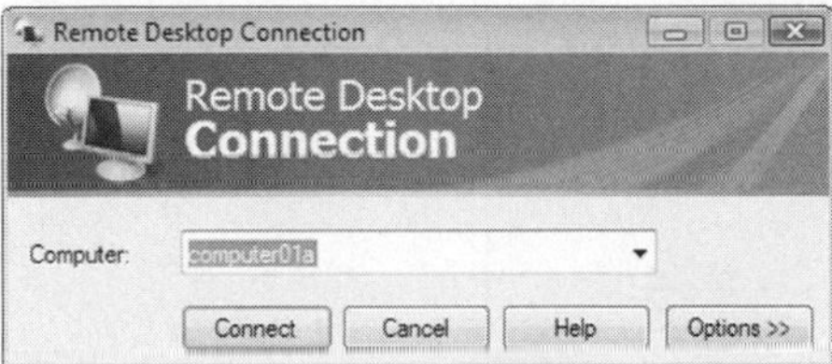

2. Click **Options.** The dialog box expands to show additional controls, as shown in Figure 11-7.

Figure 11-7

The General tab in the expanded Remote Desktop Connection dialog box

3. On the General tab, key the name of the host computer you want to access in the Computer text box. Then click the **Display** tab, as shown in Figure 11-8.

Figure 11-8

The Display tab in the Remote Desktop Connection dialog box

4. In the *Remote desktop size* box, use the slider to select the desired size for the image of the host computer's desktop that will appear on the client system. In the Colors box, select the desired color depth using the dropdown list. Then click the **Local Resources** tab, as shown in Figure 11-9.

Figure 11-9

The Local Resources tab in the Remote Desktop Connection dialog box

5. Using the controls provided, specify which of the resources on the remote computer you want to bring to your local computer, including sound, printers, clipboard, smart cards, serial ports, drives, and other Plug and Play devices. In the Keyboard box, specify how you want the client to handle the Windows key combinations you press on your local computer. Then click the **Experience** tab, as shown in Figure 11-10.

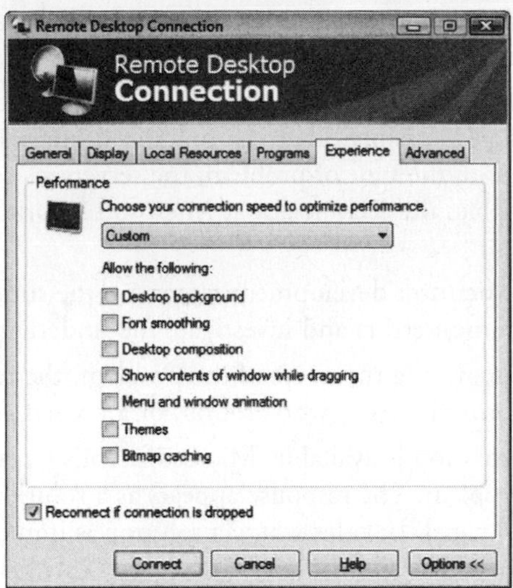

Figure 11-10

The Experience tab in the Remote Desktop Connection dialog box

6. On the Experience tab, you can enhance the performance of the Remote Desktop Connection client by eliminating nonessential visual effects from the display information transmitted over the network. Select one of the network connection speeds from the dropdown list or choose the items you want to suppress by clearing their checkboxes.
7. Click **Connect** to initiate the connection process. A Windows Security dialog box appears.
8. Supply User Name and Password values to log on to the remote computer, and then click **OK.** A Remote Desktop window appears containing an image of the remote computer's desktop.

TAKE NOTE Windows Vista also includes a Remote Desktops console (accessible from the Administrative Tools control panel) that you can use to connect to multiple Remote Desktop hosts and switch between them as needed.

Using the Problem Reports and Solutions Control Panel

Windows Vista includes a tool that you can use to report system problems directly to Microsoft's technicians.

The Problem Reports and Solutions control panel is a tool that enables Microsoft to provide assistance when your own troubleshooting attempts fail to correct a problem. The Problem Reports and Solutions control panel is the user interface for ***Windows Error Reporting (WER)***, which is the Windows Vista replacement for the Dr. Watson error handler found in earlier versions of Windows. WER is, in turn, the client component of the ***Watson Feedback Platform (WFP)***, which is a Microsoft service that collects reports about system and application errors, investigates the information in those reports, and responds to the user with possible solutions.

Windows Vista can send problem reports to Microsoft automatically, or you can configure WER to request permission to submit them. When the operating system or an application experiences a significant error, it typically terminates the offending process and displays a message box offering to submit the problem report. If you agree to send the report, the problem resolution procedure occurs in the following manner:

1. Report—The report submission process can be triggered by an operating system event, or by an application that has been designed to create a custom event type. You can also create problem reports manually in the Problem Reports and Solutions control panel.

The problem reports are transmitted to a WFP server at Microsoft as soon as an Internet connection is available.

2. Categorization—On arrival at the back-end servers, the problem is categorized, based on the event parameters and possibly other information submitted with the report, such as a memory dump. Based on the type of problem, the servers also assign the problem a Watson Bucket ID, which enables the technicians at Microsoft to prioritize issues based on the number of incidents.
3. Investigation—The Microsoft development teams use the submitted information to identify the most common errors and investigate the underlying cause.
4. Resolution—After discovering the cause of the problem, the technicians attempt to arrive at a solution in the form of a fix, a workaround, or a revised version.
5. Response—When a solution is available, Microsoft sends a response to the computers that submitted the problem. The response appears as a solution in the Problem Reports and Solutions control panel. In cases where a solution is immediately available, the entire process might be automated, and the response appears as a balloon notification almost immediately after the system submits the problem.

MORE INFORMATION

By itself, the Windows Error Reporting engine in Windows Vista can only send its problem reports directly to Microsoft. However, there is a product called Microsoft System Center Operations Manager 2007 that enterprise administrators can use to redirect the client problem submissions to an internal management server first. This way, administrators can evaluate the submitted problems first and decide which ones should be forwarded to Microsoft. They can also specify exactly how much and what types of information the clients should submit.

To open the Problem Reports and Solutions control panel, click **Start**, and then click **Control Panel > System and Maintenance > Problem Reports and Solutions**. The *Solve problems on your computer* page appears, as shown in Figure 11-11.

Figure 11-11

The Problem Reports and Solutions control panel

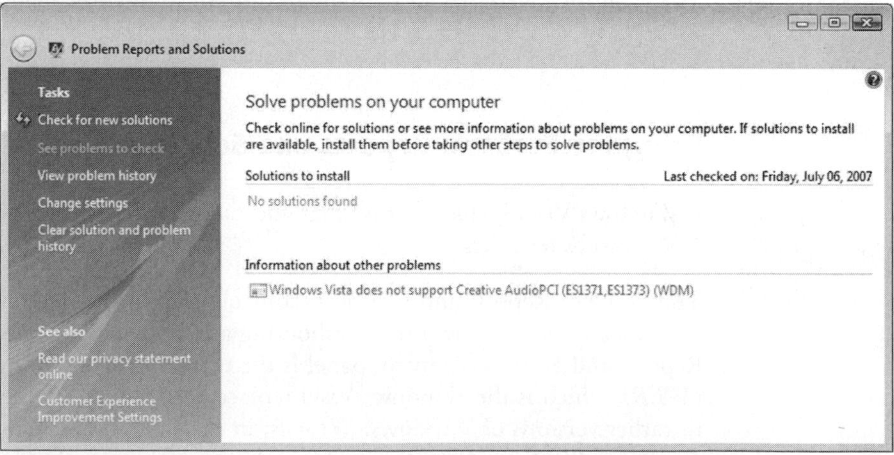

This page lists the responses that the WER client has received from Microsoft in response to the computer's problem reports. Double-clicking one of the entries displays more information, as shown in Figure 11-12.

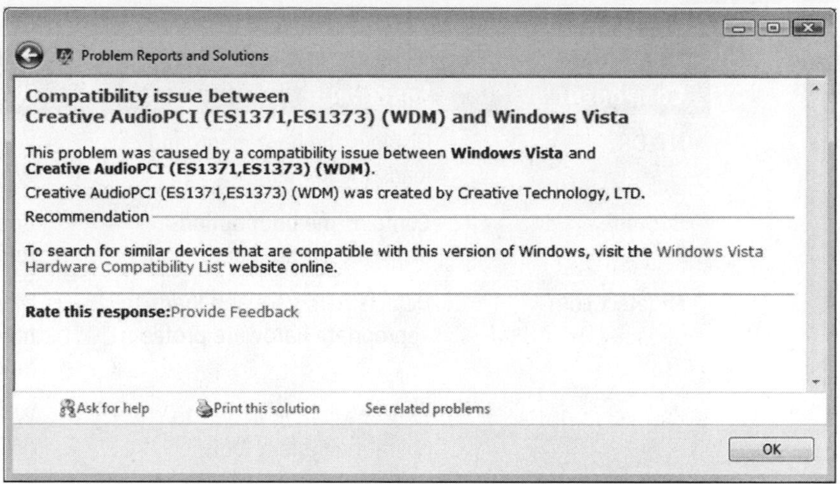
Problem Reports and Solutions
Compatibility issue between
Creative AudioPCI (ES1371,ES1373) (WDM) and Windows Vista
This problem was caused by a compatibility issue between Windows Vista and Creative AudioPCI (ES1371,ES1373) (WDM).
Creative AudioPCI (ES1371,ES1373) (WDM) was created by Creative Technology, LTD.
Recommendation
To search for similar devices that are compatible with this version of Windows, visit the Windows Vista Hardware Compatibility List website online.
Rate this response: Provide Feedback
Ask for help
Print this solution
See related problems
OK

Figure 11-12

A response from Microsoft, displayed in the Problem Reports and Solutions control panel

Using the links on the left side of the control panel, you can also see a list of the problems submitted to Microsoft, trigger a check for new solutions to outstanding problems, and configure the behavior of the client.

Troubleshooting Installation and Startup Issues

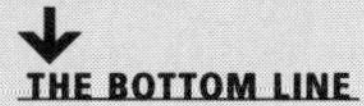

THE BOTTOM LINE

Learning the troubleshooting process is better than learning to fix specific problems. However, troubleshooting startup problems can be difficult because the usual tools are unavailable.

This lesson has so far concentrated on general troubleshooting procedures and the troubleshooting tools that Windows Vista provides. This is in keeping with the belief that, to become an efficient troubleshooter, it is better to concentrate on learning the general process than dealing with specific problems. After all, there are an unlimited number of things that can go wrong on a computer and, as the old saying goes, giving a man a fish feeds him for a day, but teaching him to fish feeds him for life.

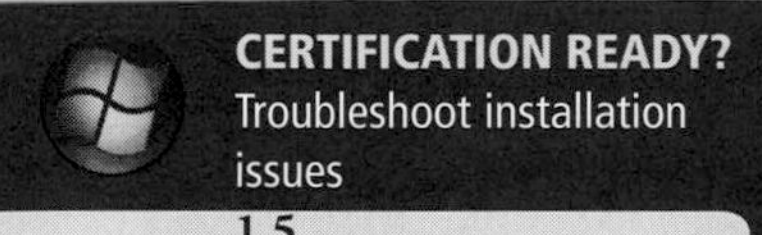

CERTIFICATION READY?
Troubleshoot installation issues
1.5

One of the more difficult types of problem to troubleshoot is one that prevents the computer from starting properly, because you don't have access to all of the troubleshooting tools included with Windows Vista. To troubleshoot a Windows Vista computer that fails to start, you must have an understanding of the startup procedure, and knowledge of the tools that are available to you.

Understanding the Windows Vista Startup Process

Windows Vista uses a startup process that is substantially different from those of previous Windows versions, and desktop technicians should be familiar with the changes.

Windows Vista introduces some significant changes to the startup procedure, when compared to Windows XP and other NT-based Windows versions. Table 11-2 lists the new components found in Windows Vista, and the Windows XP components they replace.

Table 11-2

Windows XP and Windows Vista Startup Components

WINDOWS XP COMPONENT	FUNCTION	WINDOWS VISTA COMPONENT
NTLDR	Displays the boot menu and loads the kernel	Windows Boot Manager Windows Boot Loader
Boot.ini	Contains the boot options displayed on the boot menu	Boot Configuration Data (BCD) registry file
Ntdetect.com	Detects hardware and loads the appropriate hardware profile	Merged into the kernel, as hardware profiles are no longer needed
Recovery Console	Provides limited access to operating system tools	Windows Recovery Environment (Windows RE)

The Windows Vista startup process consists of the following steps:

1. ***Power-on self test (POST)*** phase—When you first turn the computer on, it loads the BIOS or Extensible Firmware Interface (EFI) and runs a hardware self-test procedure that detects the devices installed in the system and configures them using settings stored in non-volatile memory. After the main POST, any devices with their own BIOS firmware (such as video display adapters) can run their own self-test procedures.
2. Initial startup phase—On BIOS-equipped computers, the system reads the BIOS settings to determine which hardware device it should use to boot the computer. When booting from a hard disk, the system loads the master boot record (MBR) from the disk and locates the active (bootable) partition. The system then loads and runs a stub program called Bootmgr, which switches the processor from real mode to protected mode and loads the Windows Boot Manager application. EFI computers have their own built-in boot manager, which Vista configures to run the same Windows Boot Manager application, eliminating the need for the interim disk location steps.
3. Windows Boot Manager phase—Reads the ***Boot Configuration Data (BCD)*** registry file, which contains the system's moot menu information, and provides the user with access to the boot menu, as shown in Figure 11-13. If there is only one operating system installed on the computer, the boot menu only appears when the user presses the a key just after the POST, or presses the F8 key to display the Advanced Boot Options menu. If there are multiple operating systems installed, the boot menu appears, providing the user with 30 seconds to select one of the operating systems before it loads the default.
4. Windows Boot Loader phase—Initiates the memory paging process and loads various operating system elements into memory, such as the Windows kernel, the hardware abstraction layer (HAL), the system registry hive, and boot class device drivers, but it does not actually run them.
5. Kernel loading phase—Runs the Windows Executive (consisting of the Windows kernel and the HAL), which processes the registry hive and initializes the drivers and services specified there. The kernel then starts the Session Manager, which loads the kernel-mode part of the Win32 subsystem, causing the system to switch from text mode to graphics mode. Then the kernel loads the user-mode portion of Win32, which provides applications with indirect, protected access to the system hardware. At this time, the system also performs delayed rename operations resulting from system updates that must replace files that were in use when the update was installed. Finally, the kernel creates additional virtual memory paging files and starts the Logon Manager.
6. Logon phase—Loads the Service Control Manager (SCM) and the Local Security Authority (LSA), and then presents the logon user interface (LogonUI). The interface passes the credentials supplied by the user to the LSA for authentication, and the SCM loads the Plug and Play services and drivers that are configured for autoloading. If the

authentication is successful, the Logon Manager launches Userinit.exe, which is responsible for applying group policy settings and running the programs in the Startup group, and then loads the Windows Explorer shell, which provides the Windows desktop.

Figure 11-13

The Windows Vista boot menu

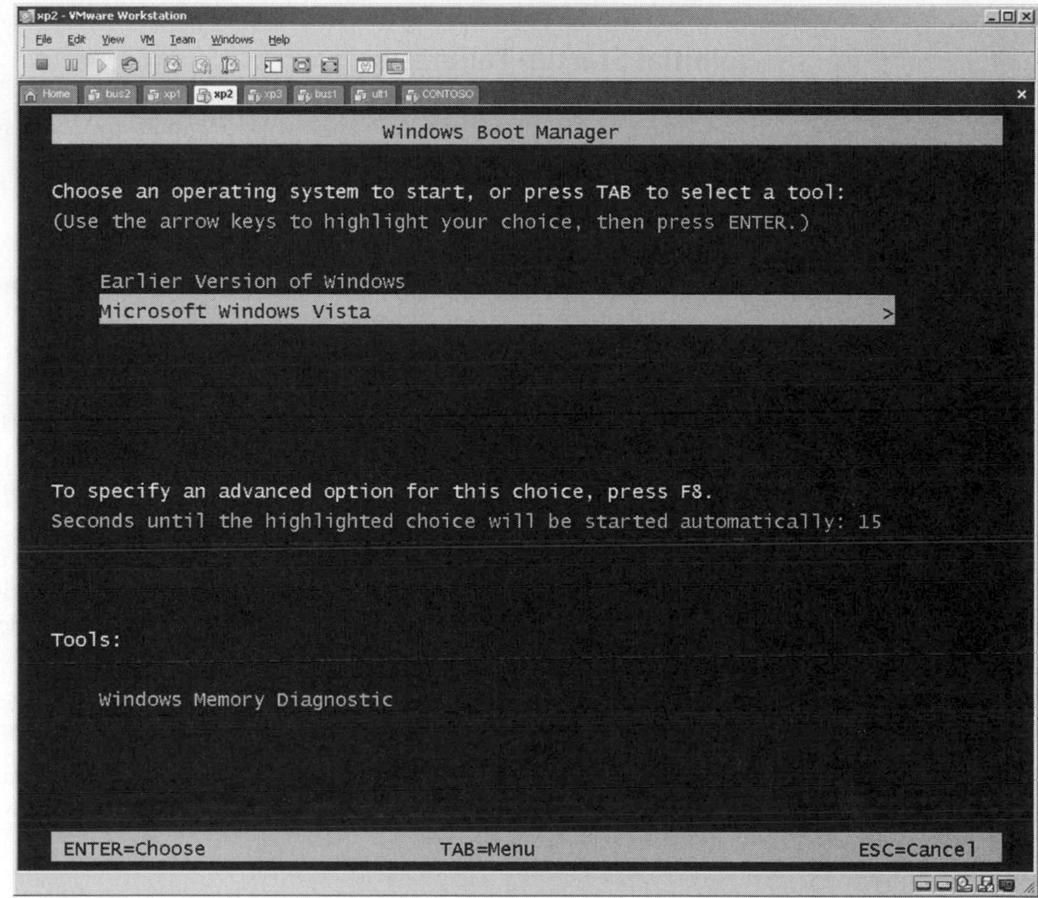

Troubleshooting Startup Failures

The first step in troubleshooting a startup failure is determining exactly where in the startup process the failure is occurring.

The symptoms of a startup failure differ depending on where in the process the failure occurs. Therefore, the first step to take when a Windows Vista computer fails to start is to determine exactly where in the startup sequence the problem is occurring.

POST Failures

One of the most fundamental questions a troubleshooter can ask is whether a problem is being caused by a hardware or a software failure. If a computer fails to make it through the POST successfully, the problem is unquestionably hardware-related. In most cases, the BIOS will display an error message or produce a series of beeps identifying the exact problem that is causing the failure. Consult the BIOS documentation for more information on its error messages and/or beep codes.

MORE INFORMATION

Some BIOS programs enable you to select between a "quick" POST or an extended "diagnostic" sequence. At the first sign of a hardware problem, you should switch to the diagnostic mode to gather as much information as possible about the problem.

Initial Startup Failures

A failure during the initial startup phase typically results in a "Non-system disk or disk error," which means that there is an issue with the BIOS configuration, the storage subsystem, or the file system. Startup failures that occur before the progress bar appears are typically caused by one of the following problems:

- Incorrect BIOS Settings—If the boot settings in the BIOS are misconfigured, the system might be attempting to boot from the wrong drive. For example, if the BIOS is configured to boot from the CD or DVD drive first, and there is no bootable disk in the drive, the computer will be unable to start.
- Hardware faults—If anyone has recently worked inside the computer's case, you might want to begin by checking the hard drive's power and data connections. Also, if there is an internal problem with the hard disk, such as corruption of the MBR, the system might not be able to locate the active partition.
- Missing startup files—If some of the required startup files are missing or damaged, the computer will fail to boot. This could be due to the installation of another operating system over Windows Vista, accidental deletion of system files, or data corruption on the hard disk.
- Data corruption—Corrupted data on a disk drive can be the result of a hardware fault, environmental factors (such as magnetic fields), or some form of malware.

Resolving these problems can require the replacement of a hardware component, but in many cases you can repair them using the specialized recovery tools provided with Windows Vista, as discussed later in this lesson.

Driver and Service Failures

The appearance of the progress bar indicates that the kernel has loaded successfully. When a startup failure occurs after the progress bar appears, but before the logon user interface appears, the problem could be hardware-related, but it is most likely due to a issue with one of the drivers or services that the kernel is attempting to load. Resolving the problem is a matter of determining which of the drivers or services is at fault.

To locate the offending driver or service, you must first attempt to get the computer started by using the Last Known Good Configuration option, Safe Mode, or other means. Then you can examine the event logs, enable the boot log, and run the System Information tool to gather information on what is affecting the startup sequence. Finally, use Device Manager or the Services console to disable the offending drivers or services. Once you are able to get the computer started in normal node, you can begin to examine the problematic driver or service, perhaps replacing them with an updated version or rolling back to a previous one.

Logon Failures

When the startup process fails after the user has supplied logon credentials, the problem is most likely due to one of the applications running from the Startup group. The simplest way to prevent the startup applications from running is to hold down the Shift key when logging on, until the icons appear on the desktop. When you do this, the startup applications do not load, but only for that session.

Once the system is started, you can try loading each of the startup applications in turn to see which one is causing the problem. After isolating the offending application, you can see about reconfiguring, upgrading, or uninstalling it, so that the problem is eliminated.

Using Recovery Tools

Windows Vista includes specialized tools for diagnosing and repairing startup problems.

Windows Vista has many tools that you can use for troubleshooting system and network problems, but if the computer fails to start, these tools are not available. Fortunately, Vista includes a special working environment that you can use when the system fails to start, as well as a selection of tools that you can use in that environment.

Using Alternate Boot Options

In many cases, just getting the computer to start can be half of the troubleshooting battle. Once the computer is started, you have access to the configuration interface and the Vista troubleshooting tools that can help you solve the problem. If the problem is hardware-related, you are unlikely to get the system started until you repair or replace the malfunctioning component. However, if the startup problem occurs after the progress bar appears, you can probably get the system started in one of the following ways:

- To suppress drivers and services—Press F8 repeatedly, immediately after the POST completes and before the progress bar appears. From the Advanced Boot Options menu, select Last Known Good Configuration or, if that does not work, one of the Safe Mode options.
- To suppress startup applications—Press the Shift key while logging on and hold it down until the icons appear on the desktop.

The Last Known Good Configuration option reverses all of the system configuration, driver, and registry changes you made since the computer last booted successfully. The Safe Mode options start the computer with a minimal set of generic drivers, just those needed to run the system. Once the system is running, you can exercise control over and gather information about the startup process using the tools covered in the following sections.

Using the Startup and Recovery Dialog Box

The Startup and Recovery dialog box provides basic controls that enable you to configure the Windows Vista startup process by modifying the BCD registry file. To open the Startup and Recovery dialog box, use the following procedure:

OPEN THE STARTUP AND RECOVERY DIALOG BOX

GET READY. Log on to Windows Vista. When the logon process is completed, close the Welcome Center window and any other windows that appear.

1. Click **Start**, and then click **Control Panel > System and Maintenance > System.** The System control panel appears.
2. Click **Advanced System Settings.** After confirming your action, the System Properties sheet appears.
3. Click the **Advanced** tab, as shown in Figure 11-14.

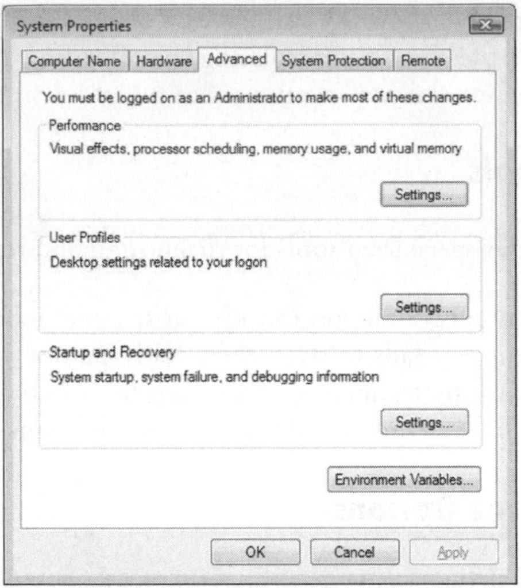

Figure 11-14

The System Properties sheet

4. In the Startup and Recovery box, click **Settings**. The Startup and Recovery dialog box appears, as shown in Figure 11-15.

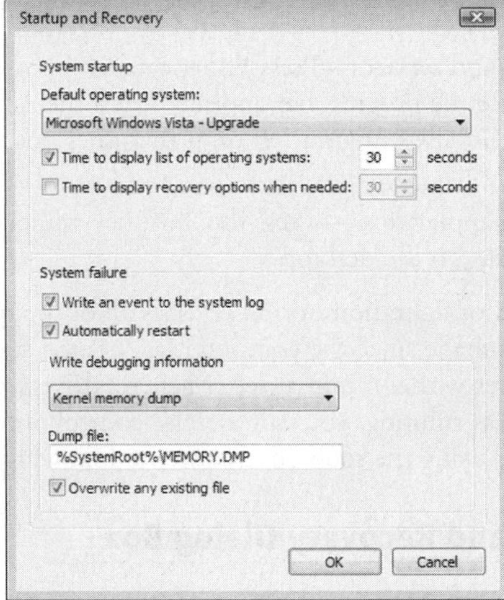

Figure 11-15

The Startup and Recovery dialog box

In this dialog box, you can specify which operating system to load on a dual boot computer, and also specify how long the boot menu and recovery options menu appear by default. You can also exercise control over the computer's logging behavior during system startup.

Using the System Configuration Tool

If you can get Windows Vista to start in Safe Mode, the System Configuration tool enables you to exercise a great deal of control over the startup process. You can select the type of startup to perform, configure a variety of BCD registry file settings, and specify individual applications and services to be omitted from the startup sequence.

MORE INFORMATION

While the System Configuration tool provides more access to the BCD registry settings than the Startup and Recovery dialog box, it is not the most comprehensive BCD editing tool available. To exercise complete control over the BCD, you must use the BCDEdit.exe tool from the command line in Windows Vista or Windows RE.

To start the System Configuration tool, click **Start**, key msconfig, and press Enter. The System Configuration dialog box appears. The dialog box contains the following tabs:

- General—Provides controls that enable you to perform a normal, diagnostic, or selective startup sequence, as shown in Figure 11-16. You can use these options to suppress specific parts of the startup process in the hope of bypassing the component causing the problem.

Figure 11-16

The General tab in the System Configuration dialog box

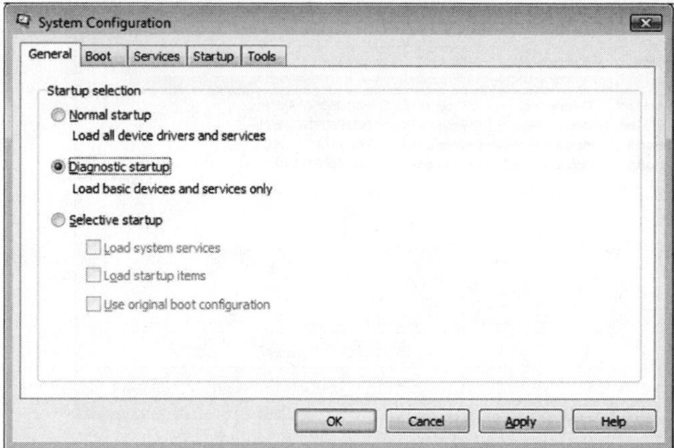

- Boot—Controls BCD registry settings that enable you to select the operating system to install and configure a limited boot sequence, as shown in Figure 11-17. Clicking *Advanced options* displays a BOOT Advanced Options dialog box, which you can use control the system hardware used during the startup sequence.

Figure 11-17

The Boot tab in the System Configuration dialog box

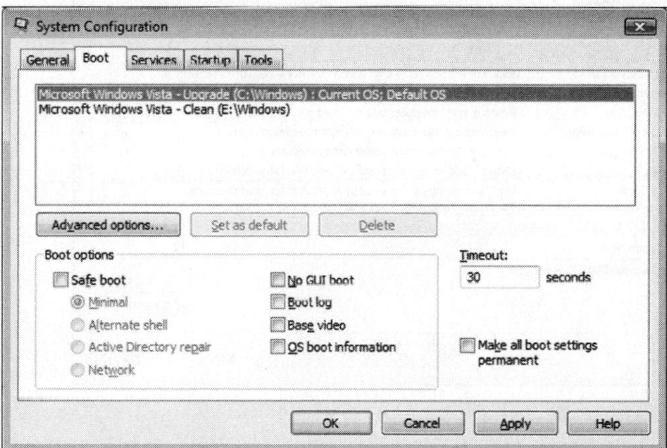

- Services—Enables you to select the services that will run during the startup sequence, as shown in Figure 11-18. By disabling all of the services and then enabling them one at a time as you repeatedly restart the computer, you can determine which service is causing a startup failure.

Figure 11-18

The Services tab in the System Configuration dialog box

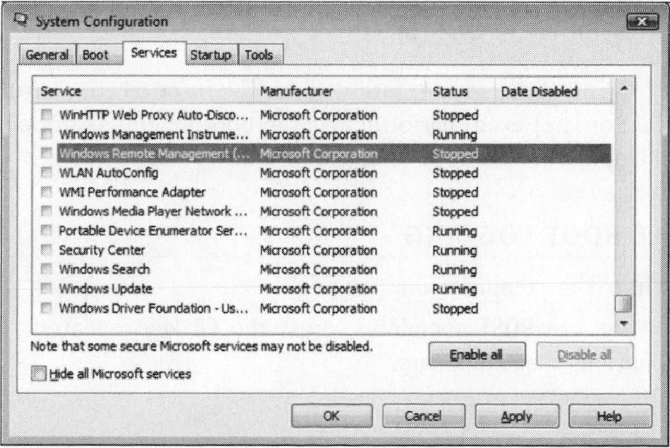

- Startup—Enables you to select the startup applications that will run during the startup sequence, as shown in Figure 11-19. By disabling all of the startup applications and then enabling them one at a time as you repeatedly restart the computer, you can determine which application is causing a startup failure.

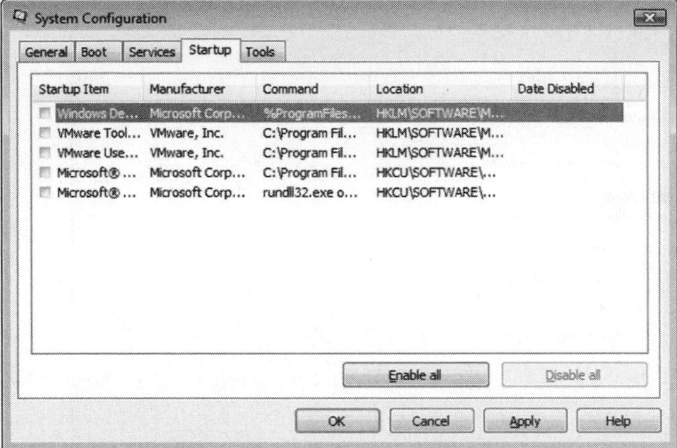

Figure 11-19

The Startup tab in the System Configuration dialog box

- Tools—Enables you to launch a variety of Windows Vista configuration and troubleshooting tools, as shown in Figure 11-20.

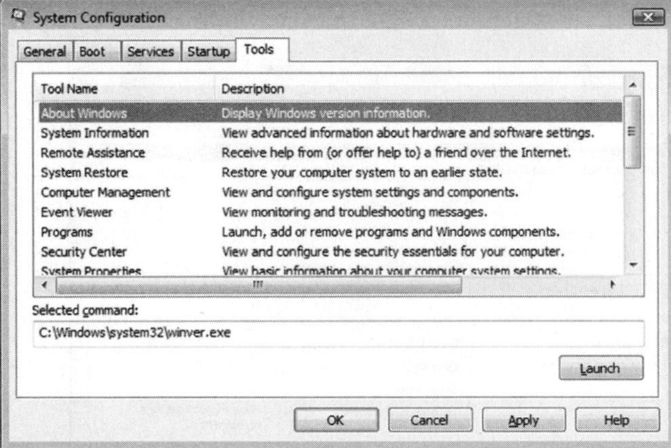

Figure 11-20

The Tools tab in the System Configuration dialog box

TAKE NOTE*

When you make changes to the system startup configuration using the System Configuration tool, Windows Vista displays a message when users log on, reminding them of the changes, so they do not forget to restore the original configuration.

Enabling Boot Logging

Boot logging gathers information about the most recent startup process and saves it to a text file for later examination. However, boot logging is not enabled by default. To enable boot logging, use the following procedure:

ENABLE BOOT LOGGING

1. Turn the computer on.
2. When the POST completes, press the **F8** key repeatedly until the Advanced Boot Options menu appears.

3. Select **Enable Boot Logging**. The system creates a log file in the \Windows folder called Ntblog.txt. The startup procedure continues, adding information to the log file as it proceeds.

The boot log contains a list of all the files that Vista attempts to load during the startup process, along with a status indicator specifying whether each file loaded successfully. If you enable boot logging during a normal startup, and then perform a Safe Mode startup, the system will append the Safe Mode startup information to the existing log. This enables you to compare the two startup sequences and determine which files are required for a successful, normal startup that are not required for a Safe Mode startup. If the Safe Mode startup is successful and a normal one is not, then one of those files must be causing the problem.

Using Windows RE

As you learned in Lesson 2, "Installing Windows Vista," the Vista installation process uses the Windows Preinstallation Environment (Windows PE) to boot the system for the first time and initiate the Setup program. Windows PE is a stripped-down operating system that, unlike the DOS environment used in previous Windows versions, supports the same drivers used in a complete Vista installation, as well as a subset of the Win32 application programming interface (API).

For computers that already have the operating system installed, Windows Vista includes the Windows Recovery Environment (Windows RE), which is essentially the same as Windows PE. By booting into Windows RE, you bypass all of the drivers, applications, and services that can be the source of a startup problem. Windows RE also provides access to a collection of recovery tools that can identify and even repair many of the problems that can prevent the system from starting.

To run Windows RE, use the following procedure:

1. Insert a Windows Vista installation DVD into the drive and restart the computer.
2. If you are prompted to do so, press any key to boot from the DVD. (If the system fails to prompt and boots from the hard disk instead, you might have to modify your system BIOS settings to use the DVD as the first boot device.) The Install Windows wizard appears.
3. Select the appropriate language and keyboard settings and click **Next**. The Install Now page appears.
4. Click **Repair Your Computer**. The program scans the computer's drives for Windows Vista installations and displays a System Recovery Options dialog box containing the results.
5. Select the instance of the operating system you want to repair, and then click **Next**. The Choose a Recovery Tool page appears.
6. Click one of the links to launch a recovery tool.

TAKE NOTE*

If Windows Vista experienced a startup failure immediately before you booted from the DVD, the Startup Repair tool will load automatically.

Using the System Recovery Tools

When you load Windows RE from the Windows Vista installation DVD, the system provides you with a choice of recovery tools, including the following:

- Startup Repair—An automated troubleshooting tool that is capable of diagnosing and repairing a variety of problems that can prevent Windows Vista from starting, including BCD problems and missing startup files. The prompts displayed by the tool vary, depending on the conditions it detects, but all of its activities are logged in a file called SRTTrail.txt, located in the \Windows\System32\LogFiles\SRT folder. When the cause of a startup problem is not immediately apparent, this should be the first tool you use.

- System Restore—Enables you to access the restore points on the computer, whether manually or automatically created, and use them to restore the system to an earlier state. This is the same functionality available in the System Restore application, accessible from the System Tools program group in Windows Vista (in normal or safe mode).
- Complete PC Restore—Enables you to perform a full restoration of your computer, using a Complete PC image you previously created.
- Windows Memory Diagnostic Tool—Tests the computer's memory for hardware errors.
- Command Prompt—Displays a command prompt, from which you can run a variety of text-based tools included with Windows RE.

SUMMARY SKILL MATRIX

IN THIS LESSON YOU LEARNED:
When troubleshooting a problem in a professional environment, whether it's a corporate enterprise network, a help desk in a retail store, or a freelance consultancy, it is important to have a set troubleshooting procedure.
The troubleshooting procedure should include the following: Establish the symptoms. Identify the affected area. Establish what has changed. Select the most probable cause. Implement a solution. Test the result. Document the solution.
Remote access technologies enable a user on one computer to effectively take control of another computer on the network.
Remote Assistance is a Windows Vista feature that enables an administrator, trainer, or desktop technician at one location to connect to a distant user's computer, chat with the user, and either view all the user's activities or take complete control of the system.
Remote Desktop is an administrative feature that enables users to access computers from remote locations, with no interaction required at the remote site.
The Problem Reports and Solutions control panel is the user interface for Windows Error Reporting (WER), which is the Windows Vista replacement for the Dr. Watson error handler found in earlier versions of Windows.
To troubleshoot a Windows Vista computer that fails to start, you must have an understanding of the startup procedure, and knowledge of the tools that are available.
The first step to take when a Windows Vista computer fails to start is to determine exactly where in the startup sequence the problem is occurring.
A failure during the initial startup phase typically results in a "Non-system disk or disk error."
When a startup failure occurs after the progress bar appears, but before the logon user interface appears, the problem is most likely due to a issue with one of the drivers or services that the kernel is attempting to load.
When the startup process fails after the user has supplied logon credentials, the problem is most likely due to one of the applications running from the Startup group.
Windows RE is a stripped-down operating system that supports the same drivers used in a complete Vista installation, as well as a subset of the Win32 application programming interface (API).
When the cause of a startup problem is not immediately apparent, the Startup Repair tool should be the first program you use.

Knowledge Assessment

Fill in the Blank

Complete the following sentences by writing the correct word or words in the blanks provided.

1. To connect to a remote computer that is unattended, you must use the Remote ______________ utility.
2. Windows Error Reporting is the client component of the ______________.
3. Microsoft prioritizes submitted problems based on the number of incidents, using an identifier called a(n) ______________.
4. Startup failures that generate a "Non-system disk or disk error" typically occur during the ______________ phase.
5. The Windows XP Boot.ini file has been replaced in Windows Vista by the ______________ file.
6. The first tool you should use when the cause of a startup problem is not immediately apparent is ______________.
7. To run the System Configuration tool, key ______________ at a command prompt.
8. The acronym for the hardware test that the computer performs when you first switch it on is called the ______________.
9. To enable boot logging, you must access the ______________ menu.
10. Startup failures that occur after the kernel is loaded and before the logon are typically caused by a problematic ______________ or ______________.

True / False

Circle T if the statement is true or F if the statement is false.

T | F 1. Remote Assistance is not designed to minimize the dangers of any person who takes control of a computer.

T | F 2. Because Remote Desktop is essentially an implementation of the Terminal Services technology built into the Windows server operating systems, you must purchase licenses to use any connections with Remote Desktop on Windows Vista.

T | F 3. If a startup problem occurs after the progress bar appears, one of the ways you might be able to get the system started is to press F8 repeatedly, immediately after the POST completes and before the progress bar appears. This action suppresses drivers, services, and startup applications.

T | F 4. To troubleshoot a Windows Vista computer that fails to start, it helps to have an understanding of the startup procedure's phases, and of the tools that are available during startup.

T | F 5. The Windows Error Reporting engine in Windows Vista can enable enterprise administrators to redirect the client problem submissions to an internal management server so that administrators can evaluate the submitted problems and decide which ones should be forwarded to Microsoft.

T | F 6. Boot logging gathers information about the most recent startup process and saves it to a text file for later examination. Boot logging is enabled by default.

T | F 7. The Last Known Good Configuration option reverses all of the system configuration, driver, and registry changes you made since the computer last booted successfully.

T | F 8. A well-organized technical support organization should have a system in place in which each problem call is registered as a trouble ticket that eventually contains a complete record of the problem and the steps taken to isolate and resolve it.

T | F 9. The Problem Reports and Solutions control panel is a tool that enables Microsoft to provide assistance when your own troubleshooting attempts fail to correct a problem.

T | F 10. Hardware-related error is a common cause of problems that might at first seem to be user-related.

Review Questions

1. Give three reasons why the Remote Assistance tool is safe to use, despite the fact that it can provide a remote user with control over a computer.
2. Place the following phases of the windows Vista startup sequence in the correct order.

    Logon phase

    Windows Boot Loader phase

    Initial startup phase

    Power-on self test (POST) phase

    Windows Boot Manager phase

    Kernel loading phase

■ Case Scenarios

Scenario #1: Assigning Troubleshooting Priorities

During a busy shift at the help desk at Litware, Inc., a call comes in at 9:05 A.M. from an angry user whose mouse is not working. At 9:07 A.M., the vice president of the Marketing department calls to report that the hard drive in the file server where the company's ad campaigns are stored has failed. At 9:15 A.M., the manager of the Order Entry department calls to report that the e-mail server that delivers the product orders generated through the company's Website is down. Between 9:25 and 9:45 A.M., four users on the LAN in the Sales department call to report that they cannot access the company intranet server containing the health insurance forms they need. As the help desk manager, which of these four problems should you address first? Explain your answer, and why you did not choose the other three.

Scenario #2: Isolating the Problem

You are a freelance computer consultant providing desktop support to a client, Ralph, with a small business network that you designed and installed. The network consists of five Windows Vista computers connected to a single switch, which is in turn connected to a DSL router, providing Internet access to all of the computers. Ralph calls to report that Internet Explorer is unable to connect to any site on the Internet.

Following are three tasks that you will ask Ralph to perform. Explain how each of the tasks can help you to isolate the component that is causing the problem.

1. Ask Ralph to open a Command Prompt window and try to ping a server on the Internet.
2. Ask Ralph to try to connect to a share on another one of the network's computers.
3. Ask Ralph to log on to one of the other computers on the network and try to access the Internet using Internet Explorer.

Working with Mobile Computers

LESSON 12

OBJECTIVE DOMAIN MATRIX

Technology Skill	Objective Domain	Objective Number
Configuring Vista Wireless Networking	Use the Network and Sharing Center to configure networking	4.1
Configuring Mobile Display Options	Configure mobile display settings	7.1
Configuring Power Options	Configure power options	7.4
Synchronizing Data	Configure mobile devices	7.2
Configuring Tablet PC Features	Configure tablet PC software	7.3

KEY TERMS

Advanced Configuration and Power Interface (ACPI)
Advanced Encryption System (AES)
DVI (Digital Visual Interface)
IEEE 802.11
Institute of Electrical and Electronic Engineers (IEEE)
multiple-input multiple-output (MIMO)
spatial multiplexing
Temporal Key Integrity Protocol (TKIP)
Wi-Fi Protected Access (WPA)
Wired Equivalent Privacy (WEP)
wireless access point (WAP)

Using Windows Vista on a Mobile Computer

Mobile computing devices present special configuration challenges for desktop technicians.

Mobile computing devices are an increasingly popular option for all classes of computer users. Today's laptop computers have performance capabilities comparable to desktops, and many people use them in place of a standard desktop. Although no special procedures or considerations are necessary to install Windows Vista on a laptop computer, desktop technicians should be aware of some special configuration settings for laptops, such as power and display options.

In addition to standard laptops, consumers have the option of purchasing tablet PCs from several manufacturers. A tablet PC looks a lot like a standard laptop except that the screen is reversible, so that it faces outwards when the user closes the lid. The screen on a tablet PC is also touch sensitive, so that a user can write directly on the LCD panel with a stylus. The standard Windows Vista editions include all of the special software needed for the tablet PC hardware, including a sophisticated handwriting recognition engine that enables the computer to interpret the stylus movements into text and commands. These features also have some specialized configuration settings.

In addition to fully capable computers using the laptop form factor, handheld devices, such as personal data assistants (PDAs), smartphones, and even music players, are taking the mobile computing world by storm. To make full use of these devices users must synchronize them with the data on their main computers, and this requires proper configuration.

The following sections examine some the configuration settings that desktop technicians should know how to use when working with mobile devices.

Using Wireless Networking

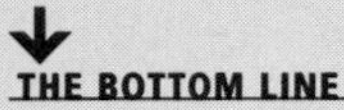

Most mobile computers sold today have wireless networking capabilities. Desktop technicians should be aware of the security issues involved in wireless networking and the configuration tasks required to support them.

Wireless networking technologies have existed for a long time, but only the improvements of the past few years have made wireless networks practical for the average user. In the past, the biggest obstacle to home and small business networking was the expense and inconvenience of installing network cables. Today, many families and organizations with multiple computers use wireless networks to share printers, data, and Internet connections, and in no situation are these wireless technologies more useful than when users are working with mobile computers.

Wireless networks enable laptop users to wander around the house or the office, sharing information and collaborating at will. Windows Vista includes full support for wireless networking but, unlike wired network connections that Vista can often install and configure automatically, wireless connections require configuration, which is a job often left to the desltop technician.

Understanding Wireless Security

Wireless networks are subject to many of the same security threats as cabled networks, but the medium they use makes it easier for attackers to penetrate them.

Establishing a wireless connection is not difficult, but establishing a secure one can be. Wired networks typically rely on physical security to protect the privacy of their communications. A potential intruder must have physical access to the network cable to connect to the network. This is not the case with wireless networks. If a wireless network is not properly secured, an intruder in a car parked outside can use a laptop to gain full access to the network's communications.

Connecting to a wireless network can grant an attacker access to resources on an organization's internal network, or it might enable the attacker to access the Internet while hiding his or her identity. Some of the specific types of attacks to which an unsecured wireless network is subject are as follows:

- Eavesdropping—Attackers can capture traffic as a wireless computer communicates with a ***wireless access point (WAP)***. Depending on the type of antennae the devices use and their transmitting power, an attacker might be able to eavesdrop from hundreds or thousands of feet away.
- Masquerading—Attackers might be able to gain access to restricted network resources by impersonating authorized wireless users. This enables the attacker to engage in illegal activities or attack hosts on remote networks while disguised with another identity.

- Attacks against wireless clients—Attackers can launch a network-based attack on a wireless computer that is connected to an ad hoc or untrusted wireless network.
- Denial of service—Attackers can jam the wireless frequencies by using a transmitter, preventing legitimate users from successfully communicating with a WAP.
- Data tampering—Attackers can delete, replay, or modify wireless communications with a man-in-the-middle attack. A man-in-the-middle attack is when an intruder intercepts network communications and modifies the contents of the packets before sending them on to their destination.

The concerns over the abuse of wireless networks are far from theoretical. Intruders have a wide variety of tools available for detecting, connecting to, and abusing wireless networks. As with most aspects of security, technologies are available that you can use to limit the vulnerabilities presented by wireless networks. Specifically, you must configure the network computers so that all wireless communications are authenticated and encrypted. This provides protection similar to that offered by the physical security of wired networks.

Evaluating Wireless Networking Hardware

The 802.11 standards published by the ***Institute of Electrical and Electronic Engineers (IEEE)*** dictate the frequencies, transmission speeds, and ranges of wireless networking products. Table 12-1 lists the ***IEEE 802.11*** standards and their capabilities.

Table 12-1

IEEE Wireless Networking Standards

IEEE Standard	Release Date	Status	Data Rate	Indoor Range	Outdoor Range
802.11a	1999	Ratified	54 Mb/sec	~30 meters	~100 meters
802.11b	1999	Ratified	11 Mb/sec	~35 meters	~110 meters
802.11g	2003	Ratified	54 Mb/sec	~35 meters	~110 meters
802.11n	2008 (Estimated)	Draft	248 Mb/sec (2×2 MIMO)	~70 meters	~160 meters

Most of the wireless networking hardware now available supports the 802.11b and 802.11g standards. There are also 802.11n products on the market, which are based on draft standards that have not yet been ratified, as well as a number of proprietary technologies that boost transmission speeds beyond those specified in the standards.

MORE INFORMATION

IEEE 802.11n equipment increases wireless networking speeds by using multiple transmitter and receiver antennae on each device in a process called ***multiple-input multiple-output (MIMO)***. For example, a device using a 2x2 MIMO format has two transmitters and two receivers, operating at different frequencies. The sending system splits its data into two signals for transmission, and the receiving device reassembles the signals into a single data stream. This process is called ***spatial multiplexing***. The only potential drawback to this arrangement is the depletion of the available frequency bandwidth by having too many devices in proximity to each other.

As a general rule, devices supporting the newer, faster standards are capable of falling back to slower speeds when necessary. For example, an 802.11g WAP will almost always support computers with 802.11b hardware as well. If you're involved in hardware evaluation or selection, compatibility problems are relatively rare, as far as these standards are concerned. The possibility of purchasing incompatible hardware is likely only if you adopt a proprietary technology or if the 802.11n definition changes substantially before it is ratified, which is unlikely.

There is, however, another compatibility factor to consider apart from the IEEE 802.11 standards, and that is the security protocols that the wireless devices support. Two main security protocols are used in the wireless LAN devices on the market today: ***Wired Equivalent Privacy (WEP)*** and ***Wi-Fi Protected Access (WPA)***. WEP has been around for some time, and is supported by virtually all wireless LAN products. WPA is comparatively recent, and some older devices do not support it.

Unfortunately, wireless devices cannot fall back from one security protocol to another. You must decide to use WEP or WPA on your network, and all of your devices must support the one you choose. WPA is inherently more secure than WEP, so it is usually preferable, but if the network has any devices that do not support WPA, you must either replace them or settle for WEP.

Using Wired Equivalent Privacy

WEP is a wireless security protocol that helps protect transmitted information by using a security setting, called a shared secret or a shared key, to encrypt network traffic before sending it. To use WEP, administrators must configure all of the devices on the wireless network with the same shared secret key. The devices use that key to encrypt all of their transmissions. Any outside party who gains possession of that key can, at the very least, read the contents of the transmitted packets, and at worst, participate on the network.

Unfortunately, the cryptography used by WEP is relatively weak, and programs that can analyze captured traffic and derive the key from it are readily available. These factors have resulted in WEP becoming one of the most frequently cracked network encryption protocols today.

In addition to its weak cryptography, another factor contributing to WEP's vulnerability is that the protocol standard doesn't provide any mechanism for automatically changing the shared secret. On wireless networks with hundreds of hosts, manually changing the shared secret on a regular basis is a practical impossibility. Therefore, on most WEP networks, the same shared secret tends to stay in place indefinitely. As with any cryptographic function, the longer a system uses the same code, the more time an attacker has to penetrate that code. A static WEP installation that uses the same permanent key gives attackers sufficient opportunity to crack the shared secret and all the time they need to gain access to the network.

If administrators could change the shared secret on a regular basis, however, they would be able to prevent an attacker from gathering enough data to crack the WEP key, and this would significantly improve WEP's privacy. There are techniques for dynamically and automatically changing the shared secret to dramatically reduce WEP's weaknesses, such as the 802.1X authentication protocol.

Selecting an Authentication Method

The initial WEP standards provided for two types of computer authentication:

- **Open system—Enables any client to connect without providing a password**
- **Shared secret—Requires wireless clients to authenticate by using a secret key**

Fortunately, choosing between open system and shared secret authentication is easy: always use open system authentication. On the surface this might seem illogical, because open system authentication does not require any proof of identity while shared key authentication requires knowledge of a secret key. However, shared secret authentication actually weakens security because most WEP client implementations use the same secret key for both authentication and WEP encryption. If a malicious user captures the authentication key and manages to penetrate its code, then the WEP encryption key is compromised as well.

Therefore, although shared secret authentication is stronger than open system for authentication, it weakens the WEP encryption. If you use open system authentication, any computer can easily join your network. However, without the WEP encryption key the unauthorized clients cannot send or receive wireless communications, and they will not be able to abuse the wireless network.

Using Wi-Fi Protected Access

Although WEP with dynamic rekeying is secure enough to meet the needs of most organizations, the protocol still has security weaknesses. WEP uses a separate static key for broadcast packets; an attacker can conceivably analyze these broadcast packets to build a map of private IP addresses and computer names.

To address these lingering weaknesses with WEP, the Wi-Fi Alliance, a consortium of the leading wireless network equipment vendors, developed Wi-Fi Protected Access (WPA). WPA can use the same authentication mechanisms and encryption algorithms as WEP, which enables manufacturers to add support for WPA to existing products with a simple software or firmware upgrade.

There are two encryption options for WPA, as follows:

- ***Temporal Key Integrity Protocol (TKIP)***—Implemented in the original WPA standard, TKIP encrypts data using the RC4 algorithm with a 128-bit key. This is the same algorithm as WEP, but TKIP virtually eliminates WEP's most exploited vulnerability by using a unique encryption key for each packet.
- ***Advanced Encryption System (AES)***—Implemented in the WPA2 standard, AES uses a different and more secure encryption algorithm, called CCMP. However, while it is possible to upgrade some legacy WEP equipment to support WPA-TKIP, most equipment cannot be upgraded to support AES. As a result, a wireless network will probably not be able to use AES encryption unless the organization chooses equipment that specifically supports it.

When you enable WPA, you establish a passphrase that is automatically associated with the dynamically generated security settings. This passphrase is stored with your network settings in the WAP and on each of your networked computers. Only wireless devices with the WPA passphrase can join the network and decrypt network transmissions.

Therefore, when configuring the security options for a wireless network, you should choose the lowest numbered option from the following list that is supported by all of your wireless devices:

1. WPA-AES
2. WPA-TKIP
3. WEP (128-bit) with 802.1X authentication
4. WEP (128-bit)
5. WEP (64-bit)
6. WEP (40-bit)

Configuring Vista Wireless Networking

Wireless networking equipment must be configured before computers can connect to the network safely and securely.

CERTIFICATION READY?
Use the Network and Sharing Center to configure networking
4.1

The process of configuring a wireless network adapter on a Windows Vista computer can vary depending on the hardware involved. Some wireless adapters are supported directly by Windows Vista, and the setup process is simply a matter of installing the hardware and letting the operating system detect it and install a device driver. However, some wireless adapters include their own configuration software, which you must install before you can configure the adapter.

To let Windows to configure the adapter, use the following procedure:

CONFIGURE A WIRELESS ADAPTER

GET READY. Install the wireless network adapter by inserting it into a PCI or PC Card slot, or connecting it to a USB port. Then start the computer and log on to Windows Vista. When the logon process is completed, close the Welcome Center window and any other windows that appear.

1. Click **Start**, and then click **Connect To**. The *Connect to a network* wizard appears, as shown in Figure 12-1.

Figure 12-1

The Connect to a network page

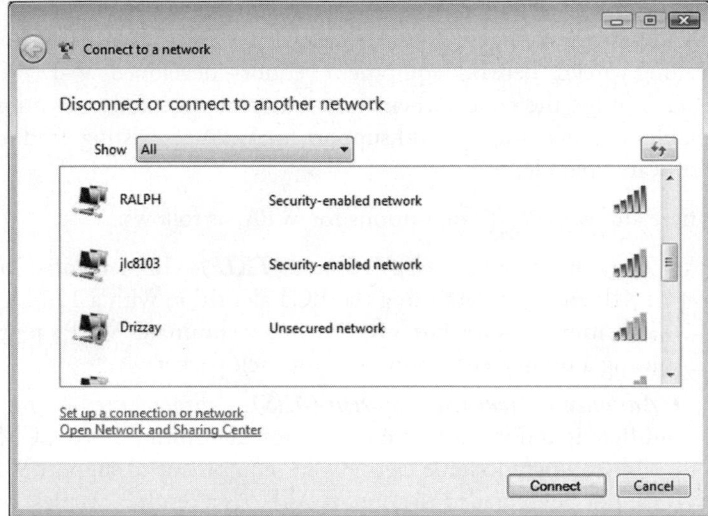

2. On the *Disconnect or connect to another network* page, the wizard displays all of the wireless networks within range of the computer. Select your network from the list and click **Connect**.
3. If the WAP is configured not to broadcast the network identifier (SSID), the *Type the network name (SSID) for the network* page appears. Key the SSID for your network in the text box, and then click **Next**.
4. If the network is encrypted, the *Type the network security key or passphrase* page appears, as shown in Figure 12-2. In the text box provided, key the security key for your network, if you're using WEP, or the passphrase, if you're using WPA. Then click **Connect**.

Figure 12-2

The Type the network security key or passphrase page

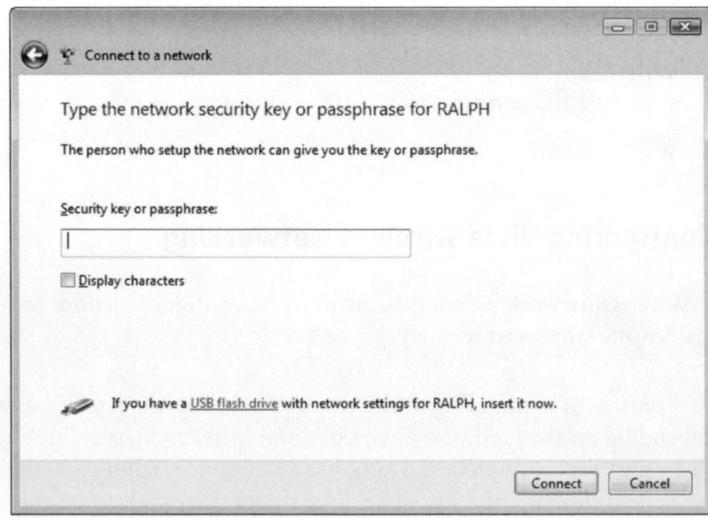

5. When the system connects to the network, the *Successfully connected to SSID* page appears. Click **Close**.

If the computer fails to connect to the wireless network, open the Status dialog box for the wireless network connection and check the Properties sheet for the network, as shown in Figure 12-3. You can do this in any of the following ways.

- In the Network and Sharing Center, click **View Status** for the wireless network connection, and then click **Wireless Properties**.
- In the Network Connections window, right-click the wireless network connection and then, from the context menu, select Status. Then click **Wireless Properties**.
- On the *Select a network to connect to* page, right-click the network and then, from the context menu, select Properties.

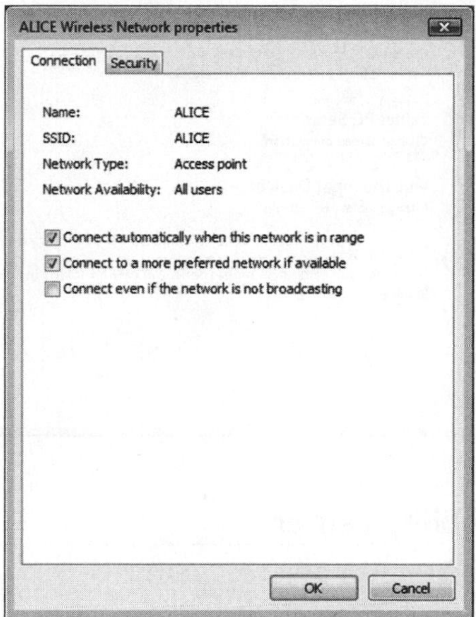

Figure 12-3

The Properties sheet for a wireless network

In most cases, wireless connection failures are due to misconfigured security settings. In the Properties sheet, you can select the security protocol and type of encryption the network uses, and specify the *Network security key* value.

Accessing Windows Mobility Controls

The Mobile PC control panel and the Windows Mobility Center provide users with convenient access to Vista's most frequently used configuration settings.

Windows Vista includes a number of special tools designed specifically for mobile PCs, and particularly laptop computers. Some of these tools take advantage of features that are unique to mobile computers, while others simply consolidate frequently used settings into a single interface.

Opening the Mobile PC Control Panel

The Mobile PC control panel gives laptop computer users quick access to all of their system controls.

Laptop computers have a special Mobile PC control panel that consolidates many of Vista's most frequently used configuration settings in one place. This provides users with rapid access to system controls, saving them time and precious battery power.

Clicking **Start > Control Panel > Mobile PC** displays the window shown in Figure 12-4, from which you can access many of the controls discussed later in this lesson.

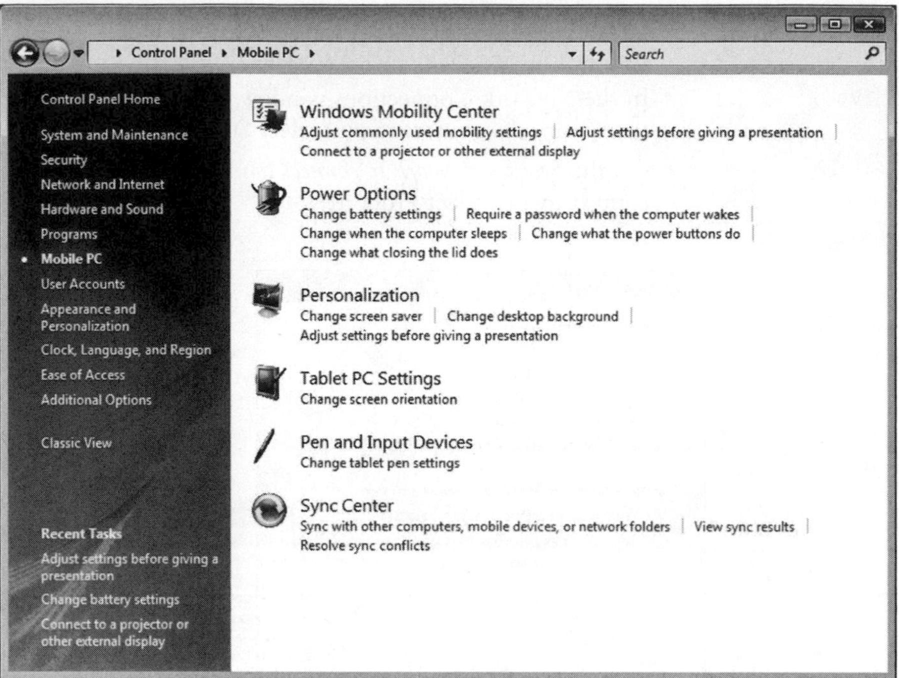

Figure 12-4

The Mobile PC control panel

Using Windows Mobility Center

Windows Mobility Center provides users with quick access to the configuration settings most commonly adjusted by mobile computer users.

Windows Mobility Center is a shell application. It performs no special functions of its own; it simply provides a central point of access for many of the configuration settings that mobile computer users need frequently. These settings are located in various control panel applets, but placing them in a single window enables users to make adjustments quickly and easily. This is particularly beneficial to business users that give presentations with their laptop computers.

To open the Windows Mobility Center on a mobile computer, click **Start > All Programs > Accessories > Windows Mobility Center** to display the window shown in Figure 12-5.

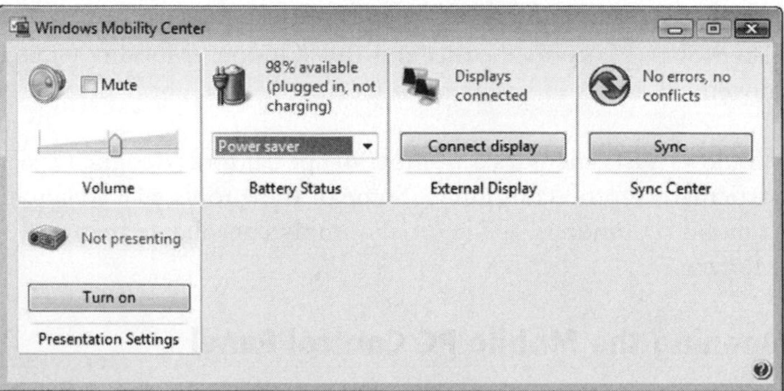

Figure 12-5

The Windows Mobility Center

The Windows Mobility Center window is divided into as many as eight tiles. The tiles that appear and the controls in them depend on the type of computer you are using, its hardware components, and the software supplied by the computer's manufacturer. You can modify configuration settings by using the controls that appear in the Windows Mobility Center window or by clicking the icon in one of the tiles to open the corresponding control panel applet.

The eight tiles that can appear in the Windows Mobility Center are as follows:

- Brightness—Enables the user to adjust the brightness of the computer's display.
- Volume—Enables the user to adjust the volume of the computer's speakers, or mute them completely.
- Battery Status—Displays the computer's current power status (AC or battery) and the battery's charge, as well as enabling the user to select one of the computer's power plans.
- Wireless Network—Displays the status of the computer's wireless network connection and enables the user to turn the wireless network adapter on or off.
- Screen Orientation—On a tablet PC, enables the user to toggle the computer's display orientation between portrait and landscape.
- External Display—Enables the user to connect an external display to the computer and modify the display settings.
- Sync Center—Enables the user to set up a sync partnership, start a sync event, or monitor the status of a sync event in progress.
- Presentation Settings—When turned on, prevents presentations from being interrupted by screen savers, alarms, and attempts to put the computer to sleep. This tile also enables the user to adjust the settings most often used during a presentation, such as the screen saver, the speaker volume, and the desktop background.

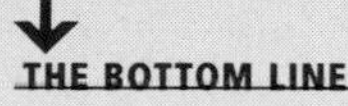

Do not confuse the Windows Mobility Center application with the Windows Vista Mobile Device Center, which is an application that enables you to synchronize data with mobile devices.

Using Windows Mobility Controls

THE BOTTOM LINE The configuration requirements of mobile computers are different from those of desktop systems.

The following sections examine the Windows Vista configuration settings that mobile computers access most often. Whether you access the settings through the standard control panel interfaces or use the Mobility Center application, the controls are essentially the same.

Configuring Mobile Display Options

To accommodate presentation audiences and other situations, mobile users are likely to adjust their display settings more frequently than desktop users.

One of the biggest benefits of mobile computing is the ability to collaborate with other users, bringing your data and your applications with you. Most laptop computers have the capability to connect an external display device, making it possible for a group of users to view the desktop without having to crowd around a single screen. Many people use this external display capability to give lectures, presentations, or demonstrations, using a variety of external display technologies.

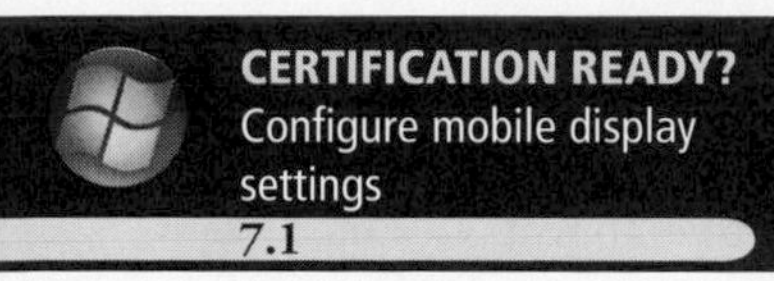

Desktop technicians should be familiar with the computer capabilities, configuration settings, and controls used to manage the display options, as discussed in the following settings.

Connecting an External Display

In most cases, the ability to connect an external display to a laptop computer depends on the system's hardware and software. Many laptops include VGA (Video Graphics Array), ***DVI (Digital Visual Interface)***, and/or S-Video connectors that enable you to attach an external display to the computer, and drivers that enable you to configure the properties of each display separately.

At its simplest, an external display can be a standard desktop monitor—analog or digital, LCD or CRT—connected to the laptop and configured to mirror the image on the laptop's own LCD display. If the computer has an S-Video jack, it is also possible to connect a similarly equipped television set. The user can then work with the computer in the normal manner, and a small group of observers can follow the user's action on the external monitor. However, for more elaborate presentations or large audiences, many users employ a display projector, which is a device that uses computer display technology to project an image on a large screen or wall.

Installing the hardware is simply a matter of connecting the external display to the computer using whatever port is provided. VGA and DVI ports are designed for computer monitors. CRTs and lower-end LCD monitors use the standard 15-pin VGA port, while many newer and more advanced LCD monitors use the 29-pin DVI connector. However, some DVI monitors come with an adapter that enables you to plug them into a computer with only a VGA port.

Laptop computers that have a VGA or DVI port for an external monitor typically have a video adapter that is capable of supporting two display configurations. This adapter, plus the device driver that goes with it, enables you to configure the displays using different resolutions, if necessary, and to choose how to use the two displays.

MORE INFORMATION

On a desktop computer, you can use either a single video adapter that supports two monitor connections, or two separate video adapters that are designed to work together. On a laptop, however, there is no way to add a second video adapter, so your computer must have an adapter that supports two displays.

Configuring Multiple Displays

When a Windows Vista computer supports two displays, the standard Display Settings dialog box is modified to contain two icons representing the two displays. By clicking one of the icons, or selecting it from the dropdown list just below the icons, you can configure each display separately.

When you run Windows Vista with two displays, you have two basic configuration choices. You can use the second monitor to display a mirror image of the first, as you would for a presentation, or you can extend the main display to the secondary monitor, creating a single large desktop. This second option enables you to move screen elements, such as icons and windows, from one monitor to the other, creating a huge work environment.

To create a single desktop out of both monitors, use the following procedure:

CONFIGURE AN EXTENDED DESKTOP

GET READY. Using a laptop computer, log on to Windows Vista. When the logon process is completed, close the Welcome Center window and any other windows that appear. Connect an external monitor to the computer, using its VGA or DVI port.

1. Click **Start**, and then click **Control Panel > Hardware and Sound > Personalization**. The *Personalize appearance and sounds* page appears, as shown in Figure 12-6.

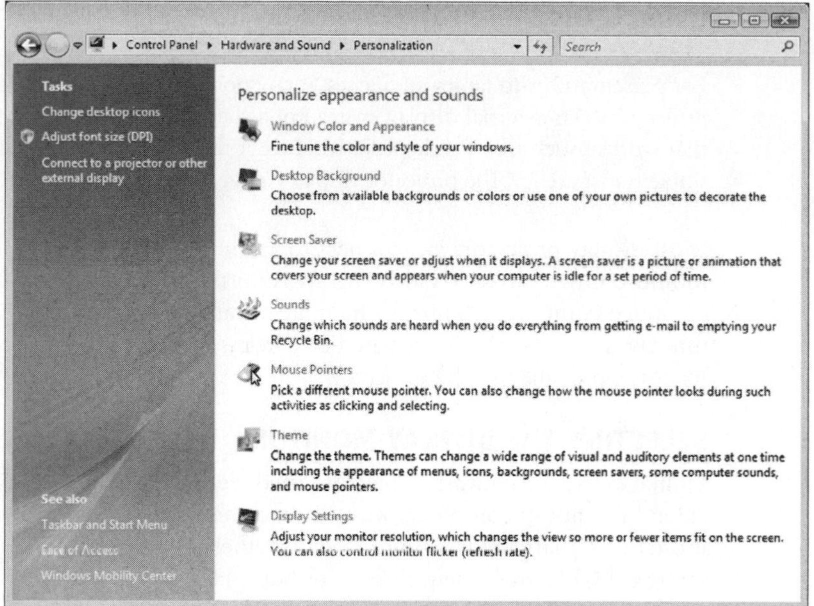

Figure 12-6

The Personalize appearance and sounds page

2. Click **Display Settings**. The Display Settings dialog box appears, as shown in Figure 12-7.

Figure 12-7

The Display Settings dialog box

3. Click the display icon for the computer's internal monitor (the one marked with a "1").
4. Make sure the *This is my main monitor* checkbox is selected.
5. Click the display icon for the external monitor (the one marked with a "2").
6. Select the Extend the desktop onto this monitor checkbox.
7. Adjust the resolution and color depth settings for the external monitor, if necessary.
8. Click **OK** to apply the settings.

TAKE NOTE*

If your external monitor is larger than the internal one, you might want to deselect the *This is my main monitor* checkbox and make the external monitor your primary display.

Depending on the size and capabilities of the external monitor, and the size of the audience that will be using it, you might want to use resolution and color depth settings that are different from those of your main monitor. Selecting one of the icons in the Display Settings dialog box enables you to configure the parameters for that display only.

TAKE NOTE*

To mirror the internal display on the external display, leave the *Extend the desktop onto this monitor* checkbox cleared.

Keep in mind, however, that using different screen resolutions on mirrored displays can have unpredictable results. If the resolution setting for your external display is substantially lower than that for the internal one, you might find yourself moving screen elements on the internal display to locations that are invisible on the external display. Always test your display configuration settings before using them in a presentation or other critical environment.

Using a Display Projector

For presentations to larger audiences, many portable computer users prefer to use a display projector as an external display, instead of a standard monitor. A display projector is a device that works much like a slide projector, except that instead of a still image generated using a single transparency, the projector displays a live image of the computer's desktop onto a screen.

Most display projectors can connect to a computer's VGA or DVI port, just like a regular monitor. Others have S-Video and RCA ports for greater flexibility in connecting to variously equipped computers. Some of the more advanced (and expensive) models can even connect directly to a network, either wired or wireless, enabling any computer on the network to send its desktop display to the projector.

SELECTING THE DISPLAY MONITOR

Unlike external monitors, projectors are designed to mirror the computer's desktop, not extend it. Laptop computers with external monitor ports typically have some sort of keyboard mechanism that enables you to select whether the computer should send the desktop to the internal LCD panel, the projector, or both. However, Windows Vista simplifies this selection process by displaying a dialog box when you connect a projector, asking you which display(s) you want to use.

CONNECTING TO A NETWORK PROJECTOR

Network projectors are a different situation, because they do not connect directly to the video display adapter, and they are not automatically detectible by Windows Vista. Instead of simply directing the monitor signal out through a VGA or DVI port, the computer uses the Remote Desktop Protocol (RDP) to transmit the monitor signals over the network to the projector device, which has the Windows Embedded CE operating system built into it.

TAKE NOTE* The Connect to a Network Projector wizard is not included in the Home Basic edition of Windows Vista.

One of the first obstacles to using a network projector with Windows Vista is that Windows Firewall, by default, blocks the port used for RDP traffic. To simplify the process of configuring the necessary firewall exceptions and locating the projector on the network, Windows Vista provides the Connect to a Network Projector wizard. Run this wizard using the following procedure:

RUN THE CONNECT TO A NETWORK PROJECTOR WIZARD

GET READY. Connect the projector to the network and configure it according to the manufacturer's instructions. Then, log on to Windows Vista. When the logon process is completed, close the Welcome Center window and any other windows that appear.

1. Click **Start > All Programs > Accessories > Connect To A Network Projector.** The Permission to Connect to a Network Projector page appears, as shown in Figure 12-8.

Figure 12-8

The Permission to Connect to a Network Projector page

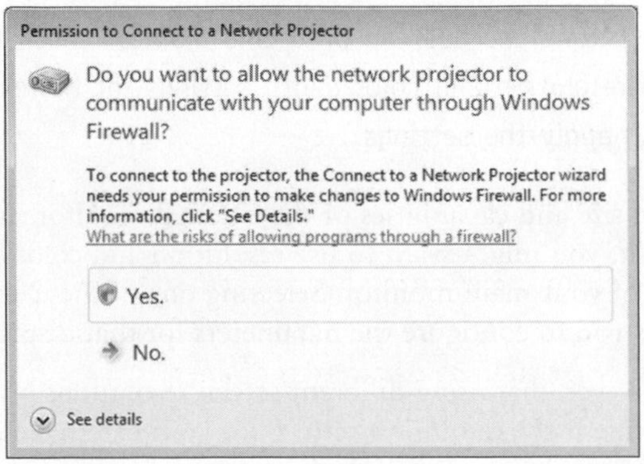

2. Click **Yes** to create exceptions in the Windows Firewall that will permit communications with the projector. The Connect to a Network Projector page appears, as shown in Figure 12-9.

Figure 12-9

The Connect to a Network Projector page

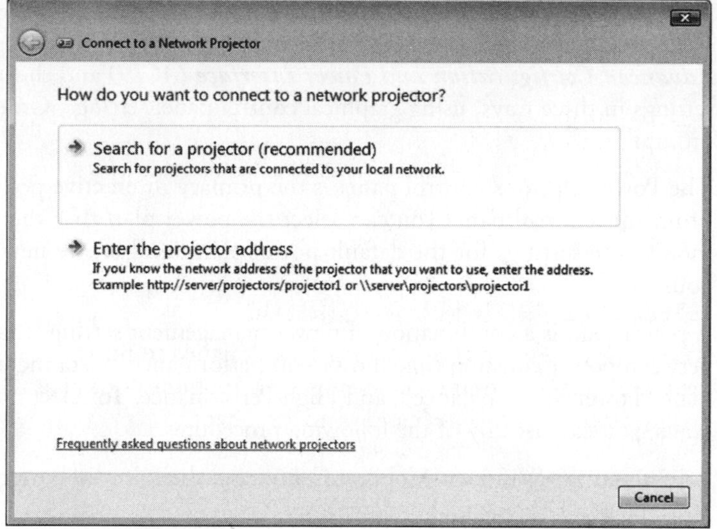

3. Click **Search for a projector**. The wizard searches for a projector on the network and prompts you for a password if one is required. You can also click **Enter the projector address** and manually supply the printer's network address and password.
4. Click **Connect** to establish the connection to the projector.

Configuring Power Options

Windows Vista enables you to fine-tune the power consumption of a mobile computer by configuring individual components to operate at lower power levels.

Power conservation is a critical issue for laptop users who rely on batteries, particularly when using the computer for a presentation. Running out of power in the middle of a demonstration could be disastrous, so it is important for users to be aware of the computer's power level and its power consumption.

To conserve battery power as much as possible, virtually all laptops made today include the hardware and firmware elements needed to dynamically adjust the power consumption of individual components. Some computer components, such as processors and LCD panels, can operate at various power levels, while other devices can be shut down completely when not in use. Windows Vista includes extensive controls called power plans that enable you to create power usage profiles for a laptop computer and assign different profiles depending on whether the computer is plugged in to an AC power source or running on batteries.

MONITORING BATTERY POWER

CERTIFICATION READY?
Configure power options
7.4

By default, the Windows Vista desktop contains a power icon in the notification area that provides the following information:

- Whether the computer is currently using AC or battery power
- When running on battery power, the percentage of the battery charge remaining and the amount of time left until the battery is drained
- The power plan currently in use

Clicking the icon enables you to change the power plan currently in use, and right-clicking the icon enables you to open the Windows Mobility Center or the Power Options control panel.

WORKING WITH POWER PLANS

Power management is the process of balancing conservation versus performance. Windows Vista includes extensive power management capabilities, including improved support for the ***Advanced Configuration and Power Interface (ACPI)*** and the ability to configure all power settings in three ways, using graphical control panel settings, Group Policy, or the command prompt.

The Power Options control panel is the primary interactive power configuration interface. From this control panel you can select the power plan that the computer should use; modify the settings for the default power plans; and create new, custom power plans of your own.

A power plan is a combination of power management settings that provides a balance between power consumption and system performance. Vista includes three default power plans: Power Saver, Balanced, and High Performance. To select one of the default power plans, you can use any of the following procedures.

- Open the Windows Mobility Center and then, in the Battery Status tile, select one of the plans from the dropdown list.
- Click **Start**, click **Control Panel > Hardware and Sound > Power Options**, and then select the radio button for the desired plan.
- Open the Mobile PC control panel, click **Power Options**, and then select the radio button for the desired plan.
- Click the power icon in the notification area, and then select one of the plans from the menu that appears.

Each power plan consists of two sets of settings, one for when the computer is plugged into an AC power source and one for when the computer is running on battery power. Table 12-2 lists the primary settings for each of the power plans.

Table 12-2

Default Power Plan Settings

POWER SETTING	POWER SAVER	BALANCED	HIGH PERFORMANCE
Turn off the display	3 minutes (battery) 20 minutes (AC)	5 minutes (battery) 20 minutes (AC)	20 minutes (battery) Never (AC)
Put the computer to sleep	15 minutes (battery) 60 minutes (AC)	15 minutes (battery) 60 minutes (AC)	60 minutes (battery) Never (AC)
Turn off hard disk	5 minutes (battery) 20 minutes (AC)	10 minutes (battery) 20 minutes (AC)	20 minutes (battery) Never (AC)
Minimum processor state	5% (battery) 5% (AC)	5% (battery) 5% (AC)	5% (battery) 100% (AC)
Maximum processor state	50% (battery) 50% (AC)	100% (battery) 100% (AC)	100% (battery) 100% (AC)
Wireless adapter power saving mode	Maximum Power Saving (battery) Maximum Performance (AC)	Maximum Performance (battery) Maximum Performance (AC)	Maximum Performance (battery) Maximum Performance (AC)

As you can see from the data in the table, all of the plans are more conservative when the computer is running on battery power, and the differences between the plan settings are incremental. There is, however, no way for the operating system to know exactly what effect the various power settings will have on a specific computer.

The LCD panel on a laptop with a large, widescreen display will obviously use more power than one with a smaller display, so turning the display off will conserve more battery power. In the same way, hard disk drives, processors, and other components can vary greatly in their power consumption levels. It is up to the user to determine what effect each of the power plans has on a specific computer.

Using the Power Options control panel, you can modify any of the individual settings in a power plan, or you can create a new power plan of your own. To create a custom power plan, use the following procedure:

CREATE A CUSTOM POWER PLAN

GET READY. Log on to Windows Vista using an account with administrative privileges. When the logon process is completed, close the Welcome Center window and any other windows that appear.

1. Click **Start**, and then click **Control Panel** > **Hardware and Sound** > **Power Options**. The Power Options control panel appears, as shown in Figure 12-10.

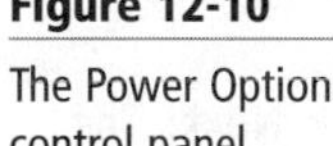

Figure 12-10

The Power Options control panel

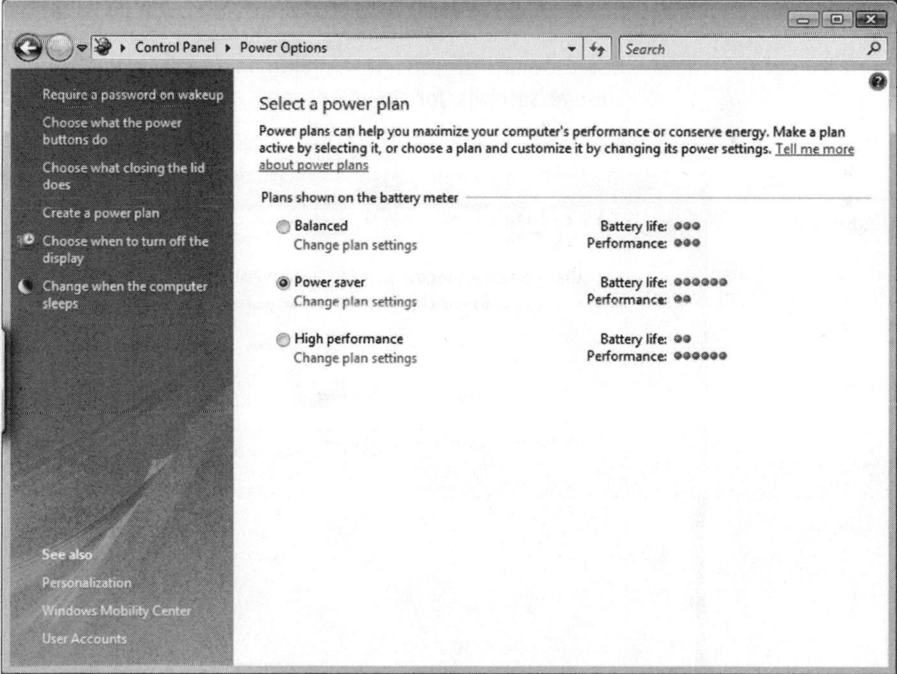

2. Click **Create a power plan**. After you confirm your action, the *Create a power plan* wizard appears, as shown in Figure 12-11.

Figure 12-11

The Create a power plan wizard

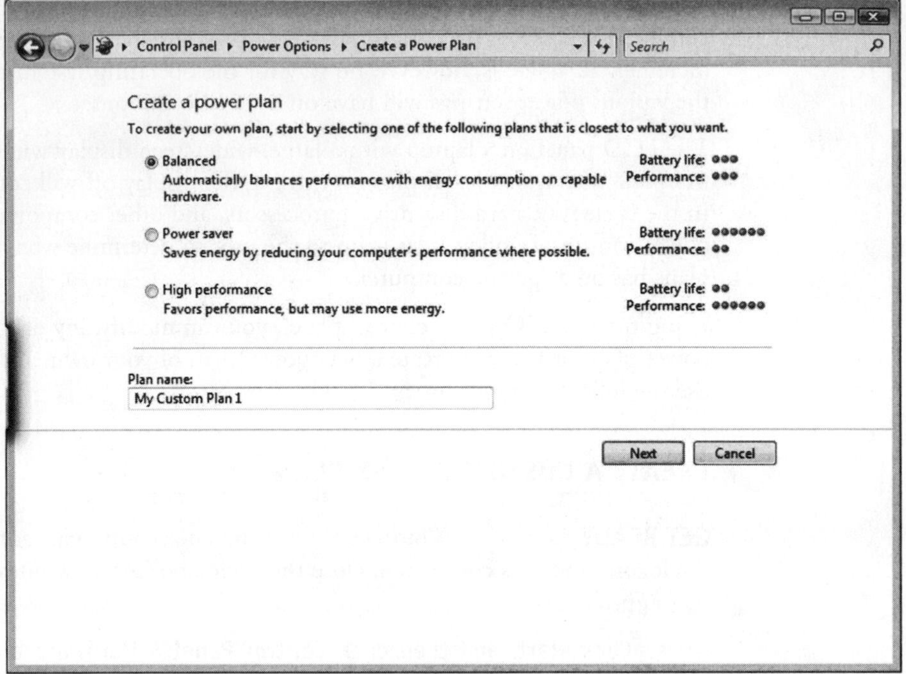

3. Select the radio button for the default power plan that will be the basis for your new plan.
4. Key a name for your power plan in the *Plan name* text box. Then click **Next**. The *Change settings for the plan* page appears, as shown in Figure 12-12.

Figure 12-12

The Change settings for the plan page

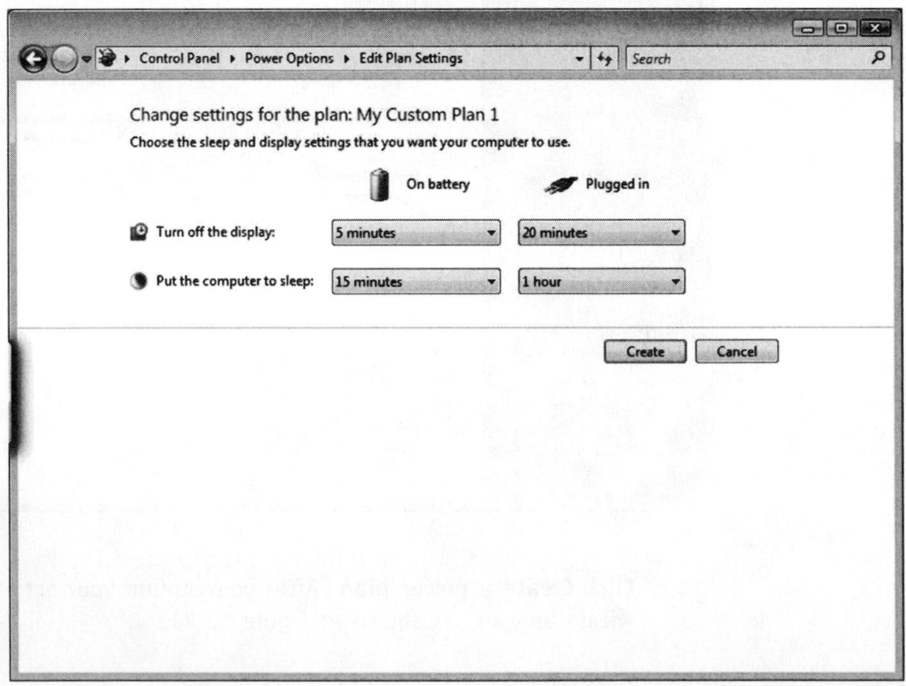

5. Modify the display and sleep settings as desired for the *On battery* and *Plugged in* power states. Then click **Create**.
6. The *Select a power plan* page appears, with the new plan you created listed as one of the options, as shown in Figure 12-13.

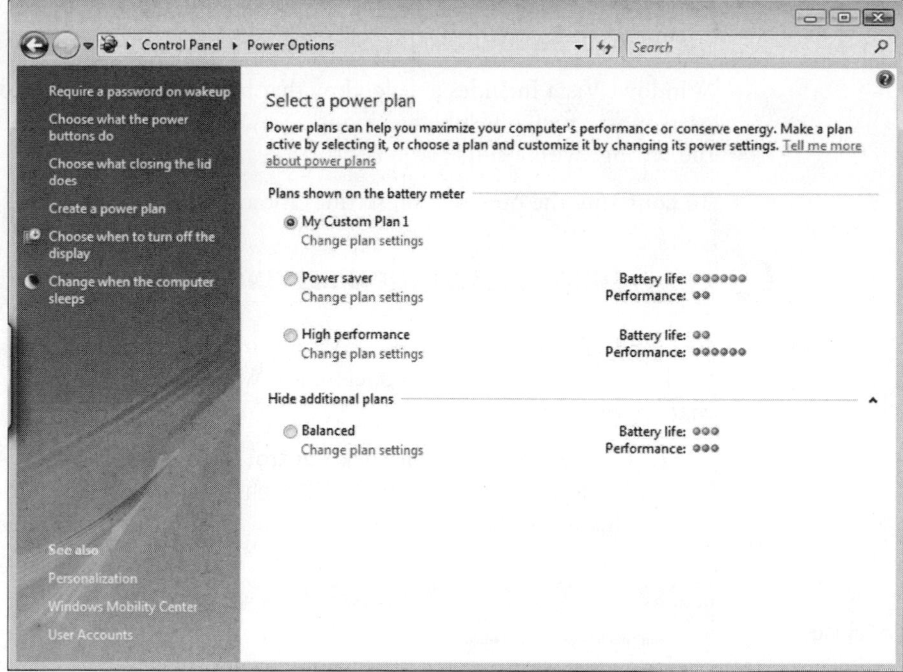

Figure 12-13

The Select a power plan page

7. Click **Change plan settings**. The *Change settings for the plan* page appears again.
8. Click **Change advanced power settings**. The *Advanced settings* dialog box appears, as shown in Figure 12-14.

Figure 12-14

The Advanced settings page

9. Modify any of the settings as desired and click **OK**.
10. Click **Save Changes** to close the *Change settings for the plan* page.

Configuring Presentation Settings

The Presentation Settings dialog box provides quick access to the most common adjustments performed by presenters.

The designers of Windows Vista have attempted to anticipate the needs of many types of computer users. For people that use their mobile computers to give presentations to an audience, few things are more unwelcome than an unexpected system event, such as an error message or a screen saver kicking in. Depending on the audience and the type of presentation, the result of problems like these can range from simple embarrassment to lost sales.

Windows Vista includes a dialog box that bundles together the configuration settings that users most often adjust before giving a presentation, and makes it possible to activate all of the settings with a single switch.

To configure the presentation settings for a computer, use the following procedure:

CONFIGURE PRESENTATION SETTINGS

GET READY. Log on to Windows Vista using an account with administrative privileges. When the logon process is completed, close the Welcome Center window and any other windows that appear.

1. Click **Start**, and then click **Control Panel > Mobile PC > Adjust Settings Before Giving a Presentation**. The Presentation Settings dialog box appears, as shown in Figure 12-15.

Figure 12-15

The Presentation Settings dialog box

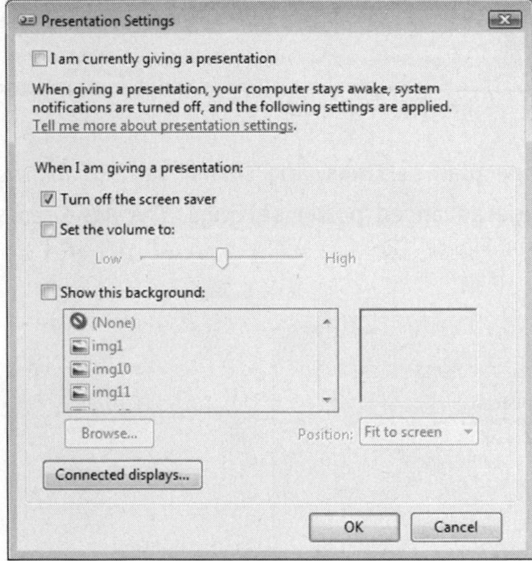

2. Use the controls to turn off the screen saver, adjust the speaker volume, or display an alternate desktop background when the Presentation Settings feature is activated.
3. Click **OK** to save your settings.

In addition to the settings in the dialog box, activating the Presentation Settings feature prevents the computer from displaying system notification messages or going to sleep. To activate the Presentation Settings feature, use one of the following procedures:

- Open the Presentation Setting s dialog box and select the *I am currently giving a presentation* checkbox.
- Open Windows Mobility Center and, in the Presentation Settings tile, click *Turn on.*

■ Using Specialized Mobile Tools

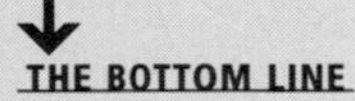

THE BOTTOM LINE

Windows Vista includes tools that enable users to take advantage of the special capabilities of their laptops and other mobile devices.

Windows Vista includes features that enable the operating system to work with specialized hardware, such as handheld devices. The following sections examine some of these features and how they accommodate the special needs and capabilities of the hardware.

Synchronizing Data

Mobile devices enable users to take their data with them wherever they go, but this creates a version control problem.

Mobile computer users often connect to a network when they are in the office, and then take their computers with them when they go home or travel on business. Once the computer disconnects from the network, however, access to the network drives and the files they contain is interrupted. Fortunately, Windows Vista includes the ability to store copies of network files on the local drive for use when the computer is disconnected. This feature is called Offline Files. Vista also makes it possible to maintain copies of files on handheld devices, such as smartphones and PDAs running Windows Mobile.

The key to this offline files capability is the synchronization process that occurs when the computer or other device reconnects to the network. Simply copying the files to the mobile device is not enough. Users would have to remember to copy their revised documents back to the network drive after reconnecting. Synchronization is a process in which Windows Vista compares the offline version of a file with the network version, and makes sure that the most recent revisions are present in both places.

Two types of synchronization are supported by Windows Vista, as follows:

- One-way synchronization—Data moves in one direction only, from the source to the destination. Any changes made to the source files are replicated to the destination, but changes to the destination files are not replicated to the source. This is recommended for scenarios such as synchronizing music files on a computer with a portable music player.
- Two-way synchronization—Data moves in both directions. Changes made to either copy of the files are replicated to the other system. In the event that both copies have changed, the system prompts the user to resolve the conflict by selecting one of the two versions. This is recommended for scenarios such as copying network-based document files to a mobile system for offline use.

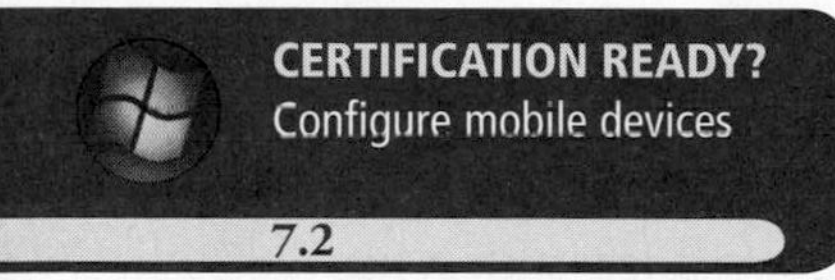

The following sections describe the tools and procedures you can use to ensure that mobile computers synchronize their data reliably.

Using Sync Center

Sync Center is an application that functions as a central control panel for all of a Windows Vista computer's synchronization partnerships, including those with network drives and mobile devices. You can use Sync Center to establish synchronization partnerships, schedule synchronizations, monitor synchronization events, and manage synchronization conflicts.

Sync partnerships are pairs of folders or devices that are configured to synchronize their data on a regular basis. You use Sync Center to create sync partnerships with mobile devices, but to synchronize a Windows Vista computer with network folders you simply browse to the folder using Windows Explorer, right-click the folder name, and select Always Available Offline from the context menu. Windows Vista then establishes the partnership and copies the contents of the selected folder to the local hard drive. Once the partnership is established, you can configure its synchronization schedule. To configure a sync partnership, use the following procedure:

CONFIGURE A SYNC PARTNERSHIP

GET READY. Log on to Windows Vista using an account with administrative privileges. When the logon process is completed, close the Welcome Center window and any other windows that appear. Then create a sync partnership with a folder on a network drive.

1. Click **Start**, and then click **Control Panel > Network and Internet > Sync Center.** The *View sync partnerships* page of the Sync Center control panel appears, as shown in Figure 12-16.

Figure 12-16

The Sync Center control panel

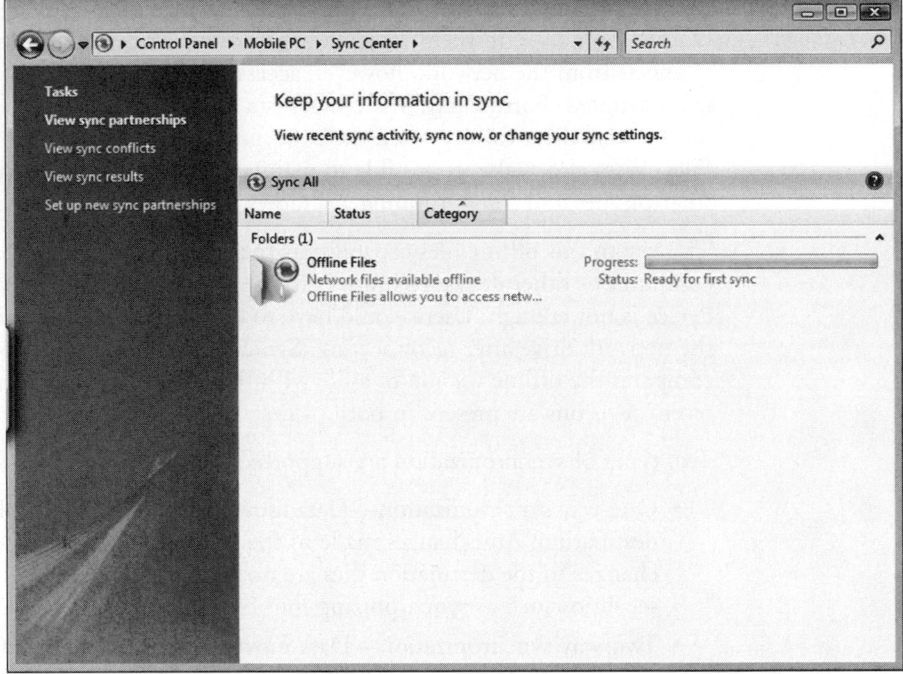

TAKE NOTE*

You can also open Sync Center from the Mobile PC control panel and from the Windows Mobility Center.

2. Select the **Offline Files** partnership, and then click **Schedule**. The Offline Files Sync Schedule wizard appears.
3. Select the network folder whose synchronization you want to schedule, and then click **Next**. The *When do you want this sync to begin?* page appears.
4. Select one of the following options, configure its properties, and then click **Next.**
   - At A Scheduled Time—Using the interface shown in Figure 12-17, specify a date and time for the synchronization and a repeat interval. You can also click **More Options** to specify conditions under which the scheduled synchronization should or should not occur.

Figure 12-17

The Sync Center Scheduled time interface

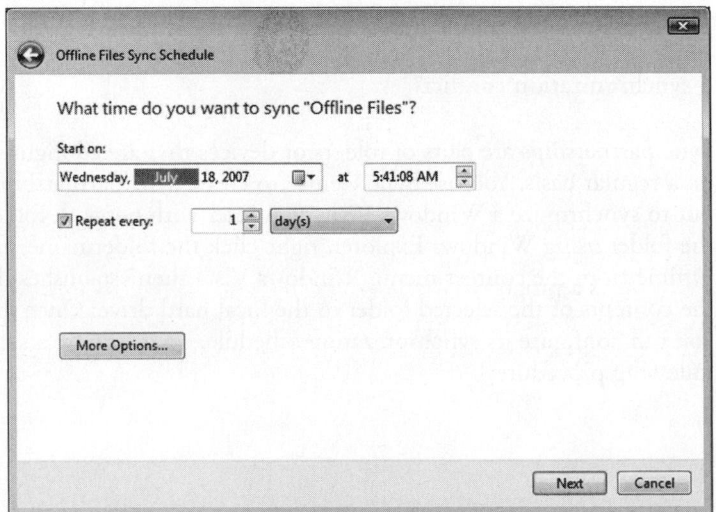

- On An Event Or Action—Using the interface shown in Figure 12-18, select an event or action that you want to trigger a synchronization, such as logging on to Windows or when the system has been idle for specified amount of time.

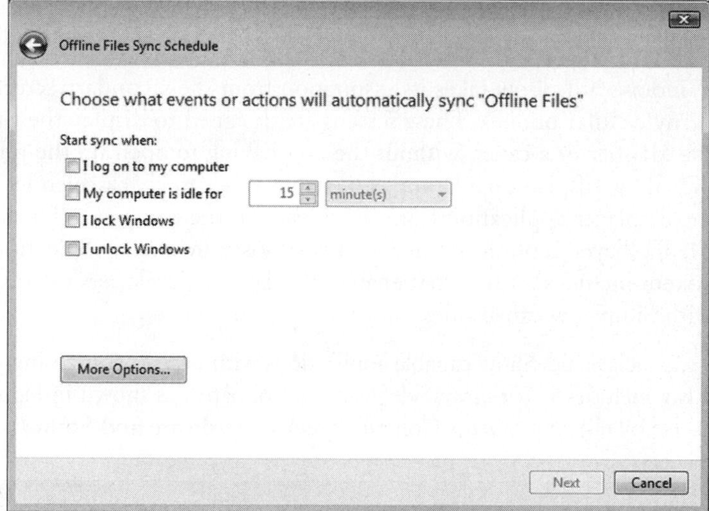

Figure 12-18
The Sync Center Event or Action interface

5. Specify a name for the schedule, and then click **Save Schedule**.

USING WINDOWS MOBILE DEVICE CENTER

Sync Center can support some mobile devices, but for devices running the Windows Mobile operating system, such as Pocket PCs, a more comprehensive tool called Windows Mobile Device Center is available. Windows Mobile Device Center is not supplied with Windows Vista; you must download it from Microsoft's Website, or use Windows Update.

TAKE NOTE*
Windows Mobile Device Center appears in Windows Update only if a supported mobile device is connected to your computer (either wirelessly using Bluetooth or by using a USB cable). To be supported, the device must be running Windows Mobile 6.0, 5.0, Windows Mobile 2003, or Windows Embedded CE 6.0.

Using Windows Mobile Device Center, you can not only synchronize data files with the mobile device, you can also synchronize certain types of application data, such as e-mail, calendar appointments, and contact information. In addition, you can use Windows Mobile Device Center to browse through the files on the mobile device, access them as needed, and manage multimedia content, such as image, audio, and video files.

Windows Mobile Device Center replaces the ActiveSync application from earlier Windows versions, and performs many of the same functions. However, the interface has been redesigned to provide a more pleasing user experience.

Introducing Windows SideShow

SideShow, a new feature in Windows Vista, is an interface that enables applications to display content on secondary displays mounted on the outside of laptops, mobile phones, handheld wireless devices, and even bags and clothing.

Windows SideShow is a new feature in Windows Vista designed to accommodate a new secondary display technology that is currently being integrated into a wide variety of products. SideShow is a programming interface that enables applications to display content on secondary displays mounted on the outside of laptops, mobile phones, handheld wireless devices, and even bags and clothing. The idea is for users to be able to access information from their computers at any time, without having to open the laptop, load an application, or even turn on the computer.

The potential for this technology is enormous. Products currently in development include refrigerators with screens that display appointment reminders, remote controls that link to your Windows Media player library, handheld electronic document readers, and even a small display that can be embedded in the fabric of a handbag or other article of clothing.

Windows SideShow takes its inspiration from the secondary screens found on the outside of many cellular phones. These screens are designed to display the time and date, or perhaps the identity of a caller, without the user having to open up the phone. In the same way, a SideShow display on a laptop can enable a user to check calender information or control a media player application from the outside of the computer. The Windows Mail and Windows Media Player applications included with Vista are already SideShow capable, and the operating system includes an API that enables third-party developers to equip their own applications with SideShow capabilities.

To associate SideShow capable applications with devices containing secondary displays, Windows Vista includes a Windows SideShow control panel, as shown in Figure 12-19, which you can access by clicking **Start > Control Panel > Hardware and Sound > Windows SideShow**.

Figure 12-19

The Windows SideShow control panel

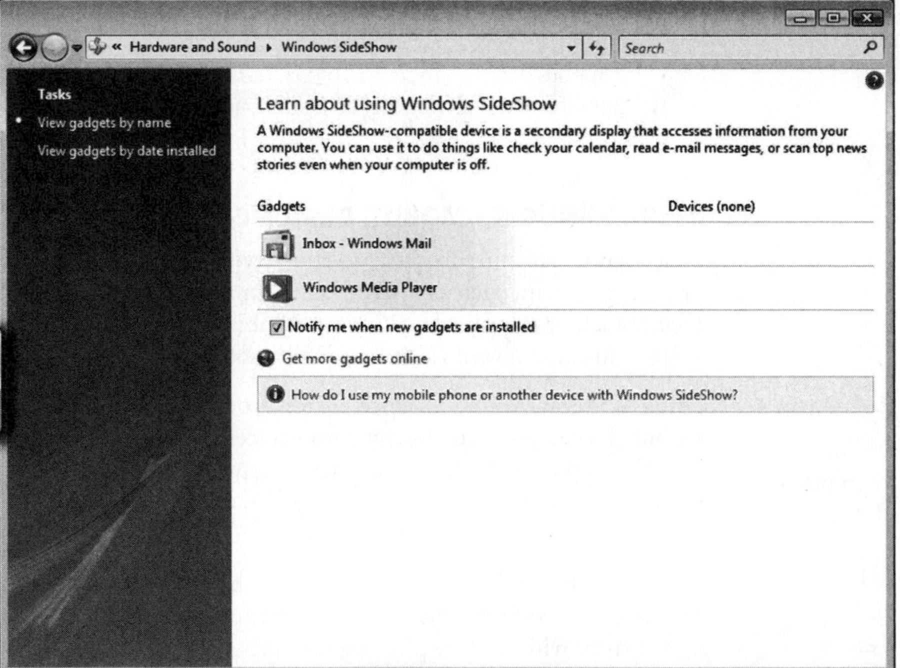

This control panel lists the currently installed gadgets, which is the term Microsoft uses for applications compatible with SideShow, and the devices containing SideShow-compatible displays that are associated with the computer. Depending on the capabilities of the display device, the control panel can provide settings that enable you to configure the appearance of the display and secure it against unauthorized access.

Configuring Tablet PC Features

Tablet PCs have a number of unique configuration settings. These include configuring pen and other input devices, the Input Panel, the handwriting recognition tool, and pen flicks.

Tablet PCs are similar to standard laptop computers, but they have some additional capabilities that require special consideration. On a tablet PC, the entire display is touch sensitive, enabling users of some machines to tap screen buttons with a finger rather than click them with a mouse. This touch sensitivity also enables users to tap, click, drag, and write directly on the screen using a stylus, which Windows Vista refers to as a pen. Windows Vista also includes handwriting recognition capabilities that convert the handwriting into digital text.

TAKE NOTE*

Windows XP has a separate Tablet PC edition that provides support for the device's special features. Windows Vista includes all of its tablet PC support in the standard operating system releases (with the exception of Windows Vista Home Basic), so a special edition is not necessary.

CERTIFICATION READY?
Configure tablet PC software
7.3

The following sections examine some of the configuration settings that are unique to tablet PCs, with which desktop technicians working on this type of computer should be familiar.

CONFIGURING PEN AND INPUT DEVICES

On a tablet PC, the pen can replace both the keyboard and the mouse (although the computer still comes with both). To use the pen effectively, users must become accustomed to its operation, and Windows Vista enables you to configure pen actions to perform specific mouse equivalents. To configure pen actions, use the following procedure:

CONFIGURE PEN ACTIONS

GET READY. Log on to Windows Vista using an account with administrative privileges. When the logon process is completed, close the Welcome Center window and any other windows that appear.

1. Click **Start**, and then click **Control Panel** > **Hardware and Sound** > **Pen and Input Devices.** The Pen and Input Devices dialog box appears, as shown in Figure 12-20.

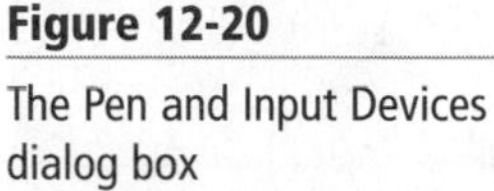

Figure 12-20

The Pen and Input Devices dialog box

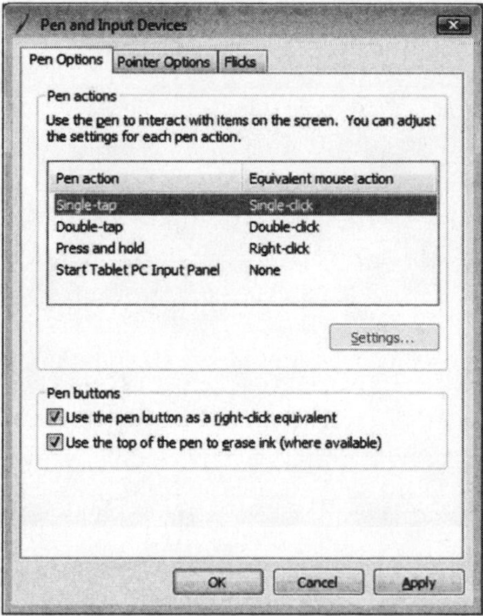

2. On the Pen Options tab, select one of the pen actions and click **Settings** to configure it. The Settings dialog boxes enables you to configure specific performance elements of the selected pen action, such as the speed of a double-tap or press-and-hold gesture. You can also configure a gesture to start the Input Panel, where you can handwrite your input with the pen.
3. In the *Pen buttons* box, select the checkboxes to enable any special features that your pen might have.
4. Click the **Pointer Options** tab and use the checkboxes to specify whether you want the computer to display visual representations of your pen actions.
5. Click **OK** to save your settings and close the dialog box.

CONFIGURING THE INPUT PANEL

Tablet PCs are designed to be able to use the pen as the computer's primary input tool. Most tablet PCs use a reversible clamshell design that enables the user to close the lid with the LCD display facing outwards. This makes it possible to hold the computer with one hand and use the pen with the other. Because the keyboard and mouse are not accessible in this configuration, the pen must be able to perform actions that are the functional equivalent of keystrokes and mouse movements.

In situations where the user is expected to enter alphanumeric information, such as a text box, a tablet PC provides an input panel. The input panel is a place in which a user can write with the pen, and the system will use handwriting recognition technology to convert the input into digital text. In addition to providing a place to write, the input panel also includes buttons for specific keystrokes and commands, and an onscreen keyboard where the user can tap letters to create input text.

By default, the input panel remains minimized to a tab on the left side of the screen. Clicking the tab opens the input panel, as shown in Figure 12-21. To configure the input panel, use the following procedure:

Figure 12-21

A tablet PC's input panel

CONFIGURE THE INPUT PANEL

GET READY. Log on to Windows Vista using an account with administrative privileges. When the logon process is completed, close the Welcome Center window and any other windows that appear.

1. Click the **Input Panel** tab on the left side of the screen. The Input Panel appears.
2. Click **Tools**, and then click **Options**. The Options dialog box appears, as shown in Figure 12-22.

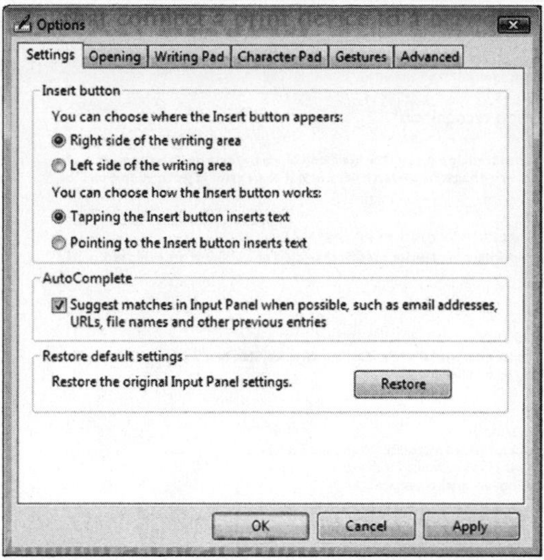

Figure 12-22

The Options dialog box

3. Click the tabs on the dialog box to configure the following options:
   - Settings—Specifies where and when the Insert button appears and controls the AutoComplete feature.
   - Opening—Specifies how, where, and when the Input Panel appears.
   - Writing Pad—Specifies the appearance and performance of the Input Panel's Writing Pad.
   - Character Pad—Specifies the appearance and performance of the Input Panel's Character Pad.
   - Gestures—Specifies the pen gestures that correspond to common editing actions, such as cross-outs, spaces, and tabs.
   - Advanced—Controls pen input security by specifying what text (such as passwords) appears on the screen as you write.
4. Click **OK** to save your settings and close the dialog box.

USING THE HANDWRITING RECOGNITION PERSONALIZATION TOOL

The most complex part of the tablet PC software in Windows Vista is the handwriting recognition engine. Because every person's handwriting is different, interpreting the input and converting it into digital text can be an extremely difficult task for the computer. Depending on how recognizable a user's handwriting is, the resulting text could have a few typos, or it could be complete gibberish.

To address this problem, Windows Vista includes a Handwriting Recognition Personalization Tool, which enables the computer to learn a user's handwriting and style and recognize specific words. To launch the tool, open the Input Panel, click Tools, and then click **Personalize Handwriting Recognition**. When the Handwriting Personalization Wizard appears, as shown in Figure 12-23, you can select one of the following personalization methods:

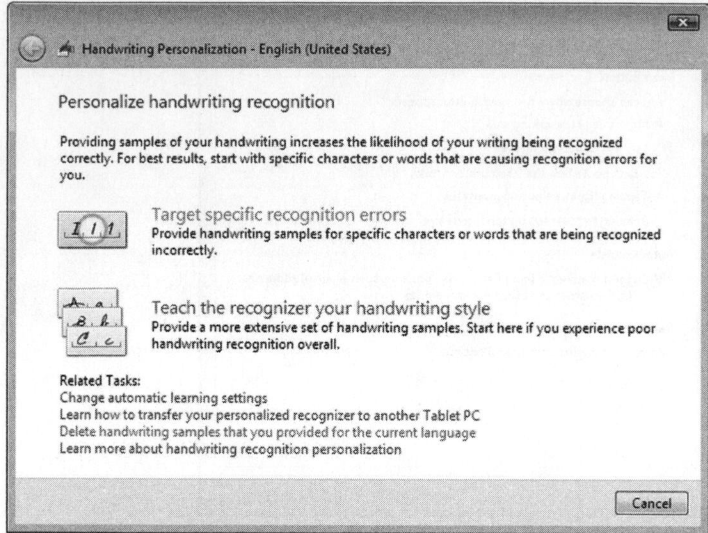

Figure 12-23

The Handwriting Personalization wizard

- Target specific recognition errors—Trains the system to recognize specific characters or words in the user's handwriting. The user keys a character or word and then handwrites it, as shown in Figure 12-24, so that the system can build a library of samples. This option is for situations in which the recognition of the user's handwriting is generally good, but occasional characters or words are consistently misinterpreted.

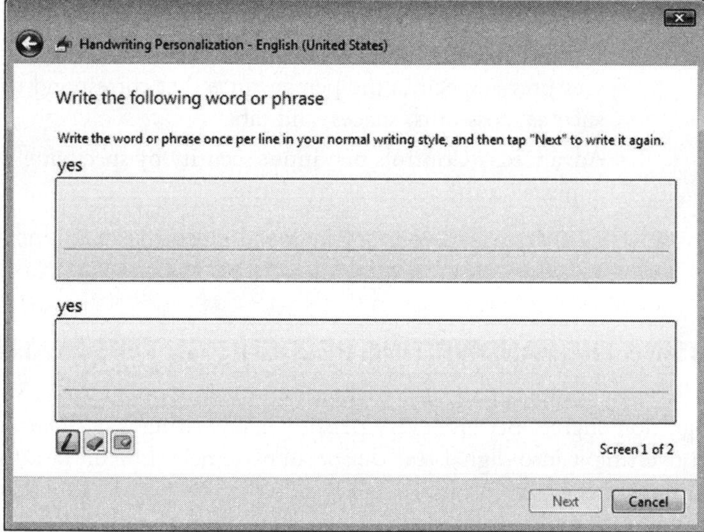

Figure 12-24

The Target Specific Recognition Errors option

- Teach the recognizer your handwriting style—Trains the system to recignize a particular user's general handwiting style. The user writes a series of sentences supplied by the computer, as shown in Figure 12-25, enabling the system to build an overall impression of the handwriting. This option is for situations in which the recognition of the user's handwriting is generally poor, and a more complete regimen is required.

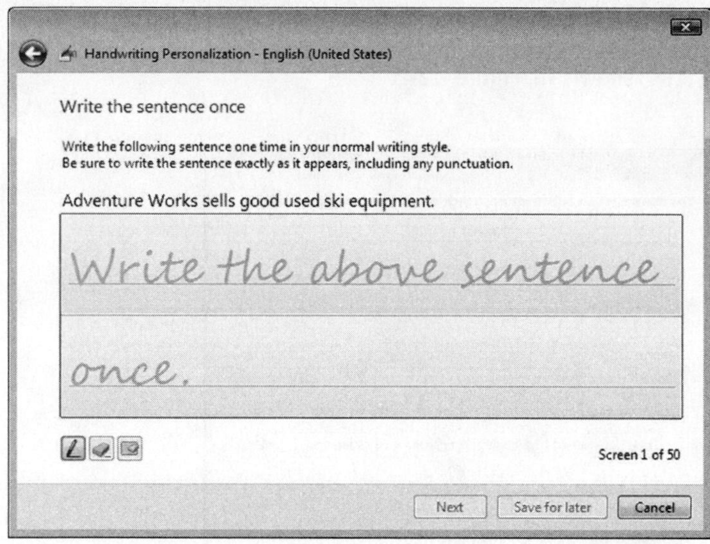

Figure 12-25

The Teach the Recognizer Your Handwriting Style option

CONFIGURING PEN FLICKS

In addition to providing handwriting input capabilities and emulating mouse actions, tablet PCs enable you to perform pen gestures called flicks, which you can configure to execute certain tasks. A flick is a short, rapid motion of the pen in a specific direction, which you can use to navigate through a document or perform other tasks. To configure pen flicks, use the following procedure:

CONFIGURE PEN FLICKS

GET READY. Log on to Windows Vista using an account with administrative privileges. When the logon process is completed, close the Welcome Center window and any other windows that appear.

1. Click **Start**, and then click **Control Panel** > **Hardware and Sound** > **Pen and Input Devices.** The Pen and Input devices dialog box appears.
2. Click the **Flicks** tab, as shown in Figure 12-26. By default, the tablet pen associates horizontal and vertical flicks with navigational commands. Use the Sensitivity slider to control how readily the system recognizes your pen flicks.

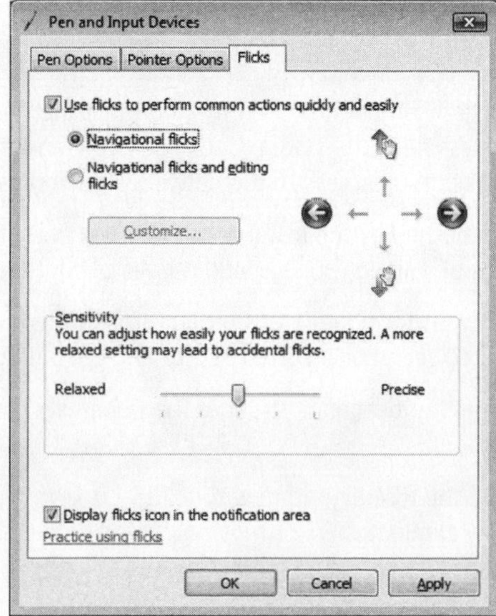

Figure 12-26

The Flicks tab of the Pen and Input Devices dialog box

3. To add editing commands, select the **Navigational flicks and editing flicks** option, and then click **Customize**. The Customize Flicks dialog box appears, as shown in Figure 12-27.

Figure 12-27

The Customize Flicks dialog box

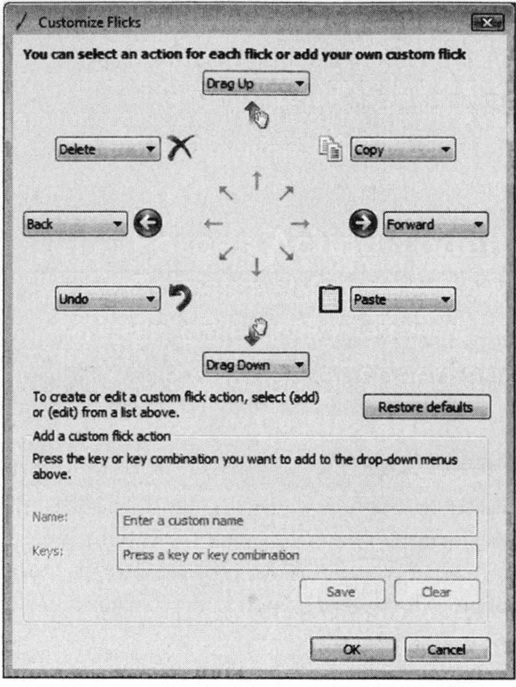

4. Use the eight dropdown lists to select the action for each directional flick. The dropdown lists contain a variety of preconfigured actions, plus an (add) action that you can use to configure a flick to generate a specific key combination, by entering values in the Name and Keys text boxes.
5. Click **OK** to close the Customize Flicks dialog box.
6. Click **OK** to close the Pen and Input Devices dialog box.

SUMMARY SKILL MATRIX

IN THIS LESSON YOU LEARNED:
Wired networks typically rely on physical security to protect the privacy of their communications. However, if a wireless network is not properly secured, an intruder in a car parked outside can use a laptop to gain full access to the network's communications.
The 802.11 standards published by the Institute of Electrical and Electronic Engineers (IEEE) dictate the frequencies, transmission speeds, and ranges of wireless networking products.
WEP is a wireless security protocol that helps protect transmitted information by using a security setting, called a shared secret or a shared key, to encrypt network traffic before sending it.
Although shared secret authentication is stronger than open system for authentication, it weakens the WEP encryption.
WPA encrypts data using the RC4 algorithm with a 128-bit key. This is the same algorithm as WEP, but TKIP virtually eliminates WEP's most exploited vulnerability by using a unique encryption key for each packet.

(continued)

Implemented in the WPA2 standard, AES uses a different and more secure encryption algorithm, called CCMP.

Laptop computers have a Mobile PC control panel, which consolidates many of Vista's most frequently used configuration settings in one place.

Windows Mobility Center is a shell application that provides a central point of access for many of the configuration settings that mobile computer users need frequently.

Most laptop computers have the capability to connect an external display device, making it possible for a group of users to view the desktop without having to crowd around a single screen.

To conserve battery power as much as possible, virtually all laptops include the hardware and firmware elements needed to dynamically adjust the power consumption of individual components.

Windows Vista includes a dialog box that bundles together the configuration settings that users most often adjust before giving a presentation and make it possible to activate all of the settings with a single switch.

Windows Vista includes the ability to store copies of network files on the local drive, for use when the computer is disconnected.

Sync Center is an application that functions as a central control panel for all of a Windows Vista computer's synchronization partnerships, including those with network drives and mobile devices.

Windows SideShow is a new feature in Windows Vista designed to accommodate a new secondary display technology that is currently being integrated into a wide variety of products.

A tablet PC's entire display is touch sensitive, enabling users to tap screen buttons with a finger, or tap, click, drag, and write directly on the screen using a stylus. Windows Vista also includes handwriting recognition capabilities that convert the handwriting into digital text.

Knowledge Assessment

Fill in the Blank

Complete the following sentences by writing the correct word or words in the blanks provided.

1. To synchronize e-mail and calendar data with a Pocket PC running Windows Mobile, you must use an application called ________________.
2. The Windows Vista feature that provides support for secondary displays is called ________________.
3. The name of the protocol that Windows Vista uses to send monitor signals to a network projector is called ________________.
4. A power plan in Windows Vista contains two sets of settings supporting the ________________ and ________________ power states.
5. The standards on which wireless LAN products are based are published by the ________________.
6. A sync partnership between a Windows Vista computer and a portable music player typically uses ________________ synchronization.
7. The slowest of the IEEE 802.11 wireless networking specifications currently in use is ________________.

8. The non-analog connection that many modern monitors now use to connect to computers is called ______________.

9. Applications that support secondary displays using Windows SideShow are called ______________.

10. A specific pen gesture that is configured to perform a navigation function on a tablet PC is called a(n) ______________.

True / False

Circle T if the statement is true or F if the statement is false.

T | F 1. Wireless networking products conforming to the IEEE 802.11g specification have the fastest transmission rates of any wireless LAN products on the market.

T | F 2. Turning on Windows Vista's Presentation Settings feature prevents system notification messages from appearing on the desktop.

T | F 3. The only ways to configure power settings in Windows Vista is through the Power Options control panel.

T | F 4. The number of tiles appearing in the Windows Mobility Center is dependent on the computer's hardware and software.

T | F 5. The Sync Center application in Windows Vista enables users to synchronize data with handheld devices and manage offline files.

T | F 6. The 802.1X standard defines a high-speed wireless networking standard.

T | F 7. WPA-TKIP is the most secure type of wireless network encryption available today.

T | F 8. The Connect to a Network Projector wizard enables you to open a port in Windows Firewall.

T | F 9. To create a customized power plan, you must copy one of the default power plans and modify its settings.

T | F 10. WEP is a relatively insecure protocol because there is no way to dynamically change the shared secret keys it uses to encrypt data.

Review Questions

1. Explain why it is preferable to use open system authentication on a wireless network using WEP, rather than shared secret authentication.

2. Explain how wireless networking products conforming to the IEEE 802.11n draft specification achieve their increases in transmission speed.

■ Case Scenarios

Scenario #1: Evaluating Wireless Security Risks

Mark Lee is a desktop technician at a large law firm. Law firms are among the slowest adopters of new technologies, and Mark's employer is no exception. The organization has, to date, not deployed a wireless network. After bringing up the benefits of wireless networks at a recent meeting with the IT staff, Mark was told that the company will not be deploying a wireless network for several years, if ever.

The lack of an IT-configured wireless network has not entirely stopped their adoption, however. Yesterday, Mark noticed a junior attorney surfing the Web with his laptop in the lunch room, without a network cable. When Mark asked the attorney how he was connected to the network, he confessed that he plugged a consumer WAP into the network port in his office.

Which of the following are potential risks of having a rogue wireless network in the office? (Choose all that apply.)

a. An attacker with a wireless network card could join their Active Directory domain.
b. An attacker could access hosts on the internal network from the lobby of the building with a wireless-enabled mobile computer.
c. An attacker could use a wireless network card to capture traffic between two wired network hosts.
d. An attacker could use the company's Internet connection from the lobby of the building with a wireless-enabled mobile computer.
e. An attacker could capture an attorney's e-mail credentials as the attorney downloads his messages across the wireless link.

Scenario #2: Establishing a Wireless Networking Policy

After evaluating the risks of a rogue wireless network, Mark Lee decides that he must convince the IT director that the company needs a wireless network security policy even if they do not want to sponsor a wireless network. Which of the following strategies would reduce the risk of a security breech resulting from a rogue wireless network? (Choose all that apply.)

a. Deploying an IT-managed WAP with WEP encryption and 802.1X authentication.
b. Publishing instructions for other employees to access the current employee-managed WAP.
c. Educating internal employees about the risks associated with wireless networks.
d. Publishing a wireless network security policy forbidding employee-managed WAPs.
e. Deploying an IT-managed WAP using open network authentication without encryption.
f. Publishing a wireless network security policy allowing employee-managed WAPs, as long as they have authentication and encryption enabled.

Appendix A
Microsoft Certified Technology Specialist (MCTS) Skills: Exam 70-620

Matrix Skill	Skill Number	Lesson Number
Installing and Upgrading Windows Vista		
Identify hardware requirements.	1.1	1
Perform a clean installation.	1.2	2
Upgrade to Windows Vista from previous versions of Windows.	1.3	2
Upgrade from one edition of Windows Vista to another edition.	1.4	2
Troubleshoot installation issues.	1.5	11
Install and configure Windows Vista drivers.	1.6	6
Configuring and Troubleshooting Post-Installation System Settings		
Troubleshoot post-installation configuration issues.	2.1	11
Configure and troubleshoot Windows Aero.	2.2	3
Configure and troubleshoot parental controls.	2.3	8
Configure Windows Internet Explorer 7+.	2.4	9
Configuring Windows Security Features		
Configure and troubleshoot User Account Control.	3.1	5
Configure Windows Defender.	3.2	8
Configure Dynamic Security for Internet Explorer 7+.	3.3	9
Configure security settings in Windows Firewall.	3.4	8
Configuring Network Connectivity		
Use the Network and Sharing Center to configure networking.	4.1	7 & 12
Troubleshoot connectivity issues.	4.2	7
Configure Remote Access.	4.3	11
Configuring Applications Included with Windows Vista		
Configure and Troubleshoot Media Applications.	5.1	9
Configure Windows Mail.	5.2	9
Configure Windows Meeting Space.	5.3	9
Configure Windows Calendar.	5.4	9
Configure Windows Fax and Scan.	5.5	9
Configure Windows Sidebar.	5.6	1 & 3
Maintaining and Optimizing Systems That Run Windows Vista		
Troubleshoot performance issues.	6.1	10
Troubleshoot reliability issues by using built-in diagnostic tools.	6.2	10 & 11
Configure Windows Update.	6.3	10
Configure Data Protection.	6.4	4

continued

MATRIX SKILL	SKILL NUMBER	LESSON NUMBER
Configuring and Troubleshooting Mobile Computing		
Configure mobile display settings.	7.1	12
Configure mobile display settings.	7.2	12
Configure mobile devices.	7.3	12
Configure tablet PC software.	7.4	12

Appendix B

LAB SETUP GUIDE

Getting Started

The *Configuring Microsoft Windows Vista* title of the Microsoft Official Academic Course (MOAC) series includes two books: a textbook and a Lab Manual. The exercises in the Lab Manual are designed for classroom use under the supervision of an instructor or a lab aide. In an academic setting, the computer classroom might be used by a variety of classes each day, so you must plan your setup procedure accordingly. For example, consider automating the classroom setup procedure and using removable fixed disks in the classroom. Use the automated setup procedure to rapidly configure the classroom environment, and remove the fixed disks after teaching this class each day.

Classroom Setup

This course should be taught in a classroom containing networked computers where students can develop their skills through hands-on experience with Microsoft Windows Vista. The exercises in the Lab Manual require the computers to be installed and configured in a specific manner. Failure to adhere to the setup instructions in this document can produce unanticipated results when the students perform the exercises.

CLASSROOM WINDOWS SERVER REQUIREMENTS

The computer running Windows Server 2003 in the classroom requires the following hardware and software:

HARDWARE REQUIREMENTS

All hardware must be on the Microsoft Windows Server 2003 Hardware Compatibility List (HCL).

- One Pentium 133 CPU (Pentium 733 or greater recommended)
- 128 MB RAM (256 or greater recommended)
- 2 GB hard disk minimum (4 GB or greater recommended)
- One CD-ROM drive
- One mouse
- One VGA display adapter and monitor (SVGA display adapter and monitor capable of displaying 256 colors recommended)
- One Ethernet network interface adapter

SOFTWARE REQUIREMENTS

All of the software listed below is required for the course:

- Microsoft Windows Server 2003 (evaluation edition available as a free download from Microsoft's website at http://technet.microsoft.com/en-us/windowsserver/bb430831.aspx)
- Microsoft PowerPoint or PowerPoint Viewer
- Microsoft Word or Word Viewer

STUDENT COMPUTER REQUIREMENTS

Each student computer requires the following hardware and software:

HARDWARE REQUIREMENTS

- 1 GHz 32-bit (x86) or 64-bit (x64) processor
- 512 MB of system memory (1 GB recommended)
- 80 GB hard drive
- DVD-ROM drive
- Network interface adapter
- For Windows Aero, support for DirectX 9 graphics with:
  - WDDM Driver
  - 128 MB of graphics memory (minimum)
  - Pixel Shader 2.0 in hardware
  - 32 bits per pixel

SOFTWARE REQUIREMENTS

All of the software listed below is required for the course.

- Windows XP Professional
- Windows Vista, Business Edition
- Microsoft PowerPoint or PowerPoint Viewer
- Microsoft Word or Word Viewer

CLASSROOM CONFIGURATION

The following configurations and naming conventions are used throughout the course and are required for completing the labs as outlined in the Lab Manual.

The classroom server is configured as a Windows Server 2003 domain controller. Use the following information for the classroom server:

- Active Directory domain name: contoso.com
- Computer name: Server01
- Fully qualified domain name (FQDN): Server01.contoso.com

The student computers are initially configured as Windows XP workstations on an isolated classroom network, with a single classroom server configured as a domain controller in a domain separate from the rest of the school network. The student computers in the domain are named Computerxx, where xx is a unique number assigned to each computer by the instructor. Each workstation will also have a corresponding user account called Studentxx, where xx is the same number assigned to the computer. During the course of the labs, the students will install Windows Vista on their computers.

SETUP INSTRUCTIONS

Before you begin, do the following:

- Read this entire document.
- Make sure you have the Instructor CD provided with the course materials and the installation disks for Microsoft Windows Server 2003, Microsoft Windows XP Professional, and Microsoft Windows Vista.

SERVER01 SETUP

Using the following setup procedure, install Windows Server 2003 on Server01 and configure it to function as a domain controller (DC) in the contoso.com domain.

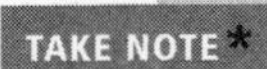

By performing the following setup instructions, your computer's hard disks will be repartitioned and reformatted. You will lose all existing data on these systems.

INSTALLING WINDOWS SERVER 2003 ON SERVER01 USING AN ANSWER FILE

In order to use the unattended answer file setup for the instructor computer, your system must meet the following configuration requirements:

- The computer's basic input/output system (BIOS) and CD/DVD-ROM must be able to boot from a CD/DVD.
- The computer's BIOS must be configured to boot from the CD/DVD-ROM drive.
- You must have a floppy disk drive in the computer.
- If your system meets these requirements, you can install the instructor computer by performing the following steps.

INSTALL WINDOWS SERVER 2003 ON SERVER01 USING AN ANSWER FILE

1. Copy the Winnt.sif file from the \\Lab Setup Guide\SetupFiles\Server01 folder on the Instructor CD-ROM to a floppy disk.
2. Insert the Windows Server 2003 Installation disk into the computer's DVD-ROM drive and restart the computer.
3. If prompted, press any key to boot from the CD/DVD-ROM drive.
4. As soon as the system begins to boot from the CD/DVD-ROM drive, insert the floppy disk with the Winnt.sif file into the floppy drive.

If your system is configured to start from floppy, you might have to remove the floppy disk upon restart. Ensure that the computer's network cable is attached; otherwise, the automated installation of Active Directory directory service might fail.

If you don't insert the floppy disk fast enough, the system will begin to prompt you with questions. If this happens, restart the computer and try again.

The installation of Windows Server 2003 should be mostly automated. During the GUI mode phase of the installation, you will see the following message: Unattended Setup Is Unable To Continue Because A Setup Parameter Specified By Your System Administrator Or Computer Manufacturer Is Missing Or Invalid. Setup Must Therefore Ask You To Provide This Information Now. Once You Have Furnished The Required Information, Unattended Setup Will Continue.

5. Click **OK**.
6. Enter the Product Key for your copy of Windows Server 2003, and then click **Next** to continue. Automated setup should finish configuring your computer at this point.

After the installation is complete, you might have to adjust your computer's regional settings, such as the time zone. If you use the answer file setup method, you can skip to the "Complete Post-Installation Tasks on Server01" section of this document.

INSTALLING WINDOWS SERVER 2003 ON SERVER01 USING THE MANUAL METHOD

If your computer has an existing 32-bit operating system installed, start the computer as usual and insert the Windows Server 2003 Installation disk. The Microsoft Windows 2003 window opens automatically. In the left pane of the window, select Install Windows Server 2003. If the Microsoft Windows 2003 window does not open automatically, run Winnt32.exe, located in the \I386 folder on the disk. This will launch the Windows Server 2003 Setup program.

TAKE NOTE*

You only need to perform a manual installation if you were unable to perform the answer file installation described in the previous section.

If your computer has an existing 16-bit operating system installed, start the computer as usual, and insert the Windows Server 2003 Installation disk. Run Winnt.exe, located in the \I386 folder on the disk. This will launch the Windows Server 2003 Setup program.

If your computer does not have an operating system installed, you might be able to boot your computer from the Windows Server 2003 Installation disk. When you boot from the disk, the Windows Server 2003 Setup program starts automatically.

If your computer will not boot from the disk, start your computer with any MS-DOS or Microsoft Windows startup floppy disk that has DVD-ROM support. Once you have started the computer and can navigate among the files on the Windows Server 2003 Installation disk, run \Winnt.exe, located in the \I386 folder on the disk. This will launch the Windows Server 2003 Setup program.

After Windows Server 2003 Setup is launched, follow the steps below to continue the installation.

INSTALL WINDOWS SERVER 2003 ON SERVER01 USING THE MANUAL METHOD

1. If you are installing the evaluation version of Windows Server 2003, a setup notification screen appears, informing you that you are about to install an evaluation version of Windows Server 2003. If this screen appears, press **Enter** to continue. The Welcome To Setup screen appears.
2. Press **Enter** to continue the installation. The Windows Server 2003 Licensing Agreement screen appears.
3. Select I Agree by pressing **F8**.
4. If another copy of Windows Server 2003 is detected, a Windows Server 2003 Setup screen informs you that you can repair the installation. If another copy of Windows Server 2003 is detected, press **Esc** to continue. The Windows Server 2003 Setup screen appears, prompting you to select an area of free space or an existing partition on which to install Windows Server 2003, create a partition, or delete a partition.
5. If any partitions exist, delete them by pressing the **D** key and following the on-screen instructions. Once the disks contain only unpartitioned space, go to the next step.
6. Make sure that the unpartitioned space on Disk 0 is selected, and then press **Enter** to continue the installation.
7. Select **Format This Partition Using The NTFS File System**, and then press **Enter** to continue. If you are prompted to insert the disk, do so, and then press **Enter** to continue. The system will perform various installation tasks and then restart when complete. A Windows Setup message box appears, and the installation continues.

TAKE NOTE*

If your computer supports booting from CD/DVD, then after Windows Server 2003 Setup restarts, the computer might try to boot from the Windows Server 2003 disk. If this happens, you should be prompted to press a key to boot from the disk. However, if Setup restarts automatically, simply remove the disk, and then restart the computer.

RUN THE GUI MODE PHASE OF WINDOWS SERVER 2003 SETUP

1. In the Regional Settings screen, make sure that the system locale, user locale, and keyboard layout are correct for your language and location, and then click **Next**. The Personalize Your Software screen appears, prompting you for your name and organization name.
2. In the Name text box, key **Server01**; in the Organization text box, key the name of your school, and then click **Next**. The Your Product Key screen appears.
3. Enter your Product Key, and then click **Next**. The Licensing Modes screen appears, prompting you to select a licensing mode. By default, the Per Server option is selected.
4. Select the **Per Device Or Per User** option, and then click **Next**. The Computer Name And Administrator Password screen appears.
5. In the Computer Name text box, key **SERVER01**. Windows Server 2003 displays the computer name in all capital letters regardless of how it is entered.
6. In the Administrator Password and Confirm Password text boxes, key **P@ssw0rd** and then click **Next**. The Date And Time Settings dialog box appears.
7. Select the appropriate date, time, and time zone, and then click **Next**. The Network Settings dialog box appears.
8. Select the **Custom Settings** option, and then click **Next**.
9. Select **Internet Protocol (TCP/IP)**, and then click the **Properties** button. The Internet Protocol (TCP/IP) Properties dialog box appears.
10. In the General tab, select the **Use The Following IP Address** option and set the following parameters:
    - IP address: **10.1.1.200**
    - Subnet mask: **255.255.0.0**
    - Default gateway: Leave this field blank.
    - Preferred DNS server: **10.1.1.200**
    - Alternate DNS server: Leave this field blank.

TAKE NOTE*

At this point, if the network interface adapter is not detected, you will have to install it manually. You might have to come back to these steps later when you are configuring.

TAKE NOTE*

If you plan to provide the classroom with Internet access, specify the IP address of the router on the classroom network in the Default Gateway field.

11. Click **OK** to close the Internet Protocol (TCP/IP) Properties dialog box.
12. Click **Next** to continue with setup. The Workgroup Or Computer Domain screen appears, prompting you to join either a workgroup or a domain.
13. Verify that the **No, This Computer Is Not On A Network, Or Is On A Network Without A Domain** option is selected and that the workgroup name is Workgroup, and then click **Next**.

Windows Setup begins copying installation files. The installation should proceed uninterrupted. Eventually the computer will restart.

COMPLETE POST-INSTALLATION TASKS ON SERVER01

TAKE NOTE*

At some point the operating system will prompt you to activate the server. When that happens, follow the steps to activate the server.

1. After the installation is completed and the computer has restarted, you should see the Welcome To Windows dialog box. Press **Ctrl+Alt+Delete** and enter the username and password you specified earlier to log on (Administrator/P@ssw0rd). The Manage Your Server dialog box appears.
2. Select the **Don't Display This Page At Logon** checkbox, and then close the Manage Your Server dialog box.

INSTALLING ACTIVE DIRECTORY ON SERVER01

You can use an automated installation file to install Active Directory. This file is named dc.txt and is located on the Instructor CD-ROM under the \Lab Setup Guide\SetupFiles\Server01 folder. You can use this file to install Active Directory by keying dcpromo /answer:D:\Lab Setup Guide\SetupFiles\Server01\dc.txt and then pressing Enter in the Run dialog box. If you would rather install Active Directory manually on the instructor computer, complete the following steps.

INSTALL ACTIVE DIRECTORY ON SERVER01

TAKE NOTE*

The command above assumes that drive D represents your CD-ROM drive. If your CD-ROM drive is referenced by a different drive letter, substitute that letter for D.

1. Click **Start**, select **Run**, key **dcpromo** and then press **Enter**. The Welcome To The Active Directory Installation Wizard appears.
2. Click **Next** to proceed with the Active Directory installation.
3. On the Operating System Compatibility page, click **Next**.
4. On the Domain Controller Type page, select **Domain Controller For A New Domain**, then click **Next**.
5. On the Create New Domain page, ensure that **Domain In A New Forest** is selected, and then click **Next**.
6. On the New Domain Name page in the Full DNS Name For New Domain box, key **contoso.com** and then click **Next**. After a few moments, the NetBIOS Domain Name page appears.
7. Verify that **CONTOSO** is the default NetBIOS name, and then click **Next**.
8. On the Database And Log Folders page, click **Next**. This will leave the log files and database in their default location.
9. On the Shared System Volume page, ensure that the **\Sysvol** folder is on a volume formatted with the NTFS file system (this should already be done), and then click **Next**.
10. On the DNS Registration Diagnostics page, view the details of the diagnostic test, ensure that the **Install And Configure The DNS Server On This Computer And Set This Computer To Use This DNS Server As Its Preferred DNS Server** option is selected, and then click **Next**.
11. On the Permissions page, click **Next** to accept the default permissions setting.
12. On the Directory Services Restore Mode Administrator Password page, key **P@ssw0rd** as the restore mode password. Confirm the password by typing it again, and then click **Next**.
13. Review the information in the Summary dialog box, and then click **Next**.
14. When the Completing The Active Directory Installation Wizard page appears, click **Finish**, and then click **Restart Now**. The computer restarts.
15. Log in using the appropriate domain administrator name and password.
16. On the This Server Is Now A Domain Controller page, click **Finish**. Active Directory is now installed on the server.

INSTALL AND CONFIGURE THE DHCP SERVER

1. On Server01, click **Start**, select **Control Panel**, and then click **Add Or Remove Programs**. The Add Or Remove Programs window appears.
2. In the left frame, click **Add/Remove Windows Components**. The Windows Components Wizard appears.
3. In the Components box, scroll down and select Networking Services (without modifying the state of the checkbox), and then click **Details**. The Networking Services dialog box appears.
4. In the Subcomponents Of Networking Services box, select the **Dynamic Host Configuration Protocol (DHCP)** checkbox.
5. Click **OK**. The Windows Components page reappears.
6. Click **Next**. The Configuring Components page shows a progress indicator as the changes you requested are made. The Completing The Windows Components Wizard page appears.
7. Click **Finish**.
8. Close the Add Or Remove Programs window.
9. Click the **Start** menu, select **Administrative Tools**, and then select **DHCP**. The DHCP console appears and server01.contoso.com is listed in the scope pane.
10. In the scope pane, expand the server01.contoso.com icon.
11. A red ↓ appears to the left of the server name.
12. Select **server01.contoso.com**, and then select **Authorize** from the Action menu.
13. Select **server01.contoso.com**, and then select **New Scope** from the Action menu. The New Scope Wizard appears.
14. Click **Next**. The Scope Name page appears.
15. In the Name text box, key **Classroom Network** and then click **Next**. The IP Address Range page appears.
16. Key **10.1.1.201** in the Start IP Address text box, and then key **10.1.1.250** in the End IP Address text box.
17. In the Subnet Mask text box, key **255.255.0.0** and then click **Next**.
18. Click **Next** to bypass the Add Exclusions page. The Lease Duration page appears.
19. Click **Next** to accept the default lease duration. The Configure DHCP Options page appears.
20. Click **Next** to accept the default **Yes, I Want To Configure These Options Now** option. The Router (Default Gateway) page appears.
21. In the IP Address text box, key **10.1.1.200**, click Add, and then click **Next**. The Domain Name And DNS Servers page appears.
22. In the IP Address text box, key **10.1.1.200** and click **Add**. Then click **Next**.
23. Click **Next** to bypass the WINS Servers page. The Activate Scope page appears.
24. Click **Next** to accept the default **Yes, I Want To Active This Scope Now** option.
25. Click **Finish** to complete the New Scope Wizard.
26. Right-click the server name in the scope pane, and then select **Authorize** from the Action menu.

TAKE NOTE

If you plan to provide the classroom with Internet access, specify the IP address of the router on the classroom network on the Router (Default Gateway) page, instead of 10.1.1.200.

PREPARE THE FILE SYSTEM

1. On the server's C: drive, create a new folder called **\VistaInstall** and copy the contents of a Windows Vista Installation disk to that folder.
2. Share the C:\VistaInstall folder using the share name **VistaInstall**, and then grant the **Everyone** special identity the **Read share permission only**.

3. On the C: drive, create a new folder called **\UpgradeAdvisor** and share it using the name **UpgradeAdvisor**. Then grant the **Everyone** special identity the **Read share permission only**.
4. Download the Windows Vista Upgrade Advisor software from Microsoft's website (http://www.microsoft.com/downloads) and copy it to the C:\UpgradeAdvisor folder.
5. Using Windows Explorer, grant the **Everyone** special identity the **Full Control NTFS permission** for the C:\VistaInstall and C:\UpgradeAdvisor folders.
6. On the C: drive, create a new folder called **\Students** and share it using the name **Students**. Then grant the **Everyone** special identity the **Full Control permission**.
7. Share the root of the C drive using the share name C, and then grant the **Everyone** special identity the **Read share permission only**.

INSTALL IIS

1. Click **Start**, select **Control Panel**, and then click **Add Or Remove Programs.**
2. Click **Add/Remove Windows Components.** The Windows Components Wizard appears.
3. In the Components list, select **Application Server**, and then click **Details**. The Application Server dialog box appears.
4. Select **Internet Information Services (IIS)**, and then click **Details**. The Internet Information Services (IIS) dialog box appears.
5. Select the following checkboxes, and then click **OK**.

   Common Files

   File Transfer Protocol (FTP) Service

   Internet Information Services Manager

   World Wide Web Service
6. Click **OK** to close the Application Server dialog box, and then click **Next**. After the installation is completed, the Completing The Windows Components Wizard appears.
7. Click **Finish**.
8. Click **Start**, select **Administrative Tools**, and then click **Internet Information Services (IIS) Manager**. The Internet Information Services (IIS) Manager console appears.
9. Expand the \FTP Sites folder, select **Default FTP Site** and then select **Properties** from the Action menu. The Default FTP Site Properties dialog box appears
10. Select the **Home Directory** tab, and then key **C:\Students** in the Local Path text box.
11. Select the **Write** checkbox, and then click **OK**.
12. Close the Internet Information Services (IIS) Manager console.

CREATE USER ACCOUNTS

1. Click **Start**, select **Administrative Tools**, and then click **Active Directory Users and Computers**. The Active Directory Users and Computers console appears.
2. Right-click the **Users** container, point to New, and select User. The New Object-User wizard appears.
3. Key **Studentxx** in the First Name and User Logon Name text boxes, where *xx* is the number assigned to the first student computer in the classroom. Then click **Next**.
4. In the Password and Confirm Password text boxes, key **P@sswOrd**.

5. Clear the **User Must Change Password At Next Logon** checkbox and select the **Password Never Expires** checkbox. Then click **Next**.
6. Click **Finish** to create the user account.
7. Double-click the **Studentxx** user object you just created. The Studentxx Properties sheet appears.
8. Click the **Profile** tab.
9. In the Home Folder box, select the **Connect** option, leave the default drive letter **Z:** selected, and key **\\server01\students\%username%** in the To text box.
10. Click **OK** to close the Studentxx Properties sheet.
11. Repeat Steps 2 to 10 to create a Studentxx user account for each computer in the classroom.
12. Right-click the **Users** container, point to **New**, and select **Group**. The New Object-Group wizard appears.
13. In the Group Name text box, key **Students**. Then click **Next**.
14. Click **Finish** to create the group.
15. Double-click the **Students** group object you just created. The Students Properties sheet appears.
16. Click the **Members** tab.
17. Click **Add**, key the name of the first Studentxx user you created, and click **OK**.
18. Repeat Step 17 to add all of the Studentxx accounts you created to the Students group.
19. Click **OK** to close the Students Properties sheet.
20. Close the Active Directory Users and Computers console.

STUDENT COMPUTER*XX* SETUP

Using the following setup procedure, install Windows XP on each student computer in the classroom.

1. If your BIOS allows you to boot from CD-ROM, set it to do so and boot the Windows XP Professional installation CD. If your computer will not boot from CD-ROM, start your computer with a floppy system disk that has CD-ROM support. At the command prompt, key **D:\I386\Winnt32.exe** (where *D:* is the drive letter of your CD-ROM) and then press **Enter**. Remove the floppy disk from the drive.
2. On the Windows XP Professional Setup screen, on the Welcome To Setup page, press **Enter**. The End-User License Agreement For Microsoft Software page appears.
3. Press **F8** to indicate that you agree to the terms of the license agreement.
4. If there is already a Windows XP installation, a repair option will be offered. If this happens, press **ESC** to install a new copy of Windows XP Professional.
5. A screen summarizing the partitions on your hard drive(s) appears. If there are any partitions on the installation hard disk, delete them by selecting them, pressing **D**, and then, when prompted, pressing **L** to confirm the delete. Repeat this process until all partitions on the installation hard drive are deleted.
6. Once only unpartitioned space exists on the installation hard drive, press **C**.
7. At the Create Partition Of Size (in MB) prompt, key **30000** and then press **Enter**.
8. Select **C: Partition1 [New (Raw)]**, and press **Enter**. (The students will configure the remaining, unpartitioned space during the labs.)
9. Verify that Format The Partition Using The NTFS File System or Format The Partition Using The NTFS File System (Quick) is selected, and then press **Enter**.

The Setup program now formats the hard drive and completes the setup tasks, which can take five minutes or more. The computer will then restart.

RUN THE GRAPHICAL USER INTERFACE PHASE OF WINDOWS XP PROFESSIONAL SETUP

The second phase of Windows XP Professional Setup uses a graphical user interface (GUI). After the restart, Windows XP Professional Setup automatically begins additional installation tasks (during which features are highlighted and the program displays an estimated time for completion). After five minutes or more, the Windows XP Professional Setup Wizard appears.

1. On the Regional And Language Options page, click **Next**.
2. On the Personalize Your Software page, in the Name text box, key **Studentxx**, where *xx* is the number assigned to the computer. Leave the Organization text box blank, or key the name of your school, if desired. Then click **Next**.
3. On the Your Product Key page, key the Windows XP product key in the Product Key text box. Click **Next**.
4. On the Computer Name And Administrator Password page, in the Computer Name text box, key **Computerxx**, where xx is the number assigned to the computer. In the Administrator Password and Confirm Password text boxes, key **P@sswOrd**. Then, click **Next**.
5. On the Date And Time Settings page, select the current date and time and your time zone. Click **Next**. Setup now performs installation tasks, and then the Network Settings page appears.
6. Select **Typical Settings**, and then click **Next**.
7. On the Workgroup Or Computer Domain page, click **Next** to accept the defaults. Windows Setup performs setup tasks, which can take 30 minutes or more. When it is done, the computer restarts.
8. After restarting, Windows might ask to adjust your display settings. In the Display Settings message box, click **OK**. In the Monitor Settings message box, click **OK**. If you do not see the Monitor Settings message box, your display settings will revert back to VGA mode in 30 seconds.
9. On the Welcome To Microsoft Windows page, click **Next**.
10. If Windows asks how you will connect to the Internet, click **Skip**.
11. On the Ready To Activate Windows page, follow the instructions to activate Windows over the Internet or by phone. Then click **Next**.
12. On the Who Will Use This Computer? page, in the Your Name text box, key **Studentxx**, where xx is the number assigned to the computer, and then click **Next**.
13. On the Thank You page, click **Finish**.

COMPLETING POST-INSTALLATION TASKS ON COMPUTER*XX*

Install the following components on each classroom Windows XP workstation:

From the Windows Update website:

- Windows Installer 3.0 (for Windows Update)
- Windows XP Service Pack 2 (if not already incorporated into your installation)
- All critical updates

From Microsoft Download Center

- .NET 3.0 Framework
- Msxml6.msi (for Upgrade Advisor)

Glossary

A

Access control entry (ACE) Each ACE consists of a security principal (that is, the name of the user, group, or computer being granted the permissions) and the specific permissions assigned to that security principal. When you manage permissions in any of the Windows Vista permission systems, you are actually creating and modifying the ACEs in an ACL.

Access control list (ACL) An ACL is a collection of individual permissions in the form of access control entries (ACEs).

Active Directory Microsoft's directory service that automates network management, such as user data, resources, and security.

Admin Approval Mode When an administrator attempts to perform a task that requires administrative access, the system switches the account from the standard user token to the administrative token.

Advanced Configuration and Power Interface (ACPI) A power management standard, developed by Microsoft, Intel, and Toshiba, which enables a computer's operating system to regulate the power consumption of specific system components, based on input received from an application, a device driver, or a user.

Advanced Encryption Standard (AES) A cryptographic algorithm used in the Wi-Fi Protected Access 2 (WPA2) wireless networking security protocol.

authentication The process by which Windows Vista verifies the identity of the person operating the computer to be the same as the user account the person is employing to gain access.

authorization The process by which an authenticated user is granted a specific degree of access to specific computer or data resources.

B

Background Intelligent Transfer Service (BITS) An HTTP-based file transfer service that downloads files using only the network's idle bandwidth. This enables Windows Update to perform downloads without affecting other applications that are using the network. BITS downloads are also resumable, in the event they are interrupted.

basic disk A basic disk uses primary partitions, extended partitions, and logical drives to organize data. A primary partition that hosts an operating system is marked as the active partition.

BitLocker A feature included with the Windows Vista Enterprise and Ultimate editions. Microsoft designed it to address the problem of data that is compromised when a computer is lost or stolen. By encrypting the entire Windows volume, including swap and hibernation files, and performing an integrity check on the boot components, the data is protected, even if someone should attempt to access the drive using another operating system.

Boot Configuration Data (BCD) In Windows Vista, a registry file that contains the information used to generate the system's boot menu. Replaces the boot.ini file used in previous Windows versions.

breadcrumb trail A new feature in Windows Explorer that contains a series of links to the selected file or folder's parent folders in the file system hierarchy. The address is essentially a trail leading back to the source. Each of the breadcrumbs functions as a link directly back to a parent level in the file system. This feature replaces the Address box used in previous Windows versions.

C

channels The Event Viewer console comes preconfigured with a large collection of component logs for Windows Vista. When you expand the Applications and Services Logs folder, you see logs for Windows applications such as Internet Explorer. Then, when you expand the Microsoft and Windows folders, you see a long list of Windows components. Each of these components has its own separate log, called a channel.

clean installation A clean installation is the simplest way to deploy Windows Vista on a new computer or a computer with a partition that you are willing to reformat (losing all of the data on the partition in the process). In a clean installation, you boot from the Windows Vista setup disk and create or select a blank partition where Vista will reside.

connection-oriented A protocol in which two communicating systems establish a connection before they transmit any data. Once the connection is established, the computers exchange packets with complex headers designed to provide error detection and correction. A connection-oriented protocol ensures bit-perfect data transmissions, but at the price of greatly increased overhead.

connectionless A protocol that does not require the establishment of a connection, nor does it perform error detection or correction. Systems simply transmit their packets to the destination, without knowing if the destination system is ready to accept data, or if it even exists. Connectionless protocols do not guarantee delivery of their data, but they operate with a very low overhead that conserves network bandwidth.

credential prompt When a standard user attempts to perform a task that requires administrative privileges, the system displays a credential prompt requesting that the user supply the name and password for an account with administrative privileges.

D

Desktop Window Manager (DWM) On a computer running the Windows Aero user experience, DWM is responsible for drawing and updating the windows that appear on the desktop. DWM is essentially a Direct3D application that uses the graphics hardware on the video adapter to render each window in an offline buffer before sending it to the display.

device driver Provides the operating system with information about a specific device so that the device can communicate with the operating system.

directory service A collection of logical objects that represent various types of network resources, including computers, applications, users, and groups. Each object consists of attributes that contain information about the object.

DirectX A collection of application programming interfaces (APIs) that provide multimedia services to application developers.

domain A set of network resources for the use of a group of users who can authenticate to the network in order to gain access to those resources.

domain controller A Windows server with Active Directory directory service installed. Each workstation computer joins the domain and is represented by a computer object. Administrators create user objects that represent human users. The main difference between a domain and a workgroup is that users log on to the domain once, rather than each computer individually.

driver signing A device driver that includes a digital signature. The signer uses a cryptographic algorithm to compute the digital signature value and then appends that value to the device driver. This process insures that the device driver comes from the authentic publisher and that someone has not maliciously altered it.

dual boot Provides access to two independent operating system installations. In a dual boot environment, both operating systems are completely independent of each other, so restrictions regarding upgrade paths do not apply.

DVI (Digital Visual Interface) A computer interface designed to provide digital connections to LCD monitors and digital projectors, using a 29-pin connector.

dynamic disk An alternative to the basic disk. The process of converting a basic disk to a dynamic disk creates a single partition that occupies the entire disk. You can then create an unlimited number of volumes out of the space in that partition. Windows Vista supports three volume types: simple, spanned, and striped.

E

elevation prompt The User Access Control message box. This confirmation prevents unauthorized processes, such as those initiated by malware, from accessing the system using administrative privileges.

encryption The translation of data, using a hash algorithm based on a secret key, into a coded form that prevents unauthorized access. Only holders of the key can translate the encrypted data back into its uncoded form.

events The primary function of the Windows Eventing engine, as always, is to record information about system activities as they occur and package that information in individual units called events.

The application you use to view the events is still an MMC snap-in called Event Viewer.

F

FAT (file allocation table) Lacks the security that NTFS provides; any user who gains access to your computer can read any file without restriction. Additionally, FAT file systems have disk size limitations: FAT32 cannot handle a partition greater than 32 GB or a file greater than 4 GB. FAT cannot handle a hard disk greater than 4 GB or a file greater than 2 GB.

filters In Windows Firewall, a feature that enables users to display rules according to the profile they are associated with, their current state, or the group to which they belong.

firewall A software routine that acts as a virtual barrier between a computer and the network to which it is attached. A firewall is essentially a filter that enables certain types of incoming and outgoing traffic to pass through the barrier, while blocking other types.

G

gadget Small applications that Windows Vista places in the Windows Sidebar, an area at the right side of the desktop. Gadgets display system information or function as push clients, continually receiving information from servers on the Internet and displaying it in a custom-designed interface, such as an analog clock or an MSNBC news headline feeder.

(GUID) globally unique identifier partition table (GPT) You can use GPT as a boot disk as long as the computer's architecture provides support for an Extensible Firmware Interface (EFI)-based boot partition. Otherwise, you can use it as a non-bootable disk for data storage only. When used as a boot disk, it differs from the master boot record in that platform operation critical data is located in partitions rather than in unpartitioned or hidden sectors.

Graphic Device Interface (GDI) Responsible for drawing the lines and curves, rendering the text fonts, and handling the color palettes used to produce the graphical windows that you see on the monitor.

graphics processing unit (GPU) A special-purpose processor designed to perform specific 3D graphics functions. The system processor could conceivably perform these functions, but the GPU can do them much faster. Offloading the graphics processing tasks to a separate chip removes a significant burden from the system processor, enabling it to concentrate on other tasks.

group A type of entity that Windows uses to represent a collection of users. System administrators can create groups for any reason and with any name, and then use them just as they would a user account. Any permissions or user rights that an administrator assigns to a group are automatically inherited by all of the members of the group.

I

IEEE 802.11 A series of standards published by the Institute of Electrical and Electronics Engineers that define wireless networking protocols using various technologies and running at various speeds.

Instant Search A box located to the right of the address box in Internet Explorer 7 in which the user can type a search string and then select a search provider from a configurable drop-down list. Network administrators can even configure the drop-down list to include internal search providers, such as Microsoft SharePoint servers.

Institute of Electrical and Electronic Engineers (IEEE) A body of engineering and electronics professionals that is best known for publishing standards defining a wide variety of networking and other technologies.

IP (Internet Protocol) address A unique 32-bit numeric address used as an identifier for a device such as a computer on a TCP/IP network.

L

language-agnostic A program module that lacks language-specific code.

M

malware A term that stands for malicious software. Malicious individuals design malware to install itself on victims' computers and then send signals to a home computer on the Internet, enabling the owner to take control of the victim's system.

mandatory user profile A read-only roaming user profile.

master boot record (MBR) A partition style that has been around as long as Windows, and is still the default partition style. Supports up to four primary partitions or three primary partitions and one extended partition, with unlimited logical drives on the extended partition.

MinWin In Windows Vista, a common core module that contains 95 percent of the operating system's functionality. All Windows Vista installations begin with the installation of the MinWin module, and are followed by the addition of a secondary module containing the functionality of the particular edition designated by the product key.

Multilingual User Interface (MUI) A set of language-specific files that allows individual users to change the user interface language of the Windows operating system according to their preferences, even on the same workstation or as a roaming user.

multiple-input multiple-output (MIMO) A technology used by IEEE 802.11n wireless networking equipment to increase transmission speeds by using multiple transmitter and receiver antennae on each device.

N

Network News Transfer Protocol (NNTP) An Internet protocol that defines communications between news servers and between news clients and servers.

NTFS permissions Controls access to the files and folders stored on disk volumes formatted with the NTFS file system. To access a file, whether on the local system or over a network, a user must have the appropriate NTFS permissions.

O

OSI (Open Systems Interconnection) reference model A theoretical teaching and design aid that splits the data networking process into seven distinct layers, each of which provides specific functions.

P

packet-switching network Local area networks are sometimes described as *packet-switching networks,* which means that the messages generated by each computer are divided up into many pieces called packets that are transmitted separately over the network.

phishing A technique that takes social engineering to a mass scale. Instead of convincing-sounding telephone callers, phishing uses convincing-looking websites that urge users to supply personal information such as passwords and account numbers.

ports In TCP/IP networking, code that identifies a particular application running on a computer, used to forward incoming traffic to the proper destination process.

Post Office Protocol 3 (POP3) The most popular type of email server. The server holds your email messages until you transfer them to your computer, after which the server deletes them.

Power On Self-Test (POST) The initial phase of a PC's startup process, in which the system detects the hardware devices installed in the system and tests them to be sure they are operating properly.

print device The actual hardware that produces hard copy documents on paper or other print media. Windows Vista supports both *local print devices,* which are directly attached to the computer's parallel, serial, Universal Serial Bus (USB), or IEEE 1394 (FireWire) ports; or *network interface print devices,* which are connected to the network, either directly or through another computer.

print server A computer (or standalone device) that receives print jobs from clients and sends them to print devices that are either locally attached or connected to the network.

Printer Control Language (PCL) A language understood by the printer. Each printer is associated with a printer driver that takes the commands generated by an application and converts them into the printer's PCL.

printer The software interface through which a computer communicates with a print device. Windows Vista supports numerous interfaces, including parallel (LPT), serial (COM), USB, IEEE 1394, Infrared Data Access (IrDA), and Bluetooth ports, and network printing services such as lpr, Internet Printing Protocol (IPP), and standard TCP/IP ports.

printer driver A device driver that converts the print jobs generated by applications into an appropriate string of commands for a specific print device. Printer drivers are designed for specific print devices and provide applications with access to all of the print device's features.

printer pool A single-print server connected to multiple-print devices. The print server can distribute large numbers of incoming jobs among several identical print devices, to provide timely service. Alternatively, you can connect print devices that support different forms and paper sizes to a single print server, which will distribute jobs with different requirements to the appropriate print devices.

private key In public key encryption, the secret key in a pair of keys, which is known only to the recipient of a message or file and used to decrypt it. The relationship between the private and the public key is that when a message is encrypted using the private key, only the public key can decrypt it. The ability to decrypt the message using the public key proves that the message originated from the holder of the private key.

protected mode An operational state that is designed to prevent attackers that penetrate the computer's defenses from accessing vital system components.

protocols Computers on a network communicate using protocols, which are nothing more than languages that all of the computers understand.

public key In public key encryption, the public key in a pair of keys, which is known to everyone and is used to encrypt a message or file. The relationship between the public and the private key is that when a message is encrypted using the public key, only the corresponding private key can decrypt it.

Q

Quick Tabs Provide a miniature visual view of the tabs for multiple open web pages in Internet Explorer 7.

R

ReadyBoost A feature that enables Windows Vista to use the storage space on a USB flash drive as additional system memory. ReadyBoost uses a flash drive to store the SuperFetch cache, thereby freeing up the system memory where the cache would ordinarily be preloaded.

Remote Desktop Protocol (RDP) The protocol used to transmit screen information, keystrokes, and mouse movements between the Remote desktop Connection client and a Remote Desktop or Terminal Services server.

roaming user profile A copy of a local user profile that is stored on a network share, so that the user can access it from any computer on the network.

router A device that connects one network to another.

RSS feed A means of pushing frequently-changing content to Internet subscribers. News sites and blogs typically maintain text-based feeds, but it is also possible for an RSS feed to push images, audio, or video content to users.

rules To filter traffic, firewalls use rules, which specify which packets are allowed to pass through the firewall and which are blocked.

S

secure desktop An alternative to the interactive user desktop that Windows normally displays. When Vista generates an elevation or credential prompt, it switches to the secure desktop, suppressing the operation of all other desktop controls and permitting only Windows processes to interact with the prompt. The object of this is to prevent malware from automating a response to the elevation or credential prompt and bypassing the human reply.

security principal The name of the user, group, or computer being granted permissions.

security zones To provide different levels of access to specific applications, Internet Explorer 7 divides the addresses accessible with the web browser into several different security zones, each of which has a different set of privileges.

shadow copy Vista creates a shadow copy of a folder or file when a system restore point is requested. In other words, the shadow copy is meant to restore a previous copy of a folder or file at a specified point.

share permissions Control access to folders over a network. To access a file over a network, a user must have appropriate share permissions and appropriate NTFS permissions.

side-by-side migration In a side-by-side migration, you run two computers simultaneously: one is the source computer containing the user profile information you want to transfer, and the other is the destination computer running Windows Vista, to which you want to transfer the profile information. When you are performing a side-by-side migration, you can use Windows Easy Transfer with the computers connected together directly, using a cable or a network, or connected indirectly, using a removable storage medium.

Simple Mail Transfer Protocol (SMTP) The Transmission Control Protocol/Internet Protocol (TCP/IP) protocol that systems use to transmit email messages between servers.

simple volume Consists of space from a single disk. Once you have created a simple volume, you can later extend it to multiple disks to create a spanned or striped volume, as long as it is not a system volume or boot volume.

Snap-in The Microsoft Management Console (MMC) is a shell application that is designed to run software modules called snap-ins. Many of Windows Vista's administrative tools take the form of MMC snap-ins. MMC is capable of loading and running multiple snap-ins at once, to create what is called a console. You can load the snap-in by itself or create your own console with any combination of snap-ins you wish.

social engineering A term used to describe any attempt to penetrate the security of a system by convincing people to disclose secret information. Many would-be attackers have realized that discovering a user's password by calling the user and asking for it is the simplest method for gaining access to their network.

socket The combination of an IP address and a port number.

spatial multiplexing The process of splitting data into two signals for transmission over different frequencies and reassembling the signals into a single data stream at the destination.

spanned volume Consists of space from at least two, to a maximum of 32, physical disks, all of which must be dynamic disks. A spanned volume is essentially a method for combining the space from multiple dynamic disks into a single large volume. If a single physical disk in the spanned volume fails, all of the data in the entire volume is lost.

special identity A placeholder for a collection of users with a similar characteristic.

spyware A type of software that gathers information about computers and their users and sends it back to another system.

striped volume Consists of space from at least two, to a maximum of 32, physical disks, all of which must be dynamic disks. The difference between a striped volume and a spanned volume is that in a striped volume, the system writes data one stripe at a time to each successive disk in the volume. If a single physical disk in the striped volume fails, all of the data in the entire volume is lost.

subnet mask In TCP/IP networking, a 32-bit value that specifies which bits of an IP address form the network identifier and which bits form the host identifier.

Superfetch An enhanced method of prefetching in which the system maintains a more detailed profile of the computer's disk usage and can make far more educated guesses about what information to include in the cache. In combination with ReadyBoost, SuperFetch can provide a substantial enhancement to a Windows Vista system's performance.

Systems Management Services (SMS) For large enterprise networks, Microsoft Systems Management Server is a comprehensive network management tool that administrators can use to deploy all types of software products, including operating system updates. SMS is by far the most advanced and customizable method of deploying updates, but it is a paid product that must be licensed for the appropriate number of clients on the network.

T

Temporal Key Integrity Protocol (TKIP) A cryptographic algorithm used in the Wi-Fi Protected Access (WPA) wireless networking security protocol.

U

Usenet A text-based messaging service that provides participants around the world with forums they use to discuss topics of interest such as operating systems, television shows, software, politics, sex, religion, and virtually every other conceivable subject.

User Account Control (UAC) A Windows Vista security feature that prevents user accounts from exercising administrative privileges unless they are specifically invoked by the user.

User rights Specific operating system tasks, such as Shut Down The System or Allow Log On Through Terminal Services, can only be performed by certain users designated by a system administrator.

V

Virtualization In Windows Vista, a backwards compatibility feature that redirects file and registry writes to protected locations, rather than letting them fail. This enables applications that are not User Account Control-compliant to function properly without compromising system security.

W

Watson Feedback Platform (WFP) A service at Microsoft that collects reports about system and application errors, investigates the information in those reports, and responds to the user with possible solutions.

Wi-Fi Protected Access (WPA) One of two main security protocols used in the wireless LAN devices on the market today. WPA is comparatively recent and more secure, but some older devices do not support it.

Windows Aero The interface element that gives the Vista desktop its glass-like, translucent look. On a Vista system running Windows Aero, the edges of all windows are translucent and contain a fuzzy image of the elements behind them.

Windows Defender Blocks the installation of software that it suspects of being spyware and monitors the computer for signs of spyware activity.

Windows Display Driver Model (WDDM) A new display driver architecture, developed by Microsoft and released for the first time in Windows Vista. WDDM provides the operating system itself, as well as the applications running on it, with access to the graphics hardware on the video display adapter. Its display drivers consist of two parts, a small kernel mode driver, and a user mode driver that does most of the work. Moving most of the code out of kernel mode protects the operating system. Display driver problems are more likely to occur in user mode, which can crash the application, but not the operating system.

Windows Error Reporting (WER) The Windows Vista replacement for the Dr. Watson error handler in earlier versions of Windows. WER is, in turn, the client component of the Watson Feedback Platform (WFP).

Windows Firewall In Windows Vista, Windows Firewall is bidirectional, meaning that it prevents unauthorized network traffic from entering the system and from leaving the system.

Windows Genuine Advantage Validating a Windows installation generates what Microsoft calls the Windows Genuine Advantage. Without a Windows installation that has been proven to be genuine, users cannot manually download free updates from the Windows Update website, obtain free downloads from the Microsoft Download Center, or use certain operating system features, including Windows Aero.

Windows Preinstallation Environment (PE) Windows Vista eliminates DOS from the installation process completely by supplying its own preinstallation environment, called Windows PE 2.0. Windows PE is a subset of Windows Vista that provides basic access to the computer's network and disk drives, so that it is possible to perform an in-place or a network installation.

Windows Recovery Environment (RE) A technician launches Windows RE if a Windows Vista computer fails to start, or if it crashes repeatedly. Windows RE is simply another name given to Windows PE on a computer with Vista already installed. In the Windows RE environment, the technician can use Vista's built-in troubleshooting utilities or run third-party or custom diagnostic tools.

Windows Server Update Services (WSUS) For medium to large networks, WSUS is a free product that conserves bandwidth by downloading updates from the Internet once and then providing them to Windows Update clients on the local network. WSUS also enables administrators to select the updates they want to release to the clients, thus giving them the opportunity to evaluate and test the updates first, and then schedule the deployment.

wipe-and-load migration In a wipe-and-load migration, you have only one computer, which initially contains the user profile settings you want to transfer. After saving the profile information to a removable storage medium, you perform a clean Windows Vista installation, wiping out all data on the drives, and then transfer the profile data from the removable medium back to the computer.

Wired Equivalent Privacy (WEP) One of two main security protocols used in the wireless LAN devices on the market today. WEP has been around for some time and is relatively insecure, but it is supported by virtually all wireless LAN products.

Wireless Access Point (WAP) Attackers can capture traffic as a wireless computer communicates with a wireless access point (WAP). Depending on the type of antennae the devices use and their transmitting power, an attacker might be able to eavesdrop from hundreds or thousands of feet away.

Index